Your future is just four parts away.

Welcome to the Becker CPA Exam Review! Congratulations on taking the first step to becoming a CPA. As the industry's leading partner in CPA Exam preparation, we know you're not just studying for an exam – you are preparing for your future. To help you get there, Becker CPA Exam Review is as close as you can get to the real thing. So let's get started.

Access Becker's CPA Exam Review course

Log in to your CPA Exam Review course anytime at **online.becker.com**. Watch our orientation video and download the mobile app to access your studies on the go. Your progress will automatically sync among all your devices, so you can pick up where you left off. For more on getting started, visit **becker.com/cpa-review/getting-started**.

Utilize the Becker resources

Make studying more organized with our study planner. With interactive tools to help you determine your ideal study schedule and to recommend your ideal exam-taking time, it's easy to plan your preparation so you're ready when exam day comes. Here are the added benefits of Becker:

- Take advantage of the personalized review sessions at the end of each unit to identify which topics you need to review and strengthen

- Access 1-on-1 academic support from our experienced CPA instructors

- Watch 400+ SkillMaster videos that coach you through task-based simulations

- Improve upon core concepts with the help of more than 1,300 flashcards

- Test your knowledge with our simulated exams – the closest thing you can get to the actual CPA Exam itself

You're not in it alone!

For tips, stories and advice, visit our blog at **becker.com/theplusside**. You can also collaborate with other Becker students studying REG on our Facebook study group at **facebook.com/groups/BeckerREGStudyGroup/**.

Submit your CPA Exam application

It takes time for your CPA Exam application to be approved – so don't wait til the last minute.

Once your CPA Exam application has been processed, your Notice to Schedule will give you a limited window of time to schedule your exam.

Your state board of accountancy sets the amount of time you have, so be sure to check your state's requirements.

Once you schedule your exam, add it to the study planner so we can share tips, strategies and more as your test date approaches.

Becker.

Join the community!

Becker.

This textbook contains information that was current at the time of printing.
Your course software will be updated on a regular basis as the content
that is tested on the CPA Exam evolves and as we improve our materials.
Note the version reference below and select your replacement textbook
under Replacement Products at **becker.com/cpa-replacement-products**
to learn if a newer version of this book is available to be ordered.

CPA Exam Review

Regulation

For Exams Scheduled
After December 31, 2019

V 3.5

COURSE DEVELOPMENT TEAM

Timothy F. Gearty, CPA, MBA, JD, CGMA . . . . Editor in Chief, Financial/Regulation (Tax) National Editor

Angeline S. Brown, CPA, CGMA. . . . . .Sr. Director, Product Management

Mike Brown, CPA, CMA, CGMA . . . . .Director, Product Management

Valerie Funk Anderson, CPA . . . . Sr. Manager, Curriculum

Stephen Bergens, CPA. . . . . Manager, Accounting Curriculum

Cheryl Costello, CPA, CGMA . . . . Sr. Specialist, Curriculum

Tom Cox, CPA, CMA . . . . Financial (GASB & NFP) National Editor

Steven J. Levin, JD . . . . .Regulation (Law) National Editor

Danita De Jane . . . . Director, Course Development

Anson Miyashiro. . . . . Manager, Course Development

Tim Munson . . . . .Project Manager, Course Development

CONTRIBUTING EDITORS

Teresa C. Anderson, CPA, CMA, MPA	Michelle Moshe, CPA, DipIFR
Katie Barnette, CPA	Peter Olinto, JD, CPA
Jim DeSimpelare, CPA, MBA	Sandra Owen, JD, MBA, CPA
Tara Z. Fisher, CPA	Michelle M. Pace, CPA
Melisa F. Galasso, CPA	Michael Potenza, CPA, JD
R. Thomas Godwin, CPA, CGMA	Jennifer J. Rivers, CPA
Holly Hawk, CPA, CGMA	Josh Rosenberg, MBA, CPA, CFA, CFP
Patrice W. Johnson, CPA	Jonathan R. Rubin, CPA, MBA
Julie D. McGinty, CPA	Michael Rybak, CPA, CFA
Sandra McGuire, CPA, MBA	Denise M. Stefano, CPA, CGMA, MBA
Stephanie Morris, CPA, MAcc	Elizabeth Lester Walsh, CPA, CITP

Permissions

Material from *Uniform CPA Examination Selected Questions and Unofficial Answers*, 1989–2019, copyright © by American Institute of Certified Public Accountants, Inc., is reprinted and/or adapted with permission.

Any knowing solicitation or disclosure of any questions or answers included on any CPA Examination is prohibited.

REGULATION

Program Attendance Record

Student: _____   Location: _____

REGULATION 1	REGULATION 2
Attendance Stamp	Attendance Stamp
REGULATION 3	**REGULATION 4**
Attendance Stamp	Attendance Stamp
REGULATION 5	**REGULATION 6**
Attendance Stamp	Attendance Stamp
REGULATION 7	**REGULATION 8**
Attendance Stamp	Attendance Stamp

IMPORTANT NOTES TO STUDENTS REGARDING "THE BECKER PROMISE"

- The attendance sheet must be stamped at the end of each class attended. This is the only acceptable record of your classroom attendance.
- An overall percentage correct of 90% or higher is required on MCQs and simulations to qualify for The Becker Promise.
- Please e-mail documentation to beckerpromise@becker.com or fax to 866-398-7375 no later than 45 days following the completion of each section.
- For Becker Promise redemption policies and procedures, visit becker.com/promise.

NOTES

REGULATION

Table of Contents

NOTES

Regulation (REG) Overview

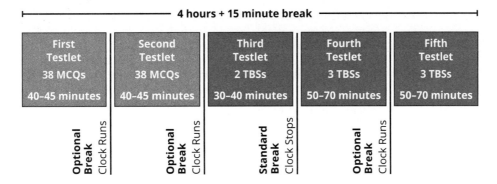

REG Exam—Summary Blueprint

Content Area Allocation	Weight
Ethics, Professional Responsibilities, and Federal Tax Procedures	10–20%
Business Law	10–20%
Federal Taxation of Property Transactions	12–22%
Federal Taxation of Individuals	15–25%
Federal Taxation of Entities	28–38%
Skill Allocation	**Weight**
Evaluation	—
Analysis	25–35%
Application	35–45%
Remembering and Understanding	25–35%

The complete REG exam blueprint appears in the back of the book.

Becker's CPA Exam Review—Course Introduction

Becker Professional Education's CPA Exam Review products were developed with you, the candidate, in mind. To that end we have developed a series of tools designed to tap all of your learning and retention capabilities. The Becker lectures, comprehensive texts, and course software are designed to be fully integrated to give you the best chance of passing the CPA Exam.

Passing the CPA Exam is difficult, but the professional rewards a CPA enjoys make this a worthwhile challenge. We created our CPA Exam Review after evaluating the needs of CPA candidates and analyzing the CPA Exam over the years. Our course materials comprehensively present topics you must know to pass the examination, teaching you the most effective tactics for learning the material.

Becker Customer and Academic Support

You can access Becker's Customer and Academic Support under Student Resources at:

http://www.becker.com/cpa-review.html

You can also access Academic Support by clicking on the Academic Support button in the Becker software. You can access customer service and technical support from Customer and Academic Support or by calling 1-877-CPA-EXAM (outside the U.S. + 1-630-472-2213).

The Uniform CPA Exam—Overview

Exam Sections

The CPA Examination consists of four sections:

Financial Accounting and Reporting

The *Financial* section consists of a four-hour exam covering financial accounting and reporting for commercial entities under U.S. GAAP, governmental accounting, not-for-profit accounting, and the differences between IFRS and U.S. GAAP.

Auditing and Attestation

The *Auditing* section consists of a four-hour exam. This section covers all topics related to auditing, including audit reports and procedures, generally accepted auditing standards, attestation and other engagements, and government auditing.

Regulation

The *Regulation* section consists of a four-hour exam, combining topics from business law and federal taxation, including the taxation of property transactions, individuals, and entities.

Business Environment and Concepts

The *Business* section consists of a four-hour exam covering general business topics, such as corporate governance, economics, financial management, information technology, and operations management, including managerial accounting.

Question Formats

The chart below illustrates the question format breakdown by exam section.

Section	Multiple-Choice Questions		Task-Based Simulations or Written Communication Tasks	
	Percentage	Number	Percentage	Number
Financial	50%	66	50%	8 TBSs
Auditing	50%	72	50%	8 TBSs
Regulation	50%	76	50%	8 TBSs
Business	50%	62	50%	4 TBSs/3 WC

Each exam will contain testlets. A testlet is either a series of multiple-choice questions, a set of task-based simulations, or a set of written communications. For example, the Regulation examination will contain five testlets. The first two testlets will be multiple-choice questions and the third, fourth, and fifth testlets will contain task-based simulations. Each testlet must be finished and submitted before continuing to the next testlet. Candidates cannot go back to view a previously completed testlet or go forward to view a subsequent testlet before closing and submitting the earlier testlet. Our mock exams contain these types of restrictions so that you can familiarize yourself with the functionality of the CPA Exam.

Exam Schedule

The computer-based CPA Exam is offered during the first two months and 10 days of each calendar quarter. Candidates can schedule an exam date directly with Prometric (www.prometric.com/cpa) after receiving a notice to schedule.

Eligibility and Application Requirements

Each state sets its own rules of eligibility for the examination. Please visit www.becker.com/state as soon as possible to determine your eligibility to sit for the exam.

Application Deadlines

With the computer-based exam format, set application deadlines generally do not exist. You should apply as early as possible to ensure that you are able to schedule your desired exam dates. Each state has different application requirements and procedures, so be sure to gain a thorough understanding of the application process for your state.

Grading System

You must pass all four parts of the examination to earn certification as a CPA. You must score 75 or better on a part to receive a passing grade and you must pass all four exams in 18 months or you will lose credit for the earliest exam that you passed.

NOTES

Individual Taxation: Part 1

Module

1 Individual Income Tax Formula

This module begins the discussion of individual income tax. The formula below provides a summary of the calculation of taxable income and federal income tax liability or refund for individuals. Ultimately, these items are reported on the individual income tax return, Form 1040.

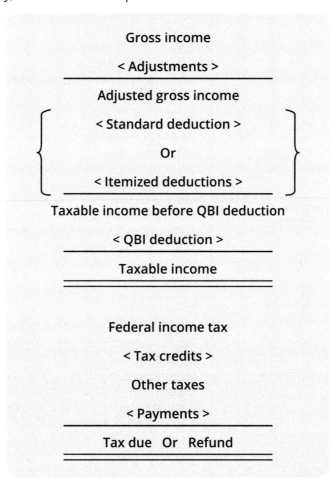

Gross income

< Adjustments >

Adjusted gross income

{ < Standard deduction >

Or

< Itemized deductions > }

Taxable income before QBI deduction

< QBI deduction >

Taxable income

Federal income tax

< Tax credits >

Other taxes

< Payments >

Tax due   Or   Refund

2 Taxable Income Formula for Individuals

Taxable income is the base for the individual income tax. The formula below demonstrates the calculation of taxable income for individual taxpayers.

Gross income
- Wages
- Interest
- Dividends
- State tax refunds
- Alimony received*
- Business income
- Capital gain/loss
- IRA income
- Pension and annuity
- Rental income/loss
- K-1 income/loss
- Unemployment compensation
- Social Security benefits
- Other income

< Adjustments >
- Educator expenses
- IRA
- Student loan interest expenses
- Health savings account
- Moving expenses**
- One-half self-employment taxes
- Self-employed health insurance
- Self-employed retirement
- Interest withdrawal penalty
- Alimony paid*

Adjusted gross income

< Itemized deductions >
- Medical (in excess of 10 percent of AGI)
- Taxes—state/local (income/sales and property, up to $10,000)
- Interest expense (Home and Investment)
- Charity (up to 60 percent of AGI)
- Casualty/theft attributable to federal disaster (in excess of 10 percent of AGI)

Taxable income before QBI deduction

< QBI deduction >

Taxable income

*Under the Tax Cuts and Jobs Act (TCJA) for all divorce or separation agreements executed after 12/31/18, alimony received will not be included in gross income and alimony paid cannot be deducted.

**Only for members of the armed forces moving pursuant to military order.

3   Filing Requirements for Individuals

3.1   Who Must File?

The first consideration when thinking about individual taxation is who must file a tax return. Generally, a taxpayer must file a return if his or her income is equal to or greater than the sum of:

1.   the regular standard deduction (except for married filing separately), plus

2.   the additional standard deduction amount for taxpayers age 65 or older or blind (except for married persons filing separately).

3.2   When to File

3.2.1   Due Date—April 15

Individual taxpayers must file on or before the 15th day of the fourth month following the close of the taxpayer's taxable year, which is April 15.

3.2.2   Extension

▪   **Automatic Six-Month Extension to October 15:** An automatic six-month extension (until October 15) is available for those taxpayers who are unable to file by the April 15 due date. The automatic six-month extension is not an extension for the payment of any taxes owed. Although granted automatically, the six-month extension must be requested by the taxpayer by filing Form 4868 by April 15.

▪   **Payment of Tax:** Even with an extension, the due date for payment of taxes remains April 15.

4   Filing Status

4.1   Single (Use the End-of-Year Test)

You are considered unmarried for the whole year if, on the last day of your tax year, you are either: unmarried or legally separated.

4.2   Joint Returns (Use the End-of-Year Test)

In order to file a joint return, the parties must be married at the end of the year, living together in a legally recognized common law marriage, or married and living apart (but not legally separated or divorced).

▪   If married during the year, a joint return may be filed, provided the parties are married at year-end. This includes same-sex couples legally married under state law (as a result of the Supreme Court case *Obergefell v. Hodges* (2015), same-sex couples have the right to marry in all states).

▪   If divorced during the year, a joint return may not be filed.

▪   If one spouse dies during the year, a joint return may be filed.

4.3   Married Filing Separately

A married taxpayer may file a separate return even if only one spouse has income for the year. In a separate property state, spouses who elect to file using the married filing separately status must separately report their own income, credits, and deductions on their own individual income tax returns. In a community property state, most of the income, deductions, credits, etc., are split 50/50.

4.4   Qualifying Widow(er) With Dependent Child

- **Two Years After Spouse's Death:** A qualifying widow(er) is a taxpayer who may use the joint tax return standard deduction and rates for each of two taxable years following the year of death of his or her spouse, unless he or she remarries. In the event of a remarriage, the surviving spouse will file a tax return (joint or separate) with the new spouse.

- **Principal Residence for Dependent Child:** The surviving spouse must pay over half the cost of maintaining a household where a dependent child lives for the whole taxable year. The dependent child must be a child (including an adopted child but not a foster child) or stepchild of the surviving spouse.

4.5   Head of Household

Head of household status entitles certain taxpayers to pay lower taxes. The lower tax results from a larger standard deduction and "wider" tax brackets.

To qualify, the following conditions must be met:

1. The individual is unmarried, legally separated, or married and has lived apart from his or her spouse for the last six months of the year as of the close of the taxable year.

2. The individual is not a "qualifying widow(er)."

3. The individual is not a nonresident alien.

4. The individual maintains as his or her home a household that, for more than half the taxable year, is the principal residence of a qualifying person, including a dependent child, parent, or relative (as discussed below).

4.5.1   A Qualifying Child

Child, stepchild, legally adopted child, foster child, brother or sister, or a descendant of one of these who meets the definition of a dependent under the qualifying children rules.

4.5.2   Father or Mother (Not Required to Live With Taxpayer)

A dependent parent is not required to live with the taxpayer, provided the taxpayer maintains a home that was the principal residence of the parent for the entire year. Maintaining a home means contributing over half the cost of upkeep. This means rent, mortgage interest, property taxes, insurance, utility charges, repairs, and food consumed in the home.

4.5.3   Dependent Relatives (Must Live With Taxpayer)

Grandparents, brothers, sisters, aunts, uncles, nephews, and nieces (as well as stepparents, parents-in-law, sisters-in-law, or brothers-in-law) qualify as relatives. A dependent relative (other than a father or mother) must live with the taxpayer. Note that cousins, foster parents, and unrelated dependents do not qualify.

4.5.4   Summary of Who Meets Head-of-Household Qualifying Person Requirement

	Qualifying Dependent	Lives With Taxpayer
Child or descendant	Yes	Yes
Parents	Yes	No
Relative	Yes	Yes

Pass Key

In order to avoid confusing the required time period for different filing statuses, just remember:

Widow/widower = Must be principal residence for dependent child for **whole** year.

Head of household = Must be principal residence for qualifying person for more than **half** a year.

5   Dependency Definitions

Certain tax benefits, such as an advantageous filing status or certain tax credits, require either a qualifying child or qualifying relative. Each category has requirements:

Qualifying Child	Or	Qualifying Relative
Close relative		**Support** test
Age limit		**Under** a specific amount of (taxable) gross income test
Residency and filing requirements		**Precludes** dependent filing a joint tax return test
Eliminate gross income test		**Only** citizens (residents of US/Canada or Mexico) test
Support test		**Relative** test Or **Taxpayer** lives with individual for whole year test

Taxpayers must obtain a Social Security number for any dependent who has attained the age of one as of the close of the tax year.

Pass Key

A taxpayer will be entitled to a family tax credit for anyone whom a taxpayer "**CARES**" for, or whom they "**SUPORT**," even if the dependent:

- was born during the year; or
- died during the year.

5.1 Qualifying Child

If the parents of a child are able to claim the child but do not, no one else may claim the child unless that taxpayer's AGI is higher than the AGI of the highest parent.

In general, a child is a qualifying child of the taxpayer if the child satisfies the following:

1. Close Relative

Under the close relationship test, to be a qualifying child of a taxpayer, the child must be the taxpayer's son, daughter, stepson, stepdaughter, brother, sister, stepbrother, stepsister, or a descendant of any of these. An individual legally adopted by the taxpayer, or an individual who is lawfully placed with the taxpayer for legal adoption by the taxpayer, is treated as a child of the taxpayer. A foster child who is placed with the taxpayer by an authorized placement agency or by judgment, decree, or other order of any court of competent jurisdiction also is treated as the taxpayer's child.

2. Age Limit

The age limit test varies depending on the benefit. In general, a child must be younger than the taxpayer, and under age 19 (or age 24 in the case of a full-time student) to be a qualifying child (although no age limit applies with respect to individuals who are totally and permanently disabled at any time during the tax year). A "full-time" student is a student who attends an educational institution for at least part of each of five months during the taxable year. An "educational institution" is one that maintains full-time faculty and a daytime program. School attendance only at night does not qualify.

3. Residency and Filing Requirements

Under the residency and filing requirement tests, a child must have the same principal place of abode as the taxpayer for more than one half of the tax year. The child also must be a citizen of the United States or a resident of the United States, Canada, or Mexico. Furthermore, the child cannot file a joint tax return for the year (unless it was filed only for a refund claim).

4. Eliminate Gross Income Test

The gross income test (see **SUPORT**) does not apply to a qualifying child.

5. Support Test

The qualifying child must not have contributed more than half of his or her own support. Support means the actual expenses incurred by or on behalf of the dependent. Scholarships received by a dependent student child or stepchild are not included in determining the student's total support. However, Social Security and state welfare payments are included in the dependent's total support, but only to the extent that such amounts are actually expended for support purposes.

5.2   Qualifying Relative

Taxpayers can apply the **SUPORT** rules to determine whether an individual meets the qualifying relative rules. In general, an individual is a qualifying relative of the taxpayer if the individual satisfies the following:

1. **Support Test**

   The taxpayer must have supplied more than one half (greater than 50 percent) of the support of a person in order to claim him or her as a qualifying relative. The same definition of support as related to a qualifying child applies.

2. **Under Gross Income Limitation**

   A person may not be claimed as a qualifying relative unless the qualifying relative's gross income is less than $4,200 (for 2019).

   ▪ **Definition of Taxable Income:** Only income that is taxable is included for the purpose of the gross income limitation.

   ▪ **Nontaxable Income**

     • Social Security (at low income levels)

     • Tax-exempt interest income (state and municipal interest income)

     • Tax-exempt scholarships

3. **Precludes Dependent Filing a Joint Return**

   A taxpayer does not meet the definition of qualifying relative if the taxpayer is a married dependent who files a joint return, unless there is no tax liability on the couple's joint return and there would not have been any tax liability on either spouse's tax return if they had filed separately.

4. **Only Citizens of the United States or Residents of the United States, Mexico, or Canada**

   The qualifying relative must be either a citizen of the United States or a resident of the United States, Mexico, or Canada.

5. **Relative**

   Children, grandchildren, parents, grandparents, brothers, sisters, aunts and uncles, nieces and nephews (as well as stepchildren, stepparents, stepbrothers or stepsisters, in-laws) can meet the definition of qualifying relative. Children include legally adopted children, foster children, and stepchildren. Foster parents and cousins must live with the taxpayer the entire year.

   Remember: A child born at any time during the year will qualify as a relative for qualifying-child or qualifying-relative purposes.

   Or:

6. **Taxpayer Lives With the Individual (if Non-relative) for the Whole Year**

   A non-relative member of a household (i.e., a person living in the taxpayer's home for the entire year) may be considered a qualifying relative provided the taxpayer's relationship with that person does not violate local law. Foster parents and cousins must live with the taxpayer the entire year because they are not regarded as relatives.

5.3 Multiple Support Agreements

Where two or more taxpayers together contribute more than 50 percent to the support of a person but none of them individually contributes more than 50 percent, the contributing taxpayers, all of whom must be qualifying relatives of (or lived the entire year with) the individual, may agree among themselves which contributor may claim the individual as a dependent for tax benefits.

- A contributor must have contributed more than 10 percent of the person's support in addition to meeting the other dependency tests in order to be able to claim him or her as a dependent.

- The joint contributors are required to file a multiple support declaration, Form 2120.

Example 1	Multiple Support Agreement

Facts: Peter, who is single and lives alone in Idaho, has no income of his own and is supported in full by the following people:

	Amount of Support	Percent of Total
Tim (an unrelated friend)	$2,400	48
Angie (Peter's sister)	2,150	43
Mike (Peter's son)	450	9
	$5,000	100%

Required: Under a multiple support agreement, Peter is considered a dependent of which of the following:

a. No one
b. Tim
c. Angie
d. Mike

Solution: Peter only meets dependency definition requirements for Angie.

	Tim	Angie	Mike
Support test	Yes	Yes	No
Under gross income	Yes	Yes	
Preclude joint filing	Yes	Yes	
Only U.S. citizens	Yes	Yes	
Relative, or	No	Yes	
Taxpayer lived with	No	N/A	

5.4   Children of Divorced Parents

- **General Rule (Custodial Parents):** Generally, the parent who has custody of the child for the greater part of the year qualifies to use the child as a dependent for tax benefit purposes (determined by a "time" test, not the divorce decree). It does not matter whether that parent actually provided more than one-half of the child's support. If the parents have equal custody during the year, the parent with the higher adjusted gross income will claim the tax benefits related to the dependent.

Question 1	MCQ-01404

Which of the following is (are) among the requirements to enable a taxpayer to be classified as a "qualifying widow(er)"?

I.   A dependent has lived with the taxpayer for six months.

II.   The taxpayer has maintained the cost of the principal residence for six months.

  a.   I only.

  b.   II only.

  c.   Both I and II.

  d.   Neither I nor II.

Question 2	MCQ-06433

Mark and Molly met at a New Year's Eve party held December 31, Year 1. They instantly bonded, fell madly in love, and were married at 11:38 p.m. that night. Identify Mark's filing status for Year 1.

  a.   Single

  b.   Married filing jointly

  c.   Head of household

  d.   Surviving spouse

NOTES

1 Gross Income Overview

The first step in determining tax liability is to compute gross income.

1.1 Gross Income Definition

Generally, gross income means all income from whatever source derived, unless specifically excluded. (For example, if the taxpayer finds $4,000 under a floorboard in his house, cannot find the owner, and keeps the money, the $4,000 is income regardless of the fact that the taxpayer did not "earn" it.)

1.2 Computation of Income (General Rule)

Except in the cases of gain derived from dealings in property (discussed below), income is determined by the amount of cash, property (FMV), or services obtained. In cases of noncash income, the amount of the income is the *fair market value* of the property or services received.

Pass Key

Event		Income	Basis
Taxable	=	FMV	FMV
Nontaxable	=	None	NBV

Example 1 — Noncash Income

Facts: A taxpayer performs services and receives a car with a fair market value of $3,000 as compensation.

Required: Determine the amount of income for the taxpayer.

Solution: The $3,000 is income to the taxpayer.

1.3 Realization and Recognition

In order to be taxable, the gain must be both realized and recognized.

- **Realization:** Realization requires the accrual or receipt of cash, property, or services, or a change in the form or the nature of the investment (a sale or exchange).

- **Recognition:** Recognition means that the realized gain must be included on the tax return (i.e., there is no provision that permits exclusion or deferral under the Internal Revenue Code).

Illustration 1   Recognition Concept

A taxpayer owns stock for which he paid $100, and the stock goes up in value to $150. There is no realized gain even though there has been an increase in the taxpayer's wealth. Gain is realized when the shares are sold for $150 or exchanged for other property worth $150. If the gain is taxable, it would also be recognized on the tax return.

1.4   Timing of Revenue Recognition

- **Accrual Method:** Under the accrual method, recognition occurs according to the rules of GAAP (with some exceptions); that is, revenue is taxable when earned.

- **Cash Method:** Under the cash method, recognition occurs in the period the revenue is actually or constructively received in cash or (FMV) property.

2   Specific Items of Income and Exclusions

2.1   Salaries and Wages

Gross income includes many forms of compensation for services.

- **Money:** All money received, credited, or available (constructive receipt).

- **Property:** The fair market value (FMV) of all property is included as gross income.

- **Cancellation of Debt:** All debts canceled are included in gross income (except for certain cancellations of mortgage debt on principal residences, which have very detailed guidelines for excluded amounts and debts canceled when insolvency exists).

Example 2   COD Income

Facts: Mary owes the bank $80,000 on an unsecured note. She satisfies the note in full with a payment of $30,000. The bank accepts this payment and forgives the remaining $50,000 of debt.

Required: Determine Mary's income as a result of the cancellation of debt.

Solution: Mary has cancellation of debt income of $50,000.

- **Bargain Purchases:** If an employer sells property to the employee for less than its fair market value, the difference is income to the employee.

- **Guaranteed Payments to a Partner:** Guaranteed payments are reasonable compensation paid to a partner for services rendered (or use of capital) without regard to the partner's ratio of income. This earned compensation is also subject to self-employment tax.

- **Taxable Fringe Benefits (Non-statutory):** The fair market value of a fringe benefit not specifically excluded by law is includable in income. For example, an employee's personal use of a company car is included as wages in an employee's income. Furthermore, the amount included is subject to employment taxes and withholding.

- **Portion of Life Insurance Premiums:** Premiums paid by an employer on a group term life insurance policy covering his employees are not income to the employees up to the cost on the first $50,000 of coverage per employee (nondiscriminatory plans only). Premiums above the first $50,000 of coverage are taxable income to the recipient and normally included in W-2 wages. (This amount is calculated from an IRS table, and it is not the entire amount of the premium in excess of the $50,000 coverage.)

2.2　Nontaxable Fringe Benefits

- **Life Insurance Coverage**

  Employees may exclude from income the value of life insurance premiums the employer pays on an employee's behalf for up to $50,000 of group-term life insurance.

- **Accident, Medical, and Health Insurance (Employer-Paid)**

  Premium payments are excludable from the employee's income when the employer paid the insurance premiums, but amounts paid to the employee under the policy are *includable in income unless such amounts are:*

  1. Reimbursement for medical expenses actually incurred by the employee; or

  2. Compensation for the permanent loss or loss of use of a member or function of the body.

- **De Minimis Fringe Benefits**

  De minimis fringe benefits are so minimal that they are impractical to account for and may be excluded from income. An example is an employee's personal use of a company computer.

- **Meals and Lodging**

  The gross income of an employee does not include the value of meals or lodging furnished to him or her in kind by the employer for the *convenience of the employer on the employer's premises.* Additionally, in order to be nontaxable, the lodging must be required as a condition of employment.

- **Employer Payment of Employee's Educational Expenses**

  Up to $5,250 may be excluded from gross income of payments made by the employer on behalf of an employee's educational expenses. The exclusion applies to both undergraduate and graduate-level education.

- **Qualified Tuition Reduction**

  Employees of educational institutions studying at the undergraduate level who receive tuition reductions may exclude the tuition reduction from income. Graduate students may exclude tuition reduction only if they are engaged in teaching or research activities and only if the tuition reduction is in addition to the pay for the teaching or research. To be excludable, tuition reductions must be offered on a nondiscriminatory basis.

▒ Qualified Employee Discounts

Employee discounts on employer-provided merchandise and service are excludable as follows:

- **Merchandise Discounts**

  The excludable discount is limited to the employer's gross profit percentage. Any excess must be reported as income.

- **Service Discounts**

  The excludable discount on services is limited to 20 percent of the fair market value of the services. Any excess discount must be reported as income.

- **Employer-Provided Parking**

  The value of employer-provided parking up to $265 (for 2019) per month may be excluded. The exclusion is available even if the parking benefit is taken by the employee in place of taxable cash compensation.

- **Transit Passes**

  The value of employer-provided transit passes up to $265 (for 2019) per month may be excluded.

▒ Qualified Pension, Profit-Sharing, and Stock Bonus Plans

- **Payments Made by Employer (Nontaxable)**

  Generally, payments made by an employer to a qualified pension, profit-sharing, or stock bonus plan are not income to the employee at the time of contribution.

- **Benefits Received (Taxable)**

  The amount that is exempt from tax (plus any income earned on such amount) is taxable to the employee in the year in which the amount is distributed or made available to the employee.

▒ Flexible Spending Arrangements (FSAs)

A *flexible spending arrangement* stems from a Section 125 employee flexible benefit plan and is a plan that allows employees to receive a pre-tax reimbursement of certain (specified) incurred expenses.

- **Pretax Deposits Into Employee's Account**

  Employees have the ability to elect to have part of their salary (generally up to $2,700 for 2019) deposited pretax into a flexible spending account designated for them. These deposits must be done via salary reduction directly by the employer, and the employee is not taxed on that income. The employee has the option to use the deposited funds to pay for qualified health care and/or qualified dependent care costs, and submits claims to the plan administrator for reimbursement.

- **Forfeit Funds Not Used Within 2½ Months After Year-End**

  An employee generally must use the money in an FSA within the plan year. Funds not used within 2½ months after the year-end are forfeited. However, this grace period only applies if the employer amended the plan accordingly. Alternatively, the employer may amend the plan to allow an employee to carry over up to $500 per year to use in the following year.

2.3 Interest Income

2.3.1 Taxable Interest Income

The items below represent taxable interest income:

- Interest from federal bonds.

- Interest from industrial development bonds.

- Interest from corporate bonds.

- Part of the proceeds from an installment sale is taxable as interest.

- Interest paid by the federal or state government for late payment of a tax refund is taxable.

- For certain taxpayers and certain bonds, the amortization of a bond premium is an offset (reduction) to the interest received and a reduction to the bond's basis, and the amortization of a bond discount is an addition to the interest received and an addition to the bond's basis.

2.3.2 Tax-Exempt Interest Income (Reportable but Not Taxable)

The following items must be reported on the tax return but are not taxable:

- **State and Local Government Bonds/Obligations:** Interest on state and local bonds/ obligations is tax-exempt. Furthermore, mutual fund dividends for funds invested in tax-free bonds are also tax-exempt.

- **Bonds of a U.S. Possession:** Interest on the obligation of a possession of the United States, such as Guam or Puerto Rico, is tax-exempt.

- **Series EE (U.S. Savings Bonds):** Interest on Series EE Savings Bonds issued after 1989 is tax-exempt when:

  - it is used to pay for higher education (reduced by tax-free scholarships) of the taxpayer, spouse, or dependents;

  - the taxpayer is over age 24 when bond is issued;

  - a married taxpayer files a joint return; and

  - the taxpayer meets certain income requirements.

  Phase-out starts when modified AGI exceeds an indexed amount. (For 2019, phase-out begins at $81,100 for single and head of household and at $121,600 for married filing jointly. When a taxpayer uses bonds for a child's education, the bonds must be registered in the taxpayer's name and/or spouse's name. The child can be listed as a beneficiary on the bond, but not as a co-owner.)

- **Veterans Administration Insurance:** Interest on insurance dividends left on deposit with the Veterans Administration Insurance is tax exempt.

2.3.3 Forfeited Interest (Adjustment) (Penalty on Withdrawal From Savings)

Forfeited interest is a penalty for early withdrawal of savings (generally on a time deposit, such as a certificate of deposit, at a bank). The bank credits the interest to the taxpayer's account and then, in a separate transaction, removes certain interest as a penalty for withdrawing the funds before maturity. The interest received is taxable on the taxpayer's income tax return, but the amount forfeited is also deductible as an adjustment in the year the penalty is incurred. Thus, the taxpayer only pays tax on the amount of interest actually received. Note, however, that the amount of forfeited interest is deducted separately and not netted with interest income on the tax return.

2.4   Dividend Income

2.4.1   Source Determines Taxability

A dividend is defined by the Internal Revenue Code as a distribution of property by a corporation out of the company's earnings and profits. The taxability of the dividend is determined by the amount of the company's earnings and profits:

- Earnings and profits → taxable dividend

- No earnings and profits and taxpayer has basis in stock → nontaxable and reduces basis of stock

- No earnings and profits and no stock basis → taxable capital gain income

2.4.2   Taxable Dividends

All dividends that represent distributions of a corporation's earnings and profits (similar to retained earnings) are includable in gross income.

- **Taxable Amount (to Shareholder Receiving)**

    - Cash = Amount received

    - Property = Fair market value

2.4.3   Special (Lower) Tax Rate for Qualified Dividends

Qualified dividends are those paid by domestic or certain qualified foreign corporations.

- **Qualified Dividends Holding Period**: To be qualified dividends, the stock must be held for more than 60 days during the 120-day period that begins 60 days before the ex-dividend date (the date on which a purchased share no longer is entitled to any recently declared dividends).

- **Disqualified Dividends Include the Following:**

    - Employer stock held by an ESOP

    - Amounts taken into account as investment income (for purposes of the limitation on investment expenses)

    - Short sale positions

    - Certain foreign corporations

    - Dividends paid by credit unions, mutual savings banks, building and loan associations, mutual insurance companies, and farmer's cooperatives.

- **Tax Rates for Qualified Dividends (2019)**

    - 15 percent—Most taxpayers

    - 0 percent—Low-income taxpayers (those in the 10 percent or 12 percent ordinary income tax bracket)

    - 20 percent—High-income taxpayers (those in the 35 percent or 37 percent ordinary income tax bracket)

2.4.4   Tax-Free Distributions

The following items are exempt from gross income:

- **Return of Capital**

    Return of capital exists when a company distributes funds but has no earnings and profits. The taxpayer will simply reduce (but not below zero) his or her basis in common stock held.

- **Stock Split**

  When a stock split occurs, the shareholder will allocate the original basis over the total number of shares held after the split.

- **Stock Dividend (Unless Cash or Other Property Option/Taxable FMV)**

  Unless the shareholder has the option to receive cash or other property (which would then be taxable at the FMV of the dividend), the basis of the shares after distribution depends on the type of stock received.

  - Same stock—original basis is divided by total shares

  - Different stock—original basis is allocated based on the relative FMV of the different stock

- **Life Insurance Dividend**

  Dividends caused by ownership of insurance with a mutual company (premium return).

2.4.5 Capital Gain Distribution

Distributions by a corporation that has no earnings and profits, and for which the shareholder has recovered his or her entire basis, are treated as taxable gross income.

2.5   State and Local Tax Refunds

The receipt of a state or local income tax refund in a subsequent year is not taxable if the taxes paid did not result in a tax benefit in the prior year.

- Itemized in prior year = State or local refund is taxable (unless a competing tax law, such as alternative minimum tax, caused the initial taxes paid to be nondeductible).

- Standard deduction used in prior year = State or local refund is nontaxable.

Illustration 2   Nontaxable and Taxable State and Local Refund

Carlos, a single individual, used the standard deduction on his Year 10 federal personal tax return. In Year 11, he received a $150 state income tax refund. The $150 tax refund is not includable in his Year 11 income because he did not itemize in Year 10 and, therefore, did not receive a tax benefit from the state income taxes paid. If he had benefitted from deducting the state taxes when paid in Year 10, a Year 11 (or later) refund of those taxes would be taxable income for federal purposes when received, regardless of whether or not the taxpayer itemized deductions in the year the refund was received.

2.6   Payments Pursuant to a Divorce

2.6.1 Alimony/Spousal Support (Income)

Under the Tax Cuts and Jobs Act (TCJA) for all divorce or separation agreements executed after 12/31/18, alimony received will not be included in gross income and alimony paid cannot be deducted. Alimony payments pursuant to divorce or separation agreements executed on or before 12/31/18 will still be included in income of the recipient and deductible by the paying spouse. To be deemed alimony under the tax law:

- payments must be legally required pursuant to a written divorce (or separation) agreement;

- payments must be in cash (or its equivalent);

- payments cannot extend beyond the death of the payee-spouse;
- payments cannot be made to members of the same household;
- payments must not be designated as anything other than alimony; and
- the spouses may not file a joint tax return.

Pass Key

On the CPA Exam, if a real date is provided (e.g., 2017 or 2018) instead of a generic date (e.g., Year 1 or Year 2), candidates should use that as a tip-off that there is a date-specific tax treatment that needs to be considered. The CPA Exam will only use real dates when it is necessary for the candidate. A clear example of this is a question about alimony in which the year is indicated so the candidate can correctly decide whether that amount is includable in income.

Candidates should also apply any assumptions given in a question and assume that the information provided in the question is material.

2.6.2 Child Support

- **Nontaxable:** If any portion of the payments is fixed by the decree or agreement as being for the support of minor children (or is contingent on the child's status, such as reaching a certain age), such portion is not deductible by the spouse making payment and is not includable by the spouse receiving payment.

- **Payment Applies First to Child Support:** If the decree or agreement specifies that payments are to be made both for alimony and for support, but the payments subsequently made fall short of fulfilling these obligations, the payments will be allocated first to child support (until the entire child support obligation is met) and then to alimony.

2.6.3 Property Settlements (Nontaxable)

If a divorce settlement provides for a lump-sum payment or property settlement by a spouse, that spouse gets no deduction for payments made, and the payments are not includable in the gross income of the spouse receiving the payment.

2.7 Business Income or Loss (Schedule C or C-EZ)

Net business income or loss from a sole proprietorship is calculated on Schedule C or Schedule C-EZ and reported on Form 1040 as a single item (the specific line item is business income or loss). Details of the profit or loss calculation from a sole proprietorship reported on an individual tax return are covered later in this unit.

2.8 Farm Income (Schedule F)

Profit or loss from farming is calculated on Schedule F and reported on Form 1040 as a single line item (the specific line item is farm income or loss). Details of the farm profit or loss calculation reported on an individual tax return are covered later in this unit.

2.9   Gains and Losses on Disposition of Property

Gain or loss on the disposition of property is measured by the difference between the amount realized and the adjusted basis. Gains and losses are given tax effect (recognized) only when the asset is sold or disposed by other means. Whether on a cash or accrual method of accounting, taxpayers who sell stock or securities on an established securities market must recognize gains and losses as of the trade date, not the settlement date. The basic formula in determining the gain or loss is as follows:

Amount realized

< Adjusted basis of assets sold >

Gain or loss realized

2.10   IRA Income

Generally, retirement money cannot be withdrawn without penalty until the individual reaches the age of 59½ (except in certain situations, covered later) or the individual elects to receive qualified equal periodic distributions over his life expectancy. A taxpayer is required to start withdrawals by the age of 70½ (this is often referred to as the "required minimum distribution" or "RMD"). Benefits are not taxable until the taxpayer receives the distribution.

2.10.1 Taxation of Distributions (Benefits)

■ **Ordinary Income (Traditional Deductible IRA Distributions)**

When a person withdraws funds from a traditional IRA for which deductions were taken at the time of contribution, the entire amount withdrawn will be taxed as ordinary income (regardless of what type of income, such as capital gain, was earned while the funds were invested).

■ **Distributions/Benefits From Nondeductible IRAs**

• **Roth IRA:** All benefits received from a Roth IRA are nontaxable if it is a "qualified distribution."

• **Traditional Nondeductible IRA:** Benefits received from a traditional nondeductible IRA are partially taxable. Distribution of principal, which is the contributions made to the plan, is nontaxable, but the earnings are taxable. The benefits received must be allocated pro rata between the taxable and nontaxable portions.

— Principal (contributions made): nontaxable

— Accumulated earnings: taxable (when withdrawn)

2.10.2 Penalty Tax (10 Percent)

Generally, a premature distribution before age 59½ is subject to a 10 percent penalty tax (in addition to regular income tax) if the individual has not met an exception.

2.10.3 Exception to Penalty Tax (Still Subject to Ordinary Income Tax)

There is no penalty if the premature distribution was used to pay:

- **Homebuyer** (first time): $10,000 maximum exclusion applies if the distribution is used toward the purchase of a first home (within 120 days of the distribution)

- **Insurance** (medical)

  - Unemployed with 12 consecutive weeks of unemployment compensation

  - Self-employed (who are otherwise eligible for unemployment compensation)

- **Medical** expenses in excess of 10 percent of AGI

- **Disability** (permanent or indefinite disability, but not temporary disability)

- **Education:** College tuition, books, fees, etc.

- *And*

- **Death**

2.10.4 Excess Contributions

Excess contributions to the plan are subject to a cumulative 6 percent excise tax each year until the excess is corrected.

2.10.5 Investment of Funds

The amounts invested in an IRA can be placed into a domestic trust or a custodial account or can be invested directly in individual annuity contracts issued by an insurance company. An individual's interest in the plan must be nonforfeitable.

2.11 Annuities

The investment amount is divided by a factor representing the number of months over which the investment will be recovered. This factor is based on the age of the annuitant at the start of the payout period. Factors range from 360 for starting ages under 56 to 160 for starting ages over 70.

Illustration 3   Annuity

General Rules: If the investment in the contract is $60,000 and the annuitant is 64 years old (the factor is 260 months per the IRS table) at the start of the payout period, then:

$$\frac{\$60,000}{260} = \$230.77 \text{ excludable from each of the first 260 payments}$$

In this example, the first $230.77 of the first 260 payments received is not taxable. Amounts of each payment in excess of $230.77 are taxable.

Live Longer Than Actuarial Payout Period: If the annuitant lives longer than 260 months, then further payments are fully taxable.

Death Before Full Recovery: If the annuitant dies before the 260 payments are collected, the unrecovered portion of the $60,000 is a miscellaneous itemized deduction on the annuitant's final income tax return.

2.12   Rental Income—Passive Activity

Net rental income or loss is calculated on Schedule E and reported as a single line item on Form 1040 (the specific line item is rental real estate, royalties, ...). Details of the calculation for income or loss from rental real estate reported on an individual tax return are covered later in this unit.

2.13   Unemployment Compensation

A taxpayer must include in gross income the full amount received for unemployment compensation.

2.14   Social Security Income

Social Security benefits received might be included in income. Taxpayers are classified into five categories depending on the level of modified adjusted gross income, or provisional income, which is defined as AGI plus tax-exempt interest plus 50 percent of Social Security benefits. Taxpayers must include in income the lesser of 50 percent (or 85 percent, depending on income) of Social Security received or 50 percent (or 85 percent, depending on income) of the excess provisional income over the threshold.

- Low Income = No Social Security benefits are taxable (income equal to or less than $25,000 for single filers or equal to or less than $32,000 for MFJ).

- Lower Middle Income = Less than 50 percent of Social Security benefits are taxable.

- Middle Income = 50 percent of Social Security benefits are taxable (income over: single $25,000/MFJ $32,000).

- Upper Middle Income = Between 50 percent and 85 percent of Social Security benefits are taxable.

- Upper Income = 85 percent of Social Security benefits are taxable (income over: single $34,000/MFJ $44,000).

2.14.1   Modified Adjusted Gross Income

Modified adjusted gross income (modified AGI), also known as provisional income, includes the following items:

- Any income excluded because of the foreign earned income exclusion.

- Any exclusion or deduction claimed for foreign housing.

- Any interest income from series EE bonds that was able to be excluded because of qualified higher education expenses.

- Any deduction claimed for student loan interest or qualified tuition and related expenses.

- Any employer-paid adoption expense that was excluded.

- Any deduction claimed for an annual (non-rollover) contribution to a regular IRA.

In other words, the above items are not taken into account in determining AGI vs. modified AGI.

2.15   Taxable Miscellaneous Income

2.15.1   Prizes and Awards

The fair market value of prizes and awards is taxable income. An exclusion from income for certain prizes and awards applies when the winner is selected for the award without entering into a contest (i.e., without any action on the winner's part) and assigns the award directly to a governmental unit or charitable organization.

2.15.2 Gambling Winnings and Losses

- **Winnings:** Gambling winnings are included in gross income.

- **Losses:** Unless the taxpayer is in the trade or business of gambling (which follows other specific reporting rules), gambling losses may only be deducted to the extent of gambling winnings. Gambling losses include the expenses the taxpayer incurred in connection with the gambling activity. The allowable amount of these gambling losses are deductible on Schedule A as an itemized deduction.

2.15.3 Business Recoveries

To decide whether a business recovery is excludable, one must determine what the damages were paid "in lieu of." Thus, if a damage award is compensation for lost profit, the award is *income*.

2.15.4 Punitive Damages

Punitive damages are fully taxable as ordinary income if received in a business context or for loss of personal reputation. Punitive damages received by an individual in a personal injury case are also taxable except in wrongful death cases where state law has limited wrongful death awards to punitive damages only.

2.16 Partially Taxable Miscellaneous Items (Scholarships and Fellowships)

- **Degree-Seeking Student:** Scholarships and fellowship grants are excludable only up to amounts actually spent on tuition, fees, books, and supplies (not room and board) provided:

  - The grant is made to a degree-seeking student;

  - No services are to be performed as a condition to receiving the grant; and

  - The grant is not made in consideration for past, present, or future services of the grantee.

- **Non-degree-Seeking Student:** Scholarships and fellowships awarded to non-degree-seeking students are fully taxable at FMV.

- **Tuition Reductions:** Graduate teaching assistants and research assistants who receive tuition reductions are taxed on the reduction if it is their only compensation, but not if the reduction is in addition to other taxable compensation.

2.17 Nontaxable Miscellaneous Items

- **Life Insurance Proceeds (Nontaxable):** The proceeds of a life insurance policy paid because of the death of the insured are excluded from the gross income of the beneficiary.

  - The interest income element on deferred payout arrangements is fully taxable.

  - If the proceeds are used to pay for long-term care, accelerated death benefits received by an insured who is terminally ill (provided there is certification that the insured is expected to die within 24 months), is chronically ill, or requires assisted living are not taxable.

  - For policies issued after August 17, 2006, if the policy is company-owned (COLI), the employer beneficiary may exclude from gross income benefits received (no more than the total amount of premiums and other amounts paid by the policyholder). Any excess received beyond the amount of premiums and other amounts paid by the policyholder would be taxable. The gross income inclusion requirement for the COLI is not applicable, however, if proper notice and consent requirements are met and any of the following situations apply:

    —The insured was a qualified highly compensated officer, director, or employee and a U.S. citizen or resident.

—Proceeds were paid to a member of the insured's family.

—The beneficiary is a family member or another individual (not the policyholder).

—The beneficiary is a trust for the benefit of the insured's family (or the estate of the insured).

- **Gifts and Inheritances (Nontaxable):** Gross income does not include property received from a gift or inheritance; however, any income received from such property (e.g., interest income, rental income, etc.) after the property is in the hands of the recipient is taxable.

- **Medicare Benefits (Nontaxable):** Exclude from gross income basic Medicare benefits received under the Social Security Act.

- **Workers' Compensation (Nontaxable):** Exclude from gross income compensation received under a workers' compensation act for personal injury or sickness.

- **Personal (Physical) Injury or Illness Award (Nontaxable):** Exclude from gross income damages received as compensation for personal (physical) injury or illness.

- **Accident Insurance: Premiums Paid by Taxpayer (Nontaxable):** Exclude from gross income all payments received (even with multiple recoveries) if the individual paid all premiums for the insurance.

- **Foreign-Earned Income Exclusion:** Taxpayers working abroad may exclude from gross income up to $105,900 (2019) of their foreign-earned income. In order to qualify for the exclusion, the taxpayer must satisfy one of the following two tests:

  1. **Bona Fide Residence Test:** The taxpayer must have been a bona fide resident of a foreign country for an entire taxable year.

  2. **Physical Presence Test:** The physical presence test requires that the taxpayer must have been present in the foreign country for 330 full days out of any 12-consecutive-month period (which may begin on any day).

Note: The exclusion cannot exceed the taxpayer's foreign earned income reduced by the taxpayer's foreign housing exclusion (maximum $16,944 in 2019, 16 percent of the foreign-earned income exclusion). Furthermore, the amount of excluded income and housing is used to determine the income tax rate (and alternative minimum tax rate) for the taxpayer for the year (i.e., although it is not taxed, the excluded income could cause other income to be taxed at higher rates, as if the excluded income were taxable).

Question 1	MCQ-01636

Clark did not itemize deductions on his Year 8 federal income tax return. In July Year 9, Clark received a state income tax refund of $900 plus interest of $10, for overpayment of Year 8 state income tax. What amount of the state tax refund and interest is taxable on Clark's Year 9 federal income tax return?

- a. $0
- b. $10
- c. $900
- d. $910

Question 2 MCQ-01620

John and Mary were divorced in 2017. The divorce decree (executed 6/30/17) provides that John pay alimony of $10,000 per year, to be reduced by 20 percent on their child's 18th birthday. During the current year, the $10,000 was paid in the following way: John paid $7,000 directly to Mary and $3,000 to Spring College for Mary's tuition. What amount of these payments should be reported as income in Mary's current year income tax return?

a. $5,600

b. $8,000

c. $8,600

d. $10,000

Question 3 MCQ-04756

DAC Foundation awarded Kent $75,000 in recognition of lifelong literary achievement. Kent was not required to render future services as a condition to receive the $75,000. What condition(s) must have been met for the award to be excluded from Kent's gross income?

I. Kent was selected for the award by DAC without any action on Kent's part.

II. Pursuant to Kent's designation, DAC paid the amount of the award either to a governmental unit or to a charitable organization.

a. I only.

b. II only.

c. Both I and II.

d. Neither I nor II.

Question 4 MCQ-01482

Klein, a master's degree candidate at Blair University, was awarded a $12,000 scholarship from Blair in Year 8. The scholarship was used to pay Klein's Year 8 university tuition and fees. Also in Year 8, Klein received $5,000 for teaching two courses at a nearby college. What amount is includable in Klein's Year 8 gross income?

a. $0

b. $5,000

c. $12,000

d. $17,000

1 Business Income or Loss, Schedule C or C-EZ

Net income from self-employment is computed on Schedule C. The net income from the sole proprietorship is then transferred to Form 1040 as one amount.

Gross business income

< Business expenses >

Profit or loss

1.1 Gross Income

Items that normally would be revenue in a trade or business or other self-employed activity (such as director or consulting fees) are included as part of gross income on Schedule C.

- Cash = Amount received (Cash Basis)
- Property = Fair market value
- Cancellation of debt

1.2 Expenses

Expenses include items that one would expect to find in business, such as:

- Cost of goods (inventory is expensed when sold).
- Salaries and commissions paid to others.
- State and local business taxes paid.
- Office expenses (e.g., supplies, equipment, and rent).
- Actual automobile expenses (depreciation expense is limited to only that portion used for business) or a standard mileage rate (58 cents per mile for 2019).
- Business meal expenses at 50 percent (when all proceeds go to benefit a charity; 100 percent may be deductible as an itemized deduction for charitable contributions).
- Depreciation of business assets.
- Interest expense on business loans (interest expense paid in advance by a cash basis taxpayer cannot be deducted until the tax year/period to which the interest relates). The deduction for business interest expense is limited to 30 percent of business income, excluding interest income, before depreciation and interest expense deductions. Disallowed business interest expense can be carried forward indefinitely. The limitation does not apply if the taxpayer's average annual gross receipts are less than $25 million for the prior three taxable years.

- Employee benefits.

- Legal and professional services.

- Bad debts actually written off for an accrual basis taxpayer only (the direct write-off method, not the allowance method, is used for tax purposes).

1.3 Nondeductible Expenses (on Schedule C)

- Salaries paid to the sole proprietor (they are considered a "draw").

- Federal income tax.

- Personal portion of:

  - Automobile, travel, and meal expenses.

  - *Interest expense:* This may be reported as an itemized deduction if mortgage interest or investment interest is paid.

  - *State and local tax expense:* Report as an itemized deduction on Schedule A.

  - *Health insurance of a sole proprietor:* Although this is not reported on Schedule C as an expense, it is reported as an adjustment to arrive at AGI.

- Bad debt expense of a cash basis taxpayer (who never reported the income).

- *Charitable contributions:* Report as an itemized deduction on Schedule A.

- Entertainment expenses

1.4 Net Business Income or Loss

1.4.1 Net Business Income Is Taxable

There are two taxes on net business income:

1. Income tax.

2. Federal self-employment (SE) tax.

  - An adjustment to income is allowed for one-half (which is 7.65 percent of up to $132,900 of self-employment income in 2019 plus 1.45 percent of self-employment income thereafter, if applicable) of SE tax (Medicare plus Social Security) paid.

  - This allows the sole proprietor the ability to "deduct" the employer portion of the SE tax as an adjustment to gross taxable income (of which the net Schedule C amount is a part).

  - All self-employment income is subject to the 2.9 percent Medicare tax.

  - Up to $132,900 in 2019 is subject to the 12.4 percent Social Security tax (i.e., a total of 15.3 percent on self-employment earnings up to $132,900 in 2019).

  - The actual SE tax is calculated on 92.35 percent of self-employment income.

Example 1	Calculation of Self-Employment Tax

Facts: Tyler earns $20,000 from his consulting business, which he runs as a sole proprietorship. This was the only income he had in the current year.

Required: Determine Tyler's self-employment tax.

Solution: Tyler's self-employment tax is $2,826 calculated as follows:

$$\$20,000 \times 92.35\% = \$18,470$$
$$\$18,470 \times 15.3\% = \$2,826$$

1.4.2 Net Taxable Loss

A business with a loss may deduct the loss against other sources of income subject to limitations. A combined excess business loss (over $500,000 for married filing jointly and $250,000 for all other taxpayers) is not allowed and must be carried forward as a net operating loss (NOL).

A net operating loss that arises in tax years beginning after December 31, 2017, only can offset up to 80 percent of taxable income in a future year, but can be carried forward indefinitely. A net operating loss that arises before then only can be carried forward 20 years, but is not subject to the 80 percent of future taxable income limitation.

1.5 Uniform Capitalization Rules

The *uniform capitalization rules* apply to all business enterprises that meet the criteria for implementation (including sole proprietorships, partnerships, and corporations) and provide guidelines with respect to capitalizing or expensing certain costs (i.e., taxes paid in connection with the acquisition of property are capitalized as part of the property's cost). In the first year of implementation, they generally cause an increase in the carrying cost of ending inventory and a decrease in operating expense. This results in an increase to taxable income. Any business that has average gross receipts of $25 million or less for the previous three years is exempt from the uniform capitalization rules.

1.5.1 Types of Property

Uniform capitalization rules apply to the following:

■ **Produced for Use:** Real or tangible personal property produced by the taxpayer for use in his or her trade or business (e.g., machine tools for use in the production line of a machine tool manufacturer).

■ **Produced for Sale:** Real or tangible personal property produced by the taxpayer for sale to his or her customers (i.e., manufacturer's inventory).

■ **Acquired for Resale:** Real or tangible personal property acquired by the taxpayer for resale (i.e., retailer's inventory).

1.5.2 Costs Required to Be Capitalized

Costs required to be capitalized include direct materials, direct labor (e.g., compensation, vacation pay, and payroll taxes), and applicable indirect costs (i.e., those to which an allocation must be applied, such as factory overhead). Examples of applicable indirect costs (capitalizable expenses) include utilities, warehousing costs, repairs, maintenance, indirect labor (e.g., supervisory), rents, storage, depreciation and amortization, insurance, pension contributions, engineering and design, repackaging, spoilage and scrap, and administrative supplies.

1.5.3 Costs Not Required to Be Capitalized

Costs not required to be capitalized include selling, advertising, and marketing expenses, certain general and administrative expenses, research, and officer compensation not attributed to production services.

1.6 Long-Term Contracts

Special tax rules are required of most taxpayers who operate under long-term contracts (exceptions exist). A long-term contract is generally defined as a contract that is incomplete at the end of a tax year in which it was started (i.e., it does not start and finish within the same tax year) and relates to the manufacture, installation, building, or construction of real or personal property.

1.6.1 Income Recognition

■ **Percentage-of-Completion Method Required for Tax for Nonexempt Long-Term Contracts**

Unless an exemption exists for a taxpayer or a contract, long-term contracts must be accounted for using the percentage-of-completion method to determine taxable income for a particular contract. (Note that a taxpayer may use other methods for other contracts if an exemption exists; thus, contracts are evaluated on a contract-by-contract basis.)

■ **Exemptions**

Certain contracts are exempt from the requirements of long-term contract income recognition for tax purposes and may use other methods (e.g., completed contract method) to calculate their taxable income under the contract for regular income tax purposes. These include:

- *Small contractors* (projects that are expected to last no more than two years and are performed by a taxpayer who has average annual gross receipts not exceeding $25 million for the three years that precede the tax year in question).

- *Home construction contractors* (where at least 80 percent of the total contract costs are related to the construction or rehabilitation of certain dwelling units, which do not include hotels, etc., where the majority of the use is on a transient basis).

1.6.2 Cost Allocation Rules

■ **Cost Allocation Rules Required for Tax on Long-Term Construction Contracts**

Unless an exemption exists for a taxpayer or a contract, those involved in long-term contracts must use cost allocation rules to account for their long-term projects. In addition to all the direct costs associated with a project, other costs that relate to the activities of the long-term contract (e.g., storage costs, production period interest, pension plan contributions, etc.) must be allocated to the cost of the long-term project. Essentially, the uniform capitalization rules discussed previously apply to long-term contracts. Note that costs associated with marketing, advertising, selling, and research and development are not subject to such cost allocation (capitalization).

Exemptions

Small contractor and home construction contractors are not required to employ the costs allocation rules identified above. However, (i) they are required to allocate production period interest related to the contract to the costs of the project; and (ii) home construction projects that are not also small constructions projects must use the uniform capitalization rules (discussed in the above section). Also, interest for the production period need not be capitalized if the total cost of the project is $1 million or less and the project is estimated to take less than 12 months to complete.

1.6.3   Production Period Defined

Start Date

For cash basis taxpayers, the starting date of production is generally the date on which the contractor incurs costs (other than the start-up engineering, design, etc., costs that are excluded from cost allocation, as discussed above) under the contract. For accrual basis taxpayers, the starting date is the later of the date for cash basis taxpayers or the date the taxpayer has incurred at least 5 percent of the total costs initially estimated under the contract.

End Date

The end date of the production period is generally the date on which the work under the contract is complete (per contract provisions) or on the date the taxpayer has incurred at least 95 percent of the total costs expected under the contract.

1.6.4   Calculation for Percentage-of-Completion Method Income Recognition

In simple terms, the amount of gross income under the contract that is recognized on the tax return is the portion of income that relates to the percentage of the contract that has been completed during the year.

Cost-to-Cost Method (to Determine Percentage)

The percentage is calculated under the cost-to-cost method, which is a ratio of the total cumulative costs incurred to date at the end of the tax year divided by the total expected costs to be incurred under the contract. This ratio provides a total "percent-complete" amount for the contract as of the end of the tax year.

Gross Income Recognition Calculation

To calculate the amount of income that will be recognized under the contract for a given tax year, multiply the ratio determined using the cost-to-cost method (above) by the total contract price and subtract the amount of income that was recognized in prior years for the contract.

1.6.5   Impact on Alternative Minimum Tax (AMT)

The details of alternative minimum tax are presented when the calculation of tax liability is discussed in more detail. Certain items should be noted with regard to the effects from long-term contracts.

- The percentage-of-completion method is required to be used for alternative minimum taxation, regardless of the method used for regular tax (except for home construction contracts).

- Even if the percentage-of-completion method is used for regular tax purposes, there are likely to be differences in the calculation of taxable income because the calculation of alternative minimum taxable income must take into account not only the method of income recognition, but also other alternative minimum tax rules (e.g., depreciation methods).

1.6.6 Miscellaneous Effects

▪ Change in Accounting Method

The method used by a taxpayer for the income recognition on a contract is deemed a "method of accounting" by the IRS and cannot be changed for the contract without consent of the IRS. Furthermore, if a taxpayer desires to sever a contract into various contracts or aggregates several contracts into one larger contract, IRS approval is generally required, and a statement explaining the changes must be attached to the original tax return for the year.

▪ "Unique" Rules for Personal Property Contracts

In order for the manufacture of personal property to qualify as a long-term contract, not only must the contract not be completed within the year it was started, but it also must be for the manufacture of a "unique" item (i.e., an item that is made specifically for a customer and could not be sold to others, is not generally part of a taxpayer's normal inventory, and requires significant preproduction costs).

▪ Related Parties

A taxpayer who performs an activity that would normally not be considered a long-term contract activity (such as engineering or design services) must report income using the percentage-of-completion method if it is incidental to or necessary to a related party's long-term contract that must be reported using the percentage-of-completion method.

2 Farming Income

A person (or entity) who engages in the management or operation of a farm with the intent of earning a profit will report income and expenses (either cash or accrual basis) using a Schedule F (which is reported on line 18 of Schedule 1 and flows to line 6 on Form 1040). Essentially, income from farming activities is treated the same as income from other business activities (which is reported on line 12 of Schedule 1 and flows to line 6 on Form 1040).

2.1 Cash Basis and Accrual Method

▪ Cash Basis

- Most farmers use the cash basis.

- Inventories of produce, livestock, etc., are *not* considered.

- Gross income includes cash and the value of all other items received from the sale of produce, livestock, etc., that has been *raised* by the farmer.

- For livestock or other items a farmer may have bought, profit is computed by subtracting the purchase price (cost) from the sales price. See line 1b of Schedule F.

- Insurance payments from crop damage are treated as income.

- Interest paid on a loan used for the farming business is deductible.

Example 2 — Farming Deduction

Facts: Bob is a cash basis sole proprietor farmer. During Year 2, Bob spends $2,100 on feed for the livestock.

Required: Determine how much Bob can deduct in Year 2 related to feed for the livestock.

Solution: Bob may deduct the entire $2,100 on his Year 2 income tax return, because he is not required to consider inventory.

- **Accrual Method**
  - The accrual method is required for certain corporate and partnership farmers as well as for all farming tax shelters.
  - Inventories must be used and maintained, and they must be taken at the start and end of the tax year. The following methods of inventory valuation for farming are accepted by the IRS:
    - —Cost.
    - —Lower of cost or market.
    - —Farm-price method (inventory is valued at the market price less the disposition costs and generally must be used for all items inventoried by the farming business, except for any livestock valued using the unit-livestock-price method).
    - —Unit-livestock-price method (uses a value for each livestock class at a standard unit price for animals within the class).
- Gross profit equals the value of inventories at year-end *plus* the proceeds received from the sales during the year, *less* the value of inventories at the beginning of the year, *less* the cost of inventory purchased during the year.

Example 3 — Farming Gross Profit Calculation

Facts: Evan has a farming business, and is required to use the accrual method. During Year 3 Evan had net sales of $75,000. Inventory at the beginning of Year 3 was $15,600 including livestock held for resale. Inventory at the end of the year was $14,200. Inventory purchases during Year, 3 including livestock, amounted to $60,000.

Required: Determine Evan's farming gross profit.

Solution: Evan's gross profit for Year 3 is $13,600, calculated as follows:

Net sales $75,000 + Ending inventory $14,200 − Beginning inventory $15,600
− Inventory purchases $60,000 = $13,600

2.2 Farm Income Averaging

Taxpayers with a qualifying farming business may be able to average some or all of the current year's farm income by spreading it out over the past three years. Farm income averaging provides farmers the opportunity to lower their tax liability during a year in which they earn a significantly higher income than in the previous three years. An individual is not required to have been engaged in a farming business in any of the base years in order to make a farm income averaging election. Schedule J is used for averaging farming income.

Illustration 1   Farm Income Averaging

In the current year, a farmer had a bountiful crop, and the income from his farming business increased significantly in Year 2 as compared with Year 1. The increased farming income resulted in the farmer being taxed at a higher rate than in the past three years. The farmer can elect to average some or all of the current year's income over the past three years.

---

3   Rental Income or Loss

3.1 General

Rental activity is reported on Schedule E. Because rental income is usually regarded as passive, rental income will be discussed in more detail when passive losses are covered. The basic formula for the determination of net rental income or loss is as follows:

> **Gross rental income**
>
> **Prepaid rental income**
>
> **Rent cancellation payment**
>
> **Improvement-in-lieu of rent**
>
> **< Rental expenses >**
>
> ---
>
> **Net rental income   Or   Net rental loss**

3.2 Rental of Residence

■ **Rented Fewer Than 15 Days**

If the residence is rented for fewer than 15 days per year, it is treated as a personal residence. The rental income is excluded from income, and mortgage interest (first or second home) and real estate taxes are allowed as itemized deductions. Depreciation, utilities, and repairs are *not* deductible.

Rented 15 or More Days

If the residence is rented for 15 or more days, and is used for personal purposes for the greater of (i) more than 14 days or (ii) more than 10 percent of the rental days, it is treated as a personal/rental residence. Expenses must be prorated between personal and rental use (see the example that follows). However, a different proration method is used for mortgage interest and property taxes (see * in the illustration that follows) than is used for other property-related expenses (e.g., utilities, insurance, depreciation, etc.). Rental use expenses are deductible only to the extent of rental income.

3.3   Nonresidence (Rental Property)

For rental property, the taxpayer includes income received from the property in gross income and deducts all expenses allocated to the rental property on Schedule E of Form 1040. As discussed later in this unit, rental losses are considered passive and will be deductible only to the extent of passive income. An exception to this rule allows an active participant in rental activity to deduct up to $25,000 of rental losses against nonpassive income.

Illustration 2   Vacation Home Rental

Julie rents her vacation home for two months and lives there for one month (during the other 11 months, Julie lives in the city). Thus, of the three-month period the vacation home is used, one-third is personal and two-thirds is rental. Assume that Julie's gross rental income is $6,000, her real estate taxes are $2,400, interest is $3,600, utilities are $4,800, and related depreciation is $7,200.

These amounts are deductible in the following order:

		Rental (Schedule E)	Personal (Schedule A)
Gross rental income		$ 6,000	–
Deduct: Taxes	$2,400		
Interest	3,600		
	$6,000 × 2/12*	(1,000)	$5,000—Schedule A
Balance		$ 5,000	
Deduct: Utilities	$4,800 × 2/3**	(3,200)	$1,600—Not Deductible
		$1,800	
Deduct: Depreciation	$7,200 × 2/3**		
	$4,800 but limited to***	(1,800)	$2,400—Not Deductible
Net income		$ 0	

  * Allocated based on rental period/total annual period.

 ** Allocated based on rental period/total annual usage.

*** The additional $3,000 ($4,800 − 1,800) is not deductible, but is carried over to next year and applied against future income from this property.

---

4 Tax Planning

Understanding the implications of the timing of income and deductions is an effective tool for maximizing the after-tax wealth of a taxpayer. Using the time value of money principles, a taxpayer can evaluate the effect of the timing of a tax decision. The two basic tax strategies, assuming that the taxpayer's tax rate remains constant, are to:

1. Defer taxable income

2. Accelerate tax deductions

However, important tax factors may change from year to year in a dynamic tax environment. These changes may be a result of a change in tax law or a change in the taxpayer's personal situation, such as retirement or opening a new business. Therefore, many other factors must be considered for tax planning. These include:

▨ Type of income

▨ Changing tax rates

▨ Type of entity

▨ Taxpayer's filing status

Example 4   Timing of Income (With Constant Tax Rates)

Facts: Jill Jones owns a small retail business. Jill is a cash-based, calendar-year taxpayer. She reports her income and expenses related to the business on Schedule C. Jill has the opportunity to make an unusually large sale in the amount of $100,000 and is trying to determine the best tax strategy regarding the timing of the sale. She can finalize the sale and receive payment on either December 31 of the current year or January 1 of next year. Jill's marginal tax rate is 30 percent in both tax years. (For all examples that follow, assume an after-tax rate of return on investments of 10 percent for present value analysis. The present value factor for one year at 10 percent is .909.)

Required: Advise Jill on whether it is optimal for the sale to be made in the current year on December 31 or next year on January 1.

Solution: If Jill finalizes the sale and receives payment on December 31 of this year, she will have to report the $100,000 of income on this year's tax return. However, if she waits to finalize the sale on January 1, then she will have income one year later on next year's tax return.

(continued)

(continued)

Compare the after-tax effect of Jill's $100,000 sale:

	Option A: $100,000 Income This Year	Option B: $100,000 Income Next Year
Income	$100,000	$100,000
Marginal tax rate	× 30%	× 30%
Tax on income	30,000	30,000
Discount factor	× 1	× .909
Present value of tax	$ 30,000	$ 27,270
Income after tax:		
Before-tax income	$100,000	$100,000
Less: Present value of tax	(30,000)	(27,270)
Income after tax	$ 70,000	$ 72,730

Option B to defer the $100,000 income to next year results in $2,730 in additional income after tax, considering the time value of money since the present value of tax paid one year later is lower than if the tax is paid in the current year.

Example 5 — Timing of Income (With Increasing Tax Rates)

Facts: Using the example above, assume that Jill's marginal tax rate is 30 percent this year but will increase to 31 percent next year under tax law.

Required: Advise Jill on whether it is optimal for the sale to be made in the current year on December 31 or next year on January 1.

Solution:

	Option A: $100,000 Income This Year	Option B: $100,000 Income Next Year
Income	$100,000	$100,000
Marginal tax rate	× 30%	× 31%
Tax on income	30,000	31,000
Discount factor	× 1	× .909
Present value of tax savings	$ 30,000	$ 28,179
Income after tax:		
Before-tax income	$100,000	$100,000
Less: Present value of tax	(30,000)	(28,179)
Income after tax	$ 70,000	$ 71,821

Although Option B is still more attractive, the increase in taxable income is only $1,821. A taxpayer must evaluate the specific facts and circumstances in his or her tax situation to effectively understand the timing effects of taxable income.

Example 6 — Timing of Deductions (With Constant Tax Rates)

Facts: Jill is planning to purchase new equipment for her retail business that costs $20,000. Jill is considering whether to purchase the equipment this year and therefore deduct the cost of the equipment on this year's tax return or purchase the equipment next year and deduct the cost of the equipment on next year's tax return. Jill's marginal tax rate is 30 percent.

Required: Determine which year Jill should purchase the equipment to provide the lowest after-tax cost.

Solution:

	Option A: Purchase $20,000 Equipment This Year	Option B: Purchase $20,000 Equipment Next Year
Tax deduction	$20,000	$20,000
Marginal tax rate	× 30%	× 30%
Tax savings	6,000	6,000
Discount factor	× 1	× .909
Present value of tax savings	$6,000	$5,454
After-tax cost of equipment:		
Before-tax cost	$20,000	$20,000
Less: Present value of tax	(6,000)	(5,454)
After-tax cost	$14,000	$14,546

Option A offers Jill the lowest after-tax cost of the equipment.

Example 7 — Timing of Deductions (With Increasing Tax Rates)

Facts: Use the same facts as above, but now assume that Jill expects that her business income will rise with the use of the new equipment. Therefore, her marginal tax rate will increase from 30 percent in the current year to 35 percent next year.

Required: Determine which year Jill should purchase the equipment to provide the lowest after-tax cost.

Solution:

	Option A: Purchase $20,000 Equipment This Year	Option B: Purchase $20,000 Equipment Next Year
Tax deduction	$20,000	$20,000
Marginal tax rate	× 30%	× 35%
Tax savings	6,000	7,000
Discount factor	× 1	× .909
Present value of tax savings	$ 6,000	$ 6,363
After-tax cost of equipment:		
Before-tax cost	$20,000	$20,000
Less: present value of tax	(6,000)	(6,363)
After-tax cost	$14,000	$13,637

With a rising tax rate next year, Option B now offers the lowest after-tax cost of the equipment.

Many factors must be considered in determining the timing of income and deductions for a taxpayer. In a changing tax environment, the facts and circumstances unique to the taxpayer must be evaluated. The examples above illustrate the effect of properly timing income and deductions to increase the after-tax wealth of a taxpayer.

Question 1   MCQ-01438

Which of the following costs is *not* included in inventory under the Uniform Capitalization rules for goods manufactured by the taxpayer?

- **a.** Research
- **b.** Warehousing costs
- **c.** Quality control
- **d.** Taxes excluding income taxes

Question 2   MCQ-01472

Baker, a sole proprietor CPA, has several clients that do business in Spain. While on a four-week vacation in Spain, Baker attended a five-day seminar on Spanish business practices that cost $700. Baker's round-trip airfare to Spain was $600. While in Spain, Baker spent an average of $100 per day on accommodations, local travel, and other incidental expenses, for total expenses of $2,800. What amount of total expense can Baker deduct on Form 1040 Schedule C, "Profit or Loss From Business," related to this situation?

- **a.** $700
- **b.** $1,200
- **c.** $1,800
- **d.** $4,100

Question 3   MCQ-01614

Nare, an accrual-basis taxpayer, owns a building which was rented to Mott under a 10-year lease expiring August 31, Year 8. On January 2, Year 2, Mott paid $30,000 as consideration for canceling the lease. On November 1, Year 2, Nare leased the building to Pine under a five-year lease. Pine paid Nare $10,000 rent for the two months of November and December, and an additional $5,000 for the last month's rent. What amount of rental income should Nare report in its Year 2 income tax return?

- **a.** $10,000
- **b.** $15,000
- **c.** $40,000
- **d.** $45,000

1 Flow-Through Business Entities

For tax purposes, business entities are either separate taxpaying entities or flow-through entities. A business entity that is a separate taxpaying entity pays tax on the income earned by the business. In contrast, a flow-through entity reports income on a tax return filed for informational purposes only. The income flows through to the owners of the entity's personal income tax return. Therefore, the tax is paid at the owner level only.

Although there are many types of legal entities, the tax system in the United States recognizes four categories of business entities:

1. **Partnership:** Flow-through entity that reports income on Form 1065

2. **S Corporation:** Flow-through entity that reports income on Form 1120S

3. **Sole Proprietorship:** Flow-through entity that reports income on Form 1040, Schedule C

4. **C Corporation:** Separate taxpaying entity that reports income on Form 1120

The coverage in this section focuses on flow-through business entities, which must provide an owner of the entity a Schedule K-1 with the income information to be reported on Form 1040. Reporting of items from Schedule C is covered earlier in this unit.

1.1 Reporting Partnership Income and Losses

A partnership is not a taxpaying entity and files an information return, Form 1065, by March 15 (extension to September 15, if necessary).

The following schedule shows which partnership items will be reported separately on Form 1065 and which will pass through to each individual partner's income tax return as separate line items to be treated by each individual according to his or her own circumstances. (Note that the details of the partnership's business income and expenses are reported only on Form 1065.) Partnership income and loss is generally allocated per the partnership agreement.

		Appears On		
		1065	K	K-1
	Business income	✓		
	< Business expenses >	✓		
	< Guaranteed Payments >			
1.	Net business income or loss*	✓	✓	✓
2.	Guaranteed payments to partners	✓	✓	✓
3.	Net "active" rental real estate income or loss		✓	✓
4.	Net "passive" rental real estate income or loss		✓	✓
5.	Interest income		✓	✓
6.	Dividend income		✓	✓
7.	Capital gains and losses		✓	✓
8.	Charitable contributions		✓	✓
9.	Section 179 (expense election)		✓	✓
10.	Investment interest expense		✓	✓
11.	Partners' health insurance premiums (reported as part of guaranteed payments)	✓	✓	✓
12.	Retirement plan contributions (Keogh Plan)**	✓	✓	✓
13.	Tax credits (reported by partnership but claimed by partners)*		✓	✓

*Net business loss limitations discussed earlier in this unit will have to be considered.

**Contributions made on behalf of employees are deductible on Form 1065 and not reported on the Schedules K and K-1; contributions for partners are not deducted on Form 1065 but are reported on Schedules K and K-1.

Pass Key

- A partner must include on his personal income tax return his distributive share of each separate "pass-through" item.

- Guaranteed payments are a business expense that reduce partnership net business income flowing through to the partners, and are also taxable income to the partner receiving the payments.

1.2   Reporting S Corporation Income and Losses

An S corporation is also not a taxpaying entity. The S corporation files an information return, Form 1120S, by March 15 (extension to September 15, if necessary). The details of the S corporation's business income and expenses are reported only on Form 1120S. Allocations to shareholders are made on a per-share, per-day basis. The following S corporation items flow through to the shareholder in a manner similar to a partnership (see Schedule K-1 for complete list):

- Ordinary business income

- Rental income/loss, which includes recapture income and unearned revenue related to rental activities

- Portfolio income (including interest, dividends, royalties, and all capital gains/losses)

- Tax-exempt interest

- Percentage depletion

- Foreign income tax

- Section 1231 gains and losses

- Charitable contributions

- Section 179 expense deduction for recovery property

- Unrecaptured Section 1250 income

- Gain (loss) from sale of collectibles

Illustration 1   Allocation on Per-Share, Per-Day Basis

The Duffy Corporation, an S corporation, is owned equally by three shareholders, Rick, Annie, and Kate. The corporation is on a calendar year basis. On February 1, Year 5, Kate sold her one-third interest in Duffy Corporation to George. For the year ended December 31, Year 5, the corporation had non-separately stated ordinary income of $120,000. For Year 5, the income of the corporation should be allocated as follows:

Rick ($120,000 × 1/3)	$ 40,000
Annie ($120,000 × 1/3)	40,000
Kate (31/365 × $40,000)	3,397
George (334/365 × $40,000)	36,603
Total	$120,000

Pass Key

Similar to a partnership, shareholders in an S corporation must include on their personal income tax return their distributive share of each separate "pass-through" item. Shareholders are taxed on these items, regardless of whether or not the items have been distributed (withdrawn) to them during the year.

1.3   S Corporation and Partnership Self-Employment Tax Difference

1.3.1   Payment for Services

Partners in a partnership (including members of a limited liability company, or LLC) are considered to be self-employed, not employees, when performing services for the partnership. Guaranteed payments are reasonable compensation paid to a partner for services rendered or use of capital without regard to his ratio of income. They are allowable tax deductions to the partnership and treated as self-employment income to the partner.

When performing services for an S corporation, shareholders are treated as employees for tax purposes. IRS rules require that S corporations pay shareholders who are also employees a reasonable compensation that is subject to payroll taxes. The S corporation pays the employer portion of payroll taxes in connection with the compensation, and the shareholder pays the employee portion of the payroll taxes on the compensation as with any other employer-employee relationship.

1.3.2   Distributive Share of Income or Loss

For a general partner of a partnership, net earnings from self-employment include the partner's distributive share of the income or loss from that trade or business. Limited partners do not pay self-employment tax on their distributive share of partnership income but only pay self-employment tax on guaranteed payments.

The allocated income from an S corporation is not subject to self-employment tax but is only subject to the shareholder's personal income tax. Being able to avoid self-employment taxes is viewed as a big advantage of operating as an S corporation in comparison to operating as a partnership.

2   Qualified Business Income Deduction for Flow-Through Business Entities

2.1   Section 199A Overview

The Tax Cuts and Jobs Act of 2017 enacted Internal Revenue Code Section 199A, which provides a deduction of up to 20 percent of qualified business income for eligible flow-through entities. The qualified business income (QBI) deduction (also known as the Section 199A deduction) is available for years beginning after December 31, 2017, to all taxpayers other than a regular C corporation. This includes individuals, trusts, and estates. The deduction is taken "below the line" or from adjusted gross income.

2.2   Definitions

1. **Qualified Business Income (QBI):** Ordinary income less ordinary deductions earned from a sole proprietorship, S corporation, limited liability company, or partnership connected to business conducted within the U.S. QBI does not include any wages earned as an employee or guaranteed payments to partners. Dividends, interest, and long-term and short-term capital gains and losses are not included. QBI for a business must be reduced by any adjustments taken to arrive at AGI that relate to that business. This includes the deductible part of the self-employment (SE) tax, deductions for qualified contributions to SE retirement plans, and SE health insurance deductions.

2. **Qualified Property:** Any tangible, depreciable property that is held by the business at the end of the year and is used at any point during the year in the production of QBI.

3. **Qualified Trade or Business (QTB):** Any business other than a Specified Service Trade or Business (SSTB).

4. **Specified Service Trade or Business (SSTB):** An SSTB is a trade or business involving direct services in the fields of health, law, accounting, actuarial science, performing arts, consulting, athletics, financial services, brokerage, including investing and investment management, trading or dealing in securities, partnership interests or commodities, and any trade in which the principal asset is the reputation or skill of one or more of its employees or owners. Engineering and architectural services are specifically excluded from the definition of SSTB.

2.3   Calculating the Deduction

The basic deduction:

$$20\% \times \text{Qualified business income (QBI)}$$

2.4   Limitations to the QBI Deduction

Limitations are applied to the QBI deduction based on the taxable income of the taxpayer and whether the business is a qualified trade or business (QTB) or a specified trade or business (SSTB). SSTBs are only eligible for the deduction if the taxpayer's taxable income is below a certain level.

Two types of limitations may apply:

■   **Limitations Based on Taxable Income Level:**

2019	
Filing Status	**Taxable Income**
Single and all other	$160,700–$210,700
Married filing jointly	$321,400–$421,400

For this purpose, taxable income equals adjusted gross income minus all below-the-line deductions other than the QBI deduction.

■   **W-2 Wage and Property Limitation:**

When applicable, the QBI deduction is limited to the greater of:

1. 50 percent of W-2 wages for the business; or

2. 25 percent of W-2 wages for the business plus 2.5 percent of the unadjusted basis, immediately after acquisition (UBIA), of all qualified property.

The W-2 wages and property limitation does not apply to real estate investment trust (REIT) or publicly traded partnership (PTP) income.

2.5   Three Categories of Taxpayers

To best understand how to apply the limitations based on taxable income and the W-2 wage and property limitation, taxpayers can be divided into three categories:

1. Taxpayers with taxable income *at or below* $160,700 (single) or $321,400 (MFJ) (2019).

2. Taxpayers with taxable income *above* $210,700 (single) or $421,400 (MFJ) (2019).

3. Taxpayers with taxable income *between* $160,700–$210,700 (single) or $321,400–$421,400 (MFJ) (2019).

Category 1: Taxpayers with taxable income at or below $160,700 (single) or $321,400 (MFJ) (2019):

> **If QTB → Full 20% QBI deduction**
>
> **If SSTB → Full 20% QBI deduction**

Basically, if a taxpayer's taxable income before the QBI deduction is under the applicable thresholds, neither the restrictive rules for SSTBs nor the W-2 wage and property limit apply. The taxpayer is eligible for the full deduction (20% × QBI). In this taxable income range, an SSTB is treated as a QTB.

Category 2: Taxpayers with taxable income above $210,700 (single) or $421,400 (MFJ) (2019):

> **If QTB → Full W-2 wage and property limitation applies**
>
> **If SSTB → No QBI deduction allowed**

Category 3: Taxpayers with taxable income within the phase-in range: $160,700–$210,700 (single) or $321,400–$421,400 (MFJ) (2019):

> **If QTB → Phase-in of W-2 wage and property limitation**
> **(if limitation is less than 20% of QBI)**
>
> **If SSTB → QBI, W-2 wages, and qualified property**
> **amounts are reduced, then phase-in of W-2 wage and**
> **property limitation using reduced amounts**

2.5.1 QTB Within the Taxable Income Phase-in Range

For taxpayers within the taxable income phase-in range, if the amount of a QTB's W-2 wage and property limitation is less than 20% of QBI, the W-2 wage and property limitation is phased in. The QBI deduction is adjusted by a "reduction amount" based on how far the taxpayer is into the phase-in range ($50,000, single, or $100,000, MFJ).

> **Reduction amount = Excess amount × Phase-in percentage**

- Excess amount is the excess of (1) tentative QBI deduction (20% of QBI) over (2) W-2 wage and property limitation.

- Phase-in percentage is the ratio of (1) taxable income in excess of the threshold amount ($160,700, single, or $321,400, MFJ) over (2) the phase-in range.

> **Reduced QBI deduction = Tentative QBI deduction (20% of QBI) – Reduction amount**

If the amount of the QTB's W-2 wage and property limitation is greater than 20% of QBI, the limitation does not apply and no reduction is required.

2.5.2 SSTB Within the Taxable Income Phase-in Range

For taxpayers within the taxable income phase-in range, QBI, W-2 wages, and qualified property amounts are first reduced to the SSTB applicable percentage of each item. SSTB applicable percentage is 100% reduced by the phase-in percentage (ratio of taxable income in excess of the threshold amount over the phase-in range).

These reduced amounts are used to determine if the W-2 wage and property limitation is phased in. If the amount of the SSTB's reduced W-2 wage and property limitation is less than 20% of the reduced QBI, the QBI deduction is adjusted in the same manner as QTB, using the reduced QBI, W-2 wages, and qualified property amounts.

If the amount of the SSTB's reduced W-2 wage and property limitation is greater than 20% of the reduced QBI, the W-2 wage and property limitation does not apply and no further reduction is required. The QBI deduction is 20% of the QBI reduced to the SSTB applicable percentage.

2.6 Overall Taxable Income Limitation to Section 199A QBI Deduction

Once the tentative QBI deduction is calculated, an overall limitation based on the taxpayer's taxable income in excess of net capital gain must be considered. For purposes of the Section 199A overall taxable income limitation, net capital gain includes the excess of net long-term capital gain (LTCG) over net short-term capital loss (STCL) and qualified dividend income. The Section 199A QBI deduction is the lesser of:

1. Combined QBI deduction for all qualifying businesses; or

2. 20% of the taxpayer's taxable income (before the QBI deduction) in excess of net capital gain.

Example 1	QTB With Taxable Income Up to $160,700

Facts: A taxpayer filing as single has the following:

Taxable income = $50,000

Net capital gains = $5,000

QBI = $40,000

Required: Calculate the Section 199A QBI deduction.

Solution:

Tentative QBI deduction = $40,000 × 20% = $8,000

W-2 wage and property limitation does not apply

Overall limit = ($50,000 taxable income – $5,000 net capital gains) × 20% = $9,000, so not limited by overall limit

Section 199A QBI deduction = $8,000

Example 2 — SSTB With Taxable Income Up to $160,700

Facts: A taxpayer filing as single has the following:

Taxable income = $50,000

Net capital gains = $15,000

QBI = $40,000

Required: Calculate the Section 199A QBI deduction.

Solution:

Tentative QBI deduction = $40,000 × 20% = $8,000

W-2 wage and property limitation and SSTB exclusion do not apply

Overall limit = ($50,000 taxable income − $15,000 net capital gains) × 20% = $7,000, so deduction is limited by overall limit

Section 199A QBI deduction = $7,000

Example 3 — QTB With Taxable Income of $210,700 or More

Facts: A taxpayer filing as single has the following:

Taxable income = $220,000

Net capital gains = $0

QBI = $100,000

Taxpayer's share of QTB's W-2 wages = $30,000

Taxpayer's share of QTB's UBIA of qualified property = $80,000

Required: Calculate the Section 199A QBI deduction.

Solution: Because the taxpayer's taxable income of $220,000 is greater than the maximum amount of $210,700 and the business is a QTB, the full W-2 wage and property limitation applies.

Tentative QBI deduction = $100,000 QBI × 20% = $20,000

W-2 wage and property limitation:

Greater of:

1. $30,000 W-2 wages × 50% = $15,000
2. ($30,000 W-2 wages × 25%) + ($80,000 UBIA of qualified property × 2.5%) = $9,500

W-2 wage and property limitation of $15,000 is less than the tentative QBI deduction of $20,000, so the QBI deduction is limited to $15,000 by the W-2 wage and property limitation.

Overall limit = $220,000 taxable income × 20% = $44,000, so not limited by the overall limit

Section 199A QBI deduction = $15,000

Example 4 — SSTB With Taxable Income of $210,700 or More

Facts: A taxpayer filing as single has the following:

Taxable income = $220,000

Net capital gains = $0

QBI = $100,000

Taxpayer's share of SSTB's W-2 wages = $30,000

Taxpayer's share of QTB's UBIA of qualified property = $80,000

Required: Calculate the QBI deduction.

Solution: Because the business is an SSTB and the taxpayer's taxable income exceeds $210,700, the taxpayer is not eligible for the QBI deduction.

Section 199A QBI deduction = $0

Example 5 — QTB With Taxable Income Between $160,700 and $210,700

Facts: A taxpayer filing as single has the following:

Taxable income = $203,200

Net capital gains = $0

QBI = $100,000

Taxpayer's share of QTB's W-2 wages = $30,000

QTB's qualified property = $0

Required: Calculate the QBI deduction.

Solution:

Tentative QBI deduction = $100,000 QBI × 20% = $20,000

W-2 wage and property limitation: $30,000 W-2 wages × 50% = $15,000 (*no qualified property*)

Because the W-2 wage and property limitation of $15,000 is less than the tentative QBI deduction of $20,000, and the taxpayer's taxable income is within the phase-in range of $160,700 to $210,700, the QBI deduction is reduced.

Phase-in percentage:

Taxable income (before QBI deduction)	$203,200
– Threshold amount (single)	<160,700>
Taxable income into the phase-in range	$ 42,500
÷ Phase-in range (single)	÷ 50,000
Phase-in percentage	85%

(continued)

(continued)

Excess amount:

Tentative 20% QBI deduction	$ 20,000
W-2 wage and property limit	<15,000>
Excess amount	$ 5,000

The limitation is applied pro rata within the taxable income phase-in range of $50,000. Because the taxpayer is 85% into the taxable income phase-in range, 85% of the W-2 wage and property limitation applies.

Reduction amount = $5,000 excess amount × 85% phase-in percentage = $4,250

Tentative QBI deduction	$ 20,000
– Reduction amount	<4,250>
Reduced QBI deduction	$ 15,750

Overall limit = $203,200 taxable income × 20% = $40,640, so not limited by the overall limit

Section 199A QBI deduction = $15,750

Example 6	SSTB With Taxable Income Between $160,700 and $210,700

Facts: A taxpayer filing single has the following:

Taxable income = $203,200

Net capital gains = $0

QBI = $100,000

Taxpayer's share of SSTB's W-2 wages = $30,000

QTB's qualified property = $0

Required: Calculate the QBI deduction.

Solution: SSTB within taxable income phase-in range of $160,700 to $210,700, so first reduce QBI, W-2 wages, and UBIA of qualified property to the SSTB applicable percentage.

Phase-in percentage:

Taxable income (before QBI deduction):	$203,200
– Threshold amount (single)	<160,700>
Taxable income into the phase-in range	$ 42,500
÷ Phase-in range (single)	÷ 50,000
Phase-in percentage	85%

(continued)

(continued)

SSTB applicable percentage = 100% – 85% phase-in percentage = 15%

Tentative QBI deduction = $100,000 QBI × 15% SSTB applicable percentage = $15,000 × 20% = $3,000

W-2 wage and property limitation (*no qualified property in this case*):

$30,000 W-2 wages × 15% SSTB applicable percentage = $4,500 × 50% = $2,250

Because the reduced W-2 wage and property limitation of $2,250 is less than the reduced tentative QBI deduction of $3,000, and the taxpayer's taxable income is within the phase-in range of $160,700 to $210,700, the QBI deduction is reduced.

Phase-in percentage:

Taxable income:	$203,200
– Threshold amount (single)	<160,700>
Taxable income into the phase-in range	$ 42,500
÷ Phase-in range (single)	÷ 50,000
Phase-in percentage	85%

Excess amount:

Reduced tentative 20% QBI deduction	$ 3,000
Reduced W-2 wage and property limit	<2,250>
Excess amount	$ 750

The limitation is applied pro rata in the taxable income phase-in range of $160,700 to $210,700. Because the taxpayer is 85% into the $50,000 taxable income phase-in range, 85% of the W-2 wage and property limitation applies.

Reduction amount = $750 excess amount × 85% phase-in percentage = $637.50

Tentative QBI deduction	$3,000.00
– Reduction amount	<637.50>
Reduced QBI deduction	$2,362.50

Overall limit = $203,200 taxable income × 20% = $40,640, so not limited by the overall limit

Section 199A QBI deduction = $2,362.50

2.7   Negative QBI Amount

2.7.1   Negative QBI With Multiple QTBs

A taxpayer may have multiple sources of business income that are eligible for the Section 199A QBI deduction. If one or more of these sources has a loss for the tax year, the losses are allocated pro rata among the qualifying businesses with positive QBI for purposes of calculating the QBI deduction. The W-2 wages and UBIA of qualified property of the business with a negative QBI are ignored, and do not get allocated or carried forward.

Illustration 2	Negative QBI With Multiple QTBs

Business A QBI $100,000   (1/3)
Business B QBI $200,000   (2/3)
Total positive QBI $300,000
Business C QBI $ (75,000) allocated 1/3 ($25,000) to A and 2/3 ($50,000) to B

Adjusted Business A QBI = $100,000 – $25,000 = $75,000

Adjusted Business B QBI = $200,000 – $50,000 = $150,000

2.7.2 Negative Total QBI Amount

If QBI for the tax year (one source or multiple sources combined) is negative, then the QBI deduction for that tax year is zero. The combined QBI loss for the tax year is carried forward and treated as a separate business for the following tax year for purposes of the Section 199A QBI deduction. The W-2 wages and UBIA of qualified property for any business with a QBI loss does not carry forward.

This carryover rule is for purposes of the Section 199A QBI deduction only and does not affect the deductibility of the loss for federal income tax purposes.

Illustration 3	Negative Total QBI Amount

Business A QBI $ 100,000
Business B QBI $ 200,000
Business C QBI $(400,000)
Combined QBI loss $(100,000) carried forward to the following year as a separate business

2.8 Aggregation Rules

An individual taxpayer may aggregate QTB (but not any SSTB) businesses if:

1. the same person, or group of persons, owns at least 50% of each business; and

2. the businesses to be aggregated satisfy at least two of the following factors:

   - Provide products/services that are the same or customarily offered together

   - Share facilities or significant centralized business elements

   - Operated in coordination with other businesses in aggregated group

The "same person or group of persons" includes members of the same family (spouse, children, grandchildren, parents) and owners in the same business entity (shareholders in S corporation, partners in a partnership).

If the taxpayer elects to aggregate businesses, then QBI, W-2 wages, and UBIA of qualifying property for all aggregated businesses must be combined for purposes of calculating the W-2 wages and property limitations.

Illustration 4	Aggregation of QTB Businesses

Maria, a single taxpayer, owns 100 percent of QTB businesses X, Y, and Z. The businesses have W-2 wages but do not have qualified depreciable property. Maria's only other source of taxable income for the year is a $750,000 salary. She does not have any net capital gains. Maria's taxable income for the year, before any Section 199A QBI deduction, is $2,400,000.

	QBI	W-2 Wages
X	$1,000,000	$ 500,000
Y	1,000,000	0
Z	2,000	500,000
Total	$2,002,000	$1,000,000

If Maria does not aggregate Businesses X, Y, and Z:

Maria's taxable income is above $210,700 (2019), so the full W-2 wage and property limitation applies for each QTB. Because the QTBs do not have qualified depreciable property, only the W-2 wages are taken into account in calculating the W-2 wage and property limitation.

Business X: Tentative QBI deduction = $1,000,000 × 20% = $200,000
W-2 wage limit = $500,000 × 50% = $250,000 (*greater than $200,000 so not limited*)
Section 199A QBI deduction for X = $200,000

Business Y: Tentative QBI deduction = $1,000,000 × 20% = $200,000
W-2 wage limit = $0 × 50% = $0 (*so no QBI deduction is allowed*)
Section 199A QBI deduction for Y = $0

Business Z: Tentative QBI deduction = $2,000 × 20% = $400
W-2 wage limit = $500,000 × 50% = $250,000 (*greater than $400 so not limited*)
Section 199A QBI deduction for Z = $400

Overall limit = $2,400,000 taxable income × 20% = $480,000, so not limited by the overall limit

Total Section 199A QBI deduction = $200,000 + $0 + $400 = $200,400

If Maria aggregates Businesses X, Y, and Z:

Maria's taxable income is above $210,700 (2019), so the full W-2 wage and property limitation applies. Because the QTBs do not have qualified depreciable property, only the W-2 wages are taken into account in calculating the W-2 wage and property limitation.

Combined X, Y, and Z Tentative QBI deduction = $2,002,000 × 20% = $ 400,400

Combined X, Y, and Z W-2 wage limit = $1,000,000 × 50% = $500,000 (greater than $400,400 so not limited)

Overall limit = $2,400,000 taxable income × 20% = $480,000, so not limited by overall limit

Section 199A QBI deduction = $400,400

3 Estates and Trusts

Estates and trusts are separate income tax paying entities. Distributions made by these entities are deductible by the entity but taxable to the recipient.

3.1 Fiduciary (Tax) Accounting

Fiduciary accounting is used in trusts and estates, and it is centered on the classification of all receipts and disbursements as either principal (corpus) or income. The rules are generally the same as the generally accepted accounting principles (GAAP) for principal and income. (A schedule showing some unusual treatments by trusts and estates is provided below.)

- The amounts taxed to the fiduciary (trust or estate) and the beneficiaries are usually determined by the classification of the receipt or disbursement as either principal or income.

- Capital gains and losses (absent written provisions to the contrary) are classified as principal and must remain with the trust (allocated to corpus) to be taxed at the trust or estate (fiduciary) level.

3.2 Income Distributed to Beneficiaries

Income distributed to beneficiaries (and reported on Schedule K-1 on Form 1041) retains the same character (e.g., tax-exempt, portfolio, passive) as the income had at the fiduciary level (which is the same as occurs in partnership taxation).

Principal vs. Income Rules			
Generally, the rules of generally accepted accounting principles apply to the determination of receipts as principal (corpus) and income.			
Receipts (Trusts and Estates)	Principal	Income	Apportion
1. Annuities			✓
2. Bonds	✓		
3. Business (sole proprietor or partnership):			
Profit		✓	
Loss	✓		
4. Change in form of principal	✓		
5. Condemnation proceeding	✓		
6. Corporate distributions			
Call for shares	✓		
Cash dividend (regular and extraordinary)		✓	
Liquidation (total or partial)	✓		
Merger, consolidation, reorganization	✓		
Proceeds of rights of property distribution		✓	
Rights to subscribe to shares or securities		✓	
Rights to subscribe to shares of securities of distributing corporation	✓		
Sales of rights of distributing corporation	✓		
Stock dividend	✓		
Stock in another corporation		✓	
Stock split	✓		

(continued)

(continued)

Receipts (Trusts and Estates)	Principal	Income	Apportion
7. Depreciation allowance	✓		
8. Depreciation and depletion expense		✓	
9. Discount on Treasury bills and certificates		✓	
10. Eminent domain proceedings	✓		
11. Employee payments (last salary; post-death bonus; death benefits)	✓		
12. Interest (apportion bond amortization to principal, rest is income)			✓
13. Insurance proceeds from damages to property	✓		
14. Prepayment penalties (except bond call premium)		✓	
15. Profit from change in form of principal (e.g., sale of building or stock for cash profit)	✓		
16. Regulated investment company:			
Ordinary income distribution		✓	
Other distributions	✓		
17. Rental income (real and personal property):			
Arrears		✓	
Prepaid or advance		✓	
18. Sale or transfer of principal	✓		
19. S corporation income	✓	✓	
20. Treasury bill and certificate discount		✓	
21. Street assessments	✓		

Question 1	**MCQ-04923**

Which of the following is both an item that is an allowable tax deduction to the partnership, reported separately on the individual partner's Schedule K-1, and then included on the partner's individual tax return?

    a. Salaries paid to non-partner employees

    b. Advertising expenditures

    c. Guaranteed payments paid to partners

    d. Depreciation on equipment used in the business

Question 2 — MCQ-08021

The Morgan Trust, a complex trust, had distributable net income (DNI) in Year 4 of $10,000. Of the $10,000 of DNI, $4,000 was distributed to trust beneficiaries. Of the $4,000 distributed, which taxpayer(s), if any, are responsible for the tax liability on the $4,000 distribution?

a. The Morgan Trust

b. The trust beneficiaries

c. The Morgan Trust and the trust beneficiaries

d. Neither the Morgan Trust nor the trust beneficiaries

Question 3 — MCQ-08057

John created a trust for the benefit of his son, Connor. John does not have the right to change any terms of the trust once established and has no right to income. All trust income is to be distributed to Connor on an annual basis. How should the trust income be reported?

a. To John, reported only on his Form 1040.

b. Reported on Form 1041, with a Schedule K-1 issued to John.

c. To Connor, reported only on his Form 1040.

d. Reported on Form 1041, with a Schedule K-1 issued to Connor.

1   Characterizations of Income

All income can be characterized and placed into one of four "baskets" of income. Understanding the baskets of income will be helpful in calculating the limitations on taxability or deductibility of various items, such as passive activity losses, capital gains and losses, and the investment interest deduction.

- **Ordinary:** Ordinary income includes salaries and wages, state and local tax refunds, alimony, IRA and pension income, self-employment income, unemployment compensation, Social Security, prizes, the taxable portion of scholarships and fellowships, gambling income, and anything not falling into one of the other three baskets.

- **Portfolio:** Portfolio income includes income a taxpayer would earn on his portfolio of assets, such as interest and dividends.

  - **Capital:** Sales of capital assets create capital gains and losses. A capital asset is generally any property (personal or business), but there are some exceptions. An explanation of the definition of capital and noncapital assets is presented when capital gains and losses are discussed in more detail in R3.

- **Passive:** The definition of "passive" generally means an activity in which a taxpayer did not actively participate (active includes working in a business, etc.). Passive losses may only offset passive income. A net passive loss is not deductible on the tax return; it is suspended and carried forward to offset future passive income (or deduct when the passive activity is disposed of).

  - **Rental Real Estate Income:** Rental income received on a property that a taxpayer owns and rents is generally deemed "passive," unless exceptions exist. Exceptions include a limited exception for rental real estate and for certain real estate professionals.

  - **Beneficiaries of Trusts and Investments in Partnerships, LLCs, and S Corporations:** Individuals (and companies) with investments in S Corporations, partnerships, limited liability companies, and beneficiary interests in trusts and estates receive a Form K-1 from the entity each year.

  If an investment in a company is deemed limited (as opposed to general) for the investor, the income from the business activities will be deemed passive for tax purposes, and the passive activity loss rules will apply. In addition, even general partners may receive passive income on their K-1s (e.g., a partnership may have a rental activity). This will be separated from regular business activities and on a different line item on the K-1 as "rental."

2 Loss Limitations (Business Type Activity)

2.1 Factors Limiting Losses

A taxpayer's loss from a rental activity or business activity is limited by four factors. This is true whether the taxpayer directly owns the rental property or business or owns a percentage of the rental or business activity through a flow-through entity such as a partnership, an LLC, or an S Corporation. A loss may be deducted only if the loss is greater than four limitations:

1. Tax basis

2. At-risk basis

3. Passive activity loss

4. Excess business loss

2.2 Tax Basis

The tax basis of an asset is essentially the taxpayer's investment in the asset adjusted for items such as income and debt. A detailed discussion on the calculation of basis will be included with the coverage of each flow-through entity in later units. Any losses not deductible in the current year because of tax basis limitation are carried forward until the taxpayer generates more tax basis to absorb the loss. Suspended losses remaining because of insufficient basis when a partner sells his or her interest are lost.

2.3 At-Risk Basis

If a taxpayer has sufficient tax basis to cover a loss, then the loss must not be greater than the taxpayer's "at-risk" amount. The amount that a taxpayer is considered "at-risk" represents the taxpayer's economic risk in the activity. Losses that have sufficient tax basis but not "at-risk" basis are carried forward until the taxpayer generates more at-risk basis or until the activity is sold. If the activity is sold, and there are any suspended at-risk losses, the taxpayer can offset the gain from the sale of the activity by the unused suspended at-risk losses.

2.4 Passive Activity Losses

A taxpayer may have sufficient tax basis and "at risk" amounts, but still not be able to deduct a loss against ordinary income.

A passive activity is any activity in which the taxpayer does not materially participate. Such activities include rental activities, interests in limited partnerships, S corporations, and most tax shelters.

2.4.1 Deductibility

A passive activity loss may not be deducted against other sources of income (active ordinary income, portfolio income, or capital gains). Passive activity losses can only be offset against passive activity income.

2.4.2 Nondeductible Passive Activity Losses

Nondeductible passive activity losses are suspended and carried forward without any time limit.

▪ Suspended losses are used to offset passive activity income in future years.

▪ If still unused, any remaining suspended passive activity losses become fully deductible in the year the activity is disposed of (sold).

▪ If the taxpayer becomes a material participant in the passive activity (therefore changing from "passive" to "active"), unused passive losses from the activity can be used to offset the taxpayer's active income in the same activity.

2.4.3 Exceptions to Passive Activity Loss Rules

An individual may deduct rental activity losses (although deduction may be limited) if either of the following two conditions are met:

▪ **Mom and Pop Exception**

- **$25,000 and "Active":** Taxpayers may deduct up to $25,000 (per year) of net passive losses attributable to rental real estate annually if the individuals are actively participating/managing and own at least 10 percent of the rental activity.

- **Carryforward:** Any excess would be carried forward indefinitely as a suspended passive activity loss.

- **Phase-out:** The $25,000 allowance is reduced by 50 percent of the excess of the taxpayer's AGI (without consideration of this loss deduction) over $100,000. The allowance is eliminated completely when AGI exceeds $150,000.

▪ **Real Estate Professional (Not Passive Activity)**

If the following two conditions are met and the taxpayer is deemed to have material participation in the activity, the rental activities are not considered passive and the taxpayer (sometimes referred to on the CPA Exam as a "real estate person") can fully deduct losses from the rental activities against other income:

- More than 50 percent of the taxpayer's personal services during the year are performed in real property businesses; and

- The taxpayer performs more than 750 hours of services in real property businesses during the year. Please note that it is generally rental real estate activity that is considered to be passive (even if the taxpayer materially participates in the activity) unless one of the two exceptions applies.

2.5 Excess Business Loss

Taxpayers are not allowed to deduct an "excess business loss" for the year. This limitation is applied after the passive activity loss limitations.

2.5.1 Excess Business Loss Calculation

An excess business loss for the year is the excess of aggregate business deductions for the year over the sum of aggregate business income for the year plus a threshold amount. For 2019, the threshold amount is $510,000 (married filing jointly) and $255,000 (all other taxpayers). Excess business losses are treated as part of the taxpayer's net operating loss carryforward. The excess business loss limitation applies to all types of business income, active or passive.

Example 1	Classification of Income

Facts: Michael has a $30,000 tax basis in a limited partnership interest. Michael's at-risk amount is $25,000. Michael is a 10 percent investment partner only and has no management responsibilities in the partnership, M. Green & Sons. Michael does not materially participate in M. Green & Sons. This year, M. Green & Sons experienced a $400,000 loss. Michael's share of the partnership loss is $40,000 (10 percent). Michael's other sources of income for the year include: $75,000 in wages; $6,000 income from a 5 percent investment in Morris & Stubbs (a different partnership in which he does not materially participate); $3,000 in long-term capital gains; and $12,000 in dividend income.

Required: Classify Michael's income into the four categories of income: Ordinary, portfolio, passive, and capital.

Solution:

Four Types of Income	
Ordinary	$75,000 wages
Portfolio	$12,000 dividend income
Passive	$6,000 income from Morris & Stubbs
Capital	$3,000 long-term capital gain

Example 2 — Tax Basis, At-Risk Basis, and Passive Activity Loss Limitation

Facts: Same facts as in Example 1.

Required: How much of Michael's $40,000 loss in M. Green & Sons is deductible in the current year?

Solution: The four factors limiting losses—tax basis, at-risk basis, passive activity loss limitation, and excess business loss limitation—must be considered.

- **Tax Basis:** Michael has a $30,000 tax basis in M. Green & Sons. He is limited to a $30,000 loss deduction as a result of his tax basis. The disallowed $10,000 loss is carried forward as a result of tax-basis limitation.

- **At-Risk:** After considering tax basis, Michael must then consider his at-risk basis in M. Green & Sons, which is $25,000. As a result of the at-risk basis, Michael can only deduct $25,000 of the $30,000 loss available after considering tax basis. The disallowed $5,000 loss due to at-risk basis limitation will be carried forward.

- **Passive Loss Limitation:** Because Michael does not actively participate in the M. Green & Sons partnership, this investment is a passive activity for him. Passive losses can only be used to offset passive income. His investment in the Morris & Stubbs partnership is also a passive activity in which he has generated $6,000 of passive income. Therefore, of the $25,000 loss available for deduction after considering at-risk basis, he can now only deduct $6,000 of loss from M. Green & Sons. The disallowed $19,000 loss due to passive loss limitation will be carried forward.

Summary Treatment of $40,000 Passive Loss From M. Green & Sons	
Deductible in the current year	$ 6,000
Tax basis: Loss carryforward	$10,000
At-risk: Loss carryforward	$ 5,000
Passive: Loss carryforward	$19,000

- **Excess business loss limitation:** No limitation applies, as the deductible loss of $6,000 is well under the threshold amount of $250,000.

Example 3 — Use of Losses When Investment Is Sold

Facts: Assume that Michael sells his interest in M. Green & Sons in the following year for a $20,000 gain.

Required: Determine how the suspended losses due to tax basis, at-risk, and passive loss limitations are treated.

Solution: The $10,000 suspended loss due to tax basis is lost. The $5,000 at-risk carryforward loss can be deducted against the $20,000 gain on sale of the partnership interest. The $19,000 passive loss is fully deductible against non-passive income in the year of disposal.

3 Loss Limitations: Capital Losses

3.1 Net Capital Loss Deduction and Loss Carryover Rules

- **$3,000 Maximum Deduction:** Individual taxpayers realizing a net long-term or short-term capital loss may only recognize (deduct) a maximum of $3,000 of the loss from other types of gross income (ordinary income, passive income, or portfolio income). A joint return of spouses is treated as one person. If the spouses file separately, the loss deduction is limited to half ($1,500).

- **Limitation:** Capital losses are limited to taxable income.

- **Excess Net Capital Loss:** Carry forward an unlimited time until exhausted. It maintains its character as long-term or short-term in future years.

- **A Personal (Nonbusiness) Bad Debt**: A personal (nonbusiness) bad debt loss is treated as a short-term capital loss in the year debt becomes totally worthless.

- **Worthless Stock and Securities:** The cost (or other basis) of worthless stock or securities is treated as a capital loss, as if they were sold on the last day of the taxable year in which they became totally worthless.

Question 1	MCQ-08220

What is the tax treatment of net losses in excess of the at-risk amount for an activity?

- **a.** Any loss in excess of the at-risk amount is suspended and is deductible in the year in which the activity is disposed of in full.
- **b.** Any losses in excess of the at-risk amount are suspended and carried forward without expiration and are deductible against income in future years from that activity.
- **c.** Any losses in excess of the at-risk amount are deducted currently against income from other activities; the remaining loss, if any, is carried forward without expiration.
- **d.** Any losses in excess of the at-risk amount are carried back two years against activities with income and then carried forward for 20 years.

Question 2	MCQ-08203

Which of the following statements regarding an individual's suspended passive activity losses is correct?

- **a.** $3,000 of suspended losses can be utilized each year against portfolio income.
- **b.** Suspended losses can be carried forward, but *not* back, until utilized.
- **c.** Suspended losses must be carried back three years and forward seven years.
- **d.** A maximum of 50 percent of the suspended losses can be used each year when an election is made to forgo the carryback period.

Question 3	MCQ-06888

In the current year, a taxpayer reports the following items:

Salary	$50,000
Income from partnership A, in which the taxpayer materially participates	20,000
Passive activity loss from partnership B	(40,000)

During the year, the taxpayer disposed of the interest in partnership B, which had a suspended loss carryover of $10,000 from prior years. What is the taxpayer's adjusted gross income for the current year?

    a. $20,000

    b. $30,000

    c. $60,000

    d. $70,000

Question 4	MCQ-08461

Dietz is a passive investor in three activities that have been profitable in previous years. The profit and losses for the current year are as follows:

	Gain/(Loss)
Activity X	$(30,000)
Activity Y	(50,000)
Activity Z	20,000
Total	$(60,000)

What amount of suspended loss should Dietz allocate to Activity X?

    a. $18,000

    b. $20,000

    c. $22,500

    d. $30,000

NOTES

Employee Stock Options

1 Overview

Corporations may grant their employees the option to purchase stock in the corporation. There are two types of employee stock options: nonqualified options and qualified options.

2 Nonqualified Options

If the option does not meet certain conditions described below for qualified stock options, it will be treated as a nonqualified option. A nonqualified option is taxed when granted if the option has a readily ascertainable value at the time of the grant. Because nonqualified options often do not have an ascertainable value, the option is generally taxed when exercised.

2.1 Definition of Readily Ascertainable Value

If the option is traded on an established market, it will have a readily ascertainable value. Otherwise, it will only have a readily ascertainable value if *all* of the following conditions are met:

- The option is transferable.
- The option is exercisable immediately in full when it is granted.
- There are no conditions or restrictions that would have a significant effect on the value.
- The fair value of the option privilege is readily ascertainable.

2.2 Employee Taxation: Readily Ascertainable Value

- If there is a readily ascertainable value, the employee recognizes ordinary income in that amount in the year granted. If there is a cost to the employee, then the ordinary income is the value of the option minus the cost.
- There is no taxation on the date of exercise. The basis of the stock is the exercise price plus any amount previously taxed on the date of grant. Any future sale of the stock could result in a capital gain or loss.
- The holding period begins with the exercise date.
- If the employee allows the options to lapse (not exercised), there is a capital loss based on the value of the options previously taxed.

2.3 Employee Taxation: Without Readily Ascertainable Value

- If no readily ascertainable value exists, the taxable event is the exercise date, not the grant date.
- On the date of exercise, the employee recognizes ordinary income equal to the "bargain element"—the difference between the fair market value of the stock and the stock option price exercised. The basis of the stock is the fair market value of the stock when stock option was exercised. Any future sale of the stock could result in a capital gain or loss.
- The holding period begins with the exercise date.
- If the options lapse, the employee can claim a capital loss equal to the cost, if any, the employee paid for the options. There are no other consequences.

2.4 Employer Taxation

Generally, an employer may deduct the value of the stock option as a business expense in the same year that the employee is required to recognize the option as ordinary income (see above).

Illustration 1   Nonqualified Stock Option

On July 1, Year 10, Bob was granted a nonqualified stock option to purchase 200 shares of his employer's stock for $12 per share. This option was selling for $4 per share on an established exchange. Bob exercised these options on August 7, Year 11. The stock was selling for $18 per share on the exercise date. On November 1, Year 12, Bob sold all of the shares for $20 per share.

Bob must report ordinary income in the amount of $800 ($4 × 200 shares) on the date of the grant in Year 10 because the option has a readily ascertainable market value.

Bob's adjusted basis in the stock is $3,200 ($2,400 exercise price + $800 recognized ordinary income). The $2,400 exercise price is 200 shares × $12.

Bob has a long-term capital gain in Year 12 in the amount of $800. This is a selling price of $4,000 (200 shares × $20) less the adjusted basis of $3,200.

Bob's employer can take a tax deduction in the amount of $800 in Year 10, the amount of ordinary income recognized by Bob.

---

3   Qualified Options

There are two types of qualified stock options, incentive stock options (ISO) and employee stock purchase plans (ESPP).

3.1   Incentive Stock Options

An ISO is usually granted to a key employee and is a right to purchase the stock at a discount.

3.1.1   Requirements

- The ISO must be granted under a plan, approved by the shareholders, that sets out the total number of shares that may be issued and who may receive them.

- The options must be granted within 10 years of the earlier of the date when the plan was adopted or approved. The options must be exercisable within 10 years of the grant date.

- The exercise price may not be less than the FMV of the stock at the date of the grant.

- The employee may not own more than 10 percent of the combined voting power of the corporation, parent, or subsidiary as of the date of the grant.

- Once exercised, the stock must be held at least two years after the grant date *and* at least one year after the exercise date.

- The employee must remain an employee of the corporation from the date the option is granted until three months (one year if due to permanent and total disability) before the option is exercised.

3.1.2 Employee Taxation

▪ Generally, there is no taxation of the option as compensation. Basis of the stock is the exercise price plus any amount paid for the option (if any).

▪ Generally, any gain or loss on a subsequent sale of the stock is capital. If the holding period requirements (covered above) are not satisfied, any gain is ordinary, up to the amount that the stock's FMV on the exercise date exceeded the option price.

▪ Generally, if the options lapse, no deduction is available as the option was not taxed in the first place. There might be a loss if any amount was paid for the option itself.

▪ An employee may exercise up to $100,000 of ISOs in a year. Any amount exercised that exceeds this will be treated as a nonqualifying option.

▪ The excess of the FMV of the stock on the exercise date less the purchase price is a preference item for alternative minimum tax.

3.1.3 Employer Taxation

Generally, an employer does not receive a tax deduction for an ISO because it is not considered compensation income to the employee.

Illustration 2   Incentive Stock Option

On July 1, Year 10, Mary was granted an Incentive Stock Option (ISO) to purchase 200 shares of her employer's stock for $120 per share. The FMV of the stock on the date of grant was $120. Mary exercised these options on August 7, Year 11. The stock was selling for $150 per share on the exercise date. On November 1, Year 12, Mary sold all of the shares for $200 per share.

Mary does not recognize any ordinary income at the date of grant because this qualified as an ISO.

Mary's adjusted basis in the stock is the exercise price of $24,000 (200 shares × $120).

Mary has a long-term capital gain in Year 12 in the amount of $16,000. This is a selling price of $40,000 (200 shares × $200) less the adjusted basis of $24,000. The holding period requirements have been met.

Mary also has an AMT preference item in Year 11 of $6,000. The FMV of stock on the date of exercise was $150, and the purchase price was $120. The excess is $30 × 200 shares.

Mary's employer receives no deduction for the granting of the option.

3.2 Employee Stock Purchase Plans

An ESPP may grant options to employees to purchase stock in the corporation.

3.2.1 Requirements

▪ The plan must be written and approved by the shareholders.

▪ An ESPP cannot grant options to any employee who has 5 percent or more combined voting power of the corporation, parent, or subsidiary.

▪ Generally, the plan must include all full-time employees other than highly compensated employees and those with less than two years employment.

▦ The option exercise price may not be less than the *lesser* of 85 percent of the FMV of the stock when granted or exercised.

▦ The option cannot be exercised more than 27 months after the grant date.

▦ No employee can acquire the right to purchase more than $25,000 of stock per year.

▦ Once exercised, the stock must be held at least two years after the grant date *and* at least one year after the exercise date.

▦ The employee must remain an employee of the corporation from the date the option is granted until three months before the option is exercised.

3.2.2 Employee Taxation

▦ Generally, there is no taxation of the option as compensation. The basis of the stock is the exercise price plus any amount paid for the option (if any).

▦ Generally, any gain or loss on a subsequent sale of the stock is capital. If the holding period requirements (covered above) are not satisfied, any gain is ordinary up to the amount that the stock's FMV on the exercise date exceeded the option exercise price.

▦ Generally, if the options lapse, no deduction is available, as the option was not taxed in the first place. There might be a loss if any amount was paid for the option itself.

▦ If the option exercise price is less than FMV of the stock on the grant date, then ordinary income is recognized when the stock is sold as the *lesser* of the difference of the FMV of the stock when sold and the exercise price, *or* the difference between the exercise price and the FMV of the stock on the grant date.

3.2.3 Employer Taxation

Generally, an employer does not receive a tax deduction for an ESPP because it is not considered compensation income to the employee.

Question 1	MCQ-07357

Which of the following statements is *not* correct?

    a. Employee stock purchase plans are a type of qualified stock option plan.

    b. The recipient of an incentive stock option will generally have to report compensation income in the year that the option is received.

    c. The employer may recognize a deductible expense for a nonqualified stock option in the same year that the employee will recognize ordinary income.

    d. For an incentive stock option, once exercised, the stock must be held at least two years after the grant date and at least one year after the exercise date.

Individual Taxation: Part 2

Module

Adjustments

1 Overview

Adjustments for AGI (often referred to as "above-the-line" deductions, or "deductions to arrive at AGI") include the following:

- Educator expenses
- IRA deduction
- Student loan interest deduction
- Health savings account deduction
- Moving expenses (only for members of the U.S. Armed Forces moving pursuant to military order)
- Deductible part of self-employment tax
- Self-employed health insurance deduction
- Deduction for contributions to certain self-employed retirement plans
- Penalty on early withdrawal of savings
- Alimony paid (only for divorce or separation agreements executed on or before 12/31/18)
- Attorney fees paid in certain discrimination and whistle-blower cases

Pass Key

The CPA Examination will often refer to "adjustments" as "deductions to arrive at adjusted gross income."

2 Educator Expenses

- Eligible educators can deduct up to $250 of qualified expenses paid. If spouses are filing jointly and both are eligible educators, the maximum deduction is $500.
- Neither spouse can deduct more than $250 of his or her qualified expenses.
- An eligible educator is a kindergarten through grade 12 teacher, instructor, counselor, principal, or aide working in a school for at least 900 hours during a school year.

- Qualified expenses include ordinary and necessary expenses paid in connection with books, supplies, equipment (including computer equipment, software, and services), and other materials used in the classroom.

  - Deductible expenses also include costs of professional development.

  - An ordinary expense is one that is common and accepted in one's educational field.

  - A necessary expense is one that is helpful and appropriate for one's profession as an educator (does not have to be required).

- Qualified expenses do not include expenses for homeschooling or for nonathletic supplies for courses in health or physical education. Qualified expenses must be reduced by the following amounts:

  - Excludable U.S. series EE and I Savings Bond interest from Form 8815.

  - Nontaxable qualified state tuition program earnings.

  - Nontaxable earnings from Coverdell education savings accounts.

  - Any reimbursements received for these expenses that were not reported in box 1 of Form W-2.

3 Individual Retirement Accounts

The three types of individual retirement accounts (IRAs) are:

- Deductible traditional IRA

- Nondeductible traditional IRA

- Roth IRA

3.1 Contributions

3.1.1 General Rule

The annual maximum contribution to IRAs is limited to the lesser of:

2019	Under age 50	Over age 50	Age 70½ and over
Unmarried	$6,000 *Or* Earned income	$7,000 *Or* Earned income	$0
Married	$12,000 ($6,000 each) *Or* Earned income of married couple	$14,000 ($7,000 each) *Or* Earned income of married couple	$0

The annual limits apply to the sum of a taxpayer's contributions to deductible IRAs, nondeductible IRAs, and Roth IRAs.

- **Earned Income Includes:**
  - Salary and wages
  - Commissions
  - Bonuses
  - Alimony (for divorce agreements executed before December 31, 2018)
  - Net earnings from self-employment

- **Earned Income Does Not Include:**
  - Interest and dividends
  - Annuity income
  - Pensions
  - Alimony (for divorce agreements executed after December 31, 2018)

3.1.2 Retirement Plan Contribution Credit

Eligible taxpayers also may be entitled to a tax credit for contributions to either a traditional IRA or a Roth IRA, subject to certain limitation (discussed later, with credits).

3.2 Deductible Traditional IRA

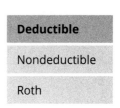

Contributions to traditional IRAs may or may not be deductible. The traditional IRA is deductible from gross income to arrive at adjusted gross income. The adjustment is allowed for a year only if the contribution is made by the due date of the tax return for individuals, which is April 15 (filing extensions are not considered).

- Earnings accumulate tax free (deferred).

- Distributions from traditional deductible IRAs are taxable as ordinary income and may be subject to applicable penalties.

- Minimum distributions are required to be taken by April 1 of the year following the year in which the taxpayer reaches age 70½.

3.2.1 Limitations on Deduction of Traditional IRA Contributions

A taxpayer's deduction for a traditional IRA contribution is limited if the taxpayer or spouse participates in an employer-sponsored plan.

- **Participation in Employer-Sponsored Retirement Plans:** If a taxpayer participates in an employer-sponsored retirement plan, AGI limitations apply to the deduction allowed for the contribution made to the traditional IRA. The allowed deductible contribution phases out proportionately within the following ranges:

Filing Status	2019 AGI Phase-out
Unmarried	$64,000–$74,000
Married filing jointly	$103,000–$123,000

- **Special Rule:** If a married taxpayer is not an active participant in an employer's retirement plan, but the spouse is, the deduction for the spouse who is not an active participant is phased out based on the following AGI limitations:

Filing Status	2019 AGI Phase-out
Married filing jointly	$193,000–$203,000 (couple's AGI)
Married filing separately	$0–$10,000 (each spouse is subject to this limitation—both the participant and the nonparticipant)

Example 1   Phase-out of Traditional IRA Deduction

Facts: Kristi, a 40-year-old single taxpayer, is an active participant in her employer's pension plan. Kristi's 2019 AGI is $66,000.

Required: Calculate Kristi's maximum IRA deduction.

Solution: Kristi's maximum 2019 IRA deduction is $4,800, calculated as follows:

2019 AGI	$ 66,000
Less phase-out threshold	(64,000)
Excess over phase-out threshold	2,000
Divided by $10,000 phase-out range	÷ 10,000
Phase-out percentage	20%
× maximum IRA deduction allowed	6,000
Phase-out amount	1,200
2019 allowed IRA deduction	$ 4,800

Question: What is Kristi's maximum IRA deduction if she does not participate in an employer-sponsored retirement plan?

Answer: $6,000. She would not be subject to the AGI limitations if she did not participate in an employer-sponsored retirement plan.

3.3 Nondeductible Traditional IRA

If a taxpayer's deduction for a contribution to a traditional IRA is limited, a nondeductible traditional IRA contribution can be made instead. The overall limitation still applies to the combined deductible and nondeductible contributions ($6,000 or earned income).

> Deductible
> **Nondeductible**
> Roth

- Earnings on nondeductible IRA contributions will accumulate tax free until withdrawn.

- Distributions from a nondeductible traditional IRA will be taxed as follows:

  - Taxable: Previously accumulated untaxed earnings

  - Nontaxable: The principal contributions (not deducted when contributed)

- Minimum distributions are required to be taken by April 1 of the year following the year in which the taxpayer reaches age 70½.

3.4 Roth IRA

▦ Contributions to a Roth IRA are not deductible when made.

▦ Earnings accumulate tax free while in a Roth IRA account.

▦ Distributions of both principal and interest are also tax free if they are qualified distributions.

Deductible
Nondeductible
Roth

3.4.1 Allowable Roth Contributions

The ability to contribute to a Roth IRA is limited by modified AGI.

Filing Status	2019 MAGI Phase-out
Unmarried	$122,000–$137,000
Married filing jointly	$193,000–$203,000
Married filing separately	$0–$10,000

3.4.2 Distributions From Roth IRA

Distributions from Roth IRAs are first considered as a tax-free return of contributions made to the plan, then earnings. Qualified distributions of earnings are not taxable. Qualified distributions must meet the following criteria:

▦ made at least five years after the first day of the year of the taxpayer's first contribution;

▦ after the taxpayer reaches age 59½;

▦ to a beneficiary after the taxpayer's death;

▦ because the taxpayer is disabled; or

▦ for use by a "first-time" homebuyer (taxpayer not owning a principal residence in the two-year period before buying this residence) to acquire a principal residence. There is a lifetime $10,000 limit on qualified distributions for this purpose.

Nonqualified distributions are taxable to the extent of earnings. The contributions are a tax-free return of capital. Required minimum distribution rules (starting on April 1 of the year after turning age 70½) do not apply to Roth IRAs.

3.5 Rollovers From Traditional to Roth IRAs

Transfers can be made from traditional IRAs to Roth IRAs. There are currently no AGI limitations that affect these transfers. Any transferred amounts that were previously deducted (and any earnings) are includable in income at the time of the rollover with no 10 percent early withdrawal penalty. Withdrawals allocable to the amounts transferred from a traditional IRA cannot be made until those amounts have been in the Roth IRA for at least five years.

3.6 Early Distribution Penalty

Distributions taken before the taxpayer reaches the age of 59½ are subject to a 10 percent penalty. The penalty applies to distributions from traditional (deductible and nondeductible) and Roth IRAs. Early distributions are exempt from penalty if used for:

▦ Qualifying medical expenses

▦ Health insurance premiums

▦ Qualified higher education expenses

▦ First-time home purchases (limited to $10,000)

IRA Summary			
	Deductible Traditional IRA	*Nondeductible Traditional IRA*	*Roth IRA*
Maximum contribution (2019):	$6,000 combined annual maximum contribution with $1,000 additional "catch up" contribution for ages 50 up to 70½; $0 for ages over 70½ (for traditional IRA only)		
Above-the-line deduction for contribution:	Yes	No	No
Withdrawals:			
• Contributions	Taxable	Nontaxable	Nontaxable
• Earnings	Taxable	Taxable	Nontaxable (if qualified distribution)

4 Student Loan Interest Expense

The adjustment for education loan interest is limited to $2,500.

■ All interest payments qualify for the adjustment.

■ It is phased out for AGI between:

2019	
Single	$70,000–$85,000
Married	$140,000–$170,000

(Must file jointly to claim the adjustment)

■ Deduction is completely phased out at AGI equal to or more than $85,000 (2019) for single taxpayers and $170,000 (for 2019) for married filing jointly.

■ A dependent may not claim the adjustment.

■ The taxpayer must be legally obligated to pay the loan (e.g., interest paid by a parent on a child's student loan will not qualify as an allowable adjustment).

■ Interest is only deductible on loans incurred by a taxpayer solely to pay for qualified education expenses (e.g., general loans such as a home equity line of credit would not qualify).

5 Health Savings Accounts

5.1 Pretax Contribution

Health savings accounts (HSAs) enable workers with high-deductible health insurance to make pretax contributions of up to $3,500 in 2019 ($7,000 for families) to cover health care costs. These amounts are increased by $1,000 for those who reach age 55 within the tax year. No contributions are allowed once a taxpayer becomes covered by Medicare Parts A or B.

5.2   Excludable Withdrawals

Any amount paid or distributed out of an HSA that is used exclusively to pay the qualified medical expense of any account beneficiary is not includable in gross income. Note that distributions for qualified drugs include only those prescribed by a physician.

- Distributions not used to pay qualified medical expenses are includable in gross income and subject to a 10 percent penalty.

5.3   High-Deductible Plan Defined

For 2019, a high-deductible health plan is a plan that has at least a $1,350 annual deductible for self-only coverage and a $2,700 deductible for family coverage. These amounts are indexed for inflation.

- **Out-of-Pocket Limitation:** Annual out-of-pocket expenses paid under the plan must be limited to $6,750 for individuals and $13,500 for families. Out-of-pocket expenses include deductibles, co-payments and other amounts (other than premiums) that must be paid for plan benefits.

- **Archer Medical Savings Account (MSA) Contributions:** No new Archer MSAs could be established after the year 2007; however, any accounts established prior to 2008 are allowed to continue.

    - Archer MSAs are similar to IRAs, but they are used for health care. Typically, they are used only if the HSA is unavailable, as HSAs are generally more flexible.

    - Qualified participants are self-employed individuals or employees of small businesses (fewer than 50 employees).

    - These accounts were designed to be and must be used in conjunction with a high-deductible ($3,500 single/$7,000 family) health insurance plan.

    - The maximum out-of-pocket expenses limit for 2019 is $4,650 single/$8,550 family.

6   Moving Expenses

Starting in 2018, moving expense deductions are only allowed for members of the Armed Forces (or spouses and dependents) on active duty who move pursuant to a military order and incident to a permanent change of station.

7   Self-Employment Tax (50 Percent)

Self-employed taxpayers with net business income are subject to two taxes: income tax and Social Security/Medicare tax. Fifty percent of the self-employed Social Security/Medicare tax is deducted to arrive at adjusted gross income.

8   Self-Employed Health Insurance (100 Percent Deductible)

Self-employed individuals may deduct all of the medical insurance premiums paid for the taxpayer, spouse, and dependents, provided that the plan is set up in the name of the self-employed individual or the individual's business.

9   Keogh (Profit-Sharing) Plans

A self-employed taxpayer subject to self-employment tax is generally allowed to set up a Keogh retirement plan.

- **Maximum Annual Deductible Amount**

    The maximum annual deductible amount is limited to the lesser of:

2019
$56,000 (indexed for inflation) *Or* 25 percent of Keogh net earnings (net earnings from self-employment)

- **Maximum Annual Addition (Contribution)**

    The maximum annual contribution may exceed the deductible amount for the year. It is limited to the lesser of:

2019
$56,000 *Or* 100 percent net earnings

- **Net Earnings (From Self-Employment)**

    Net earnings = Net earnings from self-employment (after the Keogh deduction and one-half of the self-employment tax).

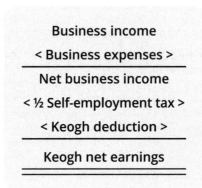

Business income

< Business expenses >

Net business income

< ½ Self-employment tax >

< Keogh deduction >

Keogh net earnings

Hint: 25 percent of self-employment income after the Keogh deduction is the mathematical equivalent of 20 percent (25% ÷ 125%) of self-employment income before the Keogh deduction.

Facts: Peter has self-employment net income (after one-half of the self-employment tax, but before any Keogh deduction) of $100,000.

Required: Calculate Peter's maximum allowable deduction to his Keogh plan for 2019.

Solution:

Gross self-employment income	$100,000
Times (shortcut)	× 20%
Maximum allowable deduction	$ 20,000*

*($100,000 − $20,000 = $80,000) × 25% = $20,000

10 Penalty on Early Withdrawal of Savings (Interest Income): Interest Forfeited

An example of forfeited interest is the interest penalty on early withdrawal of savings when funds in a certificate of deposit are withdrawn before maturity.

11 Alimony (Note That Rules Changed Starting in 2019)

Alimony payments to a former spouse are adjustments deductible to arrive at AGI only for divorce or separation agreements executed on or before December 31, 2018. The Tax Cuts and Jobs Act of 2017 eliminated both the inclusion of alimony in gross income and the deduction for alimony for any divorce or separation agreement executed after December 31, 2018.

11.1 Alimony/Spousal Support (Income to Payee/Adjustment to Payor)

Payments for the support of a former spouse are income to the spouse receiving the payments and are deductible to arrive at adjusted gross income (adjustment) by the contributing spouse. The following conditions must exist for alimony to be deductible:

- Payments must be legally required under a written divorce (or separation) decree or agreement;

- Payments must be in cash (or its equivalent);

- Payments cannot extend beyond the death of the payee-spouse;

- Payments cannot be made to members of the same household; and

- Payments must not be designated as anything other than alimony.

11.2 Child Support (Nontaxable to Payee/Nondeductible to Payor)

- **Nontaxable**

  If any portion of the payment is fixed by the decree or agreement as being for the support of minor children (or is contingent on the child's status, such as reaching a certain age), such portion is not deductible by the spouse making payment and is not includable in income by the spouse receiving payment.

■ **Payment Applies First to Child Support**

If the decree or agreement specifies that payments are to be made both for alimony and for support, but the payments subsequently made fall short of fulfilling these obligations, the payments will be allocated first to child support (until the entire child-support obligation for the year is met), and then to alimony.

11.3 Property Settlements (Nontaxable/Nondeductible)

If the divorce settlement provides for a lump-sum payment or property settlement by a spouse, that spouse gets no deduction for payments made, and the payments are not includable in the gross income of the spouse receiving the payment.

12 Attorney Fees Paid in Discrimination Cases

In certain cases, an adjustment is allowed for attorney fees paid in connection with age, sex, racial discrimination, and whistle-blower cases. The adjustment amount is limited to the amount claimed as income from the judgment. This assists some taxpayers in avoiding the alternative minimum tax (AMT) related to the deduction, which was previously reported as a miscellaneous itemized deduction (disallowed for AMT purposes).

Question 1	MCQ-01963

For the current year, Val and Pat White filed a joint return. Val earned $35,000 in wages and was covered by his employer's qualified pension plan. Pat was unemployed and received $5,000 in alimony payments (from a divorce agreement executed in 2017) for the first four months of the year before remarrying. The couple had no other income. Each contributed $5,000 to an IRA account. The allowable IRA deduction on their current year joint tax return is:

    a. $10,000

    b. $5,000

    c. $1,000

    d. $0

Question 2	MCQ-01960

The self-employment tax is:

    a. Fully deductible as an itemized deduction.

    b. Fully deductible in determining net income from self-employment.

    c. One-half deductible from gross income in arriving at adjusted gross income.

    d. Not deductible.

1 Standard Deduction

Those who do not itemize receive a standard deduction, with the amount determined based on filing status:

2019	
Single	$ 12,200
Head of household	18,350
Married filing jointly or surviving spouse	24,400
Married filing separately*	12,200
*Available only if both taxpayer and spouse do not itemize.	

1.1 Additional Deduction for Age (65 or Older) and/or Blindness

The standard deduction for a taxpayer who is age 65 or over or blind is increased by an additional amount.

2019		
	Single	*Married*
1 Qualified		
65 or blind	$1,650	$1,300
Both 65 and blind	3,300	2,600
2 Qualified		
Each 65 *or* blind		$2,600
Both 65 *and* blind		5,200

Illustration 1   Additional Standard Deduction

- Bob and Suzanne DeFilippis are both age 66 and file jointly. For tax year 2019, the standard deduction would be $27,000 ($24,400 plus $2,600 because each spouse is age 65 or over).

- For tax year 2019, Ed Joback, a blind, single taxpayer, may claim a standard deduction of $13,850 if he is blind and under age 65 ($12,200 plus $1,650), or $15,500 ($12,200 plus $3,300) if he is both blind and age 65 or over.

1.2 Standard Deduction: Dependent of Another

For 2019, the standard deduction amount is the greater of $1,100 (or the higher amount adjusted for inflation) or earned income plus $350. Thus, a dependent taxpayer with $1,300 earned income could claim a standard deduction of $1,650 ($1,300 plus $350). The dependent's standard deduction remains limited by the regular standard deduction for the tax year. Dependent taxpayers may claim the same additional standard deduction as other taxpayers for blindness and/or age 65-or-over status.

2 Itemized Deductions

Itemized deductions are referred to as "from AGI" deductions and are reported on Schedule A of an individual taxpayer's Form 1040. A taxpayer itemizes deductions when "from AGI" deductions are greater than the standard deduction. Taxpayers who are married filing separately must both take the standard deduction or itemize. One spouse cannot take the standard deduction and the other spouse itemize.

2.1 Medical Expenses

Medical
Taxes
Interest
Charity
Casualty
Misc.

2.1.1 Payments

Payments on behalf of the following individuals qualify:

- Filing taxpayer

- Spouse

- Dependent who received more than half of his or her support from the filing taxpayer

Note: The definition of "dependent" for this purpose does not consider the dependent's gross income or the joint return requirement. Thus, there is no limitation to the dependent's gross income when it relates to medical or dental expenses (however, all other dependency tests will continue to apply).

Support over 50 percent	Yes
Under $ taxable income	No
Precludes joint return	No
Only citizens	Yes
Relative *or*	Yes
Taxpayer lives with	Yes

2.1.2   Timing of Deduction

Include as potentially deductible expenses:

- Paid (cash or check) amounts during the year.

- Amounts charged to a credit card during the year (regardless of when paid).

- Payments made for a deceased spouse (deductible in the year paid, even if it is different from the year the spouse died).

- Amounts reimbursed to the taxpayer (or anyone else for the taxpayer) by hospital, health, or accident insurance must reduce otherwise allowable expense (before the 10 percent threshold is applied).

Pass Key

Individuals are typically "cash basis." Therefore, generally in order to be tax deductible, the item must have been:

- incurred as an expense
- paid or charged before year-end

2.1.3   Deductible Medical Expenses Formula

Qualified medical expenses to the extent that they exceed medical insurance reimbursement and 10 percent of the taxpayer's AGI are deductible for 2019.

> **Qualified medical expenses**
>
> **< Insurance reimbursement >**
> _____
>
> **Qualified medical expense "paid"**
>
> **< 10% AGI >**
> _____
>
> **Deductible medical expenses**
> _____

2.1.4   Types of Deductible Medical Expenses

- Medicine and prescription drugs, including Medicare part D premiums

- Doctors

- Medical and accident insurance premiums (including qualified long-term care premiums, although the deduction is limited based on the age of the taxpayer)

- Medically necessary surgery

- Transportation to medical facility

  - Actual costs

  - Allowance (20 cents per mile for 2019)

■ Physically disabled costs

• Expenses incurred by the physically disabled for the removal of structural barriers in their residences to accommodate a disability are treated as medical expenses.

2.1.5 Types of Nondeductible Medical Expenses

■ Elective surgery, elective cosmetic operations, drugs that are illegal, travel, vitamins, the part of Social Security tax paid for basic Medicare, funerals, cemetery lots, and insurance against loss of earnings due to sickness or accident (note that cosmetic surgery required due to an accident or deformity can qualify).

■ Life insurance.

■ Capital expenditures (up to the increase in FMV of the property because of the expenditure).

■ Health club memberships recommended by a doctor for general health care (it would have to be more specific to make it deductible).

■ Personal hygiene and other ordinary personal expenses (e.g., toothpaste, toiletries, over-the-counter medicines, bottled water, diaper service, maternity clothes, etc.).

2.1.6 Insurance Reimbursement

Amounts repaid to the taxpayer (or anyone else for the taxpayer) by hospital, health, or accident insurance must reduce otherwise allowable expense (before the 10 percent threshold is applied).

■ Reimbursement of expenses by an employer (or by policies provided by an employer) that exceed the total of medical or dental expenses paid by a taxpayer will be included as part of gross income.

■ Reimbursement of any expense deducted in a prior year will be included as part of gross income in the year received.

2.1.7 10 Percent AGI Test

Medical expenses, to the extent they exceed 10 percent of the taxpayer's AGI, are deductible for 2019.

2.2 State, Local, and Foreign Taxes

For cash-method taxpayers, deductible taxes are generally deductible in the year paid. For accrual-method taxpayers, taxes are generally deductible in the year in which they accrue. Itemized deductions for state and local income taxes, state and local property taxes, and sales tax are limited to $10,000 in the aggregate. In addition, foreign real property taxes, other than those incurred in a trade or business and those incurred with respect to property held as an investment, are not deductible.

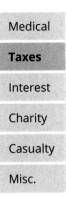

2.2.1 Real Estate Taxes (State and Local Taxes)

■ The taxpayer must be legally obligated to pay in order to deduct the taxes.

■ Prorate taxes in year of sale/purchase.

■ Taxes paid under protest are deductible. Subsequent recovery is included in gross income.

■ Real estate taxes do not include street, sewer, and sidewalk assessment taxes.

■ Taxes paid through an escrow account are deductible when paid to the taxing authority.

■ Foreign real estate taxes paid are only deductible if paid in carrying on a trade or business.

- Real estate taxes on land held for appreciation may be capitalized or deducted at the option of the taxpayer.

- Real estate taxes allocated to part of the home that is used exclusively for business may be deductible on Schedule C.

2.2.2 Personal Property Taxes (State and Local Taxes)

Personal property taxes are those assessed by state and local governments on personal property owned by the taxpayer, such as vehicles and boats. To be deductible, the tax must be based on the value of the personal property and paid during the tax year.

2.2.3 Income Taxes (State, Local, and Foreign Taxes)

- Estimated taxes paid during the year are deductible.

- Taxes withheld from paychecks during the year are deductible.

- Assessments for a prior year's tax that are paid in the current year are deductible.

- Refunds are included in gross income (if the tax was deducted in a prior year) and should not be netted against the current year itemized tax deduction.

2.2.4 Sales Tax

A taxpayer may elect to deduct either state and local income taxes or state and local general sales taxes. If the taxpayer chooses to deduct the sales tax, the amount is determined by either:

- the total of actual general sales taxes paid; or

- the relevant IRS table, plus any amount of sales tax paid for a motor vehicle, boat, or other IRS-approved items.

Note: A "tax benefit rule" applies to the impact of sales tax. If a taxpayer itemizes deductions in a year and takes a deduction for state income taxes instead of a deduction for sales taxes in that year, the tax benefit rule will calculate the taxability of the state tax refund on the extra benefit received from claiming the higher state income tax deduction instead of what would have been allowed if the state sales tax had been deducted.

2.2.5 Nondeductible Taxes

The following taxes are not deductible:

Federal taxes (including Social Security)

Inheritance taxes for states

Business (on Schedule C) and rental property taxes (on Schedule E)

Pass Key

Once again, "cash basis" taxpayers are entitled to a deduction in the year an item is paid or charged. Note that there is no "matching" to the year the tax is applicable.

2.3   Interest Expense

2.3.1   Home Mortgage Interest   `HIPPE`

Medical

Taxes

Interest

Charity

Casualty

Misc.

Deductions are allowed for "qualified residence interest" on a first or a second home (a taxpayer's principal residence and one other residence). A home that is used for personal purposes for at least 14 days in a tax year qualifies as a "second home." Mortgage interest allocated to part of the home that is used exclusively for business may be deductible on Schedule C and mortgage interest allocated to rental of the home may be deductible on Schedule E.

Interest on up to $750,000 ($375,000 MFS) of home-related indebtedness is deductible as home mortgage interest. Interest on excess principal (over $750,000, or $375,000 MFS) is treated as personal interest and, as such, is not deductible. Qualified indebtedness may be in the form of original acquisition debt or a home equity loan, but must meet the following:

- Incurred in buying, constructing, or substantially improving the taxpayer's principal and second home; and

- Secured by the home.

Points related to the debt on the home are deductible immediately. Points related to refinancing must be amortized over the period of the loan.

2.3.2   Investment Interest Expense   `HIPPE`

The investment interest deduction for individuals is limited to net (taxable) investment income.

- **Include as Investment (Taxable) Income**

  - Interest

  - Dividends (other than qualified dividends)

  - Short-term capital gains

  - Royalties (in excess of expenses)

  - Net long-term capital gains and qualified dividends (only if the taxpayer elects not to claim the reduced capital gains tax rate)

Pass Key

Any dividend income (from stock purchased with borrowed funds) that the taxpayer treats as investment income for purposes of the limitation on investment interest expense is not a qualified dividend, available for the preferential 15 percent tax rate.

- **Exclude as Investment (Taxable) Income**

  Interest expense used to purchase tax-free bonds is not deductible (because the interest earned on the bonds is not taxable).

Pass Key

An easy way to understand and remember this rule is to think of it like the limitations on gambling losses. Investments (a risk/gamble) have the limitation of not being permitted to deduct a "net investment expense."

- **Disallowed Expense: Carry Forward**

  The excess of investment interest paid over the "allowed" investment interest deducted can be carried forward indefinitely.

2.3.3 Personal (Consumer) Interest Is Not Deductible   HI**P**PE

Personal interest includes interest on:

- A personal note to a bank or person for borrowed funds

- Life insurance loans

- Bank credit cards or other revolving charge accounts

- A purchase of personal property such as autos, television sets, clothes, etc.

- Interest on federal, state, or local tax underpayments

- Interest on a home equity loan not used to improve the home

2.3.4 Prepaid Interest (Allocate to Proper Period)   HIP**P**E

Prepaid interest must be allocated over the period of the loan, even for a cash basis taxpayer. (Remember that prepaid interest received is taxable as income in the year received and is not allocated.)

2.3.5 Educational Loan Interest (Adjustment/Not Itemized Deduction)   HIPP**E**

Educational loan interest is a deduction to arrive at adjusted gross income and not an itemized deduction.

2.4 Charitable Contributions

Medical
Taxes
Interest
Charity
Casualty
Misc.

2.4.1 Definitions

- **Charity:** Items given to qualifying charitable organizations (tax deductible).

- **Gifts:** Items given to individuals (needy family) (nondeductible).

- **Political Contributions:** Items given to candidates (nondeductible).

2.4.2 Cash or FMV of Property

A charitable contribution may be in the form of cash or (FMV) property. The deduction for contributed property is usually measured by the lesser of the property's basis or its fair market value at the time the contribution is made.

2.4.3 Maximum Allowable Deduction (60 Percent of AGI)

The maximum allowable deduction for an individual is:

- Cash = 60 percent of AGI

- FMV property = 30 percent of AGI for gifts of long-term capital gain property to public charities

2.4.4 Appreciated Capital Gain Property

Special rules apply to the deductibility of gifts of long-term capital gain property.

- **Deduct at Fair Market Value**

  Appreciated property (property having a value greater than its basis) is deductible at its fair market value if it was held for more than one year.

- **30 Percent/20 Percent AGI Limit**

  A taxpayer may deduct the full value of long-term capital gain property (without paying capital gains tax on the appreciation), but the deduction may not exceed 30 percent of the taxpayer's adjusted gross income for gifts to a public charity. No more than 20 percent may be deducted for gifts of appreciated long-term capital property to a nonoperating private foundation.

- **Combination Rules**

  Always remember that in addition to the above, the total deduction for all gifts (to include long-term capital gain property, cash, and other property) may not exceed 60 percent of adjusted gross income.

Pass Key

The CPA Examination has typically tested the following rules with regard to *charitable contributions limitation*:

- Overall limit = 60 percent AGI
  - Cash—may be all 60 percent
  - General property—lesser of basis or FMV
  - Appreciated long-term capital gain property—is limited to the lesser of:
    - 30 percent of AGI
    - The remaining amount to reach 60 percent after cash contributions

2.4.5 Consideration for Contribution

The taxpayer may only deduct the excess contribution over the consideration received. Charitable organizations that receive contributions of more than $75 in exchange for services or property must provide the donor with a written statement that estimates the value of the deductible portion of the payment.

Illustration 2   Deductible Contribution

- Raffle tickets bought at a charity bazaar that have a chance of winning a prize do not give rise to a charitable deduction.
- JoAnn Veiga buys a ticket to a charity ball for $200. The actual value of attending the ball was $50. Veiga may take a charitable deduction of $150.

2.4.6 Charitable Deduction by Those Not Itemizing

Taxpayers who do not itemize deductions may not deduct charitable contributions.

2.4.7 Time for Deduction

A deduction is allowed only for the tax year in which the contribution is made:

- **Cash or Check:** Actually paid.
- **Credit Card:** When charged, a contribution made by a bank credit card is deductible in the year the charge is made, even if payment to the bank for the charge occurs the following year.

2.4.8 Contribution for Services

A taxpayer may deduct out-of-pocket expenses incurred as a result of providing services to a charity. This includes the cost of driving to and from the volunteer work. The taxpayer may take 14 cents per mile or the actual cost of gas and oil. With either method, the taxpayer may also include parking and tolls. (Note: An act of Congress is required to change the standard mileage rate for charitable contributions.)

2.4.9 Student Living in Taxpayer's Home

A charitable deduction may be taken for the expense incurred when the taxpayer takes into the home a full-time student (e.g., an exchange student). The student may not be beyond the 12th grade. The total deduction is up to $50 per month for each full month (15 or more days) the student is in the home and attending school.

2.4.10 Substantiation Requirement

Regardless of the amount of the cash contribution, taxpayers must keep records that substantiate their deductions. Either a bank record (e.g., canceled check or itemization on a bank statement with the charity's name) or a written acknowledgement from the charity is required. The acknowledgment must be obtained by the earlier of the filing date or the due date of the return.

2.4.11 Additional Substantiation Requirements for Large Noncash Contributions

For contributions of more than $500 of noncash property, the taxpayer must file Form 8283, giving certain information. In addition, taxpayers claiming more than $5,000 for any one item or group of similar items, such as a stamp collection, need a written appraisal for each such item or group donated, except that no appraisal is needed for publicly traded securities.

2.4.12 Carryover of Excess Charitable Contributions (Five Years)

All charitable contribution carryovers are applied on a first-in, first-out basis, after current year contributions are deducted, subject to the percentage of income limitations.

2.5 Casualty and Theft Losses (10 Percent AGI Test)

Casualty and theft losses of nonbusiness property are deductible to the extent that each individual loss exceeds $100 and that the aggregate of these excess losses (excess over $100) exceeds 10 percent of AGI. The $100 floor applies to each separate casualty event. The losses are only deductible if sustained in a presidentially declared disaster area. For tax years 2018–2025, the deduction for casualty and theft loss is limited to losses incurred in a federally declared disaster area.

2.5.1 Amount of Loss

The amount regarded as a casualty loss is the difference between the market value of the property immediately before the casualty and its market value immediately afterward. However, the loss may not exceed the adjusted basis of the property. Whichever amount is used must be reduced by the amount of any insurance recovery.

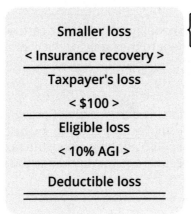

Smaller loss
< Insurance recovery >
Taxpayer's loss
< $100 >
Eligible loss
< 10% AGI >
Deductible loss

1. Lost cost/adjusted basis
2. Decreased FMV

2.5.2 Failure to Notify Insurer

A casualty loss for nonbusiness property cannot be deducted unless:

- an insurance claim was filed; or
- the losses are not covered by insurance.

2.5.3 Lost, Misplaced, or Broken Property

No casualty loss deduction is allowed for lost, misplaced, or broken property.

2.6 Miscellaneous Itemized Deductions (2 Percent AGI Test)

The Tax Cuts and Jobs Act of 2017 suspended all miscellaneous itemized deductions subject to the 2 percent floor for tax years 2018–2025.

2.7 Other Miscellaneous Deductions

The following itemized deductions are fully deductible.

2.7.1 Gambling Losses

Gambling losses remain fully deductible, but only to the extent of gambling winnings.

Medical

Taxes

Interest

Charity

Casualty

Misc.

2.7.2 Federal Estate Tax Paid on Income in Respect of a Decedent

This is estate tax that is paid by an individual because of income received by the individual as a beneficiary of an estate. The individual will include the income received as part of gross income on Form 1040 (with the same nature of income, such as interest income, as it would have been in the hands of the decedent). Estate tax will apply because the item of income was considered part of the estate for the estate's valuation (e.g., accrual of the value of a "loaded" installment note receivable). The federal estate tax paid (on Form 706) that related to the value of this income item is an allowable deduction for income tax purposes. (Estate tax is covered in detail in a later module.)

Question 1   MCQ-02011

Which of the following requirements must be met in order for a single individual to qualify for the additional standard deduction?

	Must support dependent child or aged parent	*Must be age 65 or older or blind*
a.	Yes	Yes
b.	No	No
c.	Yes	No
d.	No	Yes

Question 2   MCQ-01922

Carroll, a 35-year-old unmarried taxpayer with an adjusted gross income of $100,000, incurred and paid the following unreimbursed medical expenses:

Doctor bills resulting from a serious fall	$ 5,000
Cosmetic surgery that was necessary to correct a congenital deformity	15,000

Carroll had no medical insurance. For regular income tax purposes, what was Carroll's maximum allowable medical expense deduction, after the applicable threshold limitation, for the year?

    a. $0

    b. $10,000

    c. $15,000

    d. $20,000

Question 3	MCQ-01926

Taylor, an unmarried taxpayer, had $90,000 in adjusted gross income for the current year. During the current year, Taylor donated land to a church and made no other contributions. Taylor purchased the land 15 years ago as an investment for $14,000. The land's fair market value was $25,000 on the day of the donation.

What is the maximum amount of charitable contribution that Taylor may deduct as an itemized deduction for the land donation for the current year?

    a. $25,000

    b. $14,000

    c. $11,000

    d. $0

1 Individual Income Tax Calculation and Limitations

1.1 Individual Income Tax Rate Structure

The tax rates for individuals are 10, 12, 22, 24, 32, 35, and 37 percent.

2019 Tax Rate	Single	Head of Household	Married Filing Jointly	Married Filing Separately
10%	$0–$9,700	$0–$13,850	$0–$19,400	$0–$9,700
12%	$9,701–$39,475	$13,851–$52,850	$19,401–$78,950	$9,701–$39,475
22%	$39,476–$84,200	$52,851–$84,200	$78,951–$168,400	$39,476–$84,200
24%	$84,201–$160,725	$84,201–$160,700	$168,401–$321,450	$84,201–$160,725
32%	$160,726–$204,100	$160,701–$204,100	$321,451–$408,200	$160,726–$204,100
35%	$204,101–$510,300	$204,101–$510,300	$408,201–$612,350	$204,101–$306,175
37%	Over $510,300	Over $510,300	Over $612,350	Over $306,175

Long-term capital gains and qualified dividends are taxed at preferential tax rates, as shown in the table below.

	2019 Taxable Income			
Tax Rate	Single	Head of Household	Married Filing Jointly	Married Filing Separately
0%	$0–$39,375	$0–$52,750	$0–$78,750	$0–$39,375
15%	$39,376–$434,550	$52,751–$461,700	$78,751–$488,850	$39,376–$244,425
20%	Over $434,550	Over $461,700	Over $488,850	Over $244,425

Example 1	Calculating Individual Income Tax Liability

1. **Facts:** A taxpayer with a single filing status has $92,000 of taxable income.

   Required: Calculate the income tax liability in 2019.

   Solution:

   ($9,700 − $0) × 10% = $970

   ($39,475 − $9,700) × 12% = $3,573

   ($84,200 − $39,475) × 22% = $9,840

   ($92,000 − $84,200) × 24% = $1,872

   $970 + $3,573 + $9,840 + $1,872 = **$16,255**

2. **Facts:** A taxpayer with a head of household filing status has $60,000 of taxable income.

   Required: Calculate the income tax liability in 2019.

   Solution:

   ($13,850 − $0) × 10% = $1,385

   ($52,850 − $13,850) × 12% = $4,680

   ($60,000 − $52,850) × 22% = $1,573

   $1,385 + $4,680 + $1,573 = **$7,638**

3. **Facts:** A taxpayer with a married filing jointly filing status has $75,000 of taxable income.

   Required: Calculate the income tax liability in 2019.

   Solution:

   ($19,400 − $0) × 10% = $1,940

   ($75,000 − $19,400) × 12% = $6,672

   $1,940 + $6,672 = **$8,612**

4. **Facts:** A taxpayer with a married filing separately filing status has $50,000 of taxable income.

   Required: Calculate the income tax liability in 2019.

   Solution:

   ($9,700 − $0) × 10% = $970

   ($39,475 − $9,700) × 12% = $3,573

   ($50,000 − $39,475) × 22% = $2,316

   $970 + $3,573 + $2,316 = **$6,859**

1.1.1 Progressive Tax Rate Structure

▪ The individual income tax rate structure is a progressive tax rate structure.

▪ With a progressive tax rate structure, the marginal tax rate increases as taxable income increases.

- The tax rate applied to the next amount of incremental taxable income or deductions is the marginal tax rate.

- It is calculated as the change in tax divided by the change in taxable income.

Example 2	Increasing Marginal Tax Rate

Facts: Mark (files married filing jointly) has discovered that he will receive an additional consulting check in December 2019 that he did not expect until next year. Before the additional income, his taxable income is $70,000. After the receipt of the additional consulting income, his taxable income is $85,000.

Required: Determine Mark's marginal tax rate on the additional taxable income.

Solution:

Tax calculated on $70,000 for married filing jointly is as follows:

$($19,400 − $0) × 10\% = $1,940$

$($70,000 − $19,400) × 12\% = $6,072$

$$1,940 + $6,072 = $8,012$$

Tax calculated on $85,000 for married filing jointly is as follows:

$($19,400 − $0) × 10\% = $1,940$

$($78,950 − $19,400) × 12\% = $7,146$

$($85,000 − $78,950) × 22\% = $1,331$

$$1,940 + $7,146 + $1,331 = $10,417$$

The marginal tax rate is calculated as follows:

$($10,417 − $8,012) = $2,405$ change in tax / $15,000 change in taxable income = 16% (rounded)

---

2 Tax Credits

2.1 Tax Credits in General

Tax credits reduce personal tax liability. There are two basic types of tax credits, discussed below.

2.1.1 Personal Tax Credits

Personal tax credits may reduce personal tax liability to zero, but they may not result in a cash refund. Personal tax credits include:

- Child and dependent care credit

- Elderly and permanently disabled credit

- Education credits

  - Lifetime learning credit

  - American opportunity credit

- ▧ Retirement savings contribution credit
- ▧ Foreign tax credit
- ▧ General business credit
- ▧ Adoption credit

2.1.2 Refundable Credits

Refundable credits are subtracted from income tax liability. They may result in a cash refund when the credit exceeds tax liability owed even if no tax is withheld from wages. The following are refundable credits (or are payments that are treated as refundable credits) and are shown in the "payments" section of Form 1040:

- ▧ Child tax credit (refund is limited)
- ▧ Earned income credit
- ▧ Withholding taxes (W-2)
- ▧ Excess Social Security paid
- ▧ American opportunity credit (40 percent refundable)

2.2 Child and Dependent Care Credit

A tax credit of 20 to 35 percent of eligible expenditures:

2019 Maximum Expenditures	
One dependent	$3,000
Two or more dependents	$6,000

2.2.1 Eligible People

The child and dependent care credit is available to taxpayers who maintain a household, work, and incur eligible expenses for the care of the following eligible people:

- ▧ A dependent qualifying child who is under age 13 when the care is provided.
- ▧ Any disabled dependent of any age who is unable to care for himself, whether or not he can be claimed as a dependent, but who must meet the support test of a dependent (half of support provided for by the taxpayer).
- ▧ A spouse who is disabled and not able to take care of himself or herself.

2.2.2 Earned (Work) Income Requirement

Married taxpayers must both produce earned income from wages, salary, or net self-employment income to be eligible for the child and dependent care credit (unless one is a full-time student or physically or mentally incapacitated). The credit is computed by using the lowest of (i) the earned income of the spouse with the lesser amount, (ii) the actual child care expenditure, or (iii) the maximum amount (i.e., $3,000 or $6,000 for 2019). This lowest amount would then be multiplied by the applicable percentage to get the amount of the credit.

2.2.3 Eligible Expenses

Eligible expenditures must be for the purpose of enabling the taxpayer to be gainfully employed (i.e., allowing that person to work or look for work).

- Babysitter
- Nursery school
- Day care
- Not elementary school

2.2.4 Credit Computation

- **Maximum 35 Percent:** The maximum child care credit against the tax liability is 35 percent. In order to obtain the maximum credit, the taxpayer's adjusted gross income (AGI) must be $15,000 or less.

- **Phase-out 20 to 35 Percent:** The credit decreases by 1 percent for each $2,000 (or fraction thereof) of AGI over $15,000, but not below 20 percent.

- **Minimum 20 Percent:** The maximum child care credit at the lowest rate of 20 percent for individuals with AGI of more than $43,000 is $600 (20 percent of $3,000) or $1,200 (20 percent of $6,000) if the taxpayer has two or more qualifying dependents.

Example 3	Child and Dependent Care Credit

Facts: JoAnn Veiga is a widow with two children. In 2019, her AGI is $43,500, for which the applicable table rate is 20 percent. Her work-related expenses for a home caregiver for the children are $3,600, and $3,800 for child care at a nursery school.

Required: Calculate the amount of the child and dependent care credit for JoAnn.

Solution: JoAnn can take a child care credit of $1,200, calculated as follows:

Work-related expenses	$3,600
Nursery school expenses	3,800
Total	$7,400
Maximum allowable for two dependents	6,000
Amount of credit (20%) percentage	× 20%
Amount of credit	$1,200

2.3 Credit for the Elderly and/or Permanently Disabled

2.3.1 Eligibility

This credit of 15 percent of eligible income is available to individuals who are:

1. 65 years of age or older; or
2. under 65 and retired due to permanent disability.

2.3.2   Base Amount

The base amount used to figure the credit is as follows:

- $5,000 for a single person, widow, or widower.

- $5,000 if married filing jointly and only one spouse is a qualified individual.

- $7,500 if married filing jointly and both are qualified individuals.

- $3,750 for a qualified individual who is married filing separately.

    If a qualified individual is under age 65 and has disability income of less than $5,000, the base amount is limited to $5,000.

2.3.3   Adjusted Gross Income Limit

Eligible income is reduced by:

1.   any Social Security payments and other excludable pensions or annuities received by the taxpayer; and

2.   one half of the taxpayer's adjusted gross income that exceeds the following levels:

Single taxpayers	$ 7,500
Married persons filing jointly	$10,000
Married persons filing separately	$ 5,000

2.3.4   Summary of Credit Calculation

A taxpayer who is 65 or older starts with a tax credit for the elderly based on a specified amount that is reduced first by any Social Security payments and other excludable pensions and second by one half (50 percent) of any adjusted gross income over the stated maximum. The results, if any, are multiplied by 15 percent to arrive at the allowable tax credit. The credit is limited to the amount of tax.

Single		Joint
Single		**Joint**
5,000	**Base Amount**	7,500
(ALL)	(Social Security)	(ALL)
(½ over $7,500)	(½ Excess AGI)	(½ over $10,000)
Balance		Balance
× 15%	Rate	× 15%
Credit		Credit

Example 4	Credit for the Elderly and/or Permanently Disabled

Facts: Peter is single and 68 years old. He received the following income for the year:

Social Security received	$3,120
Taxable interest	215
Taxable part of pension	3,600
Wages from a part-time job	4,245

Required: Calculate Peter's credit for the elderly and/or permanently disabled.

Solution: His credit will be $240, computed as follows:

Peter's adjusted gross income is $8,060, calculated as follows:

Wages from part-time job	$4,245
Taxable portion of pension	3,600
Taxable interest	215
	$8,060

To calculate credit:

Base amount			$5,000
Less:			
Social Security		$3,120	
Excess AGI:	$8,060		
	(7,500)		
	560 × 50%	280	(3,400)
			$1,600
Balance			15%
Credit			$ 240

2.4 Education Tax Incentives

Assuming the requirements are met, a taxpayer has the opportunity to reduce taxes by taking advantage of the American opportunity credit (AOC), the lifetime learning credit, and/or a nontaxable distribution from a Coverdell education savings account used to pay higher education costs.

2.4.1 The American Opportunity Credit (AOC)

The American opportunity credit is available against federal income taxes for qualified tuition, fees, and course materials (including books) paid for a student's first four years of postsecondary (college) education at an eligible educational institution.

- The maximum AOC credit is $2,500 in 2019:

  - 100 percent of the first $2,000 of qualified expenses; plus

  - 25 percent of the next $2,000 of expenses paid during the year.

- The qualified expenses are on a "per student" basis and must be incurred on behalf of the:

  - taxpayer;

  - taxpayer's spouse; or

  - taxpayer's dependent.

- If a child is claimed as a dependent by a parent, expenses paid by both the parent and the child are deemed to have been made by the parent for this purpose.

- The student must be at least half-time for at least one academic period during the year.

- The credit is not available for the expenses of a student convicted of a federal or state felony drug offense in the calendar year for which expenses are incurred.

- For 2019, the credit phase-out begins with modified AGI exceeding $80,000 ($160,000 on a joint return), with full phase-out at $90,000 ($180,000 joint).

- Refundable portion: Subject to certain restrictions, 40 percent of the American opportunity credit is refundable (and the nonrefundable portion may offset both regular and alternative minimum tax). This means that up to $1,000 ($2,500 maximum credit × 40%) may be refunded.

2.4.2 The Lifetime Learning Credit ($2,000 Maximum per Year)

The lifetime learning credit is available for an unlimited number of years for qualified tuition and related expenses (except books) at eligible educational institutions.

- The credit is equal to 20 percent of qualified expenses up to $10,000.

- Qualified expenses include tuition and fees (not course materials) for undergraduate courses, graduate-level courses, certain professional degree courses, and courses to acquire or improve job skills.

- The qualified expenses are on a "per taxpayer" basis, rather than a "per student" basis, so the maximum credit is $2,000 (2019) regardless of the number of qualifying students.

- As with the American opportunity credit, expenses paid by a dependent child are treated as if made by the parent.

- For 2019, the credit phase-out begins with modified AGI exceeding $58,000 ($116,000 on a joint return), with full phase-out at $68,000 ($136,000 joint).

2.4.3 Not Limited to One Type of Credit

The taxpayer does not have to choose one type of credit on his tax return for the year. For example, a parent may claim a lifetime learning credit for the expense of one child and an American opportunity credit for the expenses of another child in the same taxable year. However, both credits can not be claimed for the same student in the same year.

2.4.4 Coverdell Education Savings Accounts

A separate education savings account may be set up to pay the qualified education expenses of a designated beneficiary.

- Contributions are nondeductible; maximum contribution per beneficiary is $2,000 annually.

- The designated beneficiary may be any child under age 18. There is no limit on the number of beneficiaries (each beneficiary has a separate account).

■ The contribution amount is phased out for taxpayers with the following modified adjusted gross income between these amounts:

2019	
Single	$95,000–$110,000
Married	$190,000–$220,000

■ Earnings accumulate tax-free while in an education savings account.

■ Distributions, both of principal and interest, are tax-free to the extent that they are used for qualified elementary, secondary, or higher education expenses of the designated beneficiary.

■ Qualified education expenses include tuition, fees, tutoring, books, room and board, supplies, and equipment.

■ Any amounts remaining when the beneficiary reaches 30 years of age must be distributed (except in the case of a special needs beneficiary). If the distribution is made directly to the beneficiary, the distributed amount is taxable to the beneficiary and subject to a 10 percent penalty. Alternatively, the balance can be rolled over tax free to another family member of the taxpayer with no penalty.

■ A taxpayer can claim the American opportunity credit or lifetime learning credit for a tax year and also exclude from gross income amounts distributed from a Coverdell education savings account. However, the distribution cannot be used for the same educational expenses for which either the American opportunity credit or the lifetime learning credit was claimed.

2.4.5 Section 529 Qualified Tuition Programs (QTP)

■ **Tax Rule:** Exempt from all federal income taxation.

■ **Definition:** A QTP is a program under which a person may purchase tuition credits or make cash contributions to an account on behalf of a beneficiary for payment of qualified higher education expenses. The program must be established and maintained by a state, state agency, or by an eligible educational institution. Eligible educational institutions generally include any accredited postsecondary educational institution, so long as contributions made to the program are held in a "qualified trust" [i.e., meets the requirements under Code Section 408(a)(2) and (5)].

■ **Qualified Costs:** Qualified higher education expenses (QHEEs) include tuition, fees, books, supplies, and equipment required by an educational institution for enrollment or attendance. These expenses also include the reasonable cost of room and board if the beneficiary is enrolled at least half-time.

■ **Tax-Free Use of Funds:** Distributions from a QTP, including cash, earnings, and in-kind distributions, may be excluded from a designated beneficiary's gross income to the extent that the distribution is used to pay for QHEEs.

2019 Education Tax Incentives: Summary

Item	General Rule	Limit	Income Phase-out
Income Exclusion			
U.S. Savings Bond—Series EE	Exclude interest income	Must pay educational expense	AGI $81,100–$96,100 (S) and $121,600–$151,600 (MFJ)
Employer-paid education expenses	Exclude from income	Up to $5,250 per year	No income limit
Scholarships	Exclude from income	Only tuition, books, and fees, not room and board	No income limit
Adjustments			
Educator expenses	Deduct above line	$500/$250	No income limit
Coverdell education savings account	Nondeductible	$2,000	AGI $95,000–$110,000 (S) and $190,000–$220,000 (MFJ)
Student loan interest deduction	Deduct above line	$2,500	AGI $70,000–$85,000 (S) and $140,000–$170,000 (MFJ)
Credits			
American opportunity credit	First four years	$2,500 per person; tuition, fees, and course materials	AGI $80,000–$90,000 (S) and $160,000–$180,000 (MFJ)
Lifetime learning credit	After first four years	$2,000 per taxpayer; tuition and fees, not course materials	AGI $58,000–$68,000 (S) and $116,000–$136,000 (MFJ)
Miscellaneous			
529 plan (qualified tuition program)	No deduction No income	Vary by state	None

2.5 Adoption Credit

A credit for qualifying expenses of adopting a child is available. The maximum adoption tax credit is:

2019	
Per child	$14,080

The adoption credit is nonrefundable, but any credit in excess of your tax liability may be carried forward for up to five years.

▨ **Phase-out**

The credit is phased out in 2019 for modified adjusted gross income over $211,160 and less than or equal to $251,160.

2019
$211,160–$251,160

▨ **Eligible Expenses**

- All reasonable and necessary expenses, costs, and fees are available for the credit.

- The credit is not available for adopting the child of a spouse or for a surrogate parenting arrangement.

- Medical expenses do not qualify as eligible expenses.

- For 2019, a taxpayer can exclude up to $14,080 of qualified adoption expenses paid by an employer (exclusion is phased out with modified AGI of $211,160–$251,160).

▨ **Timing**

The credit is claimed for years after the payment is made until the adoption is final, at which point expenses paid in the year it becomes final are claimed in that year. For foreign children adopted, no credit can be claimed until the year it becomes final. In either case, expenses paid in later years can be claimed in the year paid.

2.6 Retirement Savings Contributions Credit

For 2019, a nonrefundable tax credit that may offset both regular and alternative minimum tax is available for contributions to either a traditional IRA or Roth IRA (other eligible retirement plans are beyond the scope of the CPA Examination).

▨ **Eligible Taxpayers**

- At least 18 years old by the close of the tax year

- Not a full-time student

- Not a dependent of another taxpayer

▨ **Allowable Credit (2019 Table)**

For the year 2019, the credit is limited to the excess of the regular tax liability and the alternative minimum tax liability of the taxpayer, minus the taxpayer's nonrefundable personal credits (except the retirement savings contributions credit, the adoption credit, the foreign tax credit, and some energy credits). No carryover is allowed.

Allowable Retirement Savings Contribution Credit				
Married/Joint Income *(Over–Not Over)*	Single/MFS Income *(Over–Not Over)*	Credit Rate	Maximum Eligible Contribution *(Per Taxpayer)*	Maximum Credit
$0–$38,500	$0–$19,250	50%	$2,000	$1,000
$38,500–$41,500	$19,250–$20,750	20%	$2,000	$400
$41,500–$64,000	$20,750–$32,000	10%	$2,000	$200
Over $64,000*	Over $32,000*	0%	$2,000	-0-

*For 2019, full phase-out applies to AGI over $64,000 for MFJ; $48,000 for head of household; and $32,000 for single and MFS.

2.7 Foreign Tax Credit

A taxpayer may claim a credit for foreign income taxes paid to a foreign country or United States possession. There is a limitation on the amount of the credit an individual can obtain. In lieu of this credit, an individual can deduct the taxes as an itemized deduction.

■ **Allowable Credit**

There is no limit on foreign taxes used as a deduction; however, foreign tax credits are limited to the lesser of:

● Foreign taxes paid, or

● $$\frac{\text{Taxable income from all foreign operations}}{\text{Total taxable worldwide income}} \times \text{U.S. tax} = \text{Foreign tax credit limit}$$

■ **Carryover of Excess (Disallowed) Credit**

Any disallowed foreign tax credit may be carried over as follows:

● Carry back one year

● Carry forward 10 years

2.8 General Business Credit

2.8.1 Included Credits

The general business credit is a combination of:

■ Investment credit

■ Work opportunity credit

■ Alcohol fuels credit

■ Increased research credit (generally 20 percent of the increase in qualified research expenditures over the base amount for the year)

■ Low-income housing credit

- Qualified child care expenditures;
- Welfare-to-work credit;
- Employer-provided child care credit;
- Small employer pension plan start-up costs credit;
- Alternative motor vehicle credit
- Other infrequent (on exam) credits

2.8.2 Formula

The credit may not exceed "net income tax" (regular income tax plus alternative minimum tax less nonrefundable tax credits, other than the alternative minimum tax credit) less the greater of:

- 25 percent of regular tax liability above $25,000; or
- "tentative minimum tax" for the year.

Tentative Tax		Allowable Percentages		Allowable Amount
$0–$25,000	×	100%	=	×
Excess	×	75%	=	×
Maximum Credit Permitted				Total

2.8.3 Unused Credit Carryover

Although some limits must be applied separately, unused credits generally may be carried back one year and forward 20 years.

2.9 Work Opportunity Credit

The work opportunity credit is available to employers who hire employees from a targeted group. This credit is part of the general business credit and was extended through 2019 by the Protecting Americans From Tax Hikes Act of 2015.

2.9.1 Credit

- 40 percent of first $6,000 of first year's wages
- 40 percent of first $3,000 to certain summer youth

2.9.2 Qualified Groups

- Disabled
- 18- to- 24-year-olds from poor families
- Vietnam veterans from economically disadvantaged areas
- Certain food stamp recipients

2.10 "Child" Tax Credit

For tax years 2018–2025, taxpayers may claim a $2,000 tax credit for each "qualifying child."

2.10.1 Qualifying Child

The "**CARES**" rules on dependency definitions (discussed in R1) apply here, except that a child must be under the age of 17 (not the 19-year or 24-year age limits that "**CARES**" implies). Furthermore, the qualifying child must be a citizen, a national, or a resident of the United States.

2.10.2 Phase-out

Higher-income taxpayers must reduce the allowable child credit by $50 for each $1,000 (or fraction thereof) by which modified adjusted gross income exceeds:

■ $400,000 for a joint return;

■ $200,000 for an unmarried individual; or

■ $200,000 for married individuals filing a separate return.

2.10.3 Refundable Limit

The child tax credit is refundable to the extent of the lesser of:

■ excess child tax credit (over tax liability);

■ earned income less $2,500 (2019) multiplied by 15 percent; or

■ $1,400 per qualifying child.

2.10.4 Due Diligence Requirements

To help prevent improper claims, paid preparers are subject to due diligence requirements for returns that claim the child tax credit (similar due diligence requirements apply to returns that claim the earned income tax credit).

2.10.5 Non-child Dependent Credit

A taxpayer may claim an additional nonrefundable tax credit of $500 for each dependent who is not a qualifying child under age 17. This may include children who are age 17 and above or other dependents who meet the requirements of a qualifying relative. The non-child dependent credit is subject to the same AGI phase-outs and is not refundable.

2.11 Earned Income Credit (Refundable)

2.11.1 Eligibility

To be eligible for the earned income credit, a taxpayer must:

■ live in the U.S. (main home) for more than half the taxable year;

■ meet certain earned low-income thresholds;

■ not have more than a specified amount of disqualified income;

■ if there are no qualifying children, be over the age of 25 and under 65 (applies to both taxpayer and spouse); and

■ file a joint return with one's spouse with certain exceptions (which means that the spouse cannot be a dependent of another).

2.11.2 Earned Income

Earned income is wages, salaries, tips, other employee compensation, and earnings from self-employment. It does not include pension and annuity income. An alternative minimum tax liability will not affect an individual's earned income credit.

Pass Key

The most frequently tested issue involving the *earned income credit* is that it is a refundable credit.

2.11.3 Qualifying Child

A qualifying child is not a requirement in order to be eligible for the earned income credit. However, if the taxpayer has a qualifying child, the earned income credit percentage and allowable earned income level is higher. A qualifying child is a child who:

- is the taxpayer's son, daughter, adopted child, grandchild, stepchild, foster child, brother, sister, stepbrother, stepsister, or descendant of those individuals;

- was (at the end of the year) either under age 19 or under age 24 and a full-time student, or any age and permanently and totally disabled;

- lived with the taxpayer in the taxpayer's main home in the U.S. for more than half of the taxable year; and

- is the taxpayer's dependent (if the child is married).

2.11.4 Computing Basic Earned Income Credit

For 2019, the earned income credit table is as follows:

	No Children	One Child	Two Children	Three or More Children
Maximum earned income credit	$529	$3,526	$5,828	$6,557
Earned income required to get maximum credit	$6,920	$10,370	$14,570	$14,570
Credit rate percentage	7.65%	34%	40%	45%
Phase-out percentage	7.65%	15.98%	21.06%	21.06%
Credit phase-out for AGI or earned income (if greater) over this amount *(all taxpayers except married filing jointly)*	$8,650	$19,030	$19,030	$19,030
Credit phase-out for AGI or earned income (if greater) over this amount *(for married filing jointly)*	$14,450	$24,820	$24,820	$24,820

| Example 5 | Earned Income Tax Credit |

Facts: Karen is 26 years old. In 2019, she reported an AGI of $12,000 from her job at the local university. She is single with no dependents.

Required: Calculate the amount of earned income credit Karen can take in the current year.

Solution: Karen is eligible to take an earned income credit in the amount of $273 after phase-out.

Earned Income Tax Credit Calculation	
Earned income	$12,000
Maximum income eligible for credit	$6,920
× 7.65%	$529 [maximum credit]
$12,000 earned income − $8,650 phase-out threshold	$3,350
× 7.65% phase-out percentage	$256 [phase-out amount]
$529 maximum credit − $256 phase-out amount	$273

2.11.5 Disqualified Income

An individual cannot claim the credit if the individual has "disqualified income" exceeding $3,600 (2019). Disqualified income includes taxable and nontaxable interest, dividends, net rental and royalty income, net capital gains income, and net passive income other than self-employment income.

2.11.6 Due Diligence Requirements

To increase the prevention of improper claims, paid-preparers are subject to due diligence requirements for returns that claim the earned income tax credit.

2.12 Withholding Tax (Paycheck Credit)

All income taxes withheld from a taxpayer's paycheck are treated as a "credit" against the taxpayer's tax liability. When this credit exceeds the tax liability, a refund is provided to the taxpayer.

2.13 Excess FICA (Social Security Tax Withheld)

Excess Social Security tax withheld is treated as additional tax payments withheld.

- **Two or More Employers:** An employee who has had Social Security tax withheld in an amount greater than the maximum for a particular year may claim the excess as a credit against income tax (in the payment section), if that excess resulted from correct withholding by two or more employers.

- **One Employer:** If the excess was withheld by only one employer, the employer must refund the excess to the employee. No credit is allowed.

2.14 Small Employer Pension Plan Start-up Costs Credit

For eligible small businesses (those with 100 or fewer employees who earned at least $5,000 in the preceding tax year), a credit is allowed for 50 percent of the first $1,000 (up to $500 per year) of qualified start-up costs for establishing a new qualified pension plan for three years (starting with the year the plan was established).

■   Qualified costs include expenses to establish and administer the plan and provide information to employees regarding retirement planning.

■   If the expenses are used for the credit, they may not also be used as deductible ordinary and necessary business expenses.

■   Employers are not required to take the credit for any tax year and may be able to take the credit in the year that precedes the first year of the plan.

2.15 Small Business Health Care Tax Credit

Under the current health care tax laws:

■   A credit of up to 50 percent of the employer's costs of the plan premiums (or the average of the group's premium for small businesses within the taxpayer's state) is allowed as a credit for eligible employers, provided the employer contributes at least 50 percent of the costs of health coverage on behalf of employees enrolled in a qualified health plan offered through a Small Business Health Options Program (SHOP).

■   Smaller businesses receive the better tax benefits.

■   The credit is allowable as an offset to alternative minimum tax; however, it is not refundable, and the unused amount is carried back one year and then carried forward for 20 years. (Tax-exempt organizations, however, will receive a refund of the tax credit.)

■   The costs for family members, sole-proprietors, partners, S corporation owners with greater than 2 percent ownership, and shareholders owning more than 5 percent of corporations are excluded.

■   If the expenses were used to qualify for the credit, they are not allowable as tax deductions for employee benefits expense.

2.16 Residential Energy Credits

A maximum credit of 30 percent of qualifying solar electric or solar water heating property installed in 2018 or 2019 is allowed. The credit percentage decreases to 26 percent in 2020 and 22 percent in 2021.

2.17 Premium Tax Credit (PTC)

The premium tax credit is a refundable credit that helps eligible individuals and families with low or moderate income afford health insurance purchased through a Health Insurance Marketplace. The "credits" are available immediately when the insurance is purchased to help eligible individuals pay for their monthly health insurance premiums.

3 Estimated Tax and Inadequate Withholding

3.1 Tax Payments

A taxpayer typically makes prepayments of tax during the year. These payments reduce the amount shown as "total tax" on the tax return and result in the calculation of tax owed to the IRS or a refund owed to the taxpayer at the bottom of Form 1040. Payments include:

- Taxes withheld from paychecks (W-2 or 1099)
- Estimated taxes paid (quarterly, with extension, or applied from a prior year)
- Excess Social Security tax withheld (from two or more employers)

3.2 Estimated Taxes (Required Minimum)

A taxpayer is required to make estimated quarterly tax payments if both of the following conditions are met:

- **$1,000 or More Tax Liability**

  One condition is met if the amount of taxes owed (excess of tax liability over withholding) is expected to be $1,000 or more.

- **Inadequate Tax Estimates**

  The other condition is met if the taxpayer's withholding is less than the lesser of:

  - 90 percent of the current year's tax; or
  - 100 percent of last year's tax.
    - —This applies even if an individual files a tax return with a zero tax liability in the prior year.
    - —Exception: If a taxpayer had adjusted gross income in excess of $150,000 ($75,000 for married filing separately) in the prior year, 110 percent of the prior year's tax liability is used to compute the safe harbor for estimate payments.

3.3 Failure to Pay Estimated Taxes (Penalty)

If the taxpayer does not make proper quarterly estimated payments, a penalty may be assessed. There is no penalty due under any circumstances if the balance of tax owed at filing is under $1,000. The Internal Revenue Service may waive the penalty if the failure to pay was the result of casualty, disaster, illness, or death of the taxpayer.

3.4 Withholding Tax Treated as Estimated Payments

If, toward the end of the taxable year, a taxpayer determines that estimated payments have been insufficient to avoid a penalty, a taxpayer can increase withholding from wages, and the withholdings will be considered to have been paid evenly during the year. Such action will usually reduce or eliminate any penalty. A new W-4 will have to be completed and submitted to the taxpayer's employer.

Question 1   MCQ-02013

Mr. and Mrs. Sloan incurred the following expenses during the year when they adopted a child:

Child's medical expenses	$50,000
Legal expenses	8,000
Agency fee	3,000

Without regard to the limitation of the credit, what amount of the above expenses are qualifying expenses for the adoption credit?

   a. $16,000

   b. $11,000

   c. $10,160

   d. $5,000

Question 2   MCQ-02012

Which of the following credits can result in a refund even if the individual had no income tax liability?

   a. Credit for prior year minimum tax

   b. Elderly and permanently and totally disabled credit

   c. Earned income credit

   d. Child and dependent care credit

Question 3   MCQ-02084

Krete, an unmarried taxpayer with income exclusively from wages, filed her initial income tax return for Year 8. By December 31, Year 8, Krete's employer had withheld $16,000 in federal income taxes and Krete had made no estimated tax payments. On April 15, Year 9, Krete timely filed an extension request to file her individual tax return and paid $300 of additional taxes. Krete's Year 8 income tax liability was $16,500 when she timely filed her return on April 30, Year 9, and paid the remaining income tax liability balance.

What amount would be subject to the penalty for the underpayment of estimated taxes?

   a. $0

   b. $200

   c. $500

   d. $16,500

NOTES

1 Alternative Minimum Tax

The alternative minimum tax (AMT) is a tax designed to ensure that taxpayers who take a large number of tax-preference deductions pay a minimum amount of tax on their income. The alternative minimum tax is the excess of the tentative AMT over the regular tax.

1.1 Calculation

The alternative minimum tax is computed by first subtracting the AMT exemption amount from "alternative minimum taxable income" (AMTI) to compute the "taxable excess" AMTI or "AMT base." For all taxpayers except married taxpayers filing separately, tax is then applied at 26 percent on the first $194,800 (2019) of taxable excess AMTI and at 28 percent on all taxable excess AMTI exceeding $194,800 (2019). The alternative minimum tax is mandatory if it exceeds the regular tax.

> Regular taxable income
> ± Adjustments
> + Preferences
> _____
> Alternative minimum taxable income
> < Exemption >
> _____
> Alternative minimum tax base
> × AMT rate
> _____
> Tentative AMT tax
> < AMT foreign tax credit >
> _____
> Tentative minimum tax
> < Regular income tax >
> _____
> Alternative minimum tax
> _____

Pass Key

The CPA Examination has focused the majority of the questions concerning *individual alternative minimum tax* on the following four areas:

- The AMT exemption formula
- Distinguishing "adjustments" from "preferences"
- The AMT credit carryforward period (against regular tax)
- Credits: available to reduce AMT (not regular tax)

1.2 AMT Exemption Amounts

For 2019, the AMT exemption amount is $71,700 less [25 percent × (AMTI − $510,300)] for single taxpayers; $111,700 less [25 percent × (AMTI − $1,020,600)] for joint filers; and $55,850 less [25 percent × (AMTI − $510,300)] for married individuals filing separately. The AMT exemption cannot be less than zero.

"Joint" Exemption	(2019) $111,700
AMTI	
< $1,020,600 >	
Excess	
× 25%	
	< Reduction >
	AMT
	Exemption

Illustration 1 — Calculation of AMT Exemption

Bob and Mary file a joint return in 2019. If their AMTI is $1,118,600, their AMT exemption is $87,200 as follows:

Full MFJ exemption		$111,700
AMTI	$1,118,600	
Threshold	(1,020,600)	
Excess over threshold	98,000	
×	× 25%	(24,500)
AMT exemption		$87,200

1.3   Adjustments

Adjustments are defined in the tax code as specific items that may increase or decrease AMT, because the treatment of the item for AMT purposes is different from that for regular tax purposes. Items 1–5 are "timing differences" that may increase or decrease AMTI. Items 6–7 are items that may be included in deductions for regular tax purposes, but not for AMT purposes, and will only increase AMTI. Examples of common adjustments include:

1. **Passive** activity losses

2. **Accelerated** depreciation (post-1986 purchase)

3. **Net** operating loss of the individual taxpayer

4. **Installment** income of a dealer

5. **Contracts**—percentage completion versus completed contract

6.* **Tax** "deductions" (see 1.5 below for explanation of asterisks)

7.* **Standard deduction**

1.4   Tax Preference Items (Always "Add-Backs")

By definition in the tax code, tax preference items are always add-backs. These items will result in more income or fewer deductions being recognized for AMT versus regular tax. Examples of common tax preference items include:

1.* **Private** activity bond interest income (on certain bonds)

2.* **"Percentage** depletion" deduction (excess over adjusted basis of property)

3. **Pre**-1987 accelerated depreciation

1.5   Credit for Prior Year Minimum Tax (AMT Credit)

- Certain allowable AMT paid in a taxable year may be carried over as a credit to subsequent taxable years. It may only reduce regular tax, not future alternative minimum tax.

- The carryforward is forever.

*Asterisks Above: AMT created from certain permanent differences, identified by the asterisks, cannot be carried forward as part of the "credit." Therefore, if AMT is paid because of these items, it is never recovered.

Illustration 2   AMT Credit

In Year 2, Bart pays alternative minimum tax. His AMT credit carryover is calculated to be $5,000. If Bart is subject to AMT in a future year, this credit is not allowed to be applied to the AMT. But if Bart is not subject to AMT in a future year, he may apply this $5,000 credit against his regular tax.

1.6 Alternative Minimum Taxable Income (AMTI) Calculation

1.6.1 Regular Taxable Income (Base for Calculation)

The AMTI calculation begins with the taxpayer's regular taxable income.

1.6.2 Adjustments (Adds or Subtracts)

- **Passive** activity losses are added back, or recalculated

- **Accelerated** depreciation adjustment

    - On real property, this is the difference between regular tax depreciation and straight-line using a 40-year life for property placed in service after 1986.

    - On personal property, this is the difference between regular tax depreciation and 150 percent declining balance (with switch to straight-line). (If a taxpayer elects 150 percent declining-balance depreciation for regular tax purposes, there will be no AMT depreciation adjustment of 200 percent declining-balance eligible property.)

    - No adjustment is required for property expensed under Section 179.

- **Net** operating loss must be recomputed.

- **Installment** method may not be used by dealer for property sales.

- **Contracts** (long term)

    The difference between the percentage-of-completion method and completed-contract method or any other method of accounting is an adjustment.

Illustration 3   Adjustment Related to Contracts

Mary has a long-term construction contract in Year 1 and uses the completed-contract method for regular tax purposes. She reports income for regular tax of $20,000 in Year 4, the year the contract is completed. AMT requires the use of the percentage-of-completion method. Under this method, income would be reported as follows: $2,000 in Year 1; $5,000 in Year 2; $5,000 in Year 3; and $8,000 in Year 4.

Mary has an AMT adjustment in the amounts of $2,000 in Year 1, and $5,000 each in Years 2 and 3. These adjustments will increase AMTI because more income is being recognized for AMT purposes than for regular tax purposes. In Year 4, Mary has an adjustment of $12,000 that will decrease AMTI in Year 4. This is because regular tax recognized the entire $20,000 income in Year 4, but AMT only recognized $8,000 under percentage of completion. Because AMT recognized less income in the final year of the contract, the adjustment is a decrease to AMTI.

- **Itemized Deductions (Always "Adds" to Regular Taxable Income)**

    - **Taxes** reduced by taxable refunds (if refunds meet the tax benefit rule) are added back.

    - **Standard deductions** may not be claimed.

Illustration 4   AMT Adjustments

In Year 2, Janet has various itemized deductions. They include interest on acquisition indebtedness on her home of $11,200; state income tax deductions of $9,200; and charitable contributions of $3,000. Her total adjustments for AMT purposes are as follows:

State income taxes	$9,200
Total	$9,200

These adjustments increase AMTI because they are the disallowance of deductions that are allowed for regular tax purposes. Note that the charitable contributions and acquisition indebtedness are not adjustments for purposes of AMT.

- Other AMT Adjustments
  - Incentive stock options
  - Recalculate gain or loss on sale of depreciable assets
  - Pollution control facilities
  - Mining exploration and development costs
  - Circulation expenses
  - Research and experimental expenditures
  - (Passive) tax shelter farm activities

1.6.3 Tax Preference Items (Always "Adds" to Regular Taxable Income)

- **Private** activity bond tax-exempt interest (exceptions apply)
- **Pre**-1987 accelerated depreciation on real property and leased personal property (excess over straight-line for property placed in service before 1987)
- **"Percentage** depletion" deduction (excess over adjusted basis of property)

Illustration 5   Tax-Exempt Interest Preference Item

In Year 2, Janet has total tax-exempt interest of $15,000. Of this tax-exempt interest, $1,300 is deemed to be from private-activity bonds. Her total preference add-back for AMT purposes is $1,300.

The result here is that $15,000 tax-exempt interest is exempt from regular tax, but $1,300 of that amount must be recognized for AMT. Therefore, only $13,700 is exempt for AMT purposes ($15,000 − $1,300).

Illustration 6   AMTI Calculation

Continuing with the illustrations for Janet from above: Assume that In Year 2, Janet has regular taxable income of $60,000. From the above illustrations, her adjustments are $9,200 and her preference items are $1,300. These are both added back to taxable income to arrive at alternative minimum taxable income (AMTI) of $70,500.

Regular taxable income	$60,000
AMT adjustments	9,200
AMT preference items	1,300
AMTI	$70,500

As indicated in the previous illustrations, these items will both increase AMTI because they are eliminating deductions from the regular taxable income and adding income to the regular taxable income.

1.7   Credits

Taxpayers can reduce their AMT liability by the full amount of their nonrefundable personal tax credits.

For example, the following tax credits are permitted as a credit to reduce the alternative minimum tax:

- Child and dependent care credit
- Adoption credit
- Child tax credit
- Contributions to retirement plans credit
- Residential energy credit

2   Other Taxes

2.1   Self-Employment Tax

The self-employment tax represents the employer portion and the employee portion of FICA taxes (Social Security and Medicare) imposed on self-employment income. 100 percent of self-employment tax is collected as an "other tax" and reported in the "other taxes" section. (Note that 50 percent of this amount is reported as an adjustment to arrive at AGI.)

2.1.1   Additional Medicare Tax

The Affordable Care Act imposes an additional Medicare tax of 0.9 percent on wages in excess of $250,000 for married filing jointly; $125,000 for married filing separately; and $200,000 for all other taxpayers.

- Employers are responsible for withholding this additional tax on all wages paid to an employee that exceed $200,000 in a calendar year.
- Any amounts withheld in excess can be claimed as a credit on the taxpayer's individual income tax return.
- Additional Medicare tax is calculated on Form 8959 and reported in "other taxes" on Form 1040.

2.1.2   Net Investment Income Tax

The net investment income tax went into effect January, 1, 2013, and applies a rate of 3.8 percent to certain net investment income of individuals who have income above the statutory threshold amounts. The statutory threshold amounts are $250,000 for a filing status of married filing jointly, and $200,000 for taxpayers with a single filing status or head of household filing status.

Generally, investment income includes, but is not limited to: interest, dividends, capital gains, rental and royalty income, nonqualified annuities, and income from businesses involved in the trading of financial instruments or commodities and businesses that are passive activities to the taxpayer. Expenses allocable to the income can be deducted.

Form 8960 is used to calculate the net investment income tax in the "other taxes" section.

2.2   Tax Penalty Imposed by Individual Mandate Section of the Affordable Care Act (Repealed After 12/31/18)

The Affordable Care Act further imposes a tax penalty on certain individuals who are not covered by health insurance. This penalty is repealed after 12/31/2018.

2.3   Kiddie Tax

The net unearned income of a dependent child under 18 years of age (or, a child age 18 to under 24 who does not provide over half of his/her own support and is a full-time student) is taxed at the rates that apply to estates and trusts. Net unearned income is calculated by taking the child's total unearned income (from dividends, interest, rents, royalties, etc.) and subtracting $2,200: the child's allowable 2019 standard deduction of $1,100 (or investment expense, if greater) plus an additional $1,100 (which is taxed at the child's rate). Although the income in excess of $2,200 is taxed at the rates that apply to estates and trusts, it is nonetheless reported on the child's tax return.

Parents may elect to include on their own return the unearned income of the applicable child provided that the income is between $1,100 and $11,000 and consists solely of interest, dividends, and capital gains distributions.

2019 Child's Unearned Income	Tax Rate
$0–$1,100	0%
$1,101–$2,200	Child's rate
$2,201 and over	Estates and Trusts

Question 1   MCQ-02023

The credit for prior year alternative minimum tax liability may be carried:

    a. Forward for a maximum of five years.

    b. Back to the three preceding years or carried forward for a maximum of five years.

    c. Back to the three preceding years.

    d. Forward indefinitely.

Question 2   MCQ-02015

Don Mills, a single taxpayer, had $70,000 in taxable income in the current year. Mills had no tax preferences. His itemized deductions were as follows:

State and local income taxes	$5,000
Home mortgage interest on loan to acquire residence	6,000
Property taxes	2,000

What amount did Mills report as alternative minimum taxable income before the AMT exemption?

    a. $72,000

    b. $75,000

    c. $77,000

    d. $83,000

Question 3   MCQ-02019

Alternative minimum tax preferences include:

	Tax-Exempt Interest From Private Activity Bonds	Charitable Contributions of Appreciated Capital Gain Property
a.	Yes	Yes
b.	Yes	No
c.	No	Yes
d.	No	No

Property Taxation

Module

1 Adjusted Basis and Holding Period of Assets Sold

1.1 Purchased Property

1.1.1 Basis

Generally, the initial basis of property is the cost of such property to the taxpayer. The cost of property includes all amounts to purchase the property, prepare the property for use, and place the property into service. Examples include shipping costs, installation costs, sales taxes, and testing costs.

- Real property is land and all items permanently affixed to the land (e.g., buildings, paving, etc.).

- Personal property is all property not classified as real property.

Example 1 **Calculating Basis**

Facts: A taxpayer purchases a piece of equipment that will be used in a business. The cost of the equipment is $5,000. The shipping cost for the equipment is $500, and the cost to install the equipment is $200.

Required: Determine the basis of the equipment.

Solution: The tax basis of the piece of equipment is $5,700 ($5,000 + $500 + $200).

1.1.2 Holding Period

The holding period of purchased property begins on the date the property is acquired.

1.1.3 Reduce Basis for Accumulated Depreciation

The basis is adjusted downward for the amount of any depreciation, allowed or allowable, taken by the taxpayer with respect to that asset. The basis that has been adjusted downward by accumulated depreciation is referred to as the adjusted basis of the asset.

Example 2 **Calculating Adjusted Basis**

Facts: A taxpayer has a milling machine that was purchased for $10,000. In both Year 1 and Year 2, the taxpayer deducted $1,000 from gross income for depreciation of the machine.

Required: Determine the adjusted basis of the milling machine at the end of Year 2.

Solution: Accumulated depreciation at the end of Year 2 is $2,000 ($1,000 depreciation expense taken in Year 1 + $1,000 depreciation deduction taken in Year 2). Accordingly, the adjusted basis at the end of Year 2 would be $8,000 ($10,000 minus $2,000).

1.1.4 "Spreading" Adjustments

Although most adjustments involve an increase or decrease in the basis of the property, some spread the basis.

Illustration 1   Basis "Spreading"

Under the IRC, the receipt of a nontaxable stock dividend requires the shareholder to spread the basis of his original shares over both the original shares and the new shares received, resulting in the same total basis in the stock but a lower basis per share of stock held.

1.2   Gifted Property Basis for Gain/Loss Purposes

1.2.1   General Rule: Donor's Rollover Cost Basis

Property acquired as a gift generally retains the cost basis it had in the hands of the donor at the time of the gift. Basis is increased by any gift tax paid that is attributable to the net appreciation in the value of the gift. Gains and losses are calculated using this rollover cost basis (subject to the exception noted below).

1.2.2   Exception: Lower FMV at Date of Gift

If the fair market value at the date of the gift is lower than the rollover cost basis from the donor, the basis for the donee depends on the donee's future selling price of the asset.

- **Sale of Gifts at Price Greater Than Donor's Rollover Basis (Gain Basis):** When a taxpayer sells a gift for greater than the rollover basis, the gain shall be the difference between the sale price and that rollover basis.

Example 3   Sale of Gift at Price Greater Than Donor's Basis

Facts: Donor gives non-depreciable property worth $3,000 with an adjusted basis of $5,000 to taxpayer, who subsequently sells the property for $6,500.

Required: Determine the basis used and the gain on the sale of the property.

Solution: The taxpayer's gain will be $1,500 ($6,500 proceeds minus $5,000 basis).

- **Sale of Gift at Price Less Than Lower Fair Market Value (Loss Basis):** When a taxpayer sells the gift for less than the lower FMV at the date of the gift, the basis of the gift for purposes of determining the loss is the fair market value of the gift at the time the gift was given.

Example 4	Sale of Gift at Price Less Than Lower FMV

Facts: Donor gives property worth $3,000 having an adjusted basis of $5,000 to taxpayer, who subsequently sells the property for $1,000.

Required: Determine the basis used and the loss on the sale of the property.

Solution: The taxpayer's loss will be $2,000 ($3,000 FMV at date of gift minus $1,000). (Note that the loss may or may not be deductible on the taxpayer's income tax return, depending on the situation.)

- **Sale Less Than Rollover Cost Basis but Greater Than Lower Fair Market Value (in the Middle):** When a taxpayer sells a gift for a price less than the donor's rollover cost basis, but more than the lower fair market value at the date of gift, neither gain nor loss is recognized. The basis to the donee is the "middle" selling price.

1.2.3 Gifted Property Basis for Depreciation

- Regardless of the basis for the gain/loss (which may not be known at the time depreciation is to begin), the basis for depreciation purposes (if applicable) is the lesser of:

  - the donor's adjusted basis at the date of the gift; or

  - the fair market value at the date of the gift.

- The amount of accumulated depreciation will then reduce the taxpayer's basis calculated for gain/loss purposes (per above) before the actual gain or loss on the sale is determined.

Example 5	Determining Basis

Facts: A donor gives property worth $3,000 with an adjusted basis of $5,000 to a taxpayer.

Required: Determine the basis of the property:

- if the property is in a gain situation on sale;
- if the property is in a loss situation on sale;
- if the property is in a zero gain/loss situation on sale;
- for calculating depreciation prior to the sale.

Solution:

- For purposes of determining gain on the sale, the taxpayer's basis is $5,000.

- For purposes of determining loss on the sale, the taxpayer's basis is $3,000.

- If the taxpayer subsequently sells the property for $3,500, there is no gain or loss on the sale, and the basis is $3,500.

- For purposes of calculating depreciation on the asset (if applicable) prior to the sale, the depreciable basis is $3,000.

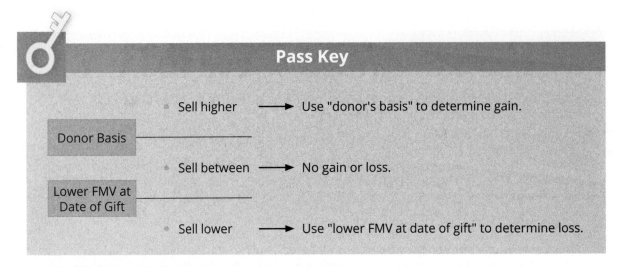

1.2.4 Holding Period

The recipient of the gift normally assumes the donor's holding period. However, under the exception above, if fair market value at the time of the gift is used (loss basis) as the basis of the gift, the holding period starts as of the date of the gift.

	General Rule: FMV Higher	Exception: FMV Lower		
	1	**2**	**3**	**4**
Donor's (rich uncle) basis	$20,000	$20,000	$20,000	$20,000
FMV at date of gift	40,000	13,000	13,000	13,000
Donee's (nephew) selling price	30,000	25,000	10,000	15,000
Donee's basis for gain/loss purposes	20,000	20,000	13,000	15,000
Taxable gain (if any)	10,000	5,000	-0-	-0-
Deductible loss (if any)	-0-	-0-	3,000	-0-

Illustration 2   Basis of Gifted Stock and Gain or Loss on Resale

1.3   Inherited Property Basis

1.3.1   General Rule: FMV at Date of Death

Property acquired by bequest or inheritance generally takes as its basis the step-up (or step-down) to the fair market value at the date of the decedent's death.

1.3.2   Alternate Valuation Date

If validly elected by the executor, the fair market value on the alternate valuation date (the earlier of six months later or the date of distribution/sale) may be used to value all of the estate property. The alternate valuation date is only available if its use lowers the entire gross estate and estate tax (although individual assets may go up or down during the period).

If the alternate valuation date is validly elected, the basis of the asset is the FMV at the earlier of:

▪ distribution date of asset; or

▪ six months after death.

Example 6 | Sale of Inherited Property

Facts: A testator died owning property worth $60,000 and in which he had a cost basis of $20,000. His son inherited the property and subsequently sold it for $55,000.

Required: Determine the loss on the sale of property.

Solution: The son will recognize a loss of $5,000 ($55,000 selling price − $60,000 basis). The built-in gain in the property at the time of the testator's death is never recognized because his son takes a basis in the land equal to the FMV at the date of death.

1.3.3 Holding Period

Inherited property is automatically considered to be long-term property regardless of how long it has actually been held.

Example 7 | Basis of Inherited Property

Facts: Assume that a taxpayer inherited property from a decedent. The FMV at the date of death was $20,000. The property was worth $15,000 six months later and was worth $22,000 when it was distributed to the taxpayer eight months later. It had a cost basis to the deceased of $5,000.

1. **Required:** What is the basis of inherited property to the taxpayer:

    a. if the alternate valuation date was not elected?

    b. if the alternate valuation date was elected?

    Solution:

    a. $20,000 (FMV at date of death)

    b. $15,000 (FMV at earlier of six months after death or date of distribution)

2. **Required:** Assuming that the beneficiary sold this property for $25,000, compute the capital gain:

    a. assuming that the alternate valuation date was not elected.

    b. assuming that the alternate valuation date was elected.

    Solution:

    a. $5,000 = 25,000 − 20,000

    b. $10,000 = 25,000 − 15,000

---

2 Capitalize or Expense

The IRS has issued regulations specifying whether and when a taxpayer must capitalize costs incurred in acquiring, maintaining, or improving tangible property. If the regulations do not require capitalization, then the costs are considered to be repairs and are expensed.

2.1 Tangible Property Must Be Capitalized

The general rule is that all tangible property that is not inventory must be capitalized, unless there is an exception.

2.1.1 Materials and Supplies

- Generally, an item that costs $200 or less or has an economic life of 12 months or less qualifies as materials and supplies.

- If the tangible property qualifies as materials and supplies, it can be deducted in the year of consumption if non-incidental, or in the year paid if incidental.

2.1.2 Amounts Paid to Acquire or Produce Property

Amounts paid or incurred to produce or acquire tangible and intangible property must be capitalized.

2.1.3 Improvements

- Improvements to a single unit of property must be capitalized if they result in a betterment to the property, adapt the property to a new or different use, or result in a restoration of the property.

- Indirect costs, such as otherwise deductible repair or removal costs, that directly benefit an improvement or are incurred by reason of an improvement, must be capitalized.

2.1.4 Single Unit of Property

- A single *unit of property* is defined as all components that are functionally interdependent. A component is functionally interdependent if the placing in service of one component is dependent on the placing in service of other components.

- A building structure is a single unit of property to the extent of the building and its structural components other than those designated as building systems (such as HVAC systems, plumbing systems, electrical systems, etc.).

- Designated building systems considered separate from the building structure include: heating, ventilation, and air-conditioning systems; plumbing systems; electrical systems; escalators; elevators; alarm and fire protection systems; security systems; and gas distribution systems.

- Any amounts paid or incurred to improve designated building systems are considered separate from the building structure and subject to the improvement rules.

2.1.5 Intangible Property

Amounts paid or incurred for acquiring, creating, or enhancing intangible property must be capitalized.

2.1.6 Holding Period

If an asset is required to be capitalized, its holding period starts as of the date the asset is completed. It is not always clear when a constructed asset is considered "completed," so detailed records should be kept as to when expenditures have been capitalized.

2.2 De Minimis Rule

Companies can make a de minimis annual expense election regarding expenditures to acquire or produce property if they have a capitalization policy in effect as of the beginning of the year. This election can also be applied to materials and supplies.

- The capitalization policy must be a written accounting policy for nontax purposes that treats as an expense in the financial statements:

  - property purchases under a certain dollar amount; and/or

  - property with an economic useful life of 12 months or less.

- If a company has an applicable financial statement, the maximum amount allowed for federal tax purposes is $5,000 per asset.

- If a company does not have an applicable financial statement, the maximum amount is $2,500 per asset after January 1, 2016.

Example 8   Capitalize vs. Expense

Facts: Center Corp. has an applicable financial statement and at the beginning of Year 1 has a written accounting policy to expense amounts paid for tangible property costing up to $10,000. During Year 1, Center pays $50,000 for eight desks.

Required: Determine Center Corp.'s amount expensed and/or capitalized for the desks for federal tax purposes.

Solution: For financial reporting purposes, Center can expense the entire $50,000 paid for the eight desks because each desk costs less than the $10,000 limit ($50,000/8 = $6,250 per desk). However, for tax purposes, Center must capitalize all of the purchases unless their economic life is less than 12 months because the de minimis rule is not met. The de minimis rule is not met because the purchases exceed $5,000 per asset.

2.3 Safe Harbors

2.3.1 Routine Maintenance

There is an elective safe harbor that allows taxpayers to expense routine maintenance that the taxpayer reasonably expects to occur more than once during the class life of the asset and does not result in a betterment.

2.3.2 Qualifying Small Taxpayers

Qualifying small taxpayers can expense costs related to an eligible building if the costs do not exceed the lesser of 2 percent of unadjusted basis of the building or $10,000.

- A qualifying small taxpayer is a taxpayer with average annual gross receipts of $10 million or less during the three preceding tax years.

- An eligible building is any building with an unadjusted basis that does not exceed $1 million.

2.4 Relief for Small Business Taxpayers

Effective for tax years beginning in 2014, small businesses can change the method of accounting under the repair regulations on a prospective basis rather than a retroactive basis. (Small businesses are those with less than $10 million in assets or less than $10 million in average annual gross receipts.)

For small businesses, the requirement to file Form 3115, Application for Change in Accounting Method, is eliminated. Form 3115 requires the taxpayer to go back in time and account for items of income and deduction as if they had always used the new method of accounting. This can be a significant amount of work for the taxpayer.

Question 1   **MCQ-01736**

Hall, a divorced person and custodian of her 12-year-old child, filed her Year 9 federal income tax return as head of a household. She submitted the following information to the CPA who prepared her Year 9 return:

In June, Year 9, Hall's mother gifted her 100 shares of a listed stock. The donor's basis for this stock, which she bought in Year 1, was $4,000, and market value on the date of the gift was $3,000. Hall sold this stock in July, Year 9 for $3,500. The donor paid no gift tax. What was Hall's reportable gain or loss in Year 9 on the sale of the 100 shares of stock gifted to her?

    a. $0

    b. $500 gain

    c. $500 loss

    d. $1,000 loss

Question 2   **MCQ-01669**

If the executor of a decedent's estate elects the alternate valuation date and none of the property included in the gross estate has been sold or distributed, the estate assets must be valued as of how many months after the decedent's death?

    a. 12

    b. 9

    c. 6

    d. 3

1 Calculation of Gain or Loss on Disposition

Generally, gain or loss realized on the sale of an asset is calculated by comparing the amount realized on the disposition to the adjusted basis of the asset being relinquished in the transaction. For certain types of transactions, the gain is realized but not recognized.

Illustration 1	Calculating Gain or Loss at Disposition

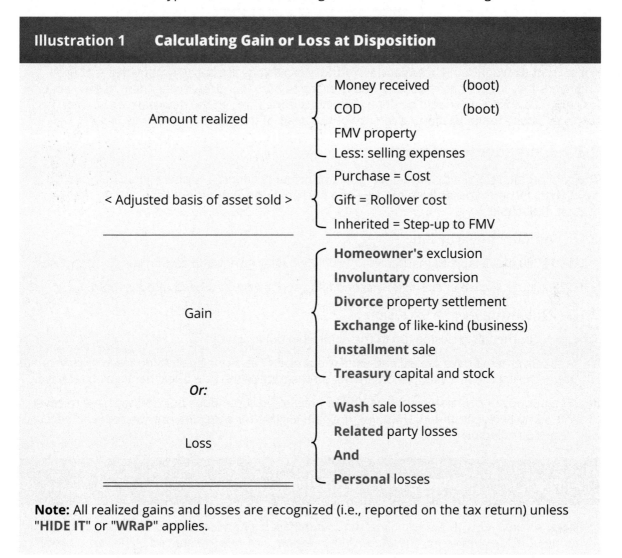

Note: All realized gains and losses are recognized (i.e., reported on the tax return) unless "**HIDE IT**" or "**WRaP**" applies.

2   Gains (Excluded or Deferred)

A gain is not taxed if the taxpayers can "**HIDE IT**" all (see Illustration 1). Gain to the extent of boot received is taxable. Boot includes the following:

- **Cash:** Kept and not reinvested
- **COD:** Excess debt assumed by buyer

$$\begin{array}{c} \text{Amount realized} \\ \underline{< \text{Adjusted basis of asset sold} >} \\ \text{Gain } Or \text{ Loss} \end{array}$$

There is a special group of transactions for which any realized gain is either excluded or not currently recognized. These special statutory provisions are based on the idea that the taxpayer's investment has not substantially changed and, therefore, recognition of the gain or loss on the transaction should be deferred. This is done through the device of *substituting* the taxpayer's basis in the property given up for the basis of the property acquired.

2.1   Homeowner's Exclusion

The gain on the sale of a taxpayer's personal principal residence may be eligible for an exclusion from gross income. Losses from the sale of a personal principal residence (a personal use asset) are not deductible.

2.1.1   Amount of Exclusion

- $500,000 is available to married couples filing a joint return and certain surviving spouses.
- $250,000 is available for single, married filing separately, and head of household.

2.1.2   Qualifying for the Exclusion

To qualify for the full exclusion (up to the applicable dollar limit):

- A taxpayer must have owned and used the property as a principal residence for two years or more during the five-year period ending on the date of the sale or exchange by a taxpayer.
- The periods of ownership and use do not have to be continuous nor do they have to cover the same two-year period. However, the gain eligible for exclusion may be reduced because of nonqualified use.

Example 1	Homeowner's Exclusion

Facts: A taxpayer with a single filing status purchased a home and lived in the home as her personal residence for one year. After one year, she was transferred by her employer to work in a new city for the next two years. During this two-year period, she continued to own the house but rented it to a tenant. After two years in the new city, she returned to live in the house for one year prior to selling it.

(continued)

(continued)

Required: Determine whether the taxpayer qualifies for the homeowner's exclusion.

Solution: The taxpayer meets both the ownership and use tests because she owned and used the house for two or more years during the five-year period prior to the sale, even though the use of the property was not in consecutive years. The taxpayer is eligible for the exclusion; however, gain eligible for exclusion may be limited because of nonqualified use by the taxpayer.

▦ Either spouse for a joint return must meet the ownership requirement, but both spouses must meet the use requirement with respect to the property. If both spouses do not meet the use requirement, one spouse may still be eligible to take the single $250,000 exclusion.

Example 2	Use Requirement for Married Taxpayers

Facts: After owning and using his home as a principal residence for three years, a taxpayer marries and his spouse moves into the home. After one year of marriage, the taxpayer and his spouse decide that they need more space and sell the home.

Required: Determine the allowable homeowner's exclusion amount.

Solution: The taxpayer meets both the ownership and use test because he has owned and used the home for at least two years prior to the sale. The spouse, however, does not meet the ownership and use test for at least two of the five years prior to the sale. On the jointly filed tax return, the maximum gain exclusion that may be claimed is $250,000.

▦ If a widow or widower sells a home that the surviving spouse owned and occupied with the decedent spouse, the surviving spouse is entitled to the full $500,000 exclusion provided that the surviving spouse sells the home within two years after the date of the decedent spouse's death.

▦ There is no age requirement to receive the exclusion.

▦ There is no requirement that the taxpayer purchase another personal residence.

▦ The exclusion is renewable.

▦ A taxpayer may use the homeowner exclusion as often as available over his or her lifetime provided he or she meets the other requirements, but the exclusion may not be used more than once every two years.

2.1.3 Hardship Provision

Taxpayers may be eligible for a reduced exclusion (not a reduced amount of gain eligible for the exclusion) if the sale is due to a change in place of employment, health, or other unforeseen circumstances, and either the exclusion has been claimed within the previous two years or the taxpayer fails to meet the ownership and use requirements. Under the hardship provision, the maximum exclusion is calculated as the number of months of qualifying ownership divided by 24 months (the minimum time period the taxpayer must own and use the home to qualify for the exclusion) multiplied by the maximum exclusion available to the taxpayer based on filing status.

To meet the hardship provision requirement for change in employment, the taxpayer's new place of employment must be at least 50 miles farther from the residence that is sold than was the distance between the taxpayer's previous place of employment and the home that is sold.

Example 3	Hardship Provision (Reduced Exclusion)

Facts: One year after purchasing her home and living in it as her principal residence, a single taxpayer was diagnosed with nontreatable cancer. The taxpayer sold her home to move in with her daughter, who would be caring for her. The taxpayer sold the home for a gain of $150,000.

Required: Determine the amount, if any, of the homeowner's exclusion available to the taxpayer.

Solution: The taxpayer is not eligible for the maximum exclusion of $250,000 because she did not meet the ownership test. The exclusion available to the taxpayer under the hardship provision is calculated as $125,000, which is 12 months (the number of months of qualifying ownership) divided by 24 months (the time period the taxpayer must own the home to qualify for the maximum exclusion) multiplied by the maximum exclusion of $250,000 available to single filing taxpayers.

2.1.4 Nonqualified Use Provision

- There is a nonqualified use provision that applies if a taxpayer has nonqualified use of the home on or after January 1, 2010.

- A nonqualified use is any use of the home other than use as a principal residence.

- If a taxpayer has a nonqualified use of the home, the exclusion amount is not adjusted, but the portion of the gain attributable to the nonqualified use is not eligible for the exclusion.

- The portion of the gain not eligible for the exclusion is the ratio of the period of nonqualified use divided by the total period of time the taxpayer owned the property.

Example 4	Reduced Homeowner's Exclusion

Facts: A taxpayer with a single filing status purchased a home and lived in the home as her personal residence for one year. After one year, she was transferred by her employer to work in a new city for the next two years. During this two-year period, she continued to own the house but rented it to a tenant. After two years in the new city, she returned to live in the house for one year prior to selling it for a gain of $50,000. The taxpayer meets both the ownership and use tests because she owned and used the house for two or more years during the five-year period prior to the sale and qualifies for the maximum $250,000 exclusion.

Required: Determine any amount of the gain that is not eligible for the homeowner's exclusion.

Solution: Because there was a period of two years of nonqualified use when the home was rented and not used by the taxpayer as her principal residence, the gain eligible for exclusion will be reduced. The gain not eligible for exclusion is $25,000, which is calculated as: 2 years of nonqualified use/4 years of ownership = 50% × $50,000 total gain. Therefore, the taxpayer will be able to take an exclusion on the sale of her home for $25,000 ($50,000 − $25,000). The remaining $25,000 gain on the sale of the home will be recognized as a capital gain by the taxpayer.

The period of nonqualified use does not include any portion of the five-year period ending on the date of the sale that is after the last date that the home was used as the principal residence of the taxpayer. This provision allows a taxpayer time to sell or rent the home without having to count the period the home is empty or rented as a nonqualified period.

Example 5	Empty House Available for Sale

Facts: A taxpayer purchased a home seven years ago and lived in it for four years. The taxpayer then moved to a new city and placed the home for sale. The home sold after being empty for three years.

Required: Determine if any of the gain on the sale is excluded.

Solution: Gain should be available for exclusion up to the maximum amount as the taxpayer owned and used the home for two years in the five years prior to the sale. The time in which the home was empty and available for sale does not disqualify the gain from exclusion treatment.

2.2 Involuntary Conversions

Nonrecognition treatment is given to gains realized on involuntary conversions of property (e.g., destruction, theft, condemnation) on the rationale that the taxpayer's reinvestment of the involuntarily received proceeds restores him to the position he held prior to the conversion. To tax him under such circumstances would produce undue hardship. If the taxpayer does not reinvest all the proceeds, the gain on the transaction will be recognized to the extent of the amount not reinvested.

2.2.1 No Gain Recognized

When no gain is recognized because of the direct conversion of the property into other similar property, the basis of the new asset is the same as the basis of the old asset (increased by any additional amounts invested).

2.2.2 Personal Property (Two Years From Year-End)

The reinvestment must occur within two years after the close of the taxable year in which any part of the gain was realized and be in property "similar or related in service or use" (i.e., the replacement property must serve the same function in the taxpayer's business as did the old property, which is a narrower standard than the "like-kind" test, discussed later). For principal residences destroyed in a federally declared disaster area, the replacement period is four years instead of two years.

2.2.3 Condemned Business Property (Three Years From Year-End)

The reinvestment must occur within three years after the close of the taxable year in which any part of the gain was realized and be in property "similar or related in service or use" (i.e., the replacement property must serve the same function in the taxpayer's business as did the old property, which is a narrower standard than the like-kind test).

The basis of property acquired as a result of an involuntary conversion will be the cost of such property decreased by the amount of any gain not recognized upon such conversion.

Example 6   Condemnation

Facts: Land owned by McIntyre had an adjusted basis of $30,000. It was condemned by the state and McIntyre received similar property from the state to replace the condemned land.

Required: Determine the basis of the new property.

Solution: The basis of the new land is $30,000.

2.2.4 Gain Recognized (Boot)

When gain is recognized because the amount received exceeds the cost of replacement, the basis of the replacement property is its cost less the gain not recognized.

Example 7   Basis Calculated When Gain Is Deferred

Facts: Crudd owned a building with an adjusted basis of $400,000. The state condemned it and awarded him $450,000. Crudd bought a new building for $440,000.

Required: Determine the gain realized, gain recognized, and the basis of the new building.

Solution: Although he realized $50,000, only $10,000 is recognized as follows:

Amount realized	$ 450,000
Adjusted basis	(400,000)
Realized gain	50,000
Recognized gain ($450,000 – $440,000)	(10,000)
Gain not recognized	$ 40,000
Cost of new building	$ 440,000
Less: gain not recognized	(40,000)
Basis of new building	$ 400,000

When the gain exceeds $100,000, property acquired from related parties and certain close relatives do not qualify as replacement property.

2.2.5 Loss Recognized

Involuntary conversion rules apply to gains only. Losses would be recognized. When the loss is recognized, the basis of the new property is its replacement cost.

Example 8   Loss Recognition

Facts: Rigoli had a factory, with a cost basis of $340,000 that was destroyed by a fire. The insurance company paid Rigoli $330,000. Rigoli used the money to buy a new plant for $500,000.

Required: Determine any loss recognized on the involuntary conversion and the basis of the new property.

Solution: The $10,000 loss is recognized, and the basis of the new factory is $500,000.

2.3 Divorce Property Settlement

When a divorce settlement provides for a lump-sum payment or property settlement, it is a nontaxable event. The basis of the property to the recipient spouse will be the carryover basis (basis in the hands of the transferor). This rule applies regardless of whether the transfer is of property separately owned by the transferor or is a division (equal or unequal) of community property. Nonrecognition rules apply even if the transferred property is subject to liabilities that exceed the adjusted basis of the property (with the exception of property held in trust).

2.4 Exchange of Like-Kind Business/Investment Real Property

Nonrecognition treatment is given to gains realized on "like-kind" exchange of real property used in the trade or business or held for investment (except real property in different countries).

2.4.1 Qualifying Property

Real property used in a trade or business or held for investment that is exchanged for other real property used in a trade or business or held for investment qualifies as like-kind. Like-kind exchanges of personal property do not qualify for like-kind exchange nonrecognition treatment.

Example 9	Property Qualifying for Nonrecognition Treatment

Facts: A taxpayer owned the building in which she ran her clothing boutique. When she retired, she sold the building and purchased an apartment building, which she held as an investment.

Required: Determine whether the taxpayer's transaction qualifies as a like-kind exchange.

Solution: Because the taxpayer exchanged real property used in a trade or business for other real property held for investment, the exchange *should qualify* for the nonrecognition treatment available to like-kind exchanges.

Example 10	Property Not Qualifying for Nonrecognition Treatment

Facts: In his business, a taxpayer owned several laptop computers and decided to exchange them with another business owner for a new desk and filing cabinet.

Required: Determine whether the taxpayer's transaction qualifies as a like-kind exchange.

Solution: Laptop computers and office furniture are both personal property. The like-kind exchange rules no longer apply to personal property, only to real property. Therefore, the exchange *would not* qualify for the nonrecognition treatment available to like-kind exchanges.

2.4.2 Timing Requirements

Additionally, there are timing requirements that must be met for a like-kind exchange to receive deferral treatment. First, the taxpayers must identify like-kind replacement property within 45 days of giving up their property. Second, like-kind property must be received by the earlier of (1) 180 days after the taxpayer transfers property in a like-kind exchange; or (2) the due date of the taxpayer's income tax return (including extensions) for the year in which the transfer occurs.

2.4.3 Gain When Boot Received

If property other than property qualifying for like-kind exchange treatment is received (cash, relief from liabilities, or nonqualifying property), the gain recognized is the lesser of the realized gain or the boot received.

Example 11 **Gain When Boot Received**

Facts: A taxpayer owns real estate held for investment that is worth $40,000 and has an adjusted basis of $25,000. The taxpayer exchanges this property for other real property worth $35,000 and $5,000 in cash.

Required: Determine the realized gain and recognized gain from the like-kind exchange.

Solution: The taxpayer's realized gain of $15,000 ($40,000 proceeds minus $25,000 basis) will be recognized only to the extent of the $5,000 cash received. The amount of gain deferred is $10,000 ($15,000 realized gain less the $5,000 gain recognized).

2.4.4 Basis Rules

The basis of the property received in a like-kind exchange in which gain is deferred is ordinarily the same as the basis of the property given up. In an exchange in which boot is received, the basis is equal to the fair market value of the property received less any deferred gain (or plus any deferred loss).

$$\text{Basis in like-kind property received when boot is received} = \text{Fair market value of like-kind property received} - \text{Deferred gain} + \text{Deferred loss}$$

Illustration 2 **Basis Calculation**

In the prior example of boot received, the taxpayer's basis in the new property equals $25,000:

FMV of property received – Deferred gain + Deferred loss = New basis

$35,000 – $10,000 + $0 = $25,000

2.4.5 Losses

Realized losses are not recognized in a like-kind exchange. All of the loss is deferred, and increases the basis in the new property.

Example 12	Like-Kind Exchange: Realized Gain/No Boot

Facts: A taxpayer trades in an attached shed used solely for business purposes for another shed to be used in the business. The shed originally cost $35,000 and is currently worth $20,000. The taxpayer has taken $18,000 of depreciation on the old shed. Assume that the shed the taxpayer wants in exchange is worth $20,000.

1. **Required:** What is the gain or loss realized by the taxpayer on the exchange?

   Solution:

   Gain/loss realized = Amount realized – Adjusted basis of property given up

   = $20,000 FMV of new shed – ($35,000 cost – $18,000 depreciation)

   = $20,000 FMV of new shed – $17,000 adjusted basis of old shed

   = $3,000 realized gain

   • Adjusted basis = Original cost – Accumulated depreciation

   • Amount realized = FMV of new property received + FMV of boot received – FMV of boot paid

2. **Required:** What is the gain or loss recognized by the taxpayer on the exchange?

   Solution:

   Gain/loss recognized = Lesser of realized gain or boot received [realized loss never recognized]

   = $0 [lesser of gain realized of $3,000 or boot received of $0]

   • Boot received = Cash received + FMV of non-like-kind property received + Net relief from liability

   • Boot paid = Cash paid + FMV of non-like-kind property paid + Net liability assumed

3. **Required:** What is the gain or loss deferred?

   Solution:

   Gain/loss deferred = $3,000 [$3,000 gain realized – $0 gain recognized]

4. **Required:** What is the taxpayer's basis in the new property received?

   Solution:

   Basis of new property = Fair market value of property received – Deferred gain + Deferred loss

   = $20,000 – $3,000 + $0

   = $17,000 basis

Example 13	Like-Kind Exchange: Realized Loss

Facts: A taxpayer trades in an old, attached shed used solely for business for another shed to be used for business. The shed originally cost $35,000 and is currently worth $20,000. Assume that the shed the taxpayer wants in exchange is worth $20,000, and that the taxpayer has taken $12,000 of depreciation on the old shed:

1. **Required:** What is the gain or loss realized by the taxpayer on the exchange?

    Solution:

    Gain/loss realized = Amount realized − Adjusted basis of property given up
    = $20,000 FMV of new shed − ($35,000 cost − $12,000 depreciation)
    = $20,000 FMV of new shed − $23,000 adjusted basis of old shed
    = $(3,000) realized loss

2. **Required:** What is the gain or loss recognized by the taxpayer on the exchange?

    Solution:

    Gain/loss recognized = $0 [realized loss is never recognized in like-kind exchange]

3. **Required:** What is the gain or loss deferred?

    Solution:

    Gain/loss deferred = $3,000 loss deferred [$3,000 loss realized − $0 loss recognized]

4. **Required:** What is the taxpayer's basis in the new property received?

    Solution:

    Basis of new property = Fair market value of property received − Deferred gain
    + Deferred loss
    = $20,000 − $0 + $3,000
    = $23,000 basis

Example 14	Like-Kind Exchange: Boot Received Greater Than Gain Realized

Facts: A taxpayer trades in an old, attached shed used solely for business for another shed to be used for business. The shed originally cost $35,000 and the taxpayer has taken $18,000 in depreciation. The old shed is currently worth $20,000. Assume that the new shed the taxpayer wants in exchange is only worth $16,500, so the other party agrees to give the taxpayer $3,500 in cash in addition to the new shed:

1. **Required:** What is the gain or loss realized by the taxpayer on the exchange?

   Solution:

   Gain/loss realized = Amount realized – Adjusted basis of property given up

   = $20,000 amount realized
   [$16,500 FMV new shed + $3,500 cash boot received]
   – $17,000 adjusted basis old shed
   [$35,000 cost – $18,000 depreciation]

   = $3,000 realized gain

2. **Required:** What is the gain or loss recognized by the taxpayer on the exchange?

   Solution:

   Gain/loss recognized = $3,000 [lesser of realized gain of $3,000 or boot received of $3,500]

3. **Required:** What is the gain or loss deferred?

   Solution:

   Gain/loss deferred = $0 gain deferred [$3,000 gain realized – $3,000 gain recognized]

4. **Required:** What is the taxpayer's basis in the new property received?

   Solution:

   Basis of new property = Fair market value of property received – Deferred gain
                             + Deferred loss

   = $16,500 – $0 + $0

   = $16,500 basis

Example 15	Like-Kind Exchange: Boot Received Less Than Gain Realized

Facts: A taxpayer trades in an old, attached shed used solely for business for another shed to be used for business. The shed originally cost $35,000 and the taxpayer has taken $18,000 in depreciation. The old shed is currently worth $20,000. Assume that the new shed the taxpayer wants in exchange is only worth $17,500, so the other party agrees to give the taxpayer $2,500 in cash in addition to the new shed:

1. **Required:** What is the gain or loss realized by the taxpayer on the exchange?

    Solution:

    Gain/loss realized = Amount realized – Adjusted basis of property given up

    = $20,000 amount realized
       [$17,500 FMV of new shed + $2,500 cash boot received]
       – $17,000 adjusted basis of old shed
       [$35,000 cost – $18,000 depreciation]

    = $3,000 realized gain

2. **Required:** What is the gain or loss recognized by the taxpayer on the exchange?

    Solution:

    Gain/loss recognized = $2,500 [lesser of realized gain of $3,000 or boot received of $2,500]

3. **Required:** What is the gain or loss deferred?

    Solution:

    Gain/loss deferred = $500 gain deferred [$3,000 gain realized – $2,500 gain recognized]

4. **Required:** What is the taxpayer's basis in the new property received?

    Solution:

    Basis of new property = Fair market value of property received – Deferred gain
                               + Deferred loss

    = $17,500 – $500 + $0

    = $17,000 basis

Example 16 — Like-Kind Exchange: Realized Gain, Boot Paid

Facts: A taxpayer trades in an old, attached shed used solely for business for another shed to be used for business. The old shed originally cost $35,000 and the taxpayer has taken $18,000 in depreciation. The old shed is currently worth $20,000. Assume that the new shed the taxpayer wants in exchange is worth $22,000, so the taxpayer agrees to give the other party $2,000 in cash in addition to the old shed:

1. **Required:** What is the gain or loss realized by the taxpayer on the exchange?

   Solution:

   Gain/loss realized = Amount realized – Adjusted basis of property given up – Cash paid

   = $22,000 amount realized [FMV of new shed]
   – $17,000 adjusted basis of old shed
   [$35,000 cost – $18,000 depreciation]
   – $2,000 cash boot paid (not received)

   = $3,000 realized gain

2. **Required:** What is the gain or loss recognized by the taxpayer on the exchange?

   Solution:

   Gain/loss recognized = $0 [lesser of realized gain of $3,000 or boot received of $0]

3. **Required:** What is the gain or loss deferred?

   Solution:

   Gain/loss deferred = $3,000 [$3,000 gain realized – $0 gain recognized]

4. **Required:** What is the taxpayer's basis in the new property received?

   Solution:

   Basis of new property = Fair market value of property received – Deferred gain
   + Deferred loss

   = $22,000 – $3,000 + $0

   = $19,000 basis of new property

2.5   Installment Sales

Under the installment method, part of the payments on a transaction are received in a tax year after the year of the sale. Revenue is reported over the period in which the cash payments are received rather than all being recognized at the time of the sale. Installment sales will be discussed in more depth later in this unit.

2.6   Treasury and Capital Stock Transactions (by Corporation)

The following corporate transactions are exempt from gain (and any losses are disallowed—essentially corporations are precluded from tax benefits or income taxes resulting from dealing in their own stock):

- Sales of stock by corporation

- Repurchase of stock by corporation

- Reissue of stock

3   Losses (Nondeductible)

"WRaP" up these losses because they are nondeductible.

3.1   Wash Sale Loss

A wash sale exists when a security (stock or bond) is sold for a loss and is repurchased within 30 days before or after the sale date. Dealers in securities are excluded from wash sale rules if the loss occurs from a transaction made in the ordinary course of business.

3.1.1   Disallowed Loss

The loss on the wash sale is disallowed for tax purposes. The wash sale disallowance only applies to losses, not gains.

3.1.2   Basis of Repurchased Security

The basis of the repurchased security is equal to the purchase price of the new security plus the disallowed loss on the wash sale (or, alternatively, the basis of the old security, less the proceeds from the sale, plus the purchase price of the new security).

3.1.3   Date of Acquisition

The date of acquisition of the repurchased security is the date of acquisition of the original security.

3.1.4   Gain

If a security is sold resulting in a gain and it is repurchased within 30 days, the taxpayer cannot use "substituted basis." Instead, the taxpayer must pay capital gains tax and use the new purchase price as the basis.

Example 17 — Inability to Use Substituted Basis

Facts: Bob DeFilippis entered into the following transactions in April:

Item	Cost	Selling Price
(A) 100 shares of XYZ stock	$22,000	$21,000
(B) 100 shares of XYZ stock	21,500	

The shares sold during the year were purchased 15 years ago. These shares were sold on April 1 and the new shares were purchased on April 25.

Required: Determine if the sale qualifies as a wash sale, the amount of any loss allowed, and the basis of the purchased stock.

Solution: Although there is a loss on the sale of $1,000 ($21,000 sales price − $22,000 cost basis), the realized loss will be disallowed because the same stock (XYZ) was purchased within 30 days of the sale. The basis of the stock in the second purchase on April 25 is now $22,500, as the disallowed wash sale loss is added to the basis ($21,500 cost + $1,000 disallowed wash sale loss).

Pass Key

The CPA Examination has often tested the wash sale rules by having the taxpayer purchase shares of the same stock 30 days *before* the sale of the stock that resulted in a loss. This is still a wash sale, and the loss is disallowed. For example, on January 4 you buy one share for $100. On March 5 you buy another share for $40. Then, on March 15, the first share is sold for $41. Although you have "realized" a $59 loss, it will not be recognized because of the wash sale rules.

3.2   Related Party Transactions

Sales between related parties are not considered "arm's-length," and the loss is generally disallowed (see discussion on related parties in module 4 for more details).

3.3   Personal Loss

No deduction is allowed for the loss on a nonbusiness disposal or loss. An itemized deduction may be available in the category of casualty (attributable to a federally declared disaster) and theft.

Question 1

MCQ-01671

In December, Year 10, Davis, a single taxpayer, purchased a new residence for $200,000. Davis lived in the new residence continuously from Year 10 until selling the new residence in July, Year 17, for $455,000. What amount of gain is recognized from the sale of the residence on Davis' Year 17 tax return?

a. $455,000

b. $255,000

c. $5,000

d. $0

Question 2

MCQ-01747

In Year 9, Joan Reed exchanged commercial real estate that she owned for other commercial real estate plus cash of $50,000. The following additional information pertains to this transaction:

Property given up by Reed

Fair value	$500,000
Adjusted basis	300,000

Property received by Reed

Fair value	450,000

What amount of gain should be recognized in Reed's Year 9 income tax return?

a. $200,000

b. $100,000

c. $50,000

d. $0

Question 3

MCQ-01742

In a "like-kind" exchange of an investment asset for a similar asset that will also be held as an investment, no taxable gain or loss will be recognized on the transaction if both assets consist of:

a. Convertible debentures.

b. Convertible preferred stock.

c. Partnership interests.

d. Rental real estate located in different states.

1 Character of Gain or Loss

When a taxpayer disposes of property, the gain or loss recognized is classified as either capital or ordinary. The character of the gain or loss is determined by the nature of the asset that is disposed.

1.1 Capital Assets

Capital assets include property (real and personal) held by the taxpayer, such as:

- Personal automobile of individual taxpayer
- Furniture and fixtures in the home of the individual taxpayer
- Stocks and securities of all types (except those held by dealers)
- Personal property of a taxpayer not used in a trade or business
- Real property not used in a trade or business
- Interest in a partnership
- Goodwill of a corporation
- Copyrights, literary, musical, or artistic compositions that have been purchased
- Other assets held for investment

1.1.1 Reporting Disposition of Capital Assets

Form 8949 was created to accumulate detailed information about each sale of various investments for taxpayers, similar to what was reported on Schedule D in the past.

Totals from Form 8949 are transferred to Schedule D, which summarizes information on Form(s) 8949.

1.2 Noncapital Assets (Ordinary Treatment Except Where Noted)

- Property normally included in inventory or held for sale to customers in the ordinary course of business.
- Depreciable personal property and real estate used in a trade or business (e.g., Section 1231, Section 1245, and Section 1250 property). May be capital or ordinary; see later discussion in the module.
- Accounts and notes receivable arising from sales or services in the taxpayer's business.
- Copyrights, literary, musical, or artistic compositions *held by the original artist*. (Exception: Sales of musical compositions held by the original artist receive capital gains treatment.)
- Treasury stock (not an ordinary asset and not subject to capital gains treatment).

2   Calculation of Gain or Loss

The basic formula for calculating gain or loss is as follows:

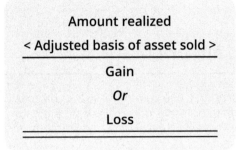

Amount realized

< Adjusted basis of asset sold >
_____

Gain

Or

Loss
_____

2.1   Amount Realized

The amount realized includes:

1. Cash received

2. Assumption of debt by buyer

3. FMV of property received

4. FMV of services received

5. Reduction by any selling expenses (e.g., broker's commissions)

Example 1 ▶ **Realized Gain**

Facts: A taxpayer conveys commercial property in which he has a basis of $70,000 and which is subject to a mortgage of $45,000 to X for $60,000 in cash, and X's assumption of the mortgage on the property.

Required: Determine the amount realized on the sale and the gain or loss realized.

Solution: The amount realized by the taxpayer is $105,000 (Debt relief of $45,000 + Cash of $60,000), and the taxpayer realizes a gain of $35,000 ($105,000 amount realized − $70,000 basis in the property).

---

3   Capital Gain and Loss Rules for Individual Taxpayers

3.1   Net Capital Gain Rules

3.1.1   Long-Term

▪ **Holding Period:** More than one year.

▪ **Tax Rate:** The tax rate is dependent on the taxpayer's taxable income and filing status:

2019 Taxable Income				
Tax Rate	Single	Head of Household	Married Filing Jointly	Married Filing Separately
0%	$0–$39,375	$0–$52,750	$0–$78,750	$0–$39,375
15%	$39,376–$434,550	$52,751–$461,700	$78,751–$488,850	$39,376–$244,425
20%	Over $434,550	Over $461,700	Over $488,850	Over $244,425

3.1.2   Short-Term

▪ **Holding Period:** One year or less.

▪ **Tax Rate:** Treated as ordinary income.

3.1.3   Unrecaptured Section 1250 Gain (25 Percent Rate Group)

Any unrecaptured section 1250 gain from depreciation of real property that is not treated as ordinary income is taxed at a maximum rate of 25 percent.

3.1.4   Collectibles and Small Business Stock (28 Percent Rate Group)

Long-term gains on collectibles, antiques, and small company (Section 1202) stock are taxed at a maximum rate of 28 percent.

3.2   Net Capital Loss Deduction and Loss Carryover Rules

3.2.1 $3,000 Maximum Deduction

Individual taxpayers realizing a net long-term or short-term capital loss may only recognize (deduct) a maximum of $3,000 of the realized loss from other types of gross income (ordinary income, passive income, or portfolio income). A joint return of spouses is treated as one person. If the spouses file separately, the loss deduction is limited to half ($1,500).

3.2.2   Excess Net Capital Loss

Carry forward for an unlimited period of time until exhausted. The loss maintains its character as long-term or short-term in future years.

3.2.3   A Personal (Nonbusiness) Bad Debt

A personal (nonbusiness) bad debt loss is treated as a short-term capital loss in the year the debt becomes totally worthless.

3.2.4   Worthless Stock and Securities

The cost (or other basis) of worthless stock or securities is treated as a capital loss, as if they were sold on the last day of the taxable year in which they became totally worthless.

3.3   Netting Procedures

Specific netting procedures for capital gains and losses are outlined in the Internal Revenue Code. Essentially, gains and losses are netted within each tax rate group (e.g., the 15 percent rate group), creating net short-term and long-term gains or losses by rate group. Resulting short-term and long-term losses then offset short-term and long-term gains (respectively) beginning with the highest tax rate group and continuing to the lower rates.

3.3.1   Short-Term Capital Gains and Losses

- If there are any short-term capital losses (this includes any short-term capital loss carryovers), they first offset any short-term gains that would be taxable at the ordinary income rates.

- Any remaining short-term capital loss is used to offset any long-term capital gains from the 28 percent rate group (e.g., collectibles).

- Any remaining short-term capital loss is then used to offset any long-term gains from the 25 percent group (e.g., unrecaptured Section 1250 gains).

- Any remaining short-term capital loss is used to offset any long-term capital gains applicable at the lower (e.g., 15 or 20 percent) tax rate group.

3.3.2   Long-Term Capital Gains and Losses

- If there are any long-term capital losses (this includes any long-term capital loss carryovers) from the 28 percent rate group, they first offset any net gains from the 25 percent rate group and then against net gains from the 15 or 20 percent rate group.

- If there are any long-term capital losses (this includes any long-term capital loss carryovers) from the 15 or 20 percent rate group, they first offset any net gains from the 28 percent rate group and then against net gains from the 25 percent rate group.

4   C Corporation Capital Gains and Loss Rules

4.1   Net Capital Gains (Long-Term and Short-Term)

Net capital gains of a corporation are added to ordinary income and taxed at the regular tax rate. There is no distinction between short-term and long-term capital gains and losses for C corporations.

- Corporations do not get the benefit of lower capital gains rates.

- Section 1231 gains are entitled to capital gains treatment (see discussion later in the module).

4.2   Net Capital Losses (Long-Term and Short-Term)

Corporations may not deduct any net capital losses from ordinary income.

- Net capital losses are carried back three years and forward five years as a short-term capital loss.

- Net capital losses are deducted from capital or Section 1231 gains. (Section 1231 gains are treated as *capital* assets used in the business and Section 1231 losses are treated as ordinary losses.)

		Excess	
	Offset Income	Carryback	Carryforward
Net operating losses	Yes*	No	Forever
Individual capital losses	$3,000	No	Forever
Corporate capital losses	No	3 years	5 years

*Limited to 80 percent of taxable income for tax years beginning after 12/31/17.

5   Long-Term Trade or Business Use Assets

5.1   Section 1231

Section 1231 assets include Section 1245 depreciable personal property, Section 1250 depreciable real property, and land. Assets must be used in the taxpayer's trade or business and held for more than 12 months to be classified as Section 1231 assets. The tax treatment of Section 1231 gains and losses depends on whether the taxpayer has a net 1231 gain or a net 1231 loss for the tax year.

5.1.1   Net 1231 Loss—Ordinary Loss Treatment

If the taxpayer's combined 1231 gains and losses for the tax year result in a net 1231 loss, the net 1231 loss is treated as an ordinary loss. The advantages of an ordinary loss over a capital loss are as follows:

- The deduction of capital losses is limited. For C corporations, capital losses can only be offset against capital gains. For individuals, estates, and trusts, the deduction of net capital losses is limited to $3,000 per year.

- The deduction of ordinary losses are not limited.

5.1.2   Net 1231 Gain—Capital Gain Treatment

If the taxpayer's combined 1231 gains and losses for the tax year result in a net 1231 gain, the net 1231 gain is treated as a long-term capital gain and netted with other long-term capital gains and losses. The advantages of a capital gain over an ordinary gain are as follows:

- For C corporations, capital gains can be used to offset capital losses.

- For individuals, net capital gains are taxed at preferential tax rates of 0, 15, or 20 percent.

However, part or all of a net 1231 gain may be treated as ordinary income under the Section 1231 five-year look-back rule.

5.1.3   Section 1231 Five-Year Look-Back Rule

When a taxpayer has a net Section 1231 gain for the year, the taxpayer must first "look back" to see if there were any net Section 1231 losses deducted as ordinary losses during the previous five years. If so, the taxpayer must "pay back" this ordinary treatment by treating the current year net Section 1231 gain as ordinary income to the extent of those prior net Section 1231 losses.

Once the ordinary benefit for a prior net Section 1231 loss has been paid back, or recaptured, the prior net Section 1231 loss will no longer cause a future net Section 1231 gain to be treated as ordinary. When doing the five-year look-back, you only look at any nonrecaptured net Section 1231 losses, starting with the oldest year in the five-year look-back period first.

| Example 2 | Section 1231 Five-Year Look-Back |

Facts: Lancaster Inc., a C corporation, purchased land that it used in its business for $100,000 in Year 1. Lancaster sold the land in Year 7 for $150,000. Lancaster had a prior unrecaptured net Section 1231 loss in Year 3 of $30,000. Lancaster had no other 1231 gains or losses in Year 7 and no other prior net 1231 gains or losses.

Required: Calculate the amount and character of the gain recognized on the sale of the land.

Solution: Recognized gain on the sale of the land is $50,000 ($150,000 sales price – $100,000 tax basis). Lancaster has no other Section 1231 gains or losses in Year 7 so it has a net 1231 gain of $50,000. Because it has a net 1231 gain for Year 7, Lancaster must look back at the prior five years (Year 2, then Year 3, Year 4, Year 5, and Year 6). In Year 3, it had a net 1231 loss of $30,000 that was deducted as an ordinary loss. There were no 1231 gains or losses in the other years in the look-back period. Lancaster took an ordinary loss deduction in Year 3, so $30,000 of the Year 7 net 1231 gain must be treated as ordinary income. The remaining gain of $20,000 is treated as a long-term capital gain.

5.2   Section 1245 (Machinery and Equipment): Gains Only

5.2.1   Business Use Personal Property

Section 1245 assets are generally depreciable personal property used in a trade or business for more than 12 months (e.g., autos, machinery, and equipment).

5.2.2   Recapture Accumulated Depreciation as Ordinary Income

Upon the sale of a Section 1245 asset:

■ the lesser of gain recognized or all accumulated depreciation taken on the asset is recaptured as ordinary income under Section 1245; and

■ any remaining gain is a Section 1231 gain.

5.3   Section 1250 (Real Property): Gains Only

5.3.1   Business Use Real Property

Section 1250 assets are depreciable real property used in a trade or business over 12 months (e.g., a warehouse or office building, but not land).

5.3.2   Section 1250 and Section 291 Depreciation Recapture for C Corporations

Section 1250 rules differ slightly from Section 1245 in that generally Section 1250 recaptures only that portion of depreciation taken on real property that is in excess of straight line. (Note: Generally Section 1250 only applies to assets placed into service under the pre-1987 accelerated methods of depreciation for real property. The current law requires real property to be depreciated under the straight-line method, so Section 1250 recapture rules no longer apply to real property.)

For C corporations, Section 291 applies to Section 1250 assets (depreciable real property) sold at a gain. Under Section 291, the amount of recapture as ordinary income is equal to 20 percent of the lesser of the recognized gain or the accumulated straight-line depreciation taken on the asset. Any remaining gain is a Section 1231 gain.

Note that Section 291 depreciation recapture only applies to C corporations, not other types of businesses.

| Example 3 | Section 291 Depreciation Recapture (C Corporation) |

Facts: Lancaster Inc., a C corporation, owned a building used in its business with an original cost basis of $100,000 and straight-line accumulated depreciation of $15,000. Lancaster sold the building for $95,000.

Required: Calculate the amount and character of the gain recognized on the sale of the building.

Solution: Recognized gain on the sale of the building is $10,000 ($95,000 sales price – $85,000 tax basis). Of the $10,000 gain, the amount recognized as ordinary income is 20 percent of the lesser of $10,000 (gain recognized) or $15,000 (accumulated depreciation on the building). Ordinary income will be: 20% × $10,000 = $2,000. The remaining gain of $8,000 will be recognized as Section 1231 gain.

5.3.3 Section 1250 Recapture for Individuals

For individual taxpayers selling Section 1250 property at a gain, the gain is characterized as a Section 1231 gain and netted with other Section 1231 gains and losses to determine if the individual taxpayer has an overall net Section 1231 gain or a net Section 1231 loss for the tax year.

However, when an individual has sold a Section 1250 asset at a gain and included the gain with other Section 1231 gains, an amount called unrecaptured Section 1250 gain equal to the lesser of (1) the recognized gain on the sale of the Section 1250 asset, or (2) the straight-line accumulated depreciation on the Section 1250 asset is taxed at a maximum rate of 25 percent. Any net 1231 gain in excess of the amount that will be taxed at 25 percent is taxed at the preferential rates of 0, 15, or 20 percent.

| Example 4 | Section 1250 Gain (Individuals) |

Facts: Lancaster Company is a sole proprietorship and is reported on Schedule C of the taxpayer's individual tax return. Lancaster owned a building with an original cost basis of $100,000 and straight-line accumulated depreciation of $15,000, resulting in a tax basis of $85,000. Lancaster sold the building for $95,000. There were no other sales of property during the tax year.

Required: Calculate the amount recognized on the sale along with the rate at which it is taxed.

Solution: Recognized gain on the sale of the building was $10,000 ($95,000 – $85,000). The amount taxed at 25 percent will be $10,000, which is the lesser of the recognized gain of $10,000 or the straight-line accumulated depreciation of $15,000. No portion of the gain will be taxed at a preferential rate of 0, 15, or 20 percent.

Flowchart of Gain or Loss From Section 1231 and 1245/1250 Assets

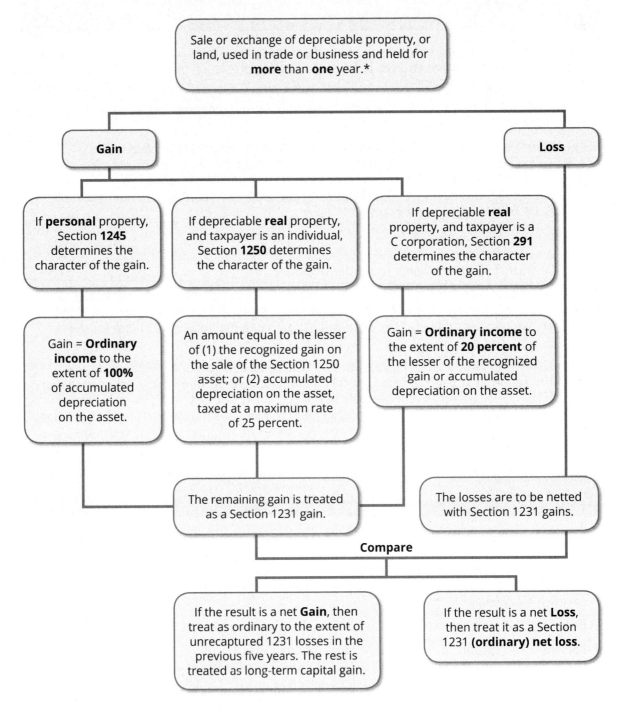

*This illustrates the general rules. Special rules are applicable to casualty and theft, involuntary conversion situations, and low-income housing.

Example 5	Application of Sections 1231 and 1245

Facts: Roberts Printing Inc. sold the following assets during the year:

Description	Selling Price	Cost	Accumulated Depreciation	Recognized Gain/Loss
Printing press	$4,000	$ 6,800	$ 3,200	$ 400 gain
Photocopier	2,600	2,500	500	600 gain
Delivery van	500	15,000	13,000	1,500 loss

1. **Required:**

   Step 1: Calculate gain or loss.

   Solution: Gain or loss is calculated by the following formula:

   Cost − Accumulated depreciation = Adjusted basis

   Compare the selling price to the adjusted basis = Gain or loss

2. **Required:**

   Step 2: Calculate depreciation recapture.

   Solution: Both the printing press and photocopier are Section 1245 personal property sold at a gain; thus, for each asset, the lesser of gain recognized or accumulated depreciation must be recaptured as ordinary income:

	Ordinary Income (Depreciation Recapture)
Printing press	$400
Photocopier	500*
Total	$900

   *Only $500 of the $600 gain is ordinary income because the ordinary income recapture is the lesser of the accumulated depreciation ($500) or gain recognized ($600).

3. **Required:**

   Step 3: Determine character of any remaining gain or loss

   Solution: Any remaining gain, after calculating the ordinary income recapture, is then netted with all Section 1231 net losses:

	Sec. 1231 Gain	Sec. 1231 Loss
Photocopier	$100	
Delivery van		$1,500

   The net result is a loss of $1,400, which is treated as a Section 1231 net loss and is deducted as an ordinary loss.

Pass Key

The CPA Examination infrequently tests on the *depreciation recapture rules*. However, when tested, the Section 1245 personal property *(machinery and equipment)* rules are typically the area. A simple rule of thumb for personal property depreciation recapture is:

- Loss = Section 1231 loss; net 1231 loss treated as ordinary loss.
- Ordinary income = Gain to extent of accumulated depreciation, and net 1231 gain to the extent of net 1231 losses in previous five years.
- Capital gain = Net Section 1231 gain after depreciation recapture and five-year look-back.

Question 1   MCQ-01761

Platt owns land that is operated as a parking lot. A shed was erected on the lot for the related transactions with customers. With regard to capital assets and Section 1231 assets, how should these assets be classified?

	Land	Shed
a.	Capital	Capital
b.	Section 1231	Capital
c.	Capital	Section 1231
d.	Section 1231	Section 1231

Question 2   MCQ-01876

Lee qualified as head of a household for Year 9 tax purposes. Lee's Year 9 taxable income was $100,000, exclusive of capital gains and losses. Lee had a net long-term loss of $8,000 in Year 9. What amount of this capital loss can Lee offset against Year 9 ordinary income?

- **a.** $0
- **b.** $3,000
- **c.** $4,000
- **d.** $8,000

6   Installment Sale

The installment method is the tax method of reporting gains (not losses) for sales made by a "nonmerchant" in personal property and "nondealer" in real estate when part of the payments are received in a tax year after the year of the sale. This installment sale method is not available for sales of stocks or securities traded on an established market. Immediate recognition can be elected by reporting all of the gain on the sale on the seller's return for the year of disposition.

6.1   Recognize When Cash Is Received

Under the installment method, revenue is reported over the period in which the cash payments are received. This method does not alter the type of gain to be reported (capital gain, ordinary income). Taxable income is calculated by multiplying the annual cash collections by the gross profit percentage.

6.2   Reportable Installment Sale Gain/Income

- Gross profit = Sales price − Adjusted basis

- Gross profit percentage = Gross profit / sales price

- Gain recognized (taxable income) = Cash collections (excluding interest) × Gross profit percentage

---

Example 6   Installment Sale Reporting

Facts: Assume that a taxpayer had $400,000 in installment sales in Year 1 and a December 31, Year 1, balance in installment notes receivable of $150,000. The taxpayer had $300,000 as its adjusted basis.

Required: Calculate gross profit, the gross profit percentage, and gain recognized in Year 1 under the installment method.

Solution: The taxpayer would calculate realized profit in Year 1 as follows:

Step 1: Gross profit	Year 1
Sales on installment	$ 400,000
Adjusted basis	(300,000)
Total gross profit	$ 100,000

Step 2: Gross profit percentage

$$\frac{\text{Gross profit}}{\text{Sales on installment}} \quad \frac{\$100,000}{\$400,000} = \underline{\underline{25\%}}$$

Step 3: Gain recognized	
Sales on installment	$ 400,000
Ending installment notes receivable	(150,000)
Collections in Year 1 (excluding interest income)	250,000
Gross profit percentage	25%
Gain recognized in Year 1	$ 62,500

6.3   Interest

The seller is required to charge interest on an installment sale. The interest is reported separately from each installment payment as ordinary income. If no interest or inadequate interest is reported by the seller, a portion of each installment payment will be treated as imputed interest and taxed at ordinary rates.

6.4   Miscellaneous

- All depreciation recaptured shall be reported in income in the year of sale.

- Net proceeds from loans that are secured by the installment obligation shall be reported as amounts received/collected.

- Gain from the sale of depreciable property to a related person is generally ineligible for installment sale reporting.

1 Related Party Provisions

The provisions of Section 267 prevent taxpayers from shifting ownership of stock or property to a related person or entity in an effort to take advantage of beneficial provisions of the Internal Revenue Code when essentially still controlling their original interest through their related party. In order to accomplish this, Section 267 lays out several "constructive ownership" rules, in which stock held by certain parties related to the taxpayer is treated as though it is actually held by the taxpayer. Note that any transaction between a personal services corporation and an employee owner are automatically classified as related parties (regardless of the ownership percentage of the employee owner).

1.1 Definition of Related Parties

Section 267 of the IRC defines related parties as:

- Brothers and sisters.

- Spouses.

- Ancestors and lineal descendants (e.g., father, son, grandfather).

- Entities that are more than 50 percent owned, directly or indirectly, by individuals, corporations, trusts and/or partnerships. Note that constructive ownership rules apply (see discussion later in the module).

- Controlled groups (any two corporations, partnerships, S corporations, or a combination of those, both more than 50 percent owned by the same party).

- Various relationships between trusts, grantors, fiduciaries, executors, and beneficiaries.

- Tax-exempt organizations (within definition of Section 501) and person controlling, directly or indirectly, such organizations.

Note: In-laws and step relationships are not related parties.

1.2 Constructive Ownership

The Section 267 attribution rules are as follows:

- **Rule 1:** Stock owned directly or indirectly by a corporation, partnership, estate, or trust is treated as owned proportionately by its shareholders, partners, or beneficiaries.

Example 1	Rule 1

Facts: Kathy owns 80 percent of Handlebars Company, which in turn owns 30 percent of ABC Company.

Required: Determine Kathy's ownership percentage in ABC Company.

Solution: Kathy is treated as owning 24 percent of ABC (80% × 30%) through her holdings of Handlebars stock.

- **Rule 2:** An individual shall be considered as owning stock owned by those family members related in accordance with Section 267.

Example 2	Rule 2

Facts: Chad owns a 30 percent interest in Wick Corp.; his wife, Kathy, owns a 20 percent interest; his grandson owns a 5 percent interest; and his nephew owns a 15 percent interest.

Required: Determine Chad's ownership in Wick Corp.

Solution: Chad is treated as owning 55 percent of Wick Corp. (30% + 20% + 5%); his nephew is not a related party under Section 267.

- **Rule 3:** Stock constructively owned by a person under Rule 1 above (proportionate attribution) shall be treated as actually owned by that person for the purposes of applying either Rule 1 or Rule 2 in other situations. However, Rule 2 (family members) cannot be applied in this manner.

Example 3	Rule 3

Facts: In Example 1 above, Kathy was treated as constructively owning 24 percent of ABC Company (80% × 30%).

Required: Determine any ownership of ABC by Kathy's husband, Chad, under constructive ownership rules.

Solution: Kathy's husband, Chad, would have to include Kathy's 24 percent of ABC with any stock in ABC he actually owns when testing Chad for loss disallowance, because Kathy's constructive holdings are treated as actual holdings for these purposes.

Example 4	Non-attribution to Other Family Members

Facts: In Example 2 above, Chad was treated as constructively owning his wife's 20 percent interest in Wick Corp.

Required: Determine whether Chad's 20 percent ownership in Wick Corp. through his wife may be attributed to other family members.

Solution: Chad's 20 percent in Wick Corp. could not also be attributed to Chad's sister, Shirley, because this would involve double attribution with family members—from Chad's wife, Kathy, to Chad, and then to Chad's sister, Shirley.

Example 5	Related Parties

Facts: Arnold Corp. owns 40 percent of Cooper Corp. and 30 percent of Diggins Corp. Diggins Corp. owns 40 percent of Cooper Corp.

Required: Determine whether Arnold and Cooper are related parties.

Solution: Under constructive ownership rules, Arnold and Cooper are related parties, as Arnold owns 52 percent of Cooper (30% × 40% = 12% constructively, plus Arnold's 40 percent direct ownership in Cooper).

1.3   Capital Gains and Related Parties

1.3.1   General Rule

Capital gains taxes are imposed on all sales of non-depreciable property (e.g., land) between all related parties, with the exception below.

1.3.2   Exception

Sales between the following related parties do not receive capital gains treatment:

- Two spouses (where basis is merely transferred).

- An individual and a 50-percent-plus controlled corporation or partnership (where the gain is taxed as ordinary income).

1.4   Capital Losses and Related Parties

Losses are disallowed on (most) related party sales transactions, even if they were made at an "arm's-length" FMV price.

1.5   Basis Rules and Related Parties

The basis (and related gain or loss) of the (second) buying relative depends on whether the second relative's resale price is higher, lower, or between the first relative's basis and the lower selling price to the second relative.

1.6   Gain and Loss Rules for Related Parties

1.6.1   Gain Rules

Gain is recognized only to the extent that the future sale price exceeds the previous relative's cost basis.

Example 6	Basis in Related Party Transaction

Facts: Ned bought stock for $20,000 that he sold to his brother, Ray, for $16,000. The $4,000 loss is disallowed. Ray then sells the stock to Bobby, an unrelated party, for $21,000.

Required: Determine Ray's basis in the stock and his recognized gain or loss on the sale to Bobby.

Solution: Ray's recognized gain from the sale is $1,000, calculated as follows:

Ray's selling price		$ 21,000
Less: Ray's cost	$16,000	
Disallowed loss	4,000	
Ray's basis		(20,000)
Ray's gain		$ 1,000

1.6.2 Loss Rules

Loss is recognized only to the extent that the sale price to the unrelated party is lower than the acquiring relative's original purchase price in the asset (FMV).

1.6.3 No Gain or Loss Rules

No gain or loss is recognized when the sale price to the unrelated party is between the original cost basis and related party purchase price.

1.7 Holding Period and Related Parties

The holding period starts with the new owner's period of ownership.

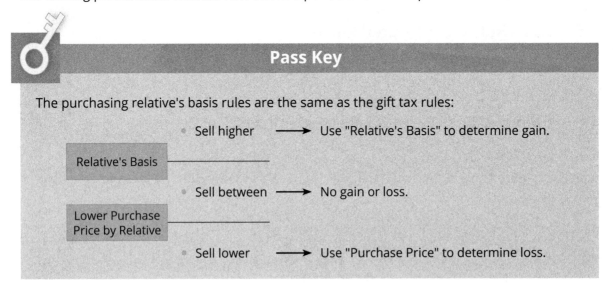

Pass Key

The purchasing relative's basis rules are the same as the gift tax rules:

- Sell higher → Use "Relative's Basis" to determine gain.

Relative's Basis

- Sell between → No gain or loss.

Lower Purchase Price by Relative

- Sell lower → Use "Purchase Price" to determine loss.

2　Below-Market Loans and Imputed Interest

Section 7872 of the IRC seeks to prevent parties from offering below-market interest rates on loans that could be particularly appealing to related parties. If Section 7872 applies, the loan is re-characterized as an arm's-length transaction in which the lender made a loan to the borrower in exchange for a note requiring payment of interest at the applicable federal rate (AFR; these are published regularly by the IRS).

Individuals who make a below-market loan generally must report any foregone interest as interest income. The borrower may be able to deduct the foregone interest, unless it is personal interest.

2.1　Loans Affected by Imputed Interest Rules

The below-market loan provisions apply to the following loans:

- **Gifts:** Any below-market loan which is a gift loan.
- **Compensation-Related Loans:** Any below-market loan directly or indirectly between:
  - an employer and an employee; or
  - an independent contractor and a person for whom the independent contractor provides services.
- **Corporation-Shareholder Loans:** Any below-market loan directly or indirectly between a corporation and any shareholder of such corporation.
- **Tax-Avoidance Loans:** Any below-market loan for which a principal purpose of the interest arrangement is the avoidance of any federal tax.
- **Other Below-Market Loans:** To the extent provided in regulations, any below-market loan that is not otherwise described, if the interest arrangements of the loan have a significant effect on any federal tax liability of the lender or the borrower.
- **Loans to Qualified Continuing Care Facilities:** Any loan to any qualified continuing care facility, pursuant to a continuing care contract.

2.2　De Minimis Exception

- **Gift Loans Between Individuals:** In the case of any gift loan directly between individuals, the imputed interest rules shall not apply to any day on which the aggregate outstanding amount of loans between individuals does not exceed $10,000.
- **Compensation-Related and Corporate-Shareholder Loans:** The imputed interest rules shall not apply to any day on which the aggregate outstanding amount of loans between the borrower and lender does not exceed $10,000 for loans that are compensation-related or corporate-shareholder loans.

2.3　Special Rules for Gift Loans Not in Excess of $100,000

For gift loans between individuals, if the outstanding loans between the lender and borrower total $100,000 or less, the foregone interest to be included in income by the lender and deducted by the borrower is limited to the amount of the borrower's net investment income for the year. If the borrower's net investment income is $1,000 or less, the foregone interest is treated as zero.

2.4 Calculation of Foregone Interest

Foregone interest is calculated by the following:

The amount of interest that would be payable for that period if the loan's interest accrued at the applicable federal rate (AFR) and was payable annually on December 31, minus any interest actually payable on the loan for the period.

Example 7 — Imputed Interest

Facts: Mike loans $200,000 to his sister, Angie, payable in 10 years at an annual interest rate of 1 percent. The AFR issued by the IRS for long-term loans is 2.24 percent.

Required: Determine whether Mike's loan to Angie qualifies as a below-market loan and, if so, calculate the imputed interest income to Mike.

Solution: The loan appears to be a gift loan between individuals because interest is charged at below-market rates. This is a loan to which Section 7872 applies and imputed interest will be charged.

Imputed interest is $2,480, calculated as follows:

- Interest required under AFR: $4,480 (2.24% × $200,000), less
- Interest payable under the loan: $2,000 (1% × $200,000) = $2,480

Question 1 — MCQ-01726

In Year 3, Fay sold 100 shares of Gym Co. stock to her son, Martin, for $11,000. Fay had paid $15,000 for the stock in Year 1. Subsequently in Year 3, Martin sold the stock to an unrelated third party for $16,000.

What amount of gain from the sale of the stock to the third party should Martin report on his Year 3 income tax return?

- a. $0
- b. $1,000
- c. $4,000
- d. $5,000

1 Depreciation

Depreciation is an annual allowance given to a trade or business for exhaustion, wear and tear, and normal obsolescence of assets used in trade or business. An asset's basis must be reduced by the depreciation allowed (or allowable) for a particular year, even if depreciation was not claimed by the taxpayer for that particular year. The depreciation method typically used for federal income tax purposes is the Modified Accelerated Cost Recovery System (MACRS).

1.1 Definitions

- **Real Property (Land and Buildings):** Real property is defined as land and all items permanently affixed to the land (e.g., buildings, paving, etc.).

- **Personal Property (Machinery, Equipment, and Automobiles):** Personal property is all property not classified as real property.

1.2 MACRS: Property Other Than Real Property

1.2.1 Types of Property

3-year 200% Class:	ADR (asset depreciation range) midpoints of 4 years and less. Excludes automobiles and light trucks, includes racehorses more than 2 years old and other horses more than 12 years old, and special tools.
5-year 200% Class:	ADR midpoints of more than 4 years and less than 10 years. Includes automobiles, light trucks, computers, and copiers.
7-year 200% Class:	ADR midpoints of 10 years and more, and less than 16 years. Includes office furniture and fixtures, equipment, property with no ADR midpoint not classified elsewhere, and includes railroad track.
10-year 200% Class:	ADR midpoints of 16 years and more, and less than 20 years. Includes boats and water transportation equipment.
15-year 150% Class:	ADR midpoint of 20 years and more, and less than 25 years. Includes sewage treatment plants, telephone distribution plants, qualified improvement, restaurant and retail property, and comparable equipment used for the two-way exchange of voice and data communications.
20-year 150% Class:	ADR midpoint of 25 years and more, other than real property with an ADR midpoint of 27.5 years and more, including sewer pipes. Includes certain farm buildings and municipal sewers.

1.2.2 MACRS Depreciation Rules Method

For 3-, 5-, 7-, and 10-year MACRS property (other than real property) placed in service after January 1, 1987, MACRS is computed using the 200 percent declining balance method. For 15- and 20-year property, MACRS is computed using the 150 percent declining balance method.

1.2.3 Salvage Value (Ignored)

Salvage value is ignored under MACRS.

1.2.4 Half-Year Convention

In general, a *half-year convention* applies to personal property, under which such property placed in service or disposed of during a taxable year is treated as having been placed in service or disposed of halfway through the year. A personal property asset is allowed six months of depreciation in the year of acquisition and disposition, regardless of the date on which it is acquired or disposed.

1.2.5 Mid-quarter Convention

If more than 40 percent of depreciable personal property is placed in service in the last quarter of the year, the mid-quarter convention must be used (identify the MACRS table with "mid-quarter" as the applicable convention to calculate depreciation).

Example 1   **MACRS Depreciation**

The following example illustrates the factors that are used to calculate MACRS depreciation expense under the half-year convention. Remember that salvage value is ignored. Generally, the calculation of MACRS depreciation expense for an entity that has been in operation for the entire year is to take the purchase price (plus improvements) and multiply that amount by the applicable MACRS factor. Proration is not applicable in the general case and only applies to short tax years (i.e., when the entity begins operations some period of time into the tax year).

Assume a company that started business in Year 1 purchased office furniture on February 14, Year 3, at a price of $10,000. Further assume that this was the only purchase of assets in the year (reason: avoid possibly applying the mid-quarter convention rules) and that no special depreciation rules apply. Office equipment is MACRS 7-year property. The depreciation expense for Year 3 for the office equipment would be $10,000 × 0.1429 (per the table, below) = $1,429. The depreciation expense for Year 4 would be $10,000 × 0.2449 = $2,449. Note that the expense is lower in the first year due to the half-year convention. The sum of the factors for a type of asset will equal 100. Note that the calculation of MACRS depreciation expense is quite simple once you can identify the applicable factor.

(continued)

(continued)

MACRS Depreciation Table

Applicable depreciation method: 200 or 150 percent declining balance switching to straight line
Applicable recovery period: 3, 5, 7, 10, 15, 20 years
Applicable convention: Half-year

If The Recovery Year Is	And The Recovery Period Is					
	3-year	*5-year*	*7-year*	*10-year*	*15-year*	*20-year*
1	33.33	20	14.29	10	5	3.75
2	44.45	32	24.49	18	9.5	7.219
3	14.81	19.2	17.49	14.4	8.55	6.677
4	7.41	11.52	12.49	11.52	7.7	6.177
5		11.52	8.93	9.22	6.93	5.713
6		5.76	8.92	7.37	6.23	5.285
7			8.93	6.55	5.9	4.888
8			4.46	6.55	5.9	4.522
9				6.56	5.91	4.462
10				6.55	5.9	4.461
11				3.28	5.91	4.462
12					5.9	4.461
13					5.91	4.462
14					5.9	4.461
15					5.91	4.462
16					2.95	4.461
17						4.462
18						4.461
19						4.462
20						4.461
21						2.231

1.3   MACRS: Real Property

Salvage value should be ignored when computing MACRS depreciation on real property.

1.3.1   Residential Rental Property (27.5-Year Straight-Line)

Examples of *residential rental property* include apartments and duplex rental homes.

1.3.2   Nonresidential Real Property (39-Year Straight-Line)

Examples of *nonresidential real property* (real property that is not residential rental property and that does not have an ADR midpoint of more than 27.5 years) include office buildings and warehouses.

1.3.3   Land

Land is not depreciable and should be removed from the total cost of real property when calculating depreciation.

1.3.4 Mid-month Convention

Straight-line depreciation is computed based on the number of months the property was in service. One half month is taken in the month the property is placed in service. One half month is taken for the month in which the property is disposed of.

Example 2	Mid-month Convention

Facts: Leigh Corp. placed a new office building into service on April 6 of Year 1. The adjusted basis of the office building is $100,000.

Required: Calculate the depreciation on the office building for Year 1.

Solution: Leigh figures the straight-line depreciation rate for the building by dividing 1 by 39 years. The result is 0.02564. The depreciation for a full year is $2,564 ($100,000 × 0.02564). Under the mid-month convention, the property is treated as placed in service in the middle of April, allowing 8.5 months of depreciation for the year. Expressed as a decimal, the fraction of 8.5 months divided by 12 months is 0.7083. The first-year depreciation for the building is $1,816 ($2,564 × 0.7083).

1.4 Expense Deduction in Lieu of Depreciation (Section 179 Expense)

Each tax year, a taxpayer may elect to deduct, as an expense in lieu of depreciation, a fixed amount of depreciable (machinery, equipment, computer software, etc.) property.

1.4.1 Limitations on Immediate Expensing

The limit is $1,020,000 for new or used personal property that is acquired from an unrelated party during the year in 2019.

■ The maximum amount is reduced dollar for dollar by the amount of property placed in service during the taxable year that exceeds $2,550,000 in 2019. This amount will be indexed for inflation.

■ The deduction is not permitted when a net loss exists or if the deduction would create a net loss.

■ SUVs: Section 179 limits the cost of a sport utility vehicle (SUV) that may be expensed to $25,500. An SUV is defined as a four-wheeled vehicle with a gross vehicle weight of more than 6,000 pounds but less than 14,000 pounds, not including heavy pickup trucks, vans, and small buses.

Example 3	Section 179 Deduction

Facts: Nicholas Inc. placed into service $50,000 of five-year property in Year 1. Assume that Nicholas Inc. is not subject to the taxable income limitation for a Section 179 expense. Year 1 MACRS rate for five-year property from MACRS depreciation tables = 20%.

Required: Compare Nicholas' MACRS depreciation expense to its Section 179 expense if Nicholas elects to take the full amount of Section 179 expense against the property.

Solution: MACRS: $50,000 × 20% = $10,000 depreciation deduction. Section 179: $50,000. The property placed into service is within Section 179 expensing and property limits, so the entire amount is deductible this year (given that Nicholas is not in a net loss situation). Electing Section 179 yields the greatest deduction. (Note that if the taxpayer is in a loss position or sees the need for greater deductions in the future, depreciating the asset under normal MACRS convention would be best).

1.5   Bonus Depreciation

Bonus depreciation is extended through 2026. Under bonus depreciation rules, a taxpayer can expense an additional percentage of qualified property that is placed into service in the current year.

- Qualified property is new or used personal property with a recovery period of 20 years or less. A property is only qualified if the acquiring taxpayer had not previously used the acquired property and so long as the property is not acquired from a related party.

- The bonus depreciation percentage is 100 percent for property placed in service during years 2018 through 2022, but then phases down to 80 percent in 2023, 60 percent in 2024, 40 percent in 2025, and 20 percent in 2026. The 100 percent rate is extended retroactively to property acquired and placed in service after September 27, 2017.

- An $8,000 additional first-year depreciation for vehicles on which bonus depreciation is claimed is allowed.

- Bonus depreciation is not an adjustment for, or a preference for, AMT purposes.

- Bonus depreciation is claimed after the Section 179 expense deduction, if elected, but before the regular depreciation expense deduction.

Example 4	Bonus Depreciation and Section 179

Facts: Company A places into service $2,750,000 of seven-year MACRS property (all qualified under the rules of Section 179 and bonus depreciation).

Required: Determine the total expensing deduction for the year on the property, assuming that Company A wants the maximum deduction possible for the current year.

Solution: The order is Section 179 first, then bonus depreciation, then regular depreciation:

Section 179: $820,000 Section 179 deduction (the $1,020,000 deduction is reduced dollar for dollar by qualified property placed into service in excess of $2,550,000; so in this case, reduced by $200,000)

Bonus: $1,930,000 ($2,750,000 – $820,000 179 deduction = $1,930,000 available for bonus. $1,930,000 × 100% bonus rate = $1,930,000)

MACRS: $0 because no additional basis remains.

Total expense deduction for the year: $2,750,000 ($820,000 + $1,930,000).

1.6   Straight-Line in Lieu of Accelerated Depreciation Election

A taxpayer may choose to depreciate property on a straight-line basis, rather than use the more accelerated MACRS. A taxpayer who chooses straight-line may choose the regular recovery period or a longer alternative depreciation system (ADS) recovery period.

Pass Key

It is important for CPA Examination candidates to remember the following concepts:

Machinery and Equipment	Real Estate
• Half-year convention • Mid-quarter convention	• Mid-month convention

2 Depletion

Depletion is allowed on exhaustible natural resources, such as timber, minerals, oil, and gas. The two methods of depletion are (i) cost depletion and (ii) percentage depletion. Generally, you must use the method that results in the larger deduction. You must reduce the basis of your property by the depletion allowed or allowable, whichever is greater.

2.1 Cost Depletion (GAAP)

Under cost depletion, the remaining basis of the property is divided by the remaining number of recoverable units (tons of ore, barrels of oil) to arrive at the unit depletion rate. The deduction for depletion is the depletion unit rate multiplied by the number of units sold (not the number of units produced) for the year.

Note that the computation of the unit depletion rate is based on an estimate of the remaining unsold units. Because this estimate will likely be revised every year, the computation of the unit depletion rate must be redone every year by dividing the basis remaining at the end of the prior year by the estimated amount of unsold units remaining at the end of the prior year. Once the property is fully depleted, no further cost depletion deductions may be taken (even if not all units have yet been sold). Any remaining undepleted basis is deducted in the year that the last unit is sold.

Example 5 | Depletion Calculation

Facts: Oil property having an estimated 1,000,000 recoverable barrels at the beginning of the year has a cost basis of $1,000,000. In Year 1, 50,000 barrels were sold.

Required: Calculate the depletion deduction for Year 1.

Solution: The depletion deduction for Year 1 is $50,000, calculated as follows:

$$\frac{\$1,000,000 \text{ basis}}{1,000,000 \text{ barrels}} = \$1 \text{ per barrel}$$

$$\$1 \text{ per barrel} \times 50,000 = \$50,000 \text{ cost depletion}$$

2.2   Percentage Depletion (Non-GAAP)

To figure percentage depletion, multiply a certain percentage, (specified in the tax law for each type of natural resource), by gross income from the property during the tax year. The deduction is limited to 50 percent of taxable income (excluding depletion) from the natural resource. The allowable percentages range from 5 to 22 percent depending on the mineral or substance being extracted. Percentage depletion may be taken even after costs have been completely recovered and there is no remaining cost basis. However, any percentage depletion deduction in excess of the property's basis is an AMT preference item.

For oil and gas properties only, the overall limitation of 50 percent of taxable income from the property is increased to 100 percent (however, unless you are an independent producer or royalty owner, you generally cannot use percentage depletion for oil and gas wells).

3   Amortization

3.1   Intangibles

Intangibles such as goodwill, licenses, franchises, and trademarks may be amortized using straight-line basis over a period of 15 years, starting with the month of acquisition. (Note the difference for GAAP purposes: Intangible assets with *indefinite* lives are subject only to an impairment test, and intangible assets with *finite* lives are amortized over those lives and also subject to an impairment test).

3.2   Others

Certain items can be expensed and/or amortized on a straight-line basis over a period of years upon election to do so, regardless of their useful life. These include the following:

- Business organization and start-up costs. Each is permitted to first take off $5,000 to be expensed, and the remainder is amortized over 180 months. (The $5,000 is reduced dollar for dollar as total cost exceeds $50,000 for each item).

- Research expenses (existing trades or businesses may amortize research expenses over a 60-month period).

- Pollution-control facilities (amortized over 60 months).

- Reforestation costs (amortized over 84 months).

- Geological and geophysical costs (amortized over 24 months).

Example 6   Amortization

Facts: Royal Corp. acquired a patent with a cost of $50,000 in August of Year 1.

Required: Determine the amortization on the patent in Year 1.

Solution: $1,390, calculated as follows:

$50,000/180 = $278 Amortization allowed per month

$278 × 5 months = $1,390

---

4 Other Considerations Related to Cost Recovery Adjustments

4.1 After-Tax Cash Flows

Financial models used for capital decisions focus a financial manager on the cash flows associated with an investment and the comparison of those cash flows with expected rates and amounts of return. Because amortization, depreciation, and depletion represent declining economic value of an asset but not an actual cash flow, these noncash expense charges must be added back to net income for the calculation of after-tax cash flows.

> **After-tax cash flow = Earnings after tax + Amortization + Depletion + Depreciation**

After-tax cash flow can also be represented as Pretax cash flow × (1 − Tax rate), where pretax cash flow is calculated as pretax earnings plus noncash expenses such as amortization, depletion, and depreciation.

4.2 Tax Savings Associated With Deductions

The tax savings associated with taking amortization, depletion, or depreciation can be calculated as the amount of the expense multiplied by the marginal income tax rate for the taxpayer. This is important when considering investment in an asset.

Question 1	MCQ-02058

On August 1, Year 1, Graham purchased and placed into service an office building costing $264,000, including $30,000 for the land. What was Graham's MACRS deduction for the office building in Year 1?

    a. $9,600

    b. $6,000

    c. $3,600

    d. $2,250

Corporate Taxation

Module

NOTES

1 Comparison of Corporation to Other Business Entities

Business entities are generally classified as a corporation, limited liability company, limited partnership, partnership, or sole proprietorship.

- **Corporation**

  Formed through the filing of articles of incorporation with a state and recognized as a legal entity separate from its owners (shareholders).

- **Limited Liability Company**

  Formed through the filing of articles of organization with a state and recognized as a legal entity separate from its owners (members). A limited liability company can be taxed as a corporation, a partnership, or a sole proprietorship. (Details of limited liability companies will be discussed in a later unit.)

- **Limited Partnership**

  Often organized by a written agreement and must file a certificate of limited partnership to be recognized by the state. (Details of limited liability partnerships will be discussed in a later unit.)

- **Partnership**

  Often formed by a written agreement known as a partnership agreement between two or more partners or may be formed by oral agreement; there is no requirement to formally organize under state law as compared with a corporation. (Details of partnerships will be discussed in a later unit.)

- **Sole Proprietorship**

  Not treated as a legal entity separate from its owner (unincorporated), and owner is not required to formally organize the business in the state. Unlike corporations, individual owners of a sole proprietorship are ultimately responsible for the liabilities of the business.

	Limited Liability	Entity Taxation	Owner Taxation	Suitable for Initial Public Offering	Eligible for Qualified Business Income Deduction
Corporation	Yes	On earnings	On dividends	Yes	No
LLC	Yes	Dependent on classification	Dependent on classification	No	Yes
Partnership	Only for limited partners	None	On earnings	No	Yes
S Corporation	Yes	Not generally	On earnings, not generally on distributions	No	Yes
Sole Proprietorship	No	None	On earnings	No	Yes

2 Formation of C Corporations

C corporations are the only type of entity whose earnings are subject to double taxation (taxed once at the corporate level and again at the shareholder level when dividends are distributed). Whereas double taxation is the primary disadvantage of the corporate form, a primary advantage of this entity is the protection the corporate form offers its shareholders from liabilities of the corporation. A corporation is solely responsible for its liabilities under state law.

| **Formation** |
| Operations |
| Taxation |
| Distributions |
| Liquidation |

2.1 Corporation Tax Consequences

There is no gain or loss recognized by the corporation issuing stock in exchange for property in the following transactions:

- Formation—issuance of common stock
- Reacquisition—purchase of treasury stock
- Resale—sale of treasury stock

2.1.1 Basis of Property Corporation Receives

The general rule is that the *basis of the property* received by a corporation from the transferor/shareholder is the greater of:

1. The transferor/shareholder's adjusted basis (net book value) of the property (plus any gain recognized by the transferor/shareholder); or

2. The debt assumed by a corporation (however, the transferor may recognize gain to prevent a negative basis in stock received in exchange for the property).

Pass Key

If the aggregate adjusted basis of property contributed to a corporation by each transferor/shareholder in a tax-free incorporation exceeds the aggregate fair market value of the property transferred, the corporation's basis in the property is limited to the aggregate fair market value of the property. (This prevents the transfer of property with *built-in losses* to the corporation.)

2.2 Shareholder Tax Consequences

The shareholder contributing property in exchange for corporation common stock has no gain or loss if the following two conditions of IRC Section 351 have been met:

1. **80 Percent Control:** Immediately after the transaction, those transferors/shareholders contributing property (control group) must own at least 80 percent of the voting stock and at least 80 percent of the nonvoting stock.

2. **No Receipt of Boot:** Transfer of property must be solely in exchange for stock.

2.2.1   Recognition of Gain From Boot Received

The following items represent boot (taxable) and will trigger gain recognition (limited to the lesser of the transferor/shareholder's realized gain or fair market value of boot received) by the transferor/shareholder:

- Cash withdrawn

- Receipt of debt securities (e.g., bonds)

2.2.2   Liabilities in Excess of Basis

The amount of liabilities assumed by the corporation that exceeds the adjusted basis of the total assets transferred to the corporation is not boot (per se) but does generate gain. The recognized gain increases stock basis to prevent negative basis.

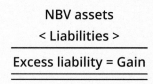

NBV assets

< Liabilities >

Excess liability = Gain

2.2.3   Shareholder's Basis of Common Stock

The shareholder's basis in common stock received from the corporation will be the total of:

- **Cash: Amount Contributed**

- **Property: Adjusted Basis (NBV)**

  - The adjusted basis of property is reduced by (1) cash and the fair market value of boot received by the shareholder, and (2) any debt on the property (e.g., COD) that is assumed by the corporation.

  - Gain is recognized by the shareholder because of boot received or contributed liabilities that are in excess of basis.

- **Services: Fair Market Value (Taxable)**

  - Ordinary income (taxable): The shareholder receiving common stock for services rendered must recognize the fair market value as ordinary income. (*Note:* A shareholder who contributes only services is not counted as part of the control group for purposes of the 80 percent control.)

Pass Key

Special Rule: Exception to General Rule

The general rule for taxable events and basis applies to corporations:

	Transactions		
Event		**Income**	**Basis**
Taxable	=	FMV =	FMV
Nontaxable	=	N-O-N-E =	NBV

Detailed Alternative Computation of Basis to Shareholder

Adjusted basis of transferred property (including cash)

+	FMV of services rendered
+	Gain recognized by shareholder
–	Cash received
–	Liabilities assumed by the corporation
–	FMV of nonmoney boot received
=	Basis of common stock

Illustration 1   Illustration of Liabilities in Excess of Basis

The ABC Company admits Tim as a one-third shareholder. Tim contributes a building that is worth $500,000 but has a basis of $100,000. There is a mortgage of $225,000 on the building, assumed by the corporation.

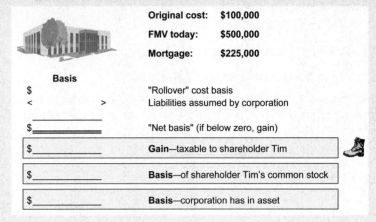

Original cost:	$100,000	
FMV today:	$500,000	
Mortgage:	$225,000	

Basis

$ _____   "Rollover" cost basis
<   > Liabilities assumed by corporation

$ _____   "Net basis" (if below zero, gain)

$ _____   **Gain**—taxable to shareholder Tim

$ _____   **Basis**—of shareholder Tim's common stock

$ _____   **Basis**—corporation has in asset

Illustration 2   Shareholder and Corporate Consequences at Formation

Olinto forms a corporation and contributes the following property:

	Adjusted Basis	Fair Market Value
Equipment	$ 40,000	$120,000
Building	20,000	40,000
Inventory	80,000	100,000
	$140,000	$260,000

Olinto receives 100 shares of stock:

1. Gain realized by Olinto

Amount realized	$260,000
Adjusted basis	(140,000)
Gain realized	$120,000

2. Gain recognized by Olinto   0

3. Olinto's stock basis

Old basis	$140,000
Less: boot	0
Add: recognized gain	0
New basis of stock	$140,000

4. Basis to corporation

Transferor's basis	$140,000
Add: gain recognized	0
Basis of assets	$140,000

Illustration 3   Corporation Formation With Contribution of Liability

Gearty forms a corporation and contributes property with a basis of $140,000 subject to a $60,000 mortgage, as shown below:

	Adjusted Basis	Fair Market Value
Assets with $60,000 mortgage	$140,000	$260,000

Gearty received 100 shares of stock with the following results:

1. Gain realized by Gearty

Amount realized	$260,000
Adjusted basis	(140,000)
Gain realized	$120,000

2. No gain recognized—no boot received/liabilities do not exceed basis.

3. Gearty's stock basis

Old basis	$140,000
Less: liability assumed by corporation	(60,000)
Add: recognized gain	0
New basis of stock	$ 80,000

4. Basis to corporation

Transferor's basis	$140,000
Add: gain recognized	0
Basis of assets	$140,000

Question 1	MCQ-04633

Which of the following forms of business can be formed with only one individual owning the business?

	Sole Proprietorship	Limited Liability Company	Partnership
a.	Yes	Yes	Yes
b.	Yes	Yes	No
c.	Yes	No	Yes
d.	No	No	No

Question 2   **MCQ-02030**

Lind and Post organized Ace Corp., which issued voting common stock with a fair market value of $120,000. They each transferred property in exchange for stock as follows:

	Property	Adjusted Basis	Fair Market Value	Percentage of Ace Stock Acquired
Lind	Building	$40,000	$82,000	60%
Post	Land	5,000	48,000	40%

The building was subject to a $10,000 mortgage that was assumed by Ace. What amount of gain did Lind recognize on the exchange?

    a. $0

    b. $10,000

    c. $42,000

    d. $52,000

1 Corporate Taxable Income

1.1 Gross Income

The concept of *gross income* is very similar for both corporations and individuals. The general rule is that income is recognized when received.

Formation

Operations

Taxation

Distributions

Liquidation

- Cash received in advance of accrual GAAP income is taxed, such as:

  - Interest income received in advance.

  - Rental income received in advance. (Nonrefundable rent deposits and lease cancellation payments are rental income when received.)

  - Royalty income received in advance.

- Some GAAP income items are not included in taxable income, such as:

  - Interest income from municipal or state obligations/bonds.

  - Certain proceeds from life insurance on the life of a corporate officer ("key person" policy) when the corporation is the beneficiary.

    —For life insurance contracts that were issued after August 17, 2006, limitations exist regarding the amount of proceeds that are excluded from income relating to company-owned life insurance (COLI) contracts, unless certain requirements are met. The general rule is that the portion of the proceeds that equals the previously paid premiums and other nondeductible amounts paid in is tax-free, and the balance is generally taxable.

- In contrast to individual taxpayers, corporate capital gains are taxed at the same rate as ordinary corporate income (i.e., no special capital gains rates apply).

1.2 Accrual Basis vs. Cash Basis

While the cash basis of accounting is used for tax purposes by most individuals, qualified personal service corporations (which are treated as individuals for purposes of these rules), and taxpayers whose average annual gross receipts do not exceed $25 million (for the prior three-year period), the accrual basis method of accounting for tax purposes is required for the following:

- The accounting for purchases and sales of inventory (and inventories must be maintained), provided the business has greater than $25 million of average annual gross receipts for the three-year period ending with the preceding tax year.

- Tax shelters.

- Certain farming corporations (other farming or tree-raising businesses may generally use the cash basis), provided the business has greater than $25 million of average annual gross receipts for the three-year period ending with the preceding tax year.

- C corporations, trusts with unrelated trade or business income, and partnerships having a C corporation as a partner, provided the business has greater than $25 million of average annual gross receipts for the three-year period ending with the preceding tax year.

1.3 Trade or Business Deductions (Ordinary and Necessary Expenses)

All of the ordinary and necessary expenses paid or incurred during the taxable year in carrying on a business are deductible. "Ordinary and necessary" means that the expenses are common (or accepted) in the particular business or profession and that they relate to the production of the current year's income.

Illustration 1   Trade or Business Deductions

Reasonable salaries, office rentals, office supplies, and traveling expenses are all deductible when incurred for business purposes.

1.3.1 Executive Compensation

A publicly held corporation may not deduct compensation expenses (whether or not performance-based) in excess of $1,000,000 paid to covered employees, which includes the CEO, CFO, and the three other most-highly compensated officers. Covered employees remain covered employees for all future years.

Entertainment expenses for officers, directors, and 10-percent-or-greater owners may be deducted only to the extent that they are included in the individual's gross income.

1.3.2 Bonus Accruals (Non-shareholder/Employees)

Bonuses paid by an accrual basis taxpayer are deductible in the tax year when all events have occurred that establish a liability with reasonable accuracy, and provided they are paid within 2.5 months of the taxpayer's year-end.

1.3.3 Bad Debts: Specific Charge-off Method

- **Accrual Basis**

  Accrual method taxpayers must use the specific charge-off method (direct write-off method) for tax purposes. Thus, most taxpayers will write off bad debts as they become worthless or partially worthless. (The allowance method is still required for financial accounting purposes, but it is not allowed for calculating the income tax deduction.)

- **Cash Basis**

  A very important point for purposes of the CPA Exam is to be aware of bad debts of cash basis taxpayers. Because a cash basis taxpayer has not included the amount in gross income, a bad debt is not deductible, except in the case of an uncollectible check that has been deposited and recorded as income.

1.3.4 Business Interest Expense

Most *interest* paid or accrued during the taxable year on indebtedness incurred for business purposes is deductible, although limitations may apply.

The deduction for business interest expense is limited to 30 percent of business income, excluding interest income, before depreciation and interest expense deductions. Disallowed business interest expense can be carried forward indefinitely. The limitation does not apply if the taxpayer's average annual gross receipts are less than $25 million for the prior three taxable years.

Prepaid interest expense must be allocated to the proper period to which it is related. Interest expense on debt incurred to purchase "tax-free" bonds is not deductible. Certain other types of interest are not deductible (beyond the scope of the exam).

1.3.5 Charitable Contributions (10 Percent of Adjusted Taxable Income Limitation)

Corporations making contributions to qualifying charitable organizations are allowed a maximum deduction of 10 percent of their taxable income, as defined below. Any disallowed charitable contribution may be carried forward for five years. Any accrual must be paid within 3.5 months of the taxable year-end to be deductible. Total taxable income for purposes of the charitable contributions limit is calculated before the deduction of:

▓ any charitable contribution deduction;

▓ the dividends-received deduction; or

▓ any capital loss carryback.

1.3.6 Business Losses or Casualty Losses Related to Business

Generally, any loss sustained during the taxable year and not compensated for by insurance or otherwise is deductible. The loss may be treated as an ordinary loss or a capital loss, depending upon the type of asset involved in the casualty. Business casualty losses are treated differently from losses by individuals in a federally declared disaster (discussed in R2).

▓ **Partially Destroyed**

For property only partially destroyed, the loss is limited to the lesser of:

• the decline in value of the property; or

• the adjusted basis of the property immediately before the casualty.

▓ **Fully Destroyed (NBV)**

For property that has been fully destroyed (i.e., a total loss), the amount of the loss is the adjusted basis of the property.

Example 1	Casualty Loss

1. **Facts:** Bad Luck Inc. had a major casualty loss in Year 1. A warehouse building was seriously damaged by a storm, and the federal government declared a major disaster for the area. The fair market value of the building before the storm was $850,000; the fair market value after the storm was $400,000. The adjusted basis of the property was $600,000. Insurance reimbursements amounted to $300,000.

   Required: Determine the amount of casualty loss that can be deducted for tax purposes.

   Solution: The amount of the casualty loss before insurance reimbursements is $450,000, which is the decline in value of the property and is less than the adjusted basis of the property. Subtracting the insurance reimbursement of $300,000, Bad Luck's deductible loss would be $150,000.

2. **Facts:** Assume the same facts above except that the property was totally destroyed.

   Required: Determine the amount of casualty loss that can be deducted for tax purposes.

   Solution: The deductible casualty loss would be $300,000 ($600,000 − $300,000). Note that the adjusted basis is used to determine the casualty loss, not the decline in value.

1.3.7 Organizational and Start-up Costs

▓ **Calculation**

A corporation may elect to deduct up to $5,000 of organizational costs and $5,000 of start-up costs. Each $5,000 amount is reduced by the amount by which the organizational or start-up costs exceed $50,000, respectively. Any excess organizational or start-up costs are amortized over 180 months (beginning with the month in which active trade or business begins).

■ **Included Costs**

Allowable organizational costs and start-up costs include fees paid for legal services in drafting the corporate charter, bylaws, minutes of organization meetings, fees paid for accounting services, and fees paid to the state of incorporation.

■ **Excluded Costs**

The costs do not include costs of issuing and selling the stock, commissions, underwriter's fees, and costs incurred in the transfer of assets to a corporation.

Pass Key

It is important for CPA candidates to remember the difference in the GAAP (financial statement) and the tax (income tax return) rule for organizational and start-up costs.

Organizational and Start-up Costs

- Tax rule: $5,000 expense maximum/180 months amortization of remainder

- GAAP rule: Expense

Example 2 — Organizational Costs

Facts: Kristi, a newly organized corporation, was formed on June 30, Year 1, and began doing business on July 1, Year 1. The corporation will have a December 31 year-end. Kristi Co. incurred the following expenses in organizing the business:

Legal fees for drafting corporate charter	$15,000
Fees paid for accounting services	5,000
Fees paid to state of incorporation	3,000
Costs of selling shares of stock	10,000
	$33,000

Required: Determine the deduction for organizational costs in Year 1.

Solution: Amortization for the six months (July 1 to December 31, Year 1) will be $5,600, calculated as follows:

Legal fees for corporate charter	$15,000
Accounting fees	5,000
Fees paid to state	3,000
Organization expenses	$23,000

$23,000

<u><5,000></u> ⟶ $5,000

$18,000   ÷ 180 mo. = $100 per mo. × 6 mo. =   600

$5,600

The deduction for organizational costs in Year 1 is $5,600. The cost of selling the shares may not be amortized; it is a reduction in the capital stock account.

1.3.8 Amortization, Depreciation, and Depletion

Goodwill, covenants not-to-compete, franchises, trademarks, and trade names must be amortized on a straight-line basis over a 15-year period beginning with the month such intangible was acquired. For depreciation and depletion, corporations use the rules covered in R3.

Pass Key

The CPA Examination often tests the candidate's ability to distinguish the GAAP (financial statements) and tax (income tax returns) rules. The difference in the treatment of purchased goodwill (years 2002 and forward) should be noted:

Purchased Goodwill

- Tax rule: Amortized on a straight-line basis over 15 years

- GAAP rule: Not amortized; test for impairment

1.3.9 Life Insurance Premiums (Expense)

- **Corporation Named as Beneficiary—Corporation Owns the Policy (Key Person):** Premiums paid by the corporation for life insurance policies on key employees are not deductible when the corporation is directly or indirectly the beneficiary.

- **Insured Employee Named as Beneficiary—Employee Owns the Policy (Fringe Benefit):** If the premiums are paid on insurance policies where the beneficiary is named by the insured employee, such premiums are deductible by the corporation as an employee benefit.

1.3.10 Business Gifts

Business gifts are deductible up to a maximum deduction of $25 per recipient per year.

1.3.11 Business Meals

Business meals are 50 percent deductible to the corporation. This includes employee travel meals, meals provided as a de minimis fringe benefit, and meals provided for the convenience of the employer.

1.3.12 Business Entertainment Expenses Not Deductible

Business entertainment expenses are not deductible.

1.3.13 Penalties and Illegal Activities Not Deductible

Bribes, kickbacks, fines, penalties, and other payments that are illegal under federal law or under a generally enforced state law are not deductible. Similarly, the top two thirds of a treble damage payment are not deductible if the taxpayer has been convicted of an antitrust violation.

1.3.14 Payments Made Related to Sexual Harassment or Sexual Abuse

Any settlement, payment, or related attorney fees related to sexual harassment or sexual abuse are not deductible if the settlement or payment is subject to a nondisclosure agreement.

1.3.15 Taxes

All state and local taxes and federal payroll taxes are deductible when incurred on property or income relating to business. Federal income taxes are not deductible. Foreign income taxes may be used as a credit.

1.3.16 Lobbying and Political Expenditures

Lobbying expenses incurred in attempting to influence local, state, or federal legislation are not deductible. Political contributions are not deductible.

1.3.17 Capital Loss Deduction Not Allowed

The $3,000 deduction for net capital losses available to individuals is not allowed to corporations. Thus, a corporation can only use capital losses to offset capital gains. Excess capital losses may be carried back three years or carried forward five years. (Details on the tax treatment of capital losses are covered in R3.)

1.3.18 Inventory Valuation Methods

In general, the tax method used for accounting purposes can be used for income tax purposes; provided the method clearly reflects income and is consistent in application (i.e., opening and closing inventories must use the same valuation method). Furthermore, all taxpayers who have inventory are required to use the accrual basis of accounting for purchases and sales unless the taxpayer has average annual gross receipts of $25 million or less during the three preceding years. A change in inventory method is considered a change in accounting method and must be approved by the IRS.

- **Basic Valuation Methods**

    - **Cost Method:** Inventories are valued at cost (including direct labor, direct materials, and attributable indirect costs), less discounts, plus freight-in. The cost methods of "prime cost" (no overhead) and "direct cost" (which includes variable overhead only) are not allowable for tax purposes.

    - **Lower of Cost or Market Method:** Inventories are valued at the lower of cost (per above) or market, which for normal goods is generally the current bid price at the date of inventory for each item in inventory (i.e., the lower amount is determined based on each item, not on the aggregate value of the inventory).

    - **Rolling-Average Method:** This method will generally not be allowed when inventories are held for long periods of time or when costs tend to fluctuate significantly (unless the taxpayer regularly recomputes costs and makes certain adjustments), as the method may not clearly reflect income in certain cases.

    - **Retail Method:** In general, the retail method will approximate the cost or the market of items in inventory by subtracting the mark-up percentage to retail from the retail price, typically from inventory that has a large volume of items.

- **Common Inventory Identification Methods (Cost-Flow Assumptions)**

    - **FIFO (First In, First Out) Method:** FIFO is the most commonly used method, unless the inventory can be specifically identified.

    - **LIFO (Last In, First Out) Method:** LIFO must be elected by the taxpayer in the first year it is used, and the taxpayer must use the same method for its financial statement purposes. Significant adjustments to inventory valuations may be required to use LIFO.

    - **Specific Identification Method**

Uniform Capitalization Rules Impact

IRC Section 263A details the uniform capitalization rules that require certain costs normally expensed be capitalized as part of inventory for tax purposes. This may cause the corporation to make an M-1/M-3 adjustment on their tax return to conform to the rules. Certain methods of accounting for inventory (such as the strict cost method) do not provide for the capitalization of the inventory costs that are required by the uniform capitalization rules. Thus, taxpayers who are subject to the uniform capitalization rules may not use certain valuation methods. Taxpayers with average annual gross receipts of $25 million or less during the three preceding years are not subject to the uniform capitalization rules and may treat these costs as supplies.

Unsalable or Unusable Goods

When inventories are deemed to be unsalable or unusable, they must be valued at their expected selling price ("bona fide selling price") within 30 days less the costs to dispose of them.

1.4   Dividends-Received Deduction

Domestic corporations are allowed a *dividends-received deduction* based on qualified dividend income. The purpose of this deduction is to prevent triple taxation of earnings (as illustrated in the diagram below). The amount of the dividends-received deduction allowed depends on the percentage of the investee corporation owned by the investor corporation. The percentage allowed may be either 50, 65, or 100 percent. The corporate shareholder must own the investee stock for at least 46 days during the 91-day period beginning on the date 45 days before the ex-dividend date of the stock to qualify for the dividends-received deduction. Below is the percentage deductions based upon stock ownership:

Percentage Ownership	Dividends-Received Deduction
0% to < 20%	50%
20% to < 80%	65%
80% or more	100%

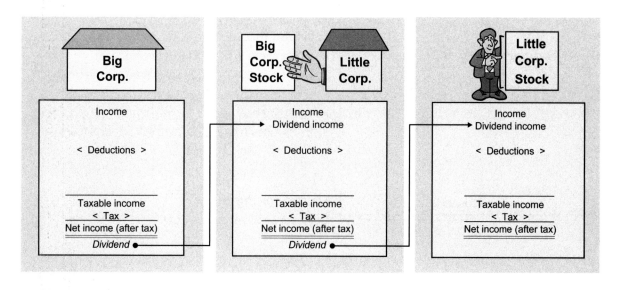

1.4.1   Taxable Income Limitation

The *dividends-received deduction* (DRD) equals the lesser of:

- 50 percent (or 65 percent) dividends received; or
- 50 percent (or 65 percent) of taxable income computed without regard to the DRD, any NOL carryforward, or any capital loss carryback.

1.4.2   Exception to Taxable Income Limitation

The *taxable income limitation* above does not apply if taking the full dividends-received deduction results in a net operating loss (NOL). See Illustration 2.

1.4.3   Summary of Corporate Taxable Income Limitations

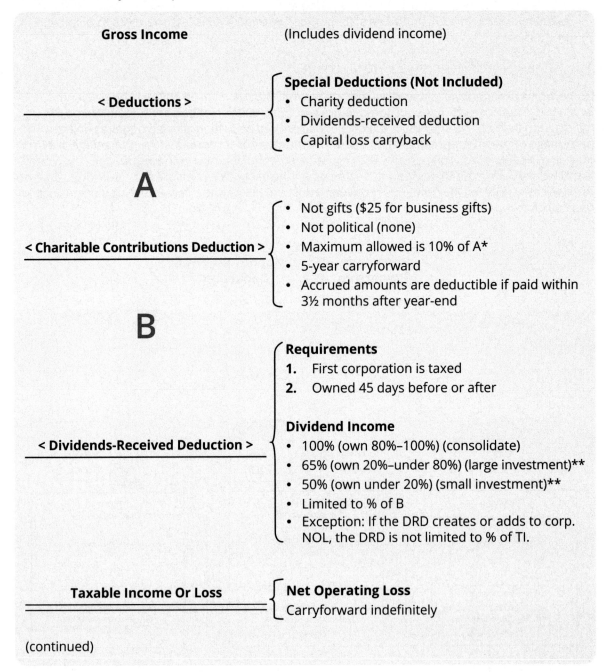

Gross Income   (Includes dividend income)

< Deductions >

Special Deductions (Not Included)
- Charity deduction
- Dividends-received deduction
- Capital loss carryback

A

< Charitable Contributions Deduction >
- Not gifts ($25 for business gifts)
- Not political (none)
- Maximum allowed is 10% of A*
- 5-year carryforward
- Accrued amounts are deductible if paid within 3½ months after year-end

B

< Dividends-Received Deduction >

Requirements
1. First corporation is taxed
2. Owned 45 days before or after

Dividend Income
- 100% (own 80%–100%) (consolidate)
- 65% (own 20%–under 80%) (large investment)**
- 50% (own under 20%) (small investment)**
- Limited to % of B
- Exception: If the DRD creates or adds to corp. NOL, the DRD is not limited to % of TI.

Taxable Income Or Loss

Net Operating Loss
Carryforward indefinitely

(continued)

*The chart indicates that the corporate charitable deduction is limited to 10 percent of "A." "A" is defined here as gross income minus deductions, with the "special deduction" not included. This is the same definition as that presented earlier in this module; the material is simply shown differently.

**The 50 percent and 65 percent deductions operate exactly the same except, of course, for the percentage differences.

Illustration 2   Dividends-Received Deduction

The Duffy Corp. owns 30 percent of the Fox Corp. (so the 65 percent dividends-received deduction, or DRD, applies). Below are alternative situations for the year. The dividends-received deduction and taxable income would be calculated as follows:

	Scenario 1	Scenario 2	Scenario 3
Gross Income			
Operating revenue	250	250	250
Dividend income	100	100	100
Total revenue	350	350	350
Less: deductions			
Total deductions, including charitable contributions	(200)	(260)	(290)
Taxable Income (TI) before DRD	150	90	60
Tentative DRD (65% × $100)	65	65	65
Limitation (65% of TI before DRD)	98	59	39
DRD	(65)	(59)*	(65)**
Taxable income	85	31	(5)

---

*Limited to lesser of 65 percent of dividends received ($100) or TI before DRD ($90) and no NOL created.

**When subtracting the full 65 percent DRD, an NOL is created, thus 65 percent of TI before DRD limitation does not apply.

1.4.4   Entities Not Eligible for the DRD

The dividends-received deduction is not available to:

- personal service corporations;
- personal holding companies; or
- (personally taxed) S corporations.

Pass Key

An easy way to remember the entities not eligible for the dividends-received deduction:

Don't take it *personally*. In addition, the DRD does not apply to dividends received from certain banks and savings institutions, RICs, REITs, public utilities, tax exempt corporations, cooperatives, or DISCs.

1.4.5 100 Percent Dividends-Received Deduction

- **Affiliated Corporations—100 Percent:** Dividends from affiliated corporations (80 percent or more common ownership) that file consolidated returns qualify for a 100 percent deduction.

- **Small Business Investment Corporations (SBICs)—100 Percent:** A 100 percent deduction is allowed for dividends received by a small business investment company. An SBIC makes equity and long-term credit available to small business concerns.

Pass Key

Don't forget the DRD percentages.

- Ownership 0% to < 20%; DRD is 50%
- Ownership 20% to < 80%; DRD is 65%
- Ownership 80% or more 100%; DRD is 100%

Question 1	MCQ-02047

In Year 1, Best Corp., an accrual basis calendar year C corporation, received $100,000 in dividend income from the common stock that it held in an unrelated domestic corporation. The stock was not debt financed and was held for over a year. Best recorded the following information for Year 1:

Loss from Best's operations	$(10,000)
Dividends received	100,000
Taxable income (before dividends-received deduction)	90,000

Best's dividends-received deduction on its Year 1 tax return was:

- **a.** $100,000
- **b.** $65,000
- **c.** $50,000
- **d.** $45,000

1 Book Income vs. Taxable Income

Differences between net income per a company's financial statements and taxable income reported on a tax return exist because of the difference between GAAP and tax law. The following chart illustrates book (or financial statement) income versus taxable income.

Formation

Operations

Taxation

Distributions

Liquidation

		Financial Statement	**Tax Return**
		Income	
		< Expense >	
Income from continuing operations before taxes		NIBT*	Gross income
		< Tax >	
		NIAT**	
Discontinued operations, net of tax	Income < expense > − Tax = NIBT	NIAT	< Deductions >
			A
			< Charity >
			B
Accounting adjustment and changes, net of tax (to retained earnings)		Net income ← M-1/M-3 Reconcile →	< Div. rec. ded. > Taxable income

  *NIBT = Net income before tax

**NIAT = Net income after tax

(*Note:* Schedule M-1 does not distinguish between temporary and permanent differences. Part II of Schedule M-3 does, however.

2 Temporary vs. Permanent Differences

- Temporary differences are items of income or expense that are recognized in one period for book but in a different period for tax. These cause timing differences between the two incomes but, in the long run, there is no difference between book and tax.

- Permanent differences are items of income or expense that are recognized for book but never recognized for tax, or vice versa. These cause permanent differences between book and taxable income.

For example, depreciation is typically calculated using a straight-line method for books but an accelerated method for tax. The difference between these two methods will create a difference in depreciation expense from year to year, but ultimately will result in the same total deduction for both book and tax. This is a temporary difference. An example of a permanent difference is municipal bond interest income, which is recognized as income for books but is always excluded for tax. This difference will never reverse.

Example 1	Temporary vs. Permanent Differences

Facts: Barnette Corporation recorded book income of $560,000 for Year 6, which included the following items of income and expense:

Straight-line depreciation expense	$8,000
Municipal bond interest	4,000

Accelerated depreciation for the year per MACRS is $12,000. In addition, royalty income of $17,000 was received in advance of being earned and appropriately not recorded for books.

Required: Reconcile book income to taxable income.

Solution:

Temporary book/tax differences

Royalty income per tax (when received)	$ 17,000	
Royalty income per book (when earned)	0	
Difference		17,000
MACRS depreciation expense (per tax)	(12,000)	
Straight-line depreciation expense (per books)	(8,000)	
Difference		(4,000)
Total temporary differences		$13,000

Permanent book/tax differences

Municipal bond interest recognized for tax	$ 0	
Municipal bond interest recognized for book	4,000	
Difference		(4,000)
Total permanent differences		$(4,000)

Reconciliation of book income to taxable income

Book income	$560,000
Income for tax but not book	17,000
Income for book but not tax	(4,000)
Deduction for tax but not book	(4,000)
Taxable income	$569,000

3 Schedules M-1 and M-3

The IRS requires that a company reconcile book/tax differences on either Schedule M-1 or Schedule M-3 (this determination is made based on the total assets of the company).

▓ Schedule M-1 does not distinguish between temporary and permanent differences.

▓ If the total assets of the company are $10 million or greater, the company is required to reconcile book and taxable income (loss) on Schedule M-3.

▓ The M-3 breaks out items of book income/expense in more detail, and distinguishes between temporary and permanent differences.

Illustration 1   Schedule M-1

**Schedule M-1
Reconciliation of Income (Loss) per Books to Taxable Income**

1	Net income (or loss) per books	$ 875,000
2	+ Federal income tax (per books)	384,500
3	+ Excess capital losses over gains	5,000
4	+ Income subject to tax not recorded on books this year:	
	+ Installment sale income	8,500
	+ Rents received in advance	15,000
5	+ Expenses recorded on books this year not on the tax return:	
	+ Book depreciation	14,000
	+ Meals in excess of 50% allowance	4,200
	+ Allowance for doubtful accounts (increase)	15,000
	+ Warranty accrual	8,500
	+ Goodwill impairment per books	5,000
	+ Pension expense accrued	12,000
	+ Penalties	1,000
6	Add lines 1 through 5	$1,347,700

(continued)

(continued)

7	– Income recorded on books this year not included on this return:		
	– Tax-exempt interest	$	3,500
	– Life insurance proceeds		100,000
8	– Deductions on this return not charged against book income this year:		
	– Tax depreciation		28,000
	– Contribution carryover		0
	– Section 179 deduction		20,000
	– Direct bad debt write-offs		8,650
	– Actual warranty costs		7,500
	– Amortization of organizational cost		500
	– Goodwill amortization per return		9,200
	– Pensions paid		11,350
9	Add lines 7 and 8	$	188,700
10	Taxable income (line 28 page 1 of Form 1120) line 6 minus line 9		$1,159,000

This is taxable income per page 1 of the tax return, before the dividends-received deduction and the NOL carryforward deduction.

3.1 Corporation Tax Summary

The following chart lists common items of income/expense on an income statement and tax return, indicating which items will result in a book/tax difference.

Corporation Tax Summary	GAAP: Financial Statements	IRC: Tax Return	Temp.	Perm.	None
Gross Income					
Gross sales	Income	Income			✓
Installment sales	Income	Income when received	✓		
Rents and royalties in advance	Income when earned	Income when received	✓		
State tax refund	Income	Income			✓
Dividends: equity method 100/65/50% exclusion	Income is subsidiary's earnings No exclusion	Income is dividends-received Excluded forever	✓	✓	
Items Not Includable in "Taxable Income"					
State and municipal bond interest	Income	Not taxable income		✓	
Life insurance proceeds	Income	Generally not taxable income		✓	
Gain/loss on treasury stock	Not reported	Not reported			✓
Ordinary Expenses					
Cost of goods sold	Currently expensed	Uniform capitalization rules			✓
Officers' compensation (top)	Expense	$1,000,000 limit			✓
Bad debt	Allowance (estimated)	Direct write-off	✓		
Estimated liability for contingency (e.g., warranty)	Expense (accrue estimated)	No deduction until paid	✓		
Interest expense: business loan	Expense	Deduct			✓
Tax-free investment	Expense	Not deductible		✓	
Contributions	All expensed	Limited to 10% of adjusted taxable income	✓	✓	✓
Loss on abandonment/casualty	Expense	Deduct			✓
Loss on worthless subsidiary	Expense	Deduct			✓
Depreciation: MACRS vs. straight-line	Slow depreciation	Fast depreciation	✓		
Section 179 depreciation	Not allowed (must depreciate)	2019 = $1,020,000	✓		
Different basis of asset	Use GAAP basis	Use tax basis		✓	
Amortization: start-up/ organizational expenses	Expense	$5,000 maximum/15 year excess	✓		
Franchise	Amortize	Amortize over 15 years	✓		
Goodwill	Impairment test	Amortize over 15 years	✓		
Depletion: percentage vs. straight-line (cost)	Cost over years	Percentage of sales	✓		
Percentage in excess of cost	Not allowed	Percentage of sales		✓	
Profit sharing and pension expense	Expense accrued	No deduction until paid	✓		
Accrued expense (50% owner/family)	Expense accrued	No deduction until paid	✓		
State taxes (paid)	Expense	Deduct			✓
Meals	Expense	Generally 50% deductible		✓	
GAAP Expense Items That Are Not Tax Deductions					
Life insurance expense (corporation)	Expense	Not deductible		✓	
Penalties	Expense	Not deductible		✓	
Entertainment	Expense	Not deductible		✓	
Lobbying/political expense	Expense	Not deductible		✓	
Federal income taxes	Expense	Not deductible		✓	
Special Items					
Net capital gain	Income	Income			✓
Net capital loss	Report as loss	Not deductible	✓		
Carryback/carryover (3 years back/5 years forward)	Not applicable	Unused loss allowed as a STCL	✓		
Related shareholder	Report as a loss	Not deductible		✓	
Net operating loss	Report as a loss	Carryover indefinitely	✓		
Research and development	Expense	Expense/amortize/capitalize	✓	✓	✓

Question 1
MCQ-02039

In Year 1, Starke Corp., an accrual basis calendar year corporation, reported book income of $380,000. Included in that amount was $50,000 municipal bond interest income, $170,000 for federal income tax expense, and $2,000 interest expense on the debt incurred to carry the municipal bonds. What amount should Starke's taxable income be as reconciled on Starke's Schedule M-1 of Form 1120, U.S. Corporation Income Tax Return?

    a. $330,000

    b. $500,000

    c. $502,000

    d. $550,000

Question 2
MCQ-02243

Would the following expense items be reported on Schedule M-1 of the corporation income tax return showing the reconciliation of income per books with income per return?

	Interest Incurred on Loan to Carry U.S. Obligations	Provision for State Corporation Income Tax
a.	Yes	Yes
b.	No	No
c.	Yes	No
d.	No	Yes

Question 3
MCQ-05301

Which of the following items should be included on Schedule M-1, Reconciliation of Income (Loss) per Books With Income per Return, of Form 1120, U.S. Corporation Income Tax Return, to reconcile book income to taxable income?

    a. Cash distributions to shareholders.

    b. Premiums paid on key-person life insurance policy.

    c. Corporate bond interest.

    d. Ending balance of retained earnings.

1 Taxation of a C Corporation

1.1 Filing Requirements

A C corporation is required to file a U.S. Corporation Income Tax Return, Form 1120, by the 15th day of the fourth month after the close of its tax year (for a December 31 corporation, the return is due by April 15). For C corporations with fiscal years ending on June 30, the new due dates will apply for tax years beginning after 12/31/25. Until then, the tax return is due by the 15th day of the third month after the close of the tax year.

| Formation |
| Operations |
| **Taxation** |
| Distributions |
| Liquidation |

1.1.1 Legal Holiday or Weekend

When the due date falls on a legal holiday or weekend, the tax return is due on the next business day.

1.1.2 Extension (Form 7004)

An extension of six months is available by filing Form 7004. C corporations with a June 30 year-end have a seven-month extension.

1.2 Estimated Payments of Corporate Tax

Corporations are required to pay estimated taxes on the 15th day of the fourth, sixth, ninth, and 12th months of their tax year. One-fourth of the estimated tax is due with each payment. Unequal quarterly payments may be made using the annualized income method. An underpayment penalty will be assessed if these payments are not made on a timely basis and the amount owed on the return is $500 or more.

1.2.1 Corporations Other Than Large Corporations

Corporations not classified as large corporations are required to pay the lesser of:

- 100 percent of the tax shown on the return for the current year; or
- 100 percent of the tax shown on the return for the preceding year.

Note: This alternative cannot be used if the corporation owed no tax for the preceding year or the preceding tax year was less than 12 months.

1.2.2 Large Corporations

A large corporation (a corporation for which taxable income was $1 million or more in any of its three preceding tax years) must pay 100 percent of the tax as shown on the current year return.

1.3 Flat Tax Rate and Taxable Income

The taxable income of a corporation is arrived at by taking gross income (basically the same items that would be included in an individual's gross income) and deducting the same business expenses that an individual would deduct. A corporation's taxable income is subject to a flat tax of 21 percent. Personal service corporations are also subject to a flat tax of 21 percent.

Regular tax
Accumulated earnings tax
Personal holding company tax

1.4 Tax Credits

1.4.1 General Business Credit

■ **Included Credits**

The general business credit consists of a combination of any of the following:

- Investment credit
- Work opportunity credit (currently extended through December 31, 2019)
- Alcohol fuels credit
- Research and development tax credit (generally 20 percent of the increase in qualified research expenditures over the base amount for the year)
- Low-income housing credit;
- Small employer pension plan start-up costs credit
- Alternative motor vehicle credit
- Other infrequent credits

■ **Formula**

The credit may not exceed "net income tax" (regular tax less nonrefundable tax credits, other than the alternative minimum tax credit) less 25 percent of net regular tax liability above $25,000.

■ **Unused Credit Carryover**

Although some limits must be applied separately, unused credits may generally be carried back one year and forward 20 years.

1.4.2 Research and Development Tax Credit (Part of General Business Credit)

■ The research and development (R&D) tax credit is designed to stimulate research and development activity of U.S. companies by reducing their after-tax cost.

■ The credit is generally calculated as 20 percent of the increase in qualified research expenditures over a defined base amount.

■ The research tax credit can also be calculated using the alternative simplified credit.

■ The R&D tax credit is first computed separately and then is subject to the limitations of the general business credit because it is a component of the general business credit.

■ "Qualified small businesses," defined as businesses with less than $5 million in annual gross receipts and having gross receipts for no more than five years, are able to use the R&D tax credit to offset the FICA employer portion of payroll tax. The amount of credit that can be used to offset payroll tax is capped at $250,000 for each eligible year.

1.4.3 Foreign Tax Credit

■ Domestic corporations that have paid or accrued qualified foreign income taxes to a foreign country or U.S. possession may generally credit those taxes against their U.S. income tax liability on foreign source income.

■ A corporation may choose annually to take either a credit or a deduction for eligible foreign taxes paid or accrued. Generally, if a corporation elects the benefits of the foreign tax credit for any tax year, no portion of the foreign taxes will be allowed as a deduction in that year or any subsequent tax year.

■ The goal of the foreign tax credit is to keep a U.S. taxpayer's worldwide effective tax rate from exceeding the U.S. statutory tax rate, which is accomplished through the foreign tax credit limitation.

■ The foreign tax credit is calculated as follows:

- **Step 1:** Determine the qualified foreign income taxes paid or accrued for the tax year. To be eligible for the credit, the foreign levy must predominantly have the nature of an income tax in the U.S. sense (taxes on wages, interest, dividends, and royalties generally qualify).

- **Step 2:** Compute the foreign tax credit limitation. This is done by multiplying the amount of pre-credit U.S. tax paid in a year by the ratio of foreign source taxable income earned to income earned from both foreign and domestic sources (worldwide taxable income).

- **Step 3:** Determine the lesser of qualified foreign taxes paid (step 1) or the foreign tax credit limitation (step 2).

■ Any unused foreign tax credits can be carried back for one year and then carried forward for 10 years.

Example 1 ▸ Foreign Tax Credit

Facts: Rowe Co., a domestic corporation, has $20 million of worldwide taxable income, including $5 million of income from foreign sources. Rowe Co. paid $2.5 million of qualified foreign taxes during the year. Assume that the U.S. tax rate is 35 percent.

Required: Determine the amount of foreign tax credit for Rowe Co.

Solution:

Step 1 (Qualified foreign taxes): $2.5 million

Step 2 (Foreign tax credit limitation): U.S. tax liability is $20 million × 35% = $7 million
  Ratio of foreign source/total taxable income is $5 million / $20 million = 25%
  Foreign tax credit limitation is $7 million × 25% = $1.75 million

Step 3 (Lesser of steps 1 and 2): $1.75 million

Rowe Co. can carry its excess unused credits ($2.5 million – $1.75 million = $750,000) back one year and forward 10 years.

1.4.4 Minimum Tax Credit

For tax years beginning after December 31, 2017, a corporation may reduce its regular tax liability (after other allowable nonrefundable credits) by its minimum tax credit (MTC) carryforward. If a corporation's MTC carryforward exceeds its regular tax (after other allowable nonrefundable credits), then the corporation is eligible for a refundable MTC.

The credit may not exceed the regular tax liability (after other allowable nonrefundable credits) plus the refundable MTC.

For tax years beginning after 2017 and before 2022, the refundable MTC is 50 percent (100 percent for tax years beginning in 2021) of the corporation's unused MTC carryforward in excess of regular tax (after other allowable nonrefundable credits) for that year.

1.5 Accumulated Earnings Tax

Regular tax
Accumulated earnings tax
Personal holding company tax

- The accumulated earnings tax is a penalty tax imposed on regular C corporations whose accumulated (retained) earnings are in excess of $250,000 if the earnings are considered to be improperly retained instead of being distributed as dividends to (high tax bracket) shareholders. The accumulated earnings tax is only paid when the IRS assesses the tax because, during an audit, it concluded that insufficient dividends were paid out compared with the amount of earnings accumulated by the corporation.

  - Regular C corporations are entitled to $250,000 of (lifetime) accumulated earnings.

  - Personal service corporations are entitled to only $150,000 of (lifetime) accumulated earnings.

  - The accumulated earnings tax is not imposed on personal holding companies (PHCs), tax-exempt corporations, or passive foreign investment corporations.

- The additional tax rate for accumulated earnings is a flat 20 percent.

- To avoid accumulation of earnings being considered unreasonable by the IRS, there must be:

  - a demonstrated specific, definite, and feasible plan for the use of accumulated earnings (reasonable needs); or

  - a need to redeem the corporate stock included in a deceased stockholder's gross estate.

- Just because the stock is widely held does not exempt it from the accumulated earnings tax. The accumulated earnings tax is not self-assessed by the corporation; it is IRS-assessed as a result of an IRS audit of the corporation.

- A dividend paid by the due date of the tax return or hypothetical "consent" dividends may reduce or eliminate the tax.

■ Calculation:

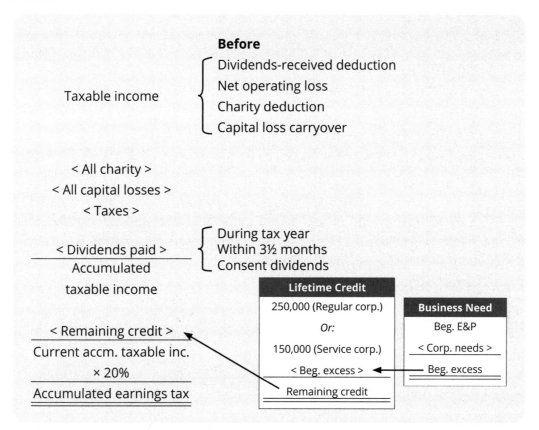

1.6 Personal Holding Company Tax

Regular tax
Accumulated earnings tax
Personal holding company tax

Personal holding companies (PHCs) are really corporations set up by high tax bracket taxpayers to channel their investment income into a corporation and shelter that income through the lower regular tax rate (21 percent) of the corporation, instead of paying their higher individual tax rates on that income.

■ **Definition of Personal Holding Company:** The tax law criteria define personal holding companies as corporations more than 50 percent owned by five or fewer individuals (either directly or indirectly at any time during the last half of the tax year) and having 60 percent of adjusted ordinary gross income consisting of:

- **Net** rent (if less than 50 percent of ordinary gross income);

- **Interest** that is taxable (nontaxable is excluded);

- **Royalties** (but not mineral, oil, gas, or copyright royalties); or

- **Dividends** from an unrelated domestic corporation.

- **Additional Tax Assessed:** Corporations deemed to be personal holding companies are taxed an additional 20 percent on personal holding company net income not distributed.

  - Taxable income must be reduced by federal income taxes and net long-term capital gain (net of tax) to determine the undistributed personal holding company income prior to the dividend paid deduction.

  - There is no penalty if net income is distributed (i.e., in the form of actual dividends or consent dividends).

  - PHCs are not subject to the accumulated earnings tax.

- **Self-Assessed Tax:** The tax is self-assessed by filing a separate Schedule 1120 PH along with Form 1120.

Question 1	MCQ-02117

Which of the following credits is a combination of several tax credits to provide uniform rules for the current and carryback-carryover years?

   a. General business credit

   b. Foreign tax credit

   c. Minimum tax credit

   d. Enhanced oil recovery credit

Question 2	MCQ-02068

The accumulated earnings tax can be imposed:

   a. On both partnerships and corporations.

   b. On companies that make distributions in excess of accumulated earnings.

   c. On personal holding companies.

   d. Regardless of the number of stockholders in a corporation.

1 Filing a Consolidated Tax Return

1.1 Overview of Filing a Consolidated Return

Filing a consolidated return is a privilege afforded to affiliated groups of corporations, and it can only be filed if all of the affiliated corporations consent to such a filing. Not all corporations are allowed the privilege of filing a consolidated return. Examples of those *denied* the privilege include S corporations, foreign corporations, most real estate investment trusts (REITs), some insurance companies, and most exempt organizations.

1.2 Initial Requirements

To be entitled to file a consolidated return, all the corporations in the group must meet the following requirements:

1. Be members of an affiliated group at some time during the tax year; and

2. Each member of the group must file a consent on Form 1122 (Authorization and Consent of Subsidiary Corporation to Be Included in a Consolidated Income Tax Return).

- Note that the act of filing a consolidated tax return by all the affiliated corporations will satisfy the consent requirement.

- The election to consolidate (which includes filing the consolidated tax return and attaching Form 1122) must be made no later than the extended due date of the parent corporation's tax return for the year.

1.3 Affiliated Group Defined

An affiliated group means that a common parent directly owns:

- 80 percent or more of the voting power of all outstanding stock; and

- 80 percent or more of the value of all outstanding stock of each corporation.

1.4 Brother-Sister Corporations

Corporations in which an individual (not a corporation) owns 80 percent or more of the stock of two or more corporations may not file consolidated returns.

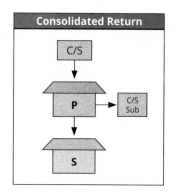
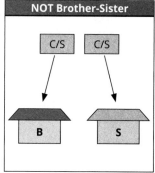

1.5   Advantages of Filing a Consolidated Return

Among the advantages of filing a consolidated return are:

- Capital losses of one corporation offset capital gains of another corporation.

- Operating losses of one corporation offset the operating profits of another corporation.

- Dividends received are 100 percent eliminated in consolidation because they are intercompany dividends.

- Certain tax deductions and tax credits may be better utilized when subject to the limitations of the overall consolidated group rather than individual members.

- A corporation's NOL carryover may be applied against the income of the consolidated group.

- Income from certain intercompany sales may be deferred.

1.6   Disadvantages of Filing a Consolidated Return

The disadvantages of filing a consolidated return include:

- Mandatory compliance with complex regulations.

- In the initial consolidated tax return year, a double counting of inventory can occur if group members had intercompany transactions.

- Losses from certain intercompany transactions may be deferred.

- Each member of the group must change its tax year to the same year as the parent corporation. A corporation joining the consolidated group may have to file a short year tax return in addition to its inclusion in the consolidated filing in the same tax year when adopting the parent corporation's tax year.

- Tax credits may be limited by operating losses of other members.

- The election to file consolidated returns is binding for future years and may only be terminated by disbanding the group or seeking permission of the Internal Revenue Service.

- Many states do not allow for the filing of consolidated tax returns, thus companies discover that they file consolidated for federal income tax purposes but must file as a separate company for state income tax purposes resulting in additional tax preparation time and expense.

Illustration 1   Eligibility to File Consolidated

1. Olinto, an individual, owns 100 percent of both corporations A and B. There is no common ownership between corporations A and B. Corporations A and B would not qualify to file consolidated returns since neither corporation is 80 percent or more owned by another corporation.

2. Corporation A owns 100 percent of corporations B and C. Corporations B and C own 60 percent and 40 percent of Corporation D respectively. A, B, C, and D could file consolidated returns. Corporation A would be considered the common parent.

1.7   Consolidated Taxable Income Calculation

Consolidated taxable income is determined using the following steps:

1. Calculate the stand-alone taxable income of each member of the group, as if the member were filing its own separate tax return.

2. Adjustments are made to each member's taxable income to remove the effects of transactions between members of the consolidated group. These include adjustments for the following:

   - Gains and losses that are deferred on intercompany sales between group members. In the year the asset is sold outside the group, a subsequent adjustment will need to be made.

   - Inventory adjustments may be required for intercompany sales.

   - Dividends received by one member from another member are excluded.

3. Gains, losses, and deductions that are required to be determined at the consolidated level are removed from each member's taxable income. This includes the following:

   - Capital gains and losses

   - Section 1231 gains and losses

   - Net operating loss (NOL)

   - Charitable contribution deduction

   - Dividends-received deduction

4. Each member's resulting taxable income from the previous steps is combined to create the group's combined taxable income.

5. The group's combined taxable income is then adjusted for the items that are required to be determined at the consolidated level (see items from step 3).

Illustration 2   Calculation of Consolidated Taxable Income

A, B, and C corporations file a consolidated tax return for Year 6. (B and C Corporations are wholly owned subsidiaries of A Corporation). Consolidated taxable income is determined as follows (see chart below):

Step 1: Calculate each member's taxable income.

Step 2: Make adjustments to eliminate intercompany transactions.

During the year, the group had the following intercompany activity that requires adjustments:

- B and C paid dividends to A of $60,000 and $30,000, respectively.

- B sold inventory to A and recorded a $50,000 intercompany profit, which needs to be excluded from B's gross receipts and deferred (until the inventory is sold to an outside party).

- C sold a piece of equipment to B and recorded a $10,000 Section 1231 gain on sale.

(continued)

(continued)

Step 3: Remove the gains, losses, and deductions that should be determined at the consolidated level.

- C's charitable contributions deduction: During the year, C paid $40,000 in contributions but was limited to $30,500 at the stand-alone level (10 percent of C's taxable income before the contributions deduction and other special deductions).

- A's dividends-received deduction: $90,000 of dividends received from B and C at 100 percent deduction; $110,000 from 30 percent owned domestic company at 65 percent deduction.

Step 4: Calculate the group's combined taxable income.

Step 5: Apply adjustments for items determined at the consolidated level.

- Charitable contributions: At the consolidated level, the contributions limitation is now $95,700 (10 percent of taxable income of $957,000), so the group may take the full $40,000 contributions deduction.

- Dividends-received deduction: The DRD is now applied on the $110,000 of dividends from the 30 percent owned corporation ($110,000 × 65% = $71,500).

| | Step 1 | | | Step 2 | Step 3 | Step 4 | Step 5 | |
	A	B	C	Adjustments	Eliminations	Combined	Cons. Adj.	Consolidated
Gross receipts	$1,500,000	$2,000,000	$1,000,000	$ (50,000)		$4,450,000		$4,450,000
Cost of goods sold	(750,000)	(1,500,000)	(650,000)	-0-	-0-	(2,900,000)	-0-	(2,900,000)
Gross profit	750,000	500,000	350,000	(50,000)		1,550,000		1,550,000
Dividends	200,000			(90,000)		110,000		110,000
Sec. 1231 gain/(loss)			10,000	(10,000)				
Other income	5,000	1,000	2,000	-0-	-0-	8,000	-0-	8,000
Total income	955,000	501,000	362,000	(150,000)		1,668,000		1,668,000
Salaries/wages	100,000	350,000	50,000			500,000		500,000
Taxes	10,000	15,000	5,000			30,000		30,000
Charitable contributions			30,500		(30,500)		40,000	40,000
Depreciation	5,000	20,000				25,000		25,000
Other deductions	4,000	150,000	2,000	-0-	-0-	156,000	-0-	156,000
Total deductions	119,000	535,000	87,500	-0-	(30,500)	711,000	40,000	751,000
Taxable Income before NOL and special deductions	836,000	(34,000)	274,500	(150,000)	30,500	957,000	(40,000)	917,000
Special deductions (dividends-received deduction)	(161,500)	-0-	-0-	-0-	161,500	-0-	(71,500)	(71,500)
Taxable Income	$ 674,500	$ (34,000)	$ 274,500	$(150,000)	$192,000	$ 957,000	$(111,500)	$ 845,500

1.8   Tax Compliance Requirements

Although supplementary attachments and schedules are required, consolidated tax returns are filed using the same Form 1120 as single filing corporations and by checking the box on page 1 indicating that the 1120 is being filed on a consolidated basis.

1.9   Tax Accounting Methods and Periods

Members of the consolidated tax group are generally permitted to continue to use the same accounting methods that were in place prior to filing as a consolidated group. An exception is certain methods which use threshold limitations applied on a consolidated basis, such as the determination of whether a corporation can use the cash method of accounting. Each member of the consolidated tax group must use the parent's tax year.

1.10   Liability for Taxes and Estimated Tax Payments

Each member of the consolidated group is jointly and severally liable for the entire consolidated tax liability, tax penalties, and interest. Estimated tax payments must be made on a consolidated basis starting with the third consolidated tax return year. Prior to the third consolidated return year, estimated tax payments can be computed and paid on either a separate or a consolidated basis.

Question 1	MCQ-06007

Which of the following groups may elect to file a consolidated corporate return?

    a. A brother-sister-controlled group.

    b. A parent corporation and all more than 10 percent-controlled partnerships.

    c. A parent corporation and all more than 50 percent-controlled subsidiaries.

    d. Members of an affiliated group.

Question 2	MCQ-02112

With regard to consolidated tax returns, which of the following statements is correct?

    a. Operating losses of one group member may be used to offset operating profits of the other members included in the consolidated return.

    b. Only corporations that issue their audited financial statements on a consolidated basis may file consolidated returns.

    c. Of all intercompany dividends paid by the subsidiaries to the parent, 50 percent are excludable from taxable income on the consolidated return.

    d. The common parent must directly own 51 percent or more of the total voting power of all corporations included in the consolidated return.

NOTES

1 Net Operating Losses

Corporations are entitled to the same net operating loss (NOL) rules as individuals. NOLs arising in tax years ending after December 31, 2017, have an indefinite carryforward period. NOLs arising in tax years ending on or before December 31, 2017, have a carryforward period of 20 years.

The following additional points should be noted when calculating the corporate NOL:

1. No charitable contribution deduction is allowed in calculating the NOL.

2. The taxable income limitation normally imposed on the dividends-received deduction does not apply if, after taking into account the full dividends-received deduction, the corporation has an NOL for the year.

3. The NOL deduction for an NOL carryover from another year is not allowed in determining a current year NOL.

4. A corporation may deduct a capital loss carryover from a current year capital gain in calculating an NOL, yet it cannot deduct a capital loss carryback against a net capital gain in determining a current year NOL.

The net operating loss (NOL) deduction is limited to 80 percent (100 percent for losses arising in tax years beginning before December 31, 2017) of taxable income prior to the NOL deduction.

Pass Key

The CPA Examination often provides answers, which relate to capital loss rules, to questions concerning net operating losses. It is important to be able to distinguish all of these tax rules:

	Offset Other Income	Carryback	Carryforward
Net operating loss (for tax years ending on or before 12/31/2017)	N/A	2	20
Net operating loss (for tax years ending after 12/31/2017)	N/A	0	Unlimited*
Corporate net capital loss	-0-	3	5
Individual net capital loss	$3,000 maximum	0	Unlimited

*Subject to 80 percent of taxable income limitation.

Example 1   NOL Utilization

Facts: Frances Corp. has gross income of $600,000 and operating expenses of $450,000. Frances Corp. has a post-12/31/2017 NOL of $175,000.

Required: Determine Frances Corp.'s NOL deduction.

Solution: Frances Corp.'s taxable income prior to the NOL deduction is calculated as gross income of $600,000 less operating expenses of $450,000, which is $150,000. The NOL deduction is limited to 80 percent of taxable income prior to the NOL deduction, which is $120,000 (80% × $150,000 = $120,000). The NOL deduction of $120,000 reduces taxable income to $30,000 with an NOL carryforward of $55,000 ($175,000 beginning NOL carryforward less $120,000 utilized NOL).

2   Capital Losses

The $3,000 deduction for net capital losses available to individuals is not allowed to corporations. Thus, a corporation can only use capital losses to offset capital gains.

■ **Capital Loss Carryover:** Net capital losses are carried back three years and forward five years. They are carried over as short-term capital losses and are applied only against capital gains.

Example 2   Capital Loss Carryover With NOL

Facts: Lane Corp. has gross income of $400,000 (including a $150,000 capital gain) and operating expenses of $500,000. Lane Corp. has an unexpired capital loss carryover of $20,000.

Required: Determine Lane Corp.'s NOL.

Solution: Lane Corp. is able to offset its capital gain of $150,000 by the capital loss carryover of $20,000. Gross income after deducting the capital loss carryover will now be $380,000. The current year NOL is calculated as $380,000 of gross income less operating expenses of $500,000, which is ($120,000). Effectively, the capital loss carryover increased the current year NOL.

Illustration 1	Net Operating Loss Calculation, Utilization of NOL, and Capital Loss Carryforwards

Loss Co. had the following items of income and deductions for the current year (Year 1):

Gross income from operations	$250,000
Dividends received (from 40% owned company)	50,000
Capital gains	10,000
Other deductions (not including dividends-received deduction)	280,000

In addition, Loss Co. has the following capital loss carryforward and NOL carryforward schedules:

Capital Loss

Tax Year Generated	Amount	Utilized	Carryforward
3 years ago	$ 8,000	$6,000	$ 2,000
Prior year	10,000		10,000
Total	$18,000	$6,000	$12,000

Net Operating Loss

Tax Year Generated	Amount	Utilized	Carryforward
19 years ago (pre-12/31/17)	$ 60,000	$40,000	$20,000
2 years ago (pre-12/31/17)	80,000	30,000	50,000
Total	$140,000	$70,000	$70,000

The net operating loss for Year 1 is calculated as follows:

Calculate taxable income (loss) before the DRD:

Gross income from operations	$ 250,000
Dividends received (from 40% owned company)	50,000
Capital gains	10,000
Capital loss carryforward*	(10,000)
Other deductions (not including dividends-received deduction)	$(280,000)
Taxable income before DRD	$ 20,000

*Because capital losses can be carried forward five years, the entire amount is available, as none have expired.

Calculate the dividends-received deduction:

Tentative DRD (65% × $50,000)	$32,500
DRD taxable income limitation (65% × $20,000)	$13,000

(continued)

(continued)

In this case, the DRD is not limited to taxable income since the entire DRD creates an NOL [$20,000 – $32,500 = ($12,500)]

Calculate the net operating loss:

Taxable income before DRD	$ 20,000
Tentative DRD (65% × $50,000)	(32,500)
Net operating loss**	$(12,500)

**Note that no NOL carryforwards from prior years were used (even though they were available), as an NOL deduction from a prior year is not allowed in the computation of the current year NOL.

The capital loss carryforward and NOL schedules should now be updated as follows:

Capital Loss

Tax Year Generated	Amount	Utilized	Expired	Carryforward
3 years ago	$ 8,000	$ 8,000		$ 0
Prior year	10,000	8,000	$0	2,000
Total	$18,000	$16,000		$2,000

Net Operating Loss

Tax Year Generated	Amount	Utilized	Expired	Carryforward
19 years ago (pre-12/31/17)	$ 60,000	$40,000	$0	$20,000
2 years ago (pre-12/31/17)	80,000	30,000	$0	50,000
Current year	12,500			12,500
Total	$152,500	$70,000		$82,500

If, in the next year, Loss Co. is in a net income position, it would need to use its NOLs from the earliest year in which NOLs were generated, as they would expire after 20 years. Note that NOLs arising in tax years ending after December 31, 2017, do not expire.

Question 1	MCQ-05271

ParentCo, SubOne, and SubTwo have filed consolidated returns since their inception. The members reported the following taxable incomes (losses) for the year:

ParentCo	$ 50,000
SubOne	(60,000)
SubTwo	(40,000)

No member reported a capital gain or loss or charitable contributions. What is the amount of the consolidated net operating loss?

- **a.** $0
- **b.** $30,000
- **c.** $50,000
- **d.** $100,000

Question 2	MCQ-02151

When a corporation has an unused net capital loss that is carried back or carried forward to another tax year:

- **a.** It retains its original identity as short-term or long-term.
- **b.** It is treated as a short-term capital loss whether or not it was short-term when sustained.
- **c.** It is treated as a long-term capital loss whether or not it was long-term when sustained.
- **d.** It can be used to offset ordinary income up to the amount of the carryback or carryover.

NOTES

7 Entity/Owner Transactions

1 Contributions to a Corporation in Exchange for Stock

1.1 Formation

As previously covered in module 1, gains and loss are generally not recognized by shareholders and corporations upon contribution of property in exchange for stock at formation when immediately after the transfer, the contributing shareholders, in aggregate, have 80 percent control of the corporation to which they transferred the property.

1.2 Subsequent Transfers of Stock

Unlike the initial formation of a corporation, it is likely that subsequent contributions will not result in 80 percent control of the corporation (e.g., only one member of the original contributing control group is now transferring assets for stock, or a new shareholder is admitted). In this case, the control test will not be met and the contribution is treated as a sale to the corporation for fair market value, resulting in gain/loss recognized by the contributing shareholder.

2 Corporate Distributions

Distributions from corporations to shareholders are taxable to such shareholders if the distributions are classified as dividends.

Formation

Operations

Taxation

Distributions

Liquidation

2.1 Dividends Defined

A dividend is defined by the Internal Revenue Code as a distribution of property by a corporation out of its earnings and profits (E&P):

Current E&P (by year-end)	⟶ Taxable dividend
Accumulated E&P (distribution date)	⟶ Taxable dividend
Return of capital (no E&P)	⟶ Tax free and reduces basis of common stock
Capital gain distribution (no E&P/no basis)	⟶ Taxable income as a capital gain

2.1.1 General Netting Rules

The general rule is that current and accumulated E&P are not netted. Dividends come from current E&P and then from accumulated E&P. If both are positive, there are no issues; distributions are dividends to the extent of the total of current and accumulated E&P. If current E&P is positive and accumulated E&P is negative, distributions are dividends to the extent of current E&P only. If current and accumulated E&P are negative, distributions are not dividends at all. *However,* if current E&P is negative and accumulated E&P is positive, the two amounts are netted, and distributions are dividends if the net is positive.

2.1.2 Dividends to Preferred vs. Common Shareholders

A dividend to a preferred shareholder is based on that shareholder's fixed percentage at purchase. Preferred shareholders are not common equity owners of a corporation, and they only get paid based on their preferred percentage; therefore, any dividend payments to a preferred shareholder are considered dividend income to the shareholder. Preferred shareholders are paid in full before common shareholders receive dividends. Common shareholders are residual owners of a corporation and share in the earnings and profits of the corporation as well as the net assets.

2.2 Source of Distributions

2.2.1 Order of Distribution Allocation

Distributions are deemed to come from current E&P first and then from accumulated E&P. Any distribution in excess of both current and accumulated E&P is treated as a nontaxable return of capital that reduces the shareholder's basis in the stock.

Illustration 1   Distribution Allocation

At December 31, Year 1, the Julie Corporation had $20,000 of accumulated E&P. For the taxable year, Year 1, Julie had current E&P (before distributions) of $25,000.

- If Julie makes distributions in Year 2 of $25,000 or less, the distribution would be a dividend out of current E&P.

- If the distribution is greater than $25,000, but less than or equal to $45,000, the distribution would be a dividend as follows: $25,000 out of current E&P and up to $20,000 out of accumulated E&P.

- If the distribution is greater than $45,000, the distribution would be a dividend of $45,000, and the excess over $45,000 is a nontaxable return of capital.

2.2.2 Matching Cash Dividends to Source

It is sometimes necessary to allocate separate cash dividends paid during the year between current and accumulated earnings and profits in order to determine the taxable income for each payment. When dividends are in excess of earnings and profits, the following allocation applies:

- **Current Earnings and Profits**

  Current earnings and profits are allocated on a pro rata basis to each distribution, regardless of the actual date of the distributions.

- **Accumulated Earnings and Profits**

  Accumulated earnings and profits are applied in chronological order, beginning with the earliest distribution.

Illustration 2   Multiple Distributions in a Year

In Year 1, Linda Corp. had current earnings and profits of $15,000 and accumulated earnings and profits of $10,000. It paid four cash dividends, in February, April, August, and November, of $7,500 each for a total of $30,000. Half of each dividend ($3,750) will be treated as having been made from current earnings and profits taxable to the shareholder to that extent. The remaining $3,750 of each dividend will be taxable as follows:

February and April: Paid from accumulated earnings and profits (taxable dividend).

August: $2,500 paid from accumulated earnings and profits (taxable dividend); $1,250 return of capital.

November: Entire amount is tax-free return of capital (up to basis of stock; amount in excess of stock basis will be taxed as capital gain).

2.3   Constructive Dividends

Some transactions, although not in the form of dividends, are treated as such when the payments are not in proportion to stock ownership. Examples include:

- Excessive salaries paid to shareholder employees.
- Excessive rents and royalties.
- "Loans" to shareholders where there is no intent to repay.
- Sale of assets below fair market value.

Note: Corporations may have an incentive to not classify the above as dividends since the transactions listed above could create a deductible expense or a loss, while a dividend payment is not a deduction to the corporation. The IRS may classify these as dividends to avoid giving the deduction to the corporation and to count them as income to the recipients.

2.4   Stock Dividends

- **Definition**

   A stock dividend is a distribution by a corporation of its own stock to its shareholders.

- **Generally Not Taxable**

   Stock dividends are generally not taxable unless the shareholder has a choice of receiving cash or other property.

- **Determination of Value**

   The value of the taxable stock dividend is the fair market value on the distribution date.

- **Allocation of Basis**

   The basis of a nontaxable stock dividend, where old and new shares are identical, is determined by dividing the basis of the old stock by the number of old and new shares.

Illustration 3   Basis Allocation After Stock Dividend

In Year 1, Linda purchased 100 shares of Conduf stock for $18,000 ($180 per share). In Year 2, the corporation declared a 50 percent stock dividend and Linda received 50 new shares. After the stock dividend, the basis of each new share is $120 ($18,000 ÷ 150 shares).

2.5   Shareholder Taxable Amount

The taxable amount of a dividend from a corporation's earnings and profits depends on what type of entity the shareholder is.

2.5.1   Individual Shareholder

- **Cash Dividends:** amount received

- **Property Dividends:** FMV of property received

2.5.2   Corporate Shareholders (Eligible for the Dividends-Received Deduction)

- **Cash Dividends:** amount received

- **Property Dividends:** FMV of property received

2.6   Corporation Paying Dividend: Taxable Amount

- **General Rule**

  The *general rule* is the payment of a dividend does not create a taxable event. A dividend is a reduction of earnings and profits (retained earnings).

- **Property Dividends**

  If a corporation distributes appreciated property, the tax results are as follows:

  - The corporation recognizes gain as if the property had been sold (i.e., FMV less adjusted basis).

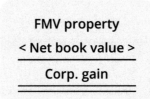

FMV property

< Net book value >

Corp. gain

  - The recipient shareholder includes the FMV of property in income as a dividend (to the extent of E&P).
  - When appreciated property is distributed, the corporation cannot recognize a loss.

Pass Key

When the CPA Examination has tested on tax issues related to corporations paying property dividends, it normally involves the following sequence of events:

1. Corporation has no E&P (dividend would not be taxable income).

2. Corporation distributes appreciated property as a dividend.

3. Corporation has a recognized gain (on property dividend).

4. Corporate gain increases/creates corporate E&P.

5. Dividend to shareholder is now taxable income (to extent of E&P).

2.7 Stock Redemption

Stock redemptions occur when a corporation buys back stock from its stockholders. If the stock redemption qualifies for sale or exchange treatment, gain or loss is recognized by the shareholder. If not, the redemption is treated as a dividend to the extent of the corporation's E&P. The corporation can recognize gain (but not loss) on any appreciated property distributed as though it had sold the property for its FMV.

▪ **Proportional:** Taxable dividend income (to shareholder-ordinary income). Generally, the corporation either redeems or cancels the stock pro rata for all shareholders.

▪ **Disproportional (Substantially Disproportionate):** Sale by shareholder subject to taxable capital gain/loss to shareholder. Disproportional means that there has been a meaningful reduction in the shareholder's ownership interest. The percentage ownership after the redemption must be less than 50 percent and must be less than 80 percent of the percentage ownership before the redemption. Percentage ownership includes what is owned by certain family members (only spouse, children, grandchildren, and parents). Regardless of family ownership, a complete 100 percent termination of shareholder's interest is considered disproportional.

▪ **Partial Liquidation of Corporation (Stock Held by a Noncorporate Shareholder):** Treated as an exchange of stock, not as a dividend.

▪ **Complete Buyout of Shareholder:** Shareholder's entire interest is redeemed, and the transaction is treated as an exchange of stock.

▪ **Redemption Not Essentially Equivalent to a Dividend:** Treated as an exchange of stock.

▪ **Redemption to Pay Estate Taxes or Expenses:** Treated as an exchange when the corporation redeems stock that has been included in the decedent's gross estate (subject to dollar and time limitations).

3   Corporation Liquidation

If a corporation is liquidated, the transaction is subject to double taxation (that is, the corporation and the shareholders must generally recognize gain or loss). Note that the corporation generally deducts its liquidation expenses (e.g., filing fees and professional fees) on its final tax return. Corporation liquidation takes two general forms: Either the corporation sells the assets and distributes the cash to the shareholders or distributes the assets to the shareholders.

| Formation |
| Operations |
| Taxation |
| Distributions |
| **Liquidation** |

3.1   Corporation Sells Assets and Distributes Cash to Shareholders

The result of this transaction is:

1.   Corporation recognizes gain or loss (as normal) on the sale of the assets; and

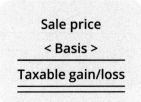

Sale price
< Basis >
_____
Taxable gain/loss

2.   Shareholders recognize gain or loss to the extent that cash exceeds adjusted basis of stock.

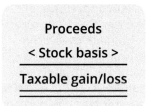

Proceeds
< Stock basis >
_____
Taxable gain/loss

3.2   Corporation Distributes Assets to Shareholders

The result of this transaction is:

1.   Corporation recognizes gain or loss as if it sold the assets for the FMV; and

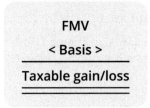

FMV
< Basis >
_____
Taxable gain/loss

2.   Shareholders recognize gain or loss to the extent that the FMV of assets received exceeds the adjusted basis of stock.

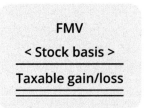

FMV
< Stock basis >
_____
Taxable gain/loss

3.3   Tax-Free Reorganizations

3.3.1   Reorganization Defined

Reorganization includes the following:

- Mergers or consolidations (Type A).
- The acquisition by one corporation of another corporation's stock, stock for stock (Type B).
- The acquisition by one corporation of another corporation's assets, stock for assets (Type C).
- Dividing of the corporation into separate operating corporations (Type D).
- Recapitalizations (Type E).
- A mere change in identity, form, or place of organization (Type F).

3.3.2   Parent/Subsidiary Liquidation

No gain or loss is recognized by either the parent corporation or the subsidiary corporation when the parent, who owns at least 80 percent, liquidates its subsidiary. The parent assumes the basis of the subsidiary's assets as well as any unused NOL or capital loss or charitable contribution carryovers.

3.3.3   Nontaxable Event

- **Corporation: Nontaxable**
  - The reorganization is a nontaxable transaction.
  - All tax attributes remain.

- **Shareholder: Nontaxable**
  - The reorganization is a nontaxable transaction.
  - The shareholder continues to retain his or her original basis.
  - The shareholder recognizes gain to the extent that he or she receives boot (cash) in the reorganization.

Pass Key

The general rule for taxable events and basis applies to reorganizations:

Taxpayer	Event	Income	Basis	Tax Attributes
Corporation	Nontaxable	N-O-N-E	NBV	No Change
Shareholder	Nontaxable	N-O-N-E	NBV	No Change

3.3.4   Continuity of Business

A reorganization is treated as a nontaxable transaction because it results in the continuation of a business in a modified form. In order to meet the "continuity requirement," the acquiring corporation must continue the business of the old entity (or entities) or use a significant portion of the old corporation's assets.

3.3.5   Control Requirement

In addition to the continuity requirement, there is a control test. Control is defined as at least 80 percent of the total voting power of all classes of stock and at least 80 percent of all other classes of stock. This is the same requirement as that of a tax-free incorporation.

3.3.6   Tax Status of Reorganizations

Reorganizations are nontaxable (except to the extent of boot received) because the shareholders have not liquidated their investment but have continued operations in a modified form.

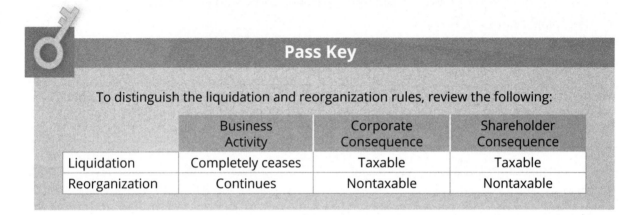

Pass Key

To distinguish the liquidation and reorganization rules, review the following:

	Business Activity	Corporate Consequence	Shareholder Consequence
Liquidation	Completely ceases	Taxable	Taxable
Reorganization	Continues	Nontaxable	Nontaxable

3.4   Worthless Stock: Section 1244 Stock (Small Business Stock)

When a corporation's stock is sold or becomes worthless, an original stockholder can be treated as having an ordinary loss (fully tax deductible) instead of a capital loss, up to $50,000 ($100,000 if married filing jointly). Any loss in excess of this amount would be a capital loss, which would offset capital gains, and then a maximum $3,000 ($1,500 if MFS) per year would be deductible.

- **Maximum Ordinary Loss Deduction**
  - Married filing jointly: $100,000
  - All other individual filers: $50,000

- **Qualifications**
  - Cash or property paid to the corporation in exchange for its first $1,000,000 of capital stock.
  - The stock must have been issued to an individual stockholder (or a partnership) for money or other property, but not stock or securities or services rendered.

3.5   Small Business Stock

3.5.1   Exclusion Amount

A noncorporate shareholder, who holds qualified small business stock for more than five years, may generally exclude 100 percent of the gain on the sale or exchange of the stock.

Maximum exclusion and limited to 100 percent of the greater of:

- 10 times the taxpayer's basis in the stock; or
- $10 million; $5 million if MFS (shareholder by shareholder basis).

3.5.2 Qualifications

Qualified corporation and must have the following:

- Stock issued after August 10, 1993.
- Acquired at the original issuance.
- C corporation only (not an S corporation).
- Less than $50 million of capital as of the date of stock issuance.
- 80 percent (or more) of the value of the corporation's assets used in the active conduct of one or more qualified trades or businesses.

3.5.3 Taxable Portion

The includable portion of the gain is taxed at regular tax rates.

Question 1   MCQ-02120

Tank Corp., which had earnings and profits of $500,000, made a nonliquidating distribution of property to its shareholders in Year 1 as a dividend in kind. This property, which had an adjusted basis of $20,000 and a fair market value of $30,000 at the date of distribution, did not constitute assets used in the active conduct of Tank's business. How much gain did Tank recognize on this distribution?

    a. $30,000

    b. $20,000

    c. $10,000

    d. $0

Question 2   MCQ-02026

Elm Corp. is an accrual basis calendar year C corporation with 100,000 shares of voting common stock issued and outstanding as of December 28, Year 1. On Friday, December 29, Year 1, Hall surrendered 2,000 shares of Elm stock to Elm in exchange for $33,000 cash. Hall had no direct or indirect interest in Elm after the stock surrender.

Additional information follows:

Hall's adjusted basis in 2,000 shares of Elm on December 29, Year 1 ($8 per share)	$16,000
Elm's accumulated earnings and profits at January 1, Year 1	25,000
Elm's Year 1 net operating loss	(7,000)

What amount of income did Hall recognize from the stock surrender?

    a. $33,000 dividend

    b. $25,000 dividend

    c. $18,000 capital gain

    d. $17,000 capital gain

NOTES

Flow-Through Entity Taxation and Multi-jurisdictional Tax Issues

Module

1 S Corporations

Small, closely held corporations, if eligible, may elect to be taxed as an S corporation, a flow-through entity taxed in a manner similar to partnerships. In effect, all the income, losses, and deductions of the corporation are passed (or flowed) through to the shareholders. Corporations whose owners elect to treat them as flow-through entities are classified as such under the Subchapter S rules of the Internal Revenue Code.

This election generally results in no corporate-level tax; however, the individuals are taxed on their share of the corporate earnings regardless of whether the corporation actually distributes the earnings to them.

1.1 Formation

- An S corporation is formed by first forming a C corporation and then making an election (agreed upon by all shareholders) on Form 2553 to be treated as an S corporation for tax purposes.

- Realized and recognized gain/loss to the corporation and shareholders upon contribution of assets in exchange for stock are computed in the same manner as for a C corporation (discussed in R4).

1.2 Property Contributions to an S Corporation

Although setting up an S corporation affords a company many tax advantages similar to those of partnerships, which will be discussed in later modules, some S corporation traits remain the same as for C corporations. Taxability of shareholder contributions to an S corporation are governed under Section 351, in the same manner as C corporations. That is, a contribution will be tax-free if it is:

1. a contribution of property (not services);

2. solely in exchange for stock; and

3. after the transfer, the shareholder (or group of shareholders transferring in an integrated transaction) has control of the corporation through 80 percent stock ownership.

Transfers falling outside of these terms will be treated as a taxable sale (gain recognized for FMV received over shareholder basis). Note that the requirements for Section 351 are fairly easily met upon formation of the S corporation but may be harder to meet upon subsequent contributions of property by individual shareholders or new shareholders.

As covered in the section discussing calculation of shareholder stock basis, contributions to the S corporation also increase the shareholder's stock basis.

Example 1	Contributions to S Corporations

Facts: Ray contributes property with FMV of $20,000 and an adjusted basis to Ray of $10,000 in exchange for stock in Falcon Corporation, an existing S corporation. Immediately after the transfer, Ray owns 20 percent of Falcon's stock.

Required: Determine the realized and recognized gain or loss on the transfer to Ray and his basis in the S corporation stock.

Solution: $10,000 recognized gain ($20,000 FMV – $10,000 adjusted basis).

Ray will have a $10,000 recognized gain. Because Ray did not have 80 percent or more ownership in Falcon after the exchange, he is required to recognize gain on the transfer.

Ray will have a $20,000 basis in Falcon ($10,000 carryover basis plus $10,000 gain recognized). Falcon's basis in the property received is also $20,000.

2 Eligibility

To qualify as an S corporation, the following requirements must be met:

1. **Qualified Corporation**

   The corporation must be a domestic corporation. An S corporation may own any interest in a C corporation (even 100 percent), but the S corporation may not file a consolidated tax return with the C corporation. An S corporation may also create a qualified S subsidiary in which the S corporation owns 100 percent of the stock; the two S corporations would file as one entity for tax purposes.

2. **Eligible Shareholders**
   * Eligible shareholders must be an individual, estate, or certain types of trusts.
   * An individual shareholder may not be a nonresident alien.
   * Qualified retirement plans, trusts, and 501(c)(3) charitable organizations may be shareholders.
   * Neither corporations nor partnerships are eligible shareholders.
   * Grantor and voting trusts are permissible shareholders.

3. **Shareholder Limit**

   There may be no more than 100 shareholders. Family members may elect to be treated as one shareholder. Family members include common ancestors, lineal descendants of common ancestors, and their current or former spouses.

4. **One Class of Stock**

   There may be no more than one class of stock outstanding. However, differences in common stock voting rights are allowed. Preferred stock is not permitted.

3   Electing S Corporation Status

3.1   When Election Takes Effect

All shareholders (voting and nonvoting) must consent to a valid election on Form 2553, which the company files with the IRS. If the election is made at any time during the entire preceding year or on or before the 15th day of the third month of the election year, the election is effective on the first day of the tax year (e.g., January 1 for a calendar-year corporation).

3.2   New Shareholders

After the election is in effect, the consent of a new shareholder is not required. The S corporation status continues unless a shareholder(s) who owns more than 50 percent of the stock affirmatively acts to terminate the election.

4   Effect of S Corporation Election on Corporation

4.1   S Corporation Tax Year

S corporations file Form 1120S and must adopt the calendar year, unless a valid business purpose for a different taxable year (fiscal year) is established. The return is due by the 15th day of the third month (March 15) after the close of the tax year.

4.2   No Tax on Corporation

Generally, there is no tax at the corporation level; all earnings are passed through to shareholders and taxed at the individual shareholder level. There are certain exceptions (see topic 4.3 below).

4.3   Certain Corporation-Level Taxes

Although S corporations generally do not pay tax, there are three different taxes that may be imposed if the S corporation was previously taxed as a C corporation.

4.3.1   LIFO Recapture Tax

C corporations that elect S status must include in taxable income for the last C corporation year the excess of inventory computed using the FIFO method over the inventory computed using the LIFO method. The resulting tax on the C corporation may be paid in four equal annual installments, the first of which is due with the final C corporation return. The remaining installments are paid by the S corporation.

4.3.2   Built-in Gains Tax

■ **Overview**

A distribution or sale of an S corporation's assets may result in a corporate-level tax on any *built-in gain*. An unrealized built-in gain results when the following two conditions occur:

- A C corporation elects S corporation status; and
- The fair market value of the corporate assets exceeds the adjusted basis of corporate assets on the election date.

The net unrealized built-in gain is the excess of the fair market value of corporate assets over adjusted basis of corporate assets at the time the corporation converts from a C corporation to an S corporation. When those assets are later disposed of, the S corporation may have to pay tax on the built-in gain. The amount of built-in gain recognized in any one year is limited to the total net unrealized built-in gain less any built-in gain previously recognized.

■ **Exemptions From Recognition of Built-in Gain**

An S corporation is exempt from a tax on built-in gains under any of the following circumstances:

- The S corporation was never a C corporation.
- The sale or transfer does not occur within five years of the first day of the first year that the S election is effective.
- The S corporation can demonstrate that the appreciation in the asset being sold or transferred occurred after the S election.
- The S corporation can demonstrate that the distributed asset was acquired after the S election.
- The total net unrealized built-in gain has been completely recognized in prior tax years.

■ **Calculation of Tax**

The tax is calculated by multiplying 21 percent (the corporate tax rate) by the lesser of the following:

- Recognized built-in gain for the current year; or
- The taxable income of the S corporation if it were a C corporation.

4.3.3 Tax on Passive Investment Income

An S corporation is subject to an income tax imposed at the corporate rate (21 percent) on the lesser of net income or excess passive investment income if the following two tests are met:

■ The S corporation has accumulated C corporation earnings and profits (i.e., accumulated earnings attributable to prior periods in which the corporation was a C corporation); and

■ Passive investment income (e.g., royalties, dividends, interest, rents, and annuities but not gains on sales of securities) exceeds 25 percent of total gross receipts.

5 Effect of S Corporation Election on Shareholders

5.1 Pass-Through of Income and/or Losses (to Shareholder/K-1)

5.1.1 Overview

Like partnerships, S corporations report both separately stated items of income and deductions and the non-separately stated items of business income or loss. Separately stated income items include dividends, interest, capital gains and losses, Section 1231 gains and losses, etc. Separately stated deductions include charitable deductions, Section 179 expenses, etc. Allocations to shareholders are made on a per-share, per-day basis.

5.1.2 Qualified Business Income Deduction

A below-the-line deduction of 20 percent of qualified business income may be available on ordinary business income flowed-through from an S corporation. This deduction is discussed in more detail in R1.

| Example 2 | Allocation on Per-Share and Per-Day Basis |

Facts: The Duffy Corporation, an S corporation, is owned equally by three shareholders, Rick, Tim, and Peter. The corporation is on a calendar-year basis. On February 1, Year 5, Peter sold his one-third interest in Duffy Corporation to George. For the year ended December 31, Year 5, the corporation had ordinary business income of $120,000 and no separately stated items.

Required: Calculate each shareholder's ordinary business income allocation for the year.

Solution: For Year 5, the income of the corporation should be allocated as follows:

Rick ($120,000 × 1/3)	$ 40,000
Tim ($120,000 × 1/3)	40,000
Peter (31/365 × $40,000)	3,397
George (334/365 × $40,000)	36,603
Total	$120,000

5.1.3 Pass-Through of Losses

- Losses are limited to a shareholder's adjusted basis in S corporation stock plus direct shareholder loans to the corporation. Shareholder guarantees do not increase basis. Any losses disallowed may be carried forward indefinitely and will be deductible as the shareholder's basis is increased.

- Losses are additionally limited to an S corporation shareholder's at-risk amount in the corporation.

  - The *at-risk* loss limitation rules for S corporations are similar to the rules for partnerships.

    — The rules limit the shareholder's loss to the amount of the risk of financial loss in the business.

    — The at-risk amount is generally equal to the shareholder's stock and debt basis.

    — A nonrecourse loan (which is a loan where the shareholder is not personally liable) can create basis for the shareholder but will not be considered in the at-risk amount.

  - The taxpayer's at-risk amount would be increased by:

    — contribution of cash or other property to the corporation;

    — loans to the corporation; and

    — allocable share of income undistributed.

  - The taxpayer's amount at risk would be reduced by:

    — allocable share of losses; and

    — distributions of cash or other property.

  - The taxpayer's amount at risk in the business entity would only increase by recourse loans but not increase by nonrecourse loans.

  - Losses are also limited by the excess business loss limitations discussed in R1.

Example 3	At-Risk Basis Calculation

Facts: Taxpayer A's stock basis in S corporation stock is $60,000. Included in the stock basis is $10,000, which Taxpayer A borrowed on a nonrecourse basis.

Required: Determine Taxpayer A's at-risk basis in the S corporation.

Solution: Taxpayer A's at-risk basis in the S corporation is $50,000. Taxpayer A can only deduct a loss from the S corporation up to the amount of the at-risk basis of $50,000. If the loan had been a recourse loan, the shareholder could deduct losses up to the full amount of the $60,000 stock basis.

5.1.4 Separately Stated Items

The following S corporation items flow through to the shareholder in a manner similar to a partnership (see Schedule K-1 for a complete list):

- Ordinary income *(not subject to FICA)*, which includes recapture income and unearned revenue not related to rental activities and mark-to-market income

- Rental income/loss, which includes recapture income and unearned revenue related to rental activities

- Portfolio income *(including interest, dividends, royalties, and all capital gains/losses)*

- Tax-exempt interest

- Percentage depletion

- Foreign income tax

- Section 1231 gains and losses

- Charitable contributions

- Expense deduction for recovery property (Section 179)

- Unrecaptured Section 1250 income

- Gain (loss) from sale of collectibles

Example 4	Ordinary Income Calculation and Separately Stated Items

Facts: Gray Corporation, an S corporation, had the following items of income and deduction for the year:

Gross income	$150,000
Cost of goods sold	70,000
Interest income	10,000
Section 1231 gain	5,000
Salary expense	40,000
Depreciation expense	10,000
Charitable contributions	5,000

Required: Calculate Gray Corporation's ordinary business income and separately stated items for the year.

Solution: Ordinary business income: $30,000 (gross income of $150,000 less COGS of $70,000, salaries of $40,000, and depreciation of $10,000)

Separately stated items:

Interest income	$10,000
Section 1231 gain	5,000
Charitable contributions	5,000

5.2   Fringe Benefits

5.2.1   Deductible Fringe Benefits

Fringe benefits for non-shareholder employees and those employee shareholders owning 2 percent or less of the S corporation are deductible by the S corporation in calculating ordinary business income.

5.2.2   Nondeductible Fringe Benefits

The cost of fringe benefits for shareholders owning over 2 percent is not deductible by the S corporation, unless the corporation includes the benefits in the employee/shareholder's W-2 income.

Pass Key

Similar to a partnership, shareholders in an S corporation must include on their personal income tax return their distributive share of each separate "pass-through" item.

Shareholders are taxed on these items, regardless of whether or not the items have been distributed (withdrawn) to them during the year.

5.3   Accumulated Adjustments Account (AAA)

The tax effects of distributions paid to shareholders of an S corporation that has accumulated earnings and profits since inception (or since the most recent electing of S status) are computed by using the accumulated adjustments account (AAA). The AAA is *zero* at the *inception* of the S corporation.

5.3.1   Increases to the AAA

The AAA is essentially increased by separately and non-separately stated income and gains (except tax-exempt income and certain life insurance proceeds).

5.3.2   Decreases to the AAA

The AAA is essentially decreased by corporate distributions (distributions may not reduce the AAA below zero), separately and non-separately stated expense items and losses (except for certain nondeductible items that do not affect the capital account), and nondeductible expenses (except life insurance premiums on a contract that is owned by the corporation and that identifies the corporation as beneficiary) that relate to income other than tax-exempt income.

5.3.3   Other Adjustments Account

The other adjustments account (OAA) is a bookkeeping account that is designed to keep a cumulative record of items which affect S corporation shareholders' basis but do not affect the AAA. These primary differences are:

- tax-exempt income and related expenses; and
- federal taxes attributable to C corporation years.

Examples of items included in the OAA include:

- tax-exempt interest on municipal bonds and related expenses;
- tax-exempt life insurance proceeds and related nondeductible premiums; and
- federal taxes paid or accrued in an S corporation year that relate to C corporation years.

After these adjustments are made, the account is reduced for any distributions made during the year. However, keep in mind that the OAA is purely an administrative account to reconcile shareholder stock basis with AAA and has no impact on the taxability of an S corporation's distributions.

5.4   Computing Shareholder Basis in S Corporation Stock

The rules for determining a shareholder's basis in S corporation stock are generally the same as for partnerships, as follows:

	Initial basis
+	Income items (separately and non-separately stated items)
+	Additional shareholder investments in corporation stock
–	Distribution to shareholders
–	Loss or expense items
=	Ending basis

Pass Key

An S corporation shareholder is permitted to deduct (on a personal income tax return) the pro rata share of the S corporation loss subject to the following limitation:

Loss limitation = Basis + Direct shareholder loans – Distributions

Illustration 1   At-Risk Amount Computation

Gearty is a shareholder in an S corporation. He contributed $12,000 in cash and land with a basis of $25,000 and a fair market value of $100,000. He also loaned the S corporation $15,000, which Gearty borrowed on a nonrecourse basis. Gearty has $10,000 as his pro rata share of S corporation income not distributed. Gearty's amount at risk would be:

$12,000 (cash contribution)

   25,000 (basis in land contributed)

   10,000 (undistributed share of income)

$47,000 At-risk amount

Gearty's at-risk amount would not include nonrecourse loans. Like basis, the at-risk amount would include the basis of property contributed, rather than the fair market value. Once his pro rata share of income is distributed, his basis, as well as at-risk amount, would be reduced.

5.5   Taxability of Distributions to Shareholders

Because S corporations are only subject to a single level of tax, distributions from an S corporation are generally not taxable to the shareholders, as the shareholder has already been taxed on the income when it passes through on the shareholder's K-1 each year. However, if an S corporation has corporate earnings and profits (E&P) which carried over from the former C corporation when the S election was made, distributions may be taxable.

The rules for determining the taxability of distributions are presented below.

	Distribution	Tax result	Treatment
	S Corporation With No C Corporation E&P		
1st	To extent of basis in stock	Not subject to tax, reduces basis in stock	Return of capital
2nd	In excess of basis of stock	Taxed as long-term capital gain (if stock held for > one year)	Capital gain distribution

Illustration 2   Taxability of Distributions With No C Corporation E&P

Feline Corporation, a calendar year S corporation since its formation in Year 1, has two equal shareholders, Carlin and Radon. During Year 5, Carlin received distributions from Feline Corporation of $22,000. At December 31, Year 5, after all adjustments to basis had been made, except for distributions, Carlin's basis in his Feline stock was $18,000. For Year 5, Carlin will treat $18,000 as a nontaxable return of capital (reduction of basis of stock) and $4,000 as a long-term capital gain.

S Corporation With C Corporation E&P

	Distribution	Tax result	Treatment
1st	To extent of AAA	Not subject to tax, reduces basis in stock	S corporation profits
2nd	To extent of C corporation E&P	Taxed as a dividend, does not reduce basis in stock	Old C corporation taxable dividend
3rd	To extent of basis of stock	Not subject to tax, reduces basis in stock	Return of capital
4th	In excess of basis of stock	Taxed as long-term capital gain	Capital gain distribution

As previously presented, "AAA" stands for *Accumulated Adjustments Account*, which essentially means the cumulative amount of S corporation income or loss (separately and non-separately stated items, excluding tax-exempt income), since the corporation most recently elected S status, less all cumulative distributions. *Distributions may not reduce AAA below zero; however, AAA may be negative from S corporation losses.*

Illustration 3   Taxability of Distributions With C Corporation E&P

The New Elect Corporation was a C corporation until it elected S status on January 1, Year 2. New Elect had accumulated E&P of $20,000 at December 31, Year 1. For the period Year 2 to Year 8, New Elect had ordinary income of $100,000 and had made shareholder distributions of $60,000. Thus, New Elect's AAA balance at December 31, Year 8, was $40,000. In Year 9, New Elect had ordinary income of $40,000 and made distributions to shareholders of $110,000. The tax result of these Year 9 items are as follows:

1. To extent of AAA ($40,000 + $40,000 = $80,000) ...... Tax-free
2. To extent of C corporation E&P ($20,000) .... Dividend
3. Excess ($10,000)... Reduces basis in stock, if in excess of basis, LTCG

6   Terminating the Election

6.1   When S Corporation Status Terminates

The S corporation status will terminate as a result of any of the following:

- Holders of a majority (greater than 50 percent) of the corporation's stock (any combination of voting and nonvoting common stock) consent to a voluntary revocation;

- The corporation fails to meet any or all of the eligibility requirements (qualifications) for S corporation status (termination effective immediately); or

- More than 25 percent of the corporation's gross receipts come from passive investment income for three consecutive years and the corporation had C corporation earnings and profits at the end of each year. The S corporation status is terminated as of the beginning of the fourth year.

Example 5	S Corporation Termination

Facts: Small Corporation is an S corporation, which has maintained a valid S election since the corporation was formed 10 years ago. In the current year, Small admits Large Corporation, a C corporation, as a 40 percent shareholder.

Required: Determine the impact of Small Corporation's admittance of Large as a shareholder on the S election.

Solution: Because Large Corporation is a C corporation, Small would no longer meet the requirements of an S corporation, and its S election would be terminated upon the admittance of Large as a shareholder.

6.2   Re-electing: Five Years

Once an S corporation election is terminated or revoked, a new election cannot be made for five years, unless the IRS consents to an earlier election. If the termination occurs in midyear, the corporation will have two short years, a short S year and a short C year. Earnings are prorated on a daily basis to each of the short years. A special election may be made to "cut off" net income at the exact date of conversion.

7   Liquidation of an S Corporation

The liquidation of an S corporation is treated the same as the liquidation of a C corporation (discussed in R4).

7.1   Consequences to an S Corporation

In a liquidating distribution, the corporation will recognize gain or loss on the distribution of property as if the property was sold at fair market value (FMV):

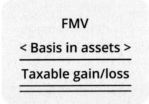

FMV

< Basis in assets >

Taxable gain/loss

Note: Distributions to related parties (as defined in Section 267) do not qualify for loss recognition.

7.2   Consequences to Shareholders

- Distributions from an S corporation in complete liquidation of the S corporation are treated as payments in exchange for stock.

- The shareholder's adjusted basis in the stock is subtracted from the amount realized (cash and FMV of property received from the corporation) to calculate the gain or loss.

- If the shareholder assumes corporate liabilities or receives property subject to a liability, the amount realized is reduced by the amount of the liabilities assumed:

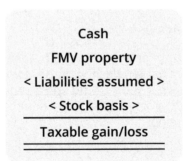

Cash

FMV property

< Liabilities assumed >

< Stock basis >

Taxable gain/loss

- The shareholder's stock basis in this calculation is determined after all of the other activity of the S corporation for the year has been taken into account (share of taxable income, etc.).

- The character of the gain/loss recognized to the shareholder will depend on the shareholder's holding period in the S corporation stock and whether the stock is a capital asset to the shareholder.

Example 6   Liquidation of S Corporation

Facts: XYZ Corp. (which is treated as an S corporation for tax purposes) makes a distribution in complete liquidation of a building with FMV of $100,000 and a basis to XYZ of $60,000 to its only shareholder, W. XYZ also had net income for the year of $10,000. W has a basis in its XYZ stock of $30,000 at the beginning of the year.

Required: Determine the tax consequences of the liquidating distribution to XYZ Corporation and to its only shareholder, W.

Solution: Consequences to XYZ: XYZ recognizes a gain of $40,000 on the distribution of the building ($100,000 FMV – $60,000 basis).

Consequences to W: W first computes its basis in XYZ stock immediately before the distribution:

Beginning basis	$30,000
Net income	10,000
XYZ gain on distribution of building	40,000
	$80,000

W's gain on the distribution is $20,000 ($100,000 FMV of building less $80,000 stock basis).

Question 1   MCQ-01966

Bristol Corp. was formed as a C corporation on January 1, Year 1, and it elected S corporation status on January 1, Year 3. At the time of the election, Bristol had accumulated C corporation earnings and profits, which have not been distributed. Bristol has had the same 25 shareholders throughout its existence. In Year 6, Bristol's S corporation election will terminate if it:

    a. Increases the number of shareholders to 100.

    b. Adds a decedent's estate as a shareholder to the existing shareholders.

    c. Takes a charitable contribution deduction.

    d. Has passive investment income exceeding 90 percent of gross receipts in each of the three consecutive years ending December 31, Year 5.

Question 2   MCQ-01955

Lane Inc., an S corporation, pays single-coverage health insurance premiums of $4,800 per year and family coverage premiums of $7,200 per year. Mill is a 10 percent shareholder-employee in Lane. On Mill's behalf, Lane pays Mill's family coverage under the health insurance plan. What amount of insurance premiums is includable in Mill's gross income?

    a. $0

    b. $720

    c. $4,800

    d. $7,200

NOTES

1 Partnerships

A partnership is a flow-through entity, which means that the income is taxed only once when it "flows through" to the partner. Unincorporated business entities such as general partnerships, limited partnerships, and limited liability companies (LLCs) are generally treated as partnerships under the Subchapter K rules of the Internal Revenue Code.

| **Formation** |
| Operation |
| Taxation |
| Distribution |
| Liquidation |

1.1 Partnership Formation

When a partnership is formed, the partners contribute money, other property, or services in return for their ownership interests. A new partner may also obtain an interest by making a contribution after the partnership is formed and already operating.

Generally, no gain or loss is recognized on a contribution of property to a partnership in return for a partnership interest.

| Example 1 | **Contribution of Property in Exchange for Partnership Interest** |

Facts: A taxpayer contributes land in exchange for a partnership interest. The land has an adjusted basis of $30,000 and FMV of $50,000 at the time of transfer.

Required: Determine the amount of gain or loss recognized to the taxpayer.

Solution: No gain is recognized to the taxpayer on the transfer.

1.1.1 Profits Interest Acquired for Services Rendered

A profits interest in a partnership represents the right to share in the future profits of the partnership. A profits interest has no liquidation value when it is received. A partner who receives a profits interest in a partnership in exchange for services rendered does not recognize ordinary income at the exchange.

| Example 2 | **Profits Interest Acquired for Services Rendered** |

Facts: A taxpayer has no property to contribute to a partnership. He receives a 20 percent profits interest in exchange for services rendered. On the day he is admitted to the partnership, the partnership's assets have a basis of $20,000 and a liquidation value of $80,000.

Required: Determine the amount of gain or loss recognized to the taxpayer.

Solution: The taxpayer will not have to recognize income at the time the profits interest is exchanged for the rendering of services.

1.2 Exceptions to Nonrecognition of Gain (Taxable Events for Partners)

▪ **Capital Interest Acquired for Services Rendered (FMV):** Capital interest in a partnership represents the right to receive a share of capital in the partnership if it liquidates. As such, it is valued at liquidation value. The value of a partnership capital interest acquired for services rendered is ordinary income to the partner. The partnership either deducts or capitalizes the value of the capital interest (according to the type of the services the partner provides).

Example 3	Capital Interest Acquired for Services Rendered

Facts: A taxpayer has no property to contribute to a partnership. He receives a 20 percent partnership capital interest in exchange for services rendered. On the day he is admitted to the partnership, the partnership's assets have a basis of $20,000 and a liquidation value of $80,000.

Required: Determine the amount of gain or loss recognized to the taxpayer.

Solution: He will recognize ordinary income of $16,000 (20 percent of $80,000).

▪ **Property Subject to a (Excess) Liability:** When property is contributed that is subject to a liability, the excess of the liabilities assumed by the other partners over the contributed basis is treated as taxable boot and is a gain to the partner.

2 Basis

2.1 Basis of Contributing Partner's Interest

The partner's original basis for a partnership interest acquired by a contribution is:

2.1.1 Initial Basis

The partner's initial basis in the partnership interest is:

▪ **Cash:** Amount contributed.

▪ **Property:** Adjusted basis (NBV).

▪ **(Liabilities):** Incoming partner's liabilities assumed by other partners is a reduction.

▪ **Services:** Fair market value (and taxable to incoming partner if issued in exchange for a capital interest).

▪ **Liabilities:** Other partners' liabilities assumed by incoming partner, loans guaranteed by the partner, or loans made by the partner to the partnership.

2.1.2 Property Subject to an (Excess) Liability

As previously mentioned, when property that is subject to a liability is contributed to a partnership and the subsequent decrease in the partner's individual liability exceeds his or her partnership basis, the excess amount is treated like taxable boot, which means there is a taxable gain to the partner.

Pass Key

In a partnership, it is important to remember to subtract only the liabilities *assumed* by the *other partners* and not the entire liability.

Illustration 1   Contributed Property With Excess Liability

Becker and Peter admit Tim to their partnership as a one-third partner. Tim contributes a building that is worth $500,000 but has a basis of $100,000. There is a mortgage of $225,000 on the building, assumed by the partnership.

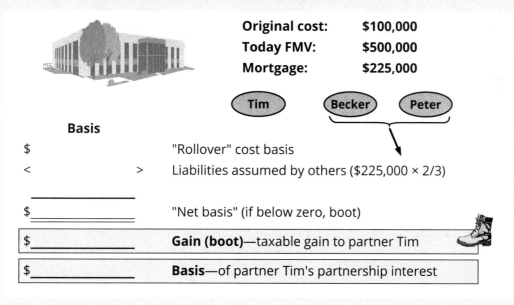

Original cost:	**$100,000**	
Today FMV:	**$500,000**	
Mortgage:	**$225,000**	

Basis

$		"Rollover" cost basis
<	>	Liabilities assumed by others ($225,000 × 2/3)
$_____		"Net basis" (if below zero, boot)
$_____		**Gain (boot)**—taxable gain to partner Tim
$_____		**Basis**—of partner Tim's partnership interest

Pass Key

A partner's capital account in a partnership can never begin with a negative balance (when liabilities assumed by partnership are greater than the adjusted basis (NBV) of assets contributed). The excess liability is treated as taxable boot, and the recognized gain increases the capital account to a "zero" starting point.

2.1.3 Holding Period of Partnership Interest

If the property was previously a capital asset or Section 1231 asset in the hands of the partner, the partner's holding period for his partnership interest includes the holding period of the property contributed. If the property is an ordinary income asset (i.e., inventory), the holding period begins on the date the property is contributed to the partnership.

2.1.4 Subsequent Transactions

■ Subsequent contributions will increase a partner's basis.

■ Subsequent withdrawals will decrease a partner's basis.

2.1.5 Partnership Income/Loss

After initial formation, the partner's basis will:

■ increase by her pro rata share of income and increase of partnership liabilities.

■ decrease by her pro rata share of losses and decrease in partnership liabilities.

2.1.6 Special Allocation: Contributed Appreciated (or Built-in Loss) Property

When a partner contributes property with an FMV that is higher or lower than the property's adjusted basis (or NBV), a built-in gain (or loss) exists at the date of contribution. Upon the subsequent sale of that property, the "built-in" gain or loss that existed at the date of contribution must be specially allocated to the contributing partner. (Note that any gains or losses that occur after the contribution date are allocated among the partners in the partnership.)

2.2 Partnership's Basis for Contributed Property

The partnership's basis in the contributed property is the contributor's basis, or carryover basis (plus any gain recognized by the incoming partner, if a special election is made). The partnership's holding period for contributed property includes the time held by the partner, regardless of the character of the contributed property.

Pass Key

- "Outside basis" is a partnership concept that refers to the basis a partner has in the ownership interest in the partnership. This partnership interest has a tax basis similar to ownership interests in other property.

- "Inside basis" refers to the basis that the partnership itself has in the assets it owns. This inside basis can come from contributions made by the partners. As a general rule, the basis of an asset contributed by a partner would carry over and be the basis of the asset in the hands of the partnership. In addition, inside basis can come from purchases the partnership makes with partnership funds.

Example 4 — Calculation of Inside and Outside Basis

Facts: In Year 1, Jeff contributes the following items in exchange for a one-third interest in KNC Partnership:

- $10,000 cash.

- Building with FMV of $300,000 and adjusted basis to Jeff of $100,000. The building is subject to a liability of $90,000.

- In Year 2, Jeff contributes another building with FMV of $600,000 and an adjusted basis to Jeff of $300,000.

- The partnership had $150,000 of net income in Year 2.

Required: Determine Jeff's initial outside basis in the partnership at Year 1, and his outside basis at the end of Year 2. Also determine the partnership's inside basis and holding period in Jeff's contributed assets.

Solution: Jeff's initial outside basis in KNC Partnership is $50,000, calculated as follows:

- $10,000 cash, plus $100,000 adjusted basis of building, less $60,000 (liabilities assumed by other partners, $90,000 × 2/3).

- KNC's inside basis in the building contributed by Jeff in Year 1 is the adjusted basis in his hands, $100,000. KNC's holding period in the building will start when the property was initially purchased by Jeff.

Jeff's basis at the end of Year 2 is $400,000, calculated as follows:

- $50,000 beginning basis, plus $300,000 adjusted basis of contributed building, plus $50,000 share of partnership income in Year 2 ($150,000 × 1/3).

- The partnership will again take a carryover basis of $300,000 and carryover holding period in the new building.

3   Partnership Operations: Partner Basis Formula

| Formation |
| **Operation** |
| Taxation |
| Distribution |
| Liquidation |

B   **Beginning Capital Account**
- Cash
- FMV services
- NBV assets
  < liability >

A   **+ % All Income**
- Ordinary
- Capital
- Tax-free

< % All Losses >

Partner may take a partnership loss as a tax deduction up to his/her basis

S   **< Withdrawals >**

Property distribution: Reduce capital account by the adjusted basis (NBV) of the distributed property; cannot go below zero in the capital account

—————————

E   **Ending Capital Account**

**+ % Liabilities
(recourse and nonrecourse)**
—————————

Year-end Basis
═════════

Pass Key

It is important to remember the difference between capital account and partnership basis:

Basis = Capital account + Partner's share of liabilities

4 Partnership Tax Returns

A partnership is not subject to income taxes, but it still must file a partnership tax return (Form 1065). A Form 1065 is an informational return (including Schedules K and K-1) that provides detailed information about partnership income and expenses and indicates the amount and type of each partner's distributive share of income (or loss). Each partner is liable only for taxes due on his distributive share of partnership income, as reported on Schedule K-1, regardless of whether the distribution is actually made to the partner.

| Formation |
| Operation |
| **Taxation** |
| Distribution |
| Liquidation |

4.1 Accounting Periods of the Partnership

- **Adoption of Partnership Tax Year**

  - **Calendar Year (Generally Required):** A partnership return is due on March 15.

  - **Fiscal Year:** A three-month deferral (October, November, December) is the maximum permitted.

- **When Partnership Terminates**

  A partnership terminates when:

  - Operations cease.

  - There are fewer than two partners (i.e., the partnership becomes a sole proprietorship).

4.2 Transactions Between Partner and Partnership

4.2.1 Partner Not Acting in Capacity of Partner

Generally, if a partner enters into a transaction (other than in her capacity as a partner) with her partnership (such as rendering services to the partnership, or sales between a partner and partnership), the transaction is deemed to have occurred between the partnership and an unrelated party, subject to the following limitations:

- **Related Party Loss (WRaP) Is Disallowed**

  As discussed in an earlier unit when addressing related party transactions (WRaP), losses (directly or indirectly) between a controlling partner (over 50 percent interest in capital or profits) and his controlled partnership from the sale or exchange of property are not allowed.

- **Related Party Gain Is Ordinary Income**

  Gains (directly or indirectly) between a controlling partner (over 50 percent interest in capital or profits) and her controlled partnership, or between two controlled partnerships, from the sale or exchange of assets shall be treated as ordinary income if the property is not a capital asset in the hands of the transferee.

4.2.2 Constructive Ownership

Ownership of capital or interest in the profits of a partnership shall be determined by certain rules of constructive ownership as defined in Section 267 of the Internal Revenue Code.

Question 1   MCQ-08044

Able, Bill, and Connor admit Dan as a 25 percent partner in the ABC&D partnership. Able, Bill, and Connor each own 25 percent. Dan contributes a parcel of land with a basis to Dan of $50,000 and a fair market value of $150,000. The land is subject to a liability of $60,000 assumed by the partnership. Able, Bill, Connor, and Dan will share profits and losses equally.

What is Dan's gain, basis in the partnership, as well as the impact on the other partners' basis upon Dan's contribution?

	Dan's Gain	*Dan's Partnership Basis*	*Impact on Basis of Other Partners*
a.	$0	$5,000	Increase by $15,000 each
b.	$10,000	$50,000	Remains the same
c.	$5,000	$45,000	Decreases by $15,000 each
d.	$0	$40,000	Remains the same

Question 2   MCQ-04917

Ball and Baig are equal partners in the firm of Games Associates. On January 1 of the current year, each partner's adjusted basis in Games was $50,000. During the year, Games borrowed $80,000, for which Ball and Baig are personally liable. Games sustained an operating loss of $30,000 for the current year. The basis of each partner's interest in Games at the end of the current year was:

- **a.** $35,000
- **b.** $50,000
- **c.** $65,000
- **d.** $75,000

1 Determination of Partner's Share of Income, Credits, and Deductions

1.1 Taxable Income

A partner must include his distributive share of partnership income (even if not received) in his tax return for his taxable year within which the taxable year of the partnership ends. For tax years beginning after December 31, 2017, the Tax Cuts and Jobs Act added a 20 percent deduction for partners for qualified business income. The deduction is below the line and is discussed in detail in R1.

Pass Key

A frequently tested concept on the CPA Examination is the timing of taxable income to a partner. An easy way to remember the timing of taxable income and basis impact is to associate the partnership interest to a *bank account*:

Event	Tax Consequence	Basis Impact
Income	Taxable	Increase
Withdrawals	Nontaxable	Decrease

1.2 Tax Losses (Limited to Tax Basis/"At Risk" and Must Clear Passive Loss Hurdle)

Tax losses generated by a partnership are deductible by the partners of the partnership and can be used to offset ordinary income. For the partner to deduct the losses, the losses must clear four hurdles:

1. tax basis;

2. at-risk amount;

3. passive activity; and

4. excess business loss

1.2.1 Losses Limited to Tax Basis

The partnership tax loss deduction is limited to the partner's adjusted basis in the partnership, which is increased by any partnership liabilities for which he is personally liable or additional capital contributions to the partnership.

1.2.2 Losses Limited to At-Risk Amount

The ability to deduct losses is limited to the partner's "at-risk" amount in the partnership. The at-risk amount is calculated in a similar manner to a partner's tax basis, but a partner's "at-risk" amount in the partnership does not include certain nonrecourse liabilities.

- **Nonrecourse Liability**

  - A partnership liability is a nonrecourse liability if no partner or related person has an economic risk of loss for that liability.

  - This is the case for a loan secured by property, where the lender's only cause for remedy if the company defaults is to foreclose on the property. In addition, all liabilities to a limited partner are nonrecourse liabilities, because the limited partner will not be personally liable for that liability with certain exceptions.

- **Recourse Liabilities**

  Recourse liabilities are those liabilities for which a partner is personally liable. In traditional partnerships, one or more general partners are responsible for all recourse liabilities. Recourse liabilities may also include any loans made directly by a partner to the partnership, or those personally guaranteed by a partner (whether a limited partner or not). For basis calculation purposes, recourse liabilities are allocated only to the partner, or partners, with liability for the debt.

Example 1	Nonrecourse and Recourse Liabilities

Facts: A partnership has $60,000 in nonrecourse liabilities and $30,000 in recourse liabilities. It has three partners (A, B, and C), each with a one-third interest in the partnership. A is the general partner, and B and C are limited partners.

Required: Calculate each partner's basis in the partnership's liabilities, including their at-risk amounts.

Solution:

Partner A: $50,000 total basis in partnership liabilities (one-third of $60,000 nonrecourse liabilities plus $30,000 of recourse liabilities, assumed as the general partner); $30,000 is at-risk.

Partner B: $20,000 total basis in partnership liabilities, none of which are at-risk (one-third of $60,000 nonrecourse liabilities).

Partner C: $20,000 total basis in partnership liabilities, none of which are at-risk (one-third of $60,000 nonrecourse liabilities).

1.2.3 Passive Loss Limitations

After applying the tax basis and at-risk limitations, the partner must then consider the passive activity loss limitations to determine whether the loss from a partnership is deductible. The passive activity loss rules limit the ability of partners involved in passive activities (such as rental or real estate or nonactive participation in a partnership) from using ordinary losses from the passive activity to reduce ordinary taxable income.

1.2.4 Excess Business Loss Limitations

The pass-through losses are also subject to the $250,000 ceiling ($500,000 for married filing jointly) on aggregate business losses (discussed in more detail in R1).

1.2.5 Carryforward of Losses

- Any unused loss resulting from the tax basis limitations can be carried forward and used in a future year when basis becomes available.

- Any unused loss resulting from the at-risk limitation can be carried forward until the partner generates additional at-risk amounts to utilize the loss or until they are used to reduce the gain from selling a partnership interest.

- Any unused loss resulting from the passive activity limitation can be carried forward until additional passive income can be generated to absorb the loss or until the taxpayer sells the activity that generates the passive loss.

- The excess business losses are carried forward as part of an NOL carryforward, which can be used to offset up to 80 percent of taxable income.

Example 2	Tax Basis, Calculation of At-Risk Amount, and Loss Limitations With Active Participation in Business

Facts: Rachel created a limited liability company (LLC), which she elected to have taxed as a partnership, to sell her handmade necklaces. Rachel had an initial cash contribution to the business of $20,000. Additionally, Rachel was allocated $5,000 of recourse debt that she had personally guaranteed and $8,000 of nonrecourse debt. In the first year of operation, Rachel was allocated $35,000 of loss from the LLC.

Required: Calculate her tax basis in the LLC. Calculate her "at-risk" amount in the LLC. Calculate how much of the loss from the LLC she can deduct on her individual tax return.

Solution: Rachel's tax basis in the LLC is $33,000 ($20,000 cash contribution + $5,000 recourse debt + $8,000 nonrecourse debt). Rachel's at-risk amount is $25,000 ($20,000 cash contribution + $5,000 recourse debt).

First, Rachel's loss is limited to her tax basis in the LLC of $33,000. Rachel must then consider the at-risk limitation. The $33,000 loss, which cleared the tax basis hurdle, is now limited to her at-risk amount of $25,000. Rachel may deduct $25,000 of the $35,000 loss. The $2,000 loss suspended by the tax basis limitation ($35,000 – $33,000) is carried forward and can only be used when additional basis is created. The $8,000 loss limited by the at-risk criteria is carried forward until the partner generates additional at-risk amounts to utilize the loss.

Example 3	Tax Basis, Calculation of At-Risk Amount, and Loss Limitations With Passive Activity

Facts: Rachel created a limited liability company (LLC), which she elected to have taxed as a partnership, to sell rental real estate. Rachel is not an active participant in the business. Rachel does not have passive income from other activities.

Rachel had an initial cash contribution to the business of $100,000. Additionally, Rachel was allocated $20,000 of recourse debt that she had personally guaranteed and $30,000 of nonrecourse debt. In the first year of operation, Rachel was allocated $50,000 of loss from the LLC.

Required: Calculate her tax basis in the LLC. Calculate her "at-risk" amount in the LLC. Calculate how much of the loss from the LLC she can deduct on her individual tax return when considering the limitations imposed by the tax basis, at-risk, and passive activity limitations.

Solution: Rachel's tax basis in the LLC is $150,000 ($100,000 cash contribution + $20,000 recourse debt + $30,000 nonrecourse debt). Rachel's at-risk amount is $120,000 ($100,000 cash contribution + $20,000 recourse debt).

When considering whether she can deduct her $50,000 loss from the partnership on her individual tax return, she easily clears the tax basis and at-risk hurdles. However, because Rachel has no passive income from other sources, she is not able to deduct any of the $50,000 loss. The loss is carried forward until she generates passive income or until she sells the LLC that has generated the loss.

1.3   Guaranteed Payments

Guaranteed payments are reasonable compensation paid to a partner for services rendered or use of capital without regard to the partner's profit- or loss-sharing ratio. They are allowable tax deductions to the partnership and taxable income to the partner.

1.3.1   Guaranteed Payments Tax Treatment

▪ **Partnership Tax Deduction:** Guaranteed payments are allowable tax deductions to the partnership for services (guaranteed salary) or for the use of capital (guaranteed interest) without regard to partnership income or profit- and loss-sharing ratios (this includes the FMV of capital partnership interests issued in exchange for services contributed).

▪ **Partner Taxable Income:** Guaranteed payments are also included on Schedule K-1, line 4, as ordinary income to the partner (they may also be included as part of net earnings from self-employment on line 14a). Guaranteed payments for services are not included in qualified business income for purposes of the Section 199A deduction for flow-through business entities, as discussed in R1.

▪ **Payments (Salaries) Not Guaranteed:** Payments that are not guaranteed are merely another way to distribute partnership profits. They are not a tax deduction to the partnership because the payments are considered partner draws or partner distributions.

1.4   Retirement Payments

Payments received by a retired partner that are not in liquidation of a partnership interest (but are merely retirement benefit payments) are treated as follows:

- Ordinary income to the recipient; and
- Deductions to the partnership.

1.5   Tax Elections

Most elections that affect the calculation of taxable income are made by the partnership. Some of these elections are:

- Organizational expenditures and start-up costs (discussed below).
- Accounting methods (cash or accrual).
- Tax year (fiscal, if not calendar).
- Depreciation methods (MACRS, straight-line, etc.).
- Elections out of installment sale treatment.
- Section 754 election for optional basis adjustment of partnership assets.

1.6   Organizational Expenditures and Start-up Costs

1.6.1   Calculation

The partnership may elect to deduct up to $5,000 each of organizational expenditures and start-up costs. Each $5,000 amount is reduced by the amount by which the organizational expenditures or start-up costs exceed $50,000, respectively. Any excess organizational expenditures or start-up costs are amortized over 180 months (beginning with the month in which the active trade or business begins).

1.6.2   Included Costs

Allowable organizational expenditures include fees paid for legal services in drafting the partnership agreement, fees paid for accounting services, and fees paid for partnership filings. Start-up costs include training costs, advertising costs, and testing costs incurred prior to the opening of the business.

1.7   Syndication Costs (Nondeductible)

Syndication costs (e.g., offering materials) are not deductible.

1.8   Calculation of "Cancellation of Debt" Income

When a partnership transfers a capital or profits interest in the partnership to a creditor in satisfaction of partnership debt, the partnership recognizes cancellation of debt income. The amount of such income is the excess of the amount of the debt discharged (canceled) over the fair market value of the partnership interest that the partnership transfers to the creditor.

2 Reporting Partnership Income and Losses (K-1)

A partner must include on a personal income tax return the partner's distributive share of each separate "pass-through" item. The reporting of these items on Form 1040 is covered in R1. The following chart (also in R1) shows which partnership items will be reported separately on Form 1065 and which will pass through to each individual partner's income tax return as separate line items to be treated by each individual partner according to his or her own circumstances.

	Appears On		
	1065	*K*	*K-1*
Business income	✓		
< Business expenses >	✓		
< Guaranteed Payments >			
1. **Net business income or loss***	✓	✓	✓
2. Guaranteed payments to partners	✓	✓	✓
3. Net "active" rental real estate income or loss		✓	✓
4. Net "passive" rental real estate income or loss		✓	✓
5. Interest income		✓	✓
6. Dividend income		✓	✓
7. Capital gains and losses		✓	✓
8. Charitable contributions		✓	✓
9. Section 179 (expense election)		✓	✓
10. Investment interest expense		✓	✓
11. Partners' health insurance premiums (reported as part of guaranteed payments)	✓	✓	✓
12. Retirement plan contributions (Keogh plan)**	✓	✓	✓
13. Tax credits (reported by partnership but claimed by partners)*		✓	✓

*Net business loss limitations discussed earlier in this unit will have to be considered.

**Contributions made on behalf of employees are deductible on Form 1065 and not reported on Schedules K and K-1; contributions for partners are not deducted on Form 1065 but are reported on Schedules K and K-1.

Example 4	Ordinary Income Calculation and Other Separately Stated Items

Facts: A partnership had the following items of income and deductions for the year:

Gross business income	$250,000
Dividend income	8,000
Salary expense	50,000
Rent expense	15,000
Depreciation expense	10,000
Section 179 expense	30,000
Charitable contributions	20,000

Required: Determine the partnership's ordinary business income or loss and separately stated items for the year.

Solution: Ordinary business income for the year is $175,000, calculated as follows:

Gross business income	$250,000 less
Salary expense	50,000 less
Rent expense	15,000 less
Depreciation expense	10,000

The separately stated items reported on Schedule K are:

Dividend income	$ 8,000
Section 179 expense	30,000
Charitable contributions	20,000

3 Reporting Partnership Losses (Limited to Basis)

Generally, a partner's distributive share of the partnership loss is allowed as an adjustment to the basis of such partner's interest in the partnership at the end of the partnership's tax year. A partner's loss in excess of basis will be a carryforward indefinitely (and remain suspended until basis is reestablished).

Example 5	Reporting Partnership Losses

Facts: On January 1, Year 1, Becker and Conviser formed a partnership with each contributing the following property:

	Basis	FMV
Becker	$30,000	$30,000
Conviser	6,000	30,000

The partners have agreed to share profits and losses equally. During Year 1, each partner withdrew $3,000; and for the year ended December 31, Year 1, the partnership's operating loss was $8,000.

(continued)

(continued)

Required: Determine how much of the operating loss each partner may deduct in Year 1.

Solution: Conviser's Year 1 loss would be limited to his basis, $3,000, calculated as follows:

	Becker	Conviser
Original contributions (NBV)	$30,000	$ 6,000
Less: withdrawals	(3,000)	(3,000)
Basis at end of tax year before loss pass-through	27,000	3,000
Each partner's share of operating loss of $8,000	$ (4,000)	(4,000)
Conviser's loss limited to basis of		(3,000)
Basis at end of tax year	$23,000	$ -0-
Excess is carried forward indefinitely until utilized against future increases in basis		$(1,000)

4   Nonliquidating Distributions

- In general, a nonliquidating distribution to a partner is nontaxable, both to the partner and the partnership.

- In general, distributions of cash or property to a partner reduce the partner's basis by the cash or adjusted basis (NBV) of the property distributed.

- In a nonliquidating distribution, the basis of property received will be the same as the basis in the hands of the partnership immediately prior to the distribution.

> Formation
>
> Operation
>
> Taxation
>
> **Distribution**
>
> Liquidation

4.1   Basis Assigned to Distributed Property

The basis of distributed property assigned may not exceed the basis of a partner's entire interest in the partnership (reduced by the amount of cash distributed in the same transaction).

- **Partnership Basis Is Greater Than Book Value of Asset**

  When a partner's basis in the partnership is *greater* than the book value of an asset received, no gain is recognized because the partner's basis in the partnership is simply reduced by the net book value of the property distributed (and a positive basis in the partnership still remains). The basis of the distributed asset to the partner will be the prior basis to the partnership.

- **Partnership Basis Is Less Than Book Value of Asset**

  If the partner's basis in the partnership is *less* than the book value of the asset received, however, there is a limit to the partnership basis reduction under the general rule. Although no gain is recognized in this case either, the partner's basis in the partnership cannot go below zero. This means that the partner's basis in the asset received as a distribution will equal his basis in the partnership just before the distribution (after any cash paid in the same transaction). The partner's remaining basis in the partnership will then be zero.

4.2 Gain on Excess Cash

Gain is recognized to the partner only to the extent that cash (including partnership liability assumed by a partner) distributed exceeds the adjusted basis of the partner's interest in the partnership immediately before the distribution. In a complete liquidation, the partner's basis for the distributed property is the same as the adjusted basis of the partner's partnership interest, reduced by any monies actually received.

Example 6 | **Basis Determination in Nonliquidating Distribution**

Facts: Olinto's adjusted basis of his interest in a partnership was $30,000. He received a nonliquidating distribution of $24,000 cash plus a parcel of land with a fair market value of $12,000 and partnership basis of $9,000.

Required: Determine Olinto's basis for the land distributed.

Solution: Olinto's basis for the land is $6,000.

Rule: The basis of property received in a distribution, other than in liquidation of a partner's interest, ordinarily will be the same as the basis in the hands of the partnership immediately prior to distribution. However, in no case may the basis of property in the hands of the partner exceed the basis of his partnership interest reduced by the amount of money distributed to him in the same transaction.

Partnership interest adjusted prior to distribution	$ 30,000
Amount of cash distributed	(24,000)
Remaining basis after cash distribution	*6,000*
Distribution of land with basis of $9,000	(6,000)
Remaining partnership interest	$ -0-

The partnership interest may not be reduced below zero. Therefore, the land has a basis of $6,000 in the hands of the partner.

---

5 Limited Partnerships

The limited partnership was designed to allow limited partners to invest in the business but not have the drawback of personal liability. A limited partnership is like a general partnership with the exception that limited partnerships have both general partners and limited partners. The key difference related to liability for general and limited partners include the following:

■ General partners have unlimited liability for the debts and obligations of the partnership.

■ Limited partners' liability is limited to the total amount of their investment in the partnership. They do not have personal liability for the debts and obligations of the partnership.

6 Limited Liability Companies

A limited liability company (LLC) is a separate legal entity from its owners. As with corporate shareholders, LLC "members" are not personally liable for the obligations of the business. All members of an LLC have "limited liability," which is different from a limited partnership, where at least one general partner is personally liable for all partnership debts.

6.1 Formation

The business owner files articles of organization with the state where the LLC is organized, which is similar to the formation of a corporation. The following list summarizes some of the key points a business owner should consider when trying to decide whether or not to organize a business as an LLC:

- An LLC provides similar protection from liabilities as a corporation but does not have the "double taxation" of a corporation if the LLC is taxed as a partnership.

- LLC members generally have the right to amend the LLC operating agreement, provide input, and manage LLCs, yet corporate shareholders generally do not have these same rights.

- An LLC cannot become a public company. It must convert to a corporation before issuing an IPO.

- S corporations have restrictions on the type and number of shareholders they may have. LLCs do not have these same restrictions.

- A sole proprietorship may become a single member LLC if it files articles of organization with a state.

6.2 Taxation

For federal income tax purposes, an LLC is treated as one of the following: a partnership, corporation, or sole proprietorship. The Internal Revenue Code does not specifically address taxation of limited liability companies. A limited liability company with at least two owners is taxed as a partnership unless an election is made to have the LLC taxed as a C corporation. Such an election is made on Form 8832, Entity Classification Election. A single member LLC, not electing to be taxed as a corporation, is considered a disregarded entity for federal income tax purposes and will be treated as a sole proprietorship.

Question 1	MCQ-01793

The adjusted basis of Jody's partnership interest was $50,000 immediately before Jody received a current distribution of $20,000 cash and property with an adjusted basis to the partnership of $40,000 and a fair market value of $35,000.

What is Jody's basis in the distributed property?

    a. $0

    b. $30,000

    c. $35,000

    d. $40,000

Question 2	MCQ-01791

The adjusted basis of Jody's partnership interest was $50,000 immediately before Jody received a current distribution of $20,000 cash and property with an adjusted basis to the partnership of $40,000 and a fair market value of $35,000.

What amount of taxable gain must Jody report as a result of this distribution?

- **a.** $0
- **b.** $5,000
- **c.** $10,000
- **d.** $20,000

NOTES

1 Section 754 Election and Section 743(b) Basis Adjustment

Partnerships have the option to make a Section 754 election when certain distributions of property from the partnership to a partner occur, or when there is a transfer of a partnership interest by sale or exchange, or upon the death of a partner.

- **Transfer of Partnership Interest**

  In the case of a Section 754 election being made by reason of sale or exchange, a Section 743(b) adjustment follows. The Section 743(b) adjustment equals the difference between the value of the outside basis to the transferee partner (e.g., purchase price) and her share of the partnership's inside basis of the assets. This adjustment, which can be either positive or negative, is prorated over the partnership assets under the rules set forth in Section 755. The goal of the adjustment is to make the transferee have an inside basis in the partnership assets equal her outside basis. The adjustment is specially allocated only to the transferee and has no effect on the partnership's income or loss. Once the election is made, it remains in effect for all future transactions (being revoked only with permission from the IRS). Alternatively, even in the absence of a Section 754 election, the IRS mandates a 743(b) adjustment when there is a substantial built-in loss at the time of purchase (inside basis exceeds outside basis by $250,000 or more).

Example 1	Transfer of Partnership Interest

Facts: Oscar purchases Bernice's 25 percent interest in Handly Partnership for $500,000. At the time of sale, Handly makes a 754 election to adjust the basis of the partnership asset. Immediately before the sale, the inside basis in the partnership asset (a building) is $1,200,000 and the fair market value is $2,000,000.

Required: Calculate the basis adjustment required under Section 743(b), and describe the consequences of a future sale of the asset.

Solution: The 743(b) basis adjustment is $200,000 ($500,000 purchase price of partnership interest less $300,000, which is Oscar's 25 percent interest in the $1,200,000 inside basis of the partnership assets), allocated entirely to Oscar. The basis adjustment is entirely a tax concept and does not impact the book value of the partnership's assets.

If the building is subsequently sold at fair market value of $2,000,000, a tax gain would be recognized in the amount of $600,000 ($2,000,000 less $1,400,000 adjusted basis with step-up). The $600,000 gain would be allocated to the other partners besides Oscar. No gain is allocated to Oscar.

2 Liquidation of a Partnership

There are three ways in which a partner may liquidate a partnership interest:

- Complete withdrawal
- Sale of partnership interest
- Retirement or death

Formation
Operation
Taxation
Distribution
Liquidation

2.1 Complete Withdrawal

In a complete liquidation, the partner's basis for the distributed property is the same as the adjusted basis of the partner's partnership interest, reduced by any monies actually received. The adjusted basis needs to be determined immediately before the partner's liquidation, after all other items of partnership income/loss and liabilities assumed have been taken into account for the year.

- **Nontaxable Liquidation**

> Beginning capital account
>
> Percentage of income < loss > up to withdrawal
> ___
> Partner's capital account
>
> Percentage of liabilities
> ___
> Adjusted basis at date of withdrawal
>
> < Cash withdrawn >
> ___
> Remaining basis to be allocated to assets withdrawn
> ___

- **Gain Recognized**

  The partner recognizes gain only to the extent that money received exceeds the partner's basis in the partnership.

- **Loss Recognized**

  The partner recognizes loss if money, unrealized receivables, or inventory are the only assets received and if the basis of the assets received is less than the partner's adjusted basis in the partnership.

Illustration 1   Liquidating Distributions: Impact on a Partner

The adjusted basis of Tag's interest in the KJT partnership is $24,000. Upon retirement, Tag receives a liquidating distribution of $5,000 in cash and $20,000 in real estate that has an adjusted basis to the partnership of $10,000. Tag will have a basis in the real estate of $19,000 (his adjusted basis of $24,000 less $5,000 cash received).

Alternative scenario: If Tag had instead received $25,000 in cash as well as the real estate, Tag would recognize a $1,000 gain (his adjusted basis of $24,000 less $25,000 cash received). The real estate received would have zero basis to Tag.

Alternative scenario: If Tag had received $20,000 in cash and no real estate, Tag would recognize a loss of $4,000 (his adjusted basis of $24,000 less $20,000 cash received), because there were no other assets distributed to allocate basis.

Pass Key

The CPA Examination will require candidates to understand the difference in basis rules for nonliquidating and liquidating distributions.

Withdrawal	Basis Used	Stopping Point
Nonliquidating	NBV asset taken	Stop at zero
Liquidating	Partnership interest	Must "zero-out" account

2.2   Consequences to a Partnership

As a result of liquidation, the partnership itself does not recognize any entity level gain or loss on the distribution of assets. Any gain/loss recognition on liquidating distributions are made at the partner level, as previously discussed. In addition, because a partnership itself is not subject to income taxes and is a "flow-through" entity, all effects of winding-up the affairs of the partnership and liquidating are passed on to the partners. This includes any gain or loss on sale of any assets sold off, expenses of liquidating the partnership, etc. All of these items will be included in the partners' adjusted basis immediately before their liquidating distributions.

3   Sale of Partnership Interest (Liquidation)

As a general rule, the partner has a capital gain or loss when transferring a partnership interest because a partnership interest is a capital asset.

■ **Gain or Loss on Transfer (General Rule: Capital)**

A partner who sells or exchanges his interest in the partnership has a recognized gain or loss. The gain or loss is measured by the difference between the amount realized for the sale and the adjusted basis of the partnership interest. If any partnership liabilities are allocated to the interest and transferred to the buyer, they are considered part of the amount realized.

■ **Capital Gain or Loss Calculation**

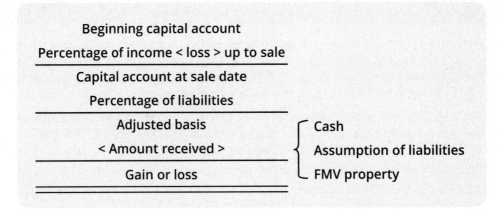

Beginning capital account

Percentage of income < loss > up to sale

Capital account at sale date

Percentage of liabilities

Adjusted basis

< Amount received >

Gain or loss

Cash
Assumption of liabilities
FMV property

Example 2	Calculating Amount Realized on Sale of Partnership Interest

Facts: Kristi sells her interest in the KJT partnership to the partnership for $15,000 cash. The partnership agrees to assume her $5,000 share in partnership liabilities.

Required: Determine the amount realized on the sale of Kristi's partnership interest.

Solution: The amount realized in the transaction is $20,000 ($15,000 plus $5,000). The $20,000 will be compared with the basis of Kristi's partnership interest in order to determine her gain or loss.

■ **Exception (Ordinary Income, Not Capital Gain)**

Any gain that represents a partner's share of "hot assets" is treated as "ordinary income," as if cash were taken. Hot assets are:

- unrealized (cash basis) receivables (as if exchanged for cash);

- appreciated inventory (as if exchanged for cash); and

- "recapture income" regarding depreciable assets owned by the partnership.

4 Retirement or Death of Partner

Payments to a retiring partner or to the interest successor of a deceased partner in liquidation of her entire partnership interest are allocated between payment for an interest in partnership assets and other payments.

■ Payments for the interest in partnership assets result in capital gain or loss.

■ If the payments are measured by partnership income, they are treated as partnership income regardless of the period over which they are paid. Thus, such payments are taxable as ordinary income to the retired partner as if he or she continued to be a partner.

■ When a partner sells his or her interest to a new partner in the middle of the tax year, the selling partner's share of partnership income or losses must be allocated pro rata (based on the date of sale) between the selling partner and the purchasing partner.

Example 3	Proration of Partnership Income

Facts: Assume that Partner A, a 20 percent partner, sells to New Partner X on March 31. The partnership reported $80,000 of partnership income for the entire tax year.

Required: Determine A's and X's shares of partnership income for the year.

Solution: Because A sold after one fourth of the year, then A will only report as his pro rata share 5 percent of the partnership's annual income ($4,000), and X will report 15 percent ($12,000).

5 Liquidation of an LLC

The liquidation of an LLC and the consequences to its members will be treated the same as either a corporation or a partnership, whichever form the LLC elected to take for federal income tax purposes upon formation. (Corporate liquidations are covered in a previous unit.)

Question 1	MCQ-01802

On December 31 of the current year, after receipt of his share of partnership income, Clark sold his interest in a limited partnership for $30,000 cash and relief of all liabilities. On that date, the adjusted basis of Clark's partnership interest was $40,000, consisting of his capital account of $15,000 and his share of the partnership liabilities of $25,000. The partnership has no unrealized receivables or substantially appreciated inventory. What is Clark's gain or loss on the sale of his partnership interest?

    a. Ordinary loss of $10,000.

    b. Ordinary gain of $15,000.

    c. Capital loss of $10,000.

    d. Capital gain of $15,000.

Question 2

MCQ-01796

The adjusted basis of Vance's partnership interest in Lex Associates was $180,000 immediately before receiving the following distribution in complete liquidation of Lex:

	Basis to Lex	Fair Market Value
Cash	$100,000	$100,000
Real estate	70,000	96,000

What is Vance's basis in the real estate?

   a. $96,000

   b. $83,000

   c. $80,000

   d. $70,000

Question 3

MCQ-05960

Baker is a partner in BDT with a partnership basis of $60,000. BDT made a liquidating distribution of land with an adjusted basis of $75,000 and a fair market value of $40,000 to Baker. What amount of gain or loss should Baker report?

   a. $35,000 loss

   b. $20,000 loss

   c. $0

   d. $15,000 gain

Question 4

MCQ-05981

Fern received $30,000 in cash and an automobile with an adjusted basis and market value of $20,000 in a proportionate liquidating distribution from EF Partnership. Fern's basis in the partnership interest was $60,000 before the distribution. What is Fern's basis in the automobile received in the liquidation?

   a. $0

   b. $10,000

   c. $20,000

   d. $30,000

1 Affiliated Groups and Transfer Pricing

An affiliated group of businesses having operations in several countries and conducting sales between affiliates could have a pricing structure that (i) intentionally or unintentionally understates income in some or all of those countries, including the United States; and (ii) results in some countries not receiving as much income tax.

Illustration 1	Sales Between Affiliates

Holding Company, a U.S.-based company, owns 100 percent of the stock of three subsidiaries, each in a different country:

- M Company, a manufacturer in Country M having an income tax rate of 10 percent

- W Company, a wholesaler and distributor in Country W having an income tax rate of 20 percent

- R Company, a retailer in the U.S. having an income tax rate of 30 percent

Facts:

1. Country M and Country W use the U.S. dollar for their currencies.

2. M Company manufactures and sells widgets both to W Company and to unrelated parties. W Company sells those widgets at wholesale to unrelated parties. W Company also sells those widgets to R Company. R Company sells the widgets at retail to unrelated parties for $9 per widget.

3. M Company's cost of goods sold is $1 per widget.

Assumptions: For purposes of this example (and to simplify this example), assume the following:

1. None of the subsidiaries has any selling, general, or administrative expenses.

2. Countries M and W do not impose any withholding on dividends paid by companies in those countries to shareholders in other countries.

3. There is no income tax on dividends received.

Set forth below is how Holding Company, in order to minimize income taxes, would ideally want to structure each sale between the subsidiaries:

	M Company	W Company	R Company	Consolidated Corporate Group
Tax rate:	10%	20%	30%	
Sales	$9.00	$9.00	$9.00	$9.00
COGS	(1.00)	(9.00)	(9.00)	(1.00)
EBT	$8.00	$0	$0	$8.00
Tax	(0.80)	0	0	(0.80)
N.I.	$7.20	$0	$0	$7.20

(continued)

(continued)

Although Country M's taxing authorities would not be displeased with this pricing structure (as the corporate group's entire profit is subject to Country M's income tax), the IRS (and the taxing authorities in Country W) would not be pleased with this pricing structure because the corporate group is not paying any income tax to the United States (or to Country W).

To address this situation, the Internal Revenue Code (Sections 482 and 6662(e)(3)) provides the IRS with the authority (i) to adjust the income and deductions (including COGS) of M Company, W Company, and R Company to prevent evasion of taxes or to clearly reflect income; and (ii) to impose penalties with respect to those adjustments. As a result, with respect to R Company's sales of widgets, the IRS would most likely reduce R Company's COGS, and R Company would then pay income tax to the U.S. Treasury.

Additional Explanatory Note: The corporate group knows that every widget that the group (via R Company) sells to end users/customers will bring the group $9. So, if we ignore IRC Section 482, the group wants to set up an intercompany pricing arrangement that will minimize the group's income taxes due, per sale, to all countries. The best way to do so is to have M sell to W at $9; next W sells to R at $9; and then R sells to the end customer at $9. In this manner, the entire profit of the corporate group is reported by M, the company subject to the lowest income tax rate.

1.1 Definitions

- A "controlled taxpayer" is any one of two or more taxpayers owned or controlled directly or indirectly by the same interests, and the definition includes a taxpayer that owns or controls the other taxpayers.

- "Uncontrolled taxpayer" means any one of two or more taxpayers not owned or controlled directly or indirectly by the same interests.

- "Controlled" includes any kind of control, direct or indirect, whether legally enforceable or not, and however exercisable or exercised, including control resulting from the actions of two or more taxpayers acting in concert or with a common goal or purpose. A presumption of control arises if income or deductions have been arbitrarily shifted.

- For purposes of the IRS's authority to make these adjustments with respect to controlled transactions, "taxpayer" means any person, organization, or business, whether or not subject to any tax imposed by the IRC.

- "Controlled transaction" or "controlled transfer" means any transaction or transfer between two or more members of the same group of controlled taxpayers.

- "Uncontrolled transaction" means any transaction between two or more taxpayers that are not members of the same group of controlled taxpayers.

- "Uncontrolled comparable" means the uncontrolled transaction or uncontrolled taxpayer that is compared, under any applicable pricing methodology, with a controlled transaction or with a controlled taxpayer. (Example: Under the comparable profits method, an uncontrolled comparable is any uncontrolled taxpayer from which data are used to establish a comparable operating profit.)

1.2 IRS Distribution/Apportionment/Allocation

To prevent the evasion of taxes or to clearly reflect the income of two or more organizations, trades, or businesses that are directly or indirectly owned by the same interests, the Internal Revenue Code (IRC) authorizes the IRS to adjust (the IRC uses "distribute, apportion, or allocate") upward or downward the gross income, deductions, credits, and allowances between or among such organizations, trades, or businesses.

These organizations, trades, or businesses need not be incorporated, organized in the United States, or affiliated. The IRS's authority to make these adjustments also extends to members of an affiliated group that file a consolidated U.S. income tax return.

1.3   Arm's-Length Standard

The IRS adjustments, necessary to determine "true taxable income" (as opposed to the taxable income that the taxpayer reported on the taxpayer's income tax return), apply to controlled transactions and controlled transfers. The purpose of these adjustments is to assure that reported prices (as adjusted per this authority given to the IRS) that one affiliate ("controlled taxpayer") charges to another affiliate yield results that are consistent with the results that would have been realized if uncontrolled taxpayers had engaged in the same transaction under the same circumstances (the "arm's-length" standard).

1.3.1   Consistent Results

A controlled transaction or controlled transfer meets the arm's-length standard if the results of the transaction or the transfer are consistent with the results that would have been realized if uncontrolled taxpayers had engaged in the same transaction or transfer under the same circumstances (the "arm's-length" result).

1.3.2   Comparable Transactions and Standards of Comparability

Because identical transactions can rarely be located, whether a transaction produces an arm's-length result generally will be determined by reference to the results of comparable transactions. Various standards of comparability (applicable pricing methodologies) are allowable and are set forth in U.S. Treasury regulations. The most common pricing methods are listed below.

- **Comparable Uncontrolled Price (CUP):** Only for tangible property (sales, purchases, and leases).
    - CUP based upon reference to published market data.
- **Comparable Uncontrolled Transaction (CUT):** Only for intangible property (regarding royalty payments).
- **Resale Price:** Tangible property only.
- **Cost Plus:** Tangible property only.
- **Comparable Profits Method:** Based upon operating margin, gross margin, return on assets, or return on capital.

1.4   Transfer Pricing Issues

The IRS often makes adjustments when there are transfer pricing issues. Transfer pricing issues exist under the following circumstances:

- A U.S.-based taxpayer transfers, sells, purchases, or leases tangible property or intangible property to or from an affiliate that either:
    - is not subject to U.S. income tax; or
    - does not file a consolidated income tax return with the U.S.-based taxpayer.
- A U.S.-based taxpayer enters into loan agreements or service contracts with an affiliate that either:
    - is not subject to U.S. income tax; or
    - does not file a consolidated income tax return with the U.S.-based taxpayer.

- A U.S.-based taxpayer shares costs with an affiliate that either:
  - is not subject to U.S. income tax; or
  - does not file a consolidated income tax return with the U.S.-based taxpayer.

1.5   IRS Options

These adjustments include the ability of the IRS to do the following:

- Modify the basis of assets; and

- Require the taxpayer to recognize income with respect to an otherwise tax-free transaction (such as a tax-free, like-kind exchange or a tax-free incorporation of a business).

1.6   Authority of the IRS to Make Adjustments

The IRS's authority to make these adjustments extends to any case in which, either by inadvertence or design, the taxable income of a controlled taxpayer is other than what the taxable income would have been if the taxpayer had been dealing at arm's-length with an uncontrolled taxpayer.

- This authority is not limited to cases of improper accounting, fraud, sham transactions, or devices and schemes designed to reduce or avoid tax by shifting or distorting income, deductions, credits, or allowances.

- However, the courts will reverse such adjustments if the controlled taxpayer shows that the results of its transactions are within an arm's-length range established by two or more uncontrolled comparable transactions based upon a single pricing method.

1.7   Limited Right of a Controlled Taxpayer to Make Adjustments

A controlled taxpayer has a limited right to make these same adjustments.

- If necessary to reflect arm's-length pricing, in a timely filed income tax return, a controlled taxpayer may report the result of controlled transactions and of controlled transfers based upon prices different from those actually charged.

- With respect to (i) untimely filed income tax returns, and (ii) amended income tax returns, the taxpayer cannot make any such adjustments which result in decreasing taxable income.

1.8   Avoidance of Penalties

A taxpayer may owe additional federal income tax due to IRS adjustments with respect to controlled transactions and controlled transfers. The taxpayer can generally avoid the "substantial valuation misstatement" penalty and the "gross valuation misstatement" penalty if any one or more of the following circumstances apply:

1.8.1   Section 482 Study Based on Allowable Pricing Methods

The taxpayer may prepare and document a "Section 482 study" based upon allowable pricing methods set forth in the U.S. Treasury regulations.

- The taxpayer must determine that the prices for controlled transactions and controlled transfers are in accordance with the allowable pricing methods set forth in the U.S. Treasury regulations and that the taxpayer's use of such method was reasonable.

- The documented study must be completed no later than the date the taxpayer files the federal income tax return.

1.8.2   Section 482 Study Not Based on Allowable Pricing Methods

The taxpayer may prepare and document a "Section 482 study" that is not based upon allowable pricing methods set forth in the U.S. Treasury regulations.

- The taxpayer must establish that none of such pricing methods was likely to result in a price that would clearly reflect income, that the taxpayer used another pricing method to determine such price, and that such other pricing method was likely to result in a price that would clearly reflect income.

- The documented study must be completed no later than the date the taxpayer files the federal income tax return.

1.8.3   Transactions Solely Between Foreign Corporations

Penalties may be avoided if any portion of such net increase in federal income tax is attributable to any transaction solely between foreign corporations unless, in the case of any such corporations, the treatment of such transaction affects the determination of income from sources within the United States or taxable income effectively connected with the conduct of a trade or business within the United States.

1.9   Competent Authority

- In certain circumstances, the taxpayer can request that the IRS and the taxing officials in the other country or countries together ascertain the appropriate transfer price so that the taxpayer group is not taxed twice on the same income.

- Such a request is a "request for competent authority," and the taxpayer may make this request any time after an IRS action results in taxation that is inconsistent with the provisions of any applicable treaty.

1.10   Advance Pricing Agreement Program

The IRS website states:

> In early 2012, the Advance Pricing Agreement (APA) Program merged with that portion of the Office of the U.S. Competent Authority (USCA) that resolves transfer pricing cases under the mutual agreement procedures of the United States' bilateral income tax conventions to form the Advance Pricing and Mutual Agreement (APMA) Program. APMA's mission is to resolve actual or potential transfer pricing disputes in a timely, principled, and cooperative manner. (https://www.irs.gov/Businesses/Corporations/APMA, accessed May 2016.)

- An APA normally requires agreement on the following issues:

    - Choosing a transfer pricing method (TPM).

    - Selecting comparable uncontrolled companies or transactions (comparables).

    - Deciding on the years over which comparables' results are analyzed.

    - Adjusting the comparables' results because of differences with the tested party.

    - Constructing a range of arm's-length results.

    - Testing the results during the APA period.

    - Agreeing on critical assumptions.

- Often two or more approaches to certain issues are possible, and there may be no clear basis for preferring one approach over another. In such situations, the IRS may give the taxpayer the taxpayer's preferred treatment of some issues if the taxpayer agrees to the IRS using its preferred treatment of other issues.

2 State Income Tax Considerations

In addition to federal income tax, a company is also subject to tax in its state of residence, as well as in any state in which it has nexus.

2.1 Definition of Nexus

Nexus is defined as the minimum level of contact a taxpayer may have with a jurisdiction to be subject to its tax. This is typically caused by a company having property, payroll, or sales within a state, and is determined under the laws of each state, which may vary as to what particular activity will trigger nexus in the state. However, federal law offers some protection to companies where state taxation is concerned.

2.2 Federal Limitations on a State's Right to Impose Income Tax

- Under Public Law No. 86-272, federal law prohibits a state and its political subdivisions (counties, cities, etc.) from imposing a net income tax on a person's net income derived from interstate commerce occurring within the state's borders when the following three circumstances are present:

  - The only business activity of the person within the state consists of the solicitation of orders for sales of tangible personal property;

  - Those orders are sent outside the state for acceptance or rejection; and

  - If those orders are accepted, they are filled by shipment or delivery from a point outside the state.

- "Person" includes individuals, corporations, partnerships, and limited liability companies.

- The prohibition against the state's imposing a net income tax does not apply to the following:

  - Individuals who are domiciled in, or are residents of, the state; and

  - Corporations which are incorporated under the laws of that state (note that the "prohibition-does-not-apply" portion of this federal law does not address either partnerships organized under the laws of that state or limited liability companies organized under the laws of that state).

  - Companies that are soliciting sales of service or other products that do not qualify as tangible personal property.

- The federal law applies only to prohibit a state from imposing a net income tax if the three circumstances above are present. This law does not apply to:

  - sales and use taxes;

  - franchise taxes; and

  - gross receipts taxes (sometimes called business and occupation taxes or commercial activity taxes).

- Because this federal law limits the right of a state to tax net income that a person earns within the state, most, if not all, states:

  - narrowly define "solicitation"; and

  - resolve in favor of the state all ambiguities under the federal law.

- The following are examples of activities that may trigger nexus in a state in which a company operates:

  - Owning or leasing tangible personal or real property.

  - Sending employees into the state for training or work.

  - Soliciting sales in a state.

  - Providing installation, maintenance, etc., to customers within a state (even through a third party).

  - Accepting or rejecting sales orders within the state, or accepting returns.

Example 1	Determination of Nexus

Facts: Hundley Corporation sells computers and is incorporated and resides in California. In addition to California, Hundley solicits sales in Oregon, Arizona, and Colorado. It provides installation services to its customers in Arizona, and it conducts employee training at a facility in Colorado.

Required: Determine with which states Hundley has nexus.

Solution:

- California (state of residence and incorporation)

- Arizona (provides installation services to customers)

- Colorado (conducts employee training)

Hundley likely will be protected from nexus in Oregon by P.L. 86-272, as its only activity in the state is solicitation of sales for tangible personal property.

2.3 State Allocation and Apportionment of Federal Taxable Income

Once nexus is established, the next step is for the company to determine how much of its total federal income or loss should be taxable by each state. This is accomplished through the rules of allocation and apportionment. Although the terms allocation and apportionment are almost always used in the same phrase, they each perform a separate function, and it is important to note the difference between the two. Generally, most states require that corporations (and sometimes, partnerships) use federal taxable income before the NOL deductions and before the dividends-received deduction as the starting point for allocation and apportionment calculations. For corporations, this amount is shown on line 28 on page 1 of the IRS Form 1120.

2.3.1 Allocation of Nonbusiness Income

Generally, allocable items of income are "nonbusiness" income. That is, the income does not relate to the primary business activities of the corporation within the state. "Allocation" refers to the process of removing the nonbusiness income from the line 28 total and assigning it entirely to the state where it should be taxed, which is generally the state of the taxpayer's commercial domicile (or, residence).

Example 2	Allocation of Nonbusiness Income

Facts: A corporation selling shoes at retail in two states has invested excess cash, which is not working capital, in high-grade stocks and bonds. The corporation plans to liquidate the investment in 10 years and use the proceeds to pay for the construction in 10 years of a planned distribution center.

Required: Determine whether the investment income from the stocks and bonds should be classified as business income or allocated as nonbusiness income.

Solution: Because the investment in stocks and bonds does not relate to the primary business activities of the corporation, in this situation, the corporation may be able to allocate entirely to the corporation's home state all dividend income and interest income (and capital gain or loss from the liquidation). No other state would be able to tax these items of nonbusiness income.

2.3.2 Apportionment of Business Income

- The portions of line 28 income which are not allocated entirely to one state are apportioned to all the states in which the corporation does business. Generally, apportionable items of income are "business" income. That is, the income does relate to the primary business activities of the corporation within the state.

- The income apportioned to a state is usually the product of:
  - the apportionment factor (based on the corporation's percentage of property, payroll, and sales in the state); and
  - the portion of line 28 income which is apportionable, business income (line 28 income less allocated income).

2.3.3 Calculation of Apportionment Factor

- Each state dictates exactly how the apportionment factor should be determined in that state, and the methods vary slightly from state to state. However, the standard apportionment factor formula that is used by many states is calculated in the following manner:

$$\left(\frac{\text{Property and rent expense located within the state}}{\text{Total property}} + \frac{\text{Payroll paid to employees within the state}}{\text{Total payroll}} + \frac{\text{Sales from sources within the state}}{\text{Total sales}} \right) \div 3$$

Example 3	**Allocation and Apportionment**

Facts: A corporation has commercial domicile in Kansas and has the following breakdown of property, payroll, and sales in the states where it operates:

Property:	**Payroll:**	**Sales:**
Kansas: $400,000	Kansas: $40,000	Kansas: $300,000
Missouri: $50,000	Missouri: $30,000	Missouri $400,000
Oklahoma: $30,000	Oklahoma: $20,000	Oklahoma: $200,000
Nebraska: $20,000	Nebraska: $10,000	Nebraska: $100,000
Total: $500,000	Total: $100,000	Total: $1,000,000

The portion of line 28 income representing allocable dividends and interest income (nonbusiness income) described above is $10,000; the remaining portion of line 28 income is $100,000 and relates to business income (and thus is apportionable income). So, total line 28 income is $110,000.

Required: Determine the corporation's taxable income in each state with nexus.

Solution: In order to determine taxable income for each state, first calculate their apportionment factors.

Kansas:
Property factor: 80% ($400,000 / $500,000)
Payroll factor: 40% ($40,000 / $100,000)
Sales factor: 30% ($300,000 / $1,000,000)
Total factor: 50% [(80% + 40% + 30%) / 3]

Missouri:
Property factor: 10% ($50,000 / $500,000)
Payroll factor: 30% ($30,000 / $100,000)
Sales factor: 40% ($400,000 / $1,000,000)
Total factor: 27% [(10% + 30% + 40%] / 3)

Oklahoma:
Property factor: 6% ($30,000 / $500,000)
Payroll factor: 20% ($20,000 / $100,000)
Sales factor: 20% ($200,000 / $1,000,000)
Total factor: 15% [(6% + 20% + 20%] / 3)

Nebraska:
Property factor: 4% ($20,000 / $500,000)
Payroll factor: 10% ($10,000 / $100,000)
Sales factor: 10% ($100,000 / $1,000,000)
Total factor: 8% [(4% + 10% + 10%] / 3)

In this situation, the home state of Kansas could tax $60,000 of the corporation's line 28 amount: (i) $10,000 nonbusiness income allocated entirely to the home state; and (ii) $50,000 apportioned to the home state (50% apportionment factor × $100,000 apportionable business income).

The remaining states have taxable income as follows:
Missouri: $27,000 (27% apportionment factor × $100,000 apportionable business income)
Oklahoma: $15,000 (15% apportionment factor × $100,000 apportionable business income)
Nebraska: $8,000 (8% apportionment factor × $100,000 apportionable business income)

2.4 State Income Taxes and Controlled Taxpayers

Most states do not have a statute similar to the IRC's statute authorizing the IRS to make controlled taxpayer adjustments with respect to transfer pricing issues. However, many states do have a statute allowing the state taxing authority to require a combination of income of related members if such combination will better reflect the extent of business done within the state.

Illustration 2	State Taxing Authority Combining Income of Related Members

Hold Company, located solely in Delaware, owns 100 percent of the stock of OP Company, operating solely in State X. Hold Company's only business is (i) owning the stock of OP Company and (ii) lending money to OP Company. Hold Company and OP Company file a U.S. consolidated income tax return. Because of Hold Company's limited activities, under Delaware law and under State X law, Hold Company is not liable for income tax to either state. Because OP Company operates solely in State X, OP Company is not liable for state income tax in Delaware.

At the end of each business day, OP Company declares and pays a dividend equal to all of OP Company's cash on hand at the end of that day. At the beginning of each next business day, Hold Company lends to OP Company sufficient cash for OP Company's operations for that day. The interest rate is an arm's-length rate. Under the terms of the loan agreement, OP Company does not have to repay any principal for 10 years.

As a result of Hold Company's daily loans to OP Company, each year OP Company incurs deductible interest expenses of $10,000,000. Because Hold Company and OP Company file a U.S. consolidated income tax return, the interest expense incurred by OP Company and the interest income recognized by Hold Company offset each other. Because the interest rate that Hold Company charges OP Company is an arm's-length rate and because the two corporations file a U.S. consolidated income tax return, the IRS makes no transfer pricing, controlled taxpayer adjustments.

Because of the daily dividends paid to Hold Company followed by the daily loan from Hold Company to OP Company, on a "separate return" basis, OP Company's line 28 income has been reduced by OP Company's $10,000,000 interest expense; so OP Company's income subject to tax by State X also has been reduced by $10,000,000 (State X bases its state income tax on the taxpayer's separate return line 28 amount).

However, if State X taxing officials have the authority to combine OP Company and Hold Company, the state tax benefit of OP Company's $10,000,000 interest expense deduction will be offset by Hold Company's $10,000,000 interest income. The combined line 28 amount will now reflect the true income of OP Company, and OP Company will pay to State X the appropriate amount of state income tax.

3   Entity Classification and Sourcing of Income

3.1   Entity Classification

A foreign entity is generally classified as either a foreign branch or a foreign subsidiary:

▪ **Foreign branch:** This is an unincorporated foreign entity that is viewed as an extension of the domestic corporation. It is not a separate legal entity; however, earnings from the branch are generally taxed by the foreign host country as well. Federal tax consequences related to a foreign branch are:

- Profits (or losses) earned by the branch are treated as being earned directly by the domestic corporation and are accordingly taxed in full when earned. This allows any losses incurred by the foreign branch to offset domestic income earned by the U.S. company.

- A credit against taxes is allowed for the lesser of foreign tax imposed by the branch's host country or the foreign tax credit limitation.

- Remittance of branch profits back to the domestic corporation is generally not a taxable event for federal tax purposes, as the profits are taxed when earned (one exception would be any related foreign currency exchange gains or losses that occur upon repatriation). However, the foreign host country may impose a branch profits tax, which is basically a withholding tax on branch income remitted back to the domestic corporation.

▪ **Foreign subsidiary:** This is a separate legal entity, incorporated under the laws of the foreign host country. Accordingly, the subsidiary profits are taxed by the host country. Federal tax consequences related to the foreign subsidiary are:

- Income earned by the subsidiary is not taxed until the earnings are brought back to the United States in the form of a dividend. In this way, the U.S. company has control over when foreign profits are recognized.

- Certain types of income earned are not allowed to be deferred and are subject to immediate taxation (e.g., passive investment income).

- Because the foreign subsidiary is a separate legal entity and taxation on profits may be deferred, it is important that transactions between the U.S. parent and foreign subsidiary follow the rules of transfer pricing (discussed earlier), or penalties will be imposed.

3.2   Sourcing of Income

3.2.1   Sourcing Rules for Gross Income and Deductions

Sourcing rules determine whether income and deductions are generated from sources within or outside the United States. For non-U.S. persons, the sourcing rules help to provide limitations on the income that is subject to U.S. taxation. For U.S. persons, the sourcing rules help to determine the income that is included in the numerator as foreign taxable income.

The IRC identifies nine items of income that should be treated as sources of income from within the United States:

1. **Interest:** Interest from the United States or the District of Columbia and interest on bonds, notes, or other interest-bearing obligations of noncorporate residents or domestic corporations.

2. **Dividends:** The source of dividends is generally determined by the residence of the corporation paying the dividend.

3. **Personal Services:** Compensation for labor or personal services performed in the United States; there is a special exception for individuals temporarily performing services in the U.S. They must meet the following requirements:

    *   The labor or services are performed by a nonresident alien individual temporarily present in the United States for a period or periods not exceeding a total of 90 days during the taxable year;

    *   Such compensation does not exceed $3,000 in the aggregate; and

    *   The compensation is for labor or services performed as an employee of or under a contract with:

        —a nonresident alien, foreign partnership, or foreign corporation, not engaged in trade or business within the United States; or

        —an individual who is a citizen or resident of the United States, a domestic partnership, or a domestic corporation, if such labor or services are performed for an office or place of business maintained in a foreign country or in a possession of the United States by such individual, partnership, or corporation.

4. **Rents and Royalties:** Rentals or royalties from property located in the United States or from any interest in such property, including rentals or royalties for the use of or for the privilege of using in the United States patents, copyrights, secret processes and formulas, goodwill, trademarks, trade brands, franchises, and other like property.

5. **Disposition of U.S. Real Property Interest:** Gains, profits, and income from the disposition of a United States real property interest.

6. **Sale or Exchange of Inventory Property:** Gains, profits, and income derived from the purchase of inventory property outside the United States (other than within a possession of the United States) and its sale or exchange within the United States.

7. **Underwriting Income:** Amounts received as underwriting income (as defined in Section 832(b)(3)) derived from the issuing (or reinsuring) of any insurance or annuity contract.

8. **Social Security Benefits**

9. **Guarantees:** Amounts received, directly or indirectly, from:

    *   a noncorporate resident or domestic corporation for the provision of a guarantee of any indebtedness of such resident or corporation, or

    *   any foreign person for the provision of a guarantee of any indebtedness of such person, if such amount is connected with income which is effectively connected (or treated as effectively connected) with the conduct of a trade or business in the United States.

After the determination of the source of the income (U.S. or foreign), a taxpayer may be required to allocate and apportion allowable deductions to determine U.S. taxable income and foreign source taxable income. The foreign source taxable income will be used to calculate the foreign tax credit limitation.

Question 1	MCQ-02232

Foreign income taxes paid by a corporation:

    a.   May be claimed either as a deduction or as a credit, at the option of the corporation.

    b.   May be claimed only as a deduction.

    c.   May be claimed only as a credit.

    d.   Do not qualify either as a deduction or as a credit.

NOTES

1 U.S. Taxation of Foreign Transactions

1.1 Worldwide Tax System

The U.S. tax system is classified as a worldwide tax system because citizens and residents are generally subject to tax on their worldwide income. Some provisions, however, allow for the exemption of certain foreign income, which instead follows a territorial-style approach (described below).

1.2 Territorial Tax System

Under a territorial tax system, a nation only taxes its citizens and residents on income earned inside its borders. Income earned outside the country's borders is not subject to tax.

Taxation is based on whether a person is actually present in the country and deriving income from within its borders. This is referred to as source-country taxation.

Most countries that are members of the Organization for Economic Cooperation and Development (OECD) employ a territorial-style tax system.

In December 2017, the U.S. government passed the Tax Cuts and Jobs Act (TCJA). The act allows certain U.S. corporations earning dividend income outside U.S. borders to take a 100 percent dividends-received deduction against such income, thereby exempting the income from U.S. taxation.

1.3 Taxation of Noncitizens and Nonresidents

Taxation of noncitizens and nonresidents generally requires a connection or nexus to the country. Most nations have rules that define "substantial presence" within the country and rules that determine when income is treated as "effectively connected" to the country. The rules provide thresholds for triggering the taxation of foreign persons.

2 Foreign Tax Credit

Under a worldwide tax system, the primary mechanism for mitigating double taxation is the foreign tax credit. The United States allows U.S. taxpayers to take a foreign tax credit for income taxes paid to a foreign government.

2.1 Foreign Tax Credit Limitation

As discussed in R4, if a U.S. taxpayer earns income in a foreign jurisdiction with a higher tax rate than the United States, no residual taxes will be paid to the U.S. government, but the foreign tax credit will be limited to the amount of U.S. taxes attributable to the foreign-source income. This helps ensure that the U.S. tax liability tied to income earned in the United States is not offset by an unlimited foreign tax credit.

The limitation calculation is as follows:

$$\text{Pre-credit U.S. tax on total taxable income} \times \frac{\text{Foreign source income}}{\text{Total taxable income}}$$

2.2   Separate Limitation Calculations

Foreign income is sourced into separate categories to prevent a company from using excess credits from high-tax foreign business profits to offset low-taxed passive investment income. The foreign tax credit limitation must be applied separately to each of the following categories of income:

- Passive category income (dividends, interest, rents, royalties)
- General category income (active business income)
- Foreign branch income
- Global intangible low-taxed income

2.3   Calculating the Foreign Tax Credit Limitation by Category

Once the income is sourced, the company applies a separate foreign tax credit (FTC) limitation to each category of income. The formula for computing the separate category limitations is the same as that for computing the overall limitation, except the numerator is now the separate category of income:

$$\text{Pre-credit U.S. tax on total taxable income} \times \frac{\text{Separate category foreign income}}{\text{Total taxable income}}$$

- As discussed in R4, the foreign tax credit is allowed for a foreign tax that the U.S. deems to be an income tax; this does not include sales taxes, value added taxes, property taxes, or customs taxes.
- The credit allowed for that category is the lesser of the limitation for that category or the foreign taxes related to that category. The total FTC is then the sum of the credits allowed for all categories.
- A corporation calculates and reports its foreign tax credit on Form 1118 Foreign Tax Credit—Corporations, and individuals, estates, and trusts use Form 1116 Foreign Tax Credit (Individual, Estate, and Trust).
- As previously mentioned in R4, taxpayers can elect to deduct foreign taxes rather than claim the credit, which can be a good decision if the taxpayer does not expect to utilize the credit in the 10-year carryforward period.

3 Participation Exemption or Dividends-Received Deduction

Under a territorial tax system, the primary mechanism for mitigating double taxation is a participation exemption or dividends-received deduction.

▪ A participation exemption allows the taxpayer to exempt foreign income from taxation.

▪ A dividends-received deduction (DRD) allows the taxpayer to offset dividend income from foreign sources with a deduction.

▪ Unlike a worldwide tax system, no residual taxes are imposed on a taxpayer earning income in a low-tax jurisdiction, meaning the taxpayer is subject to the same rate of tax as other persons operating in the foreign jurisdiction.

For taxable years beginning after December 31, 2017, a U.S. corporation is allowed to exempt foreign-source dividend payments from U.S. taxation by taking a 100 percent dividends-received deduction against such income if it owns 10 percent or more of the dividend-paying foreign corporation.

▪ No residual tax is imposed on dividend repatriations from foreign jurisdictions and the U.S. government will not collect taxes on the foreign income.

▪ A 10 percent shareholder that is not a U.S. corporation is not eligible for the DRD.

3.1 Special Rules

▪ No foreign tax credit or deduction is allowed on dividends that benefit from the 100 percent dividends-received deduction.

▪ The deduction is subject to a holding period requirement, which requires that the U.S. corporation hold the foreign corporation stock for more than 365 days during the 731-day period beginning 365 days before the ex-dividend date.

▪ Certain income is not eligible for the 100 percent dividends-received deduction:

● Subpart F income

● Global intangible low-taxed income

● Income invested in U.S. property

● Income subject to the transition tax

4 Foreign Activities of U.S. Persons (Outbound Transactions)

When a U.S. person invests abroad, it is considered an outbound transaction. The income earned outside U.S. borders is generally referred to as foreign-source income.

The definition of a U.S. person includes:

▪ U.S. citizen

▪ U.S. resident alien

▪ U.S. partnership

▪ U.S. corporation

▪ U.S. trusts and estates

U.S. persons can generally defer U.S. taxes on foreign-source income until such income is repatriated to the United States (e.g., in the form of a dividend). The benefit of deferral usually applies to income earned abroad through active operations.

4.1 Anti-deferral Rules

The United States has two anti-deferral regimes that result in the current taxation of foreign-source income:

- Passive foreign investment company regime

- Controlled foreign corporation rules/Subpart F regime

4.1.1 Passive Foreign Investment Company (PFIC)

A foreign entity is a PFIC if it meets a gross income or asset test:

- The income test classifies an entity as a PFIC if 75 percent or more of the foreign corporation's gross income is passive (e.g., dividends, interests, rents, royalties).

- The asset test classifies an entity as a PFIC if at least 50 percent of the foreign corporation's total assets are passive assets (e.g., assets that produce passive income).

Direct and indirect U.S. shareholders of a PFIC are subject to PFIC rules, and PFIC undistributed earnings are subject to U.S. taxation under one of three methods (designed to eliminate benefit of deferral):

1. Qualified electing fund

2. Mark-to-market method

3. Excess distribution method

4.1.2 Subpart F Income

The United States generally does not tax foreign business profits earned through a foreign subsidiary until the subsidiary repatriates those earnings as a dividend.

- For taxable years beginning before December 31, 2017, the deferral of such income allowed U.S. companies to compete in foreign markets without being subject to U.S. residual taxes until the time of repatriation.

- For taxable years beginning after December 31, 2017, U.S. corporations receive a 100 percent dividends-received deduction for foreign-source dividends paid by a controlled foreign corporation.

The benefits of deferral and the exemption of foreign-source dividends create opportunities for shifting income to low-tax jurisdictions to avoid U.S. taxes. The controlled foreign corporation rules (Subpart F) are intended to curb this behavior. The rules include the following:

- A foreign corporation is considered a controlled foreign corporation (CFC) if more than 50 percent of its stock is owned by U.S. shareholders.

- A U.S. shareholder is any U.S. person owning at least 10 percent of the foreign corporation's stock (vote or value). Constructive rules apply in this determination.

- Subpart F only applies to a foreign corporation that qualifies as a CFC.

- When both the PFIC and Subpart F rules apply, the Subpart F rules supersede the PFIC rules.

Example 1	Overlap Between PFIC Rules and Subpart F Rules

Facts: Company ABC (a U.S. company) is a 12 percent owner in a foreign corporation, D, whose primary source of income is investments (80 percent of gross income). The other shareholders of D include six U.S. persons each owning 10 percent (60 percent total) and a foreign person who owns 28 percent.

Required: Determine the tax treatment of ABC's investment in D.

Solution: In this scenario, D qualifies as both a CFC (owned 72 percent by 10 percent U.S. shareholders) and a PFIC (with 80 percent passive gross income). Because the Subpart F rules supersede PFIC rules, D will be treated as a CFC instead of a PFIC and ABC's income from D will be subject to Subpart F rules, resulting in immediate income recognition of D's Subpart F income.

4.1.3 Foreign Base Company Income

The main purpose of Subpart F is to discourage taxpayers from using foreign corporations to defer U.S. taxes by accumulating income in foreign "base" companies located in low-tax jurisdictions. The rules define this "bad income" as foreign base company income.

Foreign base company income includes passive income (i.e., highly mobile investment-type income that can easily be shifted to a low-tax jurisdiction) or active income tied to a related party.

A U.S. shareholder of a controlled foreign corporation generating foreign base company income is taxed on a current basis (no deferral and no DRD) with respect to the shareholder's pro rata share of such income.

4.2 Global Intangible Low-Taxed Income Tax

The Tax Cuts and Jobs Act created a new tax on global intangible low-taxed income (GILTI), and it applies to taxable years beginning after December 31, 2017.

The GILTI tax is a minimum tax imposed on certain low-taxed income that is intended to reduce the incentive to relocate CFCs to low-tax jurisdictions.

After determining a CFC's Subpart F income, U.S. shareholders must determine whether they are subject to tax on the CFC's global intangible low-taxed income (GILTI). U.S. shareholders are taxed in a manner similar to Subpart F inclusions and U.S. corporations are allowed a special deduction.

4.2.1 Deduction Amount

For 2018–2025, the deduction amount is 50 percent of GILTI (37.5 percent for 2026 and later). The taxpayer is also allowed to take a foreign tax credit for up to 80 percent of the foreign taxes deemed paid.

4.2.2 Inclusion Amount

The GILTI inclusion is equal to the U.S. shareholder's share of the CFC's net income, reduced by the excess of: (i) 10 percent of the CFC's aggregate adjusted basis in depreciable tangible property used in its trade or business, over (ii) the CFC's net interest expense.

The CFC's aggregate adjusted basis in depreciable, tangible property is measured using the average amount determined at the close of each quarter.

Example 2	Global Intangible Low-Taxed Income Inclusion and Deduction

Facts: Hughes Corp. (a U.S. corporation) owns 15 percent of EKM Corp. (a CFC). EKM's net income for Year 1 is $1,500,000 and the adjusted basis of its tangible property at the end of each quarter is $1,000,000 (first quarter), $1,250,000 (second quarter), $1,225,000 (third quarter), and $1,150,000 (fourth quarter).

Required: Determine Hughes Corp.'s GILTI inclusion and deduction.

Solution: EKM Corp.'s GILTI income is its net income ($1,500,000) less 10 percent of its average adjusted basis of depreciable tangible property: 10% × [($1,000,000 + $1,250,000 + $1,225,000 + $1,150,000)/4] = $115,625. EKM Corp.'s GILTI income is $1,384,375, which is $1,500,000 less $115,625.

Because Hughes Corp. is a 15 percent U.S. shareholder, it will include 15 percent of EKM Corp.'s GILTI income, 15% × $1,384,375 = $207,656.

Hughes Corp. is eligible for a 50 percent GILTI deduction because it is a corporate shareholder. Its GILTI deduction is $103,828, which is $207,656 × 50%.

4.3 Earnings Invested in U.S. Property

Each U.S. shareholder of a CFC must include in income their pro rata share of:

1. Subpart F income; and

2. earnings invested in U.S. property.

These provisions were enacted to deter U.S. taxpayers from repatriating non-Subpart F earnings from a CFC through loans and other investments in U.S. property in a tax-free manner.

- The impact of these rules is that a U.S. shareholder is taxed on the pro rata share of any increase in the earnings of the CFC invested in U.S. property.

- The term "U.S. property" includes tangible property located in the United States, stock of a domestic corporation, an obligation of a U.S. person, or any right to use a patent or copyright in the United States.

- The calculation compares average adjusted basis of such property for the tax year with adjusted basis at the end of the previous year and uses the close of each quarter as a measuring date.

Example 3	Earnings Invested in U.S. Property

Facts: Blue Corp., a CFC with no prior U.S. property investments, makes a $1 million loan to its U.S. parent in the second quarter of Year 1. The loan remains outstanding at the end of Year 1.

Required: Determine Blue Corp.'s increase in earnings invested in U.S. property in Year 1.

Solution: Blue Corp. has an increase of $750,000 invested in U.S. property.

$$0 \text{ million} = \text{First quarter}$$
$$\$1 \text{ million} = \text{Second quarter}$$
$$\$1 \text{ million} = \text{Third quarter}$$
$$\underline{\$1 \text{ million} = \text{Fourth quarter}}$$
$$\$3 \text{ million}/4 \text{ quarters} = \$750,000$$

Each U.S. shareholder would be taxed currently on their pro rata share of Blue Corp.'s increased investment in U.S. property during the taxable year.

4.4   Previously Taxed Income

The current taxation of a CFC's undistributed earnings is coordinated with both the taxation of actual dividend distributions made by the CFC and the taxation of dispositions of the CFC's stock.

A U.S. shareholder can exclude distributions of a CFC's earnings and profits that were previously-taxed income (PTI) to U.S. shareholders as a result of a Subpart F inclusion, GILTI inclusion, or an investment in U.S. property.

4.5   Transition Tax

The Tax Cuts and Jobs Act created a territorial-style system for certain U.S. corporations by allowing a 100 percent dividends-received deduction for foreign-source dividends from controlled foreign corporations (CFCs).

- The transition to this new system requires all U.S. shareholders to pay a one-time tax on the CFC's previously untaxed foreign earnings.

- For the last taxable year beginning before January 1, 2018, a one-time deemed repatriation tax is imposed on accumulated, untaxed earnings of foreign corporations and is taken into account by all U.S. shareholders who own 10 percent or more of the CFC.

- An exception permits S corporations to defer the tax until the S corporation liquidates, ceases doing business, or the stock of the S corporation is transferred.

4.5.1   Classification of Untaxed Earnings

The CFC's untaxed earnings are divided into two groups:

1. Cash/cash equivalents, which are taxed at 15.5 percent.

2. All other earnings, which are taxed at 8.0 percent.

4.5.2 Tax Payments

U.S. shareholders can elect to pay the transition tax in eight installments over eight years, pursuant to a specified schedule.

Transition Tax Installment Period	Tax Liability Due
Year 1	8%
Year 2	8%
Year 3	8%
Year 4	8%
Year 5	8%
Year 6	15%
Year 7	20%
Year 8	25%
	100%

4.6 Base Erosion and Anti-Abuse Tax (BEAT)

The Tax Cuts and Jobs Act created the base erosion and anti-abuse tax (BEAT) to impose a minimum tax on large U.S. corporations (average annual gross receipts of at least $500 million for the three-year taxable period ending with the preceding taxable year) with a significant amount of deductible payments to related foreign affiliates (3 percent or higher of total deductions) because such deductions reduce the U.S. tax base. The BEAT is effective for taxable years beginning after December 31, 2017, and is imposed on a U.S. corporation's modified taxable income.

Modified taxable income is regular taxable income calculated without:

- the allowance of deductions for amounts paid or accrued to related foreign persons; or

- depreciation or amortization deductions with respect to property acquired from related foreign persons.

The following rules also apply:

- Deductible payments to a CFC are added back in calculating a taxpayer's modified taxable income even if they are included in the taxpayer's income as Subpart F income.

- The tax rate is 5 percent for taxable years beginning in 2018, 10 percent for taxable years beginning in 2019–2025, and 12.5 percent for years beginning in 2026 or later.

- The BEAT does not apply to individuals, S corporations, regulated investment companies (RICs), or real estate investment trusts (REITs).

- In general, the 10 percent BEAT tax will begin to apply when payments to foreign affiliates exceed taxable income by more than 10 percent. The BEAT applies to the extent that it exceeds the regular tax liability (reduced by most credits).

4.7   Foreign-Derived Intangible Income Deduction

The Tax Cuts and Jobs Act created a new deduction for certain export activities. Under the new provision, a U.S. corporation can get a deduction for a portion of its foreign-derived intangible income (FDII). FDII is income from transactions involving non-U.S. persons located outside the U.S., including:

- the sale of property sold by the taxpayer to any person who is not a U.S. person and is for foreign use;

- services provided by the taxpayer to any person or with respect to property, not located within the U.S.; and

- property sold to a related party who is not a U.S. person, provided the property is ultimately sold by the related party to an unrelated party who is not a U.S. person, and the property is used outside the U.S.

The deduction amount is 37.5 percent for years beginning before 2026 (reduced to 21.875 percent for years after 2026). The deduction for FDII is available only to C corporations that are not RICs or REITs.

5   U.S. Activities of Foreign Persons (Inbound Transactions)

A foreign person's investment in the United States is considered an inbound transaction. The United States taxes foreign persons on income derived in the United States, which is referred to as U.S.-source income.

The definition of a foreign person includes:

- Nonresident alien individuals

- Foreign corporations

- Foreign partnerships

- Foreign trusts

- Foreign estates

- Any other person who does not meet the definition of a U.S. person

A foreign person's U.S.-source income falls into one of two categories—business income or nonbusiness income.

5.1   Business Income

A foreign person engaged in a U.S. trade or business is subject to U.S. taxation on income effectively connected with the U.S. trade or business. Business income is taxed on a net basis (gross income less allowed deductions and expenses) at U.S. graduated rates.

A foreign person with a U.S. trade or business must file Form 1120-F U.S. Income Tax Return of a Foreign Corporation to report the income earned by the U.S. branch.

If a foreign person organizes U.S. business activities under a U.S. subsidiary, instead of a branch, then the U.S. subsidiary will be taxed as a U.S. corporation reporting all its income on Form 1120 U.S. Corporation Income Tax Return.

| Example 4 | Taxation of Foreign Person Business Income |

Facts: British Bunting Inc., a British company, has a U.S. branch in Austin, Texas. The branch makes routine sales to U.S. customers. The gross profits of the U.S. branch are $100 and the cost of goods sold are $40.

Required: Determine British Bunting's U.S. taxable income.

Solution: British Bunting's U.S. taxable income is $60 ($100 gross profit less $40 cost of goods sold), which will be taxed at U.S. graduated tax rates.

5.2   Nonbusiness Income

Nonbusiness income (investment-type income, such as dividends and interest) is taxed on a gross basis (deductions and expenses are prohibited) at a 30 percent statutory withholding rate. Withholding rates may be reduced by income tax treaties.

A foreign person's nonbusiness income is subject to U.S. withholding taxes under one of two regimes.

5.2.1   U.S. Withholding Tax Regimes for Nonbusiness Income

There are two types of withholding tax regimes for nonbusiness income:

1.   Fixed, Determinable, Annual, or Periodic Income (FDAP)

2.   Foreign Account Tax Compliance Act of 2010 (FATCA)

FDAP deals with the withholding on foreign persons' investment-type income (e.g., dividends, interest, royalties):

- FDAP income includes dividends, interest, royalties, and compensation from personal services. Such income is taxed on a gross basis at a statutory rate of 30 percent.

- Withholding ensures the collection of taxes from foreign persons, over whom the IRS would typically not have the jurisdiction to tax.

- The U.S. person controlling the payment of U.S. source income to the foreign person is responsible for withholding the appropriate amount of tax on such payment.

FATCA deals with withholding tax on foreign entities for failure to provide information to U.S. recipients:

- The purpose of FATCA is to help combat tax evasion tied to U.S. persons investing in foreign entities (e.g., deposits in foreign banks).

- FATCA imposes a 30 percent withholding tax on foreign entities that do not provide information about U.S. persons on Form 8966 FATCA Report.

- FATCA applies to foreign financial institutions and nonfinancial foreign entities but does not apply to payments made to nonresident aliens (i.e., foreign individuals), foreign governments, international organizations, and certain retirement funds.

5.3   Foreign Person Treated as U.S. Resident

Foreign persons are usually only taxed on their U.S.-source income. However, a foreign individual may be treated as a U.S. resident, which means the individual is subject to U.S. taxation on worldwide income.

5.3.1 Green Card Test

A foreign individual is considered a resident of the United States if he or she is a lawful, permanent resident of the United States in accordance with U.S. immigration laws.

5.3.2 Substantial Presence Test

A foreign individual is considered a resident of the United States if he or she is substantially present in the United States for:

- at least 31 days during the current year; and
- at least 183 days for a three-year period, applying a weighted average:
  - Days in current year × 1
  - Days in immediate preceding year × ($\frac{1}{3}$)
  - Days in next preceding year × ($\frac{1}{6}$)

Example 5 ▸ Substantial Presence Test

Facts: Esther, a citizen of the United Kingdom, stayed in the United States for 122 days in each of the last three years: Year 1, Year 2, and Year 3.

Required: Determine whether Esther is treated as a U.S. resident for Year 3.

Solution: Esther is treated as a U.S. resident because she is present in the United States for more than 31 days during Year 3, and she is present for at least 183 days for the three-year period beginning in Year 1, after applying a weighted average:

Year 3:	122 days × 1	=	122 days
Year 2:	122 days × ($\frac{1}{3}$)	=	40.67 days
Year 1:	122 days × ($\frac{1}{6}$)	=	20.33 days
		Total	183 days

5.3.3 First-Year Election

A foreign person is considered a resident of the United States if the individual elects to be treated as a U.S. resident and meets the following requirements:

- Present for 31 consecutive days in the current year;
- Present 75 percent of the days in the current year (beginning day 1 of the 31 consecutive days); and
- Meets substantial presence test for the *succeeding* year.

The election is made by filing an extension for the first year or by filing an amended return for the first year.

---

6 Expatriation

6.1 Mark-to-Market Regime for Individuals

The mark-to-market tax regime is imposed on covered expatriates who renounce their U.S. citizenship and satisfy one of the following three tests:

1. **Tax Liability Test:** Average annual net income tax liability for five preceding taxable years exceeds indexed threshold ($162,000 for 2017; $165,000 for 2018; $168,000 for 2019).

2. **Net Worth Test:** Net worth of $2 million or more on date of expatriation.

3. **Compliance Test:** The individual failed to comply with U.S. federal tax obligations for five preceding taxable years.

6.1.1 Calculation of Tax

- All property of the "covered expatriate" is treated as sold on the day before the expatriation date with any gain arising from the deemed sale taken into account in the taxable year of the deemed sale.

- A $600,000 exclusion (indexed for inflation) is allowed.

- A taxpayer may elect to defer payment of tax attributable to property deemed sold [Section 877A(b)].

Example 6 — Exit Tax

Facts: Cathleen is a U.S. citizen who has lived in the United States her entire life. She is the founder of Cupcakes Inc., a U.S. company. Her stock in the company is worth $7 million and her basis in the stock is $250,000. In 2016, Cathleen renounces her citizenship and moves to Bermuda. Assume that the mark-to-market gain exclusion for 2016 is $693,000.

Required: Determine Cathleen's U.S. tax consequences of this action.

Solution: Cathleen qualifies as a covered expatriate because her net worth exceeds $2 million. She will be treated as if she sold her stock at fair market value the day before her expatriation. Cathleen's long-term capital gain is $6,057,000 ($7,000,000 stock fair market value less $250,000 stock basis less $693,000 exclusion).

6.2 Expatriated Entity Rules for Corporations

When a U.S. company decides to reorganize its operations under a foreign parent to reduce its U.S. tax obligations, it is considered an expatriated entity.

Expatriated entities fall into one of two categories for U.S. tax purposes:

1. Continue to be treated as U.S. corporations if former U.S. shareholders own 80 percent or more of interests in the new foreign parent; or

2. Denied certain tax attributes such as net operating losses and foreign tax credits to offset "inversion gain" if former U.S. shareholders own 60 percent but less than 80 percent of interests in the new foreign parent.

The TCJA also includes provisions to reduce a U.S. company's incentive to expatriate:

▥ Dividends received by a U.S. corporation from a surrogate foreign corporation are not eligible for the 100 percent dividends-received deduction.

▥ Any individual shareholder who receives a dividend from a corporation that is a surrogate foreign corporation is not entitled to the lower rates on qualified dividends.

7 Tax Treaties

Tax treaties are bilateral income tax conventions entered into by the United States and a foreign country.

▥ Tax treaties carry the same weight as domestic law and often modify otherwise applicable U.S. tax rules.

▥ Tax treaties modify the rules for investment-type income by reducing the withholding rate below 30 percent.

▥ Tax treaties also modify statutory rules related to business income, residency, and source-of-income rules.

▥ The U.S. treaty network includes income tax conventions with approximately 60 countries. Most of these countries have a comprehensive income tax system in place.

Question 1   MCQ-08766

Alpert Corp. (a U.S. corporation) manufactures dental equipment in Arizona. It makes sales of dental equipment during the year to the following customers:

   I.   Rupert Corp. (a foreign corporation) for use in its dental centers in Texas

  II.   Janis Corp. (a foreign corporation) for use in its dental centers in Canada

 III.   Rogers Corp. (a foreign corporation and related party) for use in its dental centers in Mexico

 IV.   Commodore Corp. (a U.S. corporation) for use in its dental centers in Canada

Which transactions increase Alpert Corp.'s foreign-derived intangible income?

   a.   I and II

   b.   II only

   c.   I, II, and III

   d.   II and IV

Question 2	MCQ-08767

Which of the following payments to a foreign person is not subject to U.S. withholding tax requirements?

    a. An interest payment from a savings account at a U.S. bank

    b. A dividend payment from a U.S. corporation

    c. A customer payment for the sale of inventory within the U.S.

    d. A payment to a foreign financial institution that does not provide information about U.S. persons

Other Entity Taxation, Professional Responsibilities, and Federal Tax Procedures

Module

1 Separate Entities

Trusts and estates are separate entities, often called fiduciaries. Each has been created under a fiduciary relationship in which assets (called principal or "corpus") have been transferred to the entity so that a person with fiduciary responsibility for the entity can hold legal title to the property for the benefit of named "beneficiaries."

1.1 Separate Taxpaying Entities

Estates and trusts are separate income tax paying entities, and distributions made by these entities are deductible by the entity yet taxable to the recipient. Because amounts are not taxed at both the estate or trust level and the recipient level, double taxation is avoided. In this way, estates and trusts are said to be conduits.

1.2 Fiduciaries

A fiduciary is a person in a position of special trust and confidence toward another who does one or both of the following:

■ Holds property for which another person has beneficial title or interest; and/or

■ Receives and controls income of another.

Note: Examples of fiduciary are the trustee (of a trust) and the executor (of an estate).

1.3 Taxation of Estates

Estates are subject to two separate taxes:

■ **Income Tax:** Income tax is due annually based on income earned during the year while the estate is in existence.

■ **Estate Tax:** The estate tax is a one-time-only transfer tax based on the value of the decedent's estate (taxed to the estate before the property is transferred).

2 Income Taxation Rules for Estates and Trusts

2.1 Income Tax Returns (Form 1041)

Estates and trusts file income tax returns, just as an individual taxpayer would file an income tax return.

In contrast to individuals, the income of an estate or trust is taxed at either the entity or beneficiary level depending on whether the income is allocated to principal or to distributable net income, and whether the income is distributed to the beneficiaries. (See R1 for a complete discussion on taxation of income distributed to beneficiaries.)

2.2 Distributable Net Income (DNI)

Distributable net income (DNI) is a limitation on the amount the trust or estate can deduct with respect to distributions to beneficiaries. Below is the general calculation of DNI:

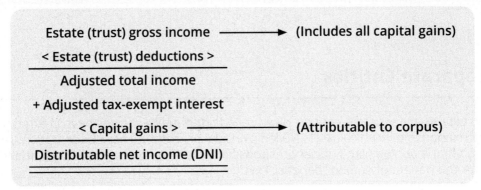

2.3 Trust Definitions and Rules

■ **Gross Income**

Gross income is generally determined in the same manner as for individuals. It includes capital gains.

■ **Deductions**

Deductions are allowed for ordinary and necessary expenses incurred in:

- Carrying on a trade or business

- Production of income

- Management or conservation of income-producing property (including the trustee's or executor's fees)

- Determination, collection, or refund of any tax

- Contributions to a charity (an unlimited charitable deduction is allowed if such contributions are provided for in a will)

■ **Adjusted Tax-Exempt Interest**

Generally, adjusted tax-exempt interest is the amount of tax-exempt interest income reduced by:

- interest expense related to the tax-exempt interest; and

- other investment expenses related to tax-exempt interest.

■ **Tax Credits**

Generally, tax credits allowed to individuals are allowed to fiduciaries (trusts and estates). The tax credits typically must be apportioned between the fiduciary and the beneficiaries based on the income allocable to each.

■ **Income Distributed to the Beneficiaries**

Income distributed to the beneficiaries (and reported on Schedule K-1 on Form 1041) retains the same character (e.g., tax exempt, portfolio, passive, etc.) as the income had at the fiduciary level. The reporting of income distributed to beneficiaries on the beneficiaries' individual income tax returns is covered in more detail in R1.

2.4   Income Distribution Deduction

The income distribution deduction equals the lesser of:

1.   Actual distribution to beneficiary

   Or:

2.   DNI (less adjusted tax-exempt interest)

> ### Pass Key
>
> When the CPA Examination tests on income taxation rules for trusts and estates, one of the most frequently tested concepts is "distributable net income" and the related income distribution deduction.

2.5   Annual Estate Income Tax Return

An estate is a legal entity that comes into existence upon the death of an individual and continues to exist until all assets of the estate are distributed. Complex estates can exist for a number of years. During the time that the decedent's affairs are being managed, income is generated and expenses are paid. Thus, the estate is a taxable entity.

Estate and Trust Tax Rates			
If Taxable Income Is			
Over	**But Not Over**	**The Tax Is**	**Of the Amount Over**
$0	$2,600	10%	$0
$2,600	$9,300	$260.00 + 24%	$2,600
$9,300	$12,750	$1,868.00 + 35%	$9,300
$12,750	–	$3,075.50 + 37%	$12,750

The above rates do not reflect the 20 percent maximum tax rate on net long-term capital gains.

Note that the top rate is reached very quickly. Once the estate is liquidated and all assets distributed, the estate is no longer required to file a Form 1041 income tax return.

- **Required When Annual Gross Income Exceeds $600**

  - An estate is not required to file a Form 1041 income tax return if the annual gross income is no more than $600.

  - No standard deduction is allowed.

- **Tax Year**

  - A calendar year tax return is due on April 15.

  - A fiscal year tax return is due on the 15th day of the fourth month after year-end.

- **Estimated Payments**

  An estate is not required to make estimated tax payments for its first two tax years.

2.6 Annual Trust Income Tax Return

Trusts are subject only to income tax and are considered separate tax-paying entities. Trusts are classified as either simple or complex.

2.6.1 Calendar Year

All trusts, except tax-exempt trusts, must use a calendar year.

Pass Key

An easy way to remember the filing requirements for trust and estate income tax years:

- **Trusts** = Year-end (I "trust" you will remember December 31 is year-end)
- **Estates** = Anytime (the government lets you die "anytime")

2.6.2 Distributable Net Income (DNI)

A trust may deduct amounts distributed to beneficiaries up to the amount of the trust's DNI (less adjusted tax-exempt interest). The following table lists deductions that may be taken to arrive at DNI that are exclusive to trusts (not estates).

Deductions (Trusts Only)	Principal	Income
1. Expenses		
• Current management of principal and application of income		✓
• Incurred in connection with principal	✓	
• Investing and reinvesting principal	✓	
• Ordinary, in the administration, management, or preservation of trust property (e.g., real estate taxes)		✓
• Preparation of property for sale or rental	✓	
2. Extraordinary Repairs: An allowance for depreciation may be established	✓	

2.6.3 Simple Trusts

- A simple trust only makes distributions out of current income; it cannot make distributions from the trust corpus (principal).

- A simple trust is required to distribute all of its income currently.

- A simple trust cannot take a deduction for a charitable contribution.

- A simple trust is entitled to a $300 exemption in arriving at its taxable income.

Example 1	Calculating Trust Taxable Income

Facts: The Reinus Trust, a simple trust, is required to make distributions only out of trust income. For Year 6, the trust had taxable interest income of $1,000 and made a $1,000 distribution to L.H. Riggs, the sole beneficiary of the trust.

Required: Calculate Reinus Trust's taxable income for Year 6.

Solution: As calculated below, the trust will have no taxable income.

Interest income of trust	$ 1,000
Less: distribution deduction	(1,000)
Taxable income before exemption	$ 0

2.6.4 Grantor Trusts

- In a grantor trust, the grantor (the individual who established the trust) retains control over the trust assets.

- A grantor trust is considered a disregarded entity for income tax purposes. Any taxable income or deduction of a grantor trust is reported on the income tax return of the grantor.

- A grantor trust can be a qualified shareholder of an S corporation.

- A grantor trust is generally included in the taxable estate of the grantor upon his or her death.

Example 2	Grantor-Type Trust

Facts: The Pat Foster Trust is a grantor-type trust. In the current year, the Pat Foster Trust sold 500 shares of XYZ stock for $60 per share. The trust's basis in the XYZ stock was $40 per share.

Required: Determine the amount of income from the sale of XYZ stock which must be reported on the Pat Foster Trust's Form 1041 tax return.

Solution: The income in connection with the sale of the XYZ stock will not be reported on a trust tax return, Form 1041, but instead will be reported on the individual income tax return of Pat Foster, because the grantor trust is a disregarded entity.

2.6.5 Complex Trusts

All trusts that are not simple trusts are complex trusts. A trust may be simple one year and complex the next.

- A complex trust may accumulate current income.

- A complex trust may distribute principal.

- A complex trust may deduct charitable contributions.

- A complex trust is permitted an exemption of $100 in arriving at its taxable income.

Example 3	Complex Trust

Facts: The Goldstein Trust, a complex trust, had gross rental income of $25,000 and taxable interest income of $10,000 for Year 1. The trust also incurred a deductible trustee fee of $1,000 and rental property expenses of $3,000. The trust plans to make a $28,000 distribution to its beneficiaries in Year 1.

Required: Calculate the trust's taxable income for Year 1.

Solution: The trust's taxable income for Year 1 will be $2,900, as calculated below:

Rental income		$ 25,000
Taxable interest income		10,000
		35,000
Less:		
Trustee fee	$ 1,000	
Rental property expenses	3,000	(4,000)
Adjusted total income		31,000
Less: income distribution deduction—lower of		
DNI (less adjusted tax-exempt interest)	31,000	
or		
Distributions (less tax-exempt income)	28,000	(28,000)
Less: exemption		(100)
Taxable income		$ 2,900

2.6.6 Determining Trust Tax Liability

A trust's accumulated income is taxed using the following tax rates (same as estates):

Estate and Trust Tax Rates			
If Taxable Income Is			
Over	**But Not Over**	**The Tax Is**	**Of the Amount Over**
$0	$2,600	10%	$0
$2,600	$9,300	$260.00 + 24%	$2,600
$9,300	$12,750	$1,868.00 + 35%	$9,300
$12,750	–	$3,075.50 + 37%	$12,750

The above rates do not reflect the 20 percent maximum tax rate on net long-term capital gains (net long-term capital gains reduced by net short-term capital losses).

Question 1   **MCQ-01812**

Astor, a cash basis taxpayer, died on February 3. During the year, the estate's executor made a distribution of $12,000 from estate income to Astor's sole heir and adopted a calendar year to determine the estate's taxable income. The following additional information pertains to the estate's income and disbursements for the year:

Estate income:	
Taxable interest	$65,000
Net long-term capital gains allocable to corpus	5,000
Estate disbursements:	
Administrative expenses attributable to taxable income	14,000
Charitable contributions from gross income to a public charity, made under the terms of the will	9,000

For the calendar year, what was the estate's distributable net income (DNI)?

    a. $39,000

    b. $42,000

    c. $58,000

    d. $65,000

Question 2   **MCQ-01813**

Gem Trust, a simple trust, reported the following items of income and expenses during the current year:

Interest income from corporate bonds	$4,000
Taxable dividend income	2,000
Trustee fees allocable to income	1,500

What is Gem's distributable net income (DNI) for the year?

    a. $6,000

    b. $4,500

    c. $2,500

    d. $500

NOTES

1 Unified Estate and Gift Tax (Transfer Tax)

The estate tax and gift tax have been unified into a single transfer tax. Not all gifts are subject to the gift tax.

1.1 Lifetime Gifts

- Certain gifts, discussed later in this module, qualify for an unlimited exclusion.

- In addition, for 2019, gifts of $15,000 or less per year/per donee are excluded.

- For 2019, a lifetime combined exclusion of $11,400,000 is allowed per individual for gifts and the taxpayer's estate. Any gifts made over the allowed amount per year ($15,000 for 2019) reduce this lifetime exclusion. This exclusion also applies to the estate of the taxpayer.

1.2 Transfers at Time of Death

- Certain transfers made at time of death, discussed later in the module, are excluded from the estate tax.

- The unified exclusion for gifts and estates is $11,400,000 per individual for 2019. This effectively allows married taxpayers to have a combined unified exclusion of $22,800,000.

2 The Estate Tax (Form 706)

The estate tax is a transfer tax rather than an income tax. It is imposed on the value of property transferred by the decedent at death.

- An estate must file IRS Form 706 if the gross value of the estate plus historical taxable gifts by the decedent exceed $11,400,000 (2019).

- Form 706 must be filed within nine months after the decedent's death (unless an extension is requested).

2.1 Gross Estate

The gross estate includes the value at the date of death (or at an alternate valuation date, which is the earlier of the date the property is distributed to the heirs or six months after the date of death) of all the decedent's worldwide property, including real property, personal tangible property, and intangible property. The gross estate also includes the fair market value of the decedent's share of jointly held property.

- If property is owned jointly (50/50) with a spouse, include 50 percent of fair market value of jointly owned property in gross estate.

- If property is owned in an arrangement other than 50/50, include 100 percent less other owner's percentage contribution in gross estate.

- Insurance proceeds (if the deceased/estate is the beneficiary or had incidence of ownership at death).

■ Incomplete gifts (joint accounts) [Gift = Drawn upon].

■ Revocable transfers:

   ● No future interest.

   ● Trust in which children receive property in the future.

■ All property entitled to be received (income in respect of a decedent).

Estate Transfer Tax

Gross Estate	⎧ FMV property ⎪ Insurance proceeds ⎨ Incomplete gifts ⎪ Revocable transfers ⎩ Income in respect of decedent
< Nondiscretionary deductions >	⎧ Medical expenses ⎪ Administrative expenses ⎪ Outstanding debts ⎨ Claims against the estate ⎪ Funeral expenses ⎪ Indebtedness of property ⎩ Certain taxes (e.g., taxes before death and state death taxes)
Adjusted gross estate	
< Discretionary deductions >	⎧ Charitable bequests, unlimited ⎩ Marital deduction, unlimited
Taxable estate	
Adjusted taxable gifts	⎧ Post-1976 gifts that were taxed ⎩ No double tax because subtracted later in this computation
Tentative tax base at death	
× Uniform tax rates	{ The "uniform tax rates" apply to both taxable gifts and estates
Tentative estate tax	
< Gift taxes payable >	⎧ Reduction by gift taxes payable on gifts made after 1976 ⎩ This eliminates double taxation of these gifts
Gross estate tax	*Credit* **2019: $4,505,800**
< Applicable credit >	⎧ This credit amount is equal to the tax, before credits, on an ⎩ $11,400,00 tentative tax base at death
Estate tax due	

Pass Key

Estates follow the same general rule for taxable events and basis as with individual and partnership taxation:

Taxpayer	Event	Taxed	Basis
Estate	Taxable	FMV	FMV
Beneficiary	Nontaxable	N-O-N-E	NBV (FMV from estate)

2.2   Estate Deductions

The gross estate is reduced by deductions that include:

2.2.1   Medical Expenses

Alternatively, medical expenses (not funeral expenses, because they are not deductible for income tax purposes) paid out of the estate may be deducted on the final income tax return of the decedent (Form 1040), subject to the applicable AGI floor. This option is available provided:

- the expenses are paid within one year of death;
- the expenses are not deducted on the decedent's Form 706; and
- the executor files an appropriate waiver.

2.2.2   Administrative Expenses

An estate is allowed to deduct expenses of administering and settling the estate on Form 706. (Alternatively, as in situations in which there is no taxable estate, the executor of the estate may deduct those expenses on the estate's Form 1041.)

- Outstanding debts of decedent
- Claims against the estate
- Funeral costs
- Certain taxes

2.2.3   Charitable Deduction (Unlimited)

Unlimited transfers to charitable, scientific, educational, and religious organizations that are termed *discretionary deductions*.

2.2.4   Marital Deduction (Unlimited)

Unlimited transfers to the decedent's spouse.

2.3   Transfer Tax Rate

The transfer tax rate schedule is applied to total transfers. Lifetime taxable gifts and transfers at death are taxed on a cumulative basis.

2.3.1   Applicable Credit

The applicable credit on the 2019 exemption amount of $11,400,000 is $4,505,800. This is the estate tax liability calculated on a tax base of $11,400,000 in 2019.

2.3.2 Applicable Exclusion Amount

The IRC calls this $11,400,000 amount the "applicable exclusion amount." However, this amount is not subtracted in calculating the tentative tax base at death; rather, the estate computes the estate tax on the tentative tax base at death and then reduces that tax by the $4,505,800 (2019) applicable credit. The net result is generally an estate tax due equal to: 40% tax rate × [tentative tax base at death – $11,400,000].

2.3.3 Deceased Spouse's Unused Exclusion

For decedents who die in 2019, the estate of a surviving spouse may be able to use, in addition to the $4,505,800 applicable credit (based on the $11,400,000 applicable exclusion amount), an additional credit based on the unused exclusion amount of the surviving spouse's predeceased spouse. The unused exclusion amount is generally the predeceased spouse's applicable exclusion amount minus the portion of that exclusion amount that the predeceased spouse's estate used to offset estate tax otherwise due.

Example 1	Exclusion

Facts: Lee and Pat are married to each other. Lee dies in 2019. The Lee estate's tentative tax base at death is $10 million. The Lee estate claims an "applicable credit" equal to the estate tax, before credits, on $10 million.

The executor of the Lee estate timely elects to allow the Pat estate—when Pat dies—to use the Lee estate's unused exclusion amount of $1,400,000. Pat, who has never made any lifetime gifts, dies later that year with a tentative tax base at death of $15 million.

Required: Determine the exclusion amount and estate tax on the Pat estate.

Solution: The Pat estate's exclusion amount will be $12,800,000, which is the sum of $11,400,000 available to the Pat estate plus the $1,400,000 that is the Lee estate's unused exclusion amount.

The Pat estate's applicable credit will be equal to the tax on $12,800,000, and the net estate tax due will be $880,000: 40% tax rate × ($15,000,000 – $12,800,000).

2.4 Other Credits

Other credits that reduce the gross estate tax include:

■ **Foreign Death Taxes**

■ **Prior Transfer Taxes (Prior Gift Taxes Paid)**

Gift taxes paid on gifts made after 1976 are technically not a credit but are subtracted from the tentative estate tax to arrive at the gross estate tax.

3 The Gift Tax (Form 709)

The gift tax is a transfer tax payable by certain donors of gifts. Its main purpose is to make the donor liable for the tax that would have been payable as estate tax at the donor's death. This reflects the theory that had the gift not been made, the asset would have been included in the donor's estate and would have been taxable. This means that an individual subject to gift tax, usually only a donor who gives more than $15,000 (or $30,000 if married and gift splitting is elected) to a single donee in a year must file a gift tax return Form 709, which includes keeping track of total lifetime taxable gifts to date.

Gifts of future interests (see discussion later in the section) are also subject to gift tax, without exemption, and must file Form 709. The estate tax return is considered the final gift tax return for purposes of computing the tax.

3.1 Taxable Gifts

Every transfer of money or property, whether real or personal, tangible or intangible, for less than adequate or full consideration in money is a gift.

3.1.1 Annual, Inflation-Adjusted Exclusion

In determining the amount of gifts made in a calendar year, the donor may exclude the first $15,000 of gifts made to each donee. This annual exclusion is not available for a gift of a future interest (i.e., a gift that can only be enjoyed by the donee at some future date), even if the donee does receive a current ownership interest in the gift. A gift by either spouse may be treated as made one-half by each. This gift splitting creates a $30,000 exclusion per donee.

3.1.2 Unlimited Exclusion

▪ **Payments Made Directly to an Educational Institution**

   Amounts paid on behalf of a donee for tuition paid directly to an educational organization are allowed an unlimited exclusion from gift tax.

▪ **Payments Made Directly to a Health Care Provider for Medical Care**

   Fees paid directly to a health care provider for medical care of the donee are allowed an unlimited exclusion from gift tax.

▪ **Charitable Gifts**

▪ **Marital Deduction**

   In order to qualify for a marital deduction, there may not be a terminable interest in the property unless the property qualifies as qualified terminable interest property (QTIP). In order to qualify as QTIP property: (1) the donee spouse must be entitled to all income from the property for his or her lifetime; (2) no one other than the donee spouse may receive any distributions of income or principal from the property for his or her lifetime; (3) the donee spouse must have the right to require that the subject property be made productive; and (4) the property must be subject to payment of its pro rata share of estate taxes upon the death of the surviving spouse.

Example 2	Marital Deduction

Facts: When Jim and Nina became engaged in April Year 1, Jim gave Nina a ring that had a fair market value of $50,000. After their wedding in July Year 1, Jim gave Nina $75,000 in cash so that Nina could have her own bank account. Both Jim and Nina are U.S. citizens.

Required: What was the amount of Jim's Year 1 marital deduction?

Solution: $75,000 was Jim's marital deduction for Year 1.

Rule: Transfers between spouses are not subject to taxation for gift tax or income tax purposes. The $75,000 transfer was after the date of marriage and would be eligible for the unlimited marital deduction. The $50,000 transfer prior to marriage was not eligible for the marital deduction. It would, however, be subject to the annual gift tax exclusion.

3.2   Gifts: Present vs. Future Interest

3.2.1   Definition

The postponement of a right to use, possess, or enjoy the property distinguishes a future interest from a present interest.

- A present interest qualifies for the annual exclusion and in most instances would be removed from the estate.

- A future interest (or a present interest without ascertainable value) does not qualify for the annual exclusion and, unless the required time period has passed, will not be removed from the estate. Because a gift of a future interest does not qualify for the annual exclusion, the donee is generally required to file Form 709 regardless of the amount of the future interest.

3.2.2   Future Interest Gifts

Examples of future interest gifts include:

- reversions (gifting assets and later getting the property back);

- remainders (distributed at some future time);

- trust income interests where accumulation of income by a trustee is mandatory and accumulations are distributed at some future time at the discretion of the trustee; and

- present interests without ascertainable value.

3.2.3   Present Interest Gifts

Examples of present interest gifts include:

- outright gifts of cash or property;

- trust income interests where annual or more frequent distribution is mandatory;

- life estates (ownership of the right to use property presently but not ownership of the property itself);

- estates for a term certain;

- bonds or notes (even though interest is not payable until maturity); and

- unrestricted transfers of life insurance policies.

3.3   Gifts: Complete vs. Incomplete Gifts

Complete gifts qualify for the annual exclusion and, in most cases, are not considered part of the gross estate at death. However, incomplete gifts are included in the gross estate for purposes of computing the estate tax.

3.3.1   Complete Gifts

A gift is considered complete (and is subject to gift tax):

- even though the donee is not yet born, provided his identity can later be ascertained.

- despite the possibility that the property may revert to the donor at some future time.

3.3.2   Incomplete Gifts

A gift is not considered complete (and is not subject to the gift tax) if it is conditional or revocable.

3.3.3   Conditional Gifts

A gift is conditional if it is subject to conditions precedent and will not be provided until the conditions have been met (e.g., a recipient will not get the gift unless he graduates from a four-year accredited college).

3.3.4   Revocable Gifts

A gift is revocable if the donor reserves the right to revoke the gift or change the beneficiaries. The gift is complete when those rights terminate by reason other than the donor's death.

3.4   Recipients: Nontaxable

The recipient of a gift pays no gift tax, and the gift does not represent taxable income to the recipient. (The general rule for the basis of gifts received is that the basis to the recipient equals the donor's basis plus gift tax paid due to the appreciation in value inherent in the gift.)

3.5   Calculating Taxable Gifts

The "total amount of gifts" equals the aggregate value of all gifts made during the calendar year less the applicable annual $15,000 ($30,000 if married and gift splitting) exclusion per donee.

Example 3	Calculating Taxable Gifts

Facts: Between January 1, Year 1, and March 31, Year 1, Jack Smith made the following gifts: $15,000 in cash to Adele; a sculpture valued at $4,000 to Barry; and 100 shares of common stock valued at $400 per share in Zorro Corp., a publicly held corporation, to Christine. Smith made no other gifts during the quarter.

Required: Calculate Jack's total amount of taxable gifts for the quarter.

Solution: The total amount of $25,000 in taxable gifts is calculated as shown in the following chart.

Donee	Value of Gift	Available Exclusion	Taxable Amount of Gift
Adele	$15,000	$15,000	$ 0
Barry	4,000	4,000	0
Christine	40,000	15,000	25,000
			$25,000

Jack would owe gift tax only if the amount of Jack's cumulative (all years) taxable gifts exceeds $11,400,000. However, Jack must file a gift tax return because the value of at least one of his gifts exceeds the $15,000-per-donee exclusion amount.

Pass Key

In order to apply the annual exclusion to a gift, the gift must be all of the following:

- A present interest
- Complete
- Under $15,000/$30,000 per donee (unless paid directly for medical expenses and/or education expenses and/or paid to charities)

The tax due on current gifts is determined as follows:

Gross Gifts in a Calendar Year (at FMV)

Less: exclusion of $15,000 per donee per year

Less: unlimited marital deduction of gift to donor's spouse

Less: charitable gifts

= Taxable gifts this year

Plus: taxable gifts of prior years

= Cumulative lifetime gifts

Tax on Cumulative Lifetime Gifts (Calculate)

Less: gift tax paid on prior gifts

Less: applicable credit

= Tax due on current gifts

4 Generation-Skipping Transfer Tax (GSTT)

The generation-skipping transfer tax is designed to prevent an individual from escaping an entire generation of gift and estate tax. This is a separate tax that is imposed in addition to federal estate and gift tax. The tax applies when individuals transfer property to a person who is two or more generations younger than the donor or transferor. Either the trustee or the transferor pays the GSTT.

The IRC provides that the GSTT rate is equal to the highest estate and gift tax rate in effect. For 2019, the exemption amount is $11,400,000. Married couples can "split" the generation-skipping transfer and thus obtain a maximum total exemption of $22,800,000 for 2019.

Question 1　　　　　　　　　　　　　　　　　　　　　MCQ-01903

On February 1, Year 3, Hall learned that he was bequeathed 500 shares of common stock under his father's will. Hall's father had paid $2,500 for the stock 10 years ago. Fair market value of the stock on February 1, Year 3, the date of his father's death, was $4,000 and had increased to $5,500 six months later. The executor of the estate elected the alternate valuation date for estate tax purposes. Hall sold the stock for $4,500 on June 1, Year 3, the date that the executor distributed the stock to him. How much income should Hall include in his Year 3 individual income tax return for the inheritance of the 500 shares of stock that he received from his father's estate?

- a. $5,500
- b. $4,000
- c. $2,500
- d. $0

Question 2　　　　　　　　　　　　　　　　　　　　　MCQ-01817

Under the provisions of a decedent's will, the following cash disbursements were made by the estate's executor:

I.　A charitable bequest to the American Red Cross.

II.　Payment of the decedent's funeral expenses.

What deduction(s) is (are) allowable in determining the decedent's taxable estate?

- a. I only.
- b. II only.
- c. Both I and II.
- d. Neither I nor II.

Question 3　　　　　　　　　　　　　　　　　　　　　MCQ-01891

In the current year, Sayers, who is single, gave an outright gift of $50,000 to a friend, Johnson, who needed the money to pay medical expenses. In filing the current year gift tax return, Sayers was entitled to a maximum exclusion of:

- a. $0
- b. $15,000
- c. $30,000
- d. $50,000

NOTES

1 Types of Tax-Exempt Organizations Allowed Under the Internal Revenue Code

1.1 Overview

Although not generally subject to income taxation, most exempt organizations are still required to file information returns with the U.S. Department of the Treasury and have other detailed reporting and record keeping requirements. Furthermore, instances will exist in which the exempt organization will owe tax for certain types of "unrelated" income the organization derives.

1.2 Section 501(c)(1) Organization

This type of corporation is organized under an act of Congress as a U.S. instrumentality and does not require an application; however, it must be declared exempt under the Internal Revenue Code or the organizing legislation. An example would be a federal credit union. Note that these organizations do not have an annual filing requirement either, unlike other tax-exempt organizations.

Note: Almost all other exempt organizations must make written application for exempt status, be approved by the IRS, become incorporated, and issue capital stock. Furthermore, the articles of organization must limit the purpose of the entity to the charitable/exempt purpose.

1.3 Section 501(c)(2) Organization

This type of corporation is organized for the exclusive purpose of holding title to property, collecting income from that property, and turning over the net income to an exempt organization (i.e., holding corporations for exempt organizations). A 501(c)(2) corporation issues capital stock and otherwise acts as a corporation (e.g., there is no limit on salaries, other than "reasonableness"). Organizations seeking tax-exempt status under Section 501(c)(2) must file Form 1024 to apply, and include the organization's articles of incorporation and bylaws in its application.

1.4 Section 501(c)(3) Organization

1.4.1 General

This is the most common type of exempt organization and includes a community chest; a community fund; a foundation organized and operated exclusively for religious, charitable, scientific, public safety testing, literary, or educational purposes; or a foundation organized to foster national or international amateur sports competitions (only if none of the activities involve the providing of athletic facilities or equipment) or to prevent cruelty to children or animals. The organization must apply for tax-exempt status using Form 1023 and be approved by the IRS to be listed as an exempt organization. Other disclosures, such as the organization's articles of incorporation, bylaws, or financial records vouching for the organization's tax-exempt activities, are typically required to be included in the application with Form 1023.

1.4.2   Requirements (Penalty Is the Loss of Tax-Exempt Status)

* No part of the net earnings may benefit any private shareholder or individual.

* A substantial part of the activities of the organization may not be nonexempt activities (e.g., carrying on propaganda or otherwise attempting to influence legislation).

* The organizations may not directly participate or intervene in any political campaign.

1.5   Section 509 Private Foundations

1.5.1   Included Organizations

Section 509 private foundations include all Section 501(c)(3) organizations other than those specifically excluded. Essentially, the exclusions separate 501(c)(3) organizations into two groups: private foundations and public charities. A foreign corporation may qualify as a private foundation.

1.5.2   Excluded Organizations ("Public Organizations")

The following four categories are not private foundations:

* Maximum (60 percent-type) charitable deduction donees

* Broadly publicly supported organizations receiving more than one third of their annual support from members of the public and less than one third from investment income and unrelated business income

* Supporting organizations

* Public safety testing organizations

1.5.3   Required Returns

An annual information return (Form 990-PF) that discloses substantial contributors and amounts of contributions received must be filed with the IRS.

1.5.4   Termination

* **Involuntary Termination**

    Private foundations will terminate when they become public charities (*they cannot be both*). Furthermore, termination by the IRS will result if the foundation commits repeated violations or a willful and flagrant violation of any of the private foundation provisions.

* **Voluntary Termination**

    Private foundation status need not be permanent. Voluntary termination may be achieved by notifying the IRS of the plan to terminate, subject to a termination tax payback of the value of its aggregate tax benefits or its net assets, whichever is lower. Alternatively, without a tax payback, a foundation may elect to distribute all of its assets to an organization qualifying for the maximum 50 percent deduction or it may operate as a public charity itself for at least five years.

    Note: A private foundation may have a charter that limits its exempt purpose, and it is not required to distribute all of its net assets to any public charity.

2 Unrelated Business Income (UBI)

2.1 Definition

Unrelated business income (UBI) is the gross income from any unrelated trade or business "regularly" carried on, minus business deductions directly connected therewith. UBI is:

- derived from an activity that constitutes a trade or business;
- regularly carried on; and
- not substantially related to the organization's tax-exempt purposes.

Note: The CPA Exam will attempt to confuse the candidate by asking questions regarding "unrelated" activities. Be aware that an unrelated business does not include any activity where all of the work is performed by unpaid workers (volunteers); thus, the fact that the organization uses unpaid workers makes the business or activity "related" and not taxable. Furthermore, articles made by disabled persons as part of their rehabilitation are deemed "related" and are not taxable.

2.2 Ownership Limitation

Statutory restrictions on unrelated business ownership limit to 20 percent the combined ownership of a business enterprise by a private foundation and all disqualified persons. Furthermore, any excess holdings that are not divested are taxed. If third parties (those who are not disqualified persons) have effective control of the business enterprise, the foundation (together with the disqualified persons) may own up to 35 percent.

2.3 Taxation of UBI

Although an organization may have tax-exempt status, it may become subject to regular corporate income tax on income from a business enterprise that is not related to its tax-exempt purpose (UBI). Note that the fact that an activity results in a loss does not exclude the activity from the definition of an unrelated business (if expenses exceed income, a net operating loss (NOL) exists, which is subject to the carryover provisions of net operating losses).

- **Tax Filing and Estimated Taxes**

  The organization must file a Form 990-T for taxable unrelated business income. The exempt organization must comply with the requirements in the tax law for corporations regarding estimated tax payments.

- **$1,000 Specific Deduction**

  An organization is allowed a $1,000 specific deduction from unrelated business income; thus, only UBI in excess of $1,000 is subject to tax.

- **Separate Calculation for Each Unrelated Trade or Business**

  An organization with more than one unrelated trade or business must calculate the UBI for each unrelated trade or business.

■ **Excluded Items of Income**

In addition to the $1,000 specific deduction, the following types of income are excluded from tax:

- Royalties, dividends, interest, and annuities (except those derived from controlled organizations).

- Rents from real property and rents from personal property leased with real property (if less than 50 percent is attributable to the personal property), other than income from debt-financed property.

- Gains and losses on the sale or exchange of property not held primarily for sale to customers in the ordinary course of trade or business.

- Income from research of a college or hospital.

- Income of labor unions (and agricultural or horticultural organizations) used to establish a retirement home, hospital, or similar exclusive-use facilities.

- Activities limited to exempt organizations by state law (e.g., bingo games).

- The value of securities loaned to a broker and the income received by a lender of securities to a broker, provided the identical securities are returned to the lender.

- Income from the exchange or rental of membership lists of tax-exempt charitable organizations.

2.4 Membership Organizations

Certain *membership organizations* (e.g., social clubs and homeowners' associations) are usually taxed on gross income less deductions for "exempt function income" (dues, fees, and charges for providing facilities and services for members, dependents, and guests). Thus, if a social club makes a profit, that profit is generally taxable.

2.5 "Feeder Organizations"

An organization operated primarily for the purpose of carrying on a trade or business for profit cannot claim tax exemption on the grounds that all of its profits are payable to exempt organizations. It must rely on its own activities and exempt nature to gain tax exemption. This type of "feeder organization" is taxed on its entire income—not just the portion it designates as unrelated business income.

2.6 Annual Return Requirement

2.6.1 General

An annual information return (Form 990) stating gross income, receipts, contributions, disbursements, etc., is required of most organizations exempt from tax under Code Section 501 and is open to public inspection. Section 501(c)(3) organizations must also include a Schedule A—Supplementary Information. Form 990-EZ may be filed if the exempt organization has gross receipts less than $200,000 and total year-end assets of less than $500,000.

2.6.2 Exceptions

Other than 501(c)(1) organizations (as previously discussed), three primary types of exempt organizations do not have an annual filing requirement of a Form 990/990-EZ information return with the IRS.

- **Religious or Internally Supported Organizations:** Churches and exclusively religious activities of a religious order or internally supported auxiliaries are exempt from filing.

- **Certain Organizations That Normally Have Less Than $5,000 in Gross Receipts:** Certain organizations that normally have less than $5,000 in gross receipts for the year are exempt from filing an annual information return. Those organizations include educational organizations, religious organizations, public-type charities, fraternal organizations, and those organized to prevent cruelty to children or animals. Although they do not have an annual information filing requirement of a Form 990/990-EZ, there may be other reporting requirements (similar to those for Form 990-N, discussed below) with which they must comply.

- **Organizations That Normally Have Less Than $50,000 in Gross Receipts:** If an organization has gross receipts of less than $50,000, a Form 990 or 990-EZ is not required to be filed. A simple electronic "postcard" (Form 990-N) is filed with the IRS and requires only the following information: (i) the tax identification number of the organization; (ii) the tax year of the organization; (iii) the legal name, physical address, and Internet address (if applicable) of the organization; (iv) the name and address of the principal officer of the organization; and (v) a statement that the annual gross receipts of the organization regularly do not exceed the $50,000 limit.

2.7 Penalties

Penalties apply for failure to file a required tax form (including a 990-N) and failing to comply with the requirements and disclosures of the exempt organization. Furthermore, if an organization fails to file the required return for three consecutive years, the tax-exempt status of the organization will be automatically revoked, effective on the original filing due date of the third annual return or notice.

2.8 Retaining Tax-Exempt Status

In order to protect its tax-exempt status, an exempt organization must timely file its required annual returns and should not:

- organize or operate for the benefit of any private interests;

- devote a substantial part of its activities to attempting to influence legislation;

- participate or intervene in any political campaign on behalf of, or in opposition to, any candidate for public office; and

- be organized for or conduct activities that are illegal or violate fundamental public policies.

Any of these activities could result in harsh penalties or revocation of tax-exempt status. Revocation may also occur in the event of new legislation which deems the activities of the previously tax-exempt organization ineligible.

2.9   Resuming Tax-Exempt Status After Revocation

▪ If an organization has had its tax-exempt status revoked and wishes to have that status reinstated, it must file an application for exemption and pay the appropriate user fee even if it was not required to apply for exempt status initially.

▪ If the IRS determines that the organization meets the requirements for tax-exempt status, it will issue a new determination letter. In most cases, the effective date of reinstated exemption will be the date that the organization's exemption application was submitted to the IRS. However, organizations that have had their tax-exempt status automatically revoked because they did not file their returns for three consecutive years may choose to request that reinstatement be retroactive to the effective date of revocation. The IRS will grant retroactive reinstatement of exemption under certain limited circumstances.

▪ Within 15 months of automatic revocation, the organization must complete one or more of the following (depending on the severity of the missed filings):

  • File all required documents for reinstatement (e.g., Form 1024 or 1023).

  • File all annual returns that were required and caused revocation.

  • Submit a statement citing reasonable cause for not filing one of the three consecutive years of missed tax returns.

If the organization applies for retroactive reinstatement after 15 months, it may only be granted retroactive reinstatement if it establishes in the statement reasonable cause for not filing all three years' tax returns.

Question 1	MCQ-06188

During Year 1, Help Others Inc., an exempt organization, derived income of $15,000 from conducting bingo games. Conducting bingo games is legal in Help Others' locality and is confined to exempt organizations in Help Others' state. Which of the following statements is true regarding this income?

  a. The entire $15,000 is subject to tax at a lower rate than the corporate income tax rate.

  b. The entire $15,000 is exempt from tax on unrelated business income.

  c. Only the first $5,000 is exempt from tax on unrelated business income.

  d. Because Help Others Inc. has unrelated business income, it automatically forfeits its exempt status for Year 1.

1   Overview

Treasury Department Circular 230 is the IRS publication entitled, "Regulations Governing Practice before the Internal Revenue Service." The publication addresses the practice before the IRS with regard to the following:

▪ rules governing the authority to practice before the IRS;

▪ the duties and restrictions relating to practice before the IRS;

▪ the sanctions for violation of the regulations; and

▪ the rules applicable to disciplinary proceedings.

1.1   Subparts

The publication is divided into subparts addressing such practice as follows:

Subpart A	Rules Governing Authority to Practice
Subpart B	Duties and Restrictions in Practice before the IRS
Subpart C	Sanctions for Violating the Regulations
Subpart D	Rules Applicable to Disciplinary Proceedings
Subpart E	General Provisions

Note: Most states, with the exception of California, do not regulate either tax preparers (those who prepare tax returns) or tax practitioners.

2   Authority to Practice

The rules governing practice before the IRS apply to:

▪ Attorneys

▪ Certified public accountants

▪ Enrolled agents

▪ Enrolled actuaries

▪ Enrolled retirement plan agents

▪ Individuals providing appraisals used in connection with tax matters (e.g., charitable contributions; estate and gift assets; fair market value for sales gain; etc.)

- Unlicensed individuals who represent taxpayers before the examination, customer service, and the Taxpayer Advocate Service in connection with returns they prepared and signed

- Individuals rendering written advice with respect to an entity plan or arrangement that has a potential for tax avoidance or evasion

3 Duties and Restrictions

3.1 Information to Be Furnished

Information to be furnished includes any IRS requested information or records:

- The practitioner may withhold information or records he believes in good faith and on reasonable grounds to be privileged.

- If the practitioner does not possess the IRS-requested information or records but knows who does, he must so inform the IRS.

3.2 Prompt Disposition of Pending Matters

No practitioner may unreasonably delay any matter before the IRS.

3.3 Assistance From or to Disbarred or Suspended Persons and Former IRS Employees

With respect to a matter before the IRS, no practitioner can knowingly and directly or indirectly accept help from or assist any person who is under disbarment or suspended from practice before the IRS or accept assistance from any former government employee where either the provisions of Circular 230 or any federal law would be violated.

3.4 Practice by Former Government Employees, Their Partners, and Their Associates

No member of a firm in which a former government employee works can represent a taxpayer where a conflict of interest may exist, unless the firm isolates the former government employee in such a way to ensure that the former government employee cannot assist in the representation.

- If an individual, while a government employee, "personally and substantially participated" in a particular matter involving specific parties, that individual can never represent or assist those parties with respect to that particular matter.

- If an individual, while a government employee, had "official responsibility" for a particular matter involving specific parties, that individual within two years after leaving government employment cannot represent those parties with respect to that particular matter. Note that the "cannot assist" language above does not apply here.

- Within one year after leaving government employment, the individual cannot appear before the IRS to influence any U.S. Treasury Department employee regarding any rule if either (i) the individual at any time "participated in the development" of the rule; or (ii) within the one year period prior to leaving government employment, the individual has "official responsibility" with respect to that rule.

3.5   Fees

A practitioner may never charge an "unconscionable fee." A contingent fee is allowable only in the following three situations before the IRS:

▪ IRS examination or audit;

▪ Claim solely for a refund of interest and/or penalties; or

▪ A judicial proceeding arising under the Internal Revenue Code.

3.6   Conflict of Interest

A practitioner may also face potential conflicts of interest with respect to various clients. Even if a conflict of interest exists, the practitioner may represent (all) clients if:

▪ the practitioner reasonably believes that he or she can competently represent the clients;

▪ no state or federal law prohibits such representation; and

▪ each affected client waives the conflict of interest in writing within 30 days after so waiving.

3.7   Advertising

A practitioner may not, with respect to any Internal Revenue Service matter, in any way use or participate in the use of any form of public communication or private solicitation containing a false, fraudulent, or coercive statement or claim, or a misleading or deceptive statement or claim.

Illustration 1   False Advertising

A small accounting firm with only CPAs advertises on a local television station. The script, which was approved by the partners of the firm, states that "Our talented staff of licensed attorneys and CPAs guarantee you the tax refund you've always wanted." This represents a likely violation of Circular 230 because the firm has falsely advertises it has licensed attorneys when it does not. Also, the advertisement includes a guarantee that could be misleading to clients.

3.8   Fee Information

Practitioners publishing a written fee schedule must honor those fees for the 30-day period following the last date that the fees were published. If additional fees may be charged for certain matters, the statement must indicate whether clients will be responsible for the costs.

3.8.1   Communicating Fee Information

▪ In the case of radio and television broadcasting, the broadcast must be recorded and the practitioner must retain a recording of the actual transmission.

▪ In the case of direct mail and e-commerce communications, the practitioner must retain a copy of the actual communication, along with a list or other description of persons to whom the communication was mailed or otherwise distributed.

▪ Copies must be retained by the practitioner for a period of at least 36 months from the date of the last transmission or use.

3.9   Best Practices for Tax Advisors

Tax advisors should provide clients the highest-quality representation by adhering to "best practices" in providing tax preparation advice or assistance in a submission to the IRS. "Best practices" include:

- Communicating with the client regarding the terms of the engagement to determine the client's purpose and use for the advice.

- Establishing the facts and arriving at a conclusion supported by the law and the facts.

- Advising the client about the importance of the conclusions reached (for example, whether the client will be able to avoid penalties).

- Acting fairly and with integrity in practice before the IRS.

- Taking reasonable steps to ensure that all members, associates, and employees of the firm follow procedures that are consistent with the above.

3.10   Client Refunds

A practitioner may not endorse or otherwise negotiate any check (including directing or accepting payment by any means, electronic or otherwise, into an account owned or controlled by the practitioner or any firm or other entity with whom the practitioner is associated) issued to a client by the government in respect of a federal tax liability.

3.11   Notary

A practitioner cannot notarize any signature of any person with respect to any matter in which the practitioner has an interest (generally by representing a taxpayer before the IRS).

4   Standards With Respect to Tax Returns and Documents, Affidavits, and Other Papers

4.1   Tax Returns

A practitioner may not willfully or recklessly sign a tax return or advise a client to take a tax position that the practitioner knows or should know lacks a reasonable basis, is an unreasonable position, is a willful attempt to understate tax liability, or recklessly or intentionally disregards the tax rules and regulations.

4.2   Documents and Other Papers

A practitioner cannot advise a client to take a tax return position on a document or other paper that will be submitted to the IRS unless the position is not frivolous. The practitioner cannot advise a client to submit any document:

- that will delay or impede the administration of federal tax law;

- that is frivolous; or

- that contains or omits information demonstrating an intentional disregard of a rule or regulation unless the practitioner also advises the client to submit a document evidencing a good faith challenge to the rule or regulation.

4.3   Reasonably Likely Penalties

The practitioner must inform the client of the following:

- Any penalties "reasonably likely" to apply with respect to a position taken on a tax return if the practitioner advised the client on the position or prepared or signed the tax return.

- Any penalties "reasonably likely" to apply with respect to any document submitted to the IRS.

- The opportunity to avoid penalties if the client discloses the position taken and the requirements for adequate disclosure.

4.4   Practitioner's Reliance Upon Client-Furnished Information

Generally, a practitioner who signs the tax return or other document may rely "in good faith without verification" upon client-furnished information. However, the practitioner cannot ignore the implications of such information; contradictory information known to the practitioner; and must make reasonable inquiries if the client-furnished information appears to be questionable or incomplete.

4.5   Knowledge of Omission by a Client

The practitioner must advise the client promptly of any noncompliance, errors, or omissions in tax returns and other documents and the consequences under the law with respect to such noncompliance, errors, or omissions.

4.6   Diligence as to Accuracy

The practitioner must exercise due diligence regarding (i) preparing returns and other documents; and (ii) determining the correctness of her/his representations to the IRS. If the practitioner relies upon the work product of another, there is a presumption that the practitioner exercised due diligence if the practitioner took reasonable care with respect to such reliance.

4.7   Return of Client Records

Generally, at the request of the client, the practitioner must return all client records. The practitioner, however, may retain copies of the records returned to a client.

Exception: If state law allows the practitioner to retain the records in the case of a fee dispute, the practitioner may do so. However, the practitioner must (i) return to the client those records that must be attached to the tax return; and (ii) allow the client to review and copy the practitioner-retained client records related to the client's federal tax obligations.

5   Written Advice

A practitioner may give written advice (including by means of electronic communication) concerning one or more federal tax matters.

The practitioner *must*:

- base the written advice on reasonable factual and legal assumptions (including assumptions as to future events);

- reasonably consider all relevant facts and circumstances that the practitioner knows or reasonably should know;

- use reasonable efforts to identify and ascertain the facts relevant to written advice on each federal tax matter;

- not rely upon representations, statements, findings, or agreements (including projections, financial forecasts, or appraisals) of the taxpayer or any other person if reliance on them would be unreasonable;

- relate applicable law and authorities to facts; and

- must not, in evaluating a federal tax matter, take into account the possibility that a tax return will not be audited or that a matter will not be raised on audit.

5.1   Definition of Federal Tax Matters

A federal tax matter, as used in this section of Circular 230, is any matter concerning the application or interpretation of:

- a revenue provision of the Internal Revenue Code;

- any provision of law impacting a person's obligations under the internal revenue laws and regulations, including but not limited to the person's liability to pay tax or obligation to file returns; or

- any other law or regulation administered by the Internal Revenue Service.

5.2   Reliance on Advice of Others

- A practitioner may only rely on the advice of another person if the advice was reasonable and the reliance is in good faith considering all the facts and circumstances.

- Reliance is not reasonable when:

  - the practitioner knows or reasonably should know that the opinion of the other person should not be relied on;

  - the practitioner knows or reasonably should know that the other person is not competent or lacks the necessary qualifications to provide the advice; or

  - the practitioner knows or reasonably should know that the other person has a conflict of interest in violation of the rules described in this part of Circular 230.

5.3   Standard of Review

- In evaluating whether a practitioner giving written advice concerning one or more federal tax matters complied with these requirements, the commissioner, or delegate, will apply a reasonable practitioner standard, considering all facts and circumstances, including, but not limited to, the scope of the engagement and the type and specificity of the advice sought by the client.

- In the case of an opinion the practitioner knows or has reason to know will be used or referred to by a person other than the practitioner in promoting, marketing, or recommending to one or more taxpayers a partnership or other entity, investment plan or arrangement a significant purpose of which is the avoidance or evasion of any tax imposed by the Internal Revenue Code, the commissioner, or delegate, will apply a reasonable practitioner standard, considering all facts and circumstances.

5.4   Competence

A practitioner must possess the necessary competence to engage in practice before the Internal Revenue Service. Competent practice requires the appropriate level of knowledge, skill, thoroughness, and preparation necessary for the matter for which the practitioner is engaged. A practitioner may become competent for the matter for which the practitioner has been engaged through various methods, such as consulting with experts in the relevant area or studying the relevant law.

6 Compliance

6.1 Procedures to Ensure Compliance With Circular 230

An individual or individuals who have principal authority for overseeing a firm's federal tax practice must take reasonable steps to ensure that the firm has adequate procedures to ensure compliance with Circular 230.

6.2 Potential Failures to Comply

▪ The individual *fails* to have adequate procedures to comply with Circular 230; there is a pattern or practice of noncompliance; and this occurs through willfulness, recklessness, or gross incompetence.

▪ The individual *fails* to ensure the *procedures for compliance are followed*; there is a pattern or practice of noncompliance; and this occurs through willfulness, recklessness, or gross incompetence.

▪ The individual knows or should know of a pattern of noncompliance and fails to take prompt action to correct the noncompliance.

7 Sanctions by the Secretary of the Treasury for Violations of the Regulations

The Secretary of the Treasury may sanction a practitioner practicing before the IRS for being incompetent or disreputable. Such conduct includes:

▪ Being convicted of (i) any federal tax law crime; (ii) any criminal offense involving dishonesty or breach of conduct; or (iii) any felony under federal or state law for conduct indicating that the practitioner is unfit to practice before the IRS.

▪ Giving false or misleading information (statements, returns, etc.) to U.S. Department of the Treasury employees or to any tribunal authorized to hear federal tax matters.

▪ Carrying out any solicitation of business prohibited by Circular 230.

▪ Willfully failing to make a tax return or willfully evading, or attempting to evade, any assessment or payment of federal tax.

▪ Willfully counseling or assisting others to evade, or attempt to evade, any assessment or payment of federal tax.

▪ Failing to timely remit to the IRS any funds received from a client for the purpose of paying any tax or other obligation owed to the U.S. government.

▪ Using threats or false accusations or offering gifts, inducements, or other favors in order to influence any official action by any IRS employee.

▪ Being disbarred or suspended from practice as an attorney, CPA, public accountant, or actuary.

▪ Knowingly helping another person practice before the IRS while that person is suspended, disbarred, or otherwise ineligible to practice before the IRS.

▪ Being contemptuously abusive, making false accusations or statements, or circulating malicious or libelous matters.

- Knowingly, recklessly, or through gross incompetence giving false opinions on questions arising under the tax laws.

- Willfully failing to sign a tax return when federal tax law requires the practitioner to sign the return (e.g., the practitioner is a "paid preparer") unless the failure is:

  - due to reasonable cause; and

  - not due to willful neglect.

- Willfully disclosing or otherwise using a tax return or tax return information where such disclosure is:

  - not authorized by the IRC;

  - contrary to the order of any court; or

  - contrary to the order of an administrative law judge in connection with a disciplinary proceeding.

- Willfully neglecting to file an e-return when the practitioner is required to do so.

- Willfully preparing or signing a tax return when the practitioner does not have a valid tax preparer ID.

- Willfully representing a taxpayer before the IRS without authorization to do so.

8   Sanctions by the IRS for Violations of the Regulations

A practitioner may be sanctioned by the IRS if the practitioner does any of the following:

- Willfully violates any part of Circular 230 (except the section on "Best practices for tax advisors").

- Recklessly or through gross incompetence violates sections 10.34 ("Standards with respect to tax returns and documents, affidavits and other papers"), 10.35 ("Competence"), 10.36 ("Procedures to ensure compliance"), or 10.37 ("Requirements for other written advice").

- Possible sanctions include censure and suspension or disbarment from practice before the IRS. The IRS may also impose monetary penalties, not exceeding the gross income derived (or to be derived) from the conduct giving rise to the penalty.

9   Petition for Reinstatement

A practitioner disbarred or suspended may petition for reinstatement before the Internal Revenue Service after the expiration of five years following such disbarment or suspension (or immediately following the expiration of the suspension period, if shorter than five years). Reinstatement will not be granted unless the Internal Revenue Service is satisfied that the petitioner is not likely to engage thereafter in conduct contrary to the regulations in this part of Circular 230, and that granting such reinstatement would not be contrary to the public interest.

Question 1   MCQ-07197

Under Circular 230, which of the following actions of a CPA tax advisor is characteristic of a best practice in rendering tax advice?

- **a.** Requesting written evidence from a client that the fee proposal for tax advice has been approved by the board of directors.
- **b.** Recommending to the client that the advisor's tax advice be made orally instead of in a written memorandum.
- **c.** Establishing relevant facts, evaluating the reasonableness of assumptions and representations, and arriving at a conclusion supported by the law and facts in a tax memorandum.
- **d.** Requiring the client to supply a written representation, signed under penalties of perjury, concerning the facts and statements provided to the CPA for preparing a tax memorandum.

Question 2   MCQ-06896

Pursuant to Circular 230, which of the following statements about the return of a client's records is correct?

- **a.** The client's records are to be destroyed upon submission of a tax return.
- **b.** The practitioner may retain copies of the client's records.
- **c.** The existence of a dispute over fees generally relieves the practitioner of responsibility to return the client's records.
- **d.** The practitioner does not need to return any client records that are necessary for the client to comply with the client's federal tax obligations.

Question 3   MCQ-06672

Leslie Ponzi has just received written tax advice from her attorney, Dewey H. Cheatem. Which of the following statements is *not* a requirement of written advice under Circular 230 of the Internal Revenue Service?

- **a.** The practitioner must base written advice on reasonable factual and legal assumptions, including assumptions as to future events.
- **b.** The practitioner must not rely on representations, statements, findings, or agreements of the taxpayer if reliance on them would be unreasonable.
- **c.** The practitioner may not provide written advice in the form of electronic communications.
- **d.** The practitioner may not, in evaluating a federal tax matter, take into account the possibility that a tax return will not be audited.

Question 4   **MCQ-02080**

Vee Corp. retained Walter, CPA, to prepare its income tax returns for Years 4–6. During the Year 6 engagement, Walter discovered that he had made a mistake on Vee's Year 4 income tax return. What is Walter's professional responsibility under Circular 230 regarding Vee's incorrect Year 4 income tax return?

    a. Amend Vee's Year 4 income tax return and submit it to the IRS.

    b. Advise Vee that the Year 4 income tax return was incorrect and recommend that Vee ignore amending its Year 4 return because the statute of limitations has passed.

    c. Advise Vee of the associated penalties that may be incurred as a result of the error.

    d. Consider withdrawing from preparation of Vee's income tax returns for Years 4–6 until the error is corrected.

Professional Responsibilities and Tax Return Preparer Penalties

1 Tax Return Preparer

1.1 Definition of Tax Return Preparer

The term "tax return preparer" means any person who prepares for compensation, or who employs one or more persons to prepare for compensation, any tax return required under the IRC, or any claim for refund of tax imposed by the IRC. The preparation of a substantial portion of a return or claim for refund shall be treated as if it were the preparation of such return or claim for refund. Any tax professional with an IRS preparer tax identification number (PTIN) is authorized to prepare federal tax returns. These individuals are often categorized as enrolled agents, certified public accountants, attorneys, annual filing season program participants, and PTIN holders.

Illustration 1 **Not a Tax Return Preparer**

A small accounting firm hires two interns each year. The interns review the data provided by the clients and enter the information into the tax return software. The interns also call to request missing information but are not permitted to offer tax advice. The returns are prepared and signed by managers in the firm. In this scenario, the interns would not be regarded as tax return preparers.

1.1.1 Does Not Include

"Tax return preparer" does not include a person who (i) merely furnishes typing, reproducing, or other mechanical assistance; (ii) prepares a return or claim for refund of the employer (or of an officer or employee of the employer); or (iii) prepares as a fiduciary (trustee, executor, etc.) a return or claim for refund for any other person.

1.2 Unlimited Representation Rights

Enrolled agents, certified public accountants, and attorneys have unlimited representation rights before the IRS. Tax professionals with these credentials may represent their clients on any matters including audits, payment/collection issues, and appeals. PTIN holders who are classified as annual filing season program participants and preparers who are PTIN holders but do not have a credential and do not participate in the annual filing season program have limited representation rights.

1.2.1 PTIN Holders With No Credentials

- Tax return preparers who have an active preparer tax identification number but no professional credentials and do not participate in the annual filing season program are authorized only to prepare tax returns.

- Effective January 1, 2016, PTIN holders who do not hold a professional credential and do not participate in the annual filing season program have no authority to represent clients before the IRS (except regarding returns they prepared and filed December 31, 2015, and prior).

1.3 Obtaining a PTIN

The IRS requires all paid tax return preparers to register with the IRS and obtain a preparer tax identification number (PTIN).

1.4 Signing and Nonsigning Tax Return Preparer

▪ **Signing Tax Return Preparer:** The individual tax return preparer who has the primary responsibility for the overall substantive accuracy of the preparation of such return or claim for refund.

▪ **Nonsigning Tax Return Preparer:** Any tax return preparer who is not a signing tax return preparer but who prepares all or a substantial portion of a return or claim for refund or offers advice (written or oral) to a taxpayer (or to another tax return preparer) when that advice leads to a position or entry that constitutes a substantial portion of the return. Factors to consider in determining whether a schedule, entry, or other portion of a return or claim for refund is a substantial portion include but are not limited to (i) the size and complexity of the item relative to the taxpayer's gross income; and (ii) the size of the understatement attributable to the item compared to the taxpayer's reported tax liability.

Illustration 2   Nonsigning Tax Return Preparer

An attorney, who is a PTIN holder, provides a spreadsheet to a CPA that shows the calculation of income to be reported on the income tax return of an estate. The income represents a substantial portion of the return, yet the attorney does not prepare any other portion of the tax return and does not sign the tax return. The attorney could be regarded as a nonsigning preparer for the return for the purpose of assessing tax return preparer penalties.

---

2   Tax Return Preparer Compliance Penalties

Individuals who meet the qualification of tax return preparers are subject to certain penalties under the Internal Revenue Code. The assessments under IRC Section 6694 are intended to ensure that the tax return preparers are in compliance with federal tax laws.

2.1   Key Terms

2.1.1   Authority

Only the following are authority for purposes of determining whether there is substantial authority (defined below) for the tax treatment of an item (note that conclusions reached in treatises, legal periodicals, legal opinions, or opinions rendered by tax professionals are not "authority"):

▪ Applicable provisions of the Internal Revenue Code and other statutory provisions.

▪ Proposed, temporary, and final regulations construing such statutes.

▪ Revenue rulings and revenue procedures, tax treaties and regulations thereunder, and U.S. Treasury Department and other official explanations of such treaties.

▪ Court cases.

▪ Congressional intent as reflected in committee reports, joint explanatory statements of managers included in conference committee reports, and floor statements made prior to enactment by one of a bill's managers.

- "General Explanations" of tax legislation prepared by the Joint [U.S. Senate and U.S. House of Representatives] Committee on Taxation (the "Blue Book").

- Private letter rulings and technical advice memoranda issued after October 31, 1976.

- Actions on decisions and general counsel memoranda issued after March 12, 1981 (as well as general counsel memoranda published in pre-1955 volumes of the Cumulative Bulletin).

- Internal Revenue Service information or press releases and notices, announcements, and other administrative pronouncements published by the Service in the Internal Revenue Bulletin.

2.1.2 Disregard

The verb "disregard" includes any careless, reckless, or intentional disregard of rules or regulations.

2.1.3 Listed Transaction

The term *listed transaction* means a reportable transaction (defined below) which is the same as, or substantially similar to, a transaction specifically identified by the Secretary of the U.S. Treasury Department as a tax avoidance transaction.

2.1.4 More-Likely-Than-Not Standard

The *more-likely-than-not standard* is met when there is a greater than 50 percent likelihood of a tax position being upheld by the courts. This standard is more stringent than the *substantial authority standard*.

2.1.5 Negligence

The term *negligence* includes any failure to make a reasonable attempt to comply with the provisions of the internal revenue laws or to exercise ordinary and reasonable care in the preparation of a tax return. *Negligence* also includes any failure by the taxpayer to keep adequate books and records or to substantiate items properly.

2.1.6 Person

Person means and includes an individual, a trust, an estate, a partnership, an association, a company, or a corporation.

2.1.7 Reasonable Basis

- Reasonable basis is a relatively high standard of tax reporting; this standard is significantly higher than not frivolous or not patently improper. The reasonable basis standard is not satisfied by a return position that is merely arguable or that is merely a colorable claim.

- If a return position is reasonably based on one or more of the authorities set forth above, the return position will generally satisfy the reasonable basis standard even though the position may not satisfy the substantial authority standard (defined below).

2.1.8 Reportable Transaction

The term *reportable transaction* means any transaction with respect to which information is required to be included with a return or statement because such transaction is of a type that the Secretary of the U.S. Treasury Department has determined as having a potential for either tax avoidance (the legal use and application of the tax laws and cases in order to reduce the amount of tax due) or tax evasion (efforts, by illegal means and methods, to not pay taxes).

2.1.9 Substantial Authority Standard

- The *substantial authority standard* is an objective standard involving an analysis of the law and application of the law to relevant facts. The substantial authority standard is less stringent than the more-likely-than-not standard (defined above).

- There is substantial authority for the tax treatment of an item only if the weight of the authorities supporting the treatment is substantial in relation to the weight of authorities supporting the contrary treatment.

- There is substantial authority for the tax treatment of an item if the treatment is supported by controlling precedent of a U.S. Court of Appeals to which the taxpayer has a right of appeal with respect to the item.

- Because this standard is an objective standard, the taxpayer's belief that there is substantial authority for the tax treatment of an item is not relevant.

2.2 Understatement Due to an Unreasonable Position [IRC Section 6694(a)]

This penalty can be assessed because of the understatement of a taxpayer's liability due to an unreasonable position taken by the taxpayer.

2.2.1 Unreasonable Position

A position is deemed unreasonable unless:

- substantial authority for the position, regardless of disclosure, exists; or

- reasonable basis for a disclosed position exists; or

- it is reasonable to believe that a tax shelter or reportable transaction position would meet the more-likely-than-not standard.

Note: IRS Form 8275 is used to disclose items and positions that are not contrary to U.S. Treasury regulations, but are not otherwise adequately disclosed on a tax return. IRS Form 8275-R is used to disclose items and positions that are contrary to U.S. Treasury regulations.

2.2.2 Penalty for Understatement Due to Unreasonable Position

Equal to the greater of $1,000 or 50 percent of the income the preparer received for tax return preparation services.

The penalty may be imposed on the preparer if:

1. a position is taken on the tax return and understates the tax liability if there is no reasonable belief that the position would be sustainable based on its merit;

2. the preparer had knowledge or should have known about the unreasonable position;

3. disclosure of the position was not made; and

4. the position lacks reasonable basis.

2.3 Understatement Due to Willful or Reckless Conduct [IRC Section 6694(b)]

A compensated preparer is liable for a penalty if the preparer's understatement of taxpayer liability on a return or claim for refund is due to the preparer's negligent or intentional disregard of rules and regulations.

2.3.1 "Willful or Reckless" Conduct

Conduct that is either:

- a willful attempt to understate the tax liability; or

- a reckless or intentional disregard of tax rules and regulations in spite of his signed declaration on the return.

2.3.2 Supporting Documentation

A preparer is not required to obtain supporting documentation unless the preparer has reason to suspect the accuracy of the information provided by the taxpayer (client). The preparer must make reasonable inquiries if the information provided by the taxpayer appears incorrect or incomplete.

2.3.3 Penalty for "Willful or Reckless" Conduct

The penalty is equal to the greater of $5,000 or 50 percent of the income the preparer derived with respect to the tax return or refund claim. The penalty is reduced by any penalty assessed because of an understatement of a taxpayer's liability as the result of an unreasonable tax position by a tax return preparer.

3 Tax Return Preparer Penalties for Unethical Behavior

Penalties assessed under IRC Section 6695 are intended to protect the taxpayer from unethical behavior.

3.1 Failure to Provide Copy to Taxpayer (IRC Sections 6695, 6701)

A preparer is required to provide to the taxpayer (client) a copy of the tax return or a copy of the refund claim no later than the time the preparer gives the taxpayer the completed return or claim. The penalty does not apply to the extent the failure is due to reasonable cause and not due to willful neglect and is $50 for each such failure (maximum penalty of $25,500 per calendar year).

3.2 Failure to Sign Return (IRC Section 6695)

The penalty is $50 for each such failure (maximum penalty of $25,500 per calendar year).

3.3 Failure to Furnish Identification Number of Preparer (IRC Section 6695)

The penalty is $50 for each such failure (maximum penalty of $25,500 per calendar year).

3.4 Failure to Properly Retain Records (IRC Sections 6695, 6107, 6060)

The tax return preparer is required to keep, for the three years following the last day of the return period, either: a copy of the return or claim or a listing of the name and ID of each taxpayer for whom the preparer prepared a return or claim. The penalty is $50 for each such failure (maximum penalty of $25,500 per return period).

3.5 Failure to File Correct Information Returns (IRC Sections 6695, 6060)

Any person who employed a tax return preparer at any time during that return period must file an information return with the IRS by July 31 immediately following the end of the return period, containing: the name, taxpayer identification number, and place of work of each tax return preparer so employed by that person. The penalty is $50 for each failure (maximum penalty of $25,500 per return period).

3.6 Negotiation of IRS Refund Check (IRC Section 6695)

Generally, any tax return preparer who endorses or otherwise negotiates an IRS refund check issued to a taxpayer other than the tax return preparer shall pay a penalty of $510 with respect to each such check. This rule does not apply to banks if the bank deposits into the taxpayer's account at such bank the full amount of the IRS refund check.

3.7 Failure to Be Diligent in Determining a Client's Eligibility for the Earned Income Credit [IRC Section 6695(g)]

3.7.1 Penalty

The penalty for failure to comply with the IRS' "due diligence" requirements with respect to determining eligibility for, or the amount of, the earned income credit is $510 for each failure.

3.7.2 Due Diligence Requirements

The due diligence requirements address (i) eligibility checklists; (ii) computation worksheets; (iii) reasonable inquires to the taxpayer; and (iv) record retention. The penalty will not apply with respect to a particular return or claim if the tax return preparer can demonstrate that the preparer's normal office procedures are reasonably designed and routinely followed to ensure due diligence compliance and the failure to meet the due diligence requirements was insolated and inadvertent.

4 Other Tax Return Preparer Penalties

4.1 Aiding and Abetting Understatement of Tax Liability [IRC Sections 6702, 6703(a)]

The penalty for aiding and abetting understatement of tax liability applies to any person, not just to tax return preparers. The IRS has the burden of proof to establish that any person is liable for this civil penalty. The penalty applies whether or not the understatement is with the knowledge or consent of the persons authorized or required to file the return, affidavit, claim, or other document.

The IRC imposes a civil penalty ($1,000 for all taxpayers except corporations and $10,000 for corporations) on any person/entity who:

- aids, assists in, procures, or advises with respect to, the preparation or presentation of any portion of a return, affidavit, claim, or other document;
- knows (or has reason to know) that such portion will be used in connection with any material matter arising under the IRC; and
- knows that such portion (if so used) would result in an understatement of the liability for tax of another person.

Note: Unless the law expressly states otherwise (as it does with this penalty), in any civil action (court hearing) the taxpayer has the burden of proof to establish by a preponderance of the evidence (more than 50 percent) that the law and the evidence do not support the position of the IRS concerning the matter in dispute. With respect to any criminal action (court proceedings regarding fines and/or imprisonment), the government has the burden of proof to establish by evidence beyond a reasonable doubt that the taxpayer is guilty of the charge(s).

4.2 Wrongful Disclosure and/or Use of Tax Return Information (IRC Sections 6713, 7216)

4.2.1 Penalty

A tax return preparer who discloses or uses information for any purpose other than to prepare a tax return shall pay a civil penalty of $250 for each such disclosure or use (maximum annual penalty shall not exceed $10,000) and be guilty of a misdemeanor and fined not more than $1,000 and/or be imprisoned for not more than one year, together with the costs of prosecution. (Note that a client may also bring civil suit against the tax preparer.)

4.2.2 Exceptions

Exceptions to the penalty and/or fine for wrongful disclosure and/or use of tax return information include:

- Disclosures allowed by any provision of the IRC and disclosures pursuant to a court order.

- Allowable uses (preparation of state and local tax returns and preparation of declaration of estimated tax).

- Disclosures and uses permitted by U.S. Treasury regulations for quality and peer reviews and administrative orders.

4.2.3 Consent of Client

Confidential client information may be disclosed to any party if the client specifically consents to the release of information.

Pass Key

Historically, the most commonly tested issues regarding the tax liability rules include:

- Endorsing and cashing refund checks. (Key: Endorsing and negotiating a client's refund check—regardless of amount—is forbidden.)

- Preparing returns that understate tax liability. (Key: Although a tax preparer cannot willfully aid in understating tax liability, the preparer has no affirmative duty to check the veracity of the facts presented by the client, with a possible exception for facts that appear implausible.)

- Disclosure of tax return information. (Key: Memorize the situations in which the tax preparer is able to disclose information without the taxpayer's consent—disclosure in all other situations without taxpayer consent is disallowed.)

5 Role of State Boards of Accountancy

5.1 Sole Power to License

- Statutes in all 50 states grant to state boards of accountancy the sole power to license certified public accountants.

- Requirements for licensure vary from state to state. They require successful completion of the CPA examination and all or some of the following:
  - A residency requirement;
  - Educational requirements; and
  - Experience requirements.
- Because a state board is the only entity that can license a CPA, the state board is also the only entity with the power to suspend or revoke a CPA's license.

5.2 Disciplinary Power of State Boards

- Although each state determines what constitutes professional misconduct by a CPA sufficient to subject the CPA to disciplinary action, there are three broad categories of misconduct.
  - Misconduct while performing accounting services (e.g., negligence, fraud, dishonesty, etc.).
  - Misconduct outside the scope of accounting services (e.g., intoxication from alcohol or drugs that significantly impairs the accountant's ability to perform accounting services, insanity, etc.).
  - Criminal conviction (e.g., commission of a felony, failure to file tax returns, crimes relating to the practice of accounting, etc.).
- After investigation of professional misconduct, the state board can conduct a formal hearing for possible disciplinary action.
  - The board must find it was more likely than not that the accountant's actions constituted professional misconduct. Proof beyond a reasonable doubt (i.e., the standard in criminal cases) is not required.
  - The accountant is entitled to due process of law.
  - All adverse state board decisions are subject to judicial review.
- There are five penalties that a state board of accountancy may impose for professional misconduct:
  - Suspension or revocation of license
  - A monetary fine
  - A reprimand or censure
  - Probation
  - Requirement for continuing professional education (CPE) courses

6 Requirements of Regulatory Agencies

6.1 The American Institute of Certified Public Accountants (AICPA) and State CPA Societies

6.1.1 The Professional Code of Conduct

The Code of Professional Conduct applies to all members of the AICPA. Many state CPA societies and state boards have incorporated all, or parts of the code.

6.1.2   Joint Ethics Enforcement Program (JEEP)

- The AICPA and 49 state societies have created the Joint Ethics Enforcement Program (JEEP) for enforcement of their codes of conduct by means of a single investigation and action.

- Investigative information is shared between the AICPA and the state societies.

- JEEP objectives also include the promotion of uniformity in the codes of conduct of the AICPA and state CPA societies and uniformity in enforcement and implementation of the codes of conduct.

6.1.3   Disciplinary Action by the AICPA and State CPA Societies

- The AICPA and state CPA societies can sanction their members, but they cannot suspend or revoke a CPA's license.

- The AICPA may suspend or terminate membership for failure to pay dues or failure to comply with membership retention requirements (e.g., practice-monitoring or continuing professional education requirements).

- Membership can be suspended or terminated without a hearing for:
    - proof of conviction of a crime punishable by imprisonment for more than one year.
    - proof of conviction for willful failure to file any income tax return.
    - proof of conviction for filing a false or fraudulent income tax return or aiding in the preparation of a false or fraudulent income tax return of a client.
    - suspension or revocation of a member's license to practice public accounting as a disciplinary measure by a government authority.

- The Professional Ethics Division of the AICPA investigates potential disciplinary matters and refers appropriate cases to the Joint Trial Board.
    - The Joint Trial Board may expel a member by a two-thirds vote.
    - The Joint Trial Board may suspend a member for up to two years or impose lesser sanctions by majority vote.

- The following are grounds for Joint Trial Board sanctions:
    - Violation of the bylaws or any rule of the Code of Conduct.
    - Declaration by a court of having committed fraud.
    - Determination by the Joint Trial Board of guilt for any act discreditable to the profession, or conviction of a criminal offense that tends to discredit the profession.
    - Declaration by a court that the CPA is insane or incompetent.
    - Suspension or revocation of a member's license to practice public accounting as a disciplinary measure by a government authority.
    - Failure to cooperate with any Professional Ethics Division disciplinary investigation.
    - Failure to comply with educational and remedial or corrective action determined to be necessary by the Professional Ethics Executive Committee within 30 days.

- Notice of disciplinary action is published in a membership periodical (i.e., CPA newsletter).

- Possible sanctions include:
    - Expulsion from the AICPA or state CPA society.
    - Suspension of membership in the AICPA or state CPA society.
    - Requirement that CPE courses be taken as a remedial measure.

6.2 Internal Revenue Service (IRS) Disciplinary Actions

6.2.1 Criminal Penalties

- The Internal Revenue Code (IRC) provides for criminal penalties for any person, including a tax return preparer, who counsels or prepares a tax return in a fraudulent or false manner with regard to any material matter.

- A person found guilty of making a false or fraudulent statement in connection with a return is guilty of a felony and may be imprisoned for not more than three years and/or fined not more than $100,000 ($500,000 for a corporation).

6.2.2 Civil Penalties

- The IRS may prohibit an accountant from practicing before the IRS.

- The IRS may impose fines for various infractions (as discussed in item 1 above).

Note: In addition to criminal and civil penalties, a person guilty of making false and fraudulent statements on a return may be subject to a malpractice suit by the taxpayer (client).

6.3 Securities and Exchange Commission (SEC)

6.3.1 Civil Penalties

- The SEC may censure, suspend, or permanently revoke an accountant's right to practice before the SEC, including the right to sign documents required by the Securities Act of 1933 and the Securities Exchange Act of 1934.

- Suspension or revocation of the right to practice before the SEC can occur if:
  - the accountant lacks the qualifications to represent others;
  - the accountant lacks character or integrity;
  - the accountant acted unethically or unprofessionally;
  - the accountant willfully violated federal security laws or regulations;
  - the accountant was convicted of a felony or convicted of a misdemeanor involving moral turpitude; or
  - the accountant's license to practice public accounting was suspended or revoked as a disciplinary measure by a government authority.

- The SEC may impose fines of not more than $100,000 ($500,000 for a firm).

- The SEC can issue cease and desist orders.

Question 1	MCQ-02187

A tax return preparer may disclose or use tax return information without the taxpayer's consent to:

- **a.** Facilitate a supplier's or lender's credit evaluation of the taxpayer.
- **b.** Accommodate the request of a financial institution that needs to determine the amount of taxpayer's debt to it, to be forgiven.
- **c.** Be evaluated by a quality or peer review.
- **d.** Solicit additional nontax business.

---

1 Audit Process

The federal income tax system is based on the self-assessment of taxes. All "persons" with taxable incomes exceeding certain amounts are required to file annual income tax returns and to timely remit taxes that are due. The audit process helps ensure that this "voluntary" assessment and payment is actually occurring.

1.1 Examination of a Return (Audit)

A return may be examined (audited) for a variety of reasons, and the examination may take place in any one of several ways. After the audit, if there are any changes to the tax payable, the taxpayer either can agree with the changes and pay the additional tax or can disagree with the changes and appeal the decision. Interest on unpaid taxes may also be due.

1.2 Selection of Returns for Audit

1.2.1 Statistical Models

The IRS utilizes statistical models (a form of discriminant analysis called the Discriminant Inventory Function System, or DIF) to select tax returns that are the most likely to contain errors and yield significant amounts of additional tax revenue upon audit.

1.2.2 Random Selection

In addition to the statistical selection of returns to be audited, a small number of additional returns are manually selected.

1.2.3 Prior Year Audit

If the taxpayer was audited in a prior year and that prior audit led to assessment of a substantial deficiency, a subsequent year may be audited.

1.2.4 Information Return Discrepancy

If information forms such as W-2s and 1099s do not match the amounts reported on a return, or if information is received from other sources on potential noncompliance, an audit may be triggered.

1.2.5 Deductions That Exceed Established Norms

If an individual's itemized deductions are in excess of norms established for certain income levels, the return may be selected for audit.

1.3 Timing of Audits

Most individual returns are audited within two years from the date of filing of the return. However, returns may be audited at any point prior to the expiration of the statute of limitations. Even then, the taxpayer may consent to extend this statute upon IRS request. Large corporations are subject to annual audits.

1.4 Review for Mathematical Errors (Correspondence Audit)

A correspondence audit arises as a result of IRS review for the following:

- Information errors (incorrect Social Security numbers or missing signatures)

- Matching issues (income reported on tax return does not match W-2 or Form 1099)

- Mathematical errors

In the case of errors, the taxpayer is typically sent a revised computation and a brief explanation of any change made along with a bill for the additional amount due or check for a refund, as appropriate. There will be no need for a formal meeting with an IRS representative. If the payment is made timely, there is no interest on the underpayment. If the required payment is not made timely, there is interest from the date of the notice.

1.5 Formal Examination (Office or Field Audit)

If a formal examination is necessary, there may be an office audit or a field audit.

1.5.1 Office Audit

An office audit is conducted by an IRS revenue agent, either in an IRS office or by correspondence, and is used for individual returns with few or no items of business income. In most cases, the taxpayer is merely required to substantiate an item of income, a deduction, or a credit.

1.5.2 Field Audit

A field audit is conducted by an IRS representative, either at the taxpayer's office or home or at the place of business of the taxpayer's representative. The IRS makes the final determination of when, where, and how the examination will take place. The taxpayer can make an audio recording of the examination interview.

1.6 After the Audit

1.6.1 Issue Resolved

Following an audit, the revenue agent may either accept the return or recommend certain changes. If agreement is reached with the taxpayer, the taxpayer signs Form 870 (Waiver of Restrictions on Assessment and Collection of Deficiency in Tax), and interest stops accumulating on the deficiency 30 days after the form is filed. The taxpayer will receive a bill for any additional taxes and interest (generally calculated from the due date of the return to the date of payment) or a check for any refund, including interest on the refund.

By signing the Form 870, the taxpayer waives the right to receive certain statutory notices and to petition the U.S. Tax Court and waives the right to the appeal process. The signing of the Form 870 normally closes the case, but the IRS may assess additional deficiencies if necessary.

1.6.2 Unresolved Issues

If agreement cannot be reached at the revenue agent level, the taxpayer receives a copy of the Revenue Agent's report and a 30-day letter (preliminary notice) notifying the taxpayer of the right to appeal. The taxpayer has 30 days to request an administrative appeal with an appeals officer (appeals conference).

1.6.3 Fast-Track Remediation

Small business owners and self-employed individuals can resolve their tax disputes through a process called fast-track remediation. The goal for resolution within fast-track remediation is 60 days. A trained mediator from the IRS Office of Appeals is assigned to help the taxpayer and the IRS reach an agreement on the disputed issue(s). Fast-track remediation is not available for issues for which there is no legal precedent in the courts, for which the courts in different jurisdictions have rendered differing decisions, and in other specialized situations. If, at the end of the fast-track mediation process, the issue remains unresolved, the normal appeals process is still available.

2 Appeals Process

2.1 Appeals Conference

If agreement cannot be reached at the revenue agent level, the taxpayer receives a copy of the Revenue Agent's report and a 30-day letter (preliminary notice) notifying the taxpayer of the right to appeal. The taxpayer has 30 days to request an administrative appeal with an appeals officer (appeals conference).

2.2 Office of Appeals

The goal of the appeals process handled by the IRS Office of Appeals is to resolve tax controversies without litigation. If an agreement is reached with the Appeals Division, the taxpayer signs Form 870-AD. Interest stops accruing when the form is received and accepted by the IRS. This settlement is normally considered binding on both parties. If agreement is not reached, a 90-day letter will be issued.

2.3 90-Day Letter (Notice of Deficiency)

If an appeals conference was not requested after receipt of the 30-day letter, or if the taxpayer and IRS still do not agree on the proposed adjustment after the appeals conference, a 90-day letter (notice of deficiency) is issued. The taxpayer has 90 days to pay the deficiency or file a petition with the U.S. Tax Court. If the taxpayer would like to litigate the case but prefers the case to be heard in the U.S. District Court or the U.S. Court of Federal Claims, the taxpayer must first pay the tax deficiency and then sue the IRS for refund in the court if the IRS denies the claim for refund.

3 Federal Judicial Process

When a taxpayer and the Internal Revenue Service cannot reach agreement on a tax matter administratively either with a revenue agent or with the Appeals Division, the dispute must be settled in the Federal Court system. Either the IRS or the taxpayer can initiate the process. In the Federal Court system, the U.S. Tax Court, a U.S. District Court, and the U.S. Court of Federal Claims are considered trial courts. The U.S. Court of Appeals, the Federal Court of Appeals, and the U.S. Supreme Court are considered appellate courts.

Appellate courts are limited to a review of the trial record of the lower court to determine if that lower court applied the proper law in arriving at its decision. Seldom will an appellate court disturb the trial court's determination of the facts.

The taxpayer can choose the route through the court system that he or she deems most favorable. Key concepts related to the federal judicial process include the following:

- **Burden of Proof**

  In most litigation, the party bringing the case has the burden of proof. In most civil tax cases, the taxpayer has the burden of proof. In certain situations, however, the burden of proof shifts to the IRS. The IRS has the burden of proof in any court proceeding on income, gift, estate, or generation-skipping tax with respect to factual issues provided that the taxpayer has introduced credible evidence, has maintained books and records as required, and has complied with reasonable IRS requests.

- **Doctrine of Stare Decisis**

  Like English law, American law is frequently made by judicial decisions. Under the doctrine of stare decisis, judges are required to respect the precedents established by prior judicial decisions on the same set of facts.

- **Appeal Outcomes**

  An appeal can have a number of possible outcomes. The appellate court may affirm (accept) or reverse the lower court's finding or it may send the case back to the lower court for further consideration (remand).

3.1   U.S. Tax Court

The U.S. Tax Court is a specialized trial court that hears only federal tax cases (income tax, estate tax, gift tax, or certain excise taxes), generally prior to the time that formal tax assessments are made by the IRS.

3.1.1   Small Cases Division Option

Taxpayers who file petitions with the U.S. Tax Court have the option of having the case heard before the informal Small Cases Division (small tax cases) if the amount of tax in dispute does not exceed $50,000 for any one tax year. Neither party may appeal the decision and the decision is not considered precedent in other courts.

3.1.2   No Payment Required to Petition/Trial by Judge (No Jury)

The U.S. Tax Court is the only forum in which taxpayers may litigate without first having paid the disputed tax in full. Trials are conducted before one judge who will be a tax expert, and there are no jury trials. Taxpayers are permitted to represent themselves. For a case to be heard, the taxpayer must petition the Tax Court, normally within 90 days of the IRS's mailing of a notice of deficiency (90-day letter) and demand for payment of the disputed amount. Cases cannot be taken to the Tax Court before the IRS sends out the notice of deficiency.

3.1.3   Decisions

The U.S. Tax Court issues two types of decisions: regular and memorandum. Small tax case decisions are published as Summary Opinions.

- **Regular Decision:** A regular decision normally involves a new or unusual point of law.

- **Memorandum Decision:** A memorandum decision concerns only the application of existing law or an interpretation of facts.

3.2 U.S. District Courts

The U.S. District Courts are the general trial courts of the U.S. federal court system. Both civil and criminal cases (not just tax cases) are filed in district courts. There is at least one district court for each state and other district courts for territories. Typically, a taxpayer will request a hearing before the district court that has jurisdiction over the location in which the taxpayer lives or conducts business.

3.2.1 Must First Pay Disputed Tax Liability and Sue IRS for Refund

A taxpayer who disagrees with the IRS may take his or her case to a U.S. District Court only after paying the disputed tax liability and then sue the IRS for a refund. Generally, a claim for refund must be filed within three years from the date the original return was filed or two years from the date the tax was paid, whichever is later.

3.2.2 One Judge and Jury Trial Is an Option

U.S. District Court cases are heard before one judge, not a panel of judges. The taxpayer can request a jury trial.

3.3 U.S. Court of Federal Claims

The U.S. Court of Federal Claims is a nationwide court that has jurisdiction over most claims for money damages against the United States, one type of which is tax refunds. The court has concurrent jurisdiction with U.S. District Courts when the claim is for less than $10,000, and there is a statute of limitations of six years from the time the claim arose. The taxpayer must pay the disputed tax and sue the IRS/government for a refund. The Court of Federal Claims does not allow jury trials on any matter. There are 16 judges.

Summary of U.S. Trial Court System

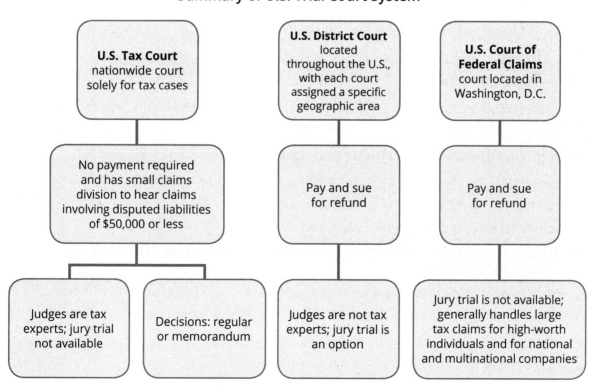

3.4 Courts of Appeals and the U.S. Court of Appeals for the Federal Circuit

The U.S. Courts of Appeals (or circuit courts) are the first level of federal appellate courts. A court of appeals hears appeals from the U.S. District Courts and the U.S. Tax Court. The U.S. Circuit Court of Appeals hears appeals from the U.S. Court of Federal Claims.

3.5 U.S. Supreme Court

The U.S. Supreme Court is the highest court in the nation and is the last level of appeal.

3.5.1 Panel of Nine Justices (No Jury)

There are nine justices (judges), who hear all cases that the Supreme Court agrees to consider (for which it grants a *writ of certiorari*) in Washington, D.C.

3.5.2 Tax Cases Are Rare

The Supreme Court seldom hears tax cases. In most cases where it does hear a tax case, it is where there is a conflict among the Courts of Appeals.

4 Taxpayer Penalties

The Internal Revenue Code contains many sections setting forth penalties, both civil and criminal, which the Internal Revenue Service can seek to impose on the taxpayer.

4.1 Earned Income Credit Penalty

The earned income credit "penalty" is more a statutory restriction on claiming the credit, rather than a penalty, per se. Taxpayers who negligently claim the earned income credit may not claim this credit for two subsequent years or for up to ten years if the claim was fraudulent.

4.2 Penalty for Failure to Make Sufficient Estimated Income Tax Payments

Taxpayers (including corporations, estates, and trusts) who do not have sufficient amounts of withholding and who do not make timely payments of estimated income tax (including self-employment tax) must pay this penalty, which accrues from the date the estimated income tax must be paid until the tax return due date without extensions.

Penalty exceptions include withholding and timely estimated payments that are:

- less than or equal to $1,000 of current year tax;
- at least 90 percent of the current year's tax;
- at least 100 percent of last year's tax (110 percent of last year's tax if last year's AGI exceeded $150,000); or
- equal to estimated current year tax based upon the "annualization of income" method.

4.3   Failure-to-File Penalty

The penalty is 5 percent of the amount of tax due for each month (or any part of) the return is late, up to a maximum of 25 percent. Other key aspects of the failure-to-file penalty are the following:

- If the return is more than 60 days late, the minimum penalty increases to the lesser of $210 or 100 percent of the tax due.

- If no tax is due, then there is no failure-to-file penalty.

- If both the failure-to-file penalty and the failure-to-pay penalty are due, the failure-to-file penalty is reduced by the amount of the failure-to-pay penalty.

- The penalty for failure to file a partnership tax return is $200 for each month or part thereof (up to a maximum of 12 months) the return is late (or required information is missing) times the numbers of persons who are partners in the partnership at any time during the year.

4.4   Failure-to-Pay Penalty

The penalty is one-half of 1 percent per month (or any part of) up to a maximum of 25 percent of the unpaid tax.

There is no penalty if at least 90 percent of the tax is paid in by the unextended due date; and the balance is paid by the extended due date.

4.5   Negligence Penalty With Respect to an Understatement of Tax (Accuracy-Related Penalty When Understatement Is Not Substantial)

- This penalty is an accuracy-based penalty for negligence or for disregard of tax rules and regulations.

- The penalty is equal to 20 percent of the understatement of tax.

- *Negligence* means any failure to make a reasonable attempt to comply with the provisions of the IRC.

- *Disregard* means careless, reckless, or intentional disregard.

- If the IRS imposes this penalty, then the IRS cannot impose either (i) the penalty for substantial underpayment of tax; or (ii) the penalty for a substantial valuation misstatement.

4.6   Penalty for Substantial Understatement of Tax (Accuracy-Related Penalty)

- The penalty is 20 percent of the understatement of tax.

  - An understatement is *substantial* if it exceeds the greater of 10 percent of the correct tax (5 percent of the correct tax if the understatement is due to the taxpayer overstating the QBI deduction) or $5,000.

  - For C corporations other than personal holding companies, an understatement is *substantial* if the amount of the understatement exceeds the lesser of (a) $10,000,000; or (b) the greater of $10,000 or 10 percent of the correct tax.

- If the IRS imposes this penalty, then the IRS cannot impose either (i) the negligence penalty with respect to an understatement of tax which is not substantial and penalty for disregard of rules or regulations; or (ii) the penalty for a substantial valuation misstatement.

4.7   Penalty for a Substantial Valuation Misstatement

▪ The penalty is 20 percent of the understatement of tax with respect to a valuation for tax purposes to the extent the understatement exceeds $5,000 ($10,000 for corporations).

▪ There are two distinct substantial valuation misstatement standards: one for IRC Section 482 transactions (related parties) and one for non-Section 482 transactions (non-related parties).

▪ Defenses for charitable contributions must include good faith, qualified appraisals, and good faith investigation of value.

▪ This penalty cannot be imposed in addition to the negligence penalty or for substantial understatement.

4.8   Fraud Penalties

▪ Both civil penalties (at least 75 percent of the understatement of tax due to fraud) and criminal penalties (as high as $100,000; $500,000 for corporations) can apply.

▪ The IRS must prove that the taxpayer willfully and deliberately attempted to evade tax.

▪ Criminal penalty and potential imprisonment subject to an inflation adjustment, top $100,000 ($500,000 for corporations), plus the IRS must prove beyond a reasonable doubt that the taxpayer criminally, willfully, and deliberately attempted to evade tax.

5   Substantiation and Disclosure of Tax Positions

There are factors which should be considered when tax positions are taken on tax returns to avoid or reduce penalties.

5.1   Frivolous Tax Return

Frivolous positions have no basis in law or other authority. Disclosure will not protect a taxpayer or a tax preparer from penalties if a tax return position is frivolous.

5.2   Reasonable Basis Standard

▪ The reasonable basis standard is a tax position that has at least a 20 percent chance of succeeding, one that is arguable but fairly unlikely to prevail in court.

▪ This standard is not met if the taxpayer fails to make a reasonable attempt to determine the correctness of a position that seems too good to be true.

▪ This standard will avoid the negligence penalty with respect to an understatement of tax that is not substantial and the penalty for disregard of rules or regulations, even if the taxpayer does not disclose the tax return position for which the taxpayer has a reasonable basis.

▪ This basis will avoid the substantial underpayment penalty only if the taxpayer disclosed the tax return position (except for tax shelters) for which the taxpayer has a reasonable basis.

5.3   Substantial Authority Standard

- The substantial authority standard is a position that has more than a one-in-three chance of succeeding but less than a more-than-50-percent chance of succeeding (the more-likely-than-not standard).

- Only analyses and reports issued by the U.S. Congress, IRS regulations, rules, and releases, and U.S. court case decisions constitute substantial authority. Tax articles and treatises do not constitute substantial authority. See discussion that follows in this module on substantial authority.

5.4   More-Likely-Than-Not Standard

The more-likely-than-not standard is met when there is a greater than 50 percent likelihood of a tax position being upheld by the courts. This standard is more stringent than the substantial authority standard.

5.5   Disclosures for Uncertain Tax Positions

Certain tax forms are used to disclose uncertain tax positions and can help taxpayer avoid understatement penalties.

- **Disclosure Statement (Forms 8275)**

  - This form is used to avoid the understatement penalty.

  - It is a statement used to disclose positions taken on a tax return that are contrary to Revenue Rulings, Revenue Procedures, or other statutory provisions (except Regulations).

  - There are three parts to the form: (1) general information; (2) detailed explanation; and (3) information about pass-through entity.

- **Regulation Disclosure Statement (Form 8275-R)**

  This form is almost identical to Form 8275 but is used to disclose positions taken on a tax return that are contrary to Treasury Regulations.

- **Reportable Transaction Disclosure Statement (Form 8886)**

  - Any taxpayer that participates in a reportable transaction and is required to file a federal tax return or information return must file Form 8886 disclosing the transaction.

  - The filing requirement applies whether or not another party, related or otherwise, has filed a disclosure for that transaction.

  - The categories of reportable transactions include the following:

    —Listed transactions

    —Confidential transactions

    —Transactions with contractual protection

    —Loss transactions

5.6 General Avoidance of Penalties

In addition to the various defenses that are available, a taxpayer generally can avoid any penalty by showing that the taxpayer:

1. had reasonable cause to support the tax return position;

2. acted in good faith; and

3. did not have willful neglect.

5.7 Interest on Penalties

Interest on many penalties begins to accrue from the tax return due date (or extended due date). (Note that interest on underpaid tax begins to accrue from the date the tax was due without extension of time to file.)

6 Substantial Authority

Only the following are authority for purposes of determining whether there is substantial authority (defined below) for the tax treatment of an item (note that conclusions reached in treatises, legal periodicals, legal opinions, or opinions rendered by tax professionals are not "authority"):

- Applicable provisions of the Internal Revenue Code and other statutory provisions.

- Proposed, temporary, and final regulations construing such statutes.

- Revenue rulings and revenue procedures, tax treaties and regulations thereunder, and U.S. Treasury Department and other official explanations of such treaties.

- Court cases.

- Congressional intent as reflected in committee reports, joint explanatory statements of managers included in conference committee reports, and floor statements made prior to enactment by one of a bill's managers.

- General Explanations of tax legislation prepared by the Joint (U.S. Senate and U.S. House of Representatives) Committee on Taxation (the "Blue Book").

- Private letter rulings and technical advice memoranda issued after October 31, 1976.

- Actions on decisions and general counsel memoranda issued after March 12, 1981 (as well as general counsel memoranda published in pre-1955 volumes of the Cumulative Bulletin).

- Internal Revenue Service information or press releases and notices, announcements, and other administrative pronouncements published by the Service in the Internal Revenue Bulletin.

Question 1   MCQ-02093

An accuracy-related penalty applies to the portion of tax underpayment attributable to:

I.   Negligence or a disregard of the tax rules or regulations.

II.   Any substantial understatement of income tax.

    a.   I only.

    b.   II only.

    c.   Both I and II.

    d.   Neither I nor II.

Question 2   MCQ-06595

John S. Loppe has not been particularly careful in preparing his income tax returns and, as a result, has substantially understated his tax. The negligence penalty with respect to understatement of tax might thus be applicable to him. The negligence penalty with respect to understatement of tax:

    a.   Is an accuracy-based penalty for negligence or for disregard of tax rules and regulations.

    b.   Is computed as 25 percent of the understatement of tax.

    c.   Defines "disregard" as any careless, reckless, or unintentional disregard of tax rules and regulations.

    d.   Is imposed in conjunction with the penalty for substantial underpayment of tax and the penalty for a substantial valuation misstatement.

Question 3   MCQ-06671

John R. Fudge is an individual taxpayer in Cut and Shoot, Texas. He has been accused of understating the tax on one of his returns and is concerned about the possibility of imprisonment if he is convicted. The understatement has nothing to do with a tax shelter. Which of the following statements is correct for his situation?

    a.   If John took a reasonable position on his tax return, he is subject to the penalty for understatement of tax but not to the penalty for substantial understatement of tax.

    b.   If there was a reasonable basis for a disclosed tax position on the tax return, and John acted in good faith, the penalty for understatement of tax would still apply if John actually did understate his tax.

    c.   If John relied on the opinion of a reputable accountant or attorney who prepared his return and furnished all relevant information, in general, he would have a reasonable basis for the tax return position and could avoid the penalties for understatement of tax.

    d.   If John's understatement of tax is a substantial understatement, the penalty is double what it would have been for a simple understatement.

Question 4   MCQ-06665

Chatham Corporation is a defendant in a lawsuit by the IRS. Which of the following statements is correct with respect to the various defenses that might be available to Chatham to avoid or reduce civil and criminal penalties that might otherwise be imposed on it?

    a.   The reasonable basis standard involves a position that is arguable but fairly unlikely to prevail in court. A numerical statement of this standard has at least a 10 percent chance of succeeding.

    b.   The substantial authority standard involves a position that has a less than 50 percent chance but more than a one-in-four chance of succeeding.

    c.   The more-likely-than-not standard involves a position that has a more than 50 percent chance of succeeding.

    d.   Reports issued by the U.S. Congress, IRS regulations, rules, and releases, and U.S. and foreign court case decisions constitute substantial authority for the substantial authority standard.

1 Legal Liabilities

Civil actions for tax malpractice are usually based on either traditional contract or traditional tort principles.

- Contract principles impose the obligation to prepare the tax return diligently and competently.

- Tort principles provide that a professional has a duty to exercise the level of skill, care, and diligence commonly exercised by other members of the profession under similar circumstances.

To prove malpractice against a tax preparer, the plaintiff must demonstrate all of the following:

1. The tax preparer owed a duty to the taxpayer.

2. There was a breach of that duty.

3. The plaintiff suffered injuries.

4. There was a determinable cause between injury suffered and the duty of the tax preparer.

1.1 Breach of Contract

If a CPA does not fulfill the terms of his engagement, the client can hold the CPA liable for breach. Contract liability generally requires *privity*, so only a party to the contract can sue under a contract theory.

Illustration 1 Tax Preparer Breach of Contract

Alan Sims has a signed engagement letter from his CPA, Joe Foster, stating that Mr. Foster's firm will prepare Alan's individual federal tax return and three state tax returns by April 1 if Alan provides all requested documentation by March 10. Alan wanted his tax returns completed by April 1 because he was leaving the country for a trip with his family. Alan's tax returns were not completed until April 30. This scenario could lead to a breach of contract claim as the tax preparer owed a duty to the taxpayer (to prepare the federal and state tax returns), and there appears to be a breach of that duty because the returns were not completed at the agreed upon date.

1.2 Commission of a Tort

CPA liability can also arise from commission of a tort. Three torts are relevant:

- negligence,

- constructive fraud (also called gross negligence), and

- fraud.

1.2.1 Negligence

As a general rule, a CPA owes a duty to his or her client not to perform work negligently. If the CPA performs negligently, he or she can be held liable for damages. Negligence requires a breach of the duty to exercise due care. The standard of care owed by a CPA is to perform with the same skill and care expected of ordinarily prudent CPAs under the circumstances.

1. **Elements in General**

   To make out a case for negligence, the plaintiff must show:

   - the defendant owed a duty of care to the plaintiff;

   - the defendant breached that duty by failing to act with due care;

   - the breach caused plaintiff's injury; and

   - damages.

2. **To Whom Is the Duty Owed?**

   - A CPA's duty to act with reasonable care generally runs only to clients and to any person or *limited* foreseeable class of persons whom the CPA knows will be relying on the CPA's work.

   - A minority of states follows the *Ultramares* decision, which limits CPA liability more narrowly to persons in privity of contract with the CPA (clients) and intended third-party beneficiaries.

1.3 Fraud and Constructive Fraud (Gross Negligence)

CPA liability can also arise through fraud or constructive fraud.

1.3.1 Elements of Fraud (Intentional Misrepresentation)

Actual fraud has five elements:

1. A misrepresentation of material fact;

2. Intent to deceive (knowing the statement was false);

3. Actual and justifiable reliance by plaintiff on the misrepresentation;

4. An intent to induce plaintiff's reliance on the misrepresentation; and

5. Damages.

Illustration 2   Tax Preparer Fraud

Mark Waters, CPA, owned Peach Tax Services Inc. and for three years intentionally misreported deductions on his clients' tax returns and electronically filed hundreds of incorrect federal income tax returns with the IRS to generate fraudulent refunds.

1.3.2 Elements of Constructive Fraud (Gross Negligence)

Constructive fraud has the same elements as actual fraud, except instead of intentionally deceiving, the defendant acts recklessly (i.e., makes a statement without knowing whether it is true or false).

1.3.3 To Whom Is the CPA Liable?

- A CPA's liability for fraud and constructive fraud is much broader than a CPA's liability for negligence. The CPA can be held liable to anyone who proves the above elements.

- Privity is not a defense to fraud. Liability is not limited to persons in privity, third-party beneficiaries or a limited class of persons who foreseeably rely.

Illustration 3   Summary of "Levels of Fault"

1. **"Reasonable care"** ("due care") is taken = No negligence = Not liable

2. **Lack of reasonable care** = Ordinary negligence

   The CPA is liable to anyone he or she knows or reasonably should expect will rely on his/her work.

3. **Lack of even slight care** = Gross negligence or constructive fraud

4. **Actual fraud** = Actual intent to deceive

5. **Criminal fraud** = Actual intent to deceive*

   Levels 1 through 4 are *civil* in nature. Only level 5 is *criminal*.

* Note the conduct that forms the basis of a level 4 civil fraud action is the same conduct that forms the basis for a criminal prosecution (level 5) by the government.

1.3.4 Damages

Damages associated with tax return preparation malpractice have multiple components including the following:

- **Taxes**: Because the filing of the tax return and payment of taxes is ultimately the responsibility of the taxpayer, the tax that a taxpayer owes is not normally a recoverable damage amount. In some situations, the tax practitioner can be held liable for the amount by which taxes were overpaid if the overpayment cannot be reclaimed through the filing of an amended return.

- **Penalties:** Courts often award damages associated with penalties imposed because of mistakes reported on tax returns.

- **Interest:** Amounts equal to the interest owed by the taxpayer may be awarded by the courts to the extent that the taxpayer has suffered actual damages related to the interest charged.

- **Costs Incurred to Correct Tax Returns:** Damages may include fees that will be incurred to file amended returns and/or challenge penalties that have been assessed.

- **Consequential Damages:** This category of potential damages includes lost investment or income opportunities for taxpayers as a result of tax preparer's mistake.

2 Privileged Communications, Confidentiality, and Privacy Acts

The rules of evidence protect information exchanged in certain confidential relationships (e.g., attorney-client, doctor-patient) by granting an evidentiary privilege—information exchanged within the scope of the relationship may not be disclosed as evidence in court without the consent of the privilege holder.

2.1 Privileged Communications

Privileges available to CPAs can include the following:

- **Attorney-Client Privilege:** This privilege is potentially available when the CPA has been engaged by the attorney prior to aid the attorney in providing legal services because the expertise of a CPA is needed.

- **Work Product Privilege:** This privilege can protect tangible materials produced in preparation for litigation as requested by an attorney but not to the communication between the attorney and accountant about the product.

- **Tax Practitioner-Taxpayer Privilege:** This privilege applies to tax advice from a tax practitioner that would qualify under the attorney-client privilege. The Tax Practitioner Privilege applies only to federally authorized tax practitioners under the IRC Section 7525. State law may vary.

2.2 Tax Practitioner Privilege

IRC Section 7525 provides that some communication between taxpayers and federal authorized tax practitioners is regarded as privileged. IRC Section 7525 provides that the same common law protections of confidentiality that apply to a communication between a taxpayer and an attorney also apply to a communication between a taxpayer and any federally authorized tax practitioner (to the extent the communication would be considered a privileged communication if it were between a taxpayer and an attorney). The tax practitioner privilege may only be asserted in any noncriminal tax matter before the Internal Revenue Service and any noncriminal tax proceeding in federal court brought by or against the United States.

2.2.1 Federally Authorized Tax Practitioner

The phrase *federally authorized tax practitioner* means any individual who is authorized under federal law to practice before the Internal Revenue Service. It is a category that includes certified public accountants, enrolled agents, and enrolled actuaries.

2.2.2 Not Applicable to Communications Regarding Tax Shelters

The tax practitioner privilege shall not apply to any written communication between a federally authorized tax practitioner and:

- any person;

- any director, officer, employee, agent, or representative of the person; or

- any other person holding a capital or profits interest in the person; and

...in connection with the promotion of the direct or indirect participation of the person in any tax shelter.

2.3   Workpapers

Workpapers belong to the accountant (or accountant's firm) that prepares them, not the client. The accountant is prohibited from showing the workpapers to anyone without the client's permission, except in the following situations:

- In response to a subpoena relevant to a court case.
- To a prospective purchaser of the CPA's practice, as long as the prospective purchaser does not disclose the confidential information.
- To a state CPA society voluntary quality-control review panel, when requested.
- In defense of a lawsuit brought by a client.
- To be used in defense of an official investigation by the AICPA/state trial board.
- When GAAP requires disclosure of such information in the financial statements.

Pass Key

Note that, although a CPA may allow a prospective purchaser to review confidential workpapers, the CPA may not turn over the workpapers to a purchaser without the client's permission.

Question 1   **MCQ-01445**

Which of the following statements is generally correct regarding the liability of a CPA who negligently gives an opinion on an audit of a client's financial statements?

- **a.** The CPA is only liable to those third parties who are in privity of contract with the CPA.
- **b.** The CPA is only liable to the client.
- **c.** The CPA is liable to anyone in a class of third parties whom the CPA knows will rely on the opinion.
- **d.** The CPA is liable to all possible foreseeable users of the CPA's opinion.

Question 2   **MCQ-01452**

Which of the following statements is correct regarding a CPA's workpapers? The workpapers must be:

- **a.** Transferred to another accountant purchasing the CPA's practice even if the client hasn't given permission.
- **b.** Transferred permanently to the client if demanded.
- **c.** Turned over to any government agency that requests them.
- **d.** Turned over pursuant to a valid federal court subpoena.

NOTES

Business Law: Part 1

Module

1 Creation of the Agency Relationship

Agency is a legal relationship in which one person or entity (the principal) appoints another person or entity (the agent) to act on his or her behalf.

1.1 Requisites for Creation

1.1.1 Principal With Capacity and Consent

As a general rule, all that is required to create an agency relationship is a principal with contractual capacity (i.e., not a minor and not incompetent) and consent of the parties (i.e., the parties agree to act as principal and agent).

1. Writing

- A writing generally is not required to create an agency relationship, even if the contract that the agent is to enter on the principal's behalf must be evidenced by a writing under the Statute of Frauds.

- However, many states require a written agency agreement if the agent is to buy or sell an interest in land for the principal.

- Note that a contract to find a buyer or seller (normal real estate broker's agreement) and a contract to build a house are contracts for services. An oral agency involving such transactions is valid.

- Agency agreements that cannot be performed in one year must be evidenced by a writing.

2. Capacity

Only the principal must be competent. The agent need not have capacity. Thus, a minor or mentally incompetent person can be appointed as an agent.

3. Consideration

Consideration is not required to form an agency relationship.

Pass Key

The examiners often ask what is necessary to create an agency. Generally, all you need is consent and a principal with capacity. A writing is necessary only if the agent will enter into land sale contracts. Thus, an answer that says a writing is required or the agent's authority must be signed by the principal usually is wrong.

1.1.2 Power of Attorney

- A power of attorney is a written authorization of agency.

- The agent under a power of attorney is referred to as an "attorney in fact." But the agent need not be a lawyer. It just means that the agent has the power to act on behalf of the principal.

- Generally only the principal is required to sign the power of attorney. There is no requirement that the *agent* sign the instrument.

- The agent's authority is normally limited to specific transactions.

1.2 Rights and Duties Between Principal and Agent

Certain duties are implied in every agency relationship.

1.2.1 Duties of Agent to Principal

The agent has whatever duties are expressly stated in the contract. The agent also owes the following four duties:

1. Duty of Loyalty

An agent owes the principal a duty of loyalty; the agent must act solely in the principal's interest in connection with the agency. An agent breaches this duty when she has interests adverse to the principal (e.g., the agent obtains kickbacks from a third party).

Illustration 1 Duty of Loyalty

Petshop hired Andy as its store manager and gave Andy authority to purchase pets for the store. Andy occasionally purchased dogs from Tremendous Dogs. When Andy bought dogs from Tremendous, it paid Andy 5 percent of the purchase price as incentive to do more business. Petshop was unaware of the payments, which Andy kept. Andy has breached his duty of loyalty and can be forced to turn over his profit to Petshop.

---

2. Duty of Obedience

An agent must obey all reasonable directions of the principal.

Illustration 2 Duty of Obedience

Paul hires Audrey as his purchasing agent for televisions, but instructs Audrey not to disclose to sellers that she is working for Paul. If Audrey discloses to a seller that she is working for Paul, she breaches her duty of obedience and will be liable to Paul for any damages the disclosure caused.

---

3. Duty of Reasonable Care

An agent owes the principal a duty to carry out the agency with reasonable care (i.e., the duty not to be negligent).

4. Duty to Account

Unless otherwise agreed, the agent has a duty to account to the principal for all property and money received and paid out when acting on behalf of the principal. The agent cannot commingle the principal's property with the agent's property.

5. Subagent

If an agent is authorized to hire a subagent, the subagent owes a duty of care to both the agent and the principal.

1.2.2 Principal's Remedies

If an agent breaches the duties she owes to the principal, the principal can recover damages from the agent:

1. Tort Damages

The principal can recover tort damages from the agent if the agent negligently or intentionally breached a duty owed to the principal.

2. Contract Damages

If the agent was compensated, the principal can collect contract damages. If the agent did not receive consideration, a contract was not formed and so contract damages are not available.

3. Recovery of Secret Profits

If the agent obtained a secret profit, as in Illustration 1, above, the principal can recover the secret profit, usually by imposing a constructive trust on the profit.

4. Withhold Compensation

If the agent committed an intentional tort or intentionally breached her duty to her principal, the principal may refuse to pay the agent.

1.2.3 Duties of Principal to Agent

In addition to any duties expressed in the agency agreement, the principal owes the agent the following duties:

1. Compensation

Unless the agent has agreed to act gratuitously, the principal has an implied duty to give the agent reasonable compensation.

2. Reimbursement/Indemnification

The principal also has an implied duty to reimburse (i.e., indemnify) the agent for all expenses incurred in carrying out the agency.

3. Remedies of the Agent

If the principal breaches her duties to the agent, the agent can bring an action against the principal for any damages caused. If the relationship is not contractual, however, the agent may not seek the contract remedy of specific performance. The agent has a *duty to mitigate* damages (e.g., a wrongfully fired agent must seek comparable work to replace lost income).

1.2.4 Power to Terminate Relationship

Because an agency relationship is consensual, either party generally has the power to terminate the relationship at any time. However, the parties don't necessarily have the *right* to terminate at any time.

Illustration 3   Termination at Will

Porthos hires Athos as his purchasing agent for nine months, at a salary of $2,000 per month. Either party can terminate the agency the next day, but a wrongful termination will be a breach of contract.

1.2.5 Agency Coupled With an Interest

Only the agent (not the principal) can terminate an agency coupled with an interest. This arises where the agent has an interest in the subject matter of the agency, such as where the agency power is given as security. In effect, the agent has paid for the right to be appointed as the agent, usually by giving credit. Death, incapacity, or bankruptcy of the principal will not end an agency coupled with an interest.

Illustration 4   Agency Coupled With Interest

Paul borrows $20,000 from Alex, promising to pay Alex within a year and appointing Alex as his agent to sell Blackacre if Paul fails to pay. Alex's agency is coupled with an interest. However, if Paul hires Alex to sell Blackacre in exchange for a 5 percent commission, Paul has the power to terminate the agency at any time because Alex has not acquired an interest in Blackacre.

---

2   Agent's Power to Contractually Bind Principal

An agent's power to bind a principal can arise through:

- a grant of actual authority;
- apparent authority or estoppel; or
- ratification.

2.1 Actual Authority

Actual authority (sometimes called "real authority" or simply "authority") is the authority the *agent reasonably believes* he possesses because of the principal's communications to the agent. An agent with actual authority has the power and the right to bind the principal to contracts with third parties. Actual authority can be either *express* or *implied*.

2.1.1 Express Actual Authority

Actual authority includes all powers that the principal expressly grants within the "four corners" of the agency agreement.

2.1.2 Implied Actual Authority

Authority that the agent could reasonably believe is implied along with the express grant is called implied actual authority. This includes the authority to do things *reasonably necessary* to carry out the agency (e.g., a person hired to manage a business will usually have authority to hire employees, buy merchandise, etc.).

Pass Key

The examiners have tested on the implied authority of a business manager a number of times. The key is to remember that the manager is there to run the business, not destroy it. Thus, she has authority to hire and fire employees, purchase inventory, and pay business debts. She has no implied authority to sell or mortgage business fixtures or other property of the principal (other than inventory). Also remember that generally an agent does not have implied authority to borrow money on the principal's behalf—such authority must be expressed.

2.1.3 Termination of Actual Authority Can Occur By:

1. **Act of the Parties**

   Termination of an agency can occur through the acts of either the principal (a revocation) or the agent (a renunciation). If the termination violates the parties' contract, damages could be available. If the agency is coupled with an interest, only the agent has the power to terminate the agency relationship.

2. **Accomplishment of Objective or Expiration of Stated Period**

   - If the agency is for a limited purpose (e.g., Phil appoints Andrea to purchase Blackacre for him), actual authority is terminated when the objective is accomplished (i.e., Andrea purchases Blackacre).

   - If the agency is for a stated period (e.g., six months), actual authority is terminated upon expiration of the period. If no time is stated, the actual authority terminates after a reasonable time.

3. **Termination of Actual Authority**

   Actual authority is terminated automatically, by operation of law upon any of the following events:

   - *death* of either the principal or the agent;

   - *incapacity* of the principal;

   - *discharge* in bankruptcy of the principal;

   - *failure* to acquire a necessary license;

   - *destruction of the subject matter* of the agency (e.g., Paula hires Alex to purchase an antique car, which is destroyed before it can be purchased); or

   - *subsequent illegality* (e.g., Hister, a U.S. corporation, hires Alex to sell certain raw materials to a company in Asia. Subsequently, the Asian company is nationalized by the government where it is located. The government then makes it illegal for the company to purchase materials from companies outside of Asia).

Pass Key

Termination of agency by operation of law is a heavily tested issue. Be sure to memorize the above list.

2.2   Apparent Authority

Even though an agent might not have actual authority, there are situations in which the agent will nevertheless have the *power* (but not the right) to bind the principal, either because the principal's conduct has caused *third parties to reasonably believe* that the agent had authority or because the principal was negligent and so will be estopped from denying that the agent had authority. This power to bind the principal is known as apparent authority.

2.2.1   Principal's Conduct

Note that apparent authority requires a holding out *by the principal* or negligent inaction *by the principal.* The purported agent's mere representation that she is an agent is not sufficient to establish apparent authority.

2.2.2   Distinguish From Actual Authority

Apparent authority is based on the third party's reasonable belief that the agent has the power to bind the principal. Actual authority arises from the *agent's* reasonable belief that the agent has the power to bind the principal, not from the third party's belief. In either case, the principal is bound. However, if the agent lacked actual authority, the principal can hold the agent liable for acting without authority.

- **From Position:** A principal who holds another out as his agent vests the agent with the power to enter into all transactions that a reasonable third party would believe a person in the agent's position would have.

Illustration 5	Apparent Authority From Position

Pam hires Alex to manage her pet store. Alex has the apparent authority to hire and fire employees, make deposits, etc.

- **Not Affected by Secret Limiting Instructions:** A principal who issues secret instructions to the agent will limit the agent's *actual* authority but not the agent's *apparent* authority. Apparent authority is based on the third party's reasonable beliefs, and secret instructions are unknown to the third party.

Illustration 6	Apparent Authority Not Affected by Secret Limiting Instructions

Pam hires Alex to manage her pet store. It is customary in the area for pet store managers to have actual authority to purchase inventory (pets). Pam tells Alex that he may purchase pets for the store, but may not purchase a pet for more than $200. Tom, a dog breeder, offers to sell Pomeranian puppies to the pet store for $250 each, and Alex accepts. Alex has apparent authority to purchase the puppies, but not actual authority. Thus, Pam will have to pay Tom for the puppies, but can hold Alex liable for any loss that results.

- **General vs. Special Agent:** A general agent will perform a series of transactions involving a continuity of service. A special agent will perform one or more transactions *not* involving continuity of service. Therefore, the general agent has broader apparent authority than a special agent.

Illustration 7	Apparent Authority of General vs. Special Agent

Pam hires Alex to manage her pet store. Pam also hires Jordan to distribute advertising brochures at the city park on the day of the annual Art in the Park festival. Alex is a general agent, and Jordan is a special agent. Alex has broader apparent authority than Jordan.

- **Termination of Apparent Authority:** When a principal terminates an agent's *actual* authority, the agent will continue to have *apparent* authority until the principal notifies third parties who might have known of the agency. *Actual notice* must be given to terminate apparent authority to old customers. *Constructive notice* (e.g., an ad in a newspaper) must be given to terminate apparent authority as to potential customers who may have known of the agency but who had not done business with the agent. If an agent's authority is terminated by operation of law, apparent authority also is terminated by operation of law and no notice is needed.

Illustration 8	Termination of Apparent Authority

Allen has been Patty's office manager for 10 years and has regularly purchased office supplies from Terri. Patty fires Allen, but does not notify Terri. If Allen purchases more office supplies from Terri purportedly on Patty's behalf, Terri can make Patty pay for the supplies because of Allen's apparent authority.

2.3 Ratification

Ratification allows a principal to choose to become bound by a previously unauthorized act of his or her agent.

2.3.1 Requirements

1. The agent must have indicated that she was acting on behalf of the principal (if the third party did not believe that the agent was acting for a principal, there can be no ratification).

2. All material facts must be disclosed to the principal.

3. The principal must ratify the entire transaction—there can be no partial ratification.

4. Ratification does not require consideration, and the principal need not notify the third party of the ratification (because the third party already thinks he has a contract with the principal).

2.3.2 May Ratify Expressly or Impliedly

The principal may ratify expressly, or may ratify impliedly by accepting the benefits of the contract when there is an opportunity to reject them.

2.3.3 What May Be Ratified?

Generally, any act may be ratified unless performance would be illegal; the third party withdraws prior to ratification; or there has been a material change of circumstance so that it would not be fair to hold the third party liable.

2.3.4 Who May Ratify?

Only the purported principal may ratify. The agent cannot take over the contract. Only a disclosed principal may ratify. An undisclosed principal cannot ratify.

2.4   Contractual Liability

2.4.1   Principal Liable if Agent Had Authority or Principal Ratified

The principal will be bound by the agent's acts if the agent acted with actual authority or apparent authority, or if the principal ratified the transaction. The principal's liability does not depend on whether the principal's existence or identity was disclosed.

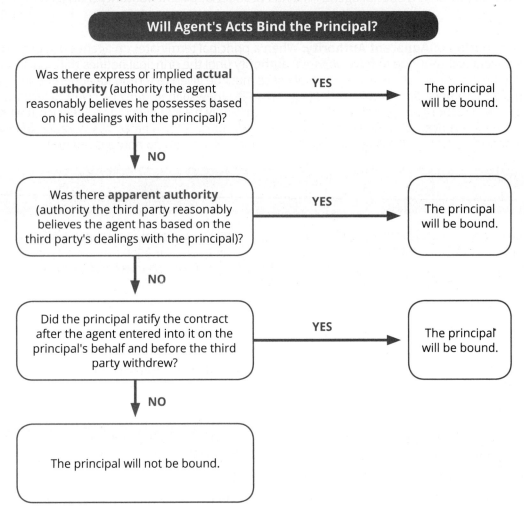

2.4.2   Agent's Liability

1. **Disclosed Principal (Agent Not Liable if Authorized)**

   If the agent discloses the existence and identity of the principal (a disclosed principal situation), the third party cannot hold an authorized agent liable on the contract. Every person representing himself as an agent impliedly warrants that he has the authority he purports to have. If, in fact, the agent has no such authority, the third party can hold the agent liable for any damages caused based on breach of this implied warranty.

2. **Partially Disclosed and Undisclosed Principal (Agent Liable)**

   If the principal's identity is not disclosed to the third party (a partially disclosed principal situation), or neither the existence nor the identity of the principal is disclosed to the third party (an undisclosed principal situation), the agent is liable on the contract with the third party.

- **Third Party's Election:** The third party can hold either the principal or the agent (but not both) liable if the principal was undisclosed or partially disclosed. The third party must elect whom to hold liable.

- **No Apparent Authority With an Undisclosed Principal:** If the principal is undisclosed, there can be no apparent authority because there is no holding out of the agent by the principal.

- **No Effect on Actual Authority:** The fact that the principal is undisclosed has no effect on the agent's actual authority since actual authority arises from the communications between the principal and the agent.

Pass Key

The examiners often ask about undisclosed principal situations. There are a few key points to remember.

- The principal is bound if the agent had authority. It is irrelevant whether the principal was disclosed, partially disclosed, or undisclosed. If the agent did not have authority, the principal is bound only if he ratifies.

- The agent can be held personally liable if the principal is partially disclosed (identity is not disclosed) or undisclosed (neither identity nor existence are disclosed).

2.4.3   Third Party's Liability

1.   Generally Only Principal Can Hold Third Party Liable

As a general rule, only the principal (not the agent) can hold the third party liable on a contract the agent entered into on the principal's behalf, even if the principal's existence or identity were not disclosed.

Illustration 9   Third Party's Liability

Ann entered into a contract with Top Corp. to purchase televisions on behalf of Paul. Paul instructed Ann to enter into the contract in her own name without disclosing that she was acting on behalf of Paul. If Top Corp. repudiates the contract, Paul may hold Top liable even though it did not know it was dealing with Paul.

2.   Exceptions

The principal cannot hold the third party liable where:

- the principal's *identity was fraudulently* concealed (e.g., if the third party indicates that she will not do business with the principal, the principal cannot get around this by dealing through an agent); or

- the performance to the principal would *increase the burden* on the third party (e.g., Big Rubber Company cannot employ Small Rubber Company as an agent to enter into a rubber requirements contract without disclosing that the contract is for Big Rubber Company).

3   Tort Liability

3.1   In General: Respondeat Superior

1.   As a general rule, a principal is not liable for the torts committed by his agent—only the agent is liable.

2.   However, there is an exception for employers. Under the doctrine of respondeat superior, an employer can be liable for an employee's torts committed within the scope of employment.

3.   This does not relieve the agent of liability. The injured person may sue both the employer under respondeat superior and the agent.

3.2   Employer-Employee Relationship

An employer (or master) is liable only for torts of an employee (or servant) and is usually not liable for torts of independent contractors.

1.   Right to Control Manner of Performance Is Key

The most important factor in determining whether a person is an employee or an independent contractor is the right of the principal to *control* the manner in which the person performs. An employer has the right to control employees, but has little control over the methods used by independent contractors.

2.   Additional Factors

Where right to control is not clear, the courts look to other factors, such as whether the worker has a business of his own, provides his own tools and facilities, length of the employment (short or definite vs. long or indefinite), basis of compensation, and the degree of supervision.

- A clear example of an employee is one who works full time for the employer, uses the employer's facilities or tools, is compensated on a time basis, and is subject to the supervision of the principal.

- A clear example of an independent contractor is one who has a calling of her own and who uses her own facilities or tools, is hired for a particular job, is paid a given amount for that job, and who follows her own discretion in carrying out the job. For example, a CPA who performs an audit for a corporation is an independent contractor.

3.3   Scope of Employment

An employer is not liable to an injured party merely because an employee caused the injury—the injury must also have occurred within the *scope of the employment*. That is, the injury must have occurred while the employee was working for the employer within the time and geographic area in which the employee was to work.

1.   Activities

The conduct causing the injury need not actually have been authorized by the employer; rather the conduct need only be (i) of the *same general type* the employee was hired to perform; and (ii) actuated, at least in part, by a desire to serve the employer.

Illustration 10   Liability of Employer for Employee

Although a bar owner might not authorize a bouncer to beat up boisterous customers, the owner nevertheless can be held liable if this occurs because the conduct is of the same general nature as the bouncer's job.

- **Intentional Torts**

    The employer usually is liable only for an employee's negligence and is not liable for intentional torts, since intentional torts are seldom within the scope of employment. However, where the tort is authorized or where use of force is authorized (as with a bouncer), the employer can be liable.

- **Crimes**

    An employer generally is not liable in tort for an employee's conduct that constitutes a serious crime (e.g., carrying an illegal weapon).

Pass Key

The examiners often ask about a principal's liability for its agent's torts. Remember, if the agent is an employee and committed a tort while trying to serve the principal/ employer, the principal/employer generally will be liable unless the tort was unexpected (e.g., illegal conduct).

2. **Time and Geographic Area**

    It is not enough simply that the conduct that caused the injury was of the same general type the employee was hired to perform. The conduct must also have occurred within usual employment time and space limits. Small detours from an employer's directions (e.g., driving a few blocks out of the way, stopping for lunch, etc.) fall within the scope of the employment. Major deviations (frolic) from an employer's directions (e.g., driving 15 miles out of the way to attend a party) fall outside the scope of employment.

3. **Cannot Limit Liability by Agreement With Employee**

    An agreement between the employer and employee that the employer will not be liable for employee torts does not prevent a third party from holding the employer liable. The employer can seek reimbursement from the employee.

3.4   Employer Liability for Independent Contractors

Although the general rule is that an employer is not liable for torts committed by independent contractors, an employer can be liable for the torts of an independent contractor if the employer authorized the tortious act or if the work involved an ultra-hazardous activity.

Illustration 11   Liability of Principal for Agent's Torts

Is the agent an **employee** or an **independent contractor** (look chiefly to the extent of the principal's control over the manner and method of the agent's performance)?

Employee

Independent Contractor

Was the act **within the scope of employment** (i.e., was the employee where she was supposed to be, doing what she was supposed to be doing, with the purposes of the employer in mind)?

Generally, the principal is not liable for the torts of an independent contractor.

YES   **NO**

The principal is liable.

The principal is not liable.

Question 1   MCQ-01318

An agent will usually be liable under a contract made with a third party when the agent is acting on behalf of a (an):

	Disclosed Principal	Undisclosed Principal
a.	Yes	Yes
b.	Yes	No
c.	No	Yes
d.	No	No

Question 2   MCQ-01333

Which of the following rights will a third party be entitled to after validly contracting with an agent representing an undisclosed principal?

- **a.** Disclosure of the principal by the agent.
- **b.** Ratification of the contract by the principal.
- **c.** Performance of the contract by the agent.
- **d.** Election to void the contract after disclosure of the principal.

1 Methods of Formation

Broadly speaking, a contract is a promise that the law will enforce. Methods of contract formation include:

Pass Key

While the examiners rarely ask you to describe a contract using the descriptive terms below, it is important for you to understand them, because the examiners sometimes use them in their questions.

- **Express Contract:** A contract formed by *language*, oral or written, is an express contract.

Illustration 1   Express Contract

If Ann promises to give Barb $10 if Barb will wash Ann's car, the contract is express.

- **Implied-in-Fact Contract:** A contract formed by *conduct* is an implied-in-fact contract.

Illustration 2   Implied-in-Fact Contract

Alex goes to Doctor and tells Doctor that he is sick. Doctor examines Alex and gives him an antibiotic. Alex and Doctor have entered into a contract for Doctor's services even though no oral or written promises were exchanged. Their conduct implies their intent to enter into a contract.

- **Implied-in-Law Contract or Quasi-Contract:** A quasi-contract is not a contract at all. It is a remedy that allows a plaintiff to recover a benefit unjustly conferred upon the defendant—a remedy to *prevent unjust enrichment*.

Illustration 3   Quasi-Contract

Joanne gives Keith $10,000 as a down payment to purchase Keith's house. The contract is oral and, as will be discussed later, is unenforceable. Keith decides to back out. Joanne can recover the down payment in quasi-contract.

- **Unilateral Contract:** In a unilateral contract, there is *one promise*, which is given in exchange for performance (e.g., Ann promises to give Barb $10 if Barb will wash Ann's car). A contract is not formed until performance is completed.

- **Bilateral Contract:** In a bilateral contract, there are *two promises*—a promise is exchanged for a promise (e.g., Ann promises to give Barb $10 if Barb promises to wash Ann's car). Here, a contract is formed as soon as the promises are exchanged.

2   Sources of Contract Law

1.   Common Law

The common law is generally derived from courts. Contracts involving real estate, insurance, services, and employment (**RISE**) are governed by the common law.

2.   Uniform Commercial Code (UCC) Sales Article

The UCC is statutory law that has been widely adopted throughout the United States. Its Sales Article (Article 2) governs contracts for the sale of goods (moveable things). There are a number of special rules that apply to contracts for the sale of goods, which are reviewed in a later module.

3   Elements of a Legally Enforceable Contract

Generally, there are three requirements of a legally enforceable contract:

1. an agreement made up of an offer and an acceptance;

2. an exchange of consideration (something of legal value); and

3. a lack of defenses.

If these three requirements are met, there is an enforceable contract and remedies are available if one party breaches (i.e., does not perform as promised).

Pass Key

Notice that "a writing" is *not* a general element of a contract. Certain contracts must be evidenced by a writing (they will be discussed in this module under the Statute of Frauds portion of the Defenses section), but the general rule is that a writing is not required. Thus, if you see an answer choice on the exam saying an offer or acceptance must be in writing, scrutinize the facts carefully. If the contract is not within the Statute of Frauds, the choice probably is wrong.

3.1 Agreement (Mutual Assent) (Offer and Acceptance)

Mutual assent is often said to be agreeing to the "same bargain at the same time"—a meeting of the minds. Generally, one party will make a proposal (an offer) and the other party will agree to it (an acceptance).

3.1.1 The Offer

An offer is a statement by an offeror that gives the recipient (i.e., the offeree) the power to form a contract by accepting *before the offer is terminated*.

- **Intent to Make a Contract:** To be valid, the offer must be sufficient for a *reasonable person* to assume that the offer was a serious offer to enter into a contract. The offeror's subjective intent (i.e., whether the offeror thought he was making an offer) is irrelevant. Contract law generally follows an objective theory (would a reasonable person believe the offer was serious). Statements made in jest or frustration and understood as such by a reasonable person are not offers.

  - **Advertisements:** Widely distributed statements such as advertisements are *not* offers because they are not addressed to anyone in particular. They are usually considered only to be *invitations* seeking offers.

  - An advertisement that limits the scope of the persons who can accept (e.g., "the first five customers can buy this coffee maker for only $1") will be considered to be an offer.

Illustration 4   Advertisements

Steve places an ad in a local paper announcing the grand opening of his store and quoting the price of certain items. Such an ad is not an offer but is only an invitation seeking offers.

- **Terms Must Be Definite and Certain:** An offer must be definite and certain in its terms. What is essential depends on the type of contract involved. An offer for the sale of goods generally need only include the quantity term (e.g., "I offer to sell 100 widgets"). An offer to create a contract under common law (e.g., a contract involving services or real property) must include:

  - the *identity of the offeree* and the subject matter;
  - the *price* to be paid;
  - the *time* of performance;
  - the *quantity* involved; and
  - the *nature of the work* to be performed.

Illustration 5   Definite Terms

Alex asks Bob to repair a broken window at Alex's store within three days, at a price to be agreed upon later. The offer here will fail for indefiniteness of the price term.

3.1.2   Termination of Offer

To create a contract, an offer must be accepted before it is terminated. An offer can be terminated in a number of ways—through the act of either party (offeror: *revocation*; offeree: *rejection*) or by operation of law (e.g., by death of a party).

■   **Revocation by Offeror:** The general rule is that the offeror can revoke an offer any time before acceptance by communicating the revocation to the offeree. Except as discussed below, this is true even where the offeror promises to keep the offer open.

Illustration 6   Revocation

Maurice sent Schmit an e-mail offering to sell him a one-acre tract of commercial property for $8,000. Maurice stated that Schmit had three days to consider the offer and in the meantime the offer would be irrevocable. The next day, Maurice received a better offer from another party, and he telephoned Schmit, informing him that he was revoking the offer. This was an effective revocation.

●   The revocation can be direct (e.g., a phone call to the offeree withdrawing the offer) or *indirect*, where the offeree receives correct information that the offeror no longer wants to make the offer.

Illustration 7   Indirect Revocation

Alex offers to sell his car to Bob for $500. Bob tells Alex that he wants to think about it. The next day, Carol, a friend of Bob, drives over to Bob's house to show Bob the car she just purchased from Alex. The offer to Bob is revoked.

●   The revocation is generally effective when received by the offeree. Where revocation is by publication, it is effective when published.

●   Although the general rule is that all offers can be revoked, there is an exception to the general rule which appears with some frequency on the CPA Exam where consideration is paid to keep the offer open (called an *option contract*). An option is a distinct contract in which the promisor promises to keep an offer open in exchange for consideration from the promisee.

Pass Key

The examiners frequently use irrevocability as a wrong answer choice. They will tell you about the parties' negotiations and ask you to pick a true statement. One answer choice frequently is that the offer is "irrevocable" or "it could not be revoked because it is an option." Scrutinize the facts carefully. The key point to remember is that if consideration was not given to keep the offer open, it is not an option.

■ **Rejection by Offeree:** The offeree can terminate the offer by rejecting it. Once the offer is effectively rejected, it cannot be accepted.

● The offeree can reject expressly (e.g., by saying "no"). But more interestingly, a *counteroffer* is also considered to be both a *rejection* (which terminates the original offer) *and an offer* (of which the original offeror is now the offeree who may accept or reject).

Illustration 8   Rejection by Offeree

1. Alex offers to sell Barb his car for $450. Barb says, "No." The offer is terminated. If Barb later has a change of heart and tells Alex, "I accept," Barb has at most made a new offer. No contract is created.

2. Alex offers to sell Barb his car for $450. Barb says, "No, but I'll give you $425." Barb has rejected and made a new offer through a counteroffer.

● A rejection is effective when *received*.

Illustration 9   Rejection

On January 3, Sam sent Ben a signed letter offering to sell his warehouse for $95,000. On January 5, Ben wrote Sam a letter saying that he would not pay $95,000 because that price was too high. On January 6, Ben was advised that similar property had recently been sold for $99,000. Ben immediately e-mailed Sam an acceptance of Sam's January 3 offer. Ben's letter arrived the next day. There is a contract because a rejection is not effective until received. The rejection here arrived after the offer was accepted by e-mail.

■ **Termination by Operation of Law**

● If either of the parties dies or becomes incompetent prior to acceptance, the offer is terminated by operation of law. It is *not* necessary that the death or incompetency be communicated to the other party.

Exception: An option contract is not terminated by the death of a party.

Illustration 10   Termination

Dee offered to sell Sue a parcel of land for $300,000. If either Dee or Sue dies before the offer is accepted, the offer will terminate by operation of law. However, if Sue paid consideration for the offer (thus creating an option contract), the offer will remain open for the period of the option (i.e., Sue or Sue's estate could accept during the option period and a contract would be formed with Dee or Dee's estate).

- If the subject matter of the offer is destroyed before the offer is accepted, the offeree's power of acceptance is terminated by operation of law.

- If the subject matter of the proposed contract becomes illegal, the offer will terminate.

Illustration 11   Termination Due to Illegality

Lucky Lou offers Vegas Vernon a share in his casino business. Prior to acceptance, a law is passed banning casinos. The offer is automatically terminated.

3.1.3   The Acceptance

The acceptance is the offeree's assent to enter into a contract. Like offers, acceptances need not be in writing. An acceptance does not even require words—a simple nod of the head or fall of a gavel (in an auction) can constitute an acceptance.

- **Who May Accept:** The general rule is that only the person to whom the offer was made may accept. Thus, offers are not assignable; however, option contracts are assignable.

- **Method of Acceptance:** Generally, acceptance may be made in any manner reasonable under the circumstances (e.g., a mailed offer can usually be accepted by letter, e-mail, etc.). However, if the offeror specifies a method of communication, that method must be used. A purported acceptance utilizing another method is a counteroffer.

- **Acceptance Generally Must Be Unequivocal:** Common law contracts follow the *mirror image rule*, which requires an acceptance to mirror the offer to be effective. An attempted acceptance that changes some of the terms or adds new terms is not a valid acceptance, but rather is a counteroffer, which serves as a rejection.

- **Generally Effective Upon Dispatch—the Mailbox Rule:** Unlike revocations, acceptances are generally effective when they are *dispatched* (i.e., mailed, e-mailed, faxed, etc.) if properly addressed. This is known as the mailbox rule. It is irrelevant if a properly addressed acceptance is lost or delayed.

Illustration 12   Mailbox Rule

On February 1, Ann sends Bob a letter offering to employ Bob at Ann's auto dealership. On February 5, Bob sends Ann a letter accepting the offer. On February 6, Ann has a change of heart and calls Bob to revoke the offer. On February 7, Ann receives Bob's acceptance. A contract was formed in this case on February 5, when the acceptance was sent. Ann's attempted revocation is ineffective because it came too late (after the acceptance was sent). The date Ann received the acceptance is irrelevant. Indeed, under the mailbox rule, a contract is formed on dispatch even if the acceptance letter is never received by the offeror.

- **Method of Communication Specified:** If the offeror required that acceptances be sent by a specific method, an acceptance sent by that method is effective when it is sent.

- **No Method of Communication Specified:** If the offer did not state how acceptances were to be sent, an acceptance sent *by any reasonable means* is effective upon dispatch (e.g., letter, e-mail, fax, etc.).

- **Offeror May Opt Out:** The offeror can opt out of the mailbox rule by stating in the offer that acceptances must be received to be effective. In such cases, the acceptance must be received before the offer terminates.

Illustration 13   Mailbox Rule Violated

On November 1, Dee sent Steve an e-mail offering to sell Steve a vase. The offer provided that an acceptance must be received by 5 p.m. on November 2. At 3 p.m. on November 1, Steve sent Dee an acceptance by overnight mail, but the acceptance did not reach Dee until November 3. There is no enforceable contract because the acceptance came too late. The offer provided that the acceptance had to be received by 5 p.m. on November 2, so the mailbox rule does not apply.

Pass Key

You probably will see a mailbox rule question on your exam. Often it is coupled with a revocability issue, as in Illustration 12. The key is to approach such questions in three steps:

1. Was the offer revocable? Chances are it was, unless the offeree paid consideration to keep the offer open (an option).

2. Determine whether the mailbox rule applies (i.e., acceptance is effective on dispatch rather than receipt, unless the offer stated that an acceptance had to be received to be effective).

3. Compare any effective revocation date with the effective acceptance date. If a revocation was effective first, the offer was terminated and there is no contract. If the acceptance was effective first, there is a contract and the revocation was ineffective.

Be sure to remember, the mailbox rule only makes *acceptances* effective on dispatch; revocations, rejections, and counteroffers are effective only upon receipt.

3.2   Consideration

Consideration is the price of contracting. Both sides of the contract must be supported by legally sufficient consideration. The law will not enforce gratuitous promises. Something must be given in exchange for a promise for it to be enforceable. There are two elements of consideration: There must be *something of legal* value given by each party, and there must be a *bargained for exchange*.

3.2.1   Element of Legal Value

Something is of legal value if it constitutes either a *detriment to the promisee* or a *benefit to the promisor*. That is, the promisor's promise is supported by consideration only if the promisee agrees to do something he or she is not already obligated to do (a detriment) or the promisor will obtain some benefit. Possible items of consideration include promises to perform acts or to refrain from performing; promises to pay money; and promises to give land, goods, stock, etc.

Illustration 14   Consideration

Phil (promisor) agrees to sell Lori (promisee) his television set for $200. Phil's promise (to sell) is supported by Lori's detriment (the giving of $200). Note that consideration must be present on both sides. Thus, Lori's promise (to give $200) is supported by Phil's detriment (giving the TV).

- **Need Not Have Monetary Value:** Consideration need not have monetary value. As long as the promisee is promising to do something that he is not already obligated to do or promising to refrain from doing something that he legally could do, there is consideration.

Illustration 15   Nonmonetary Consideration

1. Father promises Daughter that he will give Daughter $500 if she names her first-born son after Father. Daughter does so. Naming the son after Father is valid consideration.

2. Joanne promises Keith that she will refrain from suing Keith for 60 days on a valid claim if Keith promises to give Joanne an option to purchase Keith's property for a specified price during the 60-day period. Both promises constitute consideration. (Joanne's promise is known as a *forbearance to sue*.)

- **Need Not Flow to Party:** Note that the consideration need not flow to one of the parties; it is sufficient to promise to do something for or give something to a third party.

Illustration 16   Consideration Flowing to a Third Party

Alex promises Becky that he will pay her $10 if she promises to wash Cindy's car. Alex's promise is sufficient consideration to support Becky's promise, even though Cindy will receive the benefit.

- **Courts Will Not Inquire Into Adequacy:** As long as the consideration is not a sham, courts will not inquire into the *adequacy* of consideration (i.e., they will not compare the relative values of the consideration exchanged). There is no requirement that the consideration exchanged be of nearly equal value. The only requirement is that the consideration be *legally sufficient*, which means of legal value, as discussed above.

- **Preexisting Legal Duties Generally Not Sufficient:** A promise to perform, or performance of, an existing duty is not sufficient consideration. Note that this means in common law contracts the price term cannot be modified unless consideration is given for the modification.

Illustration 17   **Preexisting Legal Duty**

1. Carol is under a contract to sing at a concert for Mike. Carol decides she does not want to sing. To entice Carol to sing, Mike offers to pay Carol $5,000 more if she will sing. Carol agrees and sings. Mike does not have to pay Carol the additional $5,000. There was no consideration for the promise because of the preexisting legal duty rule—Carol was already obligated to sing.

2. Smith offers a $10,000 reward for recovery of his stolen car. Jones, a police officer assigned to this case, recovers the car. Jones' performance of his official duty is not sufficient consideration.

- **Exception:** If each party offers to give something different from what was originally promised—no matter how trivial—the courts will usually enforce the promise despite the preexisting legal duty rule.

Illustration 18   **Modification by Both Parties**

The same facts apply as in part 1 of Illustration 17, except Carol offers to sing five minutes longer than she was originally obligated to. The modification is binding.

- **Honest Dispute as to Duty:** If the scope of the legal duty owed is the subject of honest dispute, then a modifying agreement relating to it will ordinarily be given effect. This is because the parties are giving up their right to sue to have the dispute settled, and forbearance to sue is valid consideration.

3.2.2 Bargained-for Exchange

Something is not consideration unless it was given in exchange for other consideration—there must be a bargained-for exchange of consideration.

- **Gift:** Promises to make a gift are unenforceable because of lack of consideration. There is no bargained-for exchange with a gift.

- **"Past" or "Moral" Consideration:** If something had already been given or performed before the promise was made, it will not satisfy the "bargain" requirement.

Illustration 19   **Moral Consideration**

A loose piece of molding fell from a building and was about to hit Sam. Sherry, seeing this, pushed Sam out of the molding's path and was herself struck by it and seriously injured. Sam promised Sherry that he would pay her $100 per month for life. There is no consideration.

Question 1   MCQ-01351

On June 15, Peters orally offered to sell a used lawn mower to Mason for $125. Peters specified that Mason had until June 20 to accept the offer. On June 16, Peters received an offer to purchase the lawn mower for $150 from Bronson, Mason's neighbor. Peters accepted Bronson's offer. On June 17, Mason saw Bronson using the lawn mower and was told the mower had been sold to Bronson. Mason immediately wrote to Peters to accept the June 15 offer. Which of the following statements is correct?

    a. Mason's acceptance would be effective when received by Peters.

    b. Mason's acceptance would be effective when mailed.

    c. Peters' offer had been revoked and Mason's acceptance was ineffective.

    d. Peters was obligated to keep the June 15 offer open until June 20.

Question 2   MCQ-01347

In determining whether the consideration requirement to form a contract has been satisfied, the consideration exchanged by the parties to the contract must be:

    a. Of approximately equal value.

    b. Legally sufficient.

    c. Exchanged simultaneously by the parties.

    d. Fair and reasonable under the circumstances.

1   Defenses

Defenses can make a contract unenforceable. Two defenses have already been discussed—lack of an agreement and lack of consideration. There are a number of other defenses that the examiners often test.

Pass Key

Defenses are the most tested area in contracts. Pay close attention to the detail below. One key to choosing the correct choice is to remember that very few defenses make a contract void (unenforceable by either party). Most defenses make a contract only *voidable* (it may be avoided at the option of the party adversely affected). Thus, if you see a choice that says a contract is void because of a certain defense, be careful—chances are good that the choice is incorrect.

1.1   Fraud

A contracting party can establish the defense of fraud if she can prove:

■ **Misrepresentation of Material Fact by Defrauding Party**

The misrepresentation must be of a *material fact*. Opinions or statements of value do not constitute facts unless made by experts.

■ **Scienter (Intent to Deceive)**

Fraud is an intentional tort. The misrepresentation must be made with scienter, an intent to deceive. This means the defrauder must make it *knowingly or intentionally*. The intent to deceive element can also be fulfilled by making the misrepresentation with a *reckless disregard for the truth*. This is called constructive fraud or gross negligence.

■ **Intent to Induce Reliance**

The purpose of the defrauding party in making the misrepresentation was to induce the victim to rely on the misrepresentation.

■ **Reasonable Reliance**

The victim did actually and reasonably rely on the misrepresentation.

■ **Damages**

The defrauder is liable to anyone who suffered a loss. The defrauded party may rescind the contract or sue for money damages, but not both.

1.2 Fraud in the Execution and Fraud in the Inducement

Fraud can also be categorized by whether or not the defrauded party knew a contract was being made.

1.2.1 Fraud in the Execution

Fraud in the execution occurs when a party is deceived into signing something that he does not know is a contract (e.g., where a ball player signs what he thinks is a fan's autograph book but is in fact a contract). Fraud in the execution makes a contract void, not voidable because there is no "meeting of the minds."

1.2.2 Fraud in the Inducement

With fraud in the inducement the defrauded party is aware she is making a contract, but terms are materially misrepresented. Most fraud is fraud in the inducement and it makes a contract voidable.

1.3 Innocent Misrepresentation

An innocent misrepresentation has all the elements of fraud *except scienter*. The misrepresentation is made innocently, not intentionally. Innocent misrepresentation makes the contract voidable by the party who relied on the misrepresentation.

1.4 Duress

Duress arises when a party's free will to contract is overcome by an *unlawful* use of a threat of harm. If the harm threatened is physical force (e.g., "sign the contract or I'll break your arm"), the contract is *void*. If the harm threatened is economic or social (e.g., "I'll fire you if you don't sign the contract" or "I'll divorce you if you don't sign the contract"), then the contract is *voidable*. However, merely taking advantage of the other person's economic condition to negotiate a favorable contract (if no threat is involved) does not constitute duress.

1.5 Undue Influence

In the case of undue influence, a party's free will to contract is overcome by the defendant's abuse of a position of trust or confidence. The person in the position of trust or confidence (e.g., a spouse, trustee, guardian, attorney, etc.) uses the position to take advantage of the other's weakness, infirmity, or distress. Undue influence makes a contract voidable.

Illustration 1   Undue Influence

Lawyer convinces Client, a mentally infirm person, to sell Lawyer Client's personal property. An undue influence defense will likely succeed.

1.6 Mutual Mistake

If *both* parties to a contract are mistaken as to a material fact regarding the contract, the adversely affected party can avoid the contract. Note, however, that this rule generally does not apply to mistakes as to value, because value generally is considered to be a matter of opinion.

Illustration 2   Mutual Mistake as to Quality

Alex and Bob enter into a contract for Alex to buy and Bob to sell Bob's designer watch for $200. Before the sale is complete, the parties discover that the watch is a fake. Alex may avoid the contract.

If the subject matter of the contract is not in existence when the contract is made and neither party knows this, the contract is void.

Illustration 3   Mutual Mistake as to Existence

Ann enters into a contract with Barb to purchase Barb's car for $1,000. Unbeknown to either party, the car was destroyed by a fire earlier in the day. There is no contract—the contract is void.

1.7 Unilateral Mistake: Voidable in Some Cases

Generally, a unilateral mistake (i.e., a mistake by one party) is *not* a defense to a contract. There is one major exception that the examiners like to test—a unilateral mistake as to a *material fact* is a defense if the other party *knew or should have known* of the mistake.

Illustration 4   Unilateral Mistake

1. Sue enters into a contract with Tyler to sell Tyler a parcel of land. Sue knows that the land cannot support a building taller than five stories, but most of the buildings in the area are only three stories. Unbeknownst to Sue, Tyler intends to build a 20-story building on the land. Tyler's unilateral mistake (as to suitability of the land) is not a defense. However, if Tyler showed Sue the plans to the building before the sale and Sue remained silent, the defense of unilateral mistake is available.

2. Phil is selecting bids from contractors for construction of a garage. One bid is substantially lower than the others (e.g., bid 1—$6,000; bid 2—$5,600; bid 3—$3,200) so that it is obvious that there is a mistake in the bid. The mistake will be a defense. Note that the bidder's negligence is irrelevant.

1.8   Illegality: Contract Generally Void

If the consideration or the subject matter of a contract is illegal, the contract generally is *void*. Examples of illegality include agreements to commit a crime or tort (e.g., to steal and sell an employer's trade secrets); agreements in restraint of trade; gambling contracts; usurious contracts; etc.

Illustration 5   Illegality

Joe enters into a contract with Jim to murder Jason in exchange for 10 kilos of cocaine. The contract is void both because the subject matter (to murder) is illegal and the consideration on the other side (cocaine) is illegal.

1.8.1   Licensing: Revenue Raising vs. Protection

If a contract is illegal because a party does not have a required license, enforceability of the contract depends on the reason for the license.

- Failure to have a license required to *protect the public* (e.g., CPAs, attorneys, doctors, realtors, etc.) makes a contract void. Even if the unlicensed party performs the contract, the party *cannot collect*.

- If the license is required merely to *raise revenue* (e.g., all vendors at a fair pay a $25 license fee), the contract is enforceable.

1.9   Minors May Generally Disaffirm Contracts

A minor (usually a person under the age of 18) may disaffirm a contract anytime while a minor, or even within a reasonable time after becoming an adult. The minor must generally return whatever she possesses when she disaffirms. Note that minority is a defense *for the minor*— the other party cannot raise the minor's minority as a defense to avoid performance.

Illustration 6   Contract With Minor

Bob, a 16-year-old, purchased a used car from Paul. Ten months later, the car was stolen and never recovered. Bob may disaffirm the contract and get his money back.

A person can become bound on the contracts he or she enters into as a minor upon reaching the age of majority by *ratifying* the contract. A contract may be ratified by:

- *failing to disaffirm* within a reasonable time after reaching majority;

- *expressly ratifying* the entire contract orally or in writing; or

- *retaining or accepting the benefits.*

Pass Key

Ratification is all or nothing; a person cannot ratify part and reject part. Also, ratification does not require consideration. Finally, note that it is the minor who has the right to disaffirm; the adult does not have a right to rescind merely because the minor may disaffirm.

1.10 Intoxication

Intoxication is a defense to a contract only if the intoxication prevents the promisor from knowing the *nature and significance* of his or her promise *and* the other party *knew of the impairment.*

Illustration 7   Intoxication

Rick and Steve have a drink at lunch and then enter into a contract. Neither party is impaired. The contract is enforceable.

1.11 Adjudicated Mental Incompetency

A contract made by a party after he is adjudicated mentally incompetent is void.

Formation Defenses: Void vs. Voidable Distinction

The defenses below go to formation. The examiners often ask whether a particular formation defense will make a contract void or voidable. This chart summarizes the rules.

Defense	Void	Voidable
Fraud in the execution	✓	
Fraud in the inducement		✓
Innocent misrepresentation		✓
Duress (physical)	✓	
Duress (economic)		✓
Undue influence		✓
Mutual mistake		✓
Unilateral mistake		✓
Illegality	✓	
Minority		✓
Intoxication		✓
Adjudicated incompetency	✓	

1.12   Statute of Limitations

A statute of limitations provides that a legal action must be commenced within a certain period of time. Generally, if the statute of limitations period has expired on a contract, it is unenforceable. It does not make a contract void, but merely bars access to judicial remedies. Although contracts statutes of limitations vary, four to six years is typical. Actions for breach usually are measured from the time the cause of action accrued (i.e., the date of the breach).

1.13   Statute of Frauds: Six Contracts Requiring a Writing

Although the general rule is that contracts need not be in writing, six contracts require some type of writing to be enforceable. Both parties need not sign the writing. Only the party to be charged (i.e., the party trying to avoid the contract) must have signed.

1.   Contracts in which the consideration is **marriage** (e.g., "If you get married, I'll buy you a house").

2.   Contracts which by their terms cannot be performed within a **year** (e.g., "I will coach your football team for the next five years").

3.   Contracts involving interests in **land** (this includes all contracts for the sale of an interest in real property—such as a contract for the sale of a house or a warehouse—and leases of real property of more than a year).

4.   Contracts by **executors** or similar representatives to pay estate debts out of personal funds.

5.   Contracts for the sale of **goods** *for $500 or more*.

6.   Contracts to act as **surety** (i.e., to pay the debt of another).

It is very important to memorize these six types of contracts, because the examiners frequently test which contracts require a writing.

Pass Key

One key to memorizing the six categories is the mnemonic device **MYLEGS** (marriage, year, land, executors, goods, and suretyship). Contracts for services can be oral regardless of price so long as they can be completed within one year.

1.13.1 Year Contracts

Contracts that cannot be performed in one year must be evidenced by a writing. In determining if a writing is required, the one-year period runs from the date of the contract, not from when performance begins. Thus, a contract to wash a car two years hence requires a writing. Only contracts impossible to perform within one year from their making require a writing. For example, a contract to work for an employer for life need not be in writing because the employee could die the next day.

1.13.2 Land Contracts

Land contracts must be evidenced by a writing, but leases of land for less than a year do not require a writing.

1.13.3 Goods for $500 or More

Contracts for the sale of goods for $500 or more must be evidenced by a writing. If a sales contract has been modified, it is the contract as it *has been modified* that determines whether a writing is required.

Illustration 8   Sale of Goods for $500 or More

Ann offers to buy 200 books from Ben at $3 each to sell in her store. This contract must be in writing. Subsequently, Ann discovers that she has room for only 150 books and so calls Ben and asks if her order can be reduced. Ben agrees. The contract need not be in writing. Conversely, if the contract was for 150 books and then was modified to 200 books, a writing would be required.

Pass Key

The examiners often try to trick you with the $500 threshold. It applies only to goods contracts. A $200 land contract must be evidenced by a writing, and so must a $400 three-year service contract, etc. If you see $500 in an answer choice, be careful. If the contract does not involve the sale of goods, the choice is probably wrong.

1.13.4 What Writing Will Suffice

The "contract" itself need not be in writing; all that is required is some writing that provides *evidence of the material terms* of the contract that is signed by the person being sued. Thus, a letter about the contract could suffice, even a letter seeking to revoke the contract. Contracts for the sale of goods generally need only have a *quantity term* and a signature. The terms may be stated in more than one document. There is no requirement that all terms be stated in a single writing.

Pass Key

Remember that the signature you are looking for is the signature of the person being sued. The other party's signature is not needed and will not do.

1.13.5 Effect of Noncompliance

Failure to satisfy the Statute of Frauds does not prevent the formation of a contract; rather, it makes the contract unenforceable by one or both of the parties.

1.14 Impossibility

If after the parties enter into a contract an event occurs that will make performance of the contract *objectively impossible* (i.e., impossible for *anyone* to perform), impossibility is available as a defense. The defense discharges the adversely affected party from any further duty to perform. Note that a mere increase in the cost of performance does not make performance impossible.

Illustration 9   Impossibility (Situation 1)

Alex contracts with Phil to have Phil manufacture *at his factory* 1,500 wrenches. Fire then destroys the factory. Phil has the defense of impossibility because no one can make wrenches at Phil's factory because it is now destroyed.

Illustration 10   Impossibility (Situation 2)

Alex contracts to buy 1,500 wrenches from Phil, a tool wholesaler. Phil's warehouse, full of tools, is then destroyed by fire. Phil must still supply Alex because performance is not objectively impossible; Phil can purchase more wrenches to sell to Alex.

If the subject matter or the specified source of the subject matter of the contract has been destroyed, the contract may be avoided due to impossibility.

Illustration 11   Impossibility (Situation 3)

Tyler enters into a contract to repair Steve's boat. Before the boat can be repaired, it is destroyed by fire. The parties can avoid the contract on impossibility grounds.

Death or incapacity of a person to perform a personal service contract will discharge the contract due to *objective impossibility*.

Illustration 12   Impossibility (Situation 4)

Dee contracts to have Bob, a famous ball player, sign autographs at Dee's store. Bob then dies. Bob (or his estate) has the defense of impossibility. Note that this is objective, not subjective, impossibility because the contract called for Bob to sign, and there no longer is a Bob.

1.15 Accord and Satisfaction and Substituted Contract

An accord is an agreement to substitute one contract for another, and satisfaction is the execution of the accord. Accord and satisfaction discharge the original duty. Until the accord is satisfied a party may sue under the original contract or the accord. A substituted contract is very similar to an accord and satisfaction case, but the duties under the original contract are discharged immediately. Whether an agreement is an accord or a substituted contract depends on the intent of the parties.

Illustration 13   Accord and Satisfaction

Alex agrees to sell his car to Steve for $450. The parties agree to substitute a contract for the sale of Alex's bike to Steve for $100. The new agreement is the accord; when it is performed is the satisfaction.

1.16 Novation

Novation is available as a defense to a party who has been released from a contract. It occurs when a new contract substitutes a new party for an old party in an existing contract. All parties must agree to the release.

Illustration 14   Novation

Sam agrees to build a garage for Barb, but then gets a more lucrative construction job. Sam asks Barb if it's OK to substitute Dee to build the garage. The parties agree to substitute Dee and release Sam. There has been a novation.

A release or agreement to discharge one of the parties without replacing that party is not a novation but rather a simple release. Such an agreement usually requires new consideration or detrimental reliance to be enforceable.

1.17 Conditions Can Affect a Party's Duty to Perform

A condition is an event, the occurrence or nonoccurrence of which will end a party's duty to perform. Conditions have different names depending on when they occur. Conditions are often preceded by "if," "subject to," or similar language.

Illustration 15   Condition

"I will pay you $10 *if* you mow my lawn." Mowing the lawn is an express condition to payment of the $10.

A condition precedent is a condition that must occur *before* the other party must perform. Conditions concurrent are conditions that must occur *simultaneously*. For example, the payment of money and exchange of goods in most face-to-face sales contracts are conditions concurrent. The parties make the exchange simultaneously. A condition subsequent is a condition that will occur after a party's duty to perform has arisen and will cut off that duty.

Illustration 16   Condition Subsequent

"If you promise to host a weekly football party, I will pay you $1,000 per year until the Bears win their third Super Bowl." Upon the Bears winning their third Super Bowl, the duty of payment is cut off.

1.18 Prevention of Performance Is a Breach

If one party prevents the other from performing contract duties, a material breach has occurred. The non-breaching party is excused from performance.

1.19 Parol Evidence Rule

- The parol (oral) evidence rule prohibits a party in a lawsuit involving a *fully integrated* written contract (i.e., a written contract that appears to be intended to reflect the entire agreement between the parties) from introducing evidence at trial of:

  - oral or written statements made prior to the written contract or oral statements made contemporaneously with the written contract; and

  - that seek to vary the terms of the written contract.

- Oral or written modifications made after the contract has been entered into (subsequent modifications) are admissible under the parol evidence rule.

Illustration 17   Parol Evidence Rule

Bob, a 16-year-old, is looking at cars on Lori's used car lot. Lori tells Bob that if Bob buys a car today, Lori will wash the car once a week at no charge for a year. Bob selects a car and the parties sign a fully integrated agreement setting out the parties, the price, the warranty, etc., but failing to mention anything about the washing agreement. Assuming Lori's statement was not fraudulent (e.g., she actually intended to provide the washings when she made the statement but later changed her mind), Bob will not be able to introduce evidence of the statement in court. However, the parol evidence rule would not prohibit Bob from introducing evidence of his age, since that is not seeking to vary the contract's terms.

Pass Key

The examiners often ask parol evidence questions. There are two key areas to examine:

1. Examiners love to test the time element in parol evidence rule questions. Remember that prior or contemporaneous statements that contradict the writing are inadmissible. Subsequent statements that contradict (or change a term) are admissible.

2. Examiners sometimes combine the parol evidence issue with a Statute of Frauds issue, usually in an oral modification fact pattern. The key is to address each issue separately. First determine whether the modification is enforceable (is the contract *as modified* within the Statute of Frauds). Then determine whether it is admissible in evidence (subsequent modifications are admissible) under the parol evidence rule.

---

2   Remedies

The last contracts issue remaining is what to do when a party fails to perform something he or she is contractually obligated to do (i.e., what to do when there is a *breach*). This is the province of remedies. At common law, if there has been a material or substantial breach, the non-breaching party can be discharged from the contract. If the breach is only minor, the non-breaching party is not discharged, but is entitled to damages.

2.1   Damages

Once there is a breach, the next step is to determine the damages to which the non-breaching party is entitled. Numerous damage measures are set out below, but the key to all of them is that they are intended to *put the non-breaching party in as good a position as he would have been had there been no breach.*

Pass Key

Even if you cannot remember a specific remedy measure, remember the goal of contract remedies and you should be able to pick the correct choice in most damages questions.

2.1.1   Compensatory Damages (Benefit of the Bargain)

The standard measure of damages for personal service contracts awards the non-breaching party enough *money* to obtain substitute performance (i.e., the difference between the cost of substitute performance and the contract price).

Illustration 18   Compensatory Damages

Bob contracts to build a garage for Barb for $5,000. Bob gets a more lucrative construction job and refuses to build Barb's garage. Barb hires Jim to build a garage for $6,000. Barb can collect $1,000 from Bob.

2.1.2   Consequential Damages if Foreseeable

In addition to the standard measure of damages, a party may also collect all damages that are *reasonably foreseeable* as a result of the breach (e.g., extra weathering of Barb's car resulting from no garage or extra storage fees).

2.1.3   Specific Performance (Used With Land or Unique Items)

Specific performance is essentially a court order that the breaching party perform or face contempt charges. It is available if interests in land or unique personal property (e.g., one-of-a-kind items, such as a patent) are involved. In such cases, money would be an inadequate remedy (a specific piece of property or unique item of personal property cannot necessarily be purchased with money).

Specific performance cannot be used to force a party to perform personal service contracts (courts consider this a form of involuntary servitude, which is prohibited by the 13th Amendment). If specific performance is available, a party can receive either specific performance or compensatory damages, but not both.

2.1.4 Liquidated Damages (Damages Agreed to in the Contract)

A liquidated damage clause is a clause in a contract that specifies what damages will be if there is a breach (e.g., forfeiture of a down payment for breach). A liquidated damage clause is enforceable if the amount is (i) *reasonable in relation to the actual harm done*, and (ii) *not a penalty*.

2.1.5 Punitive Damages

Punitive damages generally are not available for breach of contract. They are available for fraud, which is a tort cause of action.

Pass Key

Punitive damages often appear as a choice in contracts questions. It is an incorrect choice unless the question asks which remedy is not available or the cause of action is for fraud (a tort) rather than breach of contract.

2.1.6 Rescission or Cancellation

Rescission or cancellation cancels the contract and restores the parties to their former position. Rescission or cancellation is available for mutual or unilateral mistakes, fraud, and most material contract breaches. Under the common law, a party cannot rescind or cancel if a contract has been substantially performed (the doctrine of substantial performance). The non-breaching party's only remedy is monetary damages for the minor breach.

2.1.7 Limitations on Monetary Damages

In order to fairly compensate parties for harm done, the law imposes the limitations of foreseeability and mitigation on monetary damages.

- **Foreseeability**

  Consequential damages are awardable only for those damages that at the time the contract was formed a party could reasonably foresee would result from a breach.

- **Mitigation (Reasonable Efforts to Avoid Damages)**

  Under contract law, a non-breaching party cannot recover for damages that could have been reasonably avoided. The party must mitigate damages.

Question 1 — MCQ-01250

Which of the following offers of proof are inadmissible under the parol evidence rule when a written contract is intended as the complete agreement of the parties:

I.   Proof of the existence of a subsequent oral modification of the contract.

II. Proof of the existence of a prior oral agreement that contradicts the written contract.

   a. I only.

   b. II only.

   c. Both I and II.

   d. Neither I nor II.

Question 2 — MCQ-01246

To prevail on the defense of fraud in the inducement, a victim must prove that the:

   a. Defrauder was an expert with regard to the misrepresentations.

   b. Defrauder made the misrepresentations with knowledge of their falsity and with an intention to deceive.

   c. Misrepresentations were in writing.

   d. Defrauder was in a fiduciary relationship with the victim.

NOTES

1 Introduction

The Sales Article of the UCC (Article 2) applies only to sales of goods. You already know a substantial part of Sales because it generally follows common law contracts discussed earlier in this unit. This module will highlight the differences between the two. If an issue is not covered, assume that the Sales Article follows the contract rule.

1.1 Goods—Moveable Personal Property

The UCC Sales Article applies to the sale of goods, which is defined as all things moveable. This includes most tangible personal property (e.g., cars, cows, and groceries). The following are *excluded from the Sales Article* and are covered by common law contracts:

- Contracts for personal services and real estate.
- Contracts for intangible personal property, such as stock or patent rights.
- Contracts for fixtures—things attached to the land.

1.2 Merchants—Deal in Goods of the Kind Sold

A number of UCC rules depend on whether one or more of the parties are merchants. You must be careful to note the status of the parties. A merchant is one who deals in goods of the kind sold or who has special knowledge regarding the goods being sold.

The UCC is not limited to merchants. It applies to all contracts for sale of goods.

1.3 Obligation of Good Faith

The UCC imposes an obligation of good faith on both parties to a sales contract. Merchant sellers must also observe reasonable standards of fair dealing in the trade.

2 Creation of a Contract

2.1 Agreement (Mutual Assent)—Offer and Acceptance

2.1.1 Offer—Merchant's Firm Offer

Under the common law, consideration is needed to make an offer irrevocable. There is a limited exception to this rule that only arises under the UCC—merchant's firm offers. Certain offers by merchants are irrevocable without consideration. Merchant's firm offers are irrevocable for the time stated, or if no time is stated, for a reasonable time, but in *no event longer than three months*. To qualify as a merchant's firm offer:

- The seller must be a *merchant* (regularly deals in goods of the kind sold);
- The offer must be in *writing* and *signed* by the merchant; and
- The offer must give *assurances that it will be kept open* for a certain time.

Pass Key

It is important to remember that the firm offer rule applies only to offers for the sale of goods by merchants and only if the offer is in writing. The examiners often try to fool you. They may say that a merchant phones a buyer offering to sell goods and promises to keep the offer open. The firm offer rule does not apply because the offer is oral. They might say that a person writes a friend offering to sell a car and promises to keep the offer open. The firm offer rule does not apply because the seller is not a merchant. Finally, they might say that a realtor offers in writing to sell a parcel of land and promises to keep the offer open. The firm offer rule does not apply because the contract is for land, not for the sale of goods.

2.1.2 Acceptance

Under the Sales Article, an offer that does not specify the means of acceptance may be accepted by any means reasonable under the circumstances. But an offer specifying the means of acceptance must be accepted by the specified means—the offer is the master of the offer. The Sales Article modifies the common law of acceptance in the following ways.

- **Mirror Image Rule Does Not Apply Under UCC**

    Under common law contracts, the terms of an acceptance must mirror the terms of the offer or there is no contract—just a counteroffer. This is not so under the UCC. Under the Sales Article an acceptance will be effective even if it states new or different terms. Generally, under the UCC the new or different terms will be ignored unless the contract is between merchants. In a contract between merchants, the terms of the acceptance control unless the offeror objects or the changes are material.

Pass Key

Examiners like to test new or different terms in an acceptance. Remember that under the common law, the acceptance must mirror the offer. Under the Sales Article, new or different terms are ignored unless the contract is *between merchants*. Between merchants, minor changes can generally be made in the acceptance.

- **Promise to Ship or Prompt Shipment**
    - Under the Sales Article, an offer to buy goods for current or prompt shipment can be accepted by either a promise to ship or by prompt shipment, unless the offer indicates otherwise.

Illustration 1   Valid Acceptance

Bob sends Steve an order for 400 widgets at $1 per widget. Steve can accept by either promising to ship the widgets or by promptly shipping the widgets.

- If prompt shipment of goods is an acceptance, what happens if the seller ships goods that do not conform to the contract? Under the UCC, a shipment of nonconforming goods is *both an acceptance and a breach* of contract.

Illustration 2　　Acceptance and Breach of Contract

Barb orders 100 black widgets from Sam. Sam is out of black widgets, so sends 100 blue widgets. The shipment is both an acceptance and a breach of contract, and Barb may sue Sam for damages.

- If the seller reasonably notifies the buyer that nonconforming goods are shipped only as an accommodation to the buyer, the shipment is not an acceptance. It is a counteroffer.

Illustration 3　　Counteroffer

The same facts as the example above, but Sam sends a note before shipment that the blue widgets are intended only as an accommodation. Barb may accept or reject the widgets, but Sam has not breached any contract.

Pass Key

You must remember that the accommodation shipment rule applies only when shipment is used as the means of acceptance. The examiners often try to trick you by stating that a party accepts an order by promising to ship. Then the party discovers he lacks the goods and ships nonconforming goods as "an accommodation." This is a breach, not an accommodation.

2.1.3　Auctions

The UCC contains special rules regarding auctions, which are rarely tested on the exam. Just to be safe, the key points to remember are as follows:

- Generally, the bid is the offer and the fall of the hammer is the acceptance.

- Unless otherwise stated, all auctions are "with reserve," which means that the seller does not have to sell unless an adequate bid is made.

- In an auction "without reserve" the goods must be sold to the highest bidder. The goods only can be withdrawn if no bid is made within a reasonable time.

2.2　Consideration

- **Modifications Enforceable Without Consideration**

  At common law, a modification of a contract is not enforceable unless consideration is given. The UCC abandoned this rule. Under the UCC, a modification of a contract for the sale of goods is enforceable, even without consideration, as long as the modification is sought in good faith.

■ **Payment by Check**

A sales contract may be paid by check, unless the seller demands cash, in which case the seller must give the buyer a reasonable time to obtain the cash.

Illustration 4   Modification

Rick, a book distributor, offers to sell Steve, a bookstore, 100 books for $1 each. Steve accepts. Rick subsequently discovers that he will lose money on the deal, and so asks Steve if he would be willing to pay $1.05 for each book. Steve agrees. The modification is binding.

Pass Key

Be careful. This exception applies *only in the sale of goods*. If the example above were to bind books (a common law service contract), the modification would not be binding because of the preexisting duty rule.

2.3   Defenses

■ As at common law, fraud is a defense to a contract under the UCC. The defrauded party either may sue for damages or seek rescission. Under the Sales Article, a party may rescind and sue for money damages.

■ The UCC statute of limitations is four years. An action must be brought within four years of the time the cause of action accrued (from the time the contract was breached).

2.3.1   Statute of Frauds

Contracts for the sale of goods for $500 or more must be evidenced by a writing signed by the party being sued. There are four exceptions, provided below:

1. Contracts for **specially manufactured goods** (i.e., goods not generally suitable for sale to others, such as bowling shirts with a team name embroidered on them).

2. Where a merchant sends another merchant a **written confirmation** of a contract that is sufficient to bind the sender, it will also bind the recipient if she does not object within 10 days (e.g., Randy Retailer calls Wendy Wholesaler and orders $600 worth of goods, and then sends Wendy a written and signed confirmation of the order. If Wendy does not object, the confirmation is sufficient to bind Wendy even though she did not sign it). This is known as the merchant's confirmatory memo rule.

3. Contracts that parties have **admitted** in court.

4. Contracts that have been **performed**, to the extent that the performance has been accepted (e.g., an oral contract for 200 widgets at $5 each cannot be enforced, but if 150 widgets are delivered and accepted, it is enforceable to the extent of the 150 accepted widgets).

Pass Key

The exceptions to the Statute of Frauds for goods can be remembered with the mnemonic **SWAP—S**pecially manufactured goods, **W**ritten merchant's confirmatory memo, **A**dmission in court, and **P**erformance.

Illustration 5 — Specially Manufactured Goods

Sam and Ben orally agree that Sam will specially manufacture a machine for Ben for $40,000. After Sam spends $30,000 to build the machine, Ben tells Sam that he no longer needs it. Even though the contract is oral, Ben is bound because the goods were specially manufactured.

- **Price Measured as Modified**

    If a sales contract has been modified, it is the contract as it *has been modified* that determines whether a writing is required.

Illustration 6 — Modification Effective Without Writing

Able signs a contract to purchase 600 books from Baker for 90 cents each. Subsequently, Able in good faith asks that the price be reduced to 80 cents, and Baker agrees. The modification is effective without a writing because the contract as modified is for only $480.

- **What Writing Will Suffice—Quantity Only Essential Terms**

    Under the common law, the writing must include *all essential terms*. Under the UCC, terms may be omitted (e.g., if the memorandum is silent, a sale will be at a reasonable price and delivery at the seller's place of business). The only terms that cannot be omitted are the quantity term (unless the contract is an output or requirement contract) and the signature term.

- **Impossibility and Impracticability**

    Under contract law, if an event occurs that makes the contract objectively impossible to perform (i.e., no one could perform), the contract is discharged. The UCC is more lenient. Under the Sales Article, a contract will be discharged for mere impracticability. The contract need not be impossible to perform. It need only be impracticable—extremely more burdensome than anticipated because of the occurrence of an unforeseen event.

- **Failure of Agreed-Upon Method of Transportation (No Defense)**

    If the method of transportation called for in the contract is unavailable or commercially unreasonable, the seller may use a different means of transportation and the buyer must accept (e.g., if goods are to be delivered by one shipping company and that shipping company is on strike, then the seller can use a different shipping company).

3 Delivery, Risk of Loss, and Title

This section deals with the code's rules for delivery, risk of loss, and passage of title in sales contracts. These issues are commonly tested.

3.1 Delivery and Risk of Loss

As a general rule, the seller's basic duty is to hold conforming goods for the buyer and give the buyer reasonable notice to enable the buyer to take delivery. Many contracts stray from this rule. The UCC has specific rules for when and where delivery of goods is to be made, and these rules apply if the contract is silent. Risk of loss (who will bear the loss if the goods are destroyed) generally depends on the time delivery is made. Note that if goods are damaged or destroyed after risk of loss has passed to the buyer, the buyer is not discharged from the contract; rather, the buyer must still pay the contract price.

3.1.1 For Risk of Loss to Pass, Goods Must Be Identified

Title and risk of loss cannot pass until the goods are first *identified*. Goods are identified when they are marked, segregated, or in some manner identified as goods for a specific buyer.

3.1.2 As Parties Agree

The most important rule to remember is that if the parties designate when and where delivery will occur or risk of loss will pass, their agreement governs.

3.1.3 Where No Specific Agreement

The code divides cases where there is no agreement on delivery or risk of loss into two broad categories: noncarrier cases and carrier cases.

- In *noncarrier cases* the buyer will usually pick up the goods at the seller's place of business (e.g., buying goods at the grocery store).

- In *carrier cases* the parties contemplate a common carrier will be used to ship the goods (e.g., shipping goods by UPS).

1. Noncarrier Cases

- If the seller is not a merchant, risk of loss passes to the buyer upon the seller's *tender of delivery* of the goods to the buyer.

Illustration 7   Risk of Loss When Seller Is Not a Merchant

Steve is not in the business of selling computers, but agrees to sell a computer to his neighbor, Bill, for $400. Bill gave Steve the $400. When Steve tendered delivery of the computer, Bill said he would come back later to pick it up. Before Bill returns, the computer is destroyed by fire through no fault of Steve's. Steve may keep the $400 because Bill had the risk of loss when the computer was destroyed.

- With merchant sellers, risk of loss passes only upon actual delivery to the buyer (i.e., when the buyer takes physical possession).

Illustration 8   Risk of Loss When Seller Is a Merchant

The same facts as the example above, but Steve is a computer merchant. Steve must get a computer for Bill or pay damages because Steve still had the risk of loss when the computer was destroyed.

2. Carrier Cases

If a common carrier is involved, the contract is either a *shipment* contract or a *destination* contract.

- With shipment contracts, risk of loss passes to the buyer when the goods are delivered to the carrier.

- With destination contracts, risk of loss passes to the buyer when the goods reach the destination and seller tenders delivery.

Illustration 9   Shipment Contract

Brenda Corp. entered into a shipment contract with Sally Co. to purchase a used computer from Sally Co. It was understood that Sally Co. would ship the computer to Brenda Corp.'s main office. Even though Sally Co. must arrange for the shipment, Brenda Corp. bears the risk of loss during shipment, and if the computer is damaged while in transit, Brenda Corp. must still pay for the computer.

▪ FOB (Free on Board)

FOB is a delivery term. FOB means "free on board" and is always followed by a location. On the exam, it is usually FOB the seller's place of business or FOB the buyer's place of business. FOB the seller's place is a shipment contract. The seller must get the goods to the carrier for risk of loss to pass. FOB buyer's place is a destination contract. The seller must get the goods to the destination and tender delivery for risk of loss to pass.

Illustration 10   Free on Board

Ann, an appliance retailer, agreed to purchase 100 microwaves from Stan, an appliance wholesaler. The contract provided that the goods were to be shipped to Ann by common carrier *FOB Stan's loading dock.* If the microwaves are destroyed during shipment, Ann must still pay because she had the risk of loss. If the contract were *FOB Ann's store* and the microwaves were destroyed in transit, Stan would bear the loss.

▪ Effect of Breach on Risk of Loss

If the seller sends nonconforming goods (goods that do not meet the contract description), the risk of loss remains on the seller, regardless of the shipping terms, unless the buyer accepts the defective goods.

Illustration 11   Nonconforming Goods

Betsy orders 100 microwaves from Stan with the shipping terms *FOB Stan's loading dock*. Stan sends 100 toaster ovens. If the toaster ovens are destroyed in transit or shortly after the goods reach Betsy (before acceptance), Stan bears the risk of loss despite the *FOB Stan's loading dock* term.

3.1.4   Risk in Sale on Approval and Sale or Return Contracts

Under the code, *all sales are final*, unless otherwise agreed. The UCC provides for two types of nonfinal sales: sale on approval and sale or return.

1.   Sale on Approval—Risk on Seller Until Approval

In a sale on approval, the sale is not final until the buyer gives approval (i.e., a sale with a trial period). Title and risk of loss remain with the seller until the buyer approves.

Illustration 12   Sale on Approval

Stacy sells a television to Ben. The agreement provides that Ben may return the television within 30 days if he is not happy with it. During the 30-day period, Stacy bears the risk of loss until Ben indicates his acceptance. If the television is destroyed on the 15th day, and Ben has done nothing to accept, Stacy bears the loss.

2.   Sale or Return—Risk on Buyer Until Returned

A sale or return is a completed sale on delivery, but the buyer has the right to return the goods (this is sometimes called a *sale on consignment*). Risk of loss passes to the buyer when the seller completes the delivery requirements. Risk remains with the buyer until the goods are completely returned.

Illustration 13   Sale or Return Contract

Dan is a distributor of magazines. Each month, Dan sells 1,000 magazines to Richard, a retailer. The contract provides that Richard may return whatever magazines are left at the end of the month to Dan. This is a *sale or return* contract. If any magazines are stolen from Richard's store, he bears the loss.

Pass Key

The most frequently tested Article 2 issue is risk of loss. The key things to remember are:

- Risk of loss is *not* determined by who has title.

- *Noncarrier cases*: If the seller is not a merchant, risk of loss passes to buyer upon seller's tender of *delivery*. If the seller is a merchant, risk of loss only passes when the buyer gets physical *possession*.

- *Common carrier cases*: With *shipment contracts* (i.e., FOB seller's place), risk of loss passes when the seller gets the goods *to the carrier*. With *destination contracts* (i.e., FOB buyer's place), risk of loss passes when the goods *reach the destination* and seller *tenders delivery*.

- If the goods are nonconforming, risk of loss is always on the seller regardless of the shipping terms.

3.2 Title

- Title can pass at the time and place the parties agree, but before title can pass, the goods must be identified to the contract.

- If there is no agreement as to when title will pass, title passes when the seller completes her delivery requirements. The time of delivery can vary depending on the delivery term used.

- If the buyer rejects the goods, whether the rejection was rightful or wrongful, title revests in the seller. (Recall that if nonconforming goods are shipped, risk of loss remains with the seller despite the buyer's title.)

Illustration 14   Passing of Title

Bea agreed to purchase 100 blenders from Steve *FOB Steve's warehouse*. Title passes to Bea at the time the blenders are given to the carrier, because that is when delivery occurs. If the delivery term were *FOB Bea's store*, title would pass when the blenders are delivered to Bea's store.

4   Warranties

4.1   General

In sales, a seller must make a *perfect tender* (i.e., the goods and delivery must conform exactly to the contract without any defects). If the goods do not conform to the contract, the buyer may reject them. To fulfill the requirement of perfect tender, the goods must conform to all warranties. In this regard, there are four warranties that you must know:

1.   Express warranties

2.   The implied warranty of title

3.   The implied warranty of merchantability

4.   The implied warranty of fitness for a particular purpose

In reviewing the material on warranties, it is important to note how the warranty is made, who makes the warranty, and how the warranty can be disclaimed.

4.2   Express Warranties

▪   An express warranty will arise from any statement of fact or promise made by the seller, any description of the goods made by the seller, or any sample or model shown by the seller. The express warranty is that the goods will conform to the statement of fact, to the description, or to the sample or model.

▪   An express warranty can be made by any seller (not limited to merchants) and may be oral or written. Statements of value or opinions do not generally create an express warranty. The statement must involve facts. Additionally, the UCC requires that the express warranty be a *part of the basis of the bargain* (i.e., made at a time when it could have played some part in the buyer's decision to buy).

Illustration 15   Express Warranty

A statement that a car is a "1967 Ford and a beauty" creates a warranty that the car is a 1967 Ford, because this a fact. It does not create the warranty that the car is a "beauty," because this is an opinion, not a fact.

Pass Key

When examiners test express warranties, they frequently ask about the requirement that the express warranty be a part of the basis of the bargain. Look for this in express warranty questions. For example, if a used-car retailer tells a customer that the engine in a car was rebuilt, the statement creates a warranty that the engine was in fact rebuilt, if the statement was made any time before the contract is signed. If the statement was made after the contract was signed, however, no warranty is made.

4.3 Implied Warranty of Title

- Implied in every sales contract is the warranty that the seller has *good title and the right to transfer* that title. The seller also impliedly warrants that there are no unstated *encumbrances* (i.e., no unstated liens or attachments on the goods). If the seller is a merchant, he also impliedly promises that the goods do not *infringe* on any patent or trademark.

- The implied warranty of title can only be disclaimed by specific language or by circumstances that indicate the seller is not guaranteeing he has title (e.g., judicial sale). A general disclaimer cannot disclaim title (e.g., "merchandise is sold as is," "with all faults," "seller makes no warranties beyond the face of this instrument," or "I disclaim any and all warranties").

Pass Key

The examiners love the warranty of title. The key point to remember is that it cannot be disclaimed by a general disclaimer such as "as is" or "with all faults." It can be disclaimed only specifically (e.g., "I do not warrant title") or by circumstance (e.g., judicial sale).

4.4 Implied Warranty of Merchantability

- In every sale by a merchant who deals in goods of the kind being sold, there is an implied warranty that the goods are fit for *ordinary purposes*. The warranty is implied—no writing or oral promise is required.

- The implied warranty of merchantability is made only in sales by merchants. Note, however, that the buyer need not be a merchant.

- Merchantability can be disclaimed by a statement that the goods are sold "as is" or "with all faults." Absent a general disclaimer, such as "as is," merchantability can only be disclaimed by using the word "merchantability" (i.e., a purported disclaimer stating "we hereby disclaim any and all warranties" is ineffective). A disclaimer may be oral. If the disclaimer is in writing, it must be conspicuous.

4.5 Implied Warranty of Fitness for Particular Purpose

- The implied warranty of fitness for particular purpose arises when the buyer relies on any seller (does not need to be a merchant) to select goods suitable for the buyer's particular purpose. The seller must know of the particular purpose and that the buyer is relying on him or her to select the goods.

- Merchantability requires the goods to be fit for ordinary purposes. Fitness requires the goods to be fit for the buyer's specified purpose. Fitness can be made by any seller. It is not limited to merchants.

Illustration 16   Implied Warranty of Fitness

Ben goes to *Sam the used car man* and tells Sam that he wants to buy a car suitable for towing his two-ton boat. Sam selects a pickup truck for Ben. There is an implied warranty of merchantability that the truck will be fit for ordinary purposes, such as driving around town, and an implied warranty of fitness for particular purpose that the truck can tow a two-ton boat.

Fitness, like merchantability, can be disclaimed by selling the goods "as is" or "with all faults." If not disclaimed by an "as is" sale, fitness must be disclaimed by a conspicuous disclaimer. The writing need not mention fitness (e.g., "I make no warranties beyond the face of this contract" is sufficient).

Pass Key

Examiners often test on implied warranties. The following are the key things to remember:

- Any implied warranty can be disclaimed, if the correct words are used (even by merchants).

- Implied warranties arise without a writing. They are automatically implied in a sales contract.

- Differences between merchantability and fitness: The warranty of merchantability can only be made by merchants and is a warranty only that the goods will be fit for ordinary purposes. The warranty of fitness can be made by any seller, but only if the buyer is relying on the seller to pick goods suitable for a particular purpose and is a warranty that they will be fit for that purpose.

Warranties			
Type	*How Arise*	*By Whom*	*Disclaimer*
Express	By affirmation of fact, promise, description, model or sample	Any seller	Cannot disclaim
Implied			
Warranty of Title (title is good, transfer rightful, no liens or encumbrances)	By sale of goods	Any seller	By specific language or circumstances showing seller does not claim title
Warranty of Merchantability (fit for ordinary purpose)	By sale of goods of the kind regularly sold by the merchant	Merchant only	By disclaimer mentioning "merchantability" (if written disclaimer, it must be conspicuous)*
Warranty of Fitness for Particular Purpose (fit for buyer's particular purpose)	By sale of goods where seller has reason to know of particular purpose and of buyer's reliance on seller to choose suitable goods	Any seller	By conspicuous *written* disclaimer*

*These may also be disclaimed by language such as "as is"; by inspection (or refusal to inspect); or by course of dealing, course of performance, or usage of trade.

5 Remedies

5.1 Remedies of Buyer or Seller

1. Anticipatory Repudiation—Sue or Wait

Anticipatory repudiation occurs when either the buyer or seller indicates in advance of performance that he will not perform. The nonbreaching party may sue immediately, cancel the contract, demand assurances (see below), or wait until the time for performance and sue then if the other party fails to perform. The repudiating party has the right to withdraw the repudiation until the other party relies (e.g., by bringing suit).

2. Right to Demand Assurances if Reasonable Grounds Exist

Under the UCC Sales Article, if one party has reasonable grounds to believe that the other party will not perform when required, she may make a written demand for an assurance of performance from the other. Failure to give this assurance within a reasonable time is an anticipatory repudiation.

3. Punitive Damages—Not Available in Sales

Punitive damages are not available under the Sales Article.

4. Duty to Mitigate—Avoid Damages

Both buyer and seller have a duty to mitigate damages. They cannot recover for damages that could have been avoided.

5.2 Seller's Remedies

1. Seller's Right to Cancel and Sue for Damages

If the buyer breaches the contract, the seller can cancel or rescind and/or sue for damages.

2. Seller's Right to Withhold Delivery and Stop Goods in Transit

The seller may withhold delivery if the buyer has failed to make a required payment or has repudiated the contract. The seller may also stop delivery of goods in transit for the same breaches.

3. Seller's Right to Resell and Sue for Damages

If the buyer breaches, the seller has the right to resell the goods. The seller may also sue the buyer for any losses the seller may have. This is usually the *difference between the contract price and the resale price* plus any additional or incidental damages (e.g., storage fees and the cost of resale).

4. Seller's Right to Full Contract Price

The seller can collect the full contract price plus incidental damages if the goods cannot be resold for any price (often the case when the goods are specially manufactured) or if the goods are destroyed after risk of loss has passed to the buyer.

5. Liquidated Damages—Must Be Reasonable

A liquidated damages clause in a sales contract is valid if the amount is reasonable with respect to the harm done and is not a penalty. Even if there is no liquidated damage clause, if the buyer has made a down payment and breaches, the seller may keep the lesser of $500 or 20 percent of the price.

5.3 Buyer's Remedies

5.3.1 Buyer's Right to Reject for Any Nonconformity

Under the UCC, the seller must make a "perfect tender"—a delivery free from any defects. If the goods do not conform to the contract, the buyer may reject all of the goods, reject some of the goods, or accept all of the goods. The buyer may also sue for damages.

The buyer usually has the right to inspect goods prior to payment. However, the buyer may not inspect prior to payment in a COD (cash on delivery) sale.

5.3.2 Buyer's Right to Cancel or Rescind

If the goods are nonconforming, the buyer can cancel the contract and sue for damages.

5.3.3 Buyer's Right to Sue for Damages

- **For Accepted Nonconforming Goods**

  The buyer may accept nonconforming goods and sue for damages. Damages are usually the difference between the value of conforming goods and the value of the goods as delivered plus incidental and consequential damages.

- **For Rejected or Undelivered Goods**

  If the goods are undelivered or buyer rightfully rejects, the buyer may:

  - Cover (i.e., the buyer can purchase comparable goods (cover) and sue the seller for the difference between the contract price and the cost of cover).

  - Sue for the difference between the market price and the contract price plus any incidental and consequential damages.

5.3.4 Buyer's Right to Specific Performance or Replevin

Specific performance may be used in a sales contract if the goods are unique or if the buyer cannot reasonably cover. Replevin (the right to recover goods wrongfully in the hands of the seller) may be used if the goods are identified and the buyer cannot reasonably cover.

Illustration 17 **Specific Performance**

Bob, an engine assembler, contracts with Steve, a parts manufacturer, for 1,000 engine parts to be picked up by Bob on June 1. Steve has several similar contracts with other engine assemblers. By June 1, Steve has completed a run of 2,000 parts of the type Bob wants, but Steve has not identified any as the ones for Bob. When Bob arrives, Steve refuses to deliver any parts to Bob. If Bob cannot get replacement goods in time, he has a right to specific performance. If the goods had been identified to the contract, Bob could have replevied them.

5.3.5 Buyer's Rights on Seller's Insolvency

If the buyer has paid part or all of the price and the seller is insolvent, the buyer may recover the goods from the seller if the goods are identified.

6 Entrusting

If the owner of goods entrusts them to a merchant who deals in goods of the kind sold, and the merchant sells them in the ordinary course of business to a bona fide purchaser for value, the purchaser gets good title even though the merchant did not have good title. But be careful. This rule applies only if the goods were entrusted to a merchant (not, for example, a bank), and the goods were sold in the ordinary course of business (not at a bulk sale of the merchant's business).

Question 1	MCQ-01776

Under the UCC Sales Article, which of the following statements is correct concerning a contract involving a merchant seller and a non-merchant buyer?

- **a.** Whether the UCC Sales Article is applicable does not depend on the price of the goods involved.
- **b.** Only the seller is obligated to perform the contract in good faith.
- **c.** The contract will be either a sale or return or sale on approval contract.
- **d.** The contract may not involve the sale of personal property with a price of more than $500.

Question 2	MCQ-02341

Cookie Co. offered to sell Distrib Markets 20,000 pounds of cookies at $1.00 per pound, subject to certain specified terms for delivery. Distrib replied in writing as follows:

> *"We accept your offer for 20,000 pounds of cookies at $1.00 per pound, weighing scale to have valid city certificate."*

Under the UCC:

- **a.** A contract was formed between the parties.
- **b.** A contract will be formed only if Cookie agrees to the weighing scale requirement.
- **c.** No contract was formed because Distrib included the weighing scale requirement in its reply.
- **d.** No contract was formed because Distrib's reply was a counteroffer.

Question 3   **MCQ-01785**

Webstar Corp. orally agreed to sell Northco Inc. a computer for $20,000. Northco sent a signed purchase order to Webstar confirming the agreement. Webstar received the purchase order and did not respond. Webstar refused to deliver the computer to Northco, claiming that the purchase order did not satisfy the UCC Statute of Frauds because it was not signed by Webstar. Northco sells computers to the general public and Webstar is a computer wholesaler. Under the UCC Sales Article, Webstar's position is:

    a.   Incorrect because it failed to object to Northco's purchaser order.

    b.   Incorrect because only the buyer in a sale-of-goods transaction must sign the contract.

    c.   Correct because it was the party against whom enforcement of the contract is being sought.

    d.   Correct because the purchase price of the computer exceeded $500.

Question 4   **MCQ-06901**

Under the Sales Article of the UCC, which of the following statements is correct regarding the creation of express warranties?

    a.   Express warranties must contain formal words such as warranty or guarantee.

    b.   Express warranties must be part of the basis of the bargain between buyer and seller.

    c.   Express warranties are *not* enforceable if made orally.

    d.   Express warranties *cannot* be based on statements made in the seller's promotional materials.

1 Introduction

Broadly speaking, a surety is one who agrees to be liable for the debt or obligation of another. A suretyship transaction involves three parties: the creditor (i.e., the obligee), the principal debtor (i.e., obligor), and the surety.

1.1 Surety vs. Guarantor

A surety in the narrow sense of the term is directly liable on the contract and is distinguished from a guarantor, who is liable to the creditor only if the debtor does not perform his or her duty to the creditor.

Illustration 1 Surety vs. Guarantor

1. Alex loans Becky $10,000 with a June 1 due date. Cindy is surety on the note evidencing the indebtedness. On June 1, Alex, the creditor-obligee, may demand performance directly from Cindy. Cindy is liable even though Alex has not made demand upon Becky or placed Becky in default.

2. Alex loans Becky $10,000 with a June 1 due date. Cindy guarantees Becky's performance on the note evidencing the indebtedness. On June 1, Alex, the creditor-obligee, may demand performance from Cindy if and only if Becky defaults on the obligation (which usually means fails to pay).

A guarantor of collectibility is liable only if the creditor is unable to collect from the debtor after exhausting all legal remedies, including demand, suit, judgment, and exhaustion of all supplementary proceedings.

1.2 Statute of Frauds

The Statute of Frauds requires written evidence of the promise to answer for the debt of another signed by the surety. A suretyship undertaking not evidenced by a written memorandum is unenforceable.

2 The Surety's Rights

2.1 Against Creditor

After a default, a surety generally has no right to a notice of default or to have the creditor try to collect from the principal debtor or to have the creditor apply to the debt any security that the creditor has.

Pass Key

When a debtor defaults in a suretyship situation, the creditor may do any of the following in any order:

- Immediately demand payment from the surety
- Immediately demand payment from the debtor
- Immediately go after collateral, if there is any

The surety does not have the right to require the creditor to take any of the above-mentioned actions. A guarantor of collectibility would have the right to require a creditor to first proceed against the debtor or against available collateral.

Illustration 2   Surety's Rights and Obligations

Principal is in bankruptcy. Creditor holds a mortgage on Principal's factory as security on an obligation. Surety has also agreed to serve as a surety on the obligation. There will be considerable delay before Creditor can realize on the security due to the bankruptcy. Surety has no right to force Creditor to go against the collateral. Surety must pay in full. Surety is then subrogated to Creditors' rights against Principal on the mortgage (see below).

2.2 Against Principal Debtor

2.2.1 Exoneration (Suit to Compel Payment)

The principal debtor owes the surety a duty to perform. If the principal fails to pay the creditor, the surety may bring a suit for exoneration in equity to compel the principal to pay.

2.2.2 Subrogation (Enforcement of Creditor's Right Against Principal)

After paying the principal debtor's obligation, the surety may enforce (i.e., is subrogated to) any rights that the creditor had against the principal debtor. This includes the right to enforcement of any security interest and any priority in bankruptcy that the creditor had.

2.2.3 Reimbursement (Suit Against Principal After Payment)

The surety is entitled to reimbursement from his principal debtor for any amount the surety paid on behalf of the debtor. This is also called a right to "indemnification." Reimbursement should be distinguished from exoneration. In the latter, the surety compels the principal debtor to pay the creditor and the surety does not pay.

2.3 Against Cosureties

2.3.1 Defined: Two or More Sureties of the Same Obligation

Cosureties are two or more sureties of the same obligation. Cosureties are jointly and severally liable (i.e., any one or more may be liable for the entire obligation).

2.3.2 Exoneration (Suit to Compel Payment)

If it becomes necessary for the sureties to pay the creditor, one surety may compel the cosureties, by a suit in equity for exoneration, to pay their pro rata shares of the debt.

2.3.3 Contribution

On payment, a surety is entitled to contribution from the cosureties for their share of the payment. Contribution should be distinguished from exoneration in that the right of contribution arises only after the surety has already paid more than her share.

- If the contract does not specify the liability of each surety, each surety is liable for a pro rata share determined by the number of solvent sureties.

Illustration 3   Cosureties (Solvent vs. Insolvent)

There are three solvent and two insolvent sureties. Each solvent surety is liable for one-third of the debt.

- Where cosureties are obligated for varying amounts by their agreements and the debt is reduced by part payment by the principal, each cosurety remains liable for the original amount stated in the agreement. But payment of more than the pro rata share of the reduced debt entitles a cosurety to contribution from the cosureties for the excess in the proportion of the amounts of their original liability.

Illustration 4   Amounts Owed by Cosureties

C loans D $9,000, and X, Y, and Z agree to be cosureties. The maximum liability of each is: X, $6,000; Y, $3,000; and Z, $9,000. After making payments, D defaults and Z pays the entire balance of $6,000.

Z can collect a pro rata share from X and Y. X would have to contribute 6,000/18,000 of $6,000, or $2,000. Y would have to contribute 3,000/18,000 of $6,000, or $1,000.

■ If a cosurety's obligation is discharged in bankruptcy, her agreed share should not be considered in determining the pro rata share of the remaining cosureties. The cosurety is eliminated from the calculation because nothing can be collected from the cosurety.

Illustration 5   Cosurety Is Bankrupt

C loans D $9,000 and X, Y, and Z agree to be cosureties. The maximum liability for each is: X, $6,000, Y, $3,000 and Z, $9,000. After making payments, D defaults and Z pays the entire balance of $6,000.

X's debts, including his surety obligation, were previously discharged in bankruptcy. Z cannot collect anything from X. Z can collect 3,000/12,000 of $6,000 from Y, or $1,500. X was eliminated from the calculation because X was discharged in bankruptcy.

Pass Key

The examiners often ask about sureties' pro rata liability. Be sure you understand this concept.

---

3   Defenses of Surety

1. **Defrauded Principal**

   The surety may use as a defense that the principal debtor was induced to enter into the contract by the creditor's fraud. However, fraud by the principal debtor is not a good defense for the surety against the creditor unless the creditor was aware of the fraud.

2. **Duress Upon Principal**

   The surety is not liable if the principal debtor's promise was obtained by duress and the surety did not know of the duress.

3. **Illegality of the Principal's Obligation**

   The surety is not liable if the underlying obligation between the creditor and principal debtor is illegal.

4. **Discharge of Principal's Obligation**

   If the underlying obligation is paid or the principal debtor tenders performance and the creditor refuses to accept it, the surety is no longer liable. If the creditor releases the principal, the surety is discharged unless the creditor reserved her rights against the surety.

5. **Surety's Incapacity or Bankruptcy**

   The surety's own contractual incapacity (e.g., minority, adjudicated insanity, etc.) or bankruptcy is a defense for the surety.

6. Lack of Consideration

Like all contracts, the promise to serve as a surety must be supported by consideration to be enforceable. But that does not mean that the surety must be paid. An unpaid surety (called a "*gratuitous surety*") will be bound if he or she makes the promise to act as surety before consideration flows from the creditor to the principal debtor.

Illustration 6   Gratuitous Surety

A mother's gratuitous promise to serve as surety on her son's car loan is supported by consideration if the mother's promise is made before or contemporaneous with the time the seller becomes obligated to deliver the car. But if the gratuitous promise is made after the son receives the car, there is no consideration to support the promise.

---

7. Variations of the Surety's Risk

Any variation of the contract that changes a gratuitous surety's risk will discharge the gratuitous surety. A variation of a contract that changes a compensated surety's risk will discharge the surety only if the change is material and increases the surety's risk of loss.

Illustration 7   Compensated vs. Gratuitous Surety

The principal is originally obligated to build a parking lot 148 feet by 90 feet. If the principal and creditor agree to change the contract to a lot 138 feet by 90 feet, a gratuitous surety is discharged. The risk has been varied. But a compensated surety would not be discharged, both because the change does not appear to be material and because it makes performance easier (a smaller parking lot).

---

8. Extension of Time vs. Delay in Collection

If the principal debtor and creditor agree to extend time, the above rules apply (gratuitous surety discharged; compensated surety discharged if the change is material and increases risk). However, if the creditor does not agree to extend time, but rather merely delays in collection, the surety is not discharged.

9. Loss of Security

The release of security held by the creditor discharges the surety in the amount of the value of the security released. If the security is lost due to the creditor's inaction (e.g., failure to take the steps necessary to perfect it), the surety is discharged in the amount of the value of the security unless substantial and burdensome acts were required for protection of the security.

10. Release of Cosurety

A release of a cosurety without the other cosurety's consent results in the remaining cosurety losing the right of contribution against the released cosurety. Thus, the remaining surety is discharged to the extent that the surety could have recovered from the released surety.

Illustration 8	Release of Cosurety

Ingot loans Flange $50,000. Quill and West agree to act as compensated cosureties in the amount of $50,000 each. Ingot releases West without Quill's consent and Flange defaults on the entire obligation. Ingot demands payment from Quill. Quill is discharged for 50 percent of the loan, or $25,000, because this is the amount Quill could have collected from West by reason of the right of contribution.

11. No Defense Situations

The principal's fraud against the surety (e.g., the principal debtor lies to get the surety to agree) is not a defense against the creditor unless the creditor knows of the lie. The fact that the principal debtor is or has become bankrupt or incapacitated is not a defense for the surety.

4   Creditors' Rights Outside of Suretyship

When a debtor owes a creditor money and does not have sufficient funds to pay, the debtor has a few options to alleviate the debt. Besides filing a petition in bankruptcy (discussed in the bankruptcy modules), the debtor can enter into a creditors' composition or make an assignment for the benefit of creditors.

4.1   Creditors' Composition

A creditor's composition is an agreement between the debtor and at least two creditors that the debtor pays the creditors less than their full claims in full satisfaction of their claims. Contract consideration arises from the agreement by each creditor with each other to take less than his or her full claim. This procedure results in the debtor being discharged in full for the debts owed the participating creditors after the debtor has paid the agreed amount.

4.2   Assignment for the Benefit of Creditors

In an assignment for the benefit of creditors, the debtor transfers some or all of his or her property to a trustee, who disposes of the property and uses the proceeds to satisfy the debtor's debts. The debtor is not discharged from unpaid debts by this procedure since creditors do not agree to any discharge.

5   Judicial Liens and Garnishment

5.1   In General

Creditors without a security interest or mortgage in the debtor's property can gain rights in the debtor's property through imposition of a judicial lien on property in the debtor's hands or garnishment of property in the hands of a third party.

5.2   Prejudgment Attachment

Before final judgment in a suit on a debt is rendered, if the creditor has reason to believe that the debtor will not pay, the creditor can ask the court to provisionally attach a piece of the debtor's property.

1. The court then issues a writ of attachment (to the local sheriff) and the property is seized so a creditor who prevails will be assured of recovering on the judgment through sale of the property.

2. Generally, a hearing must be held before property can be attached by the court, and most courts require that a creditor post a bond for any damages that result if the creditor does not ultimately prevail in the suit.

5.3   Judicial Lien

1. If a debtor is adjudged to owe a creditor money and the judgment has gone unsatisfied, the creditor can request the court to impose a lien on specific property owned and possessed by the debtor.

2. After the court imposes the lien, it will issue a writ (e.g., a writ of attachment), usually to the local sheriff, to seize property belonging to the debtor, sell it, and turn over the proceeds to the creditor.

3. Most states protect certain property of the debtor to ensure that the debtor does not become destitute.

    - Many states provide a "homestead" exemption that excludes items of a person's household, up to a certain amount, from the liens of most creditors (the exclusion does not apply to persons with purchase money security interests ("PMSIs") in personal property or purchase money mortgages against real property).

    - When a taxpayer fails to pay federal taxes, the IRS can file a lien on all of the taxpayer's property, including property exempt from levy under state law.

5.4   Garnishment

Where a debtor is adjudged to owe a creditor money and the debtor has property in the hands of a third party (e.g., money the debtor is owed by an employer, money in a bank account, debts owed to the debtor), a writ of garnishment may be sought.

1. The writ orders the person holding the property to turn it over to the creditor or be held personally liable for the value of the property not turned over.

2. Federal law provides that Social Security payments are not subject to garnishment, execution, levy, or attachment.

3. States often limit the amount of an employee's wages that may be garnished (e.g., no more than one-fourth of an employee's weekly salary) to prevent the debtor from becoming destitute.

6   Mechanic's and Materialman's Liens

6.1   Mechanic's Liens and Artisan's Liens

Under common law, a mechanic or artisan who works on property and either improves it or repairs it automatically has a lien on the property—for the price of the repairs—for as long as the property is in the lienor's possession. These liens are possessory—they dissolve as soon as the lienor lets the owner have the property back. If a mechanic, artisan, innkeeper, etc., goes unpaid, he or she may give the owner notice of the intention to sell the retained property to pay the owner's bill. Alternatively, the lienor may foreclose on the property by filing suit.

6.2 Materialman's Lien

Materialman's liens often are imposed in favor of contractors who perform work on, or provide supplies for, real property improvements. The unpaid materialman must file a notice with the local recorder of deeds in order to preserve his or her lien.

7 Fraudulent Conveyances

A fraudulent conveyance occurs when a debtor transfers property with the intent to hinder, delay, or defraud any of her creditors. A fraudulent conveyance is void or voidable and will be set aside in a proper proceeding.

In determining if a fraudulent conveyance occurred, a court will consider whether:

1. the transfer was to an insider (e.g., relative, partner, and co-employee);
2. the debtor retained possession or control of the property transferred;
3. the transfer was not disclosed or was concealed (i.e., done secretly);
4. the transfer was of substantially all the debtor's assets;
5. the value received by the debtor for the asset was not reasonable; and
6. the debtor was insolvent or became insolvent shortly after the transfer.

8 Fair Debt Collection Practices Act (FDCPA)

The Federal Fair Debt Collection Practices Act (FDCPA) curbs abuses by collection agencies in collecting consumer debts. The act does not apply to a creditor attempting to collect its own debts; just to services that collect consumer debts for others.

8.1 Prohibited Acts

The act severely restricts collection agencies' ability to call third parties, such as relatives of the debtor, to indirectly pressure the debtor. A collection agency can contact third persons to discover a debtor's whereabouts, but may not disclose that it is a collection agency or that the debtor owes a debt. The FDCPA also prohibits:

- Contacting the debtor at inconvenient or unusual times; in most cases "convenient" times are between 8 a.m. and 9 p.m.
- Contacting the debtor directly if the debtor is represented by an attorney.
- Using harassing or abusive language in talking to the debtor (e.g., "pay or we'll break your knee caps").
- Making false or misleading claims (e.g., "we can have you thrown in jail for not paying").
- Contacting the debtor at her place of employment if the employer objects.

8.2 Remedies Under the Act

8.2.1 Debtor's Power to Terminate Contacts

A debtor has the power to terminate the collection agency's contacts by notifying the agency in writing that the debtor will not pay the debt and to stop further communication. The agency must stop communications except to inform the debtor that it is bringing a lawsuit or seeking other remedies.

8.2.2 Damages

The FDCPA gives debtors the right to sue for actual damages caused by the collection agency's misconduct. The FDCPA also provides a statutory $1,000 damage award.

8.2.3 Federal Trade Commission

The Federal Trade Commission can bring administrative enforcement actions under the act to force a collection agency to comply with the act's provisions.

Question 1   **MCQ-01878**

Which of the following rights does a surety have?

	Right to Compel the Creditor to Collect From the Principal Debtor	Right to Compel the Creditor to Proceed Against the Principal Debtor's Collateral
a.	Yes	Yes
b.	Yes	No
c.	No	Yes
d.	No	No

Question 2   **MCQ-01920**

Nash, Owen, and Polk are cosureties with maximum liabilities of $40,000, $60,000 and $80,000, respectively. The amount of the loan on which they have agreed to act as cosureties is $180,000. The debtor defaulted at a time when the loan balance was $180,000. Nash paid the lender $36,000 in full settlement of all claims against Nash, Owen, and Polk. The total amount that Nash may recover from Owen and Polk is:

   a. $0

   b. $24,000

   c. $28,000

   d. $140,000

NOTES

1 Introduction

1.1 Secured Transactions and Security Interest

Secured transactions questions generally involve credit transactions. A *debtor buys* something from a *creditor or secured party* on credit. The creditor wants to be able to rely on something other than the debtor's promise to ensure payment. A *security interest* on *collateral* is that something. A security interest is a limited right in specific personal property (the *collateral*) of the debtor that allows the creditor to take the property (commonly referred to as repossessing) if the debtor fails to fulfill the credit obligation.

1.2 Attachment and Perfection

A security interest is effective between the parties as soon as certain steps are taken to *attach* the interest. Once the interest attaches, if the debtor defaults, the creditor has some right to take the collateral from the debtor to satisfy the debt. Attachment does not provide the creditor with rights against third parties who might also have an interest in the collateral. To gain rights over third parties, a creditor must take added steps to *perfect* the security interest. Perfection basically serves as a form of notice that the creditor has a security interest in the collateral, and because of this notice, gives the creditor rights in the collateral superior to certain third parties.

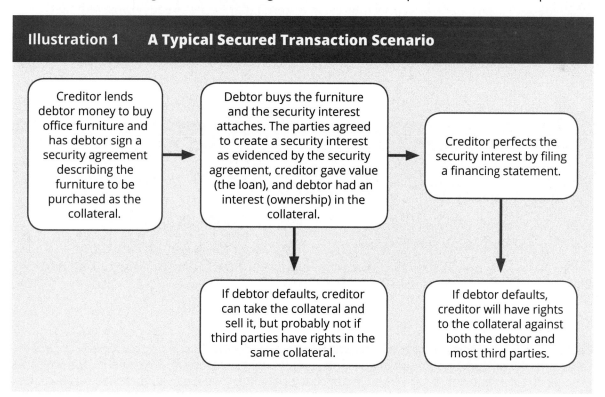

Illustration 1   A Typical Secured Transaction Scenario

Creditor lends debtor money to buy office furniture and has debtor sign a security agreement describing the furniture to be purchased as the collateral.

Debtor buys the furniture and the security interest attaches. The parties agreed to create a security interest as evidenced by the security agreement, creditor gave value (the loan), and debtor had an interest (ownership) in the collateral.

Creditor perfects the security interest by filing a financing statement.

If debtor defaults, creditor can take the collateral and sell it, but probably not if third parties have rights in the same collateral.

If debtor defaults, creditor will have rights to the collateral against both the debtor and most third parties.

1.3   Scope of Article 9, Secured Transactions

Article 9 of the Uniform Commercial Code (UCC), with certain exceptions, applies to most contractual security interests in personal property or fixtures (personal property so attached to real property as to become part of the real property) and outright sales of accounts receivable. Article 9 does not apply to security interests in land (i.e., mortgages), wage claims, and statutory liens, such as mechanic's liens.

There is a special type of security interest—a purchase money security interest (PMSI)—that has priority over all other types of security interests in the same collateral, if the PMSI is properly perfected. A PMSI arises when:

1.   a creditor sells the collateral to the debtor on credit, retaining a security interest for the purchase price; or

2.   the creditor advances funds used by the debtor to purchase the collateral.

Notice that the creditor may, but need not, be the seller of the collateral.

Illustration 2   PMSI

1.   Becky purchases a $1,000 stereo on credit from Radio Hut and signs a security agreement giving Radio Hut a security interest in the stereo. Radio Hut has a PMSI in the stereo because it supplied the credit that enabled Becky to purchase the collateral.

2.   Becky goes to Bank and asks Bank for $1,000 to purchase a stereo. Bank gives Becky the money, Becky signs a security agreement giving Bank a security interest in the stereo, and Becky buys the stereo from Radio Hut. Bank has a PMSI in the stereo because it advanced the money that was used to purchase the collateral.

3.   Becky wants to borrow $1,000 from Bank. Bank agrees to give Becky the money if Becky will give Bank a security interest in a stereo that Becky already owns. Although Bank has a security interest, it will not have a PMSI in the stereo. Becky already owned the stereo (Bank did not advance funds used to purchase the collateral).

Pass Key

Examiners frequently ask questions involving PMSI creditors. You must be able to spot PMSI creditors on the CPA Exam. Remember, a PMSI creditor exists if:

1.   the creditor sells the collateral on credit, retaining a security interest; or

2.   the creditor advances funds used by the debtor to purchase the collateral.

Simply ask—did the debtor purchase the collateral with the creditor's money or creditor's credit?

1.4   Types of Collateral

Collateral is the property subject to a security interest. Under UCC Article 9, there are four broad categories of collateral: goods, intangible and semi-intangible collateral, investment property, and proceeds. It is important to know the type of collateral you are dealing with because certain rules (e.g., how to perfect, where to perfect, and priority) depend on the type of collateral involved.

1.4.1 Goods Include

- **Consumer Goods:** Goods used for personal, family, or household purposes (e.g., a tractor used to mow the grass at home).

- **Inventory:** Goods held for sale or lease (e.g., a tractor at a farm implement store) or goods used up quickly in business, such as raw materials used in manufacturing, goods to be furnished under a service contract, and work in progress (e.g., a partially built tractor).

- **Equipment:** Goods that do not fit into another category, including durable goods used or bought for use primarily in business (e.g., a tractor used to mow the lawn at a gardening store).

Note: Whether goods are consumer goods, inventory, or equipment is determined by how the debtor uses them, not by the nature of the goods.

Illustration 3   Classifying Goods

If a debtor uses a car as a delivery vehicle for his business, it is equipment. If he uses a car for household purposes, it is consumer goods. If he buys a car to sell at his auto dealership, it is inventory.

1.4.2 Intangible Collateral Accounts

An account is any right to payment for goods, services, real property, or use of a credit card *not* evidenced by an instrument or chattel paper (e.g., the money you owe your doctor after a checkup).

1.4.3 Investment Property

Investment property includes stocks, bonds, mutual funds, etc.

1.4.4 Proceeds

Proceeds include whatever is received upon the sale, exchange, collection, or other disposition of collateral.

2   Creation (Attachment) of the Security Interest

Recall that attachment establishes the right of a creditor in collateral vis-a-vis the debtor.

2.1   Three Requisites for Attachment

1. Agreement

The parties must have an *agreement* creating the security interest evidenced by *either* an authenticated record of the security agreement, or the creditor's taking possession (a pledge) or control of the collateral.

Before the computer age, Article 9 required a security agreement to be written and signed. The term "authenticated record" includes such writings as well as their modern electronic equivalent.

A security interest in investment property, nonconsumer deposit accounts, and electronic chattel paper may be evidenced by "control." Generally, a creditor has "control" over an item if the creditor has power to make or prevent dispositions of the collateral. For example, the bank in which a nonconsumer deposit account is maintained has control over the deposit account.

2. Value

Value must be given by the secured party in exchange for the security interest (e.g., the creditor gives the debtor a loan in exchange for a security interest in the debtor's equipment—the loan is value; note that this is true even if the loan was made earlier—an antecedent debt is value, too).

3. Rights

The debtor must have rights in the collateral (usually outright ownership, but it could be something less, such as a possessory right under a rental agreement).

These three elements must coexist for the security interest to attach. Attachment will be effective when all three requisites are satisfied.

Illustration 4   Attachment

On May 1, Alex fills out a loan application, including a security agreement, from Bank to borrow $1,000 to buy a stereo. Bank tells Alex it will take five days to process the loan. On May 6, Alex obtains the money from Bank. On May 7, Alex buys the stereo. The security interest attaches on May 7 because that is the earliest date on which all three requirements for attachment were met. The agreement was made on May 1, value was given on May 6, and Alex obtained rights in the collateral on May 7.

Pass Key

A frequently tested secured transaction issue on the CPA Exam is what is or is not a requirement of attachment. There are several key points to remember:

- Because the creditor must either take possession or control of the collateral or obtain an authenticated record of a security agreement, neither is specifically required (either one will do, but one or the other must be present).

- If there is a record of the security agreement, it must be authenticated by the debtor, not the creditor.

- The debtor must have rights in the collateral, but need not necessarily own the collateral.

- A financing statement is not required. It is related to perfection, not attachment.

2.2 Property in Which Debtor Acquires Interest in Future (After-Acquired Property)

A secured party will sometimes want to obtain a security interest not only in a debtor's present property, but also in property that the debtor will obtain in the future. This is permissible. The security interest attaches to the property *as soon as the debtor acquires an interest in the property*.

2.3   Duties of Secured Party After Attachment

A secured party has a duty to file or send the debtor a termination statement when the debt is paid, confirm for the debtor the unpaid amount left on the secured debt, and to use reasonable care to preserve any collateral in the secured party's possession.

3   Perfection of the Security Interest

3.1   Introduction

To acquire the maximum priority in the collateral over other parties who may have an interest in the collateral (e.g., subsequent purchasers of the collateral, unsecured creditors, and other priority creditors), the secured party must "perfect." There are five methods of perfection:

1. Filing

2. Taking possession of the collateral

3. Control

4. Automatic perfection

5. Temporary perfection

Pass Key

The examiners like to ask about the relationship between perfection and attachment. A key point to remember is that a security interest cannot be perfected before it attaches to the collateral, but attachment and perfection can occur at the same time (e.g., by taking possession of the collateral).

3.2   Perfection by Filing

A security interest may be perfected as to all kinds of collateral except deposit accounts and money by filing a financing statement.

3.2.1   Documents to Be Filed (the Financing Statement)

The law simply requires "notice" filing—it does not require a filing of a copy of the security agreement. "Notice" is given by the filing of a "*financing statement,*" which contains the following elements:

■   The name and mailing address of the debtor and secured party;

■   An indication of the collateral covered by the financing statement; and

■   If the financing statement covers collateral related to real property (such as minerals, crops, or fixtures), a description of that real property.

Note carefully that a general description of the *type* of collateral (e.g., "inventory" or "equipment") is sufficient in the financing statement. A description of particular collateral is not necessary.

3.2.2 Debtor Must Authorize Filing

The debtor must authorize the filing of a financing statement in an "authenticated record" (i.e., the authorization cannot be oral). A debtor will be deemed to have authorized the filing if the debtor authenticates a security agreement covering the collateral that is covered by the financing statement. Generally, financing statements are filed centrally, with the secretary of state.

3.2.3 Period for Which Filing Is Effective (Five Years and It Can Be Renewed)

A financing statement is effective for five years. A financing statement can be renewed for additional five-year periods by filing a *continuation statement.*

3.2.4 Timing

A creditor can file a financing statement before all of the steps for attachment are complete. In that case, the security interest is not perfected until it attaches to the collateral. However, priority will date back to the date of filing.

3.3 Perfection by Taking Possession (Pledge)

A secured party may perfect a security interest in most types of collateral simply by taking possession of the collateral. This is similar to when a pawn shop takes an item in exchange for a loan of money. The property owner can redeem the pledged item by paying back the amount borrowed.

A security interest in accounts, deposit accounts, nonnegotiable documents, or general intangibles (e.g., a patent) cannot be perfected by possession, even if the collateral is tangibly represented (e.g., by a ledger book).

3.4 Perfection by Control

Security interests in investment property may be perfected by "control." Basically, a secured party (or other purchaser) has control of an item of investment property when the secured party has taken whatever steps are necessary to be able to have the investment property sold without further action from the owner.

If the collateral is a securities account (few people actually physically possess the stocks or bonds they own) the creditor will have control if the owner instructs the brokers or mutual fund company that the secured party now has whatever right in the account the owner has or that the broker or mutual fund company is to comply with the secured party's orders without further consent of the owner.

Illustration 5   Control

Alex borrows $100,000 from Bank. As security, Bank requires Alex to give it a security interest in his Squabb brokerage account, which has a current market value of $200,000. Bank can perfect this interest through control by having Alex instruct Squabb to follow Bank's orders regarding the account.

3.5 Automatic Perfection

Article 9 provides that a security interest can be perfected simply by the attachment of the security interest without any added requirements. This is called an *automatic perfection.* Historically, only two types of automatic perfection have appeared on the exam:

1. **PMSI in Consumer Goods**

   Recall that a PMSI arises where the creditor either sells the collateral to the debtor on credit and reserves a security interest or advances the funds that are used to purchase the collateral and reserves a security interest. The only type of PMSI that is automatically perfected is a PMSI in consumer goods. A PMSI in inventory or equipment collateral must be filed to be valid.

2. **Small-Scale Assignment of Accounts**

   A small-scale assignment of accounts (e.g., assignment of a few accounts receivable) is automatically perfected.

3.6 Temporary Perfection

3.6.1 Twenty-Day Period for Proceeds

A security interest in proceeds from original collateral is continuously perfected for 20 days from the debtor's receipt of the proceeds.

Illustration 6   **Temporary Perfection**

Sally trades in her old stereo, which is collateral for Bank's loan, for a new stereo. Bank's security interest in the new stereo is continuously perfected for 20 days from Sally's receipt of the new stereo.

3.6.2 Movement of Debtor (Four-Month Grace Period)

If the debtor moves from one state to another, perfection in the first state generally is valid for *four months* after the debtor moves to the second state. To maintain its priority, the creditor must perfect in the new state within this four-month period.

4   Priorities

4.1 Introduction

The heart of UCC Article 9 is its allocation of rights or priorities between conflicting interests in collateral. Conflicts can arise, for example, between a secured creditor and a buyer of the collateral, between creditors with a security interest in the same collateral, etc. Priorities are discussed below in the order of highest priority to lowest priority. In brief, the priority ranking is:

1. A buyer in the ordinary course of business of inventory that serves as collateral for a security agreement created by the seller; holders in due course of negotiable instruments; and holders of possessory liens;

2. The holder of a properly perfected PMSI in the collateral;

3. The holder of a perfected security interest in, or a judicial lien that has attached to, the collateral (including the lien of a trustee in bankruptcy);

4. The holder of an unperfected security interest in the collateral;

5. The debtor.

4.2 Buyers in the Ordinary Course, Holders in Due Course

4.2.1 Buyers in the Ordinary Course

A buyer who buys goods from a merchant's inventory in the ordinary course of the seller's business has the highest priority in collateral. Such a buyer takes free of a perfected security interest in the inventory, even if the buyer knows of the security interest, unless the buyer knows that the sale is in violation of the security agreement. The buyer need not be purchasing for consumer use.

Illustration 7   Buyer in the Ordinary Course

Steve, an appliance retailer, borrowed money from Friendly Bank (FB) to purchase a new line of refrigerators to sell in his store. To secure the loan, Steve gave FB a security interest in his inventory. If Becky buys a refrigerator from Steve's store, Becky takes free of FB's security interest. If Steve fails to pay FB, FB cannot repossess the refrigerator from Becky.

Pass Key

Drafters of examination questions frequently ask questions involving buyers in the ordinary course of business. Remember that a buyer in the ordinary course will always prevail over a perfected creditor, even if the buyer had knowledge of the security interest, unless the buyer knows that the sale violates the creditor's security interest.

4.2.2 Holders in Due Course and the Like

Like a buyer in the ordinary course, a holder in due course of (HDC) a negotiable instrument, or a holder to whom a negotiable document of title has been negotiated, takes priority over an earlier perfected security interest. Thus, the best way to perfect a security interest in such items is to take possession of them. Taking possession of negotiable instruments generally prevents other people from gaining status as a holder in due course or the like.

4.3 Holders of Possessory Liens: Mechanic's Liens

In most states, a repairer who does not get paid for repairing goods can place a mechanic's lien on the goods (i.e., the repairer can keep possession of the goods to ensure payment). The mechanic's lien is valid as long as the repairer keeps possession of the goods. Such possessory liens generally have priority over existing perfected security interests.

4.4 Properly Perfected PMSI

The person with the next highest priority in collateral is a holder of a properly perfected PMSI. Proper perfection depends on the nature of the collateral.

4.4.1 PMSI in Consumer Goods Automatically Perfected

As already mentioned, a PMSI in consumer goods is automatically perfected.

4.4.2 Exception: Secondhand Consumer Purchaser Without Notice

If a buyer of consumer goods resells the goods to another consumer buyer, the secondhand buyer will take free of an *automatically perfected* PMSI in consumer goods as long as the secondhand consumer buyer had no notice of the security interest. This is often called the "garage sale" rule.

Note: If the secured party filed to perfect, the secondhand buyer is subject to the security interest. Filing would give the secondhand buyer notice of the security interest.

Illustration 8	Secondhand Consumer Purchase

Becky buys a stereo for home use on credit from Steve and gives Steve a security interest in the stereo. Steve does not file a financing statement, but still has a perfected PMSI in the stereo through automatic perfection. Becky sells the stereo to her neighbor, Cindy, for use in her home. Becky stops making payments to Steve. Steve cannot repossess the stereo from Cindy. However, if Steve had filed a financing statement, he could repossess the stereo from Cindy. Even if Steve had not filed, if Cindy was using the stereo in her office, Steve could repossess. Only consumer purchasers take free of automatically perfected security interests.

Pass Key

Examiners know that you know the basic garage sale rule—a secondhand consumer purchaser usually will take free of an automatically perfected security interest in the collateral. Therefore, when they ask about this topic they usually try to trick you by telling you that the secured party filed a financing statement. Remember, if the secured party filed, the secondhand purchaser is subject to the security interest. The secured party can repossess from the secondhand purchaser because the secondhand purchaser had notice.

4.4.3 PMSI in Inventory: Prior Perfection and Notice Required for Priority

A PMSI in inventory has priority over a prior perfected security interest in the same inventory collateral only if:

- the PMSI is perfected when the debtor gets possession of the collateral (filing must occur before the inventory is delivered to debtor); and

- any secured party who has filed a security interest in the same collateral is given notice of the PMSI *before* the debtor receives the inventory.

Illustration 9	PMSI in Inventory

On March 1, First Bank (FB) loans Acme Feed Store money and takes a security interest in Acme's inventory. FB files a financing statement in the proper place. On April 1, Second Bank (SB) promises to loan Acme $10,000 to purchase cattle feed. For SB to have priority over FB, SB must file a financing statement and notify FB before Acme gets the feed.

4.4.4 Noninventory PMSI: Priority if Filing Within a 20-Day Grace Period

A PMSI in noninventory collateral (e.g., equipment) has priority over conflicting security interests in the same collateral as long as the PMSI is perfected within *20 days* after the debtor receives possession of the collateral.

■ If perfected within the 20-day grace period, perfection relates back to the day the debtor obtained possession (which means that the PMSI is superior to security interests created during the 20-day grace period).

■ There is no requirement that the secured party notify other secured parties as must be done with an inventory PMSI.

Illustration 10   Noninventory PMSI

1. As of January 2, Bank holds a perfected security interest in all of Debtor's equipment and after acquired equipment. On July 16, Dealer sells and delivers to Debtor a new piece of equipment, retaining a security interest in the equipment. On July 25, Dealer files a financing statement perfecting a security interest in the equipment. Even though Dealer knew of Bank's after-acquired property security interest, Dealer has priority as to the new piece of equipment because Dealer filed within the 20-day grace period.

2. On July 16, Dealer sells and delivers to Debtor a new piece of equipment, retaining a security interest in the equipment. On July 20, Bank loans Debtor $10,000, taking a security interest in all of Debtor's equipment, and files a financing statement covering the equipment. On July 25, Dealer files a financing statement perfecting a security interest in the new piece of equipment it sold to Debtor. Dealer has priority in the equipment it sold, because Dealer filed within the statutory 20-day period.

Pass Key

The examiners like to ask about PMSIs. There are several key points to remember:

● A PMSI in consumer goods is automatically perfected. Perfection of a security interest in other goods collateral requires filing.

● A PMSI in equipment has priority over other perfected security interests if filed anytime within 20 days of the debtor getting possession of the collateral. The perfection relates back to the date of possession.

● There is no 20-day grace period for a PMSI in inventory. To have priority, it must be perfected before the debtor gets possession and notice must be given to other perfected parties in the same collateral.

4.5   Perfected Security Interests

Perfected security interests and judicial liens that have attached have the next highest priority after properly perfected PMSIs. If there are conflicting perfected security interests or liens in the same collateral, the following rules apply:

4.5.1 Conflicting Perfected Security Interests: First to File or Perfect

When there are conflicting perfected security interests in the same collateral, priority goes to the creditor who was *first to either file or perfect*.

- Thus, if both secured parties perfected by filing, the one who filed first has priority, even if perfection was not completed upon filing.

- If one party perfected by filing and the other party perfected by some other method (e.g., by taking possession), the party who filed will have priority if he filed before the other party perfected.

Illustration 11   Competing Perfected Security Interests

1. Frank and Sam both claim a security interest in the same collateral. Frank's security interest attached on January 1 and was perfected by filing on March 1. Sam's security interest attached on February 1 and was perfected by possession on February 15. Sam's security interest is superior to Frank's interest because Sam perfected (by taking possession) before Frank filed or perfected. Note that the dates of attachment are irrelevant.

2. On May 1, First Bank (FB) took a loan application from Debtor Corp. seeking a $10,000 loan and had Debtor Inc. sign a security agreement and financing statement covering Debtor Inc.'s equipment. On May 2, FB filed a financing statement covering the transaction. On May 3, Second Bank (SB) loaned Debtor $5,000 and took possession of Debtor's bulldozer to serve as collateral. On May 4, FB loaned Debtor the requested $10,000. If Debtor defaults in paying FB, FB has priority over SB in the bulldozer because FB filed before SB perfected (by taking possession). Note that SB was the first to perfect, since its perfection was effective upon taking possession of the machine. FB's interest was not perfected until it gave Debtor Corp. the money. The first to file or perfect has priority.

Pass Key

The examiners often ask which of two perfected security interests have priority. Remember, filing or perfection dates are the dates to look at. Dates of attachment generally are irrelevant.

4.5.2 Conflict Between Perfected Security Interest and Judicial Lien

A judicial lien will have priority if it attached (i.e., the sheriff seized the property) before the security interest was perfected. If the security interest was perfected before the judicial lien attached, it has priority.

4.5.3 Trustee in Bankruptcy (Lien Creditor as of the Date of Filing)

■ A trustee in bankruptcy is treated as a hypothetical lien creditor on all of the debtor's property *as of the date the bankruptcy petition is filed*.

■ Thus, the bankruptcy trustee is subordinate to all prior perfected security interests but has priority over subsequently perfected security interests unless they have retroactive effect (e.g., PMSIs in equipment collateral).

4.6 Unperfected Security Interest (Unprotected)

Unperfected security interests have priority only over the debtor. If there are two unperfected security interests in the same collateral, the first to attach has priority.

4.7 Debtor

After default, the debtor has the lowest priority in the collateral.

Pass Key

The examiners often ask what party will have the highest priority in collateral. The order of priority is:

- Buyer in the ordinary course of business, holders in due course, and the like;

- A properly perfected PMSI holder, except in the case of a secondhand consumer purchaser of consumer goods subject to an automatically perfected PMSI;

- Perfected security interest holders and judicial lien holders once the lien has attached; and finally

- Unperfected security interests.

4.8 Priority Rules May Be Modified Contractually

Although UCC Article 9 provides rules for priority, parties entitled to priority under Article 9 may contractually subordinate their rights to the rights of other parties. Thus, if a client wishes to lend money to a debtor but all of the debtor's assets are subject to a security interest that would be superior to the client's security interest, all is not lost; the client can negotiate with the other secured creditor for a subordination agreement.

5 Rights on Default

5.1 Right to Take Possession of and Sell Collateral

The right to take possession of and sell the collateral on default is the most important and most used of the rights on default.

5.1.1 Taking Possession

The secured party may take possession by self-help without judicial process if she can do so *without a breach of the peace*.

The secured party may always take possession of the collateral by replevy action, a judicial action seeking the transfer of personal property.

5.1.2 Sale

After default and repossession, the secured party may sell or lease the collateral, either in its condition when taken or after reasonable preparation or processing. Disposition may be by either *public* (auction) or *private* sale.

- The sale or lease must be commercially reasonable in all respects: method, manner, time, place, and terms.

- The debtor and others parties must generally be given notice of the sale.

- The sale wipes out all subordinate interests, such as the interest of secured parties with lower priority, lien creditors, and the debtor's interest. A good faith purchaser of the collateral at the sale takes free of all subordinate interests, but is subject to superior interests.

- The debtor has the right to redeem by paying off the indebtedness and costs before the sale, but this right is cut off by the sale.

Pass Key

The examiners often ask about the effect of a sale of the collateral. Remember that all subordinate claims are wiped out and there is no right of redemption by subordinate security interest holders or the debtor.

5.1.3 Proceeds

Proceeds of a default sale are distributed in the following order:

1. First, to pay the expenses of repossession and sale.

2. Second, to pay creditors with a security interest in the collateral in order of priority; the creditor with the highest priority must be paid in full before any proceeds can go to the secured creditor with the next highest priority.

3. Finally, any surplus is paid to the debtor.

If sale of the collateral does not bring in enough money to pay the expenses of the sale and the debt, the secured party may bring a court action to recover the deficiency from the debtor.

5.2 Retention of Collateral in Satisfaction of Debt

- **Transactions Not Involving Consumers:** After default, a secured party may keep the collateral in full or partial satisfaction of the debt (i.e., the secured party may keep the collateral, offset its value against the debt, and seek to recover the difference from the debtor).

- **Transactions Involving Consumers:** With consumers, the secured party may keep the collateral only in full satisfaction of the debt (i.e., no deficiency may be recovered).

- **Notice Must Be Given in Full or Partial Satisfaction Cases:** In either case, the secured party must give notice of its intent to keep the collateral to the debtor and other secured parties.

- **Compulsory Disposition of Consumer Goods (60 Percent Rule):** In *consumer goods* cases in which the debtor has paid at least 60 percent of the loan, the secured party must sell the collateral *within 90 days* after repossession, unless the debtor waives this right.

5.3 Debtor's Right of Redemption (Pay All Creditors in Full)

Until the sale or discharge of the debt through retention of the collateral, the debtor may redeem the collateral by paying all of the obligations secured by the collateral plus all reasonable expenses incurred relating to the repossession.

5.4 Judicial Action (Reduce Claim to Judgment)

Instead of using self-help, on default, the secured party may bring an ordinary judicial action for the amounts due and levy on the collateral after judgment. The secured party may have the collateral seized at the same time that he or she begins the judicial action.

Question 1	MCQ-01576

Under the Secured Transactions Article of the UCC, which of the following purchasers will own consumer goods free of a perfected security interest in the goods?

    a. A merchant who purchases the goods for resale.

    b. A merchant who purchases the goods for use in its business.

    c. A consumer who purchases the goods from a consumer purchaser who gave the security interest.

    d. A consumer who purchases the goods in the ordinary course of business.

Question 2   MCQ-01621

Under the UCC Secured Transactions Article, what is the order of priority for the following security interests in store equipment?

I.   Security interest perfected by filing on April 15, 1994.

II. Security interest attached on April 1, 1994.

III. Purchase money security interest attached April 11, 1994 and perfected by filing on April 20, 1994.

    a.   I, III, II.

    b.   II, I, III.

    c.   III, I, II.

    d.   III, II, I.

Question 3   MCQ-01656

Under the UCC Secured Transactions Article, if a debtor is in default under a payment obligation secured by goods, the secured party has the right to:

	Peacefully repossess the goods without judicial process	Reduce the claim to a judgment	Sell the goods and apply the proceeds toward the debt
a.	Yes	Yes	Yes
b.	No	Yes	Yes
c.	Yes	Yes	No
d.	Yes	No	Yes

NOTES

Business Law: Part 2

Module

1   Introduction

There are six basic types of bankruptcy cases under federal law: Chapter 7, liquidation; Chapter 9, municipal debt adjustment; Chapter 11, reorganization; Chapter 12, family farmers with regular income; Chapter 13, adjustment of debts of individuals with regular income; and Chapter 15, ancillary and other cross-border cases.

1.1   Chapter 7 Liquidation: Trustee Appointed

- In a Chapter 7 liquidation case, a trustee is appointed. The trustee collects the debtor's assets, liquidates them, and uses the proceeds to pay off creditors to the extent possible.

- If the debtor is an individual (or a married couple), the debtor's debts are then discharged (i.e., the debtor is relieved from personal liability for most debts), with certain exceptions.

- If the debtor is an artificial entity (e.g., a corporation), it is dissolved. No discharge is given but the effect is the same—the debts are wiped out.

1.2   Chapter 13: Adjustment of Debts of Individuals With Regular Income

- In a Chapter 13 case, the debtor repays all or a portion of his debts over a three-year period to a maximum of a five-year period.

- Although there is not a liquidation, a Chapter 13 trustee oversees the handling of a Chapter 13 proceeding.

- At the conclusion of a Chapter 13 proceeding, the remaining debts of the debtor are discharged.

1.3   Chapter 11 Reorganization: No Liquidation, Trustee Not Required

- In a Chapter 11 reorganization case (usually used by businesses but also available to individuals), a trustee usually is not appointed.

- The debtor remains in possession of his or her assets and a plan of reorganization (i.e., a plan to pay off debts at a different time and/or amount from what was originally due) is adopted.

- Creditors are paid to the extent possible and the business continues.

Pass Key

The examiners often ask if a trustee is required for a particular type of bankruptcy. There are a few key points to remember:

- A trustee is required for Chapter 7 and Chapter 13.

- A trustee is *not required* for Chapter 11, although the court may appoint one if one is needed.

1.4   Chapter 15: Ancillary and Cross-Border Cases

Chapter 15 is the U.S. adoption of the Model Law on Cross-Border Insolvency promulgated by the United Nations. It was adopted to promote a uniform and coordinated legal regime for cross-border insolvency cases.

2   Dismissal or Conversion of a Chapter 7 Case

A Chapter 7 case by an *individual consumer* debtor may be dismissed (or with the debtor's consent converted to a case under Chapter 13) upon a finding that granting relief under Chapter 7 would constitute abuse. Abuse may be determined by a specific *means test* or by a more general *abuse test.*

2.1   Determine Whether Income Is Lower Than the State Median

If an individual filing for Chapter 7 liquidation and his or her spouse have monthly income greater than the state median income for a family of the same size, the state, any interested creditor, or the court may file a motion to dismiss the case, either under the means test or for general abuse.

2.2   Means Test

The means test is used to determine whether creditors would be better off under a Chapter 13, five-year reorganization. Sixty times the debtor's average monthly income, less allowable expenses, is compared with a high and low threshold ($8,175 and $13,650).

- If 60 times the debtor's average monthly income less allowable expenses is less than $8,175, the debtor may continue under Chapter 7.

- If 60 times the debtor's average monthly income less allowable expenses is $13,650 or more, there is a presumption of abuse and the debtor usually will have to convert the case to Chapter 13.

2.3   If Less Than $13,650, but $8,175 or More

If 60 times the debtor's average monthly income less allowable expenses is less than $13,650, but at least $8,175, a presumption of abuse will arise if the amount equals at least 25 percent of the debtor's unsecured claims not entitled to priority payment (unsecured claims entitled to priority payment will be discussed later).

2.4   Allowable Expenses

Allowable living expenses include the costs of food, clothing, and shelter as set by the IRS; expenses for health insurance and health savings plans; health care costs for family members; expenses for attending elementary or high school; and expenses related to keeping the debtor safe from family violence.

2.5   Rebutting the Presumption of Abuse

The debtor may rebut the presumption of abuse by showing special circumstances (e.g., serious illness or call to active military duty) that create additional expenses or a need to adjust current monthly income.

2.6   General Abuse Test

▪ Even if the debtor qualifies for Chapter 7, relief may be denied by a showing that the debtor acted in "bad faith" or that under the "totality of circumstances" there is abuse.

▪ If the debtor's average monthly income or the monthly income of the debtor and debtor's spouse in a joint case is at or less than the median income in the debtor's state, a Chapter 7 filing can *only* be *dismissed by the general abuse test* and *only* on motion of the *court, trustee, or bankruptcy administrator* (not a creditor).

2.7   Dismissal Upon Conviction

A court may dismiss a Chapter 7 filing by a debtor convicted of a crime involving violence or drug trafficking.

3   Who May Be a Debtor

Only a person who resides, or has a place of business, in the United States is eligible to be a debtor under the Bankruptcy Code. "Person" generally includes individuals, partnerships, corporations, and the like.

3.1   Limitation in Chapter 7 Liquidations

Railroads, savings institutions, insurance companies, banks, and small business investment companies may not file for bankruptcy under Chapter 7.

3.2   Compare Chapter 11 Reorganizations

Anyone who may be a debtor (except a stockbroker or commodity broker) under Chapter 7 may also be a debtor under Chapter 11. Additionally, a railroad may be a debtor under Chapter 11.

Although Chapter 11 is intended primarily for business debtors, an individual is eligible for relief under Chapter 11.

Pass Key

As trivial as it might seem, the key to many past bankruptcy questions was knowing who may and who may not file under the various chapters. So be sure you do not gloss over the above information.

3.3   Credit Counseling Required if Debtor Is an Individual

▪ Counseling must occur no more than 180 days before filing the bankruptcy petition.

▪ In addition, debtors filing under Chapters 7 or 13 must complete a financial management course before their debts are discharged.

4 Common Features of Chapter 7 and Chapter 11 Cases

4.1 Automatic Stay

▪ When a bankruptcy petition is filed in either a voluntary case or an involuntary case, an *automatic stay* becomes effective against most creditors.

▪ The stay stops almost all collection efforts (e.g., filing a lawsuit or simply demanding payment).

▪ The automatic stay does not apply to criminal prosecutions, paternity suits, and cases brought to establish or collect spousal or child support obligations.

4.2 Duties of Debtor

After a petition is filed, a debtor must file, among other things:

▪ A list of creditors and their addresses

▪ A schedule of assets and liabilities

▪ A schedule of current income and expenditures

▪ A statement of the debtor's financial affairs

▪ Copies of pay stubs received within 60 days before filing

▪ Copies of federal tax returns from the last tax year. If the debtor has not paid taxes for the previous tax year, he or she must do so before the bankruptcy may proceed.

Note: If an individual debtor in a voluntary Chapter 7 case fails to file any of the items specified above within 45 days after filing the petition, the case is automatically dismissed on the 46th day.

4.3 Chapter 7 and Chapter 11: Voluntary Cases

4.3.1 Debtor Files for Order of Relief

A voluntary case under Chapter 7 or Chapter 11 is commenced by the debtor filing a petition for relief.

4.3.2 Debtor Need Not Be Insolvent but Must Pass Income Tests

The debtor need not be insolvent to file. However, as previously discussed, a Chapter 7 case may be dismissed if the debtor has too much income.

4.3.3 Spouses May File Jointly

Spouses may file jointly to avoid duplicate fees.

Pass Key

Although it may seem trivial, "spouses may file jointly" often appears as a correct answer on the CPA Examination.

4.3.4 Voluntary Petition Constitutes an Automatic Order for Relief

A filed voluntary petition constitutes "an order for relief," which simply means a case may proceed unless a court orders otherwise.

4.4 Chapter 7 and Chapter 11: Involuntary Case

Unsecured creditors may petition a debtor involuntarily into bankruptcy proceedings under Chapter 7 or Chapter 11.

4.4.1 Grounds: Generally Not Paying Debts When Due

For an involuntary petition, creditors must show that the debtor generally is not paying debts as they become due.

4.4.2 Ineligible Debtors: Farmers and Charities

Farmers and nonprofit charitable organizations may not be petitioned involuntarily into bankruptcy.

4.4.3 Who Must Join Petition: Owed at Least $16,750

Only creditors who are owed, individually or in aggregate, *at least $16,750 in unsecured, undisputed debt* may petition a debtor involuntarily into bankruptcy. The number of creditors who must file depends on the debtor's total number of creditors.

- **Fewer Than 12 Creditors: One or More Owed $16,750**

  If a debtor has fewer than 12 creditors, any one or more creditors who are owed at least $16,750 in unsecured debt may file.

Illustration 1	**Who Must Join Petition**

Dee has four creditors she is not paying. Alex is owed $17,000, Bob is owed $4,000, Carla is owed $4,000, and Sam is owed $18,000, a loan secured by Dee's $20,000 car. Alex must join in an involuntary petition; Bob and Carla's claims are not sufficient. Sam may not file. Sam's claim is adequately secured.

- **12 or More Creditors: Three Owed $16,750**

  If a debtor has 12 or more creditors, *at least three creditors* who are owed at least $16,750 in aggregate, in unsecured, undisputed debt must join in the involuntary petition.

Pass Key

The number of creditors and amounts owed necessary to file an involuntary petition is a favorite exam issue. Two points should be noted:

- Usually, the examiners use this information to create "distracters" (i.e., wrong answers), such as "To file a *voluntary* petition, a debtor must owe at least $16,750" or "have at least 12 creditors." You should take time to memorize the $16,750 and one or three creditor minimums. Remember, they apply only to *involuntary* petitions.

- If a problem states the number of creditors that a debtor has, the examiners frequently have asked the number needed to file an involuntary petition. For example, if the question says the debtor has 19 creditors, then three or more must file. If the question says the debtor has eight creditors, then only one need file.

4.4.4 An Involuntary Petition Does Not Constitute an Order for Relief

- Unlike a voluntary petition, an involuntary petition does not constitute an order for relief. There is a gap between the filing and the order of relief called the involuntary case gap.

- The court will enter an order for relief if the debtor does not object to the petition within 20 days.

- If the debtor does object, a hearing is held to determine the debtor's solvency. The test for solvency is whether the debtor is *generally paying debts as they become due.*

- Persons who become creditors of the debtor during the involuntary case gap period are given high priority in recovering against the debtor's estate.

4.4.5 Dismissal of Petition: Damages

If creditors improperly filed an involuntary petition (e.g., insufficient number of creditors, insufficient unsecured claims, debtor was paying debts as they became due, etc.) a court may award the debtor compensatory damages, court costs, attorney's fees, and even punitive damages if bad faith can be shown.

Pass Key

Odd as it may seem, the Bankruptcy Code does not require a debtor to be insolvent to file for bankruptcy. A voluntary petition may be filed by *anyone who owes debts*, and an involuntary petition may be filed if the debtor is *generally not paying debts as they become due*, regardless of the debtor's ability to pay. An answer choice that suggests the debtor must be insolvent to file for, or be petitioned into, bankruptcy is wrong, but be sure to remember that an individual consumer debtor's Chapter 7 case may be dismissed or converted to Chapter 13 if his income is too high.

4.5 Section 341 Meeting: Creditors' Meeting

Ordinarily, within 20 to 40 days after the order for relief, a meeting of the creditors (called a "Section 341 meeting") is held. All interested parties, including creditors, the bankruptcy trustee, and the debtor must be given notice of the meeting.

4.6 Property of the Bankruptcy Estate

4.6.1 Property Included

▨ The debtor's estate (i.e., assets available to pay off creditors) generally includes all of the debtor's real and personal property at the time of filing.

▨ The estate also includes income generated from estate property (e.g., interest from bonds that are part of the estate) received within *180 days* after the filing of the petition for relief.

▨ It also includes property the debtor receives from divorce, inheritance, or insurance within *180 days* after the filing of the petition.

▨ Leases of property may be assumed and retained by the trustee, assumed and assigned to another, or rejected by the trustee.

Pass Key

The fact that inheritance received within 180 days after the filing of a petition for relief is included in the debtor's estate has been tested often.

4.6.2 Property Excluded From Estate

▨ **Post-petition Earnings, Spendthrift Trusts, Educational IRAs, and State Tuition Program (Excluded From Debtor's Estate)**

Post-petition earnings of an individual debtor, spendthrift trusts, contributions to educational IRAs and qualified state tuition programs made at least 365 days before the petition was filed, and contributions by employees to qualified employee benefit plans are excluded from the estate.

▨ **Exempt Property: Generally Things Necessary to Live**

An *individual debtor* is entitled to exempt certain property under the Bankruptcy Code. The code also allows states to adopt their own exemptions. About two-thirds of the states have "opted out" of the federal exemption system in favor of their own.

4.6.3 Trustee's Powers as a Lien Creditor

▨ **Trustee Is a Hypothetical Lien Creditor as of Filing Date**

The trustee is treated as having a lien on all of the debtor's property the instant the bankruptcy petition is filed.

This means that the trustee has priority over all creditors except creditors with prior perfected security interests or prior statutory or judicial liens.

▨ **Caution: PMSI in Noninventory Collateral May Have Priority**

The trustee will not prevail against PMSIs in noninventory collateral that are validly perfected under state law and within 30 days after the debtor receives possession of the collateral. Recall, however, that in most states such perfection is not valid under state law unless it occurs within 20 days after the debtor receives possession of the collateral.

> ### Illustration 2   PMSI and Bankruptcy Filing
>
> On July 1, Sue sells and delivers to Dan on credit certain equipment and properly reserves a security interest in the equipment. On July 5, Dan files a petition in bankruptcy. On July 9, Sue perfects her interest in the equipment by proper filing. Sue's PMSI prevails over the bankruptcy trustee's interest.

4.6.4 Power Over Fraudulent Transfer

The trustee also has power to set aside fraudulent transfers made within two years of the filing date.

A fraudulent transfer is any transfer made with *intent* to hinder, delay, or defraud creditors or any transfer in which the debtor received *less than equivalent value* while the debtor was insolvent.

> ### Illustration 3   Fraudulent Transfer
>
> A few days before filing a voluntary petition in bankruptcy and while Debtor was insolvent, Debtor gave Friend a $5,000 cash gift. The gift can be set aside (recovered from Friend) as a fraudulent transfer.

4.6.5 Trustee Can Disaffirm Preferences

The trustee has the power to set aside preferences. When the payment is "set aside," the payment is taken back from the creditor who received it and becomes part of the bankruptcy estate.

- **A Preferential Payment Is:**
  - a *transfer* made to or for the benefit of a creditor;
  - on account of an *antecedent debt* (i.e., already existing) of the debtor;
  - made within *90 days* prior to the filing of the petition (one year if the creditor is an insider, such as an officer of the debtor organization or a close relative of the debtor);
  - made while the debtor was *insolvent*; and
  - results in the creditor *receiving more than the creditor would have received* under the Bankruptcy Code.

> ### Pass Key
>
> Preferential payment is one of the most heavily tested issues when it comes to bankruptcy questions on the CPA Exam. Be sure to memorize the definition above and the explanations above. Understanding this material is one of the keys to your success.

Transfer

A transfer includes not only the payment of money or the giving of property, but also the giving of a security interest.

Illustration 4   Preferences

Deanna, a retailer, owes Carla money. A few days before Deanna filed her bankruptcy petition, Deanna gave Carla a security interest in all of Deanna's inventory, which Carla perfects. Carla's interest can be set aside as a preference.

Antecedent (Preexisting) Debt (Rather Than a Contemporaneous Exchange)

A payment is a preference only if it is for an antecedent (preexisting) debt. *A contemporaneous exchange for new value is not a preference.*

Illustration 5   Contemporaneous Exchange for Value

A few days before Deanna, a retailer, filed for bankruptcy, she received from Alex, a supplier, six cases of goods to be put into Deanna's inventory. Deanna paid for the goods in full on their arrival. There is no preference here; this is a contemporaneous exchange for value.

Pass Key

The exception for contemporaneous exchanges for new value has often been tested on past exams.

Insolvency: Presumed During 90 Days Preceding Bankruptcy

The debtor is presumed to be insolvent during the 90 days immediately preceding the date the bankruptcy petition is filed.

Receipt of Greater Share: Creditor Received More

A preference exists only if the creditor receives more than she would receive in a bankruptcy distribution. Therefore, payment to a *fully secured* creditor is not a preference, because the creditor would have received the collateral and been paid in full anyway.

Exceptions: Transfers That Cannot Be Set Aside by Trustee

- **Transfers in the Ordinary Course of Business**

  A transfer made to repay a debt that the debtor incurred in the ordinary course of business is *not* a voidable preference.

Illustration 6   Transfers in the Ordinary Course of Business

A regular monthly installment payment will not be set aside as a preference. Similarly, payment of a current utility bill or a current lease payment does not constitute a preference.

- **PMSI Perfected Within 30 Days:** A PMSI is not a voidable preference if it is perfected within 30 days after the debtor receives possession of the collateral, although it may be invalid under state law if not perfected within 20 days of the debtor's receiving possession.

- **Consumer Payments Under $600:** The trustee may not void payments or transfers of property of less than $600 by a debtor whose debts are primarily consumer debts.

- **Domestic Support Obligations:** Bona fide payments for domestic support obligations (e.g., spousal support or child support) are not voidable preferences.

4.7 Claims Against the Estate

Claims include all rights to payment from the debtor's estate.

- To have a claim allowed (i.e., a right of payment against the debtor's estate), unsecured creditors must file a proof of claim, and shareholders must file a proof of interest with the bankruptcy court.

- Unless someone objects, a filed claim or interest will automatically be allowed by the court. An unsecured creditor who fails to timely file a claim may not take part in the distribution of the debtor's estate.

- The general rule is that a perfected security interest passes through and survives bankruptcy even if the creditor does not file a proof of claim.

4.8 Miscellaneous

The trustee can also serve as a professional (e.g., tax preparer, accountant or lawyer) for the estate if the court approves.

A trustee serving as tax preparer for the estate may receive compensation as a professional in addition to the trustee's compensation, if a court approves.

Question 1	MCQ-01348

Under the liquidation provisions of Chapter 7 of the U.S. Bankruptcy Code, certain property acquired by the debtor after the filing of the petition becomes part of the bankruptcy estate. An example of such property is:

   a. Inheritances received by the debtor within 180 days after the filing of the petition.

   b. Child support payments received by the debtor within one year after the filing of the petition.

   c. Social Security payments received by the debtor within 180 days after the filing of the petition.

   d. Wages earned by the debtor within one year after the filing of the petition.

Question 2	MCQ-01367

Deft, CPA, is an unsecured creditor of Golf Co. for $18,000. Golf has a total of 10 creditors, all of whom are unsecured. Golf has not paid any of the creditors for three months. Under Chapter 11 of the Federal Bankruptcy Code, which of the following statements is correct?

    a. Golf may not be petitioned involuntarily into bankruptcy because there are fewer than 12 unsecured creditors.

    b. Golf may not be petitioned involuntarily into bankruptcy under the provisions of Chapter 11.

    c. Three unsecured creditors must join in the involuntary petition in bankruptcy.

    d. Deft may file an involuntary petition in bankruptcy against Golf.

NOTES

1 Features of a Chapter 7 Liquidation

The goal of federal bankruptcy law is to give an honest debtor a "fresh start" financially by discharging most debts owed by the debtor. In a liquidation, a bankruptcy trustee is appointed. The trustee collects all of the debtor's nonexempt property, liquidates it, and pays off all of the debtor's creditors. Most debts of an individual are discharged (that is, the debtor is relieved from personal liability for most debts) but certain debts survive bankruptcy.

1.1 Objections to Discharge

Creditors often want to prevent debtors from receiving a Chapter 7 discharge. The code provides two kinds of ammunition for such claims: objections to discharge and nondischargeable debts. The first type of ammunition destroys the entire Chapter 7 case—none of the debtor's debts will be discharged. The second type of ammunition prevents the discharge of specific debts. The following will prevent the debtor from receiving any discharge:

- **Debtor Not an Individual**

    Technically, only individuals (i.e., real people as opposed to artificial entities, such as corporations) can receive a discharge under Chapter 7. Artificial entities seeking relief under Chapter 7 usually are dissolved at the conclusion of the case, and so their debts are wiped out.

- **Fraudulent Transfers or Concealment of Property**

    The debtor is not entitled to a discharge if she transferred, destroyed, or concealed property in the year before or after the petition was filed with intent to hinder, delay, or defraud creditors.

- **Unjustifiably Failed to Keep Books and Records**

    The debtor is not entitled to a discharge if he unjustifiably concealed, falsified, or failed to keep or preserve adequate books and records from which the debtor's financial condition or business transactions might be ascertained.

- **Prior Discharge Within Eight Years**

    A debtor is entitled to only one discharge within an eight-year period. Eight years must elapse before another discharge can be granted.

- **Commission of a Bankruptcy Crime**

    In addition to constituting federal crimes, the following acts give rise to objections to discharge when committed knowingly and fraudulently in connection with the bankruptcy case:

    - Making a false oath or account;
    - Presenting or using a false claim;
    - Giving or receiving a bribe; or
    - Withholding records or documents.

- **Failure to Explain Loss of Assets**

    A debtor who is unable to explain satisfactorily the disappearance or loss of assets is not entitled to a discharge.

- **Refusal to Obey Orders or to Answer Questions**

    If the debtor refuses to obey a lawful order of the court, a discharge is denied.

Pass Key

The examiners sometimes ask what will prevent a party from getting a discharge in bankruptcy. Historically on the exam, the most often tested reasons are the first five above.

The choice that historically has appeared most often is failure to keep records.

1.2 Exceptions to Discharge

Certain debts *of an individual* are not discharged under Chapters 7 or 11. Those debts not discharged are called the "exceptions to discharge" and include the following:

Pass Key

It is important to remember that a bankruptcy case does not discharge all debts. The examiners often ask a broad question such as, "Which of the following is true under the Bankruptcy Code?" and one of the choices often is that "all debts of the debtor are discharged." This is not true. The following debts survive bankruptcy.

- **Taxes Due Within Three Years of Filing:** Most *tax claims* (federal, state, or local) are nondischargeable if the return for the tax was due within three years before the bankruptcy petition was filed.

- **Debts Incurred by Fraud, Embezzlement, or Larceny:** Liabilities for obtaining money, property, or services by false representation or *fraud*, or through embezzlement or larceny, are not dischargeable.

- **Luxury Goods:** Consumer debts incurred for *luxury goods* (e.g., boat, jewelry, etc.) are not dischargeable if the debts aggregate over $725 to a single creditor and are incurred within 90 days of the order for relief.

- **Open-Ended Credit to Consumers:** Cash advances obtained by a consumer under an *open-ended credit plan* are presumed to be nondischargeable if the debts are incurred within 70 days of the order for relief and exceed the aggregate amount of $1,000. Thus, if a consumer makes purchases on a credit card in an amount greater than $1,000 in the 70 days before bankruptcy, the debt will survive bankruptcy.

- **Debts Undisclosed in the Bankruptcy Petition:** Any *debt not scheduled or listed* by the debtor in time to permit the creditor to file a timely proof of claim is nondischargeable, unless the creditor had notice or actual knowledge of the bankruptcy.

- **Alimony, Maintenance, Support, and Settlements From Marital Separation:** Debts owed to the debtor's spouse, former spouse, or child (in or out of wedlock) for *alimony, maintenance, or support* are nondischargeable, as are property settlements arising out of a divorce decree or separation agreement.

- **Willful and Malicious Injury:** Liabilities arising from *willful* and *malicious* injury to another are not dischargeable. However, liabilities arising from negligent torts are dischargeable.

- **Operating a Vehicle While Intoxicated:** Judgments rendered against the debtor for death or personal injury incurred as a result of *operating a motor vehicle, aircraft, or vessel while legally intoxicated* survive the debtor's discharge.

- **Fines and Penalties:** Any obligation to pay a *fine, penalty, or forfeiture* owed to a governmental unit, such as a traffic fine, survives the debtor's discharge, as do claims for court costs.

- **Educational Loans:** An *educational loan* owed to a nonprofit institution of higher education or a student loan that is made, guaranteed, insured, or funded by a government agency or commercial entity is not dischargeable, unless it would impose an "undue hardship."

- **Denial of Discharge in a Prior Bankruptcy:** If a discharge was *denied in a prior bankruptcy* or a previous discharge was waived, debts that predate the prior bankruptcy are not dischargeable in a subsequent case. This exception does not apply if the basis for denial in the prior case was that the debtor received a discharge within eight years.

Pass Key

The examiners often ask what debts will not be discharged by a bankruptcy. The key to remembering the six nondischargeable debts that most commonly appear on the exam is the word **"WAFTED"**: **W**illful and malicious injury, **A**limony, **F**raud, **T**axes, **E**ducational loans, and **D**ebts undisclosed in the bankruptcy petition.

1.3   Reaffirmation of Discharged Debts

Sometimes a debtor does not want a particular debt discharged in bankruptcy (e.g., to maintain good relations with a particular creditor). The debtor may *reaffirm* such debts only if the agreement to reaffirm the debt was made *before* the granting of the discharge.

1.4   Revocation of Discharge

A creditor or trustee may request that a discharge be revoked for the following:

- The debtor *obtained the discharge fraudulently* and the party seeking revocation did not discover the fraud until after the discharge was granted;

- The debtor acquired property that would constitute property of the estate and *knowingly and fraudulently failed to disclose this fact*;

- The debtor *failed to obey a court order or answer material questions*; or

- The debtor has not given a satisfactory explanation for a failure to make documents available in connection with an audit that may be ordered by the United States Trustee or for a material misstatement in such documents.

1.5   Distribution of the Debtor's Estate: Payment and Priorities

Once the debtor's assets have been collected and liquidated, and all objections at that level have been disposed of, the trustee will distribute the assets of the estate. There are three basic categories of claimants, *paid in the following order*:

1. Secured claimants

2. Priority claimants (which includes nine subcategories)

3. General creditors who filed their claims on time

Payments are made in full to secured claimants to the extent of the value of the collateral securing their claims (claims in excess of the collateral are treated like claims of other general creditors). Whatever is left over then is used to pay first-priority claimants in full, then second-priority claimants in full, then third-priority claimants are paid, and so on. If money is left after paying all of the priority claimants, it is then split among the general creditors who filed claims on time. If there is not sufficient money to pay all creditors at a particular level, the creditors share pro rata.

Pass Key

The priority rules are perhaps the most heavily tested rules on the CPA Exam when it comes to bankruptcy issues. Your memorization of the order of payment and the dollar limitations specified below is key for success on the exam. Most important, though, remember that payments are made first to secured creditors to the extent of the value of the collateral securing their claims and that claims in excess of the collateral are treated like claims of other general creditors.

1.   First Priority: Support Obligations to Spouse and Children

First priority goes to claims for domestic support obligations that are owed to a spouse, former spouse, or child of the debtor on the date the petition is filed.

2.   Second Priority: Administrative Expenses

The expenses of a bankruptcy administration receive second priority. Bankruptcy administration expenses include costs of preserving the estate, trustee fees, filing fees, attorney and accountant fees, etc.

3.   Third Priority: Involuntary Case Gap Claims

Claims that accrue in the ordinary course of business after an involuntary petition is filed, but before the entering of the order for relief or appointment of a trustee, receive a third priority.

4.   Fourth Priority: Wage Claims up to $13,650

Employees who have claims for wages earned within 180 days prior to the filing of the petition receive a fourth priority. However, this priority is limited to $13,650 per employee. For example, if an employee is owed $16,000 for wages, $14,000 of which was earned within 180 days prior to bankruptcy, the employee would have a $13,650 priority claim and a $2,350 nonpriority claim.

5. **Fifth Priority: Employee Benefit Plans up to $13,650**

   Claims for contributions to employee benefit plans (e.g., health insurance or pension plans) receive a fifth-level priority if they arose within 180 days prior to bankruptcy. This priority may not exceed $13,650 per employee and is reduced by the amount paid to each employee as a fourth-priority wage claim.

Pass Key

Remember that there are three restrictions on priority payments for unpaid wages and unpaid employee benefit plans:

- Only unpaid wages and unpaid employee benefit plan expenses that arose within 180 days prior to the filing are entitled to a priority. Those that arose after filing are nonpriority claims.

- Only unpaid wages and unpaid employee benefits up to $13,650 receive a priority.

- The $13,650 priority for unpaid employee benefits is reduced by any amount paid to the employee for a priority wage claim.

6. **Sixth Priority: Grain Farmers and Fishermen up to $6,725**

   Claims of grain producers or U.S. fishermen against a debtor who operates a grain storage facility or a fish produce storage or processing facility have a sixth priority up to $6,725.

7. **Seventh Priority: Consumer Deposits up to $3,025**

   Consumer claims for a deposit made to a retail business prior to the retailer's bankruptcy are entitled to a seventh-level priority to the extent of $3,025 for each consumer. For example, if a consumer made a $3,500 deposit for furniture to be delivered, but the seller files a bankruptcy petition prior to delivery, the consumer is entitled to a $3,025 seventh-priority and a $475 nonpriority claim.

8. **Eighth Priority: Tax Claims**

   Most tax claims are entitled to an eighth-level priority.

9. **Ninth Priority: Personal Injury Claims Arising From Intoxicated Driving**

   Claims for death or personal injury arising from the operation of a motor vehicle or vessel by the debtor while the individual was legally intoxicated have a ninth priority.

Pass Key

The examiners frequently ask questions requiring candidates to prioritize debts. Remember that properly perfected secured creditors are paid up to the value of their collateral. They are unsecured, nonpriority creditors for any deficiency. The order of payment for the nine priority creditors can be learned with the mnemonic **SAG-WEG-CTI**.

- **S** = **Support** obligations to spouse and children
- **A** = **Administrative** expenses of bankruptcy proceeding
- **G** = **Gap** creditors
- **W** = **Wages** up to $13,650 for each employee if earned within 180 days prior to filing
- **E** = **Employee** benefit plan contributions up to $13,650 for each employee, reduced by wage claims, if earned within 180 days prior to filing
- **G** = **Grain** farmers' and fishermen's claims up to $6,725
- **C** = **Consumer** deposits for goods paid for but not delivered up to $3,025
- **T** = **Taxes**
- **I** = **Injury** claims caused by intoxicated driving

10. Nonpriority Claims

Any money that is left after paying the secured creditors and the priority claimants is used to pay the general unsecured creditors who timely filed, pro rata. If any assets are remaining after paying general creditors who timely filed, creditors who filed late receive payment.

Example 1 | Calculation of Cash Distribution

Facts: Rivers has been involuntarily petitioned into bankruptcy. The following are claims and expenses against Rivers' estate:

Claims and expenses	
Fees earned by bankruptcy trustee	$15,000
Claims by secured creditors	5,000
Fees earned by attorneys for bankruptcy estate	10,000
Claims by Rivers' employees for wages earned within 180 days of the filing of the bankruptcy petition	2,000

Required: Calculate the amount to be distributed to the trustee if cash available for distribution is $15,000.

(continued)

(continued)

Solution:

Total cash available for distribution	$15,000
Less: secured claims	(5,000)
Cash available for priority claimants	**$10,000**

Because total administrative expenses ($15,000 trustee fee plus $10,000 attorneys' fee = $25,000) exceed cash available ($10,000), the cash available is prorated between the administrative claimants.

Since wage claims are a lower category, the employees would receive nothing. The trustee's distribution is calculated as follows:

$$\text{Trustee's distribution} = \frac{\text{Trustee's claim}}{\text{Total administrative expense}} \times \text{Remaining cash available}$$

$$= \frac{\$15,000}{\$25,000} \times \$10,000$$

$$= \frac{3}{5} \times \$10,000$$

$$= \$6,000$$

Pass Key

It is important to understand the relationship between the exceptions to discharge and payment priorities. Some items are both a priority and an exception; other items are one, but not the other. Payment is made according to the priority rules (without regard to whether the debt is excepted from discharge). After all possible payments have been made, any remaining debts are discharged unless they are one of the exceptions to discharge. In some cases, a debt that is an exception to discharge will have been paid in the distribution process. For example:

- If creditors are paid in full through the eighth priority (tax claims, etc.), then the fact that a tax claim is an exception to discharge is irrelevant because it has been paid.

- If, however, payment is made only through the sixth priority, then any unpaid seventh priority (consumer deposits) claims are discharged (because they are not on the exception list). Any unpaid eighth-priority (tax) claims are not discharged because they are an exception to discharge.

2   Features of Reorganization Cases Under Chapter 11

2.1   Creation of Creditors' Committee

In a Chapter 11 case, shortly after the order for relief is effective, a committee of *unsecured* creditors is appointed, usually consisting of willing persons holding the *seven largest unsecured claims* against the debtor.

A person engaged in business other than real estate with debts not exceeding about $2.6 million can elect to be treated as a small business. Such a debtor can request that a creditors' committee not be appointed.

2.2   Equity Security Holders' Committee

If the debtor is a corporation, an equity security holders' (i.e., stockholders) committee may be appointed consisting of the seven largest holders of the equity securities to ensure that the equity security holders receive adequate representation. The committees can consult with the debtor, investigate the debtor's finances, participate in preparing the reorganization plan, etc.

2.3   Debtor Generally Remains in Possession

In a Chapter 11 reorganization case, committees are appointed to consult with and advise the debtor, but a trustee generally is *not* appointed.

Instead, the debtor remains in possession of the debtor's assets because the debtor is presumed to be in the best position to run the business.

Pass Key

The examiners like to ask about the trustee in a Chapter 11 case. Remember the general rule that a trustee usually is not appointed in a Chapter 11 case; the debtor usually remains in possession of the estate's assets.

2.4   Chapter 11 Reorganization Plan

The debtor may file a reorganization plan under Chapter 11 any time during the bankruptcy case. Unless a trustee has been appointed, the debtor has an *exclusive right* to file a plan during the first *120 days* after the order for relief is effective. Other interested parties (e.g., creditors) may file a plan if:

- a trustee has been appointed;

- the debtor has not filed a plan within 120 days after the order for relief became effective; or

- the debtor has filed a plan but has not obtained the acceptance of every impaired class (e.g., creditors whose claims are reduced by the plan or will be paid later than contracted for) within *180 days* after entry of the order for relief.

2.4.1   Contents of the Plan

A Chapter 11 plan must, among other things:

- classify all claims (e.g., secured, first priority, second priority, impaired, unimpaired, etc.);

- describe the treatment to be accorded each impaired class;

- treat each claimant within a particular class identically; and

- establish ways to implement the plan.

2.4.2   Acceptance of the Plan by Creditors

- Any creditor or equity security holder who has filed a claim against the debtor's estate must be given an opportunity to *accept* or reject the plan.

- A class of impaired claims is deemed accepted if it is accepted by creditors holding at least *two-thirds in amount* and *more than one-half in number* of the allowed claims.

- A class of impaired interests (e.g., equity security holders) is deemed to have accepted the plan if it is accepted by equity security holders having at least two-thirds in amount of the allowed claims.

2.4.3   Confirmation of the Plan by Court

- The court will confirm the plan if it meets certain conditions, such as being accepted by all impaired classes, providing for payment in full for priority administrative expenses and gap claims, and the plan is feasible (i.e., has a reasonable chance of succeeding).

- A plan can be confirmed by the court even if it is not accepted by *all* impaired classes if at least one impaired class has accepted, and the court finds that the plan is not unfairly discriminatory and is fair and equitable with respect to any dissenting impaired classes. This is called a *cram down*.

2.5   Effects of Confirmation

- A confirmed Chapter 11 plan is binding on all creditors, equity security holders, and the debtor regardless of whether they accept the plan.

- Generally, once confirmed the debtor pays debts according to the plan.

- Unless the order provides otherwise, confirmation discharges the debtor from all pre-confirmation debts (except that debts not discharged under Chapter 7 are also not discharged under Chapter 11).

- Confirmation also terminates the automatic stay.

3   Features of a Chapter 15 Case

3.1   Commencement of Ancillary Proceeding

A Chapter 15 ancillary case is commenced by a "foreign representative" filing a petition for recognition of a "foreign proceeding." This operates as the principal door of a foreign representative to U.S. courts.

- The petition must show the existence of the foreign proceeding and the appointment and authority of the foreign representative.

- After notice and a hearing, the U.S. court is authorized to issue an order recognizing the foreign proceeding as either a "foreign main proceeding" (i.e., a country where the debtor's main interests are located) or a "foreign non-main proceeding" (i.e., a country other than one where the debtor's main interests are located).

Upon recognition of a foreign main proceeding, the automatic stay and other provisions of the Bankruptcy Code take effect in the United States.

The U.S. court is authorized to issue preliminary relief as soon as the petition for recognition is filed.

3.2   Foreign Representative's Powers

The foreign representative is authorized to operate the debtor's business. Once recognized, a foreign representative may seek additional relief from the bankruptcy court and is authorized to bring a full-blown (as opposed to ancillary) bankruptcy case under Chapters 7 or 11. The foreign representative may participate in a pending U.S. insolvency case and may intervene in any other U.S. case in which the debtor is a party.

3.3   Prohibition Against Discrimination

Chapter 15 prohibits discrimination against foreign creditors (except certain foreign government and tax claims, which may be governed by treaty).

3.4   Requirements of Notice and Cooperation

Chapter 15 requires notice to foreign creditors concerning a U.S. bankruptcy case, including notice of the right to file claims. Under Chapter 15, U.S. courts and trustees must "cooperate to the maximum extent possible" with foreign courts and foreign representatives.

Question 1	MCQ-01382

Which of the following types of claims would be paid first in the distribution of a bankruptcy estate under the liquidation provisions of Chapter 7 of the U.S. Bankruptcy Code if the petition was filed July 15, Year 3?

    a. A secured debt properly perfected on March 20, Year 3.

    b. Inventory purchased and delivered August 1, Year 3.

    c. Employee wages due April 30, Year 3.

    d. Federal tax lien filed June 30, Year 3.

Question 2	MCQ-01373

Under the reorganization provisions of Chapter 11 of the U.S. Bankruptcy Code, after a reorganization plan is confirmed, and a final decree closing the proceedings entered, which of the following events usually occurs?

    a. A reorganized corporate debtor will be liquidated.

    b. A reorganized corporate debtor will be discharged from all debts except as otherwise provided in the plan and applicable law.

    c. A trustee will continue to operate the debtor's business.

    d. A reorganized individual debtor will not be allowed to continue in the same business.

1 Introduction

The two major securities acts that you must know are the Securities Act of 1933 and the Securities Exchange Act of 1934. The 1933 act regulates original issuances of securities, and the 1934 act regulates purchases and sales after initial issuance.

1.1 Security Defined (Any Investment Contract)

A good rule of thumb for determining whether something is a security is to ask whether the investor expects to take part in the management of the business. If the investor is passive—i.e., *relies solely on the management of others to make money*—the investment most likely is a security.

- Stocks, bonds, debentures, oil well interests, stock options, collateral trust certificates, warrants, and *limited* partnership interests are deemed securities and investment contracts.

- Certificates of deposit and general partnership interests are generally *not* deemed to be securities. In the case of general partners, each partner is expected to participate in running the business.

2 The Securities Act of 1933

2.1 Introduction

2.1.1 Purpose: Provide Investors With Sufficient Investment Information

The goal of the Securities Act of 1933 is to *assure that investors have sufficient information* on which to make an informed investment decision. It accomplishes this goal by requiring most issuers to register new issues of securities with the Securities and Exchange Commission (SEC) (unless an exemption applies) and *provide prospectuses* containing material information regarding the securities to prospective investors. The SEC does not guarantee the accuracy of this information, evaluate the offering's financial merits, or give assurances against loss.

Pass Key

A number of questions on the CPA Examination have asked about the purpose of the 1933 act. Remember that the SEC does not assure the accuracy of the information filed or evaluate the financial merits of the securities being offered. It merely assures the presence of information necessary for investors to make informed decisions.

2.1.2 Those Required to Register: Issuers, Underwriters, and Dealers

The registration requirements of the 1933 act only apply to issuers, underwriters, and dealers.

- **Issuer:** The entity whose securities are being sold.
- **Underwriter:** An intermediary who sells an issuer's securities to the general public or to dealers.
- **Dealer:** One who sells or trades securities on a full- or part-time basis.

2.2 The Registration Statement

Most securities cannot be sold unless they are first registered with the SEC. The registration statement consists of two parts. Part I is the prospectus. Part II contains detailed information regarding the securities to be issued.

2.2.1 Part I: The Prospectus (a Written Offer to Sell Securities)

In broad terms, the 1933 act defines "prospectus" as any written, radio, or television offer to sell securities. The prospectus in Part I of the registration statement (called a "statutory prospectus") summarizes important information contained in Part II. Unless an issuance is exempt, each investor must receive a copy of the prospectus *before or contemporaneous with* every sale of the security.

2.2.2 Part II: Information That Must Be Included About the Securities Being Issued

- **Audited Balance Sheet and Profit and Loss Statement**

    The registration statement must include a balance sheet dated not more than *90 days* before the filing, and a profit and loss statement of the issuer's net income or loss for the preceding *five years*. The financial statements must be *certified by a public accounting firm* registered with the Public Company Accounting Oversight Board.

- **Other Material Facts Requiring Disclosure**

    The registration statement must also include a description of the issuer's business and the following (if available):

    - The *names and addresses* of the directors, officers, underwriters, and shareholders who own 10 percent or more of the company's shares.
    - The amount of stock and debt the issuer has outstanding.
    - The *principal purposes for which the offering proceeds will be used*.
    - Anything that might *affect the value of the securities* being issued (e.g., absence of an earnings history, pending litigation, etc.).

2.2.3 Shelf Registrations: Registration Statement for Future Issuances

Many issuers are almost constantly involved in issuing new securities. It would be helpful if they could prepare just one registration statement for all securities that they will offer in the future (so-called *shelf registration*). Although generally prohibited, shelf registration is permitted if the issuer has continuously filed under the 1934 act for one year (i.e., not a first-time issuer) and the information is continuously updated.

2.2.4 Effective 20 Days After Filing

The registration statement becomes effective on the *20th day* after its filing with the SEC unless the SEC issues a refusal or stop order.

2.2.5 Blue Sky Laws (State Laws Governing Stock Sales)

State laws governing stock sales are known as "blue sky" laws. However, much of state blue sky law has been preempted by federal law.

2.3   Timetable of Sales Activity

2.3.1   30 Days Before Registration (Prefiling Period): No Sales Activity Allowed

Generally, no sales activity is allowed within the 30 days before registration, unless the issuance is exempt. However, an issuer is permitted to negotiate with an underwriter. Communications made more than 30 days before a registration generally do not constitute sales activity.

2.3.2   After Registration but Before Effectiveness (Waiting Period)

There is a 20-day waiting period between registration and the filing date. Sales are generally prohibited during this period, but some sales activities are allowed:

- *Oral offers* to sell (but no written offers to sell) can be made.

- *Tombstone ads* can be made (ad identifies the security, its price, and who will execute orders).

- Preliminary *(red herring)* prospectuses can be made (similar to the statutory prospectuses, but contain a statement in red ink that they are not yet final).

- *Summary prospectuses* are allowed (but these are outmoded and seldom used).

2.3.3   After Effective Date (Post-Effective Period)

After the registration is effective (*20 days* after filing or as the SEC directs), the securities may be sold. All investors must receive a prospectus *before* or with the sale.

2.3.4   Special Rules for Some 1934 Act Reporting Companies

- **WKSIs:** There are special rules for seasoned issuers and well-known seasoned issuers (or WKSIs, pronounced wick-sees). These rules have not been tested beyond the general notion that the normal timetable does not apply to WKSIs and that there is a document called a "free writing" prospectus.

- **Free Writing Prospectus:** WKSIs and seasoned issuers may issue a free writing prospectus. Such a prospectus must include a legend that a registration statement has been filed and advising how a reader can obtain a preliminary prospectus. Copies of a free writing prospectus must be filed with the SEC before first use and must be retained for three years.

2.4   Exemptions From Registration

Not every sale of securities is covered by the 1933 act. The act has two types of exemptions: securities exemptions (securities issued by certain types of issuers) and transaction exemptions (securities issued in certain types of transactions).

2.4.1   Securities Exemptions

Section 3 of the 1933 act specifically exempts the following securities from the registration requirements; the following securities never have to be registered:

- Securities issued by banks and savings and loans (e.g., CDs)

- Securities issued by not-for-profit organizations

- Securities issued by the government (except for certain securities issued for proprietary rather than governmental purposes)

- Securities of regulated common carriers (e.g., securities issued by railroads)

- Short-term commercial paper (notes, bonds, etc.) with a maturity date of nine months or less

- Insurance policies (but stocks, bonds, and similar securities of insurance companies are not exempt)

- Securities issued under Chapter 11 of the Bankruptcy Code

- Securities issued by a church plan or similar entity that is not an investment company

Pass Key

The examiners often ask about exemptions from the registration requirements of the 1933 act. Remember that all issues of securities must be registered unless the securities are exempt. Favorite securities exemptions on the exam appear to be securities of charitable organizations and bonds issued by municipalities for governmental purposes.

2.4.2 Transaction Exemptions

Transaction exemptions depend on the nature of the offering. Unlike the securities exemptions, which exempt a security forever, the transaction exemptions exist only for the transaction in question. If the securities are resold, they must be registered unless they qualify for another exemption.

- **Casual Sales Exempt: Not an Issuer, Underwriter, or Dealer**

  Registration requirements apply only to issuers, underwriters, and dealers. Sales by others are considered casual sales and are exempt.

Illustration 1   Casual Sale of Securities

Dee, a practicing CPA, owns 10,000 shares of General Motors stock and decides to sell them. She need not register. This is a casual sale. Dee is not the issuer, an underwriter, or a dealer.

- **Exchanges With Existing Holders and Corporate Reorganizations**

  The 1933 act provides an exemption when an issuer exchanges securities with its existing holders, provided no commission is paid (e.g., stock dividends and stock splits). There is also an exemption for government-approved exchanges that occur as a result of corporate reorganization.

- **Intrastate Sales**

  Section 3(a)(11) of the 1933 act provides an exemption for securities offered and sold only to persons who are residents of the issuer's state (i.e., the state in which it is doing business). The SEC has adopted two rules to implement this exemption: Rule 147 and Rule 147A.

  - **Rule 147**

    Under Rule 147, the entire issue must be offered and sold only to residents of that state; the issuer must do at least 80 percent of its business in that state; purchasers cannot resell the securities for six months to nonresidents of that state; and general solicitation is prohibited.

  - **Rule 147A**

    —Like Rule 147, Rule 147A is intended to provide a transaction exemption for sales of securities made in only one state.

    —However, Rule 147A recognizes the existence of the Internet and allows offers to be made through general Internet advertising, as long as the offer includes a prominent disclosure that sales will be made only to residents of the state of the offering.

—Moreover, unlike Rule 147, Rule 147A does not require issuers to be residents of the state of the offering.

—Like Rule 147, Rule 147A provides that a purchaser cannot resell the securities to a nonresident for six months.

2.4.3 Private Offering Exemptions: Regulation D

Regulation D exempts "private" offerings, and the SEC has two private offering exemptions under Regulation D: Rules 504 and 506 (there was a Rule 505 exemption as well, but that rule has been repealed). The exemptions share certain general conditions, but each also has specific conditions.

General Conditions That Apply to Rules 504 and 506

- **General Solicitation Sometimes Prohibited: Limitation of General Advertisements**

  Regulation D is intended for private offerings. Thus, the regulation has a general rule prohibiting general advertising of the securities sold under Regulation D. However, there are exceptions.

- **Immediate Resale to Public Prohibited**

  The purchasers may not immediately reoffer securities issued under Regulation D to the public. The issuer must insure that purchasers will hold for long-term investment (one year or more), not resale. Before the year is up, such securities are "restricted," and the buyer cannot resell them unless the resale falls under Regulation D or another exemption.

- **Bad Actor Disqualification**

  Issuers are disqualified from using Rules 504 and 506 (as well as Regulation Crowdfunding, discussed below) if they are affiliated with "covered persons" who have been convicted of, or are subject to court or administrative sanctions for, securities fraud or violations of similar laws (such as postal fraud laws), typically within the previous five years.

  —**Covered Persons Defined**

    The term *covered persons* includes: the issuer, including its predecessors and affiliated issuers; directors, officers, general partners, or managing members of the issuer; beneficial owners of 20 percent or more of the issuer's outstanding voting equity securities, calculated on the basis of voting power; promoters connected with the issuer in any capacity at the time of sale; and persons compensated for soliciting investors, including the general partners, directors, officers or managing members of any such solicitor.

  —**Good Faith and Good Cause Exceptions**

    An issuer will not be disqualified from making an offering under Rules 504 or 506 (or Regulation Crowdfunding) if the issuer can demonstrate that it did not know and, in the exercise of reasonable care, could not have known that a covered person with a disqualifying event participated in the offering. An issuer may also seek a waiver from disqualification from the Securities and Exchange Commission upon a showing of good cause that disqualification is not necessary under the circumstances.

- **SEC Must Be Informed Within 15 Days**

  The SEC must be notified of the issuance of securities under Regulation D within 15 days after the first sale.

■ **Requirements of Rule 504: $5 Million Limit**

To be exempt under Rule 504, the issuance of securities *may not exceed $5 million* within a 12-month period. Rule 504 has *no limitation on the number or type of purchasers* and generally *does not require any specific disclosure* to investors prior to the sale. If the Rule 504 offering is registered under state law, the general prohibition against general advertising does not apply.

■ **Requirements of Rule 506: Unlimited Dollar Amount**

Under Rule 506, there is no limit on the amount (dollar value) of stock that may be sold.

- Securities issued under Rule 506 may be sold to *any number of accredited investors and 35 or fewer unaccredited but sophisticated investors* . An accredited investor is one such as an institutional investor, a bank, officers or directors of the issuer, or an individual with a four-year average net worth of at least $1 million, excluding the value of the individual's home. An investor is sophisticated if the issuer reasonably believes that the unaccredited investor has sufficient knowledge and experience in financial matters to be capable of evaluating the risks of the investment.

- Because of the limitation on unaccredited purchasers, the issuer must also make reasonable efforts to ensure that the purchasers are buying for themselves and not for others.

- If only accredited investors purchase, no disclosure is required and the prohibition on general advertising does not apply if the issuer takes reasonable steps to verify that the purchasers are accredited. If there are any unaccredited investors, *all* investors must be given at least an annual report containing audited financial statements.

Pass Key

The examiners often try to trick you with the 35 unaccredited investor limit. Watch for fact patterns that state that Regulation D offerings cannot be made to more than 35 investors. Such a choice is incorrect because generally there is no limit on the number of unaccredited investors under Rule 504. Moreover, the 35 investor limit under Rule 506 applies only to unaccredited investors—there can be any number of accredited investors. Note also that the limitation goes to the number of actual purchasers and not to the number of offerees.

Summary Chart: Regulation D		
	Rule 504	*Rule 506*
Is general advertising allowed?	Sometimes	Sometimes
Notice required to SEC?	15 days	15 days
Reoffers to public prohibited?	Yes	Yes
Dollar limitation	$5 million	None
Limits on unaccredited buyers?	No limit	Up to 35, who must be sophisticated
Limits on accredited buyers?	No limit	No limit

2.4.4   Regulation Crowdfunding

▪ **Introduction**

Regulation Crowdfunding provides a transaction exemption for issuances of securities made through a crowdfunding process (widespread Internet solicitations of small amounts from numerous investors).

▪ **Issuer Limits**

Only issuers with assets of $25 million or less are eligible, and an issuer may not sell more than $1.07 million in securities under Regulation Crowdfunding within a 12-month period.

▪ **Investor Limits**

No investor may invest in aggregate more than $107,000 in Regulation Crowdfunding offerings within a 12-month period.

- **Income or Net Worth Less Than $107,000**

  If an investor's annual income or net worth is less than $107,000, then the investor's investment in any single Regulation Crowdfunding offering is limited to the *greater* of:

  1. $2,200; or

  2. 5 percent of the *lesser* of the investor's annual income or net worth.

- **Income and Net Worth of $107,000 or More**

  If an investor's annual income *and* net worth both are equal to or greater than $107,000, then the investor's investment limit in any single Regulation Crowdfunding offering is 10 percent of the *lesser* of the investor's annual income or net worth.

- Spouses may calculate net worth and income jointly.

▪ **Transaction Must Be Through One Online Intermediary**

Each Regulation Crowdfunding offering must be exclusively conducted through one online platform. Issuers may rely on the intermediary to determine that the aggregate amount of securities purchased by an investor does not cause the investor to exceed the investment limits unless the issuer actually knows that an investment would cause the investor to exceed the investment limits.

▪ **Ineligibility**

Certain companies are not eligible to use the Regulation Crowdfunding exemption, including:

1. Non-U.S. companies;

2. Companies that already are Exchange Act reporting companies;

3. Companies that are disqualified under Regulation Crowdfunding's disqualification rules (discussed below);

4. Companies that have failed to comply with the annual reporting requirements under Regulation Crowdfunding during the two years immediately preceding the filing of the offering statement; and

5. Companies that have no specific business plan or have indicated that their business plan is to engage in a merger or acquisition with an unidentified company or companies.

Required Disclosures

An issuer conducting a Regulation Crowdfunding offering must electronically file a Form C *offering statement* with the SEC and the intermediary facilitating the offering, which must include:

1. Information about officers, directors, and owners of 20 percent or more of the issuer;

2. A description of the issuer's business and the use of proceeds from the offering;

3. The price to the public of the securities or the method for determining the price;

4. The target offering amount, the deadline to reach the target offering amount, and whether the issuer will accept investments in excess of the target offering amount;

5. Related-party transactions; and

6. A discussion of the issuer's financial condition and financial statements.

Financial Statement Requirements

For Issuers Offering $107,000 or Less

Financial statements of the issuer and information from the issuer's federal income tax returns, *certified by the principal executive officer*. However, if financial statements that have been reviewed or audited by an independent public accountant are available, the issuer must provide those, in which case, the financial statements will not need to include the information reported on the issuer's federal income tax returns or the certification of the principal executive officer.

For Issuers Offering More Than $107,000 but Not More Than $535,000

Financial statements *reviewed by an independent public accountant*. However, if financial statements of the issuer are available that have been audited by an independent public accountant, the issuer must provide those financial statements instead and will not need to include the reviewed financial statements.

Issuers Offering More Than $535,000

— **For First-Time Regulation Crowdfunding Issuers:** Financial statements *reviewed by an independent public accountant*, unless audited financial statements of the issuer are available.

— **For Issuers That Have Previously Sold Securities in Reliance on Regulation Crowdfunding:** Financial statements *audited by an independent public accountant*.

Duty to Update

An offering that has not yet been completed or terminated must be updated on Form C/A to disclose material changes or additions. When an offering is updated, the issuer must reconfirm outstanding investment commitments within five business days or the investors' commitments will be considered canceled.

Progress Updates

An issuer must provide an update on its progress toward meeting the target offering amount within five business days after reaching 50 percent and 100 percent of its target offering amount. However, if the intermediary provides frequent target updates on its platform, then the issuer will need to file only a final Form C-U to disclose the total amount of securities sold in the offering.

Annual Reports

An issuer that sold securities in a Regulation Crowdfunding offering must provide an annual report on Form C-AR no later than 120 days after the end of its fiscal year. The annual report must include information similar to what is required in the offering statement, but neither an audit nor a review of the financial statements is required.

Limits on Advertising and Promoters

An issuer may not advertise the terms of a Regulation Crowdfunding offering except in a notice that directs investors to the intermediary's platform and includes no more than the following information:

1. A statement that the issuer is conducting an offering pursuant to Section 4(a)(6) of the Securities Act, the name of the intermediary through which the offering is being conducted, and a link directing the potential investor to the intermediary's platform;

2. The terms of the offering, which means the amount of securities offered, the nature of the securities, the price of the securities, and the closing date of the offering period; and

3. The name of the issuer of the security; the address, phone number, and website of the issuer; the e-mail address of a representative of the issuer; and a brief description of the business of the issuer.

An issuer *may* communicate with investors and potential investors about the terms of the offering through the intermediary's platform. The issuer must identify itself as the issuer and persons acting on behalf of the issuer must identify their affiliation with the issuer in all communications on the intermediary's platform.

An issuer is allowed to compensate others to promote its crowdfunding offerings through communication channels provided by an intermediary, but only if the issuer takes reasonable steps to ensure that the promoter clearly discloses the compensation with each communication.

Restrictions on Resale

Securities purchased in a crowdfunding transaction generally cannot be resold for a period of *one year*, unless the securities are transferred:

1. To the issuer of the securities;

2. To an "accredited investor";

3. As part of a registered offering; or

4. To a member of the purchaser's family or the equivalent, to a trust controlled by the purchaser, or in connection with the death or divorce of the purchaser or other similar circumstance.

Bad Actor Disqualification

The same "bad actor" rules discussed under Rules 504 and 506, above, apply to offerings under Regulation Crowdfunding.

2.4.5 Regulation A (Simplified Filing)

■ **Introduction**

Regulation A was modified in 2015, and the modified regulation is often referred to as Regulation A+. Unlike Regulation D, Regulation A is not a registration exemption, but rather is a simplified form of registration designed to allow small companies to make public offerings more quickly and with less cost than is required using full registration. Companies using Regulation A file an *offering statement*, which consists of a *notification* and an *offering circular*. Companies may "test the waters" (TTW) first before filing, if offers are preceded or accompanied by a *preliminary offering circular*.

■ **Companies That May Not Use Regulation A**

Regulation A is intended to allow small companies to make initial public offerings. The following companies may not use Regulation A:

1. SEC reporting companies;

2. Companies planning to merge with or acquire an unidentified company;

3. Companies seeking to sell interests in oil, gas, or other mineral rights; and

4. Companies disqualified by the SEC.

■ **Two Tiers Under Regulation A**

There are two offering tiers under Regulation A: Tier 1 and Tier 2. Similarities and differences are summarized in the following chart:

	Tier 1	Tier 2
Dollar limitations	Up to $20 million within a 12-month period; not more than $6 million of the offers to sell can be from security holders who are affiliates of the issuer	Up to $50 million within a 12-month period; not more than $15 million of the offers to sell can be from security holders who are affiliates of the issuer
Investor limitations	None	Unaccredited investors may not invest more than the greater of 10 percent of their income or 10 percent of their net worth; unaccredited entities may not invest more than 10 percent of their revenue or assets, whichever is greater
States may require review	Yes; in coordination with SEC review	No; state review is preempted by Regulation A
Is general solicitation allowed?	Yes	Yes
Must financials be audited?	No, just "reviewed"	Yes (audited financials and balance sheets from the past two years are required)
Must filings be updated?	No	Yes (annual, semiannual, and current event reports must be filed)

2.5   Liability Under the 1933 Act

2.5.1   In General: Liability Under Sections 11, 12, and 17

■   **Section 11: Civil Liability for Misstatement**

Section 11 imposes civil liability for misstatements, whether or not intentional, in registration statements.

■   **Section 12: Civil Antifraud Section of the 1933 Act**

Section 12 imposes civil liability if a required registration was not made; if a prospectus was not given to all investors or if materially false statements were made or omitted in connection with sales or offers to sell. The immediate purchaser may sue for damages or for rescission (i.e., the purchaser may sell the security back to the issuer and recover the price paid). The purchaser need not prove scienter or reliance (which will be discussed below).

■   **Section 17: Criminal Antifraud Section of the 1933 Act**

Section 17 imposes criminal penalties against anyone who uses any type of fraud in connection with the issuance of a security. Section 17 is enforced by the SEC and prosecuted by the U.S. Department of Justice.

2.5.2   Section 11 Liability

Examiners have focused their attention on the provisions of Section 11.

■   **Elements of a Section 11 Cause of Action**

Section 11 makes *anyone* who signs a registration statement liable for all damages caused by *any* misstatement of material fact in the registration statement. A person wishing to sue under Section 11 need only show:

- The plaintiff *acquired the stock* (need not be the initial purchaser).

- The plaintiff *suffered a loss* (i.e., suffered damages).

- The registration statement contained a *material misrepresentation or material omission of fact.*

Note that the plaintiff need not prove an intent to deceive, or negligence, or reliance on the part of the defendant. Finally, note that damages are the only remedy—rescission is not available.

Pass Key

Section 11 is a heavily tested issue. The key is to remember that the plaintiff need only prove that he or she acquired the stock; suffered a loss; and a material misstatement or material omission of fact. The plaintiff need not prove any type of intent (scienter) or negligence. Neither must the plaintiff prove reliance on the false statement.

■   **Who May Be Liable?**

Anyone who signs a registration statement may be liable under Section 11. Independent CPAs audit the financial statements in a registration statement and attest to their accuracy. Thus, the signing CPA is liable for material misstatements in the registration statement that result in loss.

Illustration 2   Who Is Liable?

While conducting an audit, Annie, CPA, failed to detect material misstatements included in the client's financial statements. Annie's unqualified opinion was included in the financial statements in the registration statement for a public offering of securities. Annie knew that the financial statements would be used for this purpose. Penny purchases the securities and incurs damages. Penny can sue Annie for damages.

■ **Due Diligence Defense**

Defendants, other than issuers, are not liable if they can prove that they used *due diligence* (called the due diligence defense). Due diligence means that the defendant had reasonable grounds to believe the facts in the registration statement were true and no material facts were omitted (e.g., an auditor can defend that he or she complied with GAAS).

Pass Key

The due diligence defense has often been tested , especially with regard to the activities of CPAs.

■ **Misstatement Did Not Cause Plaintiff's Damages**

It also is a defense to liability under Section 11 if the defendant can prove that the misstatement did not cause the plaintiff's damages. This includes cases when the misstatement was not material or when the plaintiff knew of the untruth or omission in the statement at the time she purchased her securities.

3   The Securities Exchange Act of 1934

3.1   Introduction

While the Securities Act of 1933 is concerned with the initial issuance of securities, the 1934 Securities Exchange Act is concerned with exchanges (e.g., sales, purchases, etc.) of securities after they are issued.

The 1934 act has registration and reporting provisions that apply only to certain companies and antifraud provisions that apply to all purchasers and sellers, regardless of registration. The SEC can seek suspension or revocation of a company's registered securities for violation of the 1934 act's registration or reporting requirements. Note, however, that prosecution for criminal violations of the 1934 act are undertaken by the Department of Justice and not by the SEC.

3.2   Registration Requirements

The 1934 act requires the following to register with the SEC:

■ Any companies whose shares are traded on a national exchange.

■ Companies that have more than $10 million in assets and at least 2,000 shareholders, in any outstanding class.

- Companies that have more than $10 million in assets and at least 500 shareholders who are not accredited, in any outstanding class.

- National stock exchanges, brokers, and dealers.

Pass Key

On past exams, conditions that subject a corporation to the reporting requirements of the Securities Exchange Act of 1934 have been a key issue. Be sure to memorize the information above.

3.2.1 Information Required in Registration Statement

The registration statement must include the company's financial structure; nature of its business and outstanding securities; the names and remuneration of directors, officers, underwriters, and 10 percent or more shareholders; outstanding options; and material contracts. The registration statement must also include financial statements audited by a public accounting firm registered with the Public Company Accounting Oversight Board.

3.2.2 Exemptions

Securities of investment companies, savings and loans, and charitable organizations are exempt.

Pass Key

Examiners frequently ask about *reporting companies*, those companies required to register under the 1934 act. Remember that registration is required if the shares are sold on a national exchange. Registration is equally required if the company has (i) at least 2,000 shareholders or at least 500 unaccredited shareholders; and (ii) more than $10 million in assets.

3.3   Reporting Requirements

3.3.1   Companies Required to Report

Two categories of companies are required to make reports. These companies are referred to as *reporting companies*.

- All companies required to register under the 1934 act must report, as discussed above.

- Any issuer that must register under the 1933 act must also report.

3.3.2 Periodic Business Reports

Companies registered under the 1933 act or the 1934 act are required to file the following *periodic reports*:

- *Form 10-K* (*Form 10-KSB* for small businesses) is a required report that must be filed annually within 60 days (for large corporations—90 days for small businesses) of the end of the fiscal year. It must contain material facts concerning management or otherwise affecting the value of the company's securities and financial statements certified by independent accountants.

- *Form 10-Q* (*Form 10-QSB* for small businesses) is a quarterly report filed within 40 days for large corporations (45 days for small ones) of the end of the first three quarters of each fiscal year. It must contain reviews of interim financial information by independent CPAs.

- *Form 8-K* must be filed within four days after a major change in the company, such as a change in control, disposition of major assets, change in officers or directors, resignation of directors, etc.

3.3.3 5 Percent or More Owners

Any person acquiring 5 percent or more beneficial ownership in any equity security registered under the 1934 act must file a report with the SEC, the issuer, and the exchange on which the security is traded. The report must include background information about the purchaser, the source of her funds, and her purpose in buying.

3.3.4 Tender Offers

A tender offer is an offer to all shareholders to purchase stock for a specific price for a specified period of time. Any party making a tender offer to purchase 5 percent or more of the shares of a class of securities registered under the 1934 act must file a report with the SEC, the issuer, and the exchange on which the shares are traded. The report must include background information about the purchaser, the source of her funds, and her purpose in buying.

3.3.5 Insiders

Insiders are officers, directors, more than 10 percent stockholders, accountants, or attorneys of a company registered under the 1934 act. Insiders must file a report with the SEC disclosing their holdings in the reporting company and make monthly updates. The 1934 act also limits insider trading by imposing absolute liability on any insider who makes a profit on the purchase or sale of a reporting company's stock within a six-month period (called short swing profits).

3.3.6 Proxy

A proxy solicitation is a written request for permission to vote a shareholder's shares at a shareholder meeting. Proxy solicitations in reporting companies must be reported to the SEC. If directors are to be elected at a meeting for which management is seeking proxies, an annual report with an audited balance sheet and profit and loss statement must be sent to all shareholders entitled to vote.

Proxy statements must be sent to all shareholders disclosing all facts that are pertinent to the matter on which the shareholders will vote. Proxy statements and any other documents that will be sent to shareholders as part of the proxy solicitation must be filed with the SEC. Shareholders have a right to have proposals proper for consideration at the shareholders' meeting included in management's proxy solicitation.

3.3.7 Section 18 Liability

Under Section 18, a person can be held liable for intentionally making false and/or misleading statements in a registration statement or any report required under the 1934 act. Because liability is imposed only for intentional misconduct, good faith and a lack of knowledge of a statement's falsity are defenses to an action under Section 18.

Pass Key

Candidates must know the three periodic reports (10-K, 10-Q, and 8-K). Frequently, examiners only ask the names of the other required reports. These may be learned by the memory device "5 percent **TIP**" (5 percent for 5 percent or more owners must report; **T** for **tender** offers must be reported; **I** for **insider** trading must be reported; and **P** for **proxy** solicitations and Proxy statements must be reported).

3.4 Antifraud Provisions: Rule 10b-5

3.4.1 In General

Rule 10b-5, promulgated by the SEC under Section 10(b) of the 1934 act, prohibits fraud in connection with the purchase or sale of any security. Rule 10b-5 applies whether or not the securities are of a registered company. Anyone who sells or buys securities using fraud can be liable. A violation of Rule 10b-5 can result in civil damages, an SEC injunction action, or criminal fines and penalties.

3.4.2 General Elements of Cause of Action

To recover damages for a violation of Rule 10b-5, a plaintiff must prove:

▪ **Plaintiff Bought or Sold Securities**

Rule 10b-5 applies only if the plaintiff bought or sold securities.

▪ **Plaintiff Suffered a Loss**

The plaintiff must prove that he or she suffered a loss as a result of the fraud.

▪ **Material Misrepresentation or Material Omission of Fact**

The plaintiff must prove the defendant made a material misrepresentation or material omission of fact in connection with the sale.

Illustration 3	Fraud in Purchase and Sale of Shares

Dee calls Pete and tells him that she holds Bigco stock with a market value of $50, but she will sell it to him for $25 per share. In fact, the stock's market value is $15. Pete buys Dee's stock. The fraud here was in connection with a purchase and sale.

Illustration 4	Fraud Not in Connection With Purchase or Sale

Pete is Bigco's largest stockholder. To keep Pete from selling Bigco stock, Dee, the president of Bigco, tells Pete she is about to announce that Bigco had large profits during the past year. In fact, Bigco incurred huge losses. Pete holds onto his stock, and the value of his stock plummets after Dee announces the loss. The fraud was not in connection with a purchase or sale of stock since Pete neither bought nor sold any shares.

- **Scienter (Intent to Deceive or Reckless Disregard for the Truth)**

  The plaintiff must show scienter (i.e., the defendant *intended* to deceive or made false statements with a *reckless disregard for the truth*).

  Negligence on the part of the defendant is not sufficient to satisfy this element.

Pass Key

The intent required for a Rule 10b-5 violation has been the focus of a number of past exam questions. Note that similar intent is not required to prove a violation of Rule 11 under the Securities Act of 1933. This difference has been the key to a number of the questions.

- **Reliance**

  The plaintiff must have relied on the defendant's misrepresentation.

- **Interstate Commerce**

  The plaintiff must show that a means of interstate commerce was involved. Any use of the mail or phones or a national securities exchange is sufficient to satisfy this element.

Illustration 5   CPA Liability for False Statements

Becky, a CPA, audited financial statements of Harco. Becky intentionally gave an unqualified opinion on the financial statements even though she discovered material misstatements. The financial statements and Becky's unqualified opinion were included in a registration and prospectus for an original offering of Harco stock. Becky can be held liable for a violation of Rule 10b-5 (and also under Section 11 of the 1933 act).

Pass Key

It is key to recognize the differences between an action under Section 11 of the 1933 act and under Rule 10b-5.

- Section 11 of 1933 requires no proof of scienter, reliance, or negligence. The plaintiff need only show that he acquired the stock and suffered a loss, and that there was a material misrepresentation or material omission of fact in the registration statement.

- Rule 10b-5 of the 1934 act requires proof of both scienter and reliance. The plaintiff must show that she bought or sold the stock; suffered a loss; a material misrepresentation; or material omission of fact, scienter, and reliance.

- Proof of negligence is insufficient under Rule 10b-5.

3.4.3   Insider Trading Under Rule 10b-5

Under Rule 10b-5, it is illegal for a person to trade on the basis of "inside" information if the person would breach a duty of trust owed to the issuer of the security or the shareholders of the issuer. Basically, inside information is any material, nonpublic information about the security or the issuer.

Typically, a securities issuer's insiders, such as directors, officers, controlling shareholders, and employees of the issuer will be held to owe a duty of trust and confidence. But outsiders, such as an issuer's CPAs, attorneys, and even printers, may also be held to owe a duty of trust. A private person injured by a violation of Rule 10b-5 can bring an action against the person violating the rule for any actual damages (not punitive damages) or seeking rescission of the transaction. The SEC can impose fines and seek criminal penalties.

Comparison of the Antifraud Provisions of the 1933 and 1934 Acts		
Elements of Proof	*1933 Act (Sections 12 and 17)*	*1934 Act (Section 10b)*
Source of misleading statement or omission	Must be in registration statement	Can be any written or oral statement or omission
Transactions covered	Issuance of a security	Sale or purchase of a security
Securities covered	Securities covered by the registration statement	Any securities, whether or not publicly traded or registered
Plaintiffs	Any person acquiring the security; SEC	Any purchaser or seller of the security; SEC
Defendants	• Every person who signed the registration statement • Directors • People named in the registration statement • Experts (including accountants)	Anyone responsible for the false statement or omission, or who trades on the basis of material, nonpublic information and who breaches a duty of trust and confidence by so trading
Materiality	False statement or omission must be material	False statement or omission must be material
Loss	Must prove	Must prove
Reliance	Need **not** prove	Must prove
Causation	Need **not** prove	Must prove
Scienter	Need **not** prove	Must prove
Knowledge of false statement or omission	Plaintiff cannot know of false statement or omission	Plaintiff cannot know of false statement or omission
Remedies	Rescission or monetary damages (Section 12); criminal damages (Section 17)	Rescission or monetary damages

Question 1 MCQ-01386

Dean Inc., a publicly traded corporation, paid a $10,000 bribe to a local zoning official. The bribe was recorded in Dean's financial statements as a consulting fee. Dean's unaudited financial statements were submitted to the SEC as part of a quarterly filing. Which of the following federal statutes did Dean violate?

    a. Federal Trade Commission Act

    b. Securities Act of 1933

    c. Securities Exchange Act of 1934

    d. North American Free Trade Act

Question 2 MCQ-01385

An original issue of transaction exempt securities was sold to the public based on a prospectus containing intentional omissions of material facts. Under which of the following federal securities laws would the issuer be liable to a purchaser of the securities?

I.   The anti-fraud provisions of the Securities Act of 1933.

II.   The anti-fraud provisions of the Securities Exchange Act of 1934.

    a. I only.

    b. II only.

    c. Both I and II.

    d. Neither I nor II.

Question 3 MCQ-01390

Under the Securities Act of 1933, which of the following statements most accurately reflects how securities registration affects an investor?

    a. The investor is provided with information on the stockholders of the offering corporation.

    b. The investor is provided with information on the principal purposes for which the offering's proceeds will be used.

    c. The investor is guaranteed by the SEC that the facts contained in the registration statement are accurate.

    d. The investor is assured by the SEC against loss resulting from purchasing the security.

1 Worker Classification

It is important for a business to properly determine whether a person performing services for the business is an employee or an independent contractor. All of the payroll issues discussed below arise only in an employer-employee setting and do not apply when dealing with an independent contractor.

When determining whether a worker is an employee or an independent contractor, no one factor is determinative; it is a weighing process.

Businesses must consider:

- Whether the business controls (or at least has the right to control) what the worker does and how he or she performs the work (right to control the manner and method of the work indicates an employee);

- Whether the worker owns his or her own business, tools, and the like (indicative of an independent contractor);

- Whether the worker is paid by the job (indicative of an independent contractor), or hourly or by salary (indicative of an employee);

- Whether the job is of limited duration (indicative of an independent contractor) or ongoing or continuous (indicative of an employee); and

- Whether the worker receives benefits (indicative of an employee).

2 Federal Insurance Contributions Act (FICA)

The Federal Insurance Contributions Act (FICA) provides workers and their dependents with benefits in case of death, disability, or retirement.

2.1 Participation

All full-time and part-time employees must participate in the program. The self-employed must also participate if their net profit exceeds $400 in a year. Very few workers are exempt (e.g., certain government workers and ministers).

2.2 Funding

FICA is funded by taxing income earned from labor (e.g., wages, salaries, tips, bonuses, commissions, etc.). FICA is funded by *both employers and employees*, including self-employed individuals.

2.2.1   Employer Responsibility

Employers must match their employees' contributions to FICA. Employers are *responsible for paying the tax and withholding* the employee's contribution.

- An employer that fails to withhold the employee's contribution is liable to pay the employee's half, but has a right to reimbursement from the employee. If an employer voluntarily pays the employee's share, it is deductible for the employer and taxable income for the employee.

- Penalties apply to employers who fail to make timely FICA deposits or who fail to supply their federal taxpayer identification number.

2.2.2   Employee Responsibility

For 2019, employees were liable to make FICA contributions of 6.2 percent of their *gross wages* of up to $132,900 and Medicare contributions of 1.45 percent of their entire gross wages. Individuals with income exceeding a threshold amount ($200,000 single and $250,000 married filing jointly) are liable for an additional Medicare tax of 0.9 percent of their entire gross wages. Gross wages include *all earned income*, such as salary, bonuses, and commissions. Gifts, interest, dividends, etc., are not wages.

2.2.3   Self-Employed Person Responsibility

Self-employed individuals pay into FICA through the self-employment tax, which is equal to the employer's and the employee's contribution (15.3 percent). It is imposed only on net profits and only if the net profits exceed $400 in a year.

Pass Key

The examiners often ask what income is subject to FICA. It is key to remember that an employee's *gross wages* are subject, and that a self-employed person's *net profits* are subject.

2.3   Deductibility by Employer

The employer's contribution is deductible as an ordinary business expense. The employee's contribution is *not* deductible by the employee. Because a self-employed person pays both contributions, one-half of the self-employment tax is deductible in arriving at adjusted gross income.

2.4   Benefits

FICA provides a number of benefits, including disability pay, retirement pay, survivor's benefits, dependent's benefits, and medical benefits under Medicare (not Medicaid, which is a state-run program). Benefits are available to all covered employees regardless of whether they are receiving benefits from a private plan. Employees may not opt out of Social Security, even if they are covered by a private plan.

Pass Key

The most important things to remember about Social Security for exam purposes are:

- The employer must pay the tax and collect an employee's portion of the tax.

- All income derived from labor is taxed; unearned income is not taxed.

- All employees are subject to the tax up to a maximum dollar amount for the Social Security with no limit on the Medicare; self-employment income is subject to both employer and employee taxation for income over $400.

3   Unemployment Compensation (FUTA)

The Federal Unemployment Tax Act (FUTA) establishes a state-run system of insurance to provide income to workers who have lost their jobs. Although FUTA provides federal guidelines, the states actually administer the program, set standards, and determine payments.

3.1   Participation

All employers who have quarterly payrolls of at least $1,500 or who employ at least one person for 20 weeks in a year must participate in the system. Unlike FICA, *self-employed persons do not participate*.

Pass Key

Because most employers must participate under FUTA, the examiners often try to trick you into thinking that every employer must participate. This is not true. The $1,500 minimum or time requirements must be met.

3.2   Funding

Unemployment taxes are payroll taxes generally assessed only against the *employer*. The federal unemployment tax rate currently is 6.0 percent on the first $7,000 per year of compensation for each employee.

Employers can get a credit against the federal tax due for payments made on account of state unemployment taxes of up to 5.4 percent of the first $7,000. Moreover, the state rate can be reduced if the employer has a below-average rate of unemployment claims from prior employees.

3.3   Employer Deductibility

The employer's payment is deductible as an ordinary business expense. Because the employee generally does not pay the tax, it is not deductible by the employee.

Pass Key

When the examiners test on unemployment issues, they often test on the concept above. It is key to remember that the employer may deduct the tax (because the employer pays it), but the employee may not take a deduction.

3.4 Benefits

Unemployment benefits are generally available only when an employee's job termination was not his or her fault. Benefits are distributed to employees by the state governments. The amount paid varies from state to state, but is usually determined by how long the employee has worked and his or her former rate of pay. Note that payments are not limited to the amount that has been paid by the employer on the employee's behalf.

Pass Key

The most important things to remember about FUTA for exam purposes are:

- The *employer* must pay if it employs an employee for at least 20 weeks in a year or paid $1,500 in wages in a quarter. The employee does not pay.

- Because the employer pays, the tax is deductible as a business expense. The employee cannot deduct the payment.

- If an employer's claim rate is low, the employer *may get a deduction* for state unemployment tax.

- The employee's benefits are *not limited to the contributions* made on his behalf.

4 Workers' Compensation

Workers' compensation programs are state-run programs designed to enable employees to recover for injuries incurred while on the job. In most states, coverage is compulsory.

Employers are strictly liable regardless of fault. The only requirement is that the employee's injury occurred while acting in the scope of employment.

Pass Key

Fault is the most frequently tested issue in workers' compensation. Remember that an employee can collect even if the employee was negligent, grossly negligent, or assumed the risk. An employee cannot recover for injuries resulting from intoxication, fighting, or self-inflicted wounds. Remember, the purpose of workers' compensation is to enable employees to recover for work-related injuries regardless of negligence.

4.1   Participation

Most employers must participate in workers' compensation programs. There are exceptions for agricultural workers, domestic workers, casual workers (e.g., *temporary* office workers), public employees, and independent contractors. Some states also exempt employers who have up to only three or four employees.

4.2   Funding

The employer pays for workers' compensation by purchasing insurance from the state or a private carrier. Some states also allow employers to be self-insuring if they can prove that they are financially responsible. In most states, coverage is compulsory.

In states in which coverage is not mandatory, an employer who elects not to participate in workers' compensation gives up the common-law defenses of contributory negligence, assumption of the risk, and the fellow servant doctrine. Also, damage awards are not limited to what would be recovered under workers' compensation.

4.3   Deductibility

Workers' compensation insurance premiums are ordinary business expenses deductible by the employer. Because employees do not pay, there is no deduction for the worker.

4.4   Benefits

Workers' compensation provides benefits for any injury or disease (including aggravations of existing diseases) resulting from employment. Benefits include money for loss of income, disability, loss of limbs, prosthetic devices, medical services, burial costs, and survivors' benefits. The program works like other insurance—benefits are not limited to what was paid in on the employee's behalf.

5   Affordable Care Act

The purpose of the Affordable Care Act (ACA) is to improve access to health care in the U.S. by providing workers with access to affordable health care coverage. Health care coverage may be offered through:

- A plan provided by the employer
- A plan purchased through a Health Insurance Marketplace, where employees may qualify for financial assistance
- Coverage provided under a government-sponsored program such as Medicare, most Medicaid, and health care programs for veterans
- Direct purchase by the employee from an insurance company

5.1   Participation

Both employers and employees are required to participate:

- Certain employers must offer health care coverage or pay a penalty.
- An individual must obtain health care coverage for himself, a spouse, and tax dependents.

5.2 Funding

Both the employer and the employee contribute to the purchase of affordable coverage:

■ The employer may subsidize the cost of the coverage in order to ensure that it is affordable.

■ The employee will pay a certain amount for coverage, whether purchased through the employer or through another source.

5.2.1 Employer Responsibility

Under the ACA, employers with 50 or more full-time employees are called applicable large employers, or ALEs. ALEs are required to provide full-time employees the opportunity to purchase affordable minimum essential health care coverage for themselves and their dependents under an eligible employer-sponsored health care plan.

■ All types of employers can be ALEs, including tax-exempt organizations and government entities.

■ An employee who works for an employer on average at least 30 hours a week or 130 hours of service a month is a full-time employee.

■ Coverage is considered affordable if the employee's contribution to the plan does not exceed 9.5 percent of the employee's household income for the taxable year.

■ A dependent is an employee's child who has not reached the age of 26.

■ Employers who do not comply with the ACA will pay a penalty for failure to do so.

■ Employers are required to file annual information returns with the IRS and must also provide information to employees about coverage.

5.2.2 Employee Responsibility

The ACA comes with an "individual mandate" requiring all Americans to buy health coverage. Formerly, a penalty was imposed on persons who failed to purchase health coverage, but the penalty has been eliminated. For low-income individuals, the federal government subsidizes the cost through a tax rebate, even if the individual paid no income taxes. Employees who have minimum essential coverage will report this fact on their tax return each year.

5.3 Benefits

The ACA does not create a national health insurance plan. Rather, it sets national standards for how health insurance is structured and priced, and places new requirements on individuals and employers. Because purchasing coverage is mandatory, the ACA makes it illegal for an insurer to deny coverage to individuals with preexisting conditions or to charge more for their coverage.

5.4 Penalties for Failure to Comply With ACA

The employer must pay a fee for failure to comply with the Affordable Care Act. Note that an employer is not obligated to calculate its liability and should not make a payment without first being contacted by the IRS.

1. **Penalty Type 1:** An ALE will owe the first type of employer shared responsibility payment if it does not offer minimum essential coverage to at least 95 percent of its full-time employees (and their dependents) and at least one full-time employee receives the premium tax credit for purchasing coverage through the Health Insurance Marketplace.

   • On an annual basis, this payment is equal to $2,000 (indexed for inflation in future years) for each full-time employee, with the first 30 employees excluded from the calculation.

2. **Penalty Type 2:** Even if an ALE member offers minimum essential coverage to at least 95 percent of its full-time employees (and their dependents), it may owe the second type of employer shared responsibility payment for each full-time employee who receives the premium tax credit for purchasing coverage through the Marketplace.

   * In general, a full-time employee could receive the premium tax credit if:

     —the minimum essential coverage the employer offers to the employee is not affordable;

     —the minimum essential coverage the employer offers to the employee does not provide minimum value; or

     —the employee is not one of the at least 95 percent of full-time employees offered minimum essential coverage.

   * On an annual basis, this payment is equal to $3,000 (indexed for inflation in future years) for each full-time employee who receives the premium tax credit. The total payment in this instance cannot exceed the amount the employer would have owed had the employer not offered minimum essential coverage to at least 95 percent of its full-time employees (and their dependents).

5.5 Deductibility

None of the payments required of the employer under the employer shared responsibility provisions are tax deductible for the employer.

Question 1	MCQ-02133

Kroll, an employee of Acorn Inc., was injured in the course of employment while operating a forklift manufactured and sold to Acorn by Trell Corp. The forklift was defectively designed by Trell. Under the state's mandatory workers' compensation statute, Kroll will be successful in:

	Obtaining Workers' Compensation Benefits	*A Negligence Action Against Acorn*
a.	Yes	Yes
b.	Yes	No
c.	No	Yes
d.	No	No

Question 2	MCQ-01939

Taxes payable under the Federal Unemployment Tax Act (FUTA) are:

   a. Calculated as a fixed percentage of all compensation paid to an employee.

   b. Deductible by the employer as a business expense for federal income tax purposes.

   c. Payable by employers for all employees.

   d. Withheld from the wages of all covered employees.

NOTES

1 Summary of Entities

Nearly half of the recent Business Structures questions on the exam simply require the examinee to differentiate the attributes of the various business structures. The major attributes are summarized in the following chart. More detail regarding each business structure follows.

	Overall Summary of Entities and Their Attributes						
	Entity						
Attributes	*Sole Proprietorship*	*General Partnership/ Joint Venture*	*Limited Liability Partnership (LLP)*	*Limited Partnership*	*Limited Liability Company (LLC)*	*Corporation*	*Subchapter S Corporation*
Formation	*No formalities* Owner simply operates a business	*No formalities:* Can be formed by verbal or written agreement, or mere conduct	*Formalities:* File statement of qualification with state	*Formalities:* File Certificate of Limited Partnership with state	*Formalities:* File articles of organization with state	*Formalities:* File articles of incorporation or corporate charter with state	*Formalities:* Same as regular corporation plus file "S" election
Liability of Owners	Unlimited personal liability for all business obligations	Unlimited personal liability for all partnership obligations	Partners are generally not liable for partnership obligations, unless caused by their own negligence	**General partner:** unlimited personal liability **Limited partner:** only investment is at risk	Members generally not personally liable beyond their investment	Shareholders generally not personally liable beyond their investment	Shareholders generally not personally liable beyond their investment
Management	Sole proprietor manages directly or can appoint manager	Owners manage directly or can agree to appoint managing partner	Partners manage directly or can agree to appoint a managing partner	**General partner(s)** is (are) exclusive manager(s); **Limited partners** ordinarily do not manage	Members manage directly or can agree to appoint a manager	Managed by board of directors, which appoints officers to run day-to-day operations	Managed by board of directors, which appoints officers to run day-to-day operations
Transferability	Sole proprietor can sell business at will	Partners cannot transfer ownership interest without unanimous consent	Partners cannot transfer ownership interest without unanimous consent	Partners (whether general or limited) cannot transfer ownership interest without unanimous consent	Absent agreement otherwise, members cannot transfer ownership interest without unanimous consent	Shareholders are free to transfer ownership interest unless they agree otherwise	Shareholders generally may transfer ownership unless they agree otherwise, but cannot transfer to foreign or entity shareholders

(continued)

(continued)

Taxation*	"Flow through taxation"	"Flow through" taxation	"Flow through" taxation (but partners not managing have passive loss restrictions)	"Flow through" taxation (but limited partners have passive loss restrictions)	"Flow through" taxation (but members not managing have passive loss restrictions)	Income taxed at corporate level and taxed again to shareholders when dividends are distributed	"Flow through" taxation (but shareholders not managing have passive loss restrictions)

*Default treatment, but entities may elect to be taxed differently under the "check the box" rules.

2 Sole Proprietorship

2.1 Advantages, Implications, and Constraints of a Sole Proprietorship

A sole proprietorship is the simplest form of business ownership. One person owns the business and manages all of its affairs, and the sole proprietor is not considered an entity separate from the business. No formality is required to form a sole proprietorship, and nothing need be filed with the state in which the business operates (unless the state or city requires a business license).

- **Personal Liability**

  The sole proprietor is personally liable for all obligations of the business.

- **Duration**

  A sole proprietorship cannot exist beyond the life of the sole proprietor. It may be terminated at any time by its owner.

- **Tax Treatment**

  For tax purposes, profits and losses from the business flow through the business to the sole proprietor.

- **Transferability**

  A sole proprietor is free to transfer his interest in the sole proprietorship at will.

2.2 Choice as a Business Entity

The sole proprietorship may be a good choice of business entity when an individual wants to form a business that he or she will manage, wants to claim the income or losses from the business on personal taxes, and does not want to bother with a lot of formality. The individual risks all of his or her personal assets, however, when this type of business entity is formed.

3 General Partnership/Joint Venture

3.1 Formation

A general partnership is formed whenever two or more persons intend to carry on as co-owners a business for profit.

- Papers need not be drawn up to form a partnership.

- Nothing need be filed with the state.

- An express agreement is not required; an agreement can be implied from conduct.

Illustration 1   Formation of Partnership

Steve and Becky decide to operate a hot dog cart together. Steve agrees to pay for the cart, and Becky agrees to make and sell the hot dogs. The two also agree to split the profits. A partnership has been formed even though Steve and Becky never expressly agreed to form a partnership.

Pass Key

A very common business entities question on past exams asks simply: What type of business entity can be formed without filing organizational documents with the state? A partnership or a sole proprietorship are the only possibilities. Formation of all other business entities requires filing some sort of organizational document with the state.

3.1.1   Joint Venture Compared

Courts sometimes try to distinguish joint ventures from general partnerships, but the legal requirements and consequences, and advantages and disadvantages, of forming a joint venture generally are identical to those of a general partnership. For exam purposes, the key difference between a joint venture and a general partnership is that a joint venture is formed for a single transaction or project or a related series of transactions or projects.

3.1.2   When Intent Is Unclear: Sharing of Profits

If it is unclear whether the parties intended to enter into a partnership, an agreement to share profits gives rise to a presumption that the parties intended to form a partnership.

3.1.3   Generally, a Writing Is Not Necessary

As a general rule, a general partnership agreement need not be in writing. However, if the partners want to enforce an agreement to remain partners for longer than one year, a writing is required under the Statute of Frauds.

Pass Key

The examiners often ask what is necessary to form a general partnership. The key is to remember three simple elements: (i) two or more persons (ii) who agree (expressly or impliedly) (iii) to carry on as co-owners a business for profit. There is no requirement of a writing, even if the partnership is to own land, unless the partnership is to last for more than one year.

3.2   Not a Taxable Entity for Income Tax Purposes

Partnerships are treated as entities for most purposes (e.g., may hold property and sue and be sued in own name, etc.), but they are not taxable entities for income tax purposes.

3.3   Operation of a General Partnership

Absent an agreement to the contrary, all partners have *equal rights* to manage the partnership business. Management rights and voting power are not based on the amount contributed.

Illustration 2   Management Rights in General Partnership

Alex, Becky, Cindy, Deanna, and Elias form a general partnership—Glorious Jeans—to manufacture coffee-colored clothing. Alex contributes 40 percent of the capital, Becky contributes 30 percent of the capital, Cindy contributes 20 percent of the capital, Deanna contributes 10 percent of the capital, and Elias agrees to design all the clothes. Each partner has an equal right to participate in the management of the partnership.

3.3.1   Required Approval

Decisions regarding matters within the ordinary course of the partnership's business may be controlled by majority vote unless the partnership agreement provides otherwise. Matters outside the ordinary course of the partnership's business require consent of all the partners. Examples of areas requiring unanimous consent include:

- admitting new partners;

- confessing a judgment (admitting liability in a lawsuit) or submitting a claim to arbitration; and

- making a fundamental change in the partnership business (e.g., the sale of a partnership).

Illustration 3   Fundamental Change in Partnership Business

In the partnership described in the previous example, the decision whether to buy cloth from Supplier may be approved by any three partners, but a decision to shift production from the manufacture of clothing to the manufacture of small appliances would have to be approved by all the partners.

3.3.2   Agency Law Governs

Every partner is an agent of the partnership for the purpose of its business and the partnership is their principal. An act of a partner apparently carrying on in the ordinary course of business the business of the partnership will bind the partnership through apparent authority. If a partner acts without actual or apparent authority, the partnership can still become bound if it knows of the material facts of a transaction and assents (i.e., ratifies), either expressly or by accepting the benefits of the transaction.

3.4   Rights of Partners

3.4.1   Rights in Partnership Property

A partnership owns all money and property contributed to the partnership by the partners and all other property acquired by the partnership. Partners do not own partnership property. As a general rule, partners have no right to possess or use partnership property other than for partnership purposes. Thus:

- an individual partner may not assign or sell partnership property for his own benefit; and

- a partner's personal creditors cannot attach partnership property to satisfy an individual partner's debt.

Illustration 4   **Partnership Property vs. Personal Property**

Alex and Becky agree to form a partnership to sell antique cars. Alex contributes 10 antique cars from his collection and Becky contributes $200,000. The cars and the cash are partnership property. Alex may no longer use the cars for personal use—even if they are titled in his name—and Becky may no longer freely spend the $200,000. The cars and cash can be used only for partnership purposes.

3.4.2   Rights in Partnership Interest

A partner may assign her interest in the profits and surplus at any time. The assignee obtains the right to receive the partner's share of the profits. The assignee does not become a partner and so has no right to attend partnership meetings, inspect the partnership books and records, vote, etc. An assignee can obtain such rights only if admitted to the partnership as a partner, which generally requires the approval of all the partners.

Pass Key

The examiners like to ask about the effect of a partner transferring interest in a partnership without the consent of the other partners. The key is to remember that such a transfer does not make the assignee a partner (that can be done only with the consent of all of the partners). Thus, the transferee has no power to manage the partnership, inspect the partnership's books and records, vote, etc. Generally, the assignee's only right is to get whatever distribution the assignor would have gotten. The same rule applies to a creditor with a charging order and an heir who receives a deceased partner's interest.

- **Creditors May Attach a Partner's Interest (Called a Charging Order)**

    A creditor of an individual partner may obtain from a court a *charging order* against an individual partner's share of profits.

- **Upon Death, Heirs Are Entitled to a Deceased Partner's Share of Profits**

    When a partner dies, his or her right to profits vests in his or her heirs. The partner's right to partnership property vests in the surviving partners.

3.4.3 Right to Inspect Books and Records

Every partner has the right to inspect and copy the books and records of the partnership.

3.5   Duties and Legal Obligations of Partners

3.5.1 Fiduciary Duties Owed to Other Partners

Each partner owes a fiduciary duty to the partnership and other partners.

3.5.2 Each Partner Is Personally Liable for All Partnership Obligations

Partners are personally liable for all contracts entered into and all torts committed by other partners within the scope of partnership business or which are otherwise authorized. The partners' liability is *joint and several*. This means that each partner is personally and individually liable for the entire amount of all partnership obligations. In many states, however, a creditor cannot satisfy a judgment against an individual partner unless the partner was named in the lawsuit and the assets of the partnership are exhausted.

3.6   Profit and Loss Allocation

3.6.1 Profits

Absent an agreement to the contrary, all partners have *equal rights* to share in the profits of the partnership.

Illustration 5   Sharing of Profits

Alex, Becky, Cindy, Deanna, and Elias form a general partnership—Glorious Jeans—to manufacture coffee-colored clothing. Alex contributes 40 percent of the capital, Becky contributes 30 percent of the capital, Cindy contributes 20 percent of the capital, Deanna contributes 10 percent of the capital, and Elias agrees to design all the clothes. Alex, Becky, Cindy, Deanna, and Elias will share profits equally absent an agreement to the contrary.

3.6.2 Losses

Unless the partners agree otherwise, they share losses in the same manner as they share profits.

Illustration 6   Sharing of Losses

Assume the same facts as in the previous illustration. If there is a $100,000 loss, absent an agreement to the contrary, Alex, Becky, Cindy, Deanna, and Elias will each be responsible for $20,000 of the loss.

The examiners often ask how partners will share profits and/or losses. The key is to remember that, as with the partners' management powers, unless the partners provide otherwise, *profits and losses will be split equally*, regardless of the partners' contributions. If a partner cannot contribute his or her share of losses (e.g., because of bankruptcy or other refusal), the remaining partners must make up the share on a pro rata basis.

3.7 Distributions

Unless agreed otherwise, partners are not entitled to compensation for services rendered to the partnership.

Illustration 7   Compensation

In the previous example, if Alex, Becky, and Cindy never did any work for Glorious Jeans, and Deanna and Elias worked full time to manufacture the clothes, Deanna and Elias would have no right to be paid for their services (unless Alex, Becky, and Cindy breached an agreement to work).

3.8 Termination: Dissociation of a General Partnership

Dissociation is a change in the relationship of the partners caused by any partner ceasing to be associated in the carrying on of the business. Dissociation of a partner does not necessarily cause a dissolution and winding up of the business of the partnership. A partnership at will (i.e., one without a stated termination point) may be rightfully dissolved by a partner's notice of withdrawal or dissociation at any time.

3.8.1 Events of Dissociation

A partner is dissociated from the partnership when the partner gives notice of withdrawal, dies, becomes bankrupt, or is expelled, or if an event occurs that was set out in the partnership agreement as an event that would cause a dissociation.

3.8.2 Consequences

When a partner dissociates, his right to participate in management ceases, although the dissociated partner's apparent authority to bind the partnership will continue until third parties are given notice of the dissociation.

3.8.3 Dissociated Partner's Liability to Other Parties

Generally, a dissociated partner remains liable for the debts incurred by the partnership prior to dissociation unless there has been a release by the creditor or a novation.

A dissociated partner may be held liable for debts incurred by the partnership for up to two years after dissociation unless the partner gives notice of dissociation. If a new partner is admitted, the new partner is not personally liable for debts incurred by the partnership before becoming a partner.

3.9   Termination: Dissolution of a General Partnership

3.9.1   Events Causing Dissolution

Generally, a partnership is dissolved and its business must be wound up if the partnership is at will (i.e., has no expiration date) and a partner gives notice of withdrawal, the partners agree to dissolution, or a court orders dissolution. The death of a partner does not cause a dissolution if the remaining partners agree to continue the partnership within 90 days of the partner's death.

Pass Key

The examiners often ask about the basic characteristics of a partnership. One characteristic that has been key to several past questions is that a partnership is not of unlimited duration—because any one of the above events can trigger a dissolution.

3.9.2   Partnership Continues After Dissolution

A partnership continues to exist after dissolution until its business is wound up, at which time the partnership is terminated. For example, each partner will continue to have apparent authority to bind the partnership, and each partner will continue to be liable for the obligations of the partnership. The partnership is terminated only after the winding-up process is complete.

3.10   Distribution of Assets—Final Accounting

3.10.1 Order of Distribution

When a solvent partnership is dissolved and its assets are reduced to cash, the cash must be used to pay the partnership's liabilities in the following order:

▪ **Creditors**

   Creditors, including partners who are creditors, must be paid before the non-creditor partners receive any payments.

▪ **Partners**

   After obligations to creditors are satisfied, each partner is entitled to payment, first to return their contributions and then on account of profits.

3.10.2 Application

▪ **Amounts Due or Owed**

   To determine the amounts due or owed, deduct from the assets left upon dissolution any amounts owed to creditors (including partners who are creditors) and then deduct the amounts needed to return the partners' contributions (if not already repaid).

▪ **Divide Profit (if Any)**

   If money still remains, it is profit that must be divided among the partners. If the assets at dissolution are less than what is needed to pay the creditors and return contributions, then there is a loss that must be divided among the partners. In either case, remember that unless the partnership agreement provides otherwise, profits are divided equally among partners, and losses are divided the same as profits.

Illustration 8   Dissolution of Partnership

Alex, Becky, and Cindy contributed $30,000, $15,000, and $5,000, respectively, to the ABC Partnership. Upon dissolution, after paying all creditors, $20,000 remains. The partnership has suffered a $30,000 loss because $50,000 was contributed to capital and only $20,000 remains. The partnership agreement is silent as to how losses are to be divided, but provides that profits are to be allocated 40% to Alex, 25% to Becky, and 35% to Cindy. Because the partnership agreement is silent as to allocation of losses, they will be allocated in the same proportions as profits: 40% to Alex = $12,000 (i.e., 40% of $30,000); 25% to Becky = $7,500; and 35% to Cindy = $10,500. Thus, Alex is entitled to receive $18,000 ($30,000 capital contribution less $12,000 share of loss); Becky is entitled to receive $7,500 ($15,000 capital contribution less $7,500 share of loss), and Cindy owes $5,500 ($5,000 capital contribution less $10,500 share of loss).

Illustration 9   Partner Refuses to Pay

If there is a loss and some partners refuse to contribute, are not subject to process (i.e., are not within a court's jurisdiction), or are insolvent, the remaining partners must share the extra loss proportionally. Thus, in the illustration above, if Cindy refused to pay anything else, Alex and Becky would have to share the $5,500 loss that Cindy owes on a 4 to 2.5 basis (Alex would have to deduct an extra $3,385 from his capital and Becky would have to deduct an extra $2,115 from her capital). Of course, if Cindy is solvent, Alex and Becky can seek to recover the $5,500 from Cindy in an action for indemnification.

4   Limited Liability Partnership (Similar to General Partnership)

A limited liability partnership (LLP) is similar to a general partnership in most respects, including the sharing of profits and losses, and generally all of the advantages and disadvantages of a general partnership mentioned above apply to a limited liability partnership. Important differences are listed below.

4.1   Difference: Personal Liability

- **Partners Generally Not Liable for Acts of Fellow Partners, Employees, or Agents**

  An LLP differs from a general partnership in that a partner in an LLP is not personally liable for the obligations or liabilities of the partnership arising from errors, omissions, negligence, malpractice, or the wrongful acts committed by another partner or by an employee, agent, or representative of the LLP.

- **Liable for Own Negligence and Negligence of Those Under Direct Control**

  LLP partners are, of course, liable for their own negligence or wrongful acts and for the negligence and wrongful acts of those under their direct supervision or control.

- **Generally Not Personally Liable for Debts and Contractual Obligations**

   Generally, partners in an LLP are *not* personally liable for the debts and contractual obligations of the LLP.

4.2   Difference: Formation

- **LLP Must File With the State**

   Generally, to become an LLP the partnership must file a document with the state (called a registration, statement of qualification, application for registration, or certificate of limited liability partnership). Some states restrict LLPs only to the learned professions, such as accounting or the practice of law.

- **Contents of Certificate of Limited Liability Partnership**

   Generally, registration must provide information such as the LLP's name, the name and location of its registered office, the number of partners, a description of the partnership business, etc.

5   Limited Partnership

5.1   Nature of a Limited Partnership

A limited partnership is a partnership made up of one or more general partners (who have personal liability for all partnership debts) and one or more limited partners (whose liability for partnership debts generally is limited to their investment).

Pass Key

Examiners sometimes ask whether a limited partnership can be formed with limited liability for all partners. The answer, of course, is *no*—you need at least one general partner who has unlimited personal liability for all partnership obligations.

5.1.1   Generally No Perpetual Life

A limited partnership does not have a perpetual life, unless the partnership agreement provides otherwise.

5.1.2   Similar to a Corporation

A limited partnership can be formed only pursuant to a state statute and only by filing with the state. Limited partners are very much like shareholders. They contribute capital in exchange for a partnership interest, but they do not participate in management.

5.2   Formation of a Limited Partnership

A limited partnership can be formed only pursuant to a state statute and only by filing a certificate of limited partnership with the state.

5.3   Operation of a Limited Partnership

In a limited partnership, management is the responsibility of the general partners, just as in a general partnership.

5.3.1   General Partners

A general partner is personally liable for all partnership debts. If there is a loss, only the general partner can be held personally liable.

- A general partner may also be a limited partner at the same time.
- A general partner may be a secured or unsecured creditor of the partnership.

5.3.2   Limited Partners

A limited partner's liability is limited to his investment and unpaid capital commitments. A limited partner has no right to take part in the management of the business. He is not an agent of the business and generally cannot bind the business in contract. Nevertheless, a limited partner has a right to review the financial information and tax returns of the limited partnership.

- Under the Revised Uniform Limited Partnership Act of 1976, a limited partner who participates in control of the business is liable to any creditor who reasonably believes that she is a general partner. Under the Uniform Limited Partnership Act of 2001, partners cannot be held personally liable for participating in management. Any exam questions on this issue should specify which act applies.

  - Under both the Revised Uniform Partnership Act of 1976 and the Uniform Limited Partnership Act of 2001, a limited partner may vote on extraordinary matters without incurring liability (e.g., admission or removal of a general partner, dissolution, amending the certificate of limited partnership, sale of substantially all assets, etc.).

- Under the Revised Uniform Limited Partnership Act of 1976, limited partners' names cannot be identified with the business, or they might be considered to be general partners and lose their limited liability status. Note that this is not true under the Uniform Limited Partnership Act of 2001.

- A limited partner may assign his interest in the partnership.

  - The assignment of a limited partner's interest is like an assignment in a general partnership—the assignee has the limited partner's rights to profits.

  - Unless otherwise agreed, the assignor ceases to be a limited partner upon assignment of all of his limited partnership interest.

- A new partner can be added only upon the consent of all partners.

- A limited partner does not owe a fiduciary duty to the partnership.

5.3.3   Allocation of Profits and Losses

If the partners have agreed on how profits are shared, the agreement governs. Unless otherwise agreed, general and limited partners share profits and losses in proportion to the value of the partners' contributions. Remember, though, a limited partner is not liable for any loss beyond his or her capital contribution.

5.4   Termination of a Limited Partnership

5.4.1   Methods of Dissolution

A limited partnership may be dissolved by:

- the occurrence of the time or event stated in the partnership agreement;
- written consent of all partners (i.e., unanimous written consent to dissolve);

- withdrawal or death of a general partner; or

- judicial decree.

5.4.2 Death of a Limited Partner Does Not Cause Dissolution

Note that the death of a limited partner will not dissolve the partnership.

5.4.3 Order of Distribution of Assets

After dissolution, if the limited partnership is terminated, assets are distributed in the following order:

1. To creditors, including partners who are creditors;

2. To former partners in satisfaction of liabilities that were not paid on their withdrawal; and

3. To partners, first to return their contributions, and then to distribute profits.

5.4.4 Loss Situation

If there is a loss, only the general partners are personally liable; limited partners have no personal liability beyond their capital commitments.

6   Limited Liability Company

6.1   Nature of a Limited Liability Company

6.1.1 Basic Characteristics

An LLC is an entity designed to provide its owners, who are called members, with two main features:

- The limited liability that shareholders of a corporation enjoy (i.e., owners are not personally liable for obligations of the business entity).

- The ability to be taxed like a partnership (i.e., profits and losses flow through the LLC and are treated as the owners' personal profits and losses, unlike profits of a corporation, which are taxed at the corporate level and again when distributed to the shareholders). (Note: Under tax laws, LLCs are taxed as a partnership unless they elect to be taxed as a corporation.)

6.1.2 Controlling Law (Statute vs. Operating Agreement)

LLC members may, but need not, adopt operating agreements with provisions different from the LLC statute, and generally the operating agreements will control. The operating agreement is just that: an agreement among members regarding how they will operate or run their business. Its intent is to forestall and resolve disputes among the members. These agreements are not filed with the state. Indeed, under the Uniform Limited Liability Company Act, such operating agreements need not be in writing.

6.2   Formation of a Limited Liability Company

An LLC is formed by filing articles of organization with the secretary of state.

6.2.1 Contents of Articles

Most states require the articles to include the following:

- a statement that the entity is an LLC;

- the name of the LLC, which must include an indication that it is an LLC;

- the street address of the LLC's registered office and name of its registered agent;

- if management is to be vested in managers, a statement to that effect; and

- the names of the persons who will be managing the company.

6.2.2   Number of Members

Most states now allow one person to form an LLC.

6.3   Operation of a Limited Liability Company

6.3.1   Generally All Members May Participate in Management

Unless the articles or an operating agreement provides otherwise, all members have a right to participate in management decisions of the LLC.

- **Member-Managed Limited Liability Company**

  If the members are managing the LLC, each member is an agent of the LLC and has the power to bind the LLC by acts apparently carrying on the business of the LLC.

- **Manager-Managed Limited Liability Company**

  If management is by managers, each manager is an agent of the LLC and has the power to bind the LLC. In this case, the members are not agents of the LLC and do not have the power to bind the LLC.

6.3.2   Voting Strength Proportional to Contributions

Voting strength is proportional to contributions. For example, a member who contributed 5 percent of the LLC's current capital is entitled to 5 percent of the total vote.

6.3.3   Profit and Loss Allocated According to Contributions

Unless the articles or an operating agreement provide otherwise, profits and losses of an LLC are allocated on the basis of the members' contributions in most states. Under the Uniform Limited Liability Company Act (ULLCA), which is followed by only a few states but which is sometimes specifically tested on the exam, profits are shared equally, regardless of capital contributions.

6.3.4   Transferability of Ownership and Rights

Most statutes provide that unless the operating agreement provides otherwise, a member of an LLC may not transfer all of her interest in the LLC without the consent of all other members. A member is free to assign her interest in distributions (e.g., of profits or on dissolution) but is not free to assign any rights to manage the LLC. Thus, transferability of ownership is similar to that of a partnership.

6.3.5   Books and Records

Each member of an LLC is entitled to inspect and copy the books and records of the LLC during regular business hours.

6.4   Termination of a Limited Liability Company

An LLC will dissolve upon:

- expiration of the period of duration stated in the articles;

- the consent of all members;

- the death, retirement, resignation, bankruptcy, incompetence, etc., of a member (unless the remaining members vote to continue the business)—*these events dissociate the member*; or

- a judicial decree or administrative order dissolving the LLC for violation of law.

Question 1   MCQ-03126

The partnership agreement for Owen Associates, a general partnership, provided that profits be paid to the partners in the ratio of their financial contribution to the partnership. Moore contributed $10,000, Noon contributed $30,000, and Kale contributed $50,000. For the year ended December 31, Year 3, Owen had losses of $180,000. What amount of the losses should be allocated to Kale?

    a. $40,000

    b. $60,000

    c. $90,000

    d. $100,000

Question 2   MCQ-02996

In a general partnership, which of the following acts must be approved by all the partners?

    a.   Dissolution of the partnership

    b.   Admission of a partner

    c.   Authorization of a partnership capital expenditure

    d.   Conveyance of real property owned by the partnership

1 Corporation

1.1 Nature of a Corporation

1.1.1 Distinct Legal Entity

A corporation is a legal entity (i.e., it exists as an entity distinct from its shareholders). As a distinct legal entity, usually only the corporation is liable for corporate obligations. Generally, shareholders, directors, and officers are not personally liable for contracts made by their corporation. Neither are they liable for corporate torts, except to the extent the shareholder, officer, or director participated in the tort.

1.1.2 Taxation

■ **C Corporation**

Generally, a corporation is taxed as an entity distinct from its owners. It must pay taxes on any profits it makes. Stockholders generally do not have to pay tax on the profits of the corporation until they are distributed (e.g., as dividends under the tax laws). Such a corporation is known as a C corporation.

■ **S Corporation**

The tax laws permit certain corporations to elect to be taxed like partnerships (i.e., profits are not taxed at the corporate level but rather are treated as income of the shareholders). There are a number of restrictions on S corporations, such as:

- stock can be held by no more than 100 persons;
- shareholders must be individuals, estates, or certain trusts;
- the corporation must generally be a domestic corporation;
- there can be only one class of stock; and
- foreign shareholders are generally prohibited.

1.1.3 Owned by Shareholders but Managed by Directors

Corporations are owned by their shareholders, but unless the articles of incorporation provide otherwise, the shareholders do not run the corporation. The power to run the corporation is vested in the board of directors, which is elected by the shareholders.

1.1.4 Perpetual Life

A corporation generally has a perpetual life.

1.1.5 Freely Transferable Ownership

One of the key distinguishing characteristics of a corporation is that its owners (shareholders) are free to transfer all of their ownership rights to others, unless otherwise agreed.

1.2   Formation of a Corporation

1.2.1   Created Under Statute

Corporations are created by complying with a state incorporation statute. A majority of states follow the Revised Model Business Corporation Act, or RMBCA. This outline is based on that act.

Pass Key

A number of past corporation questions have simply asked which of four statements is true. As simple as it may seem, the key to a number of these questions has been that corporations are governed by statute.

1.2.2   Promoters Procure Capital Commitments

Promoters enter into contracts before the corporation is formed to obtain financing and things the corporation will need once formed. Promoters are personally bound on the contracts they make. The corporation is not bound unless and until the corporation adopts the contracts after the corporation is formed, either expressly or by accepting the benefits of the contracts. However, even if the corporation adopts a promoter's contract, the promoter remains liable unless there is a *novation* (an agreement that the third party will release the promoter and substitute the corporation).

1.2.3   Articles of Incorporation

Incorporators must file articles of incorporation with the state.

■   **Items Included in the Articles of Incorporation**

The articles may include anything the incorporators consider appropriate but, under the RMBCA, the articles must include:

- the name of the corporation;
- the names and address of the corporation's registered agent (i.e., the person on whom process may be served if the corporation is sued);
- the names and addresses of each of the incorporators; and
- the number of shares authorized to be issued.

Note: One or more classes of shares must have unlimited voting rights.

Pass Key

The examiners often ask what must be included in the articles of incorporation. Items not in the above list are not necessary. For example, the articles need not include a statement of the states in which the corporation is to do business or have offices, the names of the initial directors or officers, terms of office, etc. Memorize the list and do not be fooled by such other choices.

■ **Purpose Clause (Ultra Vires Act)**

A corporation may include a clause in its articles stating the business purpose for which the corporation was formed. If a corporation has a narrow purpose clause and undertakes business outside the clause (or outside the business permitted by statute), it is said to be acting "ultra vires." A director or officer who authorizes an ultra vires act may be liable to the corporation for damages caused by the act.

Illustration 1   Ultra Vires Act

If a corporation was formed to accomplish the single purpose of operating a restaurant, any action to achieve some other purpose (e.g., buying an oil and lube business) would be ultra vires.

1.2.4 Bylaws (Rules)

In addition to the articles of incorporation, a corporation generally will have bylaws containing rules for running the corporation (e.g., they may set out the authority of the corporation's officers). Bylaws are adopted by the incorporators or the board of directors and may be repealed or modified by the board of directors. They are not part of the articles of incorporation and are not required to be filed with the state.

1.2.5 Disregard of Corporate Entity (Piercing the Corporate Veil)

Courts will sometimes hold the shareholders, officers, or directors of a corporation liable because the privilege of conducting business in corporate form is being abused. This disregard of the corporate entity frequently is called "piercing the corporate veil."

Courts generally will pierce the corporate veil for any of three reasons:

1. Shareholders commingle personal funds with corporate funds or use corporate assets for personal use.

2. The corporation was inadequately (or "thinly") capitalized at the time of formation (shareholders must start the corporation with sufficient capital to reasonably meet the corporation's prospective liabilities).

3. The corporation was formed to commit fraud on existing creditors (e.g., a sole proprietor transfers all assets to a newly formed corporation so that the assets are not available to pay the sole proprietor's existing creditors).

Pass Key

Piercing the corporate veil is one of the examiners' favorite corporations issues. Be sure to memorize the three reasons for piercing: commingling personal with corporate funds, inadequate capitalization, and committing fraud on existing creditors. Be mindful of what is *not* on the list. The following do not justify piercing: incorporating as an S corporation, incorporating a partnership, and bankruptcy of a corporation that was adequately capitalized at the outset.

1.3 Financing the Corporation

Corporate capital comes from the issuance of many types of securities, including equity obligations (or stock) and debt obligations (or bonds).

1.3.1 Debt Securities (Bonds)

Bonds include secured mortgage bonds and unsecured debentures, and even bonds that may be convertible into stock (i.e., convertible bonds). Bondholders are creditors.

1.3.2 Equity Securities (Stocks)

Equity securities include shares of the corporation, stock warrants (generally, options to purchase shares granted by the corporation), and stock options (generally, options to purchase stock granted by one other than the issuing corporation). Stockholders are owners of the corporation.

- **Characteristics of Equity Securities**

    A corporation may choose to issue only one class of stock, in which case each share of stock will have the same rights. Alternatively, it may choose to issue several classes or series of stock with varying rights.

- **Consideration for Stock**

    Unless the articles provide otherwise (e.g., by setting a par value for stock), the board of directors has discretion to issue stock at any price it thinks is appropriate. Under the RMBCA, stock may be issued in exchange for any benefit to the corporation (e.g., money, property, promises to perform services in the future, promissory notes, etc.).

1.4 Shareholders: Rights, Duties, Obligations, and Authority

1.4.1 Voting Rights

Shareholders have the right to vote to elect (typically annually) or remove directors. They also have the right to vote on whether to approve fundamental changes to the corporation, such as dissolution.

- **General Rule: One Share, One Vote**

    Unless the articles of incorporation provide otherwise, each share of stock is entitled to one vote.

- **Exception: Cumulative Voting for Directors**

    The articles can give shareholders the right to cumulative voting with respect to electing directors. In cumulative voting, each share is entitled to one vote for each director position that is being filled, and the shareholder may cast the votes in any way, including casting all for a single candidate. This *helps minority shareholders gain representation on the board*.

1.4.2 Distributions (Dividends)

Generally, shareholders do not have a right to a distribution (including cash dividends and repurchases of shares) unless and until it is declared by the board of directors. Once the board declares a distribution, the shareholders are treated as unsecured creditors of the corporation to the extent of the dividend. Distributions decrease the corporation's shareholders' equity.

Pass Key

The fact that shareholders have the status of unsecured creditors once a dividend is declared has been a favorite correct answer choice on a number of past exam questions.

■ **Preferred Shareholders**

A corporation need not give each shareholder an equal right to receive distributions. Shares may be divided into classes with varying rights.

- **Noncumulative Preferred Shares**

    Shares with a preference usually are entitled to a fixed amount of money (e.g., $5 a year if the preference is a dividend preference) before distributions can be made with respect to nonpreferred shares.

- **Cumulative Preferred Shares: Dividends Carry Over to Future Years**

    With cumulative preferred shares, if a dividend is not declared in a particular year, the right to receive the preference accumulates and must be paid before nonpreferred shares may be paid any dividend.

Pass Key

Cumulative preferred dividends are an exam favorite. The key is to remember that although these dividends accumulate even if not declared, no dividend can be paid to common shareholders until all cumulative dividends are paid (even for years when dividends were not declared). No dividend is due until it is declared by the board of directors.

■ **Stock Dividends**

Stock dividends are issued from a corporation's own "authorized but unissued shares." Because no assets are distributed, the shareholders receiving the stock generally do not owe any taxes on it, the solvency of the corporation remains the same, and there is no damage to creditors and shareholders (unlike cash dividends). Thus, a stock dividend is not a distribution of corporate assets.

1.4.3   Right to Inspect Books and Records

Upon five days' written notice stating a proper purpose (one related to the shareholder's rights in the corporation), a shareholder may inspect and copy the corporation's records. The shareholder may send an attorney, accountant, or other agent to inspect.

Pass Key

The examiners often ask about shareholders' inspection rights. The key is that the shareholders (or their agents, attorneys, accountants, etc.) can inspect for any proper purpose (e.g., to start a derivative suit, to solicit shareholders to vote for certain directors, etc.), but shareholders can be denied inspection for improper purposes (e.g., to get names for a retail mailing list).

1.4.4 Preemptive Rights

When a corporation proposes to issue additional shares of stock, the current shareholders often want to purchase shares in order to maintain their proportional voting strength. The common law granted shareholders such a right, known as the "preemptive right." Under the RMBCA, preemptive rights do not exist unless the articles of incorporation provide for them.

1.4.5 Derivative Actions

When a corporation has a legal cause of action against someone but refuses to bring the action, the shareholders may have a right to bring a shareholder derivative action to enforce the corporation's rights. Such an action may be brought against directors of the corporation or outsiders.

- **Derivative Action vs. Direct Action**

  Derivative actions may be brought only to vindicate wrongs against the corporation. If a shareholder seeks to vindicate the shareholder's own rights against the corporation, a *direct* action by the shareholder against the corporation is appropriate, rather than a derivative action.

1.5 Directors: Rights, Duties, Obligations, and Authority

Among the specific duties of directors are the election, removal, and supervision of officers (directors generally review the conduct of officers and may remove an officer with or without cause); adoption, amendment, and repeal of bylaws; fixing management compensation; and initiating fundamental changes to the corporation's structure.

1.5.1 Declaration of Distributions

The board of directors has sole discretion to declare distributions to shareholders, including dividends, in the form of cash, property, or the corporation's own shares. The shareholders have no power to compel a distribution. Directors who authorize a distribution in violation of law (i.e., when the corporation is insolvent) are personally liable to the extent the distribution exceeds what would have been lawful. However, they can defend under their right to rely (which will be discussed later). Moreover, the director can recover from a shareholder who received a contribution knowing that it was unlawful.

1.5.2 Fiduciary Duties and the Business Judgment Rule

Directors are fiduciaries of the corporation and must act in the best interests of the corporation. However, directors are not insurers of the corporation's success. A director will not be liable to the corporation for acts performed or decisions made in good faith, in a manner the director believes to be in the best interest of the corporation, and with the care an ordinarily prudent person in a like position would exercise. (This is sometimes called "the business judgment rule.") Thus, directors will be liable to the corporation only for negligent acts or omissions (e.g., failure to obtain fire insurance, hiring a convicted embezzler as treasurer without performing a background check, etc.).

■ **Right to Rely**

A director is entitled to rely on information, opinions, reports, or statements (including financial statements) if prepared by any of the following:

- corporate officers, employees, or a committee of the board whom the director reasonably believes to be reliable and competent; or

- legal counsel, accountants, or other persons as to matters the director reasonably believes are within such person's professional competence.

■ **Duty of Loyalty**

Directors owe their corporation a duty of loyalty and must act in the best interests of their corporation.

- The duty of loyalty prohibits directors from competing with the corporation, but does not necessarily prohibit directors from transacting business with the corporation (e.g., by buying from or selling to the corporation). An action in which a director has a conflict of interest will be upheld only if:

  —after full disclosure the transaction is approved by a disinterested majority of the board of directors or the shareholders; or

  —the transaction was fair and reasonable to the corporation.

- The board of directors has the power to set director compensation.

■ **Indemnification**

Generally, corporations are allowed to indemnify directors for expenses for any lawsuit brought against them in their corporate capacity. The corporation may also pay any judgment imposed in a lawsuit on the director, except in a shareholder derivative suit.

1.6 Officers: Rights, Duties, Obligations, and Authority

Officers are individual agents (and employees) of the corporation who ordinarily conduct its day-to-day operations and may bind the corporation to contracts made on its behalf. Note that a person may hold more than one office.

1.6.1 Selection and Removal

Officers are selected by the directors and may be removed by the directors with or without cause. They are not elected by the shareholders.

1.6.2 Authority

Officers are corporate agents and agency rules determine their authority and power. A corporate president will generally have apparent authority to enter into contracts and act on behalf of the corporation in the ordinary course of business.

1.6.3 Fiduciary Duties and Indemnification

Corporate officers, like corporate directors, are subject to fiduciary duties and must discharge their duties in good faith and with the same care as an ordinarily prudent person in a like position. Like directors, officers may be indemnified for expenses and judgments from litigation brought against them in their corporate capacity, and they are protected by the business judgment rule.

1.6.4 May Also Serve as Directors

Officers may also serve as directors of the corporation.

1.6.5 Not Required to Be Shareholders

An officer is not required to be, but may be, a shareholder of the corporation.

Pass Key

The key to several past questions has been the power structure of corporations. Remember, the shareholders generally have no direct power to manage the corporation. They elect the board of directors, but generally, the board does not manage the corporation; instead, it appoints officers to manage on a day-to-day basis. Keep in mind that the shareholders do not elect the officers, and neither do the shareholders have the power to remove officers. Officers serve at the discretion of the board.

1.7 Fundamental Changes

Decisions regarding issues that might fundamentally change the nature of the corporation require shareholder approval through a special procedure. Such fundamental corporate changes include some amendments to the articles of incorporation, dissolutions, mergers, consolidations, share exchanges, and sales of all or substantially all of the corporation's assets.

Pass Key

Remember that the examiners often ask about fundamental corporate changes. The fundamental changes that require shareholder approval include:

Mnemonic: "**DAMS**"

Dissolution

Amendments to the articles of incorporation that materially and adversely affect the shareholders' rights

Mergers, consolidations, and compulsory share exchanges

Sale of substantially all the corporation's assets outside the regular course of business

1.7.1 General Procedure

- **Board Resolution**

    A majority of the board of directors must adopt a resolution setting forth the proposed action and submitting it for a vote at a shareholders' meeting.

- **Notice**

    The corporation must notify all shareholders even if they are not entitled to vote.

- **Shareholder Approval**

    The change must be approved by a majority of the shares voted at the meeting.

■ **Filing of Articles**

A document setting forth the action taken (referred to as "articles") must be executed by the corporation and be filed with the state.

Pass Key

The examiners often ask about fundamental corporate changes. The key points to remember are:

- The board must approve a resolution, but there is no requirement of unanimity.

- The shareholders must be given notice and an opportunity to vote on the change. Approval requires a majority of the votes cast.

■ **Right to Dissent/Appraisal Rights**

Shareholders who have a right to vote on a fundamental corporate change typically have a right to dissent/appraisal right (i.e., the right to have the corporation purchase their shares at a fair price) if the shareholder votes against the fundamental change and it is nevertheless approved.

1.7.2   Amendments to the Articles of Incorporation

The corporation may amend its articles of incorporation in any and as many respects as desired, as long as the provisions, as amended, are lawful.

1.7.3   Merger, Consolidation, and Share Exchange

■ **Definitions and Distinctions**

- **Merger**

    A merger involves one or more corporations joining with another corporation. One corporation survives the merger and continues in existence, while the other merging corporations cease to exist following the merger.

Illustration 2   Merger

XYZ Corp. merges with ABC Corp., and following the merger XYZ Corp. ceases to exist. ABC Corp. now survives, with all of the assets and shareholders that formerly belonged to XYZ Corp.

- **Consolidation**

    A consolidation involves one or more corporations joining together to form a new corporation. Each constituent corporation ceases to exist after the consolidation; only the new corporation goes on. The new corporation is liable for the debts of the old corporation.

- **Share Exchange**

    A share exchange is a transaction in which one corporation acquires all of the outstanding shares of one or more classes of stock of another corporation. Both corporations continue to exist as separate entities.

■ **Procedure in General**

Both corporations in a merger and all corporations involved in a consolidation must follow the general procedure for fundamental corporate changes set out above (board resolution, notice, approval by majority of the shares, and filing). The notice must include a summary of the plan of merger, consolidation, share exchange, etc. In a share exchange, only the corporation whose shares are being acquired need follow the fundamental change procedure. The plan of merger or share exchange must include the terms and conditions of the plan and the manner of converting the corporation's securities.

- **Merger of Subsidiary (Short-Form Merger)**

    A parent corporation owning 90 percent or more of a subsidiary corporation may merge the subsidiary into the parent without the approval of the shareholders of either corporation or the approval of the subsidiary's board. However, the parent must mail a copy of the plan to each shareholder who has not waived this right.

- **Effect of Mergers Into a Surviving Corporation**

    A corporation merged into a surviving corporation ceases to exist as a separate entity. The surviving corporation has all rights, liabilities, and obligations of the merged corporations. When a share exchange takes place, the shares are exchanged as the plan provides, and the holders are entitled only to the rights of the exchanged shares.

- **Fending Off Unwanted Takeover Attempts**

    If a corporation is faced with the prospect of being taken over and the board of directors wants to resist the takeover attempt, it may do so in a number of ways, including:

    —persuading shareholders to reject the offer;

    —suing the person or company attempting the takeover for misrepresentation or omission and obtain an injunction against the takeover;

    —merging with a white knight (a company with which the directors want to merge);

    —making a "self-tender" (an offer to acquire stock from its own stockholders and thus retain control in order to prevent a takeover);

    —paying "greenmail" (i.e., pay the person or company attempting the takeover to abandon its takeover attempt);

    —locking up the crown jewels (i.e., give a third party an option to purchase the company's most valuable assets);

    —undertaking a "scorched earth" policy (which is to sell off assets or take out loans that would make the company less financially attractive); or

    —applying "shark repellent," which means amending the articles of incorporation or bylaws to make a takeover more difficult (e.g., require a large number of shareholders to approve the merger).

1.8 Termination of a Corporation

Dissolution is a fundamental change, requiring director and shareholder approval. Dissolution can also be pursuant to a court order.

After dissolution, the corporation continues in existence for purposes of winding up. Liquidation involves the process of collecting the corporate assets, paying the expenses involved, satisfying creditors' claims, and distributing the net assets of the corporation.

1.9   Calendar Year vs. Fiscal Year

Companies typically have the option of choosing a calendar year-end (a year ending on December 31) or a fiscal year-end (one ending on any day other than December 31). For tax purposes, a fiscal year must first be approved by the IRS.

1.10   Foreign Corporation Must Qualify

A foreign corporation must obtain a certificate of authority from each state in which it does intrastate business. A foreign corporation is a corporation created under the laws of another state. Maintaining an office in the foreign state would be an example of doing business in the foreign state. But merely maintaining a bank account, collecting a debt, or hiring employees in a foreign state are not instances of doing business in the foreign state sufficient to trigger the qualification requirement.

Question 1	MCQ-03235

Under the Revised Model Business Corporation Act, which of the following statements is correct regarding corporate officers of a public corporation?

   a. An officer may not simultaneously serve as a director.

   b. A corporation may be authorized to indemnify its officers for liability incurred in a suit by stockholders.

   c. Stockholders always have the right to elect a corporation's officers.

   d. An officer of a corporation is required to own at least one share of the corporation's stock.

Question 2	MCQ-03027

Which of the following statements is a general requirement for the merger of two corporations?

   a. The merger plan must be approved unanimously by the stockholders of both corporations.

   b. The merger plan must be approved unanimously by the boards of both corporations.

   c. The absorbed corporation must amend its articles of incorporation.

   d. The stockholders of both corporations must be given due notice of a special meeting, including a copy or summary of the merger plan.

NOTES

NOTES

REGULATION 1

1. MCQ-01404

Choice "d" is correct. The requirements that enable a taxpayer to be classified as a "qualifying widow(er)" are:

1. The taxpayer's spouse died in one of the two previous years and the taxpayer did not remarry in the current tax year;

2. The taxpayer has a child who can be claimed as a dependent;

3. This child lived in the taxpayer's home for all of the current tax year;

4. The taxpayer paid over half the cost of keeping up a home for the child; and

5. The taxpayer could have filed a joint return in the year the spouse died.

2. MCQ-06433

Choice "b" is correct. Mark and Molly were *married* as of midnight on December 31, Year 1. Therefore, Mark's only options are to file as married either jointly or separately, and because "jointly" is the only option presented that qualifies, it is the correct choice.

Choices "a", "c", and "d" are incorrect, based on the above explanation.

1. MCQ-01636

Choice "b" is correct. Except for interest from state and local government bonds, interest income is fully taxable, so the $10 is included in income. Since Clark did not itemize deductions on his Year 8 federal income tax return, he did not deduct any state income taxes last year. Under the tax benefit rule, the refund is not taxable this year because Clark did not deduct the tax last year.

2. MCQ-01620

Choice "b" is correct. Alimony paid pursuant to a divorce or separation agreement executed before 12/31/18 would be income to Mary while child support would not. Funds qualify as child support only if 1) a specific amount is fixed or is contingent on the child's status (e.g., reaching a certain age); 2) it is paid solely for the support of minor children; and 3) it is payable by decree, instrument, or agreement. The actual use of the funds is irrelevant to the issue. In this case, $2,000 (20% × $10,000) qualifies as child support. The other $8,000 is alimony, which would be income to Mary. Note that for all divorce or separation agreements executed after 12/31/18, the alimony is neither taxable to the recipient nor deductible by the payor.

Choice "a" is incorrect. Take 80% of the $10,000 paid, not 80% of the $7,000 received by Mary.

Choice "c" is incorrect. Only $8,000 would be alimony per the divorce decree (80% × $10,000).

Choice "d" is incorrect. The 20% reduction when the child turns 18 makes 20% of the $10,000 payment, or $2,000, child support, which is nontaxable to Mary.

3. MCQ-04756

Choice "c" is correct. Generally, the fair market value of prizes and awards is taxable income. However, an exclusion from income for certain prizes and awards applies when the winner is selected for the award without entering into a contest (i.e., without any action on the individual's part) and then assigns the award directly to a governmental unit or charitable organization. Therefore, conditions "I" and "II" must be met in order for Kent to exclude the award from his gross income.

Choice "a" is incorrect. "II" is a necessary condition as well. See explanation above.

Choice "b" is incorrect. "I" is a necessary condition as well. See explanation above.

Choice "d" is incorrect. "I" and "II" are both necessary conditions. See explanation above.

4. MCQ-01482

Choice "b" is correct. Scholarships are nontaxable for degree-seeking students to the extent that the proceeds are spent on tuition, fees, books, and supplies. The $5,000 for teaching courses is taxable compensation for services delivered.

Choice "a" is incorrect. The $5,000 for teaching courses is taxable compensation for services delivered.

Choice "c" is incorrect. The scholarship is not taxable because Klein is a degree-seeking student and used the proceeds for tuition and fees. Furthermore, the $5,000 for teaching courses is taxable compensation for services delivered.

Choice "d" is incorrect. The scholarship is not taxable because Klein is a degree-seeking student and used the proceeds for tuition and fees.

Regulation 1, Module 3

1. MCQ-01438

Choice "a" is correct. Uniform Capitalization rules provide guidelines with respect to capitalizing or expensing certain costs. With regard to inventory, direct materials, direct labor, and factory overhead should be capitalized as part of the cost of inventory. Warehousing costs, quality control, and taxes, excluding income taxes, are all considered factory overhead items. The research should be expensed.

2. MCQ-01472

Choice "b" is correct. Baker can deduct $1,200 in total expense on Form 1040 Schedule C, calculated as follows:

Direct educational expenses	$ 700	[cost of the course]
Daily expenses for 5-day seminar	500	[$100 per day × 5]
Total educational expenses	$ 1,200	

Rule: If foreign travel is primarily personal in nature (e.g., a vacation), none of the travel expenses (e.g., round-trip airfare) incurred will be allowable business deductions, even if the taxpayer was involved in business activities while in the foreign country.

Note: It does not appear that the examiners are attempting to trick candidates on the classification of the business expenses as travel or educational. It appears that the purpose of the question is to test the candidate's ability to recognize when expenses are deductible and when they are not deductible business expenses.

Choice "a" is incorrect, as the expenses for the five-day period Baker attended the seminar were directly related to being in Spain for the additional period of time and are allowable business deductions.

Choices "c" and "d" are incorrect, per the above rule.

3. MCQ-01614

Choice "d" is correct. Prepaid rent is income when received even for an accrual-basis taxpayer. The $30,000 received as consideration for canceling the lease is in substitution for rental payments and is thus rental income. The $5,000 prepaid for the last month's rent is also rental income.

Choice "a" is incorrect. The $30,000 received as consideration for canceling the lease is in substitution for rental payments and is thus rental income. The $5,000 prepaid for the last month's rent is also rental income.

Choice "b" is incorrect. The $30,000 is in substitution of rental payments and is thus rental income.

Choice "c" is incorrect. The $5,000 prepaid for the last month's rent would also be rental income.

1. MCQ-04923

Choice "c" is correct. A partnership calculates net business income or loss and passes each partner's distributive share through on Schedule K-1. Guaranteed payments paid to partners for services rendered or for the use of capital, without regard to partnership income or profit and loss sharing ratios, are an allowable tax deduction to the partnership and are separately reported on Schedule K-1 for inclusion on the partner's tax return.

Choice "a" is incorrect. Salaries paid to non-partner employees are deducted from revenues to arrive at net business income or loss at the partnership level. Each partner's distributive share of the net income or loss is then reported on Schedule K-1.

Choice "b" is incorrect. Advertising expenditures incurred by the partnership are deducted from revenues to arrive at net business income or loss at the partnership level. Each partner's distributive share of the net income or loss is then reported on Schedule K-1.

Choice "d" is incorrect. Depreciation of assets used in the business is deducted from revenues to arrive at net business income or loss at the partnership level. Each partner's distributive share of the net income or loss is then reported on Schedule K-1.

2. MCQ-08021

Choice "b" is correct. Trusts are separate income tax-paying entities. Distributions made by trusts are deductible by the trust, but taxable to the recipient. This avoids double taxation of trust income.

Choice "a" is incorrect. Distributions by trusts of income are deductible by the trust but taxable to the recipient.

Choice "c" is incorrect. Double taxation is avoided on trust income due to the distribution deduction for trust income paid to trust beneficiaries.

Choice "d" is incorrect. All income in a trust is subject to taxation. Income retained in the trust will be taxed at the trust level only, while income distributed by the trust will be deductible at the trust level, but taxable to the beneficiaries.

3. MCQ-08057

Choice "d" is correct. Because the grantor (John) does not retain (1) beneficial enjoyment of the corpus or (2) the power to dispose of the trust income without the approval or consent of any adverse party, the trust is a separate entity for tax purposes. Therefore, the trust would be required to file a Form 1041. The 1041 would issue a schedule K-1 to the income beneficiary, in this case, Connor.

Choice "a" is incorrect. Because the grantor did not retain any control or benefit from the trust, the grantor would not be taxed on the trust income.

Choice "b" is incorrect. Although the trust would file a Form 1041, a Schedule K-1 would not be issued to John because he is not the income beneficiary.

Choice "c" is incorrect. Although the income is reportable by Connor on his individual income tax return, Form 1040 is not the only reporting requirement. The trust will have to file a Form 1041 issuing a Schedule K-1 to Connor.

1. MCQ-08220

Choice "b" is correct. Any losses in excess of the at-risk amount are suspended and carried forward without expiration and are deductible against income in future years from that activity. The at-risk amount is also referred to as basis. Note that although in the textbook we discuss this for partnerships, the concept applies to all activities that have flow through income and losses.

Choice "a" is incorrect. This is the rule for suspended passive activity losses, not suspended losses due to at-risk limitations. Any losses in excess of the at-risk amount are suspended and carried forward without expiration and are deductible against income in future years from that activity.

Choice "c" is incorrect. Losses in excess of the at-risk amount may not be deducted currently against income from other activities. Any losses in excess of the at-risk amount are suspended and carried forward without expiration and are deductible against income in future years from that activity.

Choice "d" is incorrect. Losses in excess of the at-risk amount are not carried back two years against activities with income and then carried forward for 20 years. Any losses in excess of the at-risk amount are suspended and carried forward without expiration until the taxpayer generates more at-risk basis or until the activity is sold.

2. MCQ-08203

Choice "b" is correct. Tax rules allow suspended passive losses to be carried forward, but *not* back, until utilized.

Choice "a" is incorrect. This is the rule for capital losses. It does not apply to passive losses.

Choice "c" is incorrect. This rule is not correct. There is no carryback allowed for suspended passive losses.

Choice "d" is incorrect. This rule is not correct. There is no carryback allowed for suspended passive losses.

3. MCQ-06888

Choice "a" is correct. The $50,000 salary and income from partnership activity of $20,000 are taxable. Typically, passive activity losses, whether in the current or prior years, may only be used to offset passive activity income. The exception to this is in the year the passive activity is disposed of (sold); if still unused, passive activity losses are fully deductible in the year of disposal:

	Salary	$50,000
+	Income from partnership A	20,000
−	PAL from partnership B	(40,000)
−	Loss carryover from partnership B	(10,000)
	Adjusted gross income	$20,000

4. MCQ-08461

Choice "c" is correct. For the current year, there is a net passive loss of $60,000. This should be allocated to the two activities with passive losses in the ratio of their losses to total losses. Activity X will receive an allocation of $22,500 of the net loss [$60,000 × ($30,000/$80,000)].

Choices "a", "b", and "d" are incorrect, per the above explanation.

1. MCQ-07357

Choice "b" is correct. Generally there is no recognition of compensation expense with an incentive stock option.

Choices "a", "c", and "d" are incorrect, as these are all true statements.

1. MCQ-01963

Choice "a" is correct. In 2018, taxpayers can contribute and deduct up to $5,500 per year to an IRA, and alimony paid pursuant to divorce or separation agreements executed before 12/31/18 is considered earned income for IRA purposes. For couples filing a joint return where at least one spouse is an active participant in a retirement plan, the deductible portion of the contribution is phased out. For a spouse who is an active participant, the phase-out range in 2018 begins at AGI of $101,000 and is complete at $121,000. For a spouse who is not an active participant, but is married to someone who is, the phase-out range begins at $189,000 and is complete at $199,000 (2018). The earned income for IRA purposes here is $40,000 ($35,000 + $5,000), which is below both phase-out ranges, so each spouse receives a deduction of the $5,000 contribution actually made.

Choice "b" is incorrect. Pat's alimony is deemed "earned income" for the IRA contributions. However, even if Pat had no earned income, a spouse with no earned income can deduct up to $5,500, provided the couple's combined earned income is at least $11,000.

Choice "c" is incorrect. This is the amount of the additional catch-up contribution for people age 50 and older.

Choice "d" is incorrect. When a taxpayer or taxpayer's spouse is an active participant in a pension plan at work, the full deduction is allowed if the earned income of the couple is below the phase-out ranges (as is in this case).

2. MCQ-01960

Choice "c" is correct. One half of the self-employment tax is deductible to arrive at adjusted gross income.

Choice "a" is incorrect. Self-employment tax is partially deductible to arrive at adjusted gross income.

Choice "b" is incorrect. Self-employment tax is not deductible in determining self-employment income.

Choice "d" is incorrect. Self-employment tax is partially deductible to arrive at adjusted gross income.

1. MCQ-02011

Choice "d" is correct. In order to qualify for the additional standard deduction, an individual must be age 65 or older or blind by the end of the tax year. He or she does not have to support a dependent child or aged parent.

2. MCQ-01922

Choice "b" is correct. Both medical expenses are deductible. The cosmetic surgery is not elective, because it was necessary to correct a congenital deformity.

Doctor bills	$ 5,000
Surgery	15,000
	$20,000
AGI limitation ($100,000 × 10.0%)	(10,000)
Deduction	$10,000

Choices "a", "c", and "d" are incorrect, per the computation above.

3. MCQ-01926

Choice "a" is correct. Individual taxpayers may deduct the FMV of property donated to charity. The limit is 30 percent of the taxpayer's AGI (30% × $90,000 = $27,000). The FMV of the property is $25,000 and is within the allowable amount.

1. MCQ-02013

Choice "b" is correct. The adoption fees would be qualifying expenses for the tax credit (medical expenses do not qualify).

Choice "a" is incorrect. $5,000 of the $16,000 of total expenses are not eligible.

Choice "c" is incorrect. The expenses ($8,000 + $3,000) are eligible.

Choice "d" is incorrect. Medical expenses are not eligible for the credit.

2. MCQ-02012

Choice "c" is correct. The earned income credit is refundable. Eligible taxpayers can get advance payments from their employers because the credit is assured.

3. MCQ-02084

Choice "a" is correct. Provided the taxes due after withholdings were not over $1,000, there is no penalty for underpayment of estimated taxes. Note that there would be a failure to pay penalty on the $200 that was not paid until April 30, but this is a separate penalty.

Choice "b" is incorrect. This $200 would be subject to a failure to pay penalty, but if the balance due after withholdings is not over $1,000, there is no penalty for underpayment of estimated taxes.

Choice "c" is incorrect. If the balance of tax due after withholdings is not over $1,000, there is no penalty for underpayment of estimated taxes.

Choice "d" is incorrect. The penalty for underpayment of estimated taxes is not assessed on the full amount of the income tax liability, only the unpaid amount after withholdings to the extent it exceeds $1,000.

Regulation 2, Module 4

1. MCQ-02023

Choice "d" is correct. Alternative minimum tax (AMT) paid can be claimed as a credit against other years if the tax was paid on items that increased AMT that year but will reverse in later years. The concept is the same as deferred taxes for financial accounting purposes. The credit is carried forward indefinitely.

2. MCQ-02015

Choice "c" is correct. Mills' alternative minimum taxable income starts with his taxable income ($70,000). This is increased by state and local taxes paid ($5,000) and property taxes paid ($2,000) for a total of $77,000. The home mortgage interest on a loan to acquire the residence ($6,000) does not increase alternative minimum taxable income.

Choice "a" is incorrect. State and local income taxes must be added back to Mills' taxable income in calculating alternative minimum taxable income.

Choice "b" is incorrect. Property taxes paid and deducted as itemized deductions must be added back to Mills' taxable income in calculating alternative minimum taxable income.

Choice "d" is incorrect. Home mortgage interest is not added back to Mills' taxable income to calculate alternative minimum taxable income.

3. MCQ-02019

Choice "b" is correct. Tax-exempt interest from private activity bonds (generally) and accelerated depletion, depreciation, or amortization are alternative minimum tax preference items. Charitable contributions of appreciated capital gain property are not alternative minimum tax preferences.

NOTES

1. MCQ-01736

Choice "a" is correct.

Rule: The basis of property received as a gift in the hands of the donee depends on whether the selling price of the property is more or less than the basis for gain or loss.

If the property is sold at a gain, the basis to the donee is the same as it would be in the hands of the donor. If the property is sold at a loss, the basis to the donee is the same as it would be in the hands of the donor or the FV of the property at the date of the gift, whichever is lower. In some cases, such as in this fact situation, there is neither gain nor loss on the sale of the gift, because the selling price is less than the basis for gain and more than the basis for loss.

Choices "b", "c", and "d" are incorrect, per the above rule.

2. MCQ-01669

Choice "c" is correct.

Rule: The executor can elect to use an alternate valuation date rather than the decedent's date of death to value the property included in the gross estate. The alternate date is generally six months after the decedent's death or the earlier date of sale or distribution.

Note: The valuation of the assets in an estate affects the recipient as basis of the inherited assets.

Choices "a", "b", and "d" are incorrect, per the above rule.

1. MCQ-01671

Choice "c" is correct. Provided Davis has lived in his home for two years or more out of the five years preceding his sale of his residence, as a single taxpayer he may exclude up to $250,000 of gain on its sale. The basis on the residence sold in Year 17 is equal to its cost ($200,000).

Selling price	$ 455,000
Less: basis	(200,000)
Realized gain	255,000
Less: excluded amount	(250,000)
Recognized gain	$ 5,000

Choices "a", "b", and "d" are incorrect, per the above explanation.

2. MCQ-01747

Choice "c" is correct. $50,000 is Reed's recognized gain in Year 9.

Rule: Gain is only recognized on an exchange of "like-kind" property for the lesser of the amount of "gain realized" or the amount of "boot" received in the exchange.

Fair value of property received	$ 450,000
Amount of cash (boot) received	50,000
Total amount realized	$ 500,000
Basis of property given up	(300,000)
Gain realized	$ 200,000
Gain recognized*	$ 50,000

*Gain recognized is the lesser of the amount of gain realized or amount of the boot received.

Choices "a", "b", and "d" are incorrect, per the above rule.

3. MCQ-01742

Choice "d" is correct. No taxable gain or loss will be recognized on a like-kind exchange if both assets are real estate property. Rental real estate located in different states qualifies for a like-kind exchange.

Choices "a", "b", and "c" are incorrect. In order to meet the like-kind exchange requirements for nonrecognition of gain or loss, the property exchanged must be real property. Convertible debentures, convertible preferred stock, and partnership interests are not real property.

Regulation 3, Module 3

1. MCQ-01761

Choice "d" is correct. Because the parking lot and the shed constitute real estate and depreciable assets used in a trade or business, respectively, they are not capital assets per the definition below.

Note: The parking lot and shed will fall under Section 1231 (provided they are used in the business over 12 months) and possibly Section 1250 and 1245, respectively, upon sale of the assets.

Capital assets are defined as all property held by the taxpayer, *except:*

1. Property normally included in inventory or held for sale to customers in the ordinary course of business.

2. Depreciable property and real estate used in business.

3. Accounts and notes receivable arising from sales or services in the taxpayer's business.

4. Copyrights, literary, musical, or artistic compositions held by the original artist. (Exception: Sales of musical compositions held by the original artist receive capital gain treatment.)

5. Treasury stock.

Choices "a", "b", and "c" are incorrect, per the above rule.

2. MCQ-01876

Choice "b" is correct. The capital loss deduction is limited to $3,000 per year with the excess carried forward indefinitely. In this case, Lee can deduct $3,000 against his income and carry forward the remaining $5,000.

Choices "a", "c", and "d" are incorrect, based on the above explanation.

Regulation 3, Module 4

1. MCQ-01726

Choice "b" is correct. Losses between related parties are disallowed. Therefore, Fay's $4,000 capital loss ($15,000 basis less $11,000 received) is disallowed because she sold the stock to her son, a related party. When her son sells the stock to an unrelated party, however, he can use the $4,000 disallowed loss to reduce any gain he realized from the sale (but not to create or increase a loss). His realized gain is $5,000 ($16,000 received less $11,000 basis), but he can reduce it by $4,000 to $1,000 using his mother's disallowed loss. Martin sold the stock for higher than Fay purchased it. The donor's basis ($15,000) is, therefore, used to determine gain on the sale by Martin.

Choice "a" is incorrect. Martin's gain, after reducing it by his mother's disallowed loss, is reported on his tax return.

Choice "c" is incorrect. The $4,000 disallowed loss to his mother reduces his $5,000 gain.

Choice "d" is incorrect. The $5,000 gain is reduced by his mother's $4,000 disallowed loss.

Regulation 3, Module 5

1. MCQ-02058

Choice "d" is correct. Only the building is depreciable, so the depreciable portion is $264,000 less $30,000 land, for a net of $234,000. The MACRS rules provide a 39-year life, straight-line depreciation, and a "mid-month" acquisition convention that treats the property as acquired in the middle of the month, regardless of the actual date of acquisition. Therefore, the August 1, Year 1, service date provides a half-month's depreciation for August, plus a full month for September through December, for a total of 4.5 months for Year 1. ($234,000/39 years) × (4.5/12) = $2,250.

Choice "a" is incorrect. The recovery period for nonresidential real property is 39 years and the mid-month convention is used. The building is treated as if acquired in the middle of the month, regardless of the actual date of acquisition. Depreciation may only be taken for the months after the building was placed in service.

Choice "b" is incorrect. The mid-month convention is used for real property. The building is treated as if acquired in the middle of the month, regardless of the actual date of acquisition. Depreciation may only be taken for the months after the building was placed in service.

Choice "c" is incorrect. The recovery period for nonresidential real property is 39 years.

NOTES

REGULATION 4

1. MCQ-04633

Choice "b" is correct. A sole proprietorship and (in most states) a limited liability company can be formed with only one owner. A partnership requires two or more partners.

Choices "a", "c", and "d" are incorrect, per the explanation above.

2. MCQ-02030

Choice "a" is correct. The formation of a corporation under these circumstances is a nontaxable event. Thus Lind would report zero gain upon the formation of the corporation.

Choices "b", "c", and "d" are incorrect. Because the formation of this corporation is a nontaxable event, no gain or loss would be reported by Lind.

1. MCQ-02047

Choice "d" is correct. The dividends-received deduction (DRD) is generally calculated as 50 percent of dividends received, which would be $50,000 (50% × $100,000). However, the deduction is limited to 50% × dividends-received deduction (DRD) modified taxable income. DRD modified taxable income is calculated as taxable income before the dividends-received deduction, any NOL deduction, and capital loss carryback deduction. Because the loss of $10,000 is a current year loss and not a carryover, it is not an adjustment to taxable income when calculating modified taxable income. DRD modified taxable income is $90,000. Best's DRD deduction on its Year 1 tax return is limited to $45,000 (50% × $90,000).

Choice "a" is incorrect. The 100 percent DRD is available only when 80–100 percent of the stock is owned (making these entities related).

Choice "b" is incorrect. The 65 percent DRD is used when at least 20 percent but less than 80 percent of the stock is owned.

Choice "c" is incorrect. The deduction is limited to 50 percent of the lesser of dividends-received deduction modified taxable income or the dividends received.

1. MCQ-02039

Choice "c" is correct. Municipal bond interest, the interest expense on debt incurred to carry the municipal bonds, and federal income tax expense will be adjustments to taxable income.

Reported book income	$380,000
Municipal bond interest	(50,000)
Federal income tax expense	170,000
Interest to carry municipal bonds	2,000
Taxable income	$502,000

2. MCQ-02243

Choice "b" is correct. Schedule M-1 of Form 1120 is used to reconcile the differences between book income and taxable income. Because the interest incurred on loans to carry U.S. obligations and the provision for state corporation income tax are treated the same for both book purposes and tax return purposes, no Schedule M-1 adjustment is required. However, if the interest expense were to carry nontaxable municipal obligations, then the interest would not be tax deductible and would be an adjustment on the Schedule M-1 reconciliation.

Choices "a", "c", and "d" are incorrect, per the above explanation.

3. MCQ-05301

Choice "b" is correct. Schedule M-1 reports the reconciliation of income (loss) per books to income (loss) per the tax return. (Note: It reports both permanent and temporary differences that are discussed in the Financial textbook for deferred taxes.) Items that are included on this schedule are those that are (1) reported as income for book purposes but not for tax purposes; (2) reported as an expense for book purposes but not for tax purposes; (3) reported as taxable income for tax purposes but not as income for book purposes; and (4) reported as deductible for tax purposes but not as an expense for book purposes. The only option above that falls into one of these four categories is option b. Premiums paid on a key-person life insurance policy are proper GAAP expenses for book purposes, but they are not allowable deductions for tax purposes.

Choice "a" is incorrect. Cash distributions to shareholders are not reported on the income statement for book purposes and are not deductible for tax purposes. They do not enter into the calculation of income in either case and are not reported on Schedule M-1. Cash distributions actually are reported on Schedule M-2, which is a reconciliation of unappropriated retained earnings.

Choice "c" is incorrect. Corporate bond interest is not reported differently for GAAP and tax purposes. It is included as income for GAAP purposes and for tax purposes. Therefore, no reconciliation of book income to taxable income is required for this item.

Choice "d" is incorrect. The ending balance of retained earnings is not reported on a GAAP income statement, nor is it included as part of taxable income. Therefore, it is not part of Schedule M-1. Unappropriated retained earnings are reconciled on Schedule M-2 of Form 1120.

Regulation 4, Module 4

1. MCQ-02117

Choice "a" is correct. The general business credit combines several nonrefundable tax credits and provides rules for their absorption against the taxpayer's liability.

Choice "b" is incorrect. The foreign tax credit does not combine more than one credit.

Choice "c" is incorrect. The minimum tax credit does not combine more than one credit.

Choice "d" is incorrect. The enhanced oil recovery credit does not combine more than one credit.

2. MCQ-02068

Choice "d" is correct. The imposition of the accumulated earnings tax does not depend on the number of shareholders a corporation has.

Choice "a" is incorrect. Partnerships are not liable for the accumulated earnings tax, but most corporations are potentially liable.

Choice "b" is incorrect. Corporations that make distributions in excess of accumulated earnings are not liable for the accumulated earnings tax. There would be no accumulated earnings left to tax.

Choice "c" is incorrect. Personal holding companies are not liable for the accumulated earnings tax.

Regulation 4, Module 5

1. MCQ-06007

Rule: An affiliated group of corporations may elect to be taxed as a single unit, thereby eliminating intercompany gains and losses. To be entitled to file a consolidated return, all the corporations in the group (1) must have been members of an affiliated group at some time during the tax year and (2) must have filed a consent (the act of filing a consolidated return qualifies as consent). An affiliated group means that a common parent owns (1) 80 percent or more of the voting power of all outstanding stock and (2) 80 percent or more of the value of all outstanding stock of each corporation.

Rule: *Not all corporations are allowed the privilege of filing a consolidated return.* Examples of those *denied* the privilege include S corporations, foreign corporations, most real estate investment trusts (REITs), some insurance companies, brother-sister corporations in which an individual (not a corporation) owns 80 percent or more of the stock of two or more corporations, and most exempt organizations.

Choice "d" is correct. An affiliated group of corporations may file a consolidated return (electing to be taxed as a single unit and eliminating intercompany gains and losses). This answer option comes right out and defines the entities as an "affiliated group," thereby removing the need to determine if the group is actually affiliated.

Choice "a" is incorrect. Per the above rule, not all corporations are allowed the privilege of filing a consolidated return. Examples of those denied the privilege include S corporations, foreign corporations, most real estate investment trusts (REITs), some insurance companies, *brother-sister corporations* in which an individual (not a corporation) owns 80 percent or more of the stock of two or more corporations, and most exempt organizations.

Choice "b" is incorrect. Per the above rule, an affiliated group means that a common parent owns (1) 80 percent or more of the voting power of all outstanding stock and (2) 80 percent or more of the value of all outstanding stock of each corporation. In this answer option, the parent owns partnerships, not corporations [and, even if it did own corporations, the percentage ownership is too small at "more than 10 percent"].

Choice "c" is incorrect. Per the above rule, an affiliated group means that a common parent owns (1) 80 percent or more of the voting power of all outstanding stock and (2) 80 percent or more of the value of all outstanding stock of each corporation. In this answer option, the parent owns only "more than 50 percent" of the controlled corporations.

2. MCQ-02112

Choice "a" is correct. A significant advantage of consolidated tax returns is the ability to offset gains and losses among group members as if they were a single taxpayer.

Choice "b" is incorrect. Corporations need not have audited financial statements issued on a consolidated basis to file a consolidated tax return.

Choice "c" is incorrect. 100 percent of dividends received by the parent are eliminated on a consolidated tax return.

Choice "d" is incorrect. The common parent must own directly or indirectly 80 percent of the total voting power of all corporations included in the consolidated tax return.

Regulation 4, Module 6

1. MCQ-05271

Choice "c" is correct. Net capital losses are not allowable deductions for corporations. A corporation can only use capital losses to offset capital gains. Further, the deduction for charitable contributions may be limited in some cases, and no charitable contribution deduction is allowed in calculating the NOL. The facts of this question indicate that there are no reported capital gains or losses or charitable contributions for any of the consolidated entities; therefore, we know that we are able to use the total income (loss) identified in the facts to calculate the net operating loss. When entities file consolidated income tax returns, 100 percent of their net income (losses) is consolidated. The facts do not indicate that any inter-company transactions exist; therefore, there are no elimination entries to make before consolidating the net income (loss). The consolidated net operating loss is calculated as follows:

ParentCo	$ 50,000
SubOne	(60,000)
SubTwo	(40,000)
NOL	$(50,000)

Choice "a" is incorrect. A consolidated net loss of $50,000 exists, as calculated above.

Choice "b" is incorrect. A consolidated net loss of $50,000 exists, as calculated above.

Choice "d" is incorrect. The income from ParentCo ($50,000) is netted with the losses from the subsidiaries ($100,000) to arrive at the consolidated net operating loss of $50,000.

2. MCQ-02151

Choice "b" is correct.

Rule: Unused capital losses of a corporation that are carried back or forward are treated as short-term capital losses whether or not they were short-term or long-term when sustained. Capital losses can only be used to offset capital gains up to the amount of the carryback or carryover, not ordinary income.

Choices "a", "c", and "d" are incorrect, per the above rule.

1. MCQ-02120

Choice "c" is correct. The property distributed by Tank is treated as if it were sold to the shareholder at its fair market value on the date of distribution. Tank recognizes gain to the extent of the fair market value ($30,000) over the adjusted basis ($20,000) or $10,000.

Choice "a" is incorrect. Gain is computed as the difference between the FMV and adjusted basis of the property.

Choice "b" is incorrect. Gain is not equal to the adjusted basis of the property.

Choice "d" is incorrect. Gain is recognized.

2. MCQ-02026

Choice "d" is correct. Hall's gain is the difference in the $33,000 he received for his stock and his basis of $16,000, for a gain of $17,000 which is a capital gain.

Choice "a" is incorrect. Because this is a sale of Hall's interest in Elm, this is not a dividend.

Choice "b" is incorrect. The accumulated earnings of Elm have no relationship to the stock surrender.

Choice "c" is incorrect. The amount of the capital gain calculated on the stock surrender is not based on the end of year amount of accumulated earnings and profits.

NOTES

1. MCQ-01966

Choice "d" is correct. S corporations that are former C corporations with undistributed C corporation earnings and profits are restricted in the amount of passive investment income they can realize without terminating their S election. The restriction is 25 percent of total gross receipts from passive investment income. The S election is terminated if the S corporation has passive investment income greater than 25 percent of gross receipts for three consecutive years. After three years with 90 percent of its gross receipts from passive sources, Bristol will lose its S corporation status on the first day of its Year 6 taxable year.

Choice "a" is incorrect. An S corporation can have as many as 100 shareholders.

Choice "b" is incorrect. A decedent's estate may be an S corporation shareholder.

Choice "c" is incorrect. S corporations pass their charitable contribution deductions through to shareholders.

2. MCQ-01955

Choice "d" is correct. $7,200 of insurance premiums (the amount of family coverage premiums, as indicated in the question) is includable in Mill's gross income.

Rule: Fringe benefits paid by an S corporation are deductible by the S corporation only for non-shareholder employees and those employee-shareholders owning 2 percent or less of the S corporation. Other fringe benefits paid are deductible by the S corporation if included as part of gross income from the S corporation for the individual receiving the benefits (i.e., included as part of income on the shareholder's W-2).

Choices "a", "b", and "c" are incorrect, per the above rule.

1. MCQ-08044

Choice "a" is correct. When property is contributed to a partnership that is subject to a liability, the contributing partner's basis is reduced by the amount of the liabilities assumed by the other partners. As long as the liabilities assumed by others do not exceed the basis of the property contributed, the contributing partner will not have to recognize gain at the time of the contribution.

Seventy-five percent of the partnership is owned by others. Dan is still liable for 25 percent of the property's liability, which would not reduce his basis. The liabilities assumed by others would increase the basis of each of the other partners by the amount of the liability assumed by each.

Basis of property contributed	$ 50,000	
Liabilities assumed by other partners	(45,000)	(75 percent of total liability)
Basis of contributing partner	$ 5,000	

Choices "b", "c", and "d" are incorrect, per the above explanation.

2. MCQ-04917

Choice "d" is correct. A partner's basis in his partnership interest is the combination of his capital account and his share of liabilities that he is personally liable for. The beginning basis of $50,000 should be decreased by each partner's share of the $30,000 operating loss, or $15,000, and increased for each partner's share of the liabilities, or $40,000, for current calendar year-end basis of $75,000.

Choices "a", "b", and "c" are incorrect, per the above explanation.

Regulation 5, Module 3

1. MCQ-01793

Choice "b" is correct. Jody's basis in the distributed property is $30,000, Jody's remaining basis in the partnership after the cash distribution:

Jody's partnership basis	$ 50,000
Cash distribution and Jody's basis in cash	(20,000)
	$ 30,000
Property distribution and Jody's basis in the property	(30,000)*
Jody's partnership basis after distributions	$ 0

*If the partner's basis in the partnership ($30,000) is less than the property's basis ($40,000), the partner's basis in the property is limited to her basis in the partnership ($30,000).

Choice "a" is incorrect. $0 is Jody's basis in the partnership after the distributions, not her basis in the property.

Choice "c" is incorrect. The partner's basis in distributed property is equal to the partnership's basis in the distributed property, not the fair market value. In this instance, because the partnership's basis exceeds the partner's basis in the partnership, the partner's basis is limited.

Choice "d" is incorrect. If the partner's basis in the partnership is less than the property's basis, the partner's basis in the property is limited to her basis in the partnership. Remember, the cash distributed must be subtracted from the partner's basis first.

2. MCQ-01791

Choice "a" is correct. The $20,000 current distribution of cash is first applied to Jody's $50,000 basis, reducing it to $30,000. The current distribution of property is then applied at its $40,000 basis. Because Jody's remaining basis is $30,000, only $30,000 is applied to the property distribution, resulting in $0 taxable gain to Jody and $0 remaining basis in the partnership.

Choice "b" is incorrect. First, the cash distribution is fully applied, then the property distribution is applied at adjusted basis until the partner's basis is zero. No gain is generally recognized by the partner as a result of a current distribution unless the cash distributed is in excess of the partner's basis. In that case, the excess would be a gain to the partner (to avoid a negative basis).

Choice "c" is incorrect. The $10,000 gain is not recognized because the property distributed takes on a $30,000 basis to the partner.

Choice "d" is incorrect. First, the cash distribution is fully applied, then the property distribution is applied at adjusted basis until the partner's basis is zero. No gain is generally recognized by the partner as a result of a current distribution unless the cash distributed is in excess of the partner's basis. In that case, the excess would be a gain to the partner (to avoid a negative basis).

1. MCQ-01802

Choice "d" is correct. When a partner sells his partnership interest, a capital gain or loss on the sale is recognized. To the extent that there are Section 751(a) hot assets (unrealized receivables or substantially appreciated inventory), the partner must recognize ordinary income or loss. In this case, the partnership has no Section 751 assets. The amount realized less the partner's basis in the partnership is the capital gain or loss. The amount realized is $55,000 ($30,000 cash received + $25,000 relief of debt). The partner's basis in the partnership is $40,000. Thus, the capital gain is $55,000 − $40,000, or $15,000.

Choice "a" is incorrect. Because there are no Section 751 assets, the gain or loss must be capital, not ordinary.

Choice "b" is incorrect. Because there are no Section 751 assets, the gain or loss must be capital, not ordinary.

Choice "c" is incorrect. The amount realized must include the $25,000 debt relief.

2. MCQ-01796

Choice "c" is correct. In a liquidating distribution, the $100,000 cash is applied first to the $180,000 partnership basis, reducing it to $80,000. Even though the partnership's basis in the real estate is only $70,000, Vance's basis in the real estate will be his partnership basis ($80,000) because this is the last asset distributed and it is a liquidating distribution (i.e., Vance's partnership basis must be reduced to zero). Neither Vance nor the partnership recognizes any gain or loss from the distribution.

Choice "a" is incorrect. The real estate's fair market value is not used.

Choice "b" is incorrect. $83,000 is the average of the $70,000 basis and the $96,000 fair market value. The average of the two amounts is not used.

Choice "d" is incorrect. Even though the partnership's basis in the real estate is $70,000, Vance's basis in the real estate will be stepped up to $80,000, Vance's remaining basis in the partnership. Because this is a liquidating distribution, Vance's basis in the partnership must be reduced to zero.

3. MCQ-05960

Choice "c" is correct. In a complete liquidation of a partnership, a partner (Baker) recognizes gain only to the extent that the money received (if any) exceeds that partner's adjusted basis in the partnership immediately before the distribution. In this question, there is no money distributed, so there is no gain. The partner recognizes loss if only money, unrealized receivables, or inventory are received and if the basis of the assets received is less than the partner's basis in the partnership. In this question, there is no money, unrealized receivables, or inventory distributed, so there is no loss, regardless of the partner's basis in the partnership. Even though the land has a $40,000 fair market value, Baker's basis in the land is his $60,000 partnership basis, effectively giving him a $20,000 built-in loss that he can recognize by selling the land.

Choice "a" is incorrect. The $35,000 is the difference between the $40,000 fair market value of the land and the land's $75,000 adjusted basis (to the partnership). That difference is not reported as a loss by the partner or by the partnership.

Choice "b" is incorrect. The $20,000 is the difference between the $40,000 fair market value of the land and the $60,000 partner's adjusted basis in the partnership. That amount is the partner's built-in loss in the land, but the loss is not recognized unless and until the partner sells or disposes of the land in a separate taxable transaction.

Choice "d" is incorrect. The $15,000 is the difference between the $60,000 partner's adjusted basis in the partnership and the $75,000 partnership's adjusted basis in the land. That difference is not recognized in any way.

4. MCQ-05981

Choice "d" is correct. In a complete liquidation of a partnership, the amount of cash distributed initially reduces the basis of the partner in the partnership (outside basis). In this question, the partner's $60,000 basis in the partnership is reduced to $30,000 by the $30,000 cash distribution. The $30,000 remaining partner basis in the partnership is given to the other property distributed (in this question, the only property distributed was the automobile).

Choice "a" is incorrect. The $0 indicates that the automobile was given no basis. That would happen only if the cash distributed exceeded the partner's basis in the partnership before the liquidation and distribution.

Choice "b" is incorrect. The $10,000 is the difference between the amount received in cash and the (fair) market value and basis of the automobile to the partnership. That amount does not represent the basis of the automobile after the distribution.

Choice "c" is incorrect. The $20,000 is the (fair) market value of the automobile at the date of the liquidation and distribution. That basis does not necessarily carry over to the partner.

Regulation 5, Module 5

1. MCQ-02232

Choice "a" is correct.

Rule: Foreign income taxes paid by a domestic corporation may be claimed either as a deduction or as a credit, at the option of the corporation.

Choices "b", "c", and "d" are incorrect, per the above rule.

Regulation 5, Module 6

1. MCQ-08766

Choice "b" is correct. Sales to non-U.S. persons of property for use outside the U.S. increase a corporation's foreign-derived intangible income.

Choice "a" is incorrect. Both transactions involve non-U.S. persons, but sales of property for use within the U.S. have no effect on foreign-derived intangible income.

Choice "c" is incorrect. To increase foreign-derived intangible income, the sale of property must be for use within the U.S. Sales to related parties have no effect on foreign-derived intangible income if the related party purchases the property for its own use.

Choice "d" is incorrect. To increase a corporation's foreign-derived intangible income, a sale must be to a non-U.S. person.

2. MCQ-08767

Choice "c" is correct. A customer payment for the sale of inventory within the U.S. is business income, which is taxed on a net basis and is not subject to withholding.

Choice "a" is incorrect. Interest income is considered fixed, determinable, annual, or periodic income (FDAP) and is subject to U.S. withholding tax requirements.

Choice "b" is incorrect. Dividend income is considered fixed, determinable, annual, or periodic income (FDAP) and is subject to U.S. withholding tax requirements.

Choice "d" is incorrect. A foreign financial institution that does not provide information about U.S. persons is subject to the Foreign Account Tax Compliance Act of 2010 (FATCA) and is subject to U.S. withholding tax requirements.

NOTES

1. MCQ-01812

Choice "b" is correct. The estate's distributable net income (DNI) for the calendar year is $42,000.

Rule: Absent written provisions to the contrary, capital gains and losses are classified as principal and must remain with the estate or trust (i.e., allocated to corpus) to be taxed at the estate or trust level.

Rule: All other taxable income (i.e., gross income net of deductible expenses) generated by the fiduciary assets is generally classified as distributable net income (DNI). Distributable net income is adjusted total income (line 17 on the Form 1041) with modifications for tax-exempt interest (included in DNI and allocated as tax exempt) and capital gains and losses (excluded from DNI and allocated to corpus).

Gross income:	
Taxable interest	$ 65,000
Tax-exempt interest	–
Deductible expenses:	
Administrative expenses	$(14,000)
Charitable contributions from gross income	(9,000)
Distributable net income	$ 42,000

Choices "a", "c", and "d" are incorrect, per the above rules.

2. MCQ-01813

Choice "b" is correct. Distributable net income is computed as the trust's income less any expenses allocated to income. The $6,000 of income items, less the $1,500 of income-related expenses, produces DNI of $4,500. This means that the first $4,500 of distributions from the trust are taxable income to the recipient(s), with any additional distributions being considered nontaxable distributions of trust corpus. If less than $4,500 is distributed, the amount actually distributed is taxable to the recipient, and any remaining undistributed portion of the $4,500 would be taxable at the trust level.

Choice "a" is incorrect. The income-related expenses must be subtracted from the trust income items in order to complete DNI.

Choice "c" is incorrect. Dividend income is part of the income in determining DNI.

Choice "d" is incorrect. Interest income is part of the income in determining DNI.

1. MCQ-01903

Choice "d" is correct. There is no income tax on the value of inherited property. The gain on the sale is the difference between the sales price of $4,500 and Hall's basis. Hall's basis is the alternate valuation elected by the executor. This is the value six months after date of death or date distributed if before six months. The property was distributed four months after death and the value that day ($4,500) is used for the basis. $4,500 sales price − $4,500 basis = $0.

Choice "a" is incorrect. There is no income tax on the value of inherited property.

Choice "b" is incorrect. This is the basis of the stock if the alternate date had not been used. Heirs are not taxed on inheritances. The income or loss results when inherited property is sold.

Choice "c" is incorrect. There is no income tax on the value of inherited property. The gain on the sale is the difference between the sales price of $4,500 and Hall's basis. Hall's basis is the $4,500 alternate valuation elected by the executor.

2. MCQ-01817

Choice "c" is correct. Charitable bequests to qualifying organizations and funeral expenses of the decedent are both allowable deductions in determining the taxable estate.

Choices "a", "b", and "d" are incorrect. Each of these answers reflects a wrong combination of items I and/or II. Be sure to answer each Item independently and then choose the answer choice.

3. MCQ-01891

Choice "b" is correct. Medical expenses paid directly to the health care provider qualify for an unlimited deduction, even if paid for unrelated persons. In this problem, the payment was made to the friend, not to the health care provider directly. The $15,000 annual exclusion per donee applies to all gifts other than future interests.

Choice "a" is incorrect. The $15,000 annual exclusion per donee applies to all gifts other than future interests.

Choice "c" is incorrect. An exclusion of $30,000 may have been allowed if Sayers had been married and employed the gift-splitting rules.

Choice "d" is incorrect. Medical expenses paid directly to the health care provider qualify for an unlimited deduction, even if paid for unrelated persons. In this problem, the payment was made to the friend, not to the health care provider directly, so the entire $50,000 is not excluded.

1. MCQ-06188

Choice "b" is correct. The entire $15,000 is exempt from tax on unrelated business income because the bingo games are legal and are confined to exempt organizations in that state.

Choice "a" is incorrect. If the income from bingo were considered to be "unrelated business income," the net income (after the exemption) would be subject to tax at the corporate income tax rates.

Choice "c" is incorrect. There is a $1,000 specific exemption from tax on unrelated business income, not a $5,000 exemption.

Choice "d" is incorrect. An exempt organization does not lose its exempt status just because it has unrelated business income.

1. MCQ-07197

Choice "c" is correct. Characteristic of a best practice in rendering tax advice is establishing in a tax memorandum relevant facts, evaluating the reasonableness of assumptions and representations, and arriving at a conclusion supported by the law and facts.

Choice "a" is incorrect. Circular 230's "Best Practices" do not include the tax advisor's requesting written evidence from a client that the fee proposal for tax advice has been approved by the board of directors.

Choice "b" is incorrect. Circular 230's "Best Practices" do not include the tax advisor's recommending to the client that the advisor's tax advice be made orally instead of in a written memorandum.

Choice "d" is incorrect. Circular 230's "Best Practices" do not include the tax advisor's requiring the client to supply a written representation, signed under penalties of perjury, concerning the facts and statements provided to the CPA for preparing a tax memorandum.

2. MCQ-06896

Choice "b" is correct. A tax preparer may retain copies of records returned to the taxpayer.

Choice "a" is incorrect. There is no requirement for the tax preparer to destroy client records upon submission of a tax return.

Choice "c" is incorrect. Generally, at the request of the client, the practitioner must return all client records. An exception is if state law allows the practitioner to retain the records in the case of a fee dispute, the practitioner may do so. However, the practitioner must (1) return to the client those records that must be attached to the tax return, and (2) allow the client to review and copy the practitioner-retained client records related to the client's federal tax obligation.

Choice "d" is incorrect. The general rule is to return all requested records.

3. MCQ-06672

Choice "c" is correct. Written advice does include electronic communications.

Choices "a", "b", and "d" are incorrect. Each one of these statements is a requirement for written advice under Circular 230.

4. MCQ-02080

Choice "c" is correct. Upon discovery of an error in a previously filed return the tax practitioner should promptly notify the client (either orally or in writing) of the error, noncompliance, or omission and advise the client of reasonably likely penalties.

Choice "a" is incorrect, as the tax practitioner has no responsibility (without a formal client engagement) or the authority to prepare and file a client's tax return.

Choice "b" is incorrect, as a tax practitioner cannot advise a client to disobey the law because it violates a tax practitioner's ethical responsibilities.

Choice "d" is incorrect, as Circular 230 does not stipulate that a tax practitioner should consider withdrawing from an engagement until an error is corrected.

Regulation 6, Module 5

1. MCQ-02187

Choice "c" is correct. A tax return preparer may disclose or use tax return information without the taxpayer's consent to be evaluated by a quality or peer review.

Choices "a", "b", and "d" are incorrect. They would all require the taxpayer's consent.

Regulation 6, Module 6

1. MCQ-02093

Choice "c" is correct. Accuracy-related penalties apply to the portion of tax underpayments attributable to negligence or disregard of tax rules and regulations as well as to any substantial understatement of income tax.

2. MCQ-06595

Choice "a" is correct. The negligence penalty with respect to understatement of tax is an accuracy-based penalty for negligence or for disregard of tax rules and regulations.

Choice "b" is incorrect. The negligence penalty with respect to understatement of tax is computed as 20 percent, not 25 percent, of the understatement of tax.

Choice "c" is incorrect. The negligence penalty with respect to understatement of tax defines "disregard" as any careless, reckless, or intentional, not unintentional, disregard of tax rules and regulations.

Choice "d" is incorrect. The negligence penalty with respect to understatement of tax is not imposed in conjunction with the penalty for substantial underpayment of tax and the penalty for a substantial valuation misstatement. If the negligence penalty with respect to understatement of tax is imposed, the other two penalties cannot also be imposed.

3. MCQ-06671

Choice "c" is correct. If John relied on the opinion of a reputable accountant or attorney who prepared his return and furnished all relevant information, in general, he would have a reasonable basis for the tax return position and could avoid the penalties for understatement of tax.

Choice "a" is incorrect. If John took a reasonable position on his tax return, he is subject to the penalty for understatement of tax and not to the penalty for substantial understatement of tax (both would not be applied at the same time). The exact penalty that would apply would depend on the amount of the understatement of tax.

Choice "b" is incorrect. If there was a reasonable basis for a disclosed tax position on the tax return, and John acted in good faith, the penalty for understatement of tax would not apply if John actually did understate his tax. He would still be liable for the unpaid tax, and any interest, but he would not be liable for the penalty.

Choice "d" is incorrect. If John's understatement of tax is a substantial understatement, the penalty is the same percentage as for a simple understatement.

4. MCQ-06665

Choice "c" is correct. The more-likely-than-not standard involves a position that has a more than 50 percent chance of succeeding.

Choice "a" is incorrect. The reasonable basis standard involves a position that is arguable but fairly unlikely to prevail in court. A numerical statement of this standard has at least a 20 percent chance, not a 10 percent chance, of succeeding.

Choice "b" is incorrect. The substantial authority standard involves a position that has a more than one-in-three chance, not a one-in-four chance, but a less than 50 percent chance of succeeding.

Choice "d" is incorrect. Reports issued by the U.S. Congress, IRS regulations, rules, and releases, and U.S. court case decisions, but not foreign court case decisions, constitute substantial authority for the substantial authority standard.

Regulation 6, Module 7

1. MCQ-01445

Choice "c" is correct. The majority rule (the law followed in the majority of the states) is that accountants are liable to anyone in a class (such as potential lenders or investors) of third parties whom the CPA knows will rely on the opinion of the financial statements.

Choice "a" is incorrect. This describes a more limited extent of CPA liability than is the case under the majority rule.

Choice "b" is incorrect. In all states, the CPA's liability extends beyond the client.

Choice "d" is incorrect. This describes a broader extent of liability than is the case under either the majority rule or the minority rule.

2. MCQ-01452

Choice "d" is correct. Client workpapers must be turned over pursuant to a valid federal court subpoena. Client permission is not necessary in the case of a subpoena.

Choice "a" is incorrect. Workpapers cannot be turned over to a successor purchasing the CPA's practice if the client objects. However, a prospective purchaser of the CPA's practice may review the workpapers if confidentiality is assured.

Choice "b" is incorrect. Client workpapers belong to the accountant, not to the client. They need not be turned over to the client.

Choice "c" is incorrect. Unless subpoenaed, generally the workpapers cannot be turned over to a government agency without the client's permission (there is an exception for requests from the Public Company Accounting Oversight Board with respect to workpapers for clients that are publicly held).

NOTES

Regulation 7, Module 1

1. MCQ-01318

Choice "c" is correct. An agent generally is not liable on contracts that the agent makes on the principal's behalf if the principal is disclosed, but the agent is personally liable on contracts the agent makes on behalf of the principal when the principal is undisclosed.

2. MCQ-01333

Choice "c" is correct. If the principal is undisclosed, the third party with whom the agent dealt can hold the agent liable on the contract.

Choice "a" is incorrect. A third party has no general right to discover the identity of an undisclosed principal.

Choice "b" is incorrect. A third party never has the right to force a principal to ratify a contract; only a principal has a right to choose to ratify an unauthorized contract.

Choice "d" is incorrect. As a general rule, a third party who has contracted with an agent for an undisclosed principal has no right to rescind the contract upon subsequent disclosure of the principal. Such a right exists only if the nondisclosure was fraudulent.

Regulation 7, Module 2

1. MCQ-01351

Choice "c" is correct. Peters' offer was already revoked. To be effective, an acceptance must be received before the offer is terminated. An offer may be terminated by the offeror at any time unless the offeree gave consideration to keep the offer open. Mason gave no consideration to keep the offer here open; thus Peters could revoke. An offer is considered to be revoked if the offeree obtains information from a reliable source that the subject matter of the offer has been sold. Here, Mason received the information of the sale before he attempted to accept. Therefore, his attempted acceptance came too late and was ineffective.

Choice "a" is incorrect. The normal rule for contracts is the mailbox rule—an acceptance is effective upon dispatch rather than upon receipt.

Choice "b" is incorrect. Although the normal rule is that an acceptance will be effective upon dispatch, to be effective, an acceptance must also come before the offer is terminated. Here the offer was terminated before the letter was sent because Mason received reliable information that the subject matter of the offer had already been sold.

Choice "d" is incorrect. An offer will be irrevocable only if the offeree gives consideration to keep the offer open (an option contract) or the offer is a merchant's firm offer. Here, Mason did not give consideration to keep the offer open, and firm offers must be in writing and made by a merchant, yet the offer here was oral and nothing indicates that Peters is a lawn mower merchant.

2. MCQ-01347

Choice "b" is correct. To be effective, consideration must be legally sufficient, which means something that the law recognizes as consideration.

Choice "a" is incorrect. The courts do not require contracts to be "fair," giving each party equal benefit.

Choice "c" is incorrect. There is no requirement that consideration be exchanged simultaneously. For example, in a unilateral contract, the promise is given first and the performance, which is the consideration on the other side, comes later.

Choice "d" is incorrect. The courts will not inquire into the fairness of a bargain.

Regulation 7, Module 3

1. MCQ-01250

Choice "b" is correct. The parol evidence rule prohibits evidence of prior oral or written agreements that seek to contradict the terms of a fully integrated contract (i.e., one intended as the complete agreement). Thus, II is prohibited. However, the parol evidence rule does not prohibit introduction of subsequent agreements; thus, I is not prohibited.

2. MCQ-01246

Choice "b" is correct. The common law defense of fraud requires a showing of intent to deceive. Fraud in the inducement (as opposed to fraud in the execution) merely means that the victim was deceived as to the reason for the transaction.

Choice "a" is incorrect. A person need not be an expert concerning the subject matter of the deceit to be liable for misrepresentation. The person need only knowingly lie.

Choices "c" and "d" are incorrect. Fraud in the inducement means that the victim was deceived as to the reasons for entering into the fraudulent transaction; there is no requirement that the misrepresentation have been made in writing, so "c" is incorrect. Similarly, there is no requirement of a fiduciary relationship, so "d" is incorrect.

Regulation 7, Module 4

1. MCQ-01776

Choice "a" is correct. The Sales Article applies to all contracts for the sale of goods, regardless of price.

Choice "b" is incorrect. All parties are bound by the obligation of good faith under the UCC.

Choice "c" is incorrect. The presumption is that all sales are final. A sale or return or sale on approval (both of which allow the return of the goods) is available only if the parties so provide.

Choice "d" is incorrect. The Sales Article covers all sales of goods. If the purchase price is $500 or more, a writing may be required to enforce the contract under the Sales Article's Statute of Frauds, but the Sales Article still applies.

2. MCQ-02341

Choice "a" is correct. The UCC does not follow the mirror image rule; instead, generally anything that looks like an acceptance will operate as an acceptance, even if it contains new terms. In such a case, a contract generally is formed even if the offeror fails to agree to the new terms. Thus, even though the acceptance contained an additional term regarding the weighing scale, it is an effective acceptance. Indeed, even if this contract were at common law, the acceptance probably would have been found valid. The requirement of a valid city certificate for the weighing scale probably would be considered to be an implied condition of the offer.

Thus, choices "b", "c", and "d" are incorrect.

3. MCQ-01785

Choice "a" is correct. Although the contract here requires a writing under the Statute of Frauds signed by the party to be charged, the Sales Article provides a "confirmatory memo" or "written confirmation" exception between merchants. If one merchant sends the other a memo of their contract sufficient to bind the sender, it will bind the recipient as well unless the recipient objects within a reasonable time. UCC 2-201

Choice "b" is incorrect. The party whose signature is required is the party against whom the contract is being enforced. If the seller does not want to sell, a writing signed by the seller generally is required to make the contract enforceable against the seller. UCC 2-201

Choice "c" is incorrect. Although it is true that the Statute of Frauds generally requires a writing signed by the party against whom enforcement is sought, the Sales Article has an exception (the confirmatory memo rule for contracts between merchants) which provides that between merchants, if one merchant sends the other a memo of their contract sufficient to bind the sender, it will bind the recipient as well unless the recipient objects within a reasonable time. UCC 2-201

Choice "d" is incorrect. Although the contract here requires a writing under the Statute of Frauds signed by the party to be charged, the Sales Article provides a "confirmatory memo" exception. Between merchants, if one merchant sends the other a memo of their contract sufficient to bind the sender, it will bind the recipient as well unless the recipient objects within a reasonable time. UCC 2-201

4. MCQ-06901

Choice "b" is correct. To be an express warranty, the language must be part of the basis of the bargain.

Choice "a" is incorrect. An express warranty arises from any statement of fact or promise made by the seller, any description of the goods made by the seller, or any sample or model shown by the seller at a time when it could have become part of the basis of the bargain.

Choice "c" is incorrect. An express warranty may be made orally, in writing or by conduct (e.g., the showing of a model).

Choice "d" is incorrect. Express warranties can arise from any description of the goods given to the buyer before the contract is executed.

1. MCQ-01878

Choice "d" is correct. A surety generally is primarily liable on the debt the surety agrees to backstop and has no right to compel the creditor to collect from the principal debtor or to compel the creditor to proceed against the debtor's collateral. (There is, however, a very limited right to both of these in certain circumstances.)

2. MCQ-01920

Choice "c" is correct. A cosurety has a right of contribution from cosureties. Where the debt has been reduced, each cosurety remains liable for the lesser of: (i) the reduced amount of debt or (ii) the original amount for which the cosurety has agreed to be responsible. However, the right of contribution allows each cosurety to recover from the other cosureties their pro rata share of the payment. Here, Nash satisfied the debt by paying $36,000. Proportionally, Nash was liable for 40/180 (or 2/9) of the original debt, Owen was responsible for 3/9, and Polk was responsible for 4/9. Nash's pro rata share of the $36,000 is $8,000; Owen's share is $12,000; and Polk's share is $16,000. Thus, Nash may recover $28,000.

1. MCQ-01576

Choice "d" is correct. The general rule is that a buyer takes subject to security interests in the goods bought, but one large exception to this rule is that any buyer from a merchant in the ordinary course of business usually takes free of a security interest previously given by the merchant.

Choice "a" is incorrect. A merchant buyer who purchases goods for resale owns inventory rather than consumer goods. Note that if a merchant buyer purchases inventory in the ordinary course of the seller's business, the merchant buyer generally will hold the inventory free of a perfected security interest previously given by the seller.

Choice "b" is incorrect. A merchant buyer who purchases goods for use in its business owns equipment rather than consumer goods. Note that if a buyer purchases the equipment in the ordinary course of the seller's business, the buyer generally will hold the equipment free of a perfected security interest previously given by the seller.

Choice "c" is incorrect. The general rule is that a buyer takes goods subject to security interests existing in the goods. There is an exception to this rule for consumers who, in good faith and without notice of any security interest, purchase the goods from consumers, but the exception applies only when the security interest is perfected automatically, and here we are not told how the security interest was perfected.

2. MCQ-01621

Choice "c" is correct. A PMSI in equipment has priority over a perfected security interest in the same equipment as long as the PMSI is perfected within 20 days of delivery of the collateral to the debtor. A perfected security interest has priority over an unperfected security interest. Thus, III has highest priority, I has next priority, and II has last priority.

3. MCQ-01656

Choice "a" is correct. After default, a secured creditor can peacefully repossess the goods or bring an action to reduce the claim to judgment and have the goods repossessed and sold judicially, or sell the goods and apply the proceeds toward the debt.

1. MCQ-01348

Choice "a" is correct. The estate includes income generated from estate property and property the debtor receives from a bequest, devise, inheritances, property settlement, divorce, or beneficial interest in life insurance within 180 days after filing of the petition.

Choices "b", "c", and "d" are incorrect, per the above. The income described in these choices does not become part of the bankruptcy estate.

2. MCQ-01367

Choice "d" is correct. When there are fewer than 12 unsecured creditors, any one creditor who is owed $16,750 (as adjusted for inflation) in unsecured debt or more may file an involuntary petition in bankruptcy.

Choice "a" is incorrect. The fact that there are fewer than 12 unsecured creditors means that only one creditor is needed for the involuntary petition (as long as the creditor is owed at least $16,750 in unsecured debt).

Choice "b" is incorrect. A debtor who is not paying debts as they become due is subject to being involuntarily petitioned into bankruptcy under the provisions of Chapter 11.

Choice "c" is incorrect. When there are fewer than 12 unsecured creditors, any one or more of the creditors may file the involuntary petition, but the petitioner(s) must be owed in aggregate at least $16,750 in unsecured debt.

1. MCQ-01382

Choice "a" is correct. All perfected security interests are paid first. Because the security interest here was filed more than 90 days before the bankruptcy, this event does not constitute a voidable preference.

Choice "b" is incorrect. The creditor is either an involuntary case gap creditor (third priority) or a creditor with a disallowed post-petition claim; the facts are unclear. In either case, a secured creditor would have priority.

Choice "c" is incorrect. Wage claims for wages earned within 180 days of the bankruptcy have a fourth priority. Older wage claims are treated as general unsecured claims and are paid last. In either case, the wage claims are subordinate to a perfected security interest.

Choice "d" is incorrect. If the federal government obtains a lien for taxes against the debtor's estate before the bankruptcy petition is filed, the federal tax lien is treated as a secured interest. However, this interest is subordinate to the March 20 secured claim because the March 20 interest was perfected before the tax lien attached.

2. MCQ-01373

Choice "b" is correct. After the reorganization plan is confirmed, the debtor is released from debts except as provided in the plan or by law.

Choice "a" is incorrect. The goal of a reorganization is to allow the debtor's business to continue; the business is not dissolved at the conclusion of the bankruptcy proceedings.

Choice "c" is incorrect. Generally in a reorganization the debtor remains in possession and there is no trustee. In any event, a trustee would not be left in place after the reorganization is complete. The goal of Chapter 11 is to allow the debtor's business to continue.

Choice "d" is incorrect. The goal of a reorganization is just the opposite: to allow the debtor's business to continue.

Regulation 8, Module 3

1. MCQ-01386

Choice "c" is correct. Publicly traded corporations must register with the SEC and make certain periodic reports under the 1934 act. These reports include business reports (10-K, 10-Q and 8-K), insider trading tender offers and proxy solicitations. The unaudited financials, which are part of the company's 10-Q filing, fraudulently described the bribe.

2. MCQ-01385

Choice "c" is correct. The issuer could be liable for issuing securities by means of a false statement under the 1933 act and can be liable for making false statements under the 1934 act.

Choices "a", "b", and "d" are incorrect. Each of these choices incorrectly addresses either I and/or II.

3. MCQ-01390

Choice "b" is correct. One piece of information required in a registration statement is a statement of how the funds received will be used.

Choice "a" is incorrect. Generally, the registration statement need not include a list of the issuer's current shareholders.

Choice "c" is incorrect. The SEC does not guarantee the accuracy of the facts contained in a registration statement.

Choice "d" is incorrect. The SEC does not assess the financial merit of registered securities.

Regulation 8, Module 4

1. MCQ-02133

Choice "b" is correct. Workers' compensation statutes are intended to provide strict liability insurance for injuries incurred while on the job, so Kroll will be able to recover for the injuries incurred because of the design defect, even though his employer had nothing to do with the accident. However, the trade-off is that the employee cannot bring a negligence action against the employer.

2. MCQ-01939

Choice "b" is correct. FUTA tax is payable by the employer. It is deductible as a business expense. It is not withheld and is not payable on all wages.

Choice "a" is incorrect. The FUTA tax is not a fixed rate on all compensation. It applies only up to a $7,000 ceiling.

Choice "c" is incorrect. The FUTA tax applies only to employers who have a quarterly payroll of at least $1,500 or employ at least one employee at least one day a week for 20 weeks during a year.

Choice "d" is incorrect. The employer pays FUTA tax. The tax is not withheld from employees' wages.

Regulation 8, Module 5

1. MCQ-03126

Choice "d" is correct.

Rule: When the partnership agreement is silent as to how losses will be shared, they are shared in the same manner as profits.

Application of the Rule: Here, the partnership agreement provided that profits were to be split among Moore, Noon, and Kale 1:3:5, respectively. Thus, Kale's share of the loss is $100,000 [5 × (1/9 × 180,000)].

Choices "a", "b", and "c" are incorrect, per the above rule.

2. MCQ-02996

Choice "b" is correct. As a general rule, decisions regarding matters within the ordinary course of the partnership's business may be controlled by majority vote. Matters outside the ordinary course of the partnership's business require the consent of all the partners. Admitting a new partner is an extraordinary event. Thus, unanimous consent is required.

Choice "a" is incorrect. Although dissolution is an extraordinary act, in a general partnership not for a term of years, any one partner may cause a dissolution by giving notice of the intent to withdraw.

Choice "c" is incorrect. A capital expenditure could well be within the ordinary scope of partnership business and thus would require only a majority vote.

Choice "d" is incorrect. The sale of partnership real property could easily be within the ordinary scope of partnership business (e.g., a partnership can be formed for the purpose of buying and selling real property) and thus would require only a majority vote.

1. MCQ-03235

Choice "b" is correct. A corporation may indemnify its officers for liabilities incurred in a suit by stockholders, especially if the officer prevails.

Choice "a" is incorrect. There is no restriction against serving as both a director and an officer.

Choice "c" is incorrect. The RMBCA provides that officers are to be appointed by the board unless the bylaws provide otherwise.

Choice "d" is incorrect. There is no requirement that an officer own stock in the corporation in which he or she serves.

2. MCQ-03027

Choice "d" is correct. Both corporations must give shareholders notice and a summary of the merger plan.

Choice "a" is incorrect. A merger plan need only be approved by a majority of the shareholders, not by all shareholders.

Choice "b" is incorrect. The merger plan needs to be approved only by a majority of each board of directors of the corporations.

Choice "c" is incorrect. The absorbed corporation ceases to exist; its articles need not be amended.

Blueprint

REG

Summary blueprint

Content area allocation	Weight
I. Ethics, Professional Responsibilities and Federal Tax Procedures	10–20%
II. Business Law	10–20%
III. Federal Taxation of Property Transactions	12–22%
IV. Federal Taxation of Individuals	15–25%
V. Federal Taxation of Entities	28–38%

Skill allocation	Weight
Evaluation	–
Analysis	25–35%
Application	35–45%
Remembering and Understanding	25–35%

Uniform CPA Examination Blueprints: Regulation (REG)

REG5

Area I – Ethics, Professional Responsibilities and Federal Tax Procedures (10-20%)

Content group/topic	Skill				Representative task
	Remembering and Understanding	Application	Analysis	Evaluation	
A. Ethics and responsibilities in tax practice					
1. Regulations governing practice before the Internal Revenue Service	✓				Recall the regulations governing practice before the Internal Revenue Service.
		✓			Apply the regulations governing practice before the Internal Revenue Service given a specific scenario.
2. Internal Revenue Code and Regulations related to tax return preparers	✓				Recall who is a tax return preparer.
	✓				Recall situations that would result in federal tax return preparer penalties.
		✓			Apply potential federal tax return preparer penalties given a specific scenario.
B. Licensing and disciplinary systems	✓				Understand and explain the role and authority of state boards of accountancy.
C. Federal tax procedures					
1. Audits, appeals and judicial process	✓				Explain the audit and appeals process as it relates to federal tax matters.
	✓				Explain the different levels of the judicial process as they relate to federal tax matters.
		✓			Identify options available to a taxpayer within the audit and appeals process given a specific scenario.
		✓			Identify options available to a taxpayer within the judicial process given a specific scenario.

Uniform CPA Examination Blueprints: Regulation (REG)

REG6

Regulation (REG)

Area I – Ethics, Professional Responsibilities and Federal Tax Procedures (10-20%) (continued)

C. Federal tax procedures (continued)

Content group/topic	Skill				Representative task
	Remembering and Understanding	Application	Analysis	Evaluation	
2. Substantiation and disclosure of tax positions	✓				Summarize the requirements for the appropriate disclosure of a federal tax return position.
		✓			Identify situations in which disclosure of federal tax return positions is required.
		✓			Identify whether substantiation is sufficient given a specific scenario.
3. Taxpayer penalties	✓				Recall situations that would result in taxpayer penalties relating to federal tax returns.
		✓			Calculate taxpayer penalties relating to federal tax returns.
4. Authoritative hierarchy	✓				Recall the appropriate hierarchy of authority for federal tax purposes.

D. Legal duties and responsibilities

Content group/topic	Skill				Representative task
1. Common law duties and liabilities to clients and third parties	✓				Summarize the tax return preparer's common law duties and liabilities to clients and third parties.
		✓			Identify situations which result in violations of the tax return preparer's common law duties and liabilities to clients and third parties.
2. Privileged communications, confidentiality and privacy acts	✓				Summarize the rules regarding privileged communications as they relate to tax practice.
		✓			Identify situations in which communications regarding tax practice are considered privileged.

Uniform CPA Examination Blueprints: Regulation (REG)

REG7

Regulation (REG)

Area II – Business Law (10-20%)

Content group/topic	Skill				Representative task
	Remembering and Understanding	Application	Analysis	Evaluation	
A. Agency					
1. Authority of agents and principals	✓				Recall the types of agent authority.
		✓			Identify whether an agency relationship exists given a specific scenario.
2. Duties and liabilities of agents and principals	✓				Explain the various duties and liabilities of agents and principals.
		✓			Identify the duty or liability of an agent or principal given a specific scenario.
B. Contracts					
1. Formation	✓				Summarize the elements of contract formation between parties.
		✓			Identify whether a valid contract was formed given a specific scenario.
		✓			Identify different types of contracts (e.g., written, verbal, unilateral, express and implied) given a specific scenario.
2. Performance	✓				Explain the rules related to the fulfillment of performance obligations necessary for an executed contract.
		✓			Identify whether both parties to a contract have fulfilled their performance obligation given a specific scenario.

Uniform CPA Examination Blueprints: Regulation (REG)

REG8

Regulation (REG)

Area II – Business Law (10-20%) (continued)

Content group/topic	Skill				Representative task
	Remembering and Understanding	Application	Analysis	Evaluation	
B. Contracts (continued)					
3. Discharge, breach and remedies	✓				Explain the different ways in which a contract can be discharged (e.g., performance, agreement and operation of the law).
	✓				Summarize the different remedies available to a party for breach of contract.
		✓			Identify situations involving breach of contract.
		✓			Identify whether a contract has been discharged given a specific scenario.
		✓			Identify the remedy available to a party for breach of contract given a specific scenario.
C. Debtor-creditor relationships					
1. Rights, duties and liabilities of debtors, creditors and guarantors	✓				Explain the rights, duties and liabilities of debtors, creditors and guarantors.
		✓			Identify rights, duties or liabilities of debtors, creditors or guarantors given a specific scenario.
2. Bankruptcy and insolvency	✓				Explain the rights of the debtors and the creditors in bankruptcy and insolvency.
	✓				Summarize the rules related to the different types of bankruptcy.
	✓				Explain discharge of indebtedness in bankruptcy.
		✓			Identify the rights of the debtors and the creditors in bankruptcy and insolvency given a specific scenario.
		✓			Identify the type of bankruptcy described in a specific scenario.

Uniform CPA Examination Blueprints: Regulation (REG)　　　　　　　　　　REG9

Area II – Business Law (10-20%) (continued)

Content group/topic	Skill				Representative task
	Remembering and Understanding	Application	Analysis	Evaluation	
C. Debtor-creditor relationships (continued)					
3. Secured transactions	✓				Explain how property can serve as collateral in secured transactions.
	✓				Summarize the priority rules of secured transactions.
	✓				Explain the requirements needed to create and perfect a security interest.
		✓			Identify the prioritized ordering of perfected security interests given a specific scenario.
		✓			Identify whether a creditor has created and perfected a security interest given a specific scenario.
D. Government regulation of business					
1. Federal securities regulation	✓				Summarize the various securities laws and regulations that affect corporate governance with respect to the federal Securities Act of 1933 and federal Securities Exchange Act of 1934.
		✓			Identify violations of the various securities laws and regulations that affect corporate governance with respect to the federal Securities Act of 1933 and federal Securities Exchange Act of 1934.
2. Other federal laws and regulations (e.g., employment tax, qualified health plans and worker classification)	✓				Summarize federal laws and regulations, for example, employment tax, qualified health plans and worker classification federal laws and regulations.
		✓			Identify violations of federal laws and regulations, for example, employment tax, qualified health plans and worker classification federal laws and regulations.

Regulation (REG)

Area II – Business Law (10-20%) (continued)

Content group/topic	Skill				Representative task
	Remembering and Understanding	Application	Analysis	Evaluation	
E. Business structure					
1. Selection and formation of business entity and related operation and termination	✓				Summarize the processes for formation and termination of various business entities.
	✓				Summarize the non-tax operational features for various business entities.
		✓			Identify the type of business entity that is best described by a given set of nontax-related characteristics.
2. Rights, duties, legal obligations and authority of owners and management	✓				Summarize the rights, duties, legal obligations and authority of owners and management.
		✓			Identify the rights, duties, legal obligations or authorities of owners or management given a specific scenario.

Uniform CPA Examination Blueprints: Regulation (REG)

REG11

Regulation (REG)

Area III — Federal Taxation of Property Transactions (12–22%)

Content group/topic	Skill				Representative task
	Remembering and Understanding	Application	Analysis	Evaluation	
A. Acquisition and disposition of assets					
1. Basis and holding period of assets		✓			Calculate the tax basis of an asset.
		✓			Determine the holding period of a disposed asset for classification of tax gain or loss.
2. Taxable and nontaxable dispositions		✓			Calculate the realized and recognized gain or loss on the disposition of assets for federal income tax purposes.
		✓			Calculate the realized gain, recognized gain and deferred gain on like-kind property exchange transactions for federal income tax purposes.
			✓		Analyze asset sale and exchange transactions to determine whether they are taxable or nontaxable.
3. Amount and character of gains and losses, and netting process (including installment sales)		✓			Calculate the amount of capital gains and losses for federal income tax purposes.
		✓			Calculate the amount of ordinary income and loss for federal income tax purposes.
		✓			Calculate the amount of gain on an installment sale for federal income tax purposes.
			✓		Review asset transactions to determine the character (capital vs. ordinary) of the gain or loss for federal income tax purposes.
			✓		Analyze an agreement of sale of an asset to determine whether it qualifies for installment sale treatment for federal income tax purposes.

Uniform CPA Examination Blueprints: Regulation (REG)

REG12

Regulation (REG)

Area III – Federal Taxation of Property Transactions (12-22%) (continued)

Content group/topic	Skill				Representative task
	Remembering and Understanding	Application	Analysis	Evaluation	
A. Acquisition and disposition of assets (continued)					
4. Related party transactions (including imputed interest)	✓				Recall related parties for federal income tax purposes.
	✓				Recall the impact of related party ownership percentages on acquisition and disposition transactions of property for federal income tax purposes.
		✓			Calculate the direct and indirect ownership percentages of corporation stock or partnership interests to determine whether there are related parties for federal income tax purposes.
		✓			Calculate a taxpayer's basis in an asset that was disposed of at a loss to the taxpayer by a related party.
		✓			Calculate a taxpayer's gain or loss on a subsequent disposition of an asset to an unrelated third party that was previously disposed of at a loss to the taxpayer by a related party.
		✓			Calculate the impact of imputed interest on related party transactions for federal tax purposes.
B. Cost recovery (depreciation, depletion and amortization)					
		✓			Calculate tax depreciation for tangible business property and tax amortization of intangible assets.
		✓			Calculate depletion for federal income tax purposes.
			✓		Compare the tax benefits of the different expensing options for tax depreciation for federal income tax purposes.
			✓		Reconcile the activity in the beginning and ending accumulated tax depreciation account.

Uniform CPA Examination Blueprints: Regulation (REG)   REG13

Area III – Federal Taxation of Property Transactions
(12-22%) (continued)

Content group/topic	Skill				Representative task
	Remembering and Understanding	Application	Analysis	Evaluation	
C. Estate and gift taxation					
1. Transfers subject to gift tax	✓				Recall transfers of property subject to federal gift tax.
	✓				Recall whether federal Form 709 – *United States Gift (and Generation-Skipping Transfer) Tax Return* is required to be filed.
		✓			Calculate the amount and classification of a gift for federal gift tax purposes.
		✓			Calculate the amount of a gift subject to federal gift tax.
2. Gift tax annual exclusion and gift tax deductions	✓				Recall allowable gift tax deductions and exclusions for federal gift tax purposes.
	✓				Recall situations involving the gift tax annual exclusion, gift-splitting and the impact on the use of the lifetime exclusion amount for federal gift tax purposes.
		✓			Compute the amount of taxable gifts for federal gift tax purposes.
3. Determination of taxable estate	✓				Recall assets includible in a decedent's gross estate for federal estate tax purposes.
	✓				Recall allowable estate tax deductions for federal estate tax purposes.
		✓			Calculate the taxable estate for federal estate tax purposes.
		✓			Calculate the gross estate for federal estate tax purposes.
		✓			Calculate the allowable estate tax deductions for federal estate tax purposes.

Uniform CPA Examination Blueprints: Regulation (REG)

Regulation (REG)

Area IV – Federal Taxation of Individuals (including tax preparation and planning strategies) (15-25%)

Content group/topic	Skill				Representative task
	Remembering and Understanding	Application	Analysis	Evaluation	
A. Gross income (inclusions and exclusions)					
		✓			Calculate the amounts that should be included in, or excluded from, an individual's gross income as reported on federal Form 1040 – *U.S. Individual Income Tax Return.*
			✓		Analyze projected income for use in tax planning in future years.
			✓		Analyze client-provided documentation to cetermine the appropriate amount of gross income to be reported on federal Form 1040 – *U.S. Individual Income Tax Return.*
B. Reporting of items from pass-through entities					
		✓			Prepare federal Form 1040 – *U.S. Individual Income Tax Return* based on the information provided on Schedule K-1.
C. Adjustments and deductions to arrive at adjusted gross income and taxable income					
		✓			Calculate the amount of adjustments and deductions to arrive at adjusted gross income and taxable income on federal Form 1040 – *U.S. Individual Income Tax Return.*
		✓			Calculate the qualifying business income (QBI) deduction for federal income tax purposes.
			✓		Analyze client-provided documentation to determine the validity of the deductions taken to arrive at adjusted gross income or taxable income on federal Form 1040 – *U.S. Individual Income Tax Return.*
D. Passive activity losses (excluding foreign tax credit implications)					
	✓				Recall passive activities for federal income tax purposes.
		✓			Calculate net passive activity gains and losses for federal income tax purposes.
		✓			Prepare a loss carryforward schedule for passive activities for federal income tax purposes.
		✓			Calculate utilization of suspended losses on the disposition of a passive activity for federal income tax purposes.

Uniform CPA Examination Blueprints: Regulation (REG)   REG15

Area IV – Federal Taxation of Individuals (including tax preparation and planning strategies) (15-25%) (continued)

Content group/topic	Skill				Representative task
	Remembering and Understanding	Application	Analysis	Evaluation	
E. Loss limitations					
	✓				Calculate loss limitations for federal income tax purposes for an individual taxpayer.
			✓		Analyze projections to effectively minimize loss limitations for federal income tax purposes for an individual taxpayer.
			✓		Determine the basis and the potential application of at-risk rules that can apply to activities for federal income tax purposes.
F. Filing status					
	✓				Recall taxpayer filing status for federal income tax purposes.
	✓				Recall relationships meeting the definition of dependent for purposes of determining taxpayer filing status.
		✓			Identify taxpayer filing status for federal income tax purposes given a specific scenario.
G. Computation of tax and credits					
	✓				Recall and define minimum requirements for individual federal estimated tax payments to avoid penalties.
		✓			Calculate the tax liability based on an individual's taxable income for federal income tax purposes.
		✓			Calculate the impact of the tax deductions and tax credits and their effect on federal Form 1040 – U.S. *Individual Income Tax Return.*

REG16

Regulation (REG)

Area IV – Federal Taxation of Individuals (including tax preparation and planning strategies) (15-25%) (continued)

Content group/topic	Skill				Representative task
	Remembering and Understanding	Application	Analysis	Evaluation	
H. Alternative minimum tax	✓				Recall income and expense items includible in the computation of an individual taxpayer's alternative minimum taxable income (AMTI).
		✓			Calculate alternative minimum tax (AMT) for an individual taxpayer.

Area V – Federal Taxation of Entities (including tax preparation and planning strategies) (28-38%)

Content group/topic	Skill				Representative task
	Remembering and Understanding	Application	Analysis	Evaluation	
A. Tax treatment of formation and liquidation of business entities					
	✓				Calculate the realized and recognized gain for the owner and entity upon the formation and liquidation of business entities for federal income tax purposes.
		✓			Compare the tax implications of liquidating distributions from different business entities.
		✓			Analyze the tax advantages and disadvantages in the formation of a new business entity.
B. Differences between book and tax income (loss)					
	✓				Identify permanent vs. temporary differences to be reported on Schedule M-1 and/or M-3.
		✓			Calculate the book/tax differences to be reported on a Schedule M-1 or M-3.
		✓			Prepare a Schedule M-1 or M-3 for a business entity.
		✓			Reconcile the differences between book and taxable income (loss) of a business entity.
C. C corporations					
1. Computations of taxable income, tax liability and allowable credits		✓			Calculate taxable income and tax liability for a C corporation.
		✓			Calculate the credits allowable as a reduction of tax for a C corporation.

Regulation (REG)

Area V – Federal Taxation of Entities (including tax preparation and planning strategies) (28-38%) (continued)

C. C corporations (continued)

Content group/topic	Remembering and Understanding	Application	Analysis	Evaluation	Representative task
2. Net operating losses and capital loss limitations		✓			Calculate the current-year net operating or capital loss of a C corporation.
		✓			Prepare a net operating and/or capital loss carryforward schedule for a C corporation.
			✓		Analyze the impact of the charitable contribution and/or dividends received deductions on the net operating loss calculation of a C corporation.
			✓		Analyze the impact of net operating and/or capital losses during tax planning for a C corporation.
3. Entity/owner transactions, including contributions, loans and distributions		✓			Calculate an entity owner's basis in C corporation stock for federal income tax purposes.
		✓			Calculate the tax gain (loss) realized and recognized by both the shareholders and the corporation on a contribution or on a distribution in complete liquidation of a C corporation for federal income tax purposes.
		✓			Calculate the tax gain (loss) realized and recognized on a nonliquidating distribution by both a C corporation and its shareholders for federal income tax purposes.
		✓			Calculate the amount of the cash distributions to shareholders of a C corporation that represents a dividend, return of capital or capital gain for federal income tax purposes.
			✓		Reconcile an owner's beginning and ending basis in C corporation stock for federal income tax purposes.
4. Consolidated tax returns	✓				Recall the requirements for filing a consolidated federal Form 1120 – *U.S. Corporation Income Tax Return.*
		✓			Prepare a consolidated federal Form 1120 – *U.S. Corporation Income Tax Return.*
		✓			Calculate federal taxable income for a consolidated federal Form 1120 – *U.S. Corporation Income Tax Return.*

Area V – Federal Taxation of Entities (including tax preparation and planning strategies) (28-38%) (continued)

Content group/topic	Skill					Representative task
	Remembering and Understanding	Application	Analysis	Evaluation		
C. C corporations (continued)						
5. Multijurisdictional tax issues (including consideration of local, state and international tax issues)	✓					Define the general concept and rationale of nexus with respect to multijurisdictional transactions.
	✓					Define the general concept and rationale of apportionment and allocation with respect to state and local taxation.
	✓					Explain the difference between a foreign branch and foreign subsidiary with respect to federal income taxation to a U.S. company.
	✓					Explain how different types of foreign income are sourced in calculating the foreign tax credit for federal income tax purposes.
	✓					Recall payment sources to determine federal tax withholding requirements.
	✓					Identify situations where the base erosion and anti-abuse tax (BEAT) would apply.
	✓					Identify factors that would qualify income as Foreign Derived Intangible Income (FDII).
	✓					Define the components of Global Intangible Low-Taxed Income (GILTI).
		✓				Identify situations that would create nexus for multijurisdictional transactions.
		✓				Identify the federal filing requirements of cross border business investments.
		✓				Calculate the apportionment percentage used in determining state taxable income.

Area V – Federal Taxation of Entities (including tax preparation and planning strategies) (28-38%) (continued)

Content group/topic	Skill				Representative task
	Remembering and Understanding	Application	Analysis	Evaluation	
D. S corporations					
1. Eligibility and election	✓				Recall eligible shareholders for an S corporation for federal income tax purposes.
	✓				Recall S corporation eligibility requirements for federal income tax purposes.
	✓				Explain the procedures to make a valid S corporation election for federal income tax purposes.
		✓			Identify situations in which S corporation status would be revoked or terminated for federal income tax purposes.
2. Determination of ordinary business income (loss) and separately stated items		✓			Calculate ordinary business income (loss) for an S corporation for federal income tax purposes.
		✓			Calculate separately stated items for an S corporation for federal income tax purposes.
			✓		Analyze both the accumulated adjustment account and the other adjustments account of an S corporation for federal income tax purposes.
			✓		Analyze the accumulated earnings and profits account of an S corporation that has been converted from a C corporation.
			✓		Analyze components of S corporation income/deductions to determine classification as ordinary business income (loss) or separately stated items on federal Form 1120S – U.S. Income Tax Return for an S Corporation.
3. Basis of shareholder's interest		✓			Calculate the shareholder's basis in S corporation stock for federal income tax purposes.
		✓			Analyze shareholder transactions with an S corporation to determine the impact on the shareholder's basis for federal income tax purposes.

Uniform CPA Examination Blueprints: Regulation (REG)

REG21

Regulation (REG)

Area V – Federal Taxation of Entities (including tax preparation and planning strategies) (28-38%) (continued)

Content group/topic	Skill				Representative task
	Remembering and Understanding	Application	Analysis	Evaluation	
D. S corporations (continued)					
4. Entity/owner transactions (including contributions, loans and distributions)		✓			Calculate the realized and recognized gain or loss to the shareholder of property contribution to an S corporation.
		✓			Calculate the allocation of S corporation income (loss) after the sale of a shareholder's share in the S corporation for federal income tax purposes.
			✓		Analyze the shareholder's impact of an S corporation's loss in excess of the shareholder's basis for federal income tax purposes.
			✓		Analyze the federal income tax implication to the shareholders and the S corporation resulting from shareholder contributions and loans as well as S corporation distributions and loans to shareholders.
5. Built-in gains tax	✓				Recall factors that cause a built-in gains tax to apply for federal income tax purposes.

Uniform CPA Examination Blueprints: Regulation (REG)

Regulation (REG)

Area V – Federal Taxation of Entities (including tax preparation and planning strategies) (28-38%) (continued)

Content group/topic	Skill				Representative task
	Remembering and Understanding	Application	Analysis	Evaluation	
E. Partnerships					
1. Determination of ordinary business income (loss) and separately stated items		✓			Calculate ordinary business income (loss) for a partnership for federal income tax purposes.
		✓			Calculate separately stated items for a partnership for federal income tax purposes.
			✓		Analyze components of partnership income/deductions to determine classification as ordinary business income (loss) or separately stated items on federal Form 1065 – U.S Return of Partnership Income.
2. Basis of partner's interest and basis of assets contributed to the partnership		✓			Calculate the partner's basis in the partnership for federal income tax purposes.
		✓			Calculate the partnership's basis in assets contributed by the partner for federal income tax purposes.
			✓		Analyze partner contributions to the partnership to determine the impact on the partner's basis for federal income tax purposes.
3. Partnership and partner elections	✓				Recall partner elections applicable to a partnership for federal income tax purposes.
4. Transactions between a partner and the partnership (including services performed by a partner and loans)		✓			Calculate the tax implications of certain transactions between a partner and partnership (such as services performed by a partner or loans) for federal income tax purposes.
			✓		Analyze the tax implications of a partner transaction with the partnership (such as services performed by a partner or loans) to determine the impact on the partner's tax basis for federal income tax purposes.
5. Impact of partnership liabilities on a partner's interest in a partnership		✓			Calculate the impact of increases and decreases of partnership liabilities on a partner's basis for federal income tax purposes.
			✓		Analyze the impact of partnership liabilities as they relate to the general partners and limited partners for federal income tax purposes.

Uniform CPA Examination Blueprints: Regulation (REG)

REG23

Area V – Federal Taxation of Entities (including tax preparation and planning strategies) (28–38%) (continued)

Content group/topic	Skill				Representative task
	Remembering and Understanding	Application	Analysis	Evaluation	
E. Partnerships (continued)					
6. Distribution of partnership assets		✓			Calculate the realized and recognized gains (losses) by the partnership and partners of liquidating distributions from the partnership for federal income tax purposes.
		✓			Calculate the realized and recognized gains (losses) by the partnership and partners of nonliquidating distributions from the partnership for federal income tax purposes.
		✓			Calculate the partner's basis of partnership assets received in a liquidating distribution for federal income tax purposes.
		✓			Calculate the partner's basis of partnership assets received in a nonliquidating distribution for federal income tax purposes.
7. Ownership changes	✓				Recall the situations in which a partnership would be terminated for federal income tax purposes.
		✓			Calculate the allocation of partnership income (loss) after the sale of a partner's share in the partnership for federal income tax purposes.
		✓			Calculate the revised basis of partnership assets due to a transfer of a partnership interest for federal income tax purposes.
F. Limited liability companies					
	✓				Recall the tax classification options for a limited liability company for federal income tax purposes.
G. Trusts and estates					
1. Types of trusts	✓				Recall and explain the differences between simple and complex trusts for federal income tax purposes.

Uniform CPA Examination Blueprints: Regulation (REG)

Regulation (REG)

Area V – Federal Taxation of Entities (including tax preparation and planning strategies) (28-38%) (continued)

Content group/topic	Skill				Representative task
	Remembering and Understanding	Application	Analysis	Evaluation	
G. Trusts and estates (continued)					
2. Income and deductions		✓			Calculate the total amount of income items reportable on a federal Form 1041 – *U.S. Income Tax Return for Estates and Trusts.*
		✓			Calculate the total amount of deductible expenses reportable on a federal Form 1041 – *U.S. Income Tax Return for Estates and Trusts.*
3. Determination of beneficiary's share of taxable income		✓			Calculate the beneficiary's share of taxable income from a trust for federal income tax purposes.
H. Tax-exempt organizations					
1. Types of organizations	✓				Recall the different types of tax-exempt organizations for federal tax purposes.
2. Obtaining and maintaining tax-exempt status	✓				Recall the requirements to qualify as an IRC Section 501(c)(3) tax-exempt organization.
	✓				Summarize the federal filing and disclosure requirements to obtain tax-exempt status for an organization.
	✓				Summarize the annual federal filing and disclosure requirements for a tax-exempt organization.
	✓				Explain the requirements necessary for retaining tax-exempt status.
	✓				Explain the procedures and recall the time period required to obtain tax-exempt status once the status has been revoked.
3. Unrelated business income		✓			Calculate the unrelated business income for a tax-exempt organization for federal income tax purposes.

Uniform CPA Examination Blueprints: Regulation (REG)

REG25

NOTES

401(k) Plan: A deferred compensation plan set up by an employer. A portion of a participating employee's earnings is deducted and placed in a qualified retirement plan. The employer may also contribute a matching percentage. Money in the plan is not taxed until the employee receives distributions, usually at retirement. A 401(k) plan is a defined contribution plan.

Accelerated Depreciation: A depreciation method (e.g., MACRS) that allows a greater portion of the property cost to be deducted in the first years after purchase, rather than spreading the cost evenly over the life of the asset, as with the straight-line depreciation method.

Acceptance (of an offer): The acceptance is the offeree's assent to enter into a contract. Acceptances must be unequivocal.

Accord and Satisfaction: An accord is an agreement to substitute one contractual obligation for another. Satisfaction is the performance of the accord. The original contractual duties are not discharged until the accord is satisfied. *See also* substituted contract.

Account: An account is any right to payment for goods, services, real property, or use of a credit card, not evidenced by an instrument or chattel paper.

Accredited Investor: An individual with a net worth over a four-year period that averages more than $1 million, excluding the value of the person's residence.

Accrual Accounting Method: The form of business accounting in which income is reported in the year earned, and expenses are reported in the year incurred, rather than reporting income and expenses when received or paid, respectively. A business that maintains an inventory is required to use the accrual method for purchases and sales.

Accuracy-Related Penalty: An accuracy-related penalty is a penalty based on the accuracy of tax returns. It includes (1) negligence or disregard of rules or regulations, (2) substantial understatement of income tax, (3) substantial valuation misstatement, and (4) substantial overstatement of pension liabilities. It does not include the penalty for fraud.

Active Income: Income from wages, tips, salaries, commissions, and trade or business in which the taxpayer materially participates.

Active Participation: A term the IRS uses to determine if an investor in rental real estate takes an active role in its management. The rules for active participation are much easier to meet than the material participation rules. An active participant may generally deduct up to $25,000 of rental real estate losses against other income. An active participant must not be a limited partner or own 10 percent or less of the property.

Actual Authority: The authority an agent reasonably believes that he possesses because of the principal's communications to the agent. Actual authority may be express or implied.

Actual Cash Value at Time of Loss: In insurance, the insured's recovery is limited to the actual cash value of the property at the time of loss considering such factors as the fair market value and the cost of repair or replacement less depreciation.

Ad Valorem Tax: A tax imposed on the value of property; for example, real estate taxes.

Adjusted Basis: The amount used to determine profit or loss from a property sale or exchange. The adjusted basis equals an asset's original cost, plus the cost of improvements to the asset, and minus any deductions, such as depreciation and depletion. Maintenance expenses do not affect the adjusted basis.

Adjusted Gross Income (AGI): A taxpayer's income after certain allowable adjustments from gross income, such as IRA contributions, health savings account contributions, and student loan interest, have been deducted.

Adoption Credit: A tax credit for qualifying expenses of adopting a child under age 18 or adopting a person who is physically and mentally unable to care for himself or herself. Medical expenses are not qualifying expenses.

After Acquired Property: Property that the debtor will acquire in the future.

Agency: A legal relationship in which one party (the principal) authorizes another party (the agent) to act on his behalf, giving the agent the power to bind the principal in contract and in some cases making the principal liable for the agent's torts.

Agency Coupled With an Interest: This type of agency arises when the agent has an interest in the subject matter of the agency, such as where the agency power is given as security. In effect, the agent has paid for the right to be appointed as the agent, usually by giving credit. Such agencies are not revocable by the principal.

Agent: An agent is one who acts on behalf of another (principal) and who has the power to legally bind the principal to contracts or, in some cases, tort.

Alimony: Money paid to a spouse or former spouse because of a written separation agreement, or a court order in a separate maintenance agreement, or divorce decree. Alimony and separate maintenance payments are taxable income to the recipient, and deductible to arrive at adjusted gross income for the payer for divorces and separation agreements finalized by December 31, 2018. Beginning in 2019, alimony is not a deduction and is not includable in income.

Alternative Minimum Tax (AMT): A tax originally intended to primarily affect high-income taxpayers who shelter some of their income from tax through certain tax preference items or deductions.

American Opportunity Credit: The American opportunity credit is available against federal income taxes for qualified tuition, fees, and course materials (including books) paid for a student's first four years of postsecondary education at an eligible educational institution.

Amortizable Bond Discount: When the amount paid for a bond is below its face value, taxable bond interest is increased by the amount of the bond discount amortization each year until the bond matures.

Amortizable Bond Premium: When the amount paid for a bond is over its face value, taxable bond interest is decreased by the amount of the bond premium amortization each year until the bond matures.

Amount Realized: The amount received in the sale or other disposition of property. This amount includes cash, the fair market value of property and services received, and debt assumed by the buyer.

Annuity: A contract, sold by a commercial insurance company, which pays benefits on a regular basis for a specified time. The payments include the return of the investment in the contract plus interest or other returns.

Antecedent Debt: A preexisting debt.

Anticipatory Repudiation: Anticipatory repudiation occurs when one party states before the time that performance is due under a contract that he or she will not perform. The non-breaching party may cancel the contract, sue immediately for breach, or wait until the time of performance and sue if there is a breach.

Antifraud Provision, Rule 10b-5: A section under the Securities Exchange Act of 1934 prohibiting fraud in connection with any purchase or sale of securities.

Antitrust Laws: Laws that generally prohibit businesses from engaging in conduct that could stifle free competition.

Apparent Authority: Apparent authority is agency power arising from words or conduct of a principal that, when manifested to third persons, reasonably induce them to believe that actual authority exists.

Appraisal Rights: Shareholders who are dissatisfied with most fundamental corporate changes have an opportunity to "dissent" and demand that the corporation pay them the fair value of their shares rather than remain shareholders of a fundamentally changed corporation (also called dissenter's rights).

Articles of Incorporation: The articles of incorporation are the documents that must be filed with the state to form a corporation. The articles must include: the name of the corporation; the names and address of the corporation's registered agent (on whom process may be served if the corporation is sued); the names and addresses of each of the incorporators; and the number of shares authorized to be issued.

Articles of Organization: The articles of organization are the documents that must be filed with the state to form a limited liability company (LLC). The articles must include: a statement that the entity is an LLC; the name of the LLC, which must include an indication that it is an LLC; the street address of the LLC's registered office and name of its registered agent; and, if the company is to be run by managers rather than by all members, the names of the managers.

Artisan's Lien: Under common law, a skilled craftsman (an artisan) who works on property and either improves it or repairs it automatically has a lien on the property for the price of the repair. This is referred to as an artisan's lien.

Assignment: A voluntary transfer of contract rights to a third party. The assignor is the party transferring the contract rights. The assignee is the party receiving the contract rights.

Assignment for the Benefit of Creditors: A transfer of some or all of a debtor's property to a trustee, who disposes of the property and uses the proceeds to satisfy the debtor's obligations.

At-Risk Rules: Tax laws that limit the losses a taxpayer can claim on a business investment to the amount actually at risk to lose.

Attachment (of a security interest): In the context of the Secured Transactions Article of the UCC, attachment occurs when a security interest becomes effective between a creditor and a debtor. Attachment requires an agreement between the creditor and debtor to create a security interest; the creditor must give value and the debtor must have rights in the collateral.

Authenticated Record (in secured transactions): In the context of the Secured Transactions Article of the UCC, an authenticated record is a written security agreement or intangible record (such as a computer file) that has been signed or marked electronically by a party to indicate adoption of the agreement.

Authorized Shares: When a corporation is formed, its article of incorporation must indicate the number of shares that the corporation may issue. These are the "authorized shares."

Automatic Stay: In bankruptcy proceedings, the cession of almost all collection efforts against the debtor or the debtor's property upon filing. The automatic stay does not apply to criminal proceedings or efforts to collect or modify alimony, maintenance, spousal support, or child support.

Backward Vertical Merger: A merger between a firm and one of its suppliers.

Bankruptcy: Under the federal Bankruptcy Code, the inability to pay debts as they become due.

Bankruptcy Crime: The commission of certain specified acts, which will constitute grounds for a denial of discharge in bankruptcy and also constitute a federal crime. Such acts include the making of a false oath or account, presenting or using a false claim, giving or receiving a bribe, or withholding records or documents in connection with a bankruptcy proceeding.

Base Erosion and Anti-abuse Tax (BEAT): A minimum tax on large U.S. corporations (annual gross receipts of $500 million or more) with a significant amount of deductible payments to related foreign affiliates because such deductions reduce the U.S tax base.

Basis: The amount paid for an asset plus other costs, such as sales tax, shipping, and installation, less depreciation taken. The basis will change over time and is used to determine the gain or loss upon asset disposition.

Beneficiary: The person who is entitled to receive funds or property under the terms and provisions of a will, trust, insurance policy, or security instrument.

Best Practices: Best practices for tax advisors include communicating with the client regarding the terms of the engagement; establishing the facts and arriving at a conclusion supported by the law and the facts; advising the client about the import of the conclusions reached (for example, whether the client will be able to avoid penalties); and making sure that all members, associates, and employees of the firm follow procedures that are consistent with the above.

BFP: Acronym for a "bona fide purchaser" for value. Also referred to as a good faith or innocent purchaser.

Bilateral Contract: A contract formed when one promise is exchanged for another promise (i.e., a promise for a promise). The contract is created by the exchange of promises.

Bills of Lading: Documents representing goods that are being transported by a carrier.

Blue Sky Laws: State laws governing stock sales.

Bond: A type of debt owed by governments and corporations. Bonds typically pay interest twice a year.

Bond Discount: When bonds are sold below face value, the discount is the amount by which the face value exceeds market price.

Bond Premium: When bonds are sold above face value, the premium is the amount by which the market price exceeds face value.

Bonus Depreciation: This allows the expensing of an additional percentage of qualified property that is placed in service during the current year. Bonus depreciation is taken after the Section 179 deduction and before the regular MACRS depreciation.

Book Value: The net amount of an asset's value after reduction by a related reserve; for example, accumulated depreciation or allowance for bad debts.

Boot: Cash or other property used in an exchange to make the values of property traded equal. For instance, if an old delivery truck is traded for a new model, additional cash paid is boot.

Business Judgment Rule: A director will not be liable to the corporation for acts performed or decisions made in good faith, in a manner the director believes to be in the best interest of the corporation, and with the care that an ordinarily prudent person in a like position would exercise.

Business-Use Property: Property used in a trade or business. Examples include computer equipment or a commercial kitchen.

Buyer in the Ordinary Course: A purchaser of goods from a merchant's inventory in the ordinary course of the seller's business.

Bylaws: Bylaws are rules that a corporation imposes on itself regarding the operation of the corporation. Bylaws are not part of the articles of incorporation and are not required to be filed with the state. They cannot conflict with the articles of incorporation or federal, state, or local law.

CIF (Cost, Insurance, and Freight): A shipping term that specifies that the contract price includes the cost of the goods, insurance for the goods, and freight. A CIF contract is a shipment contract.

Calendar Year: A complete tax year for most taxpayers that runs from January 1 through December 31.

Cancellation: Cancellation terminates a contract between parties and restores them to their former position. Contracts may be canceled or rescinded for mistake, fraud, and most material contract breaches. *See also* rescission.

Cancellation of Debt (COD): When a creditor forgives a debt without payment. COD is taxable as income to the debtor unless the creditor intended it as a gift or it meets certain exceptions relating to bankruptcy, insolvency, or farming.

Capital Asset: An item owned for investment or personal purposes, such as stocks or bonds. The sale of a capital asset produces a capital gain or a capital loss. Depreciable assets, inventory, and other assets used in a business are not capital assets.

Capital Gain: Profit on the sale of a capital asset. Individual taxpayers' capital gains often receive more favorable tax treatment than ordinary gains.

Capital Gain Distribution: Capital gain distributions from a corporate liquidation. The difference between an investor's basis in stock and the amount distributed to the investor at liquidation is a capital gain.

Capital Loss: Loss from the sale of a capital asset. To the extent that capital losses exceed capital gains, an individual may offset up to $3,000 in capital losses against ordinary income each year, and may carry the excess capital losses forward indefinitely until they are used up.

Carrier's Lien: A carrier of goods has a lien on the goods covered by a bill of lading for storage, transportation, and expenses reasonably incurred.

Carryback: The retroactive use of deductions or credits that cannot be taken in the current year, to reduce a prior year(s)' tax liability.

Carryforward: The use of deductions or credits that cannot be taken in the current year, to reduce a subsequent year(s)' tax liability.

Cash Accounting Method: A method of accounting under which the taxpayer generally reports income when cash is received or constructively received and reports expenses when cash payments are made. However, for fixed assets, depreciation or amortization deductions are made using the accrual method.

Cash Liquidation Distribution: A return of capital when a corporation is being partially or completely liquidated. It is nontaxable unless the total amount of the taxpayer's distribution exceeds the investment basis.

Casualty and Theft Loss: A loss caused by a hurricane, earthquake, fire, flood, theft, or similar event that is sudden, unexpected, or unusual.

Cease and Desist Orders: An administrative or judicial order prohibiting a person or entity from conducting certain specified activities.

Certificate of Authority: A certificate of authority is a document issued by a state that authorizes a foreign corporation to transact business within the state.

Certificated Securities: A stock or bond that is represented by a certificate.

Chapter 7 Liquidation: A type of bankruptcy in which a debtor's assets are sold and turned into cash, which is distributed to the appropriate creditors.

Chapter 11 Reorganization: A type of bankruptcy in which the debtor remains in possession of his or her assets and a plan to pay off debts (a plan of reorganization) is submitted.

Chapter 13 Adjustment of Debts of Individuals with Regular Income: A type of bankruptcy case in which the debtor repays all or a portion of his debts over a three- to five-year period. Although there is not a liquidation, a trustee oversees the case, and at the conclusion of the case the remaining debts of the debtor are discharged.

Chapter 15 Ancillary and Cross-Border Cases: A type of bankruptcy case commenced by a "foreign representative" filing a petition for recognition of a "foreign proceeding." This operates as the principal door of a foreign representative to U.S. courts.

Charging Order: A charging order is a court order used by a creditor of an individual partner who may obtain an interest against an individual partner's share of profits.

Charitable Contribution Deduction: An itemized deduction for contributions of cash or property to a qualified tax-exempt organization.

Charitable Organization: A tax-exempt organization recognized by the IRS as a charity.

Child Support: Payments designated for the support of a minor child under an agreement of divorce or separation. Child support is not deductible by the payer, nor is it taxable to the recipient.

Child Tax Credit: A partially refundable tax credit of up to $2,000 that is available for each qualifying child under the age of 17.

Circular 230: Circular 230 is the IRS publication entitled "Regulations Governing Practice before the Internal Revenue Service." The publication addresses the practice before the IRS of "practitioners" (attorneys, certified public accountants, enrolled agents, enrolled actuaries, enrolled retirement plan agents, and appraisers).

Civil Penalty: With respect to tax practice, a civil penalty is a fine or other judgment against a taxpayer or tax preparer for failure to comply with one or more of the elements of the federal tax law.

Closely Held Corporation: A corporation that is owned by a small group of investors or a family that is typically involved in the corporation's management.

Collateral: Property that is the subject matter of a security interest.

Commission: Employee compensation paid based on a percentage of sales made, or a fixed amount per sale.

Common Law: A body of law developed from judicial decisions or custom.

Common Stock: Common stock is a class of stock that will carry with it all rights of stock ownership.

Compensated Surety: A surety who is paid or compensated for his promise to the creditor. In order to discharge a compensated surety, the creditor must make a material change in the contract that increases the surety's risk.

Compensatory Damages: An award of money to a non-breaching party to enable him to obtain an equivalent substitute performance.

Complete Gift: A complete gift is a transfer of property in which the transferor of the property has relinquished dominion and control over the property. A gift is not considered complete if the gift is conditional or revocable.

Condition of Confidentiality: A written advice subject to a condition of confidentiality is one in which the practitioner imposes on the recipient(s) a limitation on the disclosure of the information contained in the written advice regarding the tax treatment of the item or transaction.

Conditions in Contracts: A condition is an event, the occurrence or nonoccurrence of which will end a party's duty to perform a contract.

- A condition precedent is a condition that must occur before the other party must perform.

- Concurrent conditions must occur simultaneously.

- A condition subsequent is a condition that will occur after a party's duty to perform has arisen and will cut off that duty.

Confessing a Judgment: Confessing a judgment is admitting liability in a lawsuit.

Confirmation (in a Chapter 11 case): Acceptance of a Chapter 11 plan by the bankruptcy court. Once confirmed, the debtor will pay off debts in accordance with the plan.

Conglomerate Merger: A firm acquires a company in a completely different business.

Consequential Damages: Damages that are a direct consequence of a breach and that are in addition to compensatory damages. Consequential damages are recoverable only if they are a reasonably foreseeable result of the breach.

Consideration: Consideration is the price of contracting. Both sides of a contract must be supported by something of legal value that was part of a bargained for exchange.

Consignee: One to whom goods are delivered on consignment.

Consignment: A transaction in which the owner of goods (the consignor) delivers goods to another (the consignee) for the consignee to sell. The consignee pays the consignor for the goods when the goods are sold.

Consignor: One who transfers goods on consignment.

Constructive Fraud: Constructive fraud occurs when a party induces another party to enter into a contract by making a material misrepresentation of fact. The material misrepresentation is made with a reckless disregard for the truth (also called gross negligence).

Constructive Notice: Not actual notice or knowledge, but rather notice imputed by law.

Constructive Receipt of Income: Income is deemed to have been received when it is made available, regardless of whether the taxpayer actually takes possession of it. For instance, if a taxpayer receives a check in December of Year 1 and deposits it in January Year 2, it was constructively received in Year 1.

Consumer Goods: Goods used for personal, family, or household purposes.

Continuation Statement: A financing statement can be renewed for a five-year period by filing a document called a continuation statement.

Contracts for Necessities: A contract by a minor to buy things necessary for life (i.e., food, clothing, shelter, etc.). Although minors may usually disaffirm contracts, they are bound by contracts for necessities.

Contractual Capacity: The legal ability to make a contract.

Contribution (in suretyship): Once one cosurety pays the creditor, he has the right to receive a pro rata share or contribution from all other cosureties.

Corporate Opportunity Doctrine: If a director is presented with a business opportunity that would be of interest to his corporation (e.g., he is told that land the corporation is interested in purchasing has just been put on the market), generally the duty of loyalty prohibits the director from taking the opportunity for himself.

Corporation: A corporation is a legal entity distinct from its owners (called "shareholders" or "stockholders") and managers. Corporations are created by complying with a state incorporation statute.

Corporation by Estoppel: Under the estoppel doctrine, a party who treats a business as if it were a validly formed corporation will be estopped (legally barred) from claiming in a legal preceding that the corporation was not validly formed. This applies to third parties who treat the business as a corporation as well as to the business itself.

Cosureties: Two or more sureties of the same obligation.

Counteroffer: In contracts governed by the common law, a counteroffer occurs when the offeree changes the terms of the original offer or adds new terms. A counteroffer is both a rejection of the original offer and a new offer.

Covenant Not to Sue: An agreement not to bring a lawsuit.

Coverdell Education Savings Account: A type of educational savings plan. Similar to an IRA, a qualifying taxpayer may make nondeductible contributions to a qualified account for a child under 18. The child will be able to make tax-free withdrawals when he or she incurs qualified education expenses.

Cram Down: A method of confirming a Chapter 11 bankruptcy plan that is not accepted by all impaired classes. At least one impaired class must accept and the court must find that the plan is not unfairly discriminatory and is fair and equitable with respect to any dissenting impaired classes.

Creditors' Committee: In a Chapter 11 case, shortly after the order for relief is effective, a committee of unsecured creditors is appointed. This committee usually consists of the holders of the seven largest unsecured claims against the debtor.

Creditors' Composition: An agreement between the debtor and two or more creditors that each creditor receives a portion of his claim as full payment.

Criminal Penalty: With respect to tax practice, a criminal penalty is a penalty for a severe infraction of the federal tax law. There can be substantial fines or jail terms.

Cumulative Preferred Shares: Shares with a preference usually are entitled to a fixed amount of money before distributions can be made with respect to nonpreferred shares. With cumulative preferred shares, if a dividend is not declared in a particular year, the right to receive the preference accumulates and must be paid before nonpreferred shares may be paid any dividend.

Cumulative Preferred Stock: Cumulative preferred stock is preferred stock for which the dividends accumulate if they are not declared. No dividends can be paid on the common stock until the cumulative dividends not yet paid are paid. *See also* preferred stock.

Cumulative Voting: In cumulative voting, each share is entitled to one vote for each director position that is being filled and the shareholder may cast the votes in any way, including casting all for a single candidate.

Custodial Parent: For purposes of head of household status, a custodial parent is the parent with custody of the child.

Debt Relief Agency: An agency that is paid compensation to assist consumer debtors in filing bankruptcy petitions.

Debt Securities: Debt securities are bonds. A debt security represents a creditor-debtor relationship with the corporation whereby the corporation has borrowed funds from "outside investors" and promises to repay them.

De Minimis Fringe Benefits: De minimis fringe benefits are fringe benefits that are so minimal that they are impractical to account for and may thus be excluded from income.

Dealer: In securities law, one who sells or trades securities on a full- or part-time basis.

Debenture: A debenture is an unsecured bond. *See also* subordinated debenture.

Debt Securities: Debt securities are bonds. A debt security represents a creditor-debtor relationship with the corporation whereby the corporation has borrowed funds from "outside investors" and promises to repay them.

Decedent: A person who has died.

Delegation of Duties: A transfer of contractual duties to a third party.

Dependent: *See* qualifying child *and* qualifying relative.

Derivative Action: When a corporation has a legal cause of action against someone but refuses to bring the action, the shareholders may have a right to bring a shareholder derivative action to enforce the corporation's rights. Such an action may be brought against a director of the corporation or outsiders.

Destination Contract: A type of contract in which risk of loss passes from the seller to the buyer when the seller delivers the goods to the specified destination and tenders delivery to the buyer.

Detrimental Reliance: A contract doctrine, which states that a promise made by one party and detrimentally relied upon by another can be enforced without consideration (also called promissory estoppel).

Directors: Directors are individuals with the general authority and responsibility for management of the corporation. In most corporations, the board of directors delegates the power to run the corporation on a day-to-day basis to the officers.

Disaffirm: The right to cancel or rescind a contractual obligation.

Discharge: To release from liability.

Dissenters' Rights: *See* appraisal rights.

Dissociation: Dissociation is a change in the relationship of the partners caused by any partner ceasing to be associated in the carrying on of the business. The remaining partners have the right to continue the business.

Dissolution: Upon dissolution, the partnership is terminated and the business must be wound up.

Dividends: A dividend is a distribution of corporate profits as ordered by the directors and paid to the shareholders.

Domestic Corporation: A domestic corporation is a corporation incorporated within the state.

Due Diligence Defense: Under the Securities Act of 1933, defendants other than issuers are not liable for material misrepresentations or omissions in the registration statement if they can prove they had reasonable grounds to believe, and did believe, that there were no material misrepresentations or omissions. This defense is called the due diligence defense.

Duress: Forcing someone into a contract by an unlawful use of a threat of harm. The threat can be physical, economic, or a threat of criminal action.

Duty of Loyalty: A fiduciary duty imposed by law on an agent to act solely in the principal's best interest.

Duty of Obedience: A duty imposed by law on an agent to follow all reasonable directions of the principal.

Duty of Reasonable Care: A duty imposed by law on an agent to act with ordinary care or skill (duty not to be negligent) when acting on behalf of the principal.

Earned Income: Includes wages, salaries, tips, includable in gross income, and net earnings from self-employment earnings.

Employee Stock Options: Options to purchase the stock of a corporation granted to the corporation's employees.

Employee Stock Ownership Plan (ESOP): A plan for encouraging employees to own stock in their company. Dividends paid under an employee stock ownership plan are deductible by the company, whereas ordinary dividends are not.

Employee Stock Purchase Plans (ESPP): Qualified stock options meeting specific requirements that grant options to employees to purchase stock in a corporation. Generally, these options are not taxed as compensation to the employees and the employer does not receive a tax deduction.

Equipment: Goods that are bought primarily for use in a trade or business.

Equity Securities: Equity securities are stocks. An equity security is an instrument representing an investment in the corporation whereby its holder becomes a part owner of the business.

Equity Security Holders: The holders of stock or similar securities as opposed to the holders of debt securities, such as bonds, notes, or debentures.

Equity Securities Holders Committee: In a Chapter 11 case involving a corporation, a committee of stockholders is appointed shortly after the order for relief is effective. The stockholders' committee usually consists of the seven largest holders of equity securities.

Estate Tax: The tax imposed on the transfer of a decedent's property. Estate tax is levied on the decedent's estate and not on the heir(s) receiving the property.

Exception to Discharge: Those debts of an individual that are not dischargeable in bankruptcy.

Excess Accelerated Depreciation: The difference between the total amount of accelerated depreciation taken since an asset's acquisition and the amount of straight-line depreciation had that method been used.

Excise Tax: A transaction tax imposed by federal, state, and/or local governments, typically determined by multiplying a percentage by the value. Examples of products subject to excise taxes include gasoline, air travel, and tobacco.

Executed Contract: A contract in which all duties have been performed by all parties to the contract.

Executory Contract: A contract in which duties remain to be performed by one or more parties.

Exoneration (in Suretyship): A lawsuit brought by the surety to compel the debtor to pay her debt.

Express Authority: The actual authority of an agent specifically given in the principal's written or spoken communications to the agent.

Express Contract: A contract formed by language, either oral or written.

Express Warranties (in sale of goods): Under the UCC Sales Article, an express warranty is created by a seller's statement of fact concerning the goods, description of the goods, or by showing a sample or model. The express warranty is that the goods must conform to the statement of fact, description, sample, or model.

Failure-to-File Penalty: In general, the penalty is 5 percent of the amount of tax due for each month (or any portion thereof) the return is not filed.

Failure-to-Pay Penalty: In general, the penalty is one-half of 1 percent per month (of any fraction thereof) up to a maximum of 25 percent of the unpaid tax.

Fair Debt Collection Practices Act (FDCPA): A federal law that makes illegal abusive, deceptive, and unfair debt collection by collection agencies.

Family Tax Credit: A non-refundable family credit is allowed for each person who is not a qualifying child for purposes of the child tax credit, but is a qualifying dependent under the dependency rules.

Farming Income: Farming income is income for a person or an entity engaged in the management or operation of a farm with the intent of earning a profit. This income is reported on Schedule F.

Fast-Track Remediation: Fast-track remediation is a process by which small-business owners and self-employed individuals can resolve their tax disputes (a "process for the prompt resolution of tax issues").

Federal Insurance Contribution Act (FICA): A federal law providing benefits to workers and their dependents in case of death, disability, or retirement. The act also provides for hospital insurance under the Medicare provision.

Federal Reserve (Fed): The Federal Reserve is the central bank of the United States.

Federal Unemployment Tax Act (FUTA): A federal law establishing a state-run system of insurance to provide income to workers who have lost their jobs through no fault of their own.

Federal Unemployment Tax Act (FUTA) Tax: An employment tax on employers to fund unemployment benefits. FUTA applies to 6 percent of the first $7,000 of covered annual wages per employee. The federal government allows a credit (maximum 5.4 percent) for FUTA paid to the state.

Fictitious Name Statutes: Fictitious name statutes are state laws that require persons conducting a business under an assumed name to file with the state the name under which the business is conducted and the real names and addresses of all persons conducting the business.

Fiduciary: An individual, company, or association responsible for managing another's assets. Fiduciaries include executors of wills and estates, trustees, receivers in bankruptcy, and those responsible for managing the finances of a minor. Corporate directors and officers and agents also are fiduciaries.

Fiduciary Duty: Fiduciary duty is a duty of utmost loyalty and good faith.

Final Return for Decedent: An individual's tax return filed for the year in which the individual died. The decedent's personal representative is responsible for filing a final return.

Financing Statement: A document filed with the state giving constructive notice of a security interest in specified collateral. The financing statement must contain the names and addresses of the creditor and debtor, contain a general description of the type of collateral, and be authorized by the debtor.

Fiscal Year: A 12-month year ending on a date other than December 31.

Fixture: Personal property that has become so attached to real property that it is considered to be real property as a matter of law.

FOB (Free on Board): A shipping term that specifies that the seller has risk of loss until the seller gets the goods to the FOB location.

Foreclosure: The right of the mortgagee to sell the mortgaged property on default of the debtor to satisfy the mortgage debt.

Foreign Corporation: A foreign corporation is a corporation doing business in a state other than its state of incorporation.

Foreign-Derived Intangible Income (FDII): Foreign-derived intangible income is income from transactions involving non-U.S. persons located outside the United States. A U.S. corporation may get a deduction for a portion of its FDII.

Foreign Earned Income Exclusion: Income excludable from the income of a taxpayer who lives in and earns income in a foreign country.

Forfeited Interest: Forfeited interest is a penalty for early withdrawal of savings (normally on a certificate of deposit at a bank).

Form 706: U.S. tax return form for estates and generation-skipping transfers.

Form 709: U.S. tax return form for gifts and generation-skipping transfers.

Form 843: U.S. income tax form for a claim for refund or abatement of interest, penalties, and additions to tax.

Form 990: U.S. income tax form for an organization exempt from income tax.

Form 990-EZ: U.S. income tax short-form information form for exempt organizations.

Form 990-N: U.S. income tax information form for exempt organizations (electronic notice).

Form 990-PF: U.S. income tax form for the income of a private foundation or a nonexempt charitable trust treated as a private foundation.

Form 990-T: U.S. income tax form for the business income of an exempt organization.

Form 1024: U.S. income tax form for certain types of organizations for applying for recognition under Section 501(a) for plan qualification under Section 120.

Form 1040: U.S. income tax return form for individuals.

Form 1040X: U.S. income tax form for an individual to claim a refund (from a net operating loss carryback or certain other losses) for each carryback year. It is an alternative to Form 1045.

Form 1041: U.S. income tax return form for estates and trusts.

Form 1045: U.S. income tax form for application for a refund for individuals, estates, and trusts.

Form 1065: U.S. income tax return form for partnership income.

Form 1099-DIV: A required tax reporting form received from a taxpayer's broker or company in which the taxpayer owns shares. The form reports dividends received, income tax withheld from dividends, and foreign taxes paid on dividends.

Form 1099-INT: A required tax reporting form received from a taxpayer's bank or savings institution that reports interest income and related information such as early withdrawal penalties, federal tax withheld, and foreign tax paid.

Form 1120: U.S. income tax return form for corporations.

Form 1120S: U.S. income tax form for S corporations.

Form 1120X: U.S. income tax form for a corporation to file an amended income tax return.

Form 1139: U.S. income tax form for a corporation other than an S corporation to claim a refund (from a net operating loss carryback or certain other losses) for each carryback year.

Form 2120: U.S. income tax form for a multiple support declaration.

Form 4797: U.S. income tax form for reporting the details of gains and losses from the sale, exchange, involuntary conversion, or disposition of business property.

Form 4868: U.S. income tax form for an automatic extension of time to file an individual Form 1040.

Form 6251: Alternative minimum income tax return form for individuals.

Form 6252: U.S. income tax form for installment sales income.

Form 7004: U.S. income tax form for an application for an automatic six-month extension to file certain business income tax, information, and other returns.

Form 8275: U.S. income tax form to disclose tax positions, except those taken contrary to a regulation, that are not otherwise adequately disclosed on a tax return to avoid certain penalties.

Form 8282: U.S. income tax form for information about dispositions of certain charitable deduction property by a charitable organization.

Form 8332: U.S. income tax form for the release of a claim to the exemption for a child of divorced or separated parents.

Form 8815: U.S. income tax form for the exclusion from income of interest on Series EE U.S. savings bonds issued after 1989.

Form 8824: U.S. income tax form for reporting like-kind exchanges.

Form 8868: U.S. income tax form for an exempt organization to request an automatic three-month extension to file its tax return.

Form W-2: A form used by employers to report annual wages, taxes withheld, and other information. A W-2 is sent to the taxpayer and to the IRS.

Form W-4: A form completed by an employee that an employer uses to determine the amount of income tax to withhold from the employee's paycheck.

Forward Vertical Merger: A merger between a firm and one of its customers.

Fraud: Fraud occurs when a party induces another party to enter into a contract by making a material misrepresentation of fact. The material misrepresentation must be made with scienter (made knowing that the statement was false or with a reckless disregard for the truth).

Fraud in the Execution: Fraud in the execution occurs when a party is deceived into signing something that he does not know is a contract.

Fraud in the Inducement: With fraud in the inducement, the defrauded party is aware of what he or she is signing, but was tricked into signing by a representation of false circumstances.

Fraudulent Conveyance: Transfers of property by a debtor with the intent to hinder, delay, or defraud a creditor.

Fringe Benefit: Employee compensation other than wages, tips, and salaries, such as health insurance, life insurance, and pension plans.

Fundamental Changes: Fundamental changes are modifications to a business entity that alter in a material way the way the entity operates or the owners' rights in the entity. Examples include: amendments to the articles, dissolutions, mergers, consolidations, share exchanges, and sales of all or substantially all of the entity's assets outside the regular course of the entity's business, and admitting a new general partner.

Future Interest: A future interest, for estate tax purposes, is an interest that is the unrestricted right to the use, possession, or enjoyment of property or income from the property at some future date.

Gambling Income and Losses: Income and losses from gambling, such as lotteries, bingo, and racing. Gambling income is taxable regardless of whether the gambling activity is legal or illegal. Gambling losses are only deductible to the extent of reported gambling income.

Gap Claims or Gap Creditors: Under the Bankruptcy Act, claims that accrue in the ordinary course of business after an involuntary petition is filed but before the order for relief is entered. Such claims are entitled to a third priority.

Garage Sale Rule: Under the Secured Transactions Article of the UCC, if a creditor relies on the automatic perfection of a security interest in consumer goods and the consumer debtor resells the goods to a second consumer who does not have notice of the automatically perfected security interest, the second consumer purchaser takes the collateral free of the automatically perfected security interest.

Garnishment: A legal writ ordering a third party in possession or control of money or property of a debtor to turn it over to a creditor. Failure to comply with a writ of garnishment makes the third party personally liable for the value of the property not turned over.

General Agent: An agent engaged to perform a series of transactions involving a continuity of service.

General Partner: A partner in a partnership whose liability is not limited. A general partner is usually involved in the day-to-day management of the partnership.

General Partnership: A general partnership is an association of two or more persons who agree to carry on as co-owners of a business for profit.

Generation-Skipping Transfer Tax: The generation-skipping transfer tax is a tax designed to prevent an individual from escaping an entire generation of gift and estate tax.

Gift: A property transfer for less than adequate consideration. Gifts usually occur in a personal setting, such as between family members. Gifts are excluded from income tax, but may be subject to the gift tax.

Gift Tax: Tax imposed on gifted property. The tax is imposed on the donor and is based on the fair market value of the property on the gift date. An annual exclusion and lifetime credit exempts most gifts from taxation.

Global Intangible Low-Taxed Income (GILTI): A minimum tax imposed on certain low-taxed income that is intended to reduce the incentive to relocate controlled foreign corporations to low-tax jurisdictions.

Good Faith (in the UCC): Good faith as defined by the UCC in Sales is "honesty in fact in the conduct or transaction concerned."

Goods: As defined by Article 2 of the UCC, goods are moveable, tangible personal property.

Gratuitous Surety: A surety who is not compensated for his promise to the creditor. The consideration for a gratuitous surety's promise is the promise or performance that the creditor makes to the principal debtor. If the creditor does anything to vary a gratuitous surety's risk, then the gratuitous surety's obligation is discharged.

Greenmail: When a corporation is faced with the prospect of being taken over and the board of directors wants to resist the takeover attempt, one option is to pay the person or company attempting the takeover to abandon its takeover attempt.

Gross Estate: The gross estate, for estate tax purposes, includes the value at the date of death of the property in the estate.

Gross Negligence: *See* constructive fraud.

Gross Profit Percentage: The percentage of payments received from an installment sale attributable to profit.

Guaranteed Payments to Partners: Payments that are made to partners without regard to the partnership's income or loss. These predetermined, guaranteed payments are often a form of salary for working partners, and they may be subject to self-employment tax.

Guarantor: One who promises to pay a creditor only if the debtor defaults.

Guarantor of Collectibility: One who promises to pay a creditor only if the debtor defaults and the creditor has exhausted all legal remedies against the debtor.

Health Coverage Tax Credit: The health coverage tax credit is a tax credit for 72.5 percent of health care premiums for qualified health insurance paid by certain taxpayers.

Health Savings Account (HSA): An HSA is an investment account a taxpayer owns for paying qualified medical expenses for the individual and his or her family. Contributions are made with pretax income; interest and withdrawals are tax-free; and unused funds are carried over to future years. Taxpayers must participate in a high-deductible health care plan to be eligible for an HSA.

Hobby Loss: Loss from a hobby or other activity not pursued for profit. A taxpayer can only claim hobby expenses to the extent of reported hobby income.

Implied Authority: Implied authority is a type of actual authority that is not found in the express words of the principal, but rather is inferred from the principal's words or conducts that manifest an intent that the agent be authorized to act on the principal's behalf.

Implied-in-Fact Contract: A contract formed by the conduct of the parties.

Implied-in-Law Contract: Not a real contract, but rather a legal remedy that allows a plaintiff to recover a benefit unjustly conferred upon the defendant. It is a legal remedy to prevent unjust enrichment (also called quasi-contract).

Implied Warranties (in sale of goods): An implied warranty is a duty imposed by the UCC Sales Article on sellers when goods are sold. Implied warranties include the implied warranty of title, merchantability, and fitness for a particular purpose. *See also* warranty of title *and* warranty of merchantability *and* warranty of fitness for a particular purpose.

Impossibility: A contract defense that applies if, after the parties enter into a contract, an event occurs that will make performance objectively impossible (i.e., impossible for anyone to perform).

Incentive Stock Options: Qualified stock options meeting specific requirements that are granted to key employees. Generally, these options are not taxed as compensation to the employees and the employer does not receive a tax deduction.

Income in Respect of a Decedent: Income a decedent earned, or was entitled to receive, before death. This income is included in the gross income of the survivor who receives it.

Incomplete Gift: An incomplete gift is a transfer of property where the transferor of the property has not relinquished dominion and control over the property.

Incorporator: An incorporator is the party responsible for forming the corporation by filing articles of incorporation with the state.

Indemnification: Indemnification is the duty of a business entity to reimburse those properly acting on behalf of the entity for losses incurred.

Independent Contractor: A party who contracts with another to perform a specified task and is not subject to the control of the other regarding the method of performing the assigned task (e.g., a CPA or a lawyer working for a client).

Individual Retirement Account (IRA): A retirement savings account in which a taxpayer makes an annual contribution that grows, tax-free, until retirement. Depending on the type of IRA, and the taxpayer's age and income, the contribution may be excluded from adjusted gross income, and the distribution may be nontaxable.

Injunction: A court decree ordering a party to do or refrain from doing a certain act or activity.

Innocent Misrepresentation: A misrepresentation of fact made without scienter (i.e., without an intent to deceive and not made recklessly with regard for the truth).

Insider: Under securities law, a corporate director, officer, employee, agent, or other with access to confidential information and a duty not to disclose that information; in the context of preferential payments in bankruptcy, an insider is anyone in a close relationship with the debtor.

Insider Trading: The purchase or sale of securities by persons with access to nonpublic information regarding the securities, such as a corporation's officers, directors, 10 percent or more stockholders, accountants, attorneys, etc.

Installment Sale: A sale that is divisible into multiple corresponding deliveries and payments.

Inter Vivos Trust: A lifetime trust created during the lifetime of the benefactor, as opposed to a testamentary trust created after the benefactor's death.

Interlocking Directorates: Competing companies having common directors serving on their boards of directors.

Internal Revenue Service (IRS): The tax collection branch of the U.S. Department of the Treasury that administers the Internal Revenue Code enacted by Congress.

Intrastate Sales: In securities law, an exemption from registration under the Securities Act of 1933 for securities sold or offered to be sold only to residents of a specific state.

Inventory: Goods held for sale or lease in a business or goods used up quickly in a business, such as raw materials used in manufacturing.

Investment Income: Income on investments, such as taxable and tax-exempt interest, dividends, capital gains, certain rent and royalty income, and net passive activity income.

Investment Property (in secured transactions): Investment property in the context of the Secured Transaction Article of the UCC includes stocks, bonds, mutual funds, and brokerage accounts containing such items.

Involuntary Conversion: The forced disposition of property due to a casualty, theft, condemnation, or threat of condemnation. In an involuntary conversion, the asset is forfeited and the taxpayer receives insurance proceeds or a condemnation award.

Involuntary Petition in Bankruptcy: A document filed by a debtor's creditors alleging that the debtor owes more than the threshold amount specified in the revised Bankruptcy Act and is not paying debts as they become due. If the debtor does not object or the court finds the petition to be true, it becomes an order for relief.

Issued Shares: The corporation issues some or all of the authorized shares.

Issuer (of securities): In securities law, the entity whose securities are being sold.

Joint and Several Liability: Joint and several liability is liability whereby creditors may sue partners jointly or sue partners individually.

Joint Venture: An association of persons with the intent of engaging in a single transaction or series of related transactions for profit.

Judicial Lien: An interest in property obtained by court action to secure payment of a debt.

Keogh Retirement Plan: A pension or profit-sharing plan available to self-employed individuals and their employees.

Kiddie Tax: A popular name for the tax rate imposed on the investment income of children under a specified age. Children with substantial investment income, such as interest, dividends, rents, and royalties, must pay tax on their investment income at a rate that is the same as the tax brackets applicable to trusts and estates.

Lien Creditor: A creditor with a lien on property of the debtor to secure payment of a debt.

Lifetime Learning Tax Credit: A tax credit for qualified postsecondary and job-training educational expenses. The credit is subject to income limitations.

Like-Kind Exchange: A tax-deferred exchange of real property used in a trade or business or held for investment for other real property used in a trade or business or held for investment.

Limited Liability (of shareholders, limited partners, and LLC members): Limited liability means that creditors are prevented from accessing the personal assets of the individual. Their liability is limited to their investment in the entity.

Limited Liability Company (LLC): An LLC is a form of business entity that offers its owners (called "members") one of the main advantages of the corporate form of business (i.e., they are not personally liable for the obligations of the company), the ability to be taxed like a partnership (or a corporation, if the LLC so chooses), and the option of being run like a partnership or a corporation (i.e., managed by all of the members or by managers).

Limited Liability Partnership (LLP): As with a general partnership, an LLP is an association of two or more persons who agree to carry on as co-owners of a business for profit. An LLP differs from a general partnership in that a partner in an LLP is not personally liable for the obligations or liabilities of the partnership arising from errors, omissions, negligence, malpractice, or the wrongful acts committed by another partner or by an employee, agent, or representative of the LLP. Neither are the partners liable for partnership contracts.

Limited Partner: A limited partner is a partner with limited liability as to his personal assets, risking only his investment in the limited partnership. A limited partner is not an agent of the partnership.

Limited Partnership: A limited partnership is a partnership made up of one or more general partners (who have personal liability for all partnership debts) and one or more limited partners (whose personal liability for partnership debts generally is limited to their capital contributions).

Liquidated Damages: Liquidated damages occur when the contract states in advance what damages will be if there is a breach (e.g., the parties agree the buyer will forfeit a down payment if he or she breaches). Liquidated damages are enforceable if they are reasonable to the actual harm done and not a penalty.

Listed Transaction: A listed transaction is a tax avoidance transaction. It is a reportable transaction (a transaction that is required to be reported on a return or statement attached to that return which is the same as, or substantially similar to, a transaction specifically identified by the Secretary of the U.S. Treasury as a tax avoidance transaction).

Locking up the Crown Jewels: When a corporation is faced with the prospect of being taken over and the board of directors wants to resist the takeover attempt, it will give a third party an option to purchase the company's most valuable assets.

Liquidating Distribution: Asset distribution by a corporation associated with the business' termination.

Luxury Tax: Tax imposed on expensive goods and services considered nonessential by the government.

Mailbox Rule: A contract rule that states that an acceptance is generally effective when sent (i.e., mailed, telegraphed, faxed, etc.) if properly addressed.

Marital Deduction: The marital deduction, sometimes called the unlimited marital deduction, is a deduction from the gross estate for unlimited transfers to the decedent's spouse.

Material Participation: The standard used to determine whether a taxpayer worked and was involved in a business activity on a regular basis, or was only an investor. Material participants are allowed to deduct any losses from that activity against their ordinary income whereas nonmaterial participants' loss deductions may be limited by the passive activity rules.

Materialman's Lien: Liens imposed by law in favor of contractors who perform work on, or provide supplies for, real property improvements.

Means Test: A test designed to determine whether the debtor in bankruptcy has sufficient income to repay debts using a Chapter 13 plan instead of going through a Chapter 7 liquidation.

Mechanic's Lien: Under common law, a mechanic who works on property and either improves it or repairs it automatically has a lien on the property for the price of the repair. This is referred to as a mechanic's lien.

Medical Savings Account (MSA): A medical savings account is intended to help self-employed people, employees of certain small businesses, or Medicare recipients save for and pay medical expenses that are not covered by their health insurance.

Medicare: The federal insurance program that funds medical care for people age 65 and older, and certain disabled people.

Merchant: Under the UCC in Sales, a merchant is one who deals in goods of the kind being sold or has special knowledge regarding the goods being sold.

Merger: Two or more companies join to form a single entity and one of the original companies survives.

Mid-month Convention: A cost recovery convention that assumes real property is placed in service in the middle of the month that it is actually placed into service.

Mid-quarter Convention: A cost recovery convention that assumes tangible personal property is placed in service in the middle of the quarter that it is actually placed into service. This convention applies when more than 40 percent of the property (excluding eligible real estate) is placed into service in the fourth quarter.

Mirror Image Rule: A common law contract rule that requires an acceptance to exactly match or "mirror" the offer to be effective. A purported acceptance of less than all of the terms of an offer amounts to a rejection and a counteroffer at common law.

Mitigation of Damages: Prevention of harm subsequent to a breach. Damages will not be awarded in contract law for harms that the plaintiff could have reasonably avoided. The plaintiff is under a duty to avoid or mitigate damages.

Modified Accelerated Cost Recovery System (MACRS): The depreciation method generally used since 1986 for depreciable property other than real estate. MACRS reduces an asset's basis faster than the straight-line depreciation method.

Modified AGI: Modified AGI is adjusted gross income that has been adjusted in some manner for the calculation of a credit or a limitation. AGI can be modified in various ways for various calculations. For the American opportunity tax credit, for example, modified AGI is AGI increased by income excluded from sources in Puerto Rico or certain U.S. possessions. For the exclusion of savings bond income, modified AGI is AGI determined without the deduction for higher education expenses, the savings bond interest exclusion, and several other deductions and exclusions. Modified AGI for Social Security benefits is defined differently.

Multiple Support Agreement: Generally, a taxpayer must provide more than 50 percent of a person's support for the individual to be claimed as a dependent.

Municipal Bond: A bond issued by a state or local government. Municipal bond interest is exempt from federal income tax and may or may not be subject to a state's income tax.

Mutual Mistake: In contract law, a mutual mistake is a mistake by both parties to a contract as to a material item in the contract. When a mutual mistake occurs, the adversely affected party can avoid the contract.

Negligence (Law): A tort whereby a party causes damage to another by failure to use reasonable care.

Negligence (Tax): For purposes of penalties imposed on tax return preparers, negligence includes any failure to make a reasonable attempt to comply with the provisions of the internal revenue laws or to exercise ordinary and reasonable care in the preparation of a tax return. Negligence also includes any failure by the taxpayer to keep adequate books and records or to substantiate items properly.

Net Operating Loss (NOL): A net operating loss occurs when a taxpayer's deductions exceed income for the year. NOLs generally can only be carried forward indefinitely, not back. A two-year carryback is available for certain farming losses.

Nonconforming Goods: Goods that do not exactly conform to the terms of the contract.

Noncumulative Preferred Shares: Shares with a preference usually are entitled to a fixed amount of money before distributions can be made with respect to nonpreferred shares. Unless the dividend is cumulative the right to a dividend preference is extinguished if it is not declared for that year. *See also* cumulative preferred shares.

Noncustodial Parent: For purposes of head-of-household status, a noncustodial parent is the parent without custody of the child.

Nonqualified Option: An employee stock option that does not meet incentive stock option or employee stock purchase plan requirements. A nonqualified option is taxed when granted if the option has a readily ascertainable value and is taxed when exercised if there is no readily ascertainable value.

Nonrecourse Debt: An obligation for which the debtor is not personally liable; for example, a mortgage on real estate acquired by a partnership without the assumption of mortgage liability by the partnership or any of the partners.

Nontaxable Distribution: A corporate dividend that represents a return of the taxpayer's investment in the stock, rather than an earnings distribution. A taxpayer must reduce his or her basis in the stock by the amount of the distribution.

Note: A type of negotiable instrument. A note is two-party paper. It is an unconditional written promise by a maker to pay a certain sum of money on demand or at a definite time to a payee. (Also referred to as a "promissory note.")

Novation: Novation occurs when the parties to a contract agree to replace one party to the contract with a new party. The parties agree to release or discharge the old party and look only to the new party for performance.

Obligee: The party to whom a duty of performance is owed.

Obligor: The party owing a duty of performance.

Offer: An invitation to form a contract. Offers must be seriously intended, communicated, and definite and certain in the essential terms.

Officers: Officers are parties elected by the board of directors to manage the corporation on a day-to-day basis. Officers are agents of the corporation.

Option Contract: A contract in which the offeree pays consideration to keep an offer open.

Order for Relief (in bankruptcy): In bankruptcy proceedings, the order relieves the debtor of the immediate obligation to pay debts listed in the bankruptcy petition. In a voluntary case, the petition is the order; in an involuntary case, the order will be issued after the court determines that the petition was properly filed.

Ordinary and Necessary Business Expenses: Business expenses that are fully deductible as current expenses, as opposed to unreasonable or unnecessary expenses, and capital expenditures.

Parol Evidence Rule: A contract rule that prohibits the admission of oral or written evidence that contradicts the terms of a fully integrated written contract.

Par Value: Par value is a specific face value placed on stock. Traditionally, par value stock could not be sold for less than par and the par value had to be placed into a separate account.

Patent: A patent is a federal right to protect an invention, process, or design that is: novel, useful, and not obvious to a person skilled in the area.

Partially Disclosed Principal: The person for whom an agent acts if the third party dealing with the agent has notice that the agent is acting for another (principal) but the identity of the specific principal is not given.

Participating Preferred Stock: Participating preferred stock is stock that entitles its holder to a specific payment before the common stockholders may receive a dividend and, in addition, entitles the holder to the dividend the common shareholders receive as well. *See also* preferred stock *and* cumulative preferred stock.

Partnership: An unincorporated business or investment organization having two or more owners. A partnership is not subject to tax; instead income, losses, and other tax items pass through the partnership and are attributed directly to the partners.

Passive Activity: An activity in which the taxpayer does not materially participate, such as real estate rentals and limited partnerships. Passive loss rules apply to losses from passive activities.

Passive Income: Income from a passive activity. A taxpayer can offset a passive loss against passive income, but cannot offset ordinary income with passive losses.

Passive Loss: Loss from a passive activity. Passive loss rules limit the amount of a passive loss deduction to the total of other income from passive activities. There is a $25,000-per-year exception for rental real estate activities, subject to income limitations. Passive losses that have not been used as a deduction can be carried forward to subsequent years until they are used completely, or passive losses are fully deductible in the year that the taxpayer sells or disposes of their interest in the passive activity.

Payee: The party to whom payment is made.

Payroll Tax: A tax based on an employee's wages, tips, and salaries. Part of the tax is deducted from the employee's pay; the employer pays the rest. Federal, state, and local governments collect payroll taxes for expenses such as Social Security, Medicare, unemployment compensation, and workers' compensation insurance.

Pension: A retirement plan that provides systematic payments of retirement benefits to employee participants.

Per se Violation: Per se is Latin for "in itself" or "as such." A "per se" violation is a violation that is inherently illegal by its very nature.

Percentage Depletion: A deductible expense based on the using up, or depletion, of an asset, such as underground minerals. Depletion is based on a statutory percentage applied to the gross income from the property.

Perfection: The process by which a secured creditor attains superior rights to collateral over third parties. Under the Secured Transaction Article of the UCC, the most common ways to perfect are by filing a financing statement, taking possession of the collateral, and perfection by attachment (i.e., automatic perfection).

Perfection by Attachment: The Secured Transactions Article of the UCC permits automatic perfection or perfection by attachment in certain cases. The most common type (and the only type tested on the CPA Exam) occurs with a purchase money security interest in consumer goods.

Perfection by Filing: The filing of a financing statement with the state for the purpose of giving constructive notice of a security interest to third-parties.

Perfection by Possession: A secured party may perfect a security interest in most types of collateral simply by taking possession of the collateral with the debtor's agreement that the creditor is taking possession in order to have a security interest in the collateral.

Periodic Reports: In the context of the Securities Exchange Act of 1934, all issuers required to register under the 1934 Act and all issuers required to register under the 1933 Act are required to submit three periodic reports to the SEC. These reports are Form 10-K (annual report), Form 10-Q (quarterly report), and Form 8-K (major change in the issuer).

Personal Holding Company (PHC): A corporation in which five or fewer individuals own at least 50 percent of the corporation, and 60 percent or more of adjusted ordinary gross income consists of rent, taxable interest, royalties, and dividends.

Personal Service Corporation (PSC): A corporation whose principal activity is the performance of personal services (e.g., health care, law, engineering, or consulting). The employee-owners substantially perform such services.

Personalty: Property other than real estate (i.e., land, permanent improvements to land, and buildings).

Personalty-Use Property: Property used for personal purposes, and not for use in a trade or business, or for investment purposes; for example, personal car and home furnishings.

Piercing the Corporate Veil: In some circumstances, the courts will hold the shareholders, officers, or directors of a corporation liable because the legislative privilege of conducting business in corporate form is being abused. Typical causes for piercing the corporate veil include commingling personal funds with corporate funds, inadequate capitalization, and committing fraud on existing creditors.

Pledge (in secured transactions): In the context of the Secured Transactions Article of the UCC, a pledge occurs when a creditor takes possession of collateral as security for payment of a debt.

Points: A charge paid by a borrower for taking out a loan, (i.e., prepaid interest) in which each point is one percent of the loan amount. Most points must be amortized over the life of the loan; however, points paid to acquire or make improvements to a taxpayer's main residence are deductible in the year paid.

Power of Attorney: A written authorization of agency to perform certain specified tasks.

Preemptive Rights: When a corporation proposes to issue additional shares of stock, current shareholders often want to purchase some shares in order to maintain their proportional voting strength through special rights referred to as "preemptive rights" that must be granted in the articles of incorporation.

Preexisting Legal Duty Rule: A promise to perform, or performance of, an existing duty is not sufficient consideration.

Preferential Payment: A transfer made by the debtor to or for the benefit of a creditor for an antecedent debt that resulted in the creditor receiving more than the creditor would have received under the Bankruptcy Code. The transfer must have been made within 90 days of the petition (within one year of the petition if the creditor was an insider) and made while the debtor was insolvent. Also called "voidable preference."

Preferred Stock: Preferred stock is the ownership interest in a corporation that is entitled to a distribution (e.g., of dividends or assets) before the common stockholders can receive a distribution. *See also* cumulative preferred stock *and* participating preferred stock.

Present Interest: A present interest, for estate tax purposes, is an interest that is the unrestricted right to the immediate use, possession, or enjoyment of property or income from the property.

Principal: The person in an agency relationship who appoints an agent to act on his or her behalf.

Private Activity Bond: Municipal bonds used to finance facilities used by private businesses. The interest from private activity bonds is an AMT adjustment.

Private Securities Litigation Reform Act: A federal law regulating accountants and other professionals in securities fraud cases. Among other provisions, it requires accountants to design audits to detect illegal acts, related party transactions, and whether there is substantial doubt about the ability of the issuer to continue as a going concern during the next fiscal year.

Privity of Contract: A direct relationship between the parties who have made a contract.

Proceeds (in secured transactions): In the context of the Secured Transaction Article of the UCC, proceeds refers to whatever is received from the sale, exchange, collection, or other disposition of collateral.

Profit: Profit is total revenue less total cost.

Progressive Tax: Tax that takes a larger percentage of income from high-income groups than from low-income groups; for example, federal income tax rates.

Promises Not to Compete: A promise not to conduct a business similar to the business of the promisee. Promises not to compete generally are unenforceable because they violate antitrust law. However, promises not to compete that accompany the sale of a business or in an employment contract are enforceable if they are reasonably needed and reasonable as to time and distance.

Promissory Estoppel: *See* detrimental reliance.

Promoter: A promoter is an individual who forms a corporation. The promoter is responsible for the procurement of commitments for capital that will be used by the corporation after formation. The promoter enters into contracts with third parties who are interested in becoming shareholders and might also enter into contracts for goods or services to be provided to the corporation once it is formed.

Property Tax: A tax levied by local governments, based on the value of a taxpayer's property, such as real estate and some business assets. Property tax on real estate is the main source of financing for local governments and school districts.

Proportional Tax: Tax based on the same percentage of income from all income groups. Also called a flat tax.

Prospectus: In broad terms, any written offer to sell securities. Under the Securities Act of 1933, it describes the financial operations of a business issuing securities, thus allowing investors to make informed decisions about whether to invest in the business.

Proxy: A proxy is written authorization given to a third party appointing the third party as an agent for the purpose of voting the proxy giver's stock at a stockholders' meeting.

Proxy Solicitation: A written request for permission to vote a shareholder's shares.

Proxy Statement: Under the Securities Exchange Act of 1934, a proxy solicitation is prohibited unless each person solicited is provided with a document called a proxy statement disclosing all material facts concerning the matter being submitted to their vote.

Punitive Damages: Damages awarded against a tortfeasor to punish the tortfeasor for committing a wrong, rather than to compensate the victim for injury.

Purchase Money Security Interest: A purchase money security interest is a special type of security interest that arises when a creditor sells the collateral to the debtor on credit, retaining a security interest in the collateral or when the creditor advances funds used by the debtor to purchase the collateral. A properly perfected purchase money security interest is superior to all other security interests in the same collateral.

Qualified Adoption Expenses: For the adoption credit, reasonable and necessary expenses for adopting a child, including such expenses as adoption fees, attorney's fees, and other expenses, but not including medical expenses, expenses paid for a surrogate parenting arrangement, or expenses paid to adopt a spouse's child.

Qualified Business Income (QBI) Deduction: A deduction of 20 percent of qualified business income is allowed to certain pass-through entities such as S corporations, limited liability companies, partnerships, and sole proprietorships. Also known as the Section 199A deduction.

Qualified Employee Discount: A qualified employee discount is a discount on employer-provided merchandise and service that is excludable from income.

Qualified Option: An employee stock option that meets certain requirements and is not taxed as compensation to the employee and is not deductible by the employer. Inventive stock options and employee stock purchase plans are qualified option plans.

Qualified Retirement Plan: A retirement plan approved by the IRS that allows for tax-deferred accumulation of investment income.

Qualified Tuition Reduction: A qualified tuition reduction is a tuition reduction for employees of educational institutions studying at the undergraduate level that can be excluded from income.

Qualifying Child: A qualifying child must be a close relative under age 19 (or age 24 if a full-time student) who lives with the taxpayer for more than one-half of the tax year. The child may not contribute more than one-half of his or her support.

Qualifying Relative: To be classified as a qualifying relative, the taxpayer must contribute more than one-half of the relative's support (or be part of a multiple support agreement). The relative must make less than a specified amount; be a citizen of the United States or a resident of the U.S., Canada, or Mexico; be a relative; and live with the taxpayer for the entire year.

Quasi-Contract: *See* implied-in-fact contract.

Quorum: A quorum is a minimum number of parties that must be present for a valid vote or transaction.

Ratification: The acceptance of a contract by a party that is not obligated to accept the contract.

Ratification (in agency): The acceptance by a principal of a contract entered into by an agent without authority. The agent must have purportedly been acting on behalf of the principal and the principal must know of the material facts in order for the ratification to be valid.

Readily Ascertainable Value: The value of a stock option in an established market or when certain conditions are met.

Reaffirmation of Discharged Debts: An agreement between a debtor and a creditor, in which the debtor promises to pay a debt dischargeable in bankruptcy.

Real Estate Investment Trust (REIT): A trust that invests primarily in real estate and mortgages and passes income, losses, and other tax items to its investors.

Realized Gain or Loss: The difference between the amount received in a transaction (including any property) and the adjusted basis of what was given up in the transaction. The realized gain/loss is not necessarily the same as the recognized gain/loss.

Realty: Real estate. Real property is permanent, nonmovable property, such as land and buildings.

Reasonable Basis: A tax return position with a reasonable basis is a tax return position that is reasonably based on one or more authorities.

Recognized Gain or Loss: The amount of gain or loss on a transaction that is reported for income tax purposes. In some situations, such as like-kind exchanges, the recognition of gains and losses is deferred. Therefore, the realized gain/loss is not necessarily the same as the recognized gain/loss.

Recovery of Capital Doctrine: When a taxable sale or exchange occurs, a seller may recover their investment (or other adjusted basis) in the property before recognizing the gain or loss.

Red Herring Prospectus: In securities law, a preliminary prospectus that is distributed to potential investors during the period between the filing date and the effective date.

Registered Agent: A registered agent is the person on whom process may be served if the limited partnership, LLC, or corporation is sued.

Regressive Tax: A tax that takes a larger percentage of income from low-income groups than from high-income groups.

Regulation A: Under the Securities Act of 1933, a partial exemption from registration is available for issuers of $5 million or less of securities within a 12-month period.

Regulation D: Under the Securities Act of 1933, an exemption from registration is available for private offerings. There are two specific exemptions available under Regulation D: Rules 504 and 506.

Reimbursement: The right to be paid back payments made on behalf of another (e.g., an agent has a right to reimbursement of expenses paid on behalf of a principal), and a surety who pays a creditor upon the debtor's default has a right to reimbursement from the debtor for the amount paid.

Rejection (of an offer): An offeree's refusal to accept a contract. Once an offer is rejected, it cannot be accepted.

Related Party Transaction: A transaction between related parties (e.g., family members, a majority partner, and a partnership). Tax law restricts the recognition of related party gains and losses to prevent potential tax abuse.

Release: The relinquishment or giving up of a right, claim, or privilege.

Reorganization Plan: The plan filed in a Chapter 11 case, usually by the debtor, classifying all claims, describing the treatment to be accorded each class of claims, and establishing ways to implement the plan.

Replevin: The legal right to recover goods wrongfully in the hands of another.

Reportable Transaction: A reportable transaction is any transaction with respect to which information is required to be included with a return or statement because such transaction is of a type that the Secretary of the U.S. Treasury Department has determined as having a potential for either tax avoidance (the legal use and application of the tax laws and cases in order to reduce the amount of tax due) or tax evasion (efforts, by illegal means and methods, to not pay taxes).

Required Minimum Distribution: A required minimum distribution is a distribution of retirement money in an IRA that must be withdrawn starting at age 70½.

Rescind/Rescission: Disaffirmance or cancellation of a contractual obligation that restores the parties to their former position. Contracts may be rescinded for mistake, fraud, and most material contract breaches.

Residential Energy Credit: The residential energy credit is a tax credit for 30 percent of qualifying solar electric or solar water heating property installed.

Respondeat Superior: In Latin, "let the master respond." A rule of agency law in which an employer is liable for all torts of an employee committed within the scope of employment.

Return of Capital: A distribution received from an investment that is not income, but rather a return of a portion of the investment. A return of capital is not taxable unless it exceeds the investment's basis.

Revised Model Business Corporation Act (RMBCA): The RMBCA is a uniform law governing corporations that has been adopted by a slight majority of the states.

Revised Uniform Limited Partnership Act (RULPA): The RULPA is a uniform law governing limited partnerships that has been adopted by the majority of states.

Revised Uniform Partnership Act (RUPA): The RUPA is a uniform law governing partnerships that has been adopted by the majority of states.

Revocable Gift: A revocable gift is a transfer of property in which the transferor of the property reserves the right to revoke the gift or change the beneficiaries.

Revocable Trust: A trust that can be changed or terminated at any time by its creator or another person. A revocable trust does not have the tax advantages of an irrevocable trust.

Revocation (of an offer): The withdrawal or recall of an offer by the offeror. Generally, an offeror can revoke an offer any time prior to acceptance.

Revocation of Discharge: To cancel a discharge previously given in bankruptcy.

Risk of Loss: Risk of loss determines whether a buyer or seller will bear financial responsibility if the subject matter of a contract is damaged or destroyed.

Roth IRA: An IRA in which contributions are not deductible, but qualified withdrawals are tax-free. Roth IRAs are subject to income limitations.

Royalty Income: Payment for the use and exploitation of certain kinds of property, such as artistic or literary works, patents, and mineral rights.

S Corporation: A corporation that meets certain requirements and elects not to be taxed as a C corporation (i.e., an S corporation does not pay federal income tax directly, but instead passes its income or losses and other tax items on to its shareholders, much like a partnership). Its stockholders still are shielded from personal liability for corporate acts the same as stockholders in a C corporation.

Sale on Approval: In a "sale on approval," the buyer takes possession of the goods but the sale is not final until the buyer expressly or impliedly gives approval. Title and risk of loss remain with the seller until the buyer approves.

Sale or Return: In a sale or return, the buyer takes possession of the goods and has the risk of loss while the goods are in his possession, but the buyer has a right to return the goods, even if they conform to the contract. This is often used when the buyer is reselling the seller's goods.

Schedule A (1040): Attachment to Form 1040 to claim itemized deductions.

Schedule B (1040): Attachment to Form 1040 to report interest and ordinary dividends.

Schedule C (1040): Attachment to Form 1040 to report profit or loss from business.

Schedule D (1040): Attachment to Form 1040 to report capital gains and losses.

Schedule E (1040): Attachment to Form 1040 to report income from rental real estate, trusts, royalties, partnerships, etc.

Schedule F (1040): Attachment to Form 1040 to report farming income.

Schedule K (1065): Attachment to Form 1065 to report partners' shares of income.

Schedule K-1 (1065): Attachment to Form 1065 to report individual partner's share of income.

Schedule K-1 (1120S): Attachment to Form 1120S to report individual shareholders' share of income.

Scienter: Scienter denotes a particular level of culpable conduct, specifically, conduct undertaken with intent (e.g., knowingly making a false representation of fact) or with a reckless disregard of truth.

Scope of Employment: Actions by an employee of the same general type the employee was hired to perform and actuated by an intent to further his employer's business purposes.

Scorched Earth Policy: When a corporation is faced with the prospect of being taken over and the board of directors wants to resist the takeover attempt, it will sell off assets or take out loans that would make the company less financially attractive.

Secondary Liability (in negotiable instruments): The obligation to pay a negotiable instrument if the party with primary liability does not pay. Endorsers are secondarily liable, but their liability is subject to the conditions of presentment of the negotiable instrument, dishonor, and notice of dishonor. Drawers of drafts and endorsers are the secondary liable parties.

Secondary-Line Injury: Price discrimination that causes injury to a seller's customers.

Secondary Market: Secondary markets are markets other than the primary market, where securities are traded among investors.

Section 341 Meeting of Creditors: In a bankruptcy case, a meeting of creditors held from 20 to 40 days after the order for relief is effective. All interested parties, including creditors, the bankruptcy trustee, and the debtor must be given notice of the meeting. *See also* creditors' committee.

Section 1231 Asset: Depreciable property, or non-depreciable real estate, used in a trade or business, such as equipment, vehicles, and rental real estate. In general, if Section 1231 assets are held for the required time, capital gain treatment is available, while a loss is a deductible ordinary loss.

Section 1245 Asset: Tangible personal property that is subject to the recapture of depreciation under Section 1245. Upon a taxable disposition of the property, all depreciation claimed on the property is recaptured as ordinary income, to the extent of the gain recognized. Any gain on the sale in excess of depreciation may qualify for favorable capital gains tax treatment.

Section 1250 Property: Real estate that is subject to the recapture of depreciation under Section 1250 in which some or all of the accelerated depreciation in excess of straight-line depreciation claimed on the property may be recaptured as ordinary income.

Section 179 Expense Deduction: The ability to deduct a capital expenditure in the year an asset (excluding real estate) is placed in service instead of over the asset's useful life. A Section 179 deduction is limited to the extent that it would cause a net loss.

Secured Party: A creditor who has a security interest in property.

Secured Transaction: A debt the payment of which is guaranteed by the right to sell items of the debtor's property (i.e., collateral) if payment is not otherwise made.

Securities: Investment contracts; examples include stocks, bonds debentures, oil well interests, collateral trust certificates, warrants, and limited partnership interests.

Securities Act of 1933: A federal securities law requiring filing a registration statement with the SEC and giving a prospectus to investors for public sales of securities by the issuer.

Securities Act of 1933, Section 11: Section 11 of the 1933 Act imposes civil liability for misstatements in the registration statement, whether or not the misstatements were intentional.

Securities Act of 1933, Section 12: Section 12 of the 1933 Act imposes civil liability if a required registration was not made, if a prospectus was not given to all investors, or if false statements were made in connection with sales or offers to sell.

Securities Act of 1933, Section 17: Section 17 of the 1933 Act imposes criminal liability for fraud in connection with the issuance of securities.

Securities Exchange Act of 1934: A federal securities law that is primarily concerned with exchanges of securities after they are issued.

Security Interest: An interest in property (called "collateral") given by a debtor to a creditor to guarantee payment of a debt. If the debtor does not pay, the creditor can sell the collateral to satisfy the secured obligation.

Self-Employment Tax: Social Security and Medicare taxes paid by self-employed taxpayers on the net income from their trade or business.

Self-Tender: A device a corporation may use to avoid a hostile takeover. The corporation offers to acquire stock from its own stockholders so that the company trying to take over the corporation cannot purchase sufficient stock from the stockholders to achieve the takeover.

Senior Citizen's Freedom to Work Act: A provision under Social Security permitting a reduction in retirement benefits for those returning to work after they have begun receiving benefits.

SEP Retirement Plan: A retirement plan similar to an IRA for self-employed individuals and their employees. Unlike IRAs, the employer sets up a SEP.

Series EE Bonds: U.S. Savings Bonds issued after 1979. The interest from these bonds is subject to federal income tax, but not state or local income tax. A taxpayer can elect to pay the income taxes on accrued interest each year or at the time of maturity.

Share: An ownership interest in a corporation; stock.

Share Exchange: Share exchange is a transaction in which one corporation acquires all of the outstanding shares of one or more classes of stock of another corporation. Both corporations continue to exist as separate entities.

Shareholder: A shareholder is a party owning an interest in a corporation (also called a stockholder). A shareholder has a limited right to manage.

Shark Repellent: When a corporation is faced with the prospect of being taken over and the board of directors wants to resist the takeover attempt, it will amend the articles of incorporation or bylaws to make a takeover more difficult.

Shelf Registration: An issuer of securities is required to file a registration statement for any new offering of securities. A shelf registration is registration that is valid for future issuances. In essence, the registration statement is "put on the shelf" to await securities for which it is effective.

Shipment Contract: A type of contract in which risk of loss passes from the seller to the buyer when the seller delivers the goods to the carrier.

Short-Form Merger: A short-form merger is a merger whereby a parent corporation owning 90 percent or more of a subsidiary corporation may merge the subsidiary into the parent without the approval of the shareholders of either corporation or the approval of the subsidiary's board.

Small Business Health Care Tax Credit: A tax credit for certain small employers that provide health insurance coverage for their employees.

Small Employer Pension Plan Start-up Costs Credit: A tax credit for eligible small businesses for qualified start-up costs incurred in establishing and administering an eligible employer benefit plan for their employees.

Social Security Benefits: The monthly benefits paid by the Social Security Administration to recipients.

Sole Proprietorship: In a sole proprietorship, one person owns the business and manages all of its affairs. The sole proprietor is not considered an entity separate from the business.

Special Agent: An agent engaged to perform one or more transactions not involving a continuity of service.

Special Endorsement: A signature made on the back of a negotiable instrument through which the signor makes a contract of secondary liability and names a particular person who must subsequently sign the instrument in order for it to be negotiated further.

Specific Performance: A court action filed in a contract case that seeks an order instructing the defendant to act according to the terms of the contract rather than seeking monetary damages. Specific performance is available only with respect to unique, one-of-a-kind items and never with personal service contracts.

Spousal Support: *See* alimony.

Stare Decisis: Stare decisis is the judicial doctrine under which judges are required to respect the precedents established by prior judicial decisions on the same set of facts.

Statute of Frauds: A contract rule requiring certain contracts to be evidenced by a writing. Examples of contracts requiring a writing under the Statute of Frauds include contracts in which the consideration is marriage; contracts which are impossible to perform in one year; contracts involving interests in land; contracts by executors to be personally liable for the debts of an estate; contracts for the sale of goods of $500 or more; and contracts to act as a surety (i.e., to pay the debt of another).

Statute of Limitations: A provision of law that specifies the maximum period of time in which a lawsuit may be filed to remedy a past event.

Statutory Law: A law enacted by a legislative body.

Stock: An ownership share or interest in a corporation.

Stock Dividends: Stock dividends are distributions to stockholders of the corporation's own authorized but unissued shares. A stock dividend is not a taxable event.

Stock Subscription: A stock subscription is a contract to purchase stock from a corporation.

Stockholder: *See* shareholder.

Stop Payment Order: An order by a drawer of a negotiable instrument to a drawee not to pay out on the instrument.

Straight-Line Depreciation: A depreciation method that spreads the cost or other basis of an asset evenly over its useful life.

Subrogation (in suretyship): If the debtor defaults and the surety pays the creditor, the surety may enforce any rights the creditor had against the debtor (e.g., if the creditor was a secured creditor, then the surety obtains the rights of a secured creditor upon payment). The obtaining of the creditor's rights by the surety upon payment is called the right of subrogation.

Subordinated Debenture: A subordinated debenture is a debenture that is subordinated to (lower than) other debt in terms of payment in the event of bankruptcy. Subordinated debentures may be subordinated to certain types of debt or to all other debt. *See also* debenture.

Substantial Authority: Substantial authority is when the weight of an authority for the tax treatment of an item is substantial in relation to the weight of authorities supporting a contrary treatment. Authority includes the Internal Revenue Code and other statutory provisions, regulations, revenue rulings and revenue procedures, court cases, and other sources. Conclusions reached in treatises, legal periodicals, legal opinions, or opinions rendered by tax professionals are not authority.

Substantial Performance: A common law contract doctrine providing that a party cannot cancel or rescind a contract if the individual has received most of what he bargained for. He has a duty to pay the breaching party but can collect or offset damages for the minor breach.

Substituted Contract: A substituted contract is very similar to an accord and satisfaction, but the duties under the original contract are discharged immediately (not when the accord is satisfied).

Surety: A party who guarantees the debt or obligation of another.

Suretyship: The guarantee of the debts or obligations of another.

Tax Avoidance: Tax avoidance is the legal use and application of the tax laws and cases in order to reduce the amount of tax due.

Tax Benefit Rule: A provision that limits the recognition of income from the recovery of an expense or loss properly deducted in a prior tax year to the amount of the deduction that generated a tax benefit. For instance, if a taxpayer properly deducts from the federal income tax return state taxes that were paid, and then receives a refund on some/all of those state taxes, the refund is income to the extent that it was deducted in the prior year.

Tax Evasion: Tax evasion is efforts, by illegal means and methods, to not pay taxes.

Tax Practitioner: A tax practitioner is any of the following individuals who practice before the IRS: attorneys, CPAs, enrolled agents, enrolled actuaries, and enrolled retirement plan agents.

Tax Preference Items: Items, such as accelerated depreciation, percentage depletion, or certain tax-exempt income, that are considered to have favorable tax treatment and could trigger the alternative minimum tax.

Tax Return Position: A tax return position is a position taken on the tax return that the tax preparer has advised the taxpayer to take or a position taken on the tax return that the tax preparer has concluded is appropriate based on all the material facts.

Tax Return Preparer: A tax return preparer is any person who prepares for compensation, or who employs one or more persons to prepare for compensation, any tax return required under the IRC or any claim for a refund of tax imposed by the IRC.

Tax Shelter: An investment that is planned to result in tax-favored treatment. The IRS has placed restrictions on tax shelters when the principal purpose of the activity appears to be the avoidance or evasion of taxes or when the activity might result in more deductible expenses than the investors have at risk.

Tax-Exempt Interest: Interest income, such as interest from state and municipal bonds, that is exempt from federal income tax. Even though it is not taxable, tax-exempt interest is still used for certain tax calculations, such as the earned income credit and determining taxable Social Security benefits.

Tender Offers: An offer made to all stockholders to purchase stock for a specific price for a specified period of time.

Third-Party Beneficiary Contract: A third-party beneficiary contract occurs when two parties make a contract requiring some performance to be rendered to a third party. Third-party beneficiaries may be creditor beneficiaries or donee beneficiaries.

Title: Legal ownership.

Tombstone Ad: In securities law, an advertisement that names the security, its price, and by whom orders for purchase will be executed. A tombstone ad makes known the availability of a prospectus.

Tort: Causing damage to another by a civil as opposed to a criminal wrong.

Trade Association: An association of businesses in the same industry to promote common interests.

Transaction Exemption: The existence of certain circumstances in connection with the issuance of securities specified under the Securities Act of 1933 as a condition that will relieve the issuer of the general duty to register the issuance (e.g., a small scale issuance).

Transfer Tax: Tax payable when title passes from one owner to another.

Treble Damages: An award of triple the amount of damages actually suffered.

Treasury Shares: Treasury shares are issued shares that are sometimes repurchased by the corporation (called "issued but not outstanding").

Trust: A separate, taxable entity that holds property to be managed, protected, and distributed to others.

Trustee in Bankruptcy: The legal representative of the debtor's estate in bankruptcy. The trustee is responsible for collecting, liquidating, and distributing the assets of the debtor's estate.

Ultra Vires Act: An ultra vires act is an unauthorized act. Under the RMBCA, a corporation may include a clause in its articles stating the business purpose for which the corporation was formed. A number of states require a purpose clause. If a corporation undertakes business activities outside the scope of the clause (or outside the business permitted by statute), it is said to be acting "ultra vires" and may be challenged by adversely affected parties under certain circumstances.

Underwriter: In securities law, an underwriter is an intermediary who sells an issuer's securities to the general public or to dealers.

Undisclosed Principal: The third party dealing with the agent has no notice that the agent is acting for a principal. The third party believes that he is acting with a principal, not an agent.

Undue Influence: Undue influence occurs when a party induces another to enter into a contract by overcoming his or her free will through an abuse of a position of confidence (e.g., spouse, trustee, guardian, attorney, etc.).

Unearned income: Income such as interest, dividends, capital gains, or rents, as opposed to earned income, such as wages, tips, and salaries.

Unemployment Compensation: Benefit payments paid to unemployed workers who meet certain qualification requirements. Unemployment compensation is included in gross income.

Uniform Capitalization Rules: The Uniform Capitalization Rules is a set of rules that applies to all business enterprises and that provides guidelines for capitalizing or expensing certain costs related to certain property.

Uniform Commercial Code (UCC): A series of uniform laws governing commercial transactions that has been widely adopted by legislative bodies throughout the United States.

Unilateral Contract: A contract formed when one promise is given in exchange for performance (i.e., a promise for an act). The contract is not formed until performance is completed.

Unilateral Mistake: A mistake by one party to a contract. It is not a defense unless it goes to a material fact and the other party knew or should have known of the mistake.

Unlawful Distribution: A payment by a corporation to stockholders that either makes the corporation unable to pay its debts as they become due in the regular course of business or causes the corporation's total assets to be less than its total liabilities.

Unreasonable Position: A tax position is deemed unreasonable unless there is substantial authority for the position and the position does not involve either a tax shelter or a reportable transaction, or there is a reasonable basis for the position and the position does not involve either a tax shelter or a reportable transaction, or, with respect to a tax shelter or a reportable transaction, it is reasonable to believe that the position would more likely than not be sustained on its merits.

U.S. Circuit Courts of Appeals: The U.S. Courts of Appeals (or Circuit Courts) are the first level of federal appellate courts. A Court of Appeals hears appeals from the U.S. District Courts within its federal judicial circuit and some others.

U.S. Court of Federal Claims: The U.S. Court of Federal Claims is a nationwide court that has jurisdiction over most claims for money damages against the United States, one type of which is tax refunds.

U.S. District Court: The U.S. District Courts are the general trial courts of the U.S. federal court system.

U.S. Supreme Court: The U.S. Supreme Court is the highest court in the nation and is the last level of appeal.

U.S. Tax Court: The U.S. Tax Court is a specialized trial court that hears only federal tax cases (income tax, estate tax, gift tax, or certain excise taxes), generally prior to the time that formal tax assessments are made by the IRS.

Void Contract: A contract having no legal or binding effect.

Voidable Contract: A voidable contract is one wherein one or more of the parties have the right to disaffirm, rescind, or cancel the contract.

Voidable Preference: *See* preferential payment.

Voidable Title: A transfer of title wherein one or more of the parties has the right to disaffirm, rescind, or cancel the transfer.

Voluntary Bankruptcy: A bankruptcy case filed by a debtor.

Voting Agreements: Shareholders agree among themselves to vote their shares as the majority of signers directs.

Voting Trusts: A voting trust is an agreement of shareholders under which all the shares owned by the parties to the agreement are transferred to a trustee, who votes the shares and distributes the dividends in accordance with the provisions of the voting trust agreement.

Warehouseman's Lien: A warehouseman has a lien on stored goods for storage charges, insurance, labor, and other expenses reasonably incurred in storage.

Wash Sale: The sale and repurchase of stocks or securities within a short time. Under wash sale rules, if a taxpayer sells stock at a loss, and purchases substantially identical stock within 30 days before or after the sale, the taxpayer cannot claim the loss for tax purposes.

Watered Stock: Watered stock is stock that has been issued in exchange for property worth less than the par value of the stock (the difference between the par value and the value of the property is deemed to be "water").

White Knight: If a corporation is faced with the prospect of a hostile takeover, one of its options is to find a more preferable company with which to merge. The more preferable company is called a "white knight."

Winding Up: Winding up is liquidation that involves the process of collecting the corporate or partnership assets, paying the expenses involved, satisfying creditors' claims, and distributing the net assets of the business to the appropriate party.

Workers' Compensation: A state-governed system designed to address work-related injuries. Under this system, employers assume the cost of medical treatment and wage losses arising from a worker's job-related injury or disease, regardless of who is at fault. In return, employees give up the right to sue employers, even if injuries stem from employer negligence. Workers' compensation is nontaxable.

Worthless Security: A security that becomes valueless during the year. A loss, usually capital, is allowed and is deemed to have occurred on the last day of the year.

Zero Coupon Bond: A bond that has no stated interest rate and is sold at substantially less than its face value (i.e., a discount). The value of a zero coupon bond increases every year; the taxpayer pays tax annually on this increase in value, which is recognized as interest income.

NOTES

A

NOTES